POSTCOLONIAL TRANSLOCATIONS

CROSS
CULTURES

Readings in Post / Colonial
Literatures and Cultures in English

156

ASNEL Papers 17

SERIES EDITORS

Gordon Collier   Bénédicte Ledent   Geoffrey Davis
(Giessen)   (Liège)   (Aachen)

CO-FOUNDING EDITOR
†Hena Maes–Jelinek

ASNEL Papers appear under the auspices of the
Gesellschaft für die Neuen Englischsprachigen Literaturen e.V.
(GNEL)
Association for the Study of the New Literatures in English (ASNEL)

Mark Stein, President
(English Department, University of Münster)

Formatting, layout and final editing and cover image: Gordon Collier

POSTCOLONIAL TRANSLOCATIONS

Cultural Representation and Critical Spatial Thinking

ASNEL Papers 17

Edited by
Marga Munkelt, Markus Schmitz,
Mark Stein, and Silke Stroh

Amsterdam - New York, NY 2013

COVER PHOTO:
Lisa Paul

COVER DESIGN:
based on an idea by Lisa Paul

The paper on which this book is printed meets the requirements of "ISO 9706:1994, Information and documentation - Paper for documents - Requirements for permanence".

ISBN: 978-90-420-3631-4
E-Book ISBN: 978-94-012-0901-4
© Editions Rodopi B.V., Amsterdam – New York, NY 2013
Printed in The Netherlands

Table of Contents

SECTION III
TRANSLATION AND CULTURAL REWRITING

SECTION IV
DIASPORAS, IDENTIFICATIONS, RESISTANCE

Acknowledgements

THIS VOLUME HAS ITS ORIGINS in the twentieth annual conference of GNEL/ASNEL (the Association for the Study of the New Literatures in English), which took place at the University of Münster, Germany, from 21 to 24 May 2009. We would like to thank our sponsors, the German Research Foundation (Deutsche Forschungsgemeinschaft, DFG), GNEL/ASNEL, the Routledge Annual Bibliography of English Studies, the Gesellschaft zur Förderung der Westfälischen Wilhelms-Universität zu Münster e.V., the School of Philology and the Internationalization Fund of the University of Münster, Sparkasse Münsterland Ost, and Fa. Laarmann, for their generous support.

We would also like to thank our contributors for their enthusiastic dedication to this book project. Mohini Chandra, Alana Jelinek, Martin Parker, Walid Raad, and Larissa Sansour have kindly granted permission to reproduce pictures. The cover design is based on a photograph and design idea by Lisa Paul.

The Technical Editor of ASNEL Papers and Cross/Cultures, Gordon Collier, has – as ever – worked beyond the call of duty, for which the editors are very grateful. Last but not least, we are indebted to the following people for their help with coordination, preliminary formatting, and copy-editing: Tabea Bergold, Jeyapriya Srieaswaranathan, Kerstin Strotmann, Heike Wessendorf, Natalie Wiertz, and most especially Daniel Blenke, who has been a particular source of reliability.

⌘

Illustrations and Permissions

⌘

Introduction: Directions of Translocation
— Towards a Critical Spatial Thinking
in Postcolonial Studies

MARGA MUNKELT, MARKUS SCHMITZ,
MARK STEIN, AND SILKE STROH

T HE SITES FROM WHICH POSTCOLONIAL ARTICULATIONS emerge
today and the sites at which they are consumed and in turn written
about are undergoing complex and profound changes that cannot be
accounted for exclusively in terms of colonization and decolonization. Cultural products emerge from ever more shifting grounds: Narrative fiction,
lyric poetry, drama, and film are created with a view to being marketed in
several languages and markets; authors and producers move from one geographical sphere to another; global audiences consume cultural products in
different locales, creating demands in several marketplaces; national borders
are fought over and redrawn, materially as well as textually, further undermining any sense of a stable location.

Postcolonial scholars read contemporary and historical texts across disparate geographic and temporal spaces. In the context of globalization and neo-
imperialisms, not only unequal development and political instability but also
violence and gender inequality continue to shape postcolonial realities. Nation
and narration, place and displacement, location and migration remain major
paradigms of postcolonial critique. The postcolonial lexicon, with terms such
as 'dislocation', 'migration', 'diaspora', 'exile', 'hybridity', 'third space', or
'transculturation', clearly indicates the concern of the field with placement,
movement, and interconnection.

An early occurrence of the terms 'translocal' and 'translocalism' can be
found in Don Martindale and R. Galen Hanson's *Small Town and the Nation*

(1969),[1] a sociological study which examines how traditional American ideals of far-reaching autonomy for small towns were challenged and renegotiated in relation to twentieth-century developments of increasing interdependence, economic and political centralization, and mass society. These processes are analysed through a case study of one particular small town. Martindale and Hanson use the terms 'translocal' and 'translocalism' in juxtaposition with local small-town autonomy, to signify all those developments which connect the small town to the wider world and subject it to "non-local" (19), "extra-community forces" (xv; see also 3, 8–9). Accordingly, 'translocalism' includes not only the international but also (and perhaps especially) the national level (xv; see also xiv). This study from the 1960s also discusses (then) recent developments in sociological theories of community which can be usefully related to later developments in the conceptualization of the relationship between location and identity. One of the most interesting points is an increasing dissociation of community from territoriality: i.e. territory is reduced to a merely "secondary (even at times dispensable) attribute of community" (11; see also 12–13).

More than forty years later, Ulrike Freitag and Achim von Oppen deploy 'translocality' as an intermediary term between 'local' and 'global' which, they argue, is especially suitable for studying connections that are instituted by non-dominant social actors – or by regional, cultural or national collectivities – beyond the 'North' and 'West'. Thus, Freitag and von Oppen distinguish 'translocality' from the concepts of globalization, transnationalism, and cosmopolitanism, which they consider to be too strongly associated with power elites, eurocentrism, and imperialism.[2] While the connection between the translocal and the non-dominant has been related by some to postcolonial studies, with its traditional emphasis on transcending Western/Northern perspectives and on hegemonic interpretative positions, others insist on the

---

[1] Don [Albert] Martindale & R[ussell] Galen Hanson, *Small Town and the Nation: The Conflict of Local and Translocal Forces* (Contributions in Sociology 3; Westport CT: Greenwood, 1969). Further page references are in the main text.

[2] Ulrike Freitag & Achim von Oppen, "Introduction: 'Translocality': An Approach to Connection and Transfer in Area Studies," in *Translocality: The Study of Globalising Processes from a Southern Perspective*, ed. Ulrike Freitag & Achim von Oppen (Studies in Global History 4; Leiden & Boston MA: Brill, 2010): 3–5, 10–12. See also 17–18.

continuing relevance and power effects of local configurations for an analysis of translocal phenomena.[3]

The conceptual frame and the title of the present volume have their origins in an international conference which took place at the University of Münster, Germany, from 21 to 24 May 2009. As the twentieth annual conference of the Association for the Study of the New Literatures in English (GNEL/ ASNEL), it aimed to investigate forms and functions of translocation in post-colonial cultural representations. The contributions to this book have been selected from papers which were presented and discussed at the conference. The conference location can be regarded as indicative of the changing parameters of identity in the contemporary world. In the early modern period, in 1648, Münster was one of the two cities where representatives of the European states signed the Treaty of Westphalia. Following the Thirty Years War, this European peace treaty established a 'Westphalian state system' founded on "the sovereign [...] (European) nation as the basic political unit."[4]

The notion of national territory and territorial integrity in general has increasingly functioned as a foundational reference-point for political and cultural loyalty and for international contact throughout much of modern history. While internal homogenization and community-building processes have created forms of translocation: i.e. a concentric sense of belonging to both one's

---

[3] For example, Tim Oakes & Louisa Schein, "Translocal China: An Introduction," in *Translocal China: Linkages, Identities, and the Reimagining of Space*, ed. Tim Oakes & Louisa Schein (Routledge Studies on China in Transition; London & New York: Routledge, 2006): 1–5, 7–9.

[4] Barnor Hesse, "Introduction: Un/Settled Multiculturalisms," in *Un/Settled Multiculturalisms: Diasporas, Entanglements, 'Transruptions'*, ed. Barnor Hesse (London: Zed, 2000): 20. See also S[alman] Sayyid, "Beyond Westphalia: Nations and Diasporas – the Case of the Muslim *Umma*," in *Un/Settled Multiculturalisms: Diasporas, Entanglements, 'Transruptions'*, ed. Barnor Hesse (London: Zed, 2000): 33–50; Ludger Pries, "The Approach of Transnational Social Spaces: Responding to New Configurations of the Social and the Spatial," in *New Transnational Social Spaces: International Migration and Transnational Companies in the Early Twenty-First Century*, ed. Ludger Pries (Routledge Research in Transnationalism 1; London & New York: Routledge, 2001): 3–4; and Dirk Hoerder, "Transcultural States, Nations, and People," in *The Historical Practice of Diversity: Transcultural Interactions from the Early Modern Mediterranean to the Postcolonial World*, ed. Christiane Harzig, Dirk Hoerder & Adrian Shubert (New York & Oxford: Berghahn, 2003): 21.

home town or region and the wider imagined community of the nation,[5] there have always been dynamics of translocation taking place not within, but across national boundaries. In the post-Westphalian, transnational world order, location often takes the form of translocation. Salman Sayyid suggests as much, though without using the term 'translocation' itself, when he writes:

> we are now living in a world of flows. [...] Globalization is one way of summing up the transition to this world of flows. It is a process that is intrinsically linked to the formation of dislocated communities; populations that no longer fit within the Westphalian 'container'. The container is unable to contain not only because of increased mobility but also because its own walls are becoming blurred.[6]

Similarly, Ludger Pries links contemporary trends towards transnationalism to the emergence of "pluri-locally spanned [...] social spaces."[7] In today's world, the work of the imagination: i.e. literature, the media, and other forms of cultural expression, play a crucial part in the creation of such pluri-local spaces:

> As the nation-state enters a terminal crisis [...], we can [...] expect that the materials for a post-national imaginary must be around us already. Here [...], we need to pay special attention to the relation between mass mediation and migration [...]. In particular, we need to look closely at [...] *diasporic public spheres*. Benedict Anderson did us a service in identifying the way in which certain forms of mass mediation [...] played a key role in imagining the nation [...]. There is a similar link [...] between [...] imagination and the emergence of a postnational political world."[8]

The arguably premature death-song for the nation-state notwithstanding, Arjun Appadurai's emphasis on the importance of migration and diaspora in transnational imaginaries also ties in with the lively interest in diaspora culture which is currently shown by the more general public and by academics

---

[5] Benedict Anderson, *Imagined Communities: Reflections on the Origin and Spread of Nationalism* (London: Verso, 1983). For a specific connection of these processes to the concept of 'translocation', see Oakes & Schein, "Translocal China," 4, 11.

[6] Sayyid, "Beyond Westphalia," 34. See also 35.

[7] Pries, "The Approach of Transnational Social Spaces," 3.

[8] Arjun Appadurai, *Modernity at Large: Cultural Dimensions of Globalization* (Public Worlds 1; Minneapolis & London: U of Minnesota P, 1996): 21–22.

(both in postcolonial studies and in other fields). The increase in cross-border migration, the new patterns arising from these crossings, and the formation of so-called transnational diasporic communities are widely acknowledged as some of the greatest political and cultural challenges at the beginning of the twenty-first century. These developments concern the nation-state and its institutions as much as transnational organizations and representatives of non-governmental organizations. The dynamics of transnational migration have also developed into central topoi of international discourses in the social sciences and the arts.[9]

Since the early 1980s, debates crucially shaped by migrant intellectuals have been exploring opportunities for cultural identification and political intervention outside of the nation's space–time. The search for alternative, decentred spheres of emancipatory alliances beyond conventional boundaries of ethnicity and national culture have repeatedly referenced older identity concepts such as W.E.B Du Bois's 'double-consciousness' model.[10] Meanwhile, the continual alternation between distinct strategic locations and the epistemological appreciation of marginalized diasporic perspectives have become preconditions of a postcolonial archaeology of modernity[11] and a contrapuntal completion of Western humanism.[12] The majority of scholars, however, dealing with the trope of migration in the widest sense, be it in literary studies, cultural studies, cultural anthropology, or sociolinguistics, continue to invest in an expanded critical adaptation of diasporic paradigms.[13] Notions of homeland as authentic origin or as a return destination in an essentialized cultural context have been superseded by more dynamic conceptions of abiding diasporic movements and identities. In this context, the continued hybridization and creolization of diasporic cultures have become points of departure for a transhistorical interrogation of essentialist notions of belong-

---

[9] See Linda Basch, Nina Glick Schiller & Cristina Szanton Blanc, *Nations Unbound: Transnational Projects, Postcolonial Predicaments, and Deterritorialized Nation-States* (Luxembourg: Gordon & Breach, 1994).

[10] W.E.B. Du Bois, *The Souls of Black Folk* (1903; New York: Vintage, 1990).

[11] Homi K. Bhabha, *The Location of Culture* (London & New York: Routledge, 1994).

[12] Edward W. Said, *Culture and Imperialism* (1993; New York: Vintage, 1994).

[13] For example, James Clifford, "Diasporas," *Cultural Anthropology* 9.3 (Summer 1994): 302–38; Paul Gilroy, "Diaspora," *Paragraph: A Journal of the Modern Critical Theory* 17.1 (March 1994): 207–12.

ing, both with respect to the hierarchical metropolitan model of centre and periphery and the ideologies of tricontinental nativists. Today, the lived experience of migration is considered beyond its geographico-spatial dimension – as a transgression of national ideology and discrete cultural norms.[14] While not underestimating important phenomena such as deterritorialization and globalization, a focus on home, on homeland, and on location more generally, points to the importance of emplacement – and its qualification by a homeland-and-return discourse.

The propositional contents of the concept 'translocation' overlap with but also clearly extend beyond the terms 'diaspora', 'transnationalism', 'globalization', 'transculturation', and 'multiculturalism', terms which themselves are undergoing intense scrutiny and semantic shifts. These concepts share more characteristics than their oft-berated opacity. All of them are related to praxes of social, cultural, and economic mobility across a variety of borders, seeking to address processes of cultural, political, and societal change. This implies that notions of stability of institutions and durability of conventions are being interrogated. All of these terms derive from highly charged arenas of cultural, political, secular, or religious debates, relating back to or indeed rejecting (notions of) homeland, nationalism, locality, assimilation, or monoculture.

Since the 1990s, a wide array of publications have sought to describe and make sense of the cross-border flow of humans, ideas, narratives, cultural goods, and commodities, searching for explanatory models no longer based on the unity and homogeneity of nation-states.[15] Our focus on translocal processes and phenomena, and on locations so marked, on translocations rather

---

[14] Ruth Mayer, *Diaspora: Eine kritische Begriffsbestimmung* (Bielefeld: transcript, 2005).

[15] Examples from anthropology, sociology, and migration studies are: Akhil Gupta, "The Song of the Nonaligned World: Transnational Identities and the Reinscription of Space in Late Capitalism," *Current Anthropology* 7.1 (February 1992): 63–77; Michael Kearney, "Borders and Boundaries of the State and Self at the End of Empire," *Journal of Historical Sociology* 4.1 (March 1991): 52–74; Roger Rouse, "Mexican Migration and the Social Space of Postmodernism," *Diaspora* 1.1 (Spring 1991): 8–23; Roger Rouse, "Making Sense of Settlement: Class Transformation, Cultural Struggle, and Transnationalism Among Mexican Migrants in the United States," in *Towards a Transnational Perspective on Migration: Race, Class, Ethnicity, and Nationalism Reconsidered*, ed. Nina Glick Schiller, Linda Basch & Cristina Blanc–Szanton (New York: New York Academy of Sciences, 1992): 25–52.

than the *condition* of translocality, to a certain degree chimes with a current development in diaspora studies. According to one prominent scholar, this re-invigorated field can be subdivided into four distinct phases: the sociologist Robin Cohen considers this current, fourth phase to constitute a consolidation stage. Following William Safran,[16] Cohen considers the classical or proto-typical diaspora concept to have undergone a phase of considerable expansion and to have turned into "a metaphoric designation" followed by a phase of "social constructionist critiques of diaspora"[17] before entering the current path of consolidation. Both the concept of a homeland and the notion of ethnic or religious communities were severely critiqued, opening up the diaspora concept further to wide, postmodern usage. "Social constructionist critiques were partially accommodated,"[18] writes Cohen. With acute wit, Rogers Brubaker describes the formidable semantic, conceptual, as well as disciplinary expansion and dispersion of the diaspora concept, tagging it a "'diaspora' diaspora."[19] Nevertheless, three core elements remain, according to Brubaker: "The first is [voluntary or forced] dispersion in space; the second, orientation to a 'homeland'; and the third, boundary-maintenance."[20] This strategic move of acknowledging the concept's breathtaking career and the (often very fruitful) expansions of its meaning, combined with an emphasis on the continuing importance of its original key elements, is what Cohen convincingly refers to as a consolidation.

Despite the continued importance of homelands and boundaries, recent developments in diaspora studies have increasingly highlighted those dimensions of diaspora which transcend boundaries and localities – dimensions which also play a crucial part in the "cultural dynamics of [...] deterritorialization"[21] which Appadurai identifies as a key field of inquiry. A "fresh

---

[16] For example, William Safran, "Diasporas in Modern Societies: Myths of Homeland and Return," in *Migration, Diasporas and Transnationalism*, ed. Steven Vertovec & Robin Cohen (Cheltenham: Edward Elgar, 1999): 365–80.

[17] Robin Cohen, *Global Diasporas: An Introduction* (London: Francis & Taylor, 2nd ed. 2008): 1.

[18] Cohen, *Global Diasporas*, 2.

[19] Rogers Brubaker, "The 'Diaspora' Diaspora," *Ethnic and Racial Studies* 28.1 (January 2005): 1–19, http://dx.doi.org/10.1080/0141987042000289997 (accessed 10 November 2011).

[20] Brubaker, "The 'Diaspora' Diaspora," 5.

[21] Appadurai, *Modernity at Large*, 49.

approach to the role of the imagination in social life" is indeed necessary in order to understand "the nature of locality as a lived experience in a globalized, deterritorialized world."[22] This is not only relevant with regard to Appadurai's own discipline of anthropology, but also to literary and cultural studies.[23] Here, the study of diasporic, postcolonial, and transnational literatures and cultures can make an important contribution. Thus, one of the aims of this book is to build bridges between spatial theory and the emerging concept of the translocal, on the one hand, and literary and cultural studies, on the other, by spatializing colonial and postcolonial cultural articulations.

This collection explores cultural products in their spatiality and locatedness, but it also envisages location as a dynamic process. It argues the case for establishing space more firmly and explicitly as an analytic paradigm in postcolonial studies. Moreover, it highlights the contribution of postcolonial criticism to changing concepts of space in today's globalized, transcultural world. The present introductory essay provides a preliminary sketch of concepts, connections, texts, and hypotheses. Exploring, from various angles, the uses and limits of 'translocation' as an open explanatory model for a critically spatialized postcolonial studies, it traces the spectrum of possible research directions in postcolonial translocations. Rather than a comprehensive overview or a set research agenda, this introduction should be regarded as a critical intervention designed to fuel further discussion.

1. Man and the Meanings of Translocation: Etymology, Semantics, Philosophy

The existing and evolving meanings of both 'trans-' and 'location', dependent as they are on the presence of real or imagined lines and borders, or places and spaces, denote and connote actions or sufferings of human beings. Moreover, their literal and metaphorical implications can be past- or future-oriented. The most basic alternative denotations of the term waver between unidirectional changes as opposed to multiple crossings and between crossing a line vs a space or area; 'translocation' can also indicate the results of being exiled, of not belonging, or of intermingling: i.e. fostering a productive change or transformation. Other views may be dependent on the assessment

---

[22] *Modernity at Large*, 52. See also 53, 58.

[23] This was noted by Appadurai himself; see, for example, *Modernity at Large*, 48–52, 61, 63–64.

of a human being's trans-action as a voluntary or enforced act, as a violent act or something suffered, or merely as an observed event without personal involvement.

An examination of the term 'translocation' necessitates the obvious: a separate look at the semantics and etymology of its two components, the prefix 'trans-' and the noun 'location'. Both have multiple meanings. The two definitions of 'trans' depend on its syntactic usage, and, according to the *OED*,[24] 'trans' means "across" or "beyond" when used with adjectives, but "into another place or state" when used with verbs. Similarly, the origin of 'location' is the formation of a noun of action from the Latin verb *locare* (= to locate) and can signify, among others, "The action of placing" (2.a.), "Place of settlement or residence" (6.), "The action of discovering" (7.). The selected meanings cited reveal that the main distinction is between "place or position," on the one hand, and "the action of marking or placing," on the other. Each part of 'translocation', has, thus, a stationary and a mobile meaning, and both are inextricably linked with either the positions or the activities of human beings. And 'translocation' is inevitably tied to places and spaces.

It follows that places exist only as created, shaped, and defined by human beings.[25] Thus, in contrast to the notion of space as something abstract,[26] place is not only a concrete and physical reality but also person-related – that is, subjective: Spaces become places when they are made "meaningful" by people. As the cultural geographer Tim Cresswell concludes, "this is the most straightforward and common definition of place – a meaningful location."[27] The sense of relativity is indirectly confirmed by Ulf Heuner, who distinguishes absolute space from relative space, using the latter in the sense of Cresswell's 'place' and connecting it with time.[28] Additionally, Heuner emphasizes the recent theoretical and political concerns with 'space' as a social category – especially in trade and travel or electronic communication.[29] In his

---

[24] *The Oxford English Dictionary* (2nd ed. 1989) s.v. 'trans-, *prefix*' and 'location, *n.*'. Further references are in the main text.

[25] See also Tim Cresswell, *Place: A Short Introduction* (Oxford & Malden MA: Blackwell, 2004): 1–14.

[26] Cresswell, *Place: A Short Introduction*, 8.

[27] *Place: A Short Introduction*, 7.

[28] Ulf Heuner, "Die Wiederentdeckung des Raumes," in *Klassische Texte zum Raum*, ed. Ulf Heuner (Berlin: Parodos, 2008): 7.

[29] Heuner, "Die Wiederentdeckung des Raumes," 8.

xxii   POSTCOLONIAL TRANSLOCATIONS   ⌘

classification of space into objective, subjective, and abstract space,[30] the subjective type of space is the only one that can be experienced[31] and is therefore meaning-making in Cresswell's sense.

Although Cresswell's and Heuner's elaborations are recent, the basic ideas are not newborn but, rather, revive sixteenth-century discussions of the universe (based on classical concepts) that were refined in the seventeenth and eighteenth centuries. Of interest is whether man's (or woman's) meaning-making reaches beyond him- or herself to touch other humans, places, spaces, and times. The association of etymology and semantics with metaphysical concepts and philosophical explications is reflected in varying, if not contradictory, thoughts about what it is that 'trans' refers to: Is it a border, boundary, limit, margin, or line? Is it an area, land, or space? And how can such a 'space' that is not a place be crossed and thereby possibly be changed? The earliest etymological eighteenth-century dictionary[32] includes a differentiation of absolute and relative motion and their speed. It is a fact that the original meaning of space – *spatium* – denotes a distance or gap in both measurement systems, and the motion of crossing (either to and fro or in only one direction), breaking through, overcoming, or connecting that 'gap' or 'distance' is entirely dependent on the activities of human beings.

The inherent qualities of 'trans'-compounds as being both static and dynamic, stationary and mobile, emanate from scientific and philosophical arguments concerning time and place as the components of space, and also concerning space as a phenomenon whose essence may be independent of both. It is crucial whether man is understood to possess the faculty of independent agency. In other words, the controversy concerns man's influential bringing about a 'motion' (i.e. change) or allowing it or becoming part of it (i.e. abandoning all agency). As Thomas A. Spragens, Jr. summarizes it, according to Aristotle, "all motion must involve agency,"[33] whereas Thomas Hobbes's

---

[30] See also the sub-section "Social Fabrications and Contested Terrains: Human Geography," below.

[31] "Die Wiederentdeckung des Raumes," 9.

[32] Nathan Bailey, *An Universal Etymological English Dictionary* (1721; Anglistica & Americana 52; Hildesheim & New York: Georg Olms, 1969) s.v. SPACE, MOTION (and related entries).

[33] Thomas A. Spragens, Jr., *The Politics of Motion: The World of Thomas Hobbes* (London: Croom Helm, 1973): 57.

"model of motion"[34] reduces the influential role of man by integrating him into a geometrical system, in which 'motion' is "nothing but change of place."[35] Hobbes further insists that "motion [...] is not resisted by rest, but by contrary motion."[36] Implicitly, this view doubts the static or stationary quality of 'location'. According to this theory, the impression of rest is a human deception – an idea approved of by George Berkeley: "It may be, that none of those Bodies which seem to be quiescent, are truly so: And the same thing which is moved relatively, may be really at rest."[37] Typical of the scholarly and fictional works in the Age of Enlightenment, Berkeley, supporting John Locke,[38] refutes those scholars who focus on man's being able to understand his environment through the senses, through perception rather than through abstract thinking.[39] Berkeley follows Locke's theory that "there is an *absolute Space*, which, being unperceivable to Sense, remains in it self similar and immoveable" and that "Place [is] that part of Space which is occupied by any Body."[40] Berkeley's judgment, "The Place being moved, that which is placed therein is also moved: So that a Body moving in a Place which is in Motion, doth participate the Motion of its Place,"[41] coincides with Locke's view that only relative motion or space can be perceived by man,[42] but also that space and time are inseparable.

---

[34] Spragens, *The Politics of Motion*, 59.

[35] Thomas Hobbes, *The English Works of Thomas Hobbes*, ed. William Molesworth, vol. 7 (1839–45; London: Scientia Aalen, 1962): 83–84. See also Spragens, *The Politics of Motion*, 63.

[36] Hobbes, *The English Works of Thomas Hobbes*, vol. 1: 125. See also Spragens, *The Politics of Motion*, 65.

[37] George Berkeley, *A Treatise Concerning the Principles of Human Knowledge* (1710, repr. 1734; Menston: Scolar P, 1971): 130.

[38] See John Locke, *An Essay Concerning Human Understanding*, ed. Peter H. Nidditch (1690; Oxford: Clarendon, 1975).

[39] Berkeley, *A Treatise Concerning the Principles of Human Knowledge*, 13–16.

[40] *A Treatise Concerning the Principles of Human Knowledge*, 130.

[41] *A Treatise Concerning the Principles of Human Knowledge*, 130–31.

[42] Locke, *An Essay Concerning Human Understanding*, 172. See also Berkeley, *A Treatise Concerning the Principles of Human Knowledge*: "For as hath been already observed, absolute Motion exclusive of all external Relation is incomprehensible. [...] For to denominate a Body *moved*, it is requisite, first, that it changes its Distance or Situation with regard to some other Body" (133–34).

Embedded in artistic concepts, a yoking of time and space is advocated and re-phrased by Mikhail Bakhtin, whose creation of the term 'chronotope' means 'time-space'.[43] But Bakhtin, in his discussion of narrative fiction, is particularly concerned with the motions of an individual whose "wanderings" result in his transformation or metamorphosis.[44] The scope and size of epics or novels encourage a presentation of making experiences by long-term 'wanderings' about the world. Homer's epics as well as the exodus in the Old Testament are the most prominent and influential examples, but also many nineteenth-century novels illustrate this connection between walking, the passage of time and space, and the sense of making new experiences by means of 'transgression'. Ulysses' exploration of other countries, for example, entails a new form of self-recognition, and in Thomas Hardy's novel *Jude the Obscure* (1894–95), the two protagonists' non-voluntary walking and crossing of boundaries (geographical, physical, social) within their own country is enforced by the relentlessness of social and religious conventions. In Rudolfo Anaya's most recent novel, *Randy Lopez Goes Home* (2011), the protagonist watches a tarantula cross a road and asks himself: "Why was it crossing the road? Time on the other side was the same as time on this side. Or was it?"[45] – thus phrasing the basic competition of space and time to grasp reality.

The aforementioned distinction between space and place illustrates an underlying principle of much colonial discourse: Colonial lands were often treated as 'vast empty spaces' to be there for the colonizer's taking – as *terra nullius*.[46] Protocolonial space was perceived as unoccupied, or at least it was not occupied by anything or anyone (local flora, fauna, or human population) that was regarded by the colonizer as an occupant worth mentioning, let alone

---

[43] Mikhail M. Bakhtin, "Forms of Time and of the Chronotope in the Novel: Notes toward a Historical Poetics" (1937–38), tr. Caryl Emerson & Michael Holquist, in *Problems of Literature and Esthetics* (*Voprosy literatury i estetiki*, 1975), repr. in *The Dialogic Imagination: Four Essays by M.M. Bakhtin*, ed. Michael Holquist (U of Texas Slavic Series 1; Austin: U of Texas P, 1981): 84.

[44] Bakhtin, "Forms of Time and of the Chronotope in the Novel," 111–12.

[45] Rudolfo Anaya, *Randy Lopez Goes Home: A Novel* (Norman: U of Oklahoma P, 2011): 4.

[46] As George Berkeley put it in 1710 (in general, not merely colonial, terms), "When I excite a Motion [...], if it be free or without Resistance, I say there is *Space:* But if I find a Resistance, then I say there is *Body*," and a "part of Space which is occupied by any Body" is defined as "Place" (*A Treatise Concerning the Principles of Human Knowledge*, 135, 130).

respecting. For example, traditional patterns of land-occupation among in-digenous populations in North America or Australia were discounted regular-ly by European colonizers because they did not correspond to European capitalist patterns of permanent, non-nomadic agricultural land use, private property, and clearly demarcated borders of occupied land patches. European occupation was thus considered justified because it was regarded as the only way in which these lands could be made 'fully productive' according to Euro-pean standards. Colonization of those 'vast empty spaces' took place in dis-regard of existing human populations or the existing natural environment, and usually entailed a radical transformation, or even total destruction, of these populations and environments by the colonial encounter. Only occupation and settlement by the colonizer could, according to the latter's perspective, trans-form the colony from (empty, unoccupied) 'space' to ('properly') occupied 'place'.

By contrast, other non-European colonial populations were considered to be more serious antagonists and occupants to be reckoned with. This was, for instance, the case in India, where local societies often showed greater resem-blance to European models in social organization, land use, urbanization, or large-scale state apparatuses. European discourses thus often elevated Asian colonial populations from the utterly debased rank of 'savage' to the already somewhat higher rank of 'barbarian' – still allegedly more 'primitive' than Europeans, but already possessed of some form of 'civilization' and thus more amenable to further 'improvement' and (europeanizing) 'progress'.[47] While the rights of the colonized were regularly discounted by the colonizer, their lands were not usually textualized as 'vast empty spaces' but were cate-gorized as 'places': i.e. as already occupied – although indigenous occupants and rights were regarded as inferior on account of their 'backwardness'.

The construct of *terra nullius* illustrates the manifold ways in which dif-ferent cultural perceptions, clashing material interests, and unequal power-relations have shaped the discursive and material construction of geographical

---

[47] An example of the tripartite division into savagery, barbarism, and civilization is Henry Smith Williams, "Anthropology," in the *Encyclopaedia Britannica*, 11th ed. vol. 6 (Cambridge: Cambridge U P 1910): 403–10. This division is discussed in, for ex-ample, Robert J.C. Young, *Colonial Desire: Hybridity in Theory, Culture and Race* (London & New York: Routledge 1995): 34–35. On the position of Asian peoples in such systems of categorization, see, for example, Cary J. Nederman & Takashi Shōgi-men, *Western Political Thought in Dialogue with Asia* (Lanham M D & Plymouth: Lexington 2009): 76–77.

and social spaces in colonial (but also in neocolonial) contexts. Similarly, the widespread strategy of conflating spatial and cultural distance with temporal distance, by assuming a universal teleology of historical and civilizational progress, has been instrumentalized to place Europe at the top and assign indigenous cultures of the colonies to various 'inferior' levels from where they still need to 'further develop' in order to reach the 'superior', 'more advanced' European norm. Colonized cultures thus appear as 'contemporary ancestors' that illustrate a more primitive stage of human development which Europe also once went through, but which it already left behind centuries or even millennia before. Geographical and cultural difference is thus translated into temporal/historical difference.

Although the cultural hierarchies and binarisms constructed by colonial discourse often seem to entail a clear border between Self and Other or colonizer and colonized, a border that is conceptual as well as territorial (metropolitan vs peripheral space, 'mother country' vs colony), the colonial project can in fact entail a transgression of spatial or cultural boundaries and a deterritorialization of spaces and identities which are characteristic of translocation processes. The ships and sea-voyages which were so central to many ancient and modern empires can be seen as classical spaces and vehicles of translocation. Gilles Deleuze and Félix Guattari regard the sea as a deterritorialized space par excellence, despite tendencies in the inverse direction where states seek control of the sea – for instance, through cartography and 'fleets in being'.[48] Michel Foucault specifies the dual function of the boat as a vehicle of physical and of metaphorical movement:

> the boat is a floating piece of space, a place without a place, that exists by itself, that is closed in on itself and at the same time is given over to the infinity of the sea and that [...] goes as far as the colonies [...]. The boat has been for our civilization, from the sixteenth century until the present, the great instrument of economic development [...], but has been simultaneously the greatest resource of the imagination. The ship is the heterotopia *par excellence*.[49]

---

[48] Gilles Deleuze & Félix Guattari, *A Thousand Plateaus: Capitalism and Schizophrenia*, tr. Brian Massumi (*Capitalisme et schizophrénie* 2: *Mille plateaux*, 1980; tr. 1988; London & New York: Continuum, 2004): 426–27, 524, 529–30, 551, 559–60, 623–24.

[49] Michel Foucault, "Of Other Spaces," tr. Jay Miskowiec ("Des espaces autres," in *Architecture – Mouvement – Continuité*, 1984), *Diacritics* 16.1 (Spring 1986): 27.

This concept is, if not explicitly, touched on by Gesa Mackenthun's discussion, in the present volume, of Herman Melville's *Moby-Dick*, where, despite their "ethnic and cultural differences," the sailors on Ahab's ship are "united by some metaphysical force."

In the migrations of British colonial settlers, the enclosedness of the ship and the attempt to build self-enclosed British communities after the ship's arrival in 'new' lands was connected to the illusion that cultures and societies could indeed be transplanted (or translocated) wholesale from one geographical location to another without significant modification. Colonies can thus be regarded as translocations where several spaces are brought (often conflictually) into contact with each other. One could say, with Descartes, that, geographically, the settlers had moved, whereas (because their thinking defined their cultural coordinates as fixed) in cultural terms, they had not moved; in other words, the British cultural space was perceived to extend throughout the global empire. The ambivalence of the ship as both a self-enclosed unit and a mobile unit in relation to other (and sometimes very distant) places, and its heterotopian character, can also be related to Descartes' use of the ship as a prime example to illustrate the relativity of location and movement: i.e. the fact that ideas of location, locatedness, and movement are dependent on our (selective) perception.[50]

Representations and practices of location, translocation, and space have played a crucial part in colonial and postcolonial histories and discourses. The building of empires rests on an expansion of space, and a struggle for control over space. Early stages of empire-building often entail an extension of conceptual space, or of known space. Travellers and explorers discovered hitherto unknown (or little-known) territories for themselves and for the societies they came from, produced texts and maps that charted these territories, and thus often laid important foundations for the establishment of more permanent links between their own societies and the new, foreign territories they had seen. These connections could take the form of commerce, the establishment of small trading colonies, and economic empires. They could also entail more formal control over 'alien' territory through political and administrative imperialism (as in the British case) and the establishment of full-blown (and often larger-scale) territorial colonies. The individual sense of freedom

---

[50] See René Descartes, *Principles of Philosophy*, tr. Valentine Rodger Miller & Reese P. Miller (*Principia Philosophiae*, 1644; tr. 1983; Dordrecht: Kluwer, 1991): 45.

implied in travel and mobility can easily collide with restrictive and violent practices of political and economic authorities.

In addition to the material and conceptual centrality of ships to colonial translocations, other forms of communication and traffic that have helped to shrink geographical distances and created translocations also need to be acknowledged. Next to maritime connections, it is road construction whose value in empire-building was famously recognized as early as Classical Antiquity, as its significance to the Roman Empire testifies. More recent examples include the infrastructural developments that facilitated internal colonialism in the British Isles, as in the eighteenth-century road-construction projects that helped to integrate the 'Celtic fringe' into an anglocentric modern nation-state.

The European Industrial Revolution of the nineteenth century not only effected a crucial transformation of shipping technology (through the creation of steamships that significantly reduced the duration and risks of long-distance travel and transport); it contributed further vital innovations in transport and communication that have laid foundations of the deterritorialized and globalized world we live and move in today. Among these nineteenth-century innovations, the railway effected both intra-national integration (connecting Britain's outlying 'fringes' and rural regions to London and other centres) and colonial integration (the building of railways in Africa and India). Sometimes the railway could help to bring new colonial territories more closely under control; in Canada, the westward expansion of white settlement was closely connected to the extension of the rail network in the same direction.

Socio-economic, political, and cultural transformations like decolonization and postcolonial migration have initiated and fostered further expansions and refinements of the term 'translocation'. The contributors to the present volume illustrate the great variety of its inherent and ascribed meanings. This is done, on the one hand, by deductive reasoning through analytical and critical applications of the term (and its elaboration) to a body of literature; and this is done, on the other hand, by attempted definitions that direct the textual approach and possibly result in modifications and adjustments of the term itself. Noticeably, the emphases are on either time or place or on a combination of both – not unlike the standard definitions of space. Moreover, the static or mobile qualities of translocation are negotiated to different degrees.

The notion of 'translocation' has also been used in theoretical physics. In covariant quantum field theory, translocal structures are considered effects of pluri-directional interrelations between partial energy fields. Although not detectable by traditional methods of empirical observation, these structures carry the totality of non-local kinematic information in a local region. Accordingly, traceable local procedures and their physically admissible representations do not exhaust the entire set of all dynamic procedures in a local interior sector.[51] On the level of empirical short-distance scaling, the theoretical crossover from local properties to translocal properties and the complex correlation of local observations and translocal dynamics create significant "confusion concerning the substantial identification of local properties."[52] What causes "confusion" for the scientific description of a physical system, however, provides an enriching perspective for those attempting to describe cultural translocations. Just like a physical body, a cultural representation, while being recognizable only in concrete local contexts, can carry the information of multiple correlations which go beyond the local setting. The present volume addresses precisely such pluri-local overlaps. In various ways, the contributions address postcolonial locations which cannot be grasped as coordinates in a global field of cultural articulations. They are, rather, described as places of continuing translocation – transient locations from where to see the local observing gaze as well as positionalities that cannot necessarily be steadily localized.[53] A critical consciousness of postcolonial translocations therefore requires a doubling of scepticism: first, towards the notion that scholars occupy a fixed cultural and geographical location; and, secondly, towards attempts to firmly locate objects and narratives which are in motion.

Among the contributors to this collection who attempt definitions or re-definitions, the distinction of 'translocation' either as a condition or as a process is abandoned by Lucia Krämer and developed into a concept of 'trans-locality' as the quality of "being in several places at the same time" and, when applied to Hari Kunzru's novel *Transmission*, modified into a "drawing together and pulling apart." Interconnectedness is thereby assumed to be the meaning of 'trans' (i.e. 'inter' rather than 'over' or 'across'). With a slightly different focus, Katharina Rennhak discusses "border transgressions" and "constitutive transformations" with 'trans' meaning 'within' or 'among'

---

[51] Hadi Salehi, "Translocality and a Duality Principle in Generally Covariant Quantum Field Theory," *Classical and Quantum Gravity* 17.4 (December 2000): 825–34.

[52] Salehi, "Translocality and a Duality Principle in Generally Covariant Quantum Field Theory," 834.

[53] Peter Sloterdijk, *Im Weltinnenraum des Kapitals: Für eine philosophische Theorie der Globalisierung* (Frankfurt am Main: Suhrkamp, 2006): 218.

(rather than either 'across' or 'inter'); the static quality is, according to Renn-hak, an emphasis on the "social space" created by translocation. Daria Tunca embeds her discussion of Chris Abani in the semantics of 'trans'-concepts like 'transgendering' or 'transgression'. The meaning of 'trans' as 'across, over, through' is extended by Tunca beyond the sense of violation or violence into a figurative "working through" for "overcoming trauma."

The quality of fluidity in translocation is pursued by Paloma Fresno–Calleja with two dominant meanings, "place" and "be/longing," thus giving a prominent role to people's sense of community and their "diverse degrees of be/longing." Lynda Ng illustrates the shift of meanings when 'trans' is com-pounded with 'new' words. Thus, the literal translation of 'translocal' as 'across (or beyond) the local' receives new meanings: "integration of global-ization processes into localized systems" as well as "constant movement of people and cultures across national borders." Quoting Arif Dirlik, Ng inter-prets the translocal as a mixture of realms. Here, both possible usages of 'trans' as 'inter' – i.e. within and in between – find application, but, even more importantly, result in something new. Silke Stroh's view is also oriented towards the semantics of 'space' – much more than the basic definition of movement "from one place to another" and also much more than a one-way dislocation but, rather, as a phenomenon of multiple changes. Stroh favours Jacob Edmond's[54] metaphysical use of 'translocation' as "shared location" even without "physical proximity." According to Stroh, transnationalism and transculturalism, similar to Ng's use of the translocal, imply a sense of inter-mingling and sharing "similarities in outlook and experience," of community.

Dirk Wiemann understands the term 'translocal' in relation to cosmopoli-tan ideas of transcending spatial distances and cultural boundaries. This sense is not unlike Gesa Mackenthun's interpretation of 'melting' as an image ex-pressing the "collapse of cultural difference" in Herman Melville's *Moby-Dick*. In Marga Munkelt's essay, 'translocation' implies a passage of myths and traditions not only across borders and continents, civilizations, and cul-tures but also through time. Roland Walter's contribution interprets the act of black diasporic writing itself as the resistive creation of a translocal identi-tarian space across the Americas. Markus Schmitz presents artistic–literary

---

[54] See Jacob Edmond, "A Poetics of Translocation: Yang Lian's Auckland and Lyn Hejinian's Leningrad," in *Cultural Transformations: Perspectives on Translocation in a Global Age*, ed. Chris Prentice, Vijay Devadas & Henry Johnson (Cross/Cultures 125; Amsterdam & New York: Rodopi, 2010): 105–34.

articulations of cross-cultural collisions that allow for a critical rethinking of our provisional historical and epistemic location in correlation with other locations. And Claudia Perner argues for epistemically translocating the sub-field of literary imagology by going beyond its essentialist eurocentric foundations. Starting from the changing relations of inquiry and responsibility, and drawing on diverse fictional imaginings as well as theoretical interventions from disparate fields, Diana Brydon even goes one step further: She argues for a critically "translocated postcolonialism" that radically questions the use of what she calls "zombie categories" (such as decolonization) – concepts which, in her view, impede an adequate engagement with the socio-political challenges of the twenty-first century.

2. Crossing Boundaries: Language, Literature, Canon

Similar to the multiple meanings of 'trans-', the prefix 'ex-' suggests a motion out of a territory, land, or field, but an 'ex-' from one side may imply an 'into' or 're-' on the other. It is this ambivalence that Edward Said addresses when he associates exile and banishment: "Once banished, the exile lives an anomalous and miserable life, with the stigma of being an outsider,"[55] but "exiles also cross borders, break barriers of thought and experience" (185): i.e. perform actions of liberation and independence. Said additionally recognizes the contradictory implications of borders: "Borders and barriers, which enclose us within the safety of familiar territory, can also become prisons" (185). The suffering of exiles and their feeling of loss (i.e. alienation from "language, poetic convention, or life-history" [175]), however, can be outbalanced by the experience of enrichment:

> Most people are principally aware of one culture, one setting, one home; exiles are aware of at least two, and their plurality of vision gives rise to an awareness of simultaneous dimensions, an awareness that – to borrow a phrase from music – is *contrapuntal*. (186)

The provisional paradigm of 'translocation' can help to further conceptualize and differentiate this contrapuntal or blurred awareness of national and cultural belonging expressed in the terms 'transnationalism' and 'transmigra-

---

[55] Edward W. Said, "Reflections on Exile," in *Reflections on Exile and Other Essays* (Cambridge MA: Harvard UP, 2000): 181. Further page references are in the main text.

tion'. In their important 1994 study, the anthropologists Linda Basch, Nina Glick Schiller, and Cristina Szanton Blanc suggest a definition of transnationalism which enables them to "analyze the 'lived' and fluid experiences of individuals who act in ways that challenge our previous conflation of geographic space and social identity."[56] The proposed definition makes visible how "transmigrants are transformed by their transnational practices" (5). Significantly, transmigration as a practice has a bearing on more than one location, and whereas transnationalism primarily hinges on the crossing of state borders, translocation occurs across a range of borders, be they of continents, nation-states, regions, mega-cities, towns, or, indeed, rural spaces. But, because "most transmigrants have neither fully conceptualized nor articulated a form of transnational identity" (5), it is, according to Basch et al., "only in contemporary fiction [...] that this state of 'in-betweenness' has been fully voiced" (5).

A few contemporary 'voices' may illustrate this view: Grace Nichols's short poem "Skanking Englishman between trains"[57] speaks of a chance encounter at Birmingham train station,[58] where the speaker comes across an Englishman whom she describes with the verb "skanking," i.e. by a specifically Caribbean style of dancing to reggae music. The poem makes clear that this "small yellow hair" man (33) is, on the one hand, resident in England but is, on the other, connected, and not just in the way he dances, to Caribbean rhythms, and, in effect, inhabits both cultural spaces at once – translocally. His palate, too, has been creolized in more ways than one, linguistically and culinarily: He has forgotten English food, is spoiled by "me peas and rice," and shares the Caribbean idiom with the poem's speaker (33). Inhabiting a translocation, "he was alive / he was full-o-jive / said he had a lovely Jamaican wife" (33).

---

[56] "Introduction" to *Nations Unbound: Transnational Projects, Postcolonial Predicaments, and Deterritorialized Nation-States*, ed. Linda Basch, Nina Glick Schiller & Cristina Szanton Blanc (Luxembourg: Gordon & Breach, 1994): 5. Further page references are in the main text.

[57] Grace Nichols, "Skanking Englishman Between Trains," in *The Fat Black Woman's Poems* (London: Virago, 1984): 33. Further page references are in the main text.

[58] Not unlike Arjun Appadurai, for Ulf Hannerz 'translocality' denotes heightened mobility, "world cities," and "sites with a lot of transciency." See Ulf Hannerz, "Transnational Research," in *Handbook of Methods in Cultural Anthropology*, ed. H. Russell Bernard (London & New Delhi: AltaMira, 1998): 239.

In Pauline Melville's short story "The Truth is in the Clothes,"[59] a Caribbean migrant resident in London discovers a door in her Camberwell flat which allows her direct access to her home country of Jamaica. Both the skanking Englishman and the woman with a touch of magic do not simply carry 'an elsewhere' in their heads: translocation gives their connection with the Caribbean a material grounding, it becomes a part of their lived existence rather than just a reference to an 'imaginary homeland'. In the case of the Englishman, in particular, this part can even be observed and communicated by others. In the case of Melville, the eponymous figure of the 'shape-shifter' also becomes a 'space-shifter', a forger of translocal connections.

Set in the cramped space of a one-room eatery in Hackney, north-east London, Kwame Kwei–Armah's West-End success *Elmina's Kitchen*[60] resonates with translocation throughout, although the setting might at first sight impede this. *Elmina's Kitchen* is not just the name of a Caribbean café, in turn commemorating the late founder of the establishment; the title also refers us back to the oldest European building in sub-Saharan Africa, the slave fortress Elmina Castle (now in Ghana), which stands for the violent dislocation of enslaved Africans to the New World. In the past, Deli has had trouble with the law and he now tries to run his life and his restaurant as models of honest conduct, setting an example to his juvenile son; Ashley is at first torn between his reformed father and bad-man Digger. Deli's father, the calypso-singing transmigrant trader Clifton, represents the circulating populations that pass through mega-cities like London and connect them, through their itineraries, with different points on the globe, urban or not. He passes through Elmina's Kitchen regularly to sell his Caribbean wares (and jive) to an eager audience. In a highly condensed translocal space which connects him to different generations of his family, to ancestries in the Caribbean and Africa, to different ways of living in multicultural London, Ashley nevertheless chooses Digger's flamboyant material success (achieved by way of extortion and drug dealing) over his father's moral integrity. History seems to repeat itself, as Ashley cannot extricate himself from his father's and uncle's former lives of crime.[61]

---

[59] Pauline Melville, "The Truth Is in the Clothes," in *Shape-Shifter: Stories* (London: Picador, 1991): 99–112.

[60] Kwame Kwei–Armah, *Elmina's Kitchen* (London: Methuen, 2003).

[61] Mark Stein, "Translokation und Gedächtnis: *Elmina's Kitchen* von Kwame Kwei–Armah im Kontext des Black Atlantic," in *Literatur und Migration*, ed. Heinz

Finally, the bestselling 9/11-novel *The Reluctant Fundamentalist* relies on the constant transgression of boundaries, in particular between Lahore and New York City. The novel's foregrounded translocal qualities would seem to underscore the fact that the life-story of the eponymous reluctant fundamentalist cannot be reconstructed without a constant criss-crossing of those cultural and national borders on which the story-line in turn relies. One example is the interconnection of the world of education and the global marketplace. The language of commerce subtly conveying his reproach, Changez was "sourced from around the globe"[62] along with fellow international students at Princeton University, "sifted" (4), selected, and consequently "expected to contribute our talents to your society" (152).

Carefully balancing gaps and clues, Mohsin Hamid teases his readers with the question of who in the final analysis can be considered the reluctant fundamentalist – the bearded Changez or the muted American who seems to have come after him in Lahore? Given his Ivy-League provenance, his high-flying career in New York, and his love of the elusive Erica, Changez' life is intricately bound up with the USA. But as his disaffection builds up, and after the hostile responses he endures from the attacks on the Twin Towers onwards, he attempts to free himself of Erica's and of America's attractions. He is compelled to disengage himself from the West and to renew his identification with his home – America's enemy – Pakistan. Changez no longer wants to be "a modern-day janissary, a servant of the American empire" when apparently his "own country faced the threat of war" (152). Changez's experience of translocation does not represent him as unmoored. On the contrary, his moorings tie him to more places than one, and it is the complexity of filiations and affiliations that makes this a key element of his experience.

Apart from the variety of literary practices which give voice to or paint the characters' sense (or its absence) of being 'translocated', there have been many attempts at grasping this condition theoretically. Said's "plurality of vision" and Gloria Anzaldúa's "life *sin fronteras*"[63] have particularly encouraged innovative approaches to traditional categories, classification systems,

---

Ludwig Arnold (special issue of *Text + Kritik* 9; Munich: edition text + kritik, 2006): 246–54.

[62] Mohsin Hamid, *The Reluctant Fundamentalist* (London: Hamish Hamilton, 2007): 4. Further page references are in the main text.

[63] See Gloria Anzaldúa, *Borderlands/La Frontera: The New Mestiza* (1987; San Francisco: Aunt Lute, 3rd ed. 2007): 34. Further page references are in the main text.

and conventions or rules of various kinds – also to the theory of Western literature.

The theoretical concept of 'translocation', especially in the sense of multiple crossings, switching back and forth, and transformation, has affected the evaluation as well as the composition of texts. In the past (especially Classical Antiquity, the Middle Ages, and the Renaissance), the activity of writing itself, the process of composing a text, was often compared to the crossing of a waterway, sea, or channel by ship, whereby the genre or length of a textual composition was likened to either a small boat on a river (e.g., a poem) or a big ship on the ocean (e.g., an epic): The action of composing was metaphorically phrased as setting sail.[64] The activity of writing is thus a coupling of human effort with an external motion as motivation. In both literature and language, the birth and growth of new categories question, on the one hand, the validity of traditional areas and 'borders' of classification, but they legitimize, on the other, terms like 'code-switching'[65] and paradoxically call attention to the borders intended to be overcome. A variety of expressions like 'mixed code' or 'code-alternation'[66] reflect the creation of new research fields as actions of translocation. In contrast to 'switching' (i.e. multiple linguistic movements of bilingual speakers), 'language crossing' (or 'code-crossing') implies violation. It

> refers to the use of a language which isn't generally thought to 'belong' to the speaker. Language crossing involves a sense of movement across quite sharply felt social or ethnic boundaries, and it raises issues of legitimacy.[67]

---

[64] See Ernst Robert Curtius, *European Literature and the Latin Middle Ages*, tr. Willard R. Trask (*Europäische Literatur und Lateinisches Mittelalter*, 1948; Bollingen Series XXXVI, tr. 1953; Princeton NJ: Princeton UP, 1990): 128–29 (using examples from Ovid's *Fasti, Ars amandi*, and others).

[65] See Rita Franceschini, "Code-Switching and the Notion of Code in Linguistics: Proposal for a Dual Focus Model," in *Code-Switching in Conversation: Language, Interaction and Identity*, ed. Peter Auer (London & New York: Routledge, 1998): 51–72.

[66] See Peter Auer, "Introduction: Bilingual Conversation Revisited," in *Code-Switching in Conversation: Language, Interaction and Identity*, ed. Peter Auer (London & New York: Routledge, 1998): 3, 13, 15–16.

[67] Ben Rampton, "Language Crossing and the Redefinition of Reality," in *Code-Switching in Conversation: Language, Interaction and Identity*, ed. Peter Auer (London & New York: Routledge, 1998): 291.

xxxvi   POSTCOLONIAL TRANSLOCATIONS   ⌘

Similarly, literary critics and scholars of literary theory, especially in postcolonial studies, have begun to cross boundaries and/or to expand their
'territories'. The concern with foreign cultures has questioned the inherited
division between disciplines and entailed the creation of new (scholarly or
artistic) communities. The title of an anthology like *The Space of English*[68]
documents this development. Gloria Anzaldúa's "struggle […] to change the
disciplines, to change the genres, to change how people look at a poem, at
theory or at children's books"[69] resembles Edward Said's attitude towards
qualities of 'in-betweenness' and 'exterritoriality' from which his writing
emanates.[70] Paradoxically, abandoning borders implies being aware of them
and utilizing them for the purpose of change, for a 'translocation'.

   Gloria Anzaldúa's seminal work *Borderlands/La Frontera* theoretically
and practically explores this phenomenon on a number of levels and results in
a preference for the term 'borderland' or 'borderlands', even a "no-man's
borderland" (34), as opposed to that of a borderline, thereby indicating the
absence of possession, ownership, superiority, or authority. The sense of an
area or space in which a possible transition, crossing, or mingling of elements
from two entities takes place is versified, for example, by Anzaldúa in

> Wind tugging at my sleeve
> feet sinking into the sand
> I stand at *the edge where earth touches ocean*
> where the two *overlap*
> a gentle *coming together*
> at othertimes and places a *violent clash.* (23; emphasis added)

The sense of translocation as involving distance and time: i.e. mutability and
change, "a constant state of transition" (25), is, for example, indicated in the
words and shape of

---

[68] *The Space of English*, ed. David Spurr & Cornelia Tschichold (SPELL: Swiss
Papers in English Language and Literature 17; Tübingen: Gunter Narr, 2005).

[69] Karin Ikas, "Interview with Gloria Anzaldúa by Karin Ikas," in *Borderlands/La
Frontera: The New Mestiza*, Gloria Anzaldúa (1987; San Francisco: Aunt Lute, 3rd ed.
2007): 232–33.

[70] Edward W. Said, *Beginnings: Intention and Method* (New York: Basic, 1975): 8.
See also Markus Schmitz, *Kulturkritik ohne Zentrum: Edward W. Said und die
Kontrapunkte kritischer Dekolonisation* (Bielefeld: transcript, 2008): 105.

> This land was Mexican once,
>   was Indian always
>   and is.
>   And   will be again. (25)

Importantly, however, these qualities leave fewer traces on the land itself than on the human beings who are "caught in the crossfire between camps" (216), and in order "to survive the Borderlands / you must live *sin fronteras* / be a crossroads" (217).

3. Displaced Authorities: Translation, Adaptation, Edition

Similar to the etymology of 'trans' and 'location', the semantics of 'translation' literally indicates a "removal or conveyance from one person, place, or condition to another" (*OED* 1.) and includes both the action of transferring a text from one language into the other and the resulting transformed product. Robert Young talks of the "metaphorical displacement of a text."[71] When Bottom's head, in Shakespeare's *A Midsummer Night's Dream*, is changed by Puck into an ass's head, one of his fellow handicraftsmen first cries out: "O Bottom, thou art chang'd!"[72] and another rephrases: "Thou art translated" (*Riverside*, 232; III.i.119–20). 'Translate' is here used both in a literal (physical) and a figurative (interpretative) sense and catches the semantic range of the term. In other words, translation is a noticeable change of a source that results in a new appearance but is still inevitably linked to the original. The question is whether the result is only a new and different rendition of the original product or whether it can be evaluated as either gain or loss if compared to the original.[73] This phenomenon of a possible "renovation" (*OED*, translation, *n.* II.3.a) can, interestingly, even coincide with a reduction: The verb 'translate' can signify both to "make new boots from the remains (of old ones)" and to "turn, or cut down (a garment)" (*OED*, III.4.).

---

[71] Robert J.C. Young, *Postcolonialism: A Very Short Introduction* (Oxford & New York: Oxford UP, 2003): 139.

[72] William Shakespeare, "A Midsummer Night's Dream," in *The Riverside Shakespeare*, ed. G. Blakemore Evans et al. (1974; Boston MA: Houghton Mifflin, 2nd ed. 1996): 266 (III.i.114).

[73] Robert Young addresses the traditional practices of evaluating "an original" vs "an inferior copy"; see *Postcolonialism*, 140.

As is well-known, texts composed in non-European languages are regularly 'translated' into a world language in order to reach a large readership, while postcolonial writers frequently 'translate' metropolitan texts into their cultural contexts. Both forms of translation are rewritings, however different their objectives may be. Whereas the first form intends to represent an original and to make it accessible to those who are unfamiliar with it for linguistic reasons, the second form, by contrast, assumes the audience's prior familiarity with the original and provokes a recognition of the original's value and validity as relative when the personal, sociological, political, and cultural conditions are changed or reversed in the 'translated' version.

In the English Renaissance, an age devoted to the revival of classical literature, George Chapman, for example, a playwright and poet in his own right, turned out to be much more than merely a linguistic converter in his 'translations'. The title of his Homeric renditions, *Chapman's Homer*,[74] indicates that they are "English epics" composed "within the framework of Renaissance classicism."[75] The most prominent example of a 'translation' being evaluated as superior to its 'original' is The King James Bible (1611), which exemplifies how a Hebrew original (the Hebrew Bible or Old Testament), is translated into Greek and supplemented (by the New Testament), passes through Latin into the English language, resulting, however, in two drastically different versions, which were ultimately merged into yet another rendition, the "authorized version" of King James. This product of multi-lingual and multi-cultural origin became a model not only for religious but also for political and linguistic propriety/decorum in seventeenth-century England. What is more, this version made its entrance into a number of other regions and cultures where, far removed from even its Hebrew or Greek predecessors, it was and is negotiated as God's Scripture.[76]

Paradoxically, the term 'authorized' means, in the case of the King James Bible, the opposite of what is expected: It is not a product derived from the author's own thoughts and writings (whoever that author may be) but it is, on

---

[74] *Chapman's Homer: "The Iliad", "The Odyssey" and "The Lesser Homerica"*, ed. Allardyce Nicoll (London: Routledge & Kegan Paul, 1957).

[75] George de F. Lord, "Preface," in Lord, *Homeric Renaissance: The "Odyssey" of George Chapman* (London: Chatto & Windus, 1956): 9.

[76] See Adam Nicolson, *God's Secretaries: The Making of the King James Bible* (New York: HarperCollins, 2003): esp. 247–50, and "The Bible of King James," *National Geographic* (December 2011): 36–61.

the contrary, a book influenced and shaped by a political authority.[77] Interestingly, the etymology of 'authentic' offers a range of meanings from "entitled to acceptance or belief as being reliable" in the fourteenth century to "not counterfeit" in the eighteenth century, based on Greek meanings of "genuine" or "original authority."[78] In the present collection, several contributions (by Sandra Meyer, Therese–M. Meyer, Marga Munkelt, Gundo Rial y Costas, and Markus Schmitz, for example) touch on concerns deriving from linguistic or cultural translation as well as on varying degrees of intertextual relations between different types of texts and their transformations.

The fact that texts are composed and can be transmitted as translations (or, for that matter, as edited versions) reflects the possibilities of various transformations, as would the addition or substitution of pictures and diagrams. These as well as the typography and shape of texts on the page (the separation on the page of text and annotations, for example, or in images evoked by concrete verse/shaped poetry), although having different functions and origins, contribute to what has been called "textual space,"[79] or "words in space."[80] Thinking and arguing in terms of 'space' rather than using the material identifications of pages, sheets, gatherings, or books allows thoughts across physical limits and the inclusion of other textual representations like e-books, screens, hypertexts, and the like. These are actions or products of translocation as well, and they are, among other issues, illustrated in the present volume by the essays of Markus Schmitz, Kathy–Ann Tan, and Daria Tunca, who juxtapose, relate, and compare different artistic products and assess their mutual processes of transformation.

---

[77] Robert Young calls attention to the fact that usually "translation begins as a matter of intercultural communication, but it also always involves questions of power" *(Postcolonialism*, 140).

[78] *The Oxford Dictionary of English Etymology*, ed. C.T. Onions et al. (Oxford: Clarendon, 1966).

[79] David Spurr, "The Study of Space in Literature: Some Paradigms," in *The Space of English*, ed. David Spurr & Cornelia Tschichold (S P E L L : Swiss Papers in English Language and Literature 17; Tübingen: Gunter Narr, 2005): 15–34.

[80] Lukas Erne, "Words in Space: The Reproduction of Texts and the Semiotics of the Page," in *The Space of English*, ed. David Spurr & Cornelia Tschichold (S P E L L : Swiss Papers in English Language and Literature 17; Tübingen: Gunter Narr, 2005): 99–118.

4. Genres of Translocation: Lyric Poetry, Drama, or Narrative Fiction

In contrast to Aristotle, who explains literature as imitation of reality (*mimesis*), poetry and fiction were considered to be untrue (especially in Puritan England and Colonial America) and poets to be liars.[81] More generally, the "*normative* significance" of art has been both accepted and "doubted and/or rejected,"[82] because of "the widespread belief that to assign art a privileged value entails various kinds of *cultural exclusion*."[83] This fact may account for the degrees to which the three main literary genres: i.e. lyric poetry, drama, and narrative fiction, play a role in postcolonial literature. Until the eighteenth century, lyric poetry, that is, "a short non-narrative poem, came to be identified with the essence of literature."[84] Because lyric poems do not "include such elements as characters and plot,"[85] they seem to address the recipient more directly than the genres of narration and presentation. Lyric poetry, therefore, has been regarded as the most exclusively subjective form of writing, although the speaker of a lyric poem (despite the use of the first person) is only the "figure of [a] voice."[86] Poems are also "moral statements [that] deal in human values, meanings and purposes,"[87] and they offer to the composing authors a wide range of possibilities for emotional and intellectual expression of stance or social and political criticism. However, because, in lyric poems, form and language are foregrounded and therefore the clarity of meaning is subordinated to artistic elements, they have been considered, more than the other literary genres, to be particularly challenging for their recipients. Simultaneously, because of this very feature, the subject-matter and

---

[81] "Aristotle: Poetics," ed. D.A. Russell & M. Winterbottom, in *Classical Literary Criticism* (1972; Oxford & New York: Oxford U P, 1989): 53. See also Curtius, *European Literature and the Latin Middle Ages*, 397–98.

[82] Paul Crowther, *Defining Art, Creating the Canon: Artistic Value in an Era of Doubt* (Oxford: Clarendon, 2007): 15.

[83] Crowther, *Defining Art, Creating the Canon*, 15.

[84] Jonathan Culler, *Literary Theory: A Very Short Introduction* (1997; Oxford: Oxford U P, 2nd ed. 2000): 73.

[85] M.H. Abrams, *The Mirror and the Lamp: Romantic Theory and the Critical Tradition* (1953; Oxford & New York: Oxford U P, 1971): 84–85.

[86] Culler, *Literary Theory*, 74.

[87] Terry Eagleton, *How to Read a Poem* (Malden MA & Oxford: Blackwell, 2007): 29.

contents are defamiliarized, with the effect of appearing to be more important than in ordinary diction. Owing to this very tension between "aesthetic and/or expressive effects,"[88] one might assess this genre as ideal for an imitation of orality – since "postcolonial cultures have all, in various ways, been influenced by the interrelationship between orality and literacy."[89] It is therefore surprising that the creation of lyric poetry is much less frequently utilized in postcolonial literatures than might be expected.

The handling of space and time, because of their presentation (and, to different degrees, also their perception by a reader or a spectator), is particularly relevant for an investigation of literature in relation to reality. The traditionally marked genre characteristics of narrative fiction and drama concern the form of mediation – that of narration as opposed to that of (self-)presentation – as well as forms of reception: i.e. reading vs watching. Aristotle sees the advantages of narrative fiction in the flexible handling of time, especially in its independence of the reception-time (i.e. reading).[90]

The association of the novel with time is more clearly based on the relationship between different layers of reality and art as well as between author and work, and depends less on the activity (except the reading) of the recipient.[91] Novels and stories "have the function [...] of teaching us about the world, enabling us [...] to see things from other vantage points, and to understand others' motives that in general are opaque to us."[92] But due to their length as well as to their being written in the vernacular, novels "provide a mode for social criticism. [...] They expose the predicaments of the oppressed, in stories that invite readers, *through identification*, to see certain situations as intolerable."[93] This accords with Edward Said, who explains the attraction of the novel (also to non-Western writers in whose tradition no such prose genre existed before the twentieth century) thus:

---

[88] Crowther, *Defining Art, Creating the Canon*, 1.

[89] Bill Ashcroft, Gareth Griffiths & Helen Tiffin, *Post-Colonial Studies: The Key Concepts* (London & New York: Routledge, 2000): 151.

[90] "Aristotle: Poetics," ed. Russell & Winterbottom, 82.

[91] Gérard Genette, "Time and Narrative in *A la recherche du temps perdu*," tr. Paul de Man, in *Aspects of Narrative: Selected Papers from the English Institute*, ed. J. Hillis Miller (New York & London: Columbia UP, 1971): 93–95.

[92] Culler, *Literary Theory*, 91.

[93] *Literary Theory*, 92 (emphasis added).

> One of the most urgent uses of the novel is that it enables the writer to represent characters and societies in development. These characters and societies grow and move because in the novel they are imitations of the process of engenderment and growth possible for the mind to imagine. Therefore novels are aesthetic objects that fill gaps in an incomplete world, they satisfy a human urge to add to reality, and they portray fictional characters in which one can believe.[94]

Moreover, the writer's power to 'modify reality' and anticipate changes appeals to him.[95] After all, the novelist as 'author' (derived, of course, from Latin *auctor* and *augere*) represents "inauguration, augmentation by extension, possession [and] continuity."[96]

In narrative fiction, this genre characteristic also implies the possibility to control, if not manipulate, time, space, and distance. Michel de Certeau, accordingly, asserts that stories, like literal "vehicles of [...] transportation [...], traverse and organise places; they select and link them together [...]. They are spatial trajectories."[97] He has in mind a clear differentiation between cartography and narration when suggesting: "what the map cuts up, the story cuts across."[98] His differentiation also applies to stories in the specific context of diasporic identifications across distinct geographical spaces. In the case of transmigrant diasporas, with their increased number of locations traversed, such storytelling becomes a crucial element in the construction of translocal space. This phenomenon applies to both colonial and contemporary post-independence diasporas (or settler and 'victim' diasporas). The discourses of diasporic identity tend to be orientated toward a real or imagined homeland with the erection or maintenance of boundaries to the host society. These processes lead to the creation of translocations which in turn establish complex, incomplete congruities between distinct geographical and cultural spaces.

---

[94] Edward Said, "Molestation and Authority in Narrative Fiction," in *Aspects of Narrative: Selected Papers from the English Institute*, ed. J. Hillis Miller (New York & London: Columbia UP, 1971): 48.

[95] Said, "Molestation and Authority in Narrative Fiction," 49.

[96] "Molestation and Authority in Narrative Fiction," 49.

[97] Michel de Certeau, *The Practice of Everyday Life,* tr. Steven F. Rendall (*Arts de faire: L'invention du quotidien*, vol. 1, 1980; tr. Berkeley: U of California P, 1984): 115. See also 116–30.

[98] de Certeau, *The Practice of Everyday Life*, 129.

Because, in contrast to narrative fiction, speech is the basic element of drama, its "mimetic and pragmatic" potential makes a play particularly appropriate for (political) message and (social) protest. But it demands active intellectual or imaginative involvement of the recipients, and its action must be either exemplary or resort to linguistic intensification. The opportunity to "transform the world"[99] can be seized by drama because it "helps us conceive of literature as act or event."[100] Drama as a genre illustrates the flexibility of boundaries, in the use of language (which can be either verse or prose) as well as in its possible combination with narrative elements (in epic plays, for example) and poetry. Also, the hierarchy of the three basic universal elements of drama – action (*mimesis*), speech (rhetoric/verbal expression), and perception (understanding/comment) – can vary and foreground either the action or the speech acts or can challenge the audience's perception by exposing the meaninglessness of communication[101] (for example, in the so-called absurd theatre) whereas unintelligibility in narrative texts is often presented for psychological and/or cultural reasons. Gradually, however, "the so-called three unities survive mostly in the unity of place," whereas "the former unity of action gives way to episodic and cyclic scenes because they correspond more to the presentation of the human mind."[102] Moreover, plays not deriving from the Western canon frequently rebel "against various conventions – including the conventions of linguistic variety and register" and "expose cultural bias" by, for example, foregrounding language.[103]

Although dramatic writing, like narrative fiction, "represents a fictive world and fictive human beings acting in it, [...] drama is imitation in the mode of action itself. [...] We see the action performed (not narrated) by its agents."[104] The transitional quality of a performance also creates an analogy

---

[99] Culler, *Literary Theory*, 96.

[100] *Literary Theory*, 96.

[101] See Marga Munkelt, "The Stylistics of Drama: Universal Elements," in *Language and Style: In Honour of Mick Short*, ed. Dan McIntyre & Beatrix Busse (London: Palgrave Macmillan, 2010): 146–51.

[102] Munkelt, "The Stylistics of Drama," 156.

[103] "The Stylistics of Drama," 158.

[104] W.B. Worthen, *Drama: Between Poetry and Performance* (Malden MA & Oxford: Wiley–Blackwell, 2010): xiv.

with real life in its irretrievability. On the stage,[105] space, place, and time are connected, and there is an interdependence of action (on stage) and (audience) perception. These are forms of translocation: first, the imitation of life (trans-formation) into written text; second, the translation of script into performance (action); finally, the shared theatrical experience (perception and reception of the play).

Considering the almost symbiotic relationship between drama and location, one is astonished to see that a majority of literary works concerned with aspects of postcolonial translocations seems to belong to narrative fiction. This fact is also represented in the current volume, in which most of those essays that are concerned with literature are devoted to stories or novels and only a few (Paloma Fresno–Calleja, Sandra Meyer, Marga Munkelt, Katharina Rennhak, and Daria Tunca) include poetry in their analyses, whereas drama is almost wholly neglected and touched on only by Fresno–Calleja and Munkelt. It is likewise noticeable that Anzaldúa's goal of crossing boundaries by translocating disciplines and genres remains a future-oriented project.

5. Re-turning to Space: Spatial Turns and the Translocal

At least for the last three decades, the study of space has undergone a pro-found and sustained transformation across the disciplines. The increased inter-est in the dynamics and effects of economic, political, and cultural globaliza-tion has accentuated the significance of the local in its relation to non- or translocal spaces. Today, one can hardly grasp any transnational or trans-cultural formation in a serious scholarly manner without asking, at the same time, how space and place are perceived and conceptualized within the vari-ous socio-cultural locations involved in or excluded from that very formation. That the ongoing transformation of our everyday experience of space and place has led to a fundamental destabilization of the prevailing spatial knowl-edge can be seen not only in the resurgence of human geography. Meanwhile, competing orders of spatial thinking, the cultural representation of space and place, the conditions and practice of artistic mapping, and other spatial imagi-naries have become commonplace topics in the humanities and the social sciences. Scholars from a variety of geographical and disciplinary back-

---

[105] For details concerning different types of theatres and stages, see John Lennard & Mary Lockhurst, *The Drama Handbook: A Guide to Reading Plays* (Oxford: Oxford UP, 2002), ch. 14.

grounds working on space are not only concerned with geography but also explore the role of space and spatial representations in historical narratives, social (power) relations, competing epistemologies, religious and psychological formations, politics, the audiovisual arts, or literature. Particularly in the English-speaking world, the reassertion of space has long entered academic debates beyond cultural geography and social theory.

Perhaps more than other critical discourses within the sphere of literary and cultural studies, postcolonial studies – ever since its earliest formation as an academic field in its own right – has been characterized by a particular emphasis on real and imagined geographies, competing narrative locations, travelling theories, and narrative (counter-)strategies of (re-)locating cultures.[106] That space matters in the study of literature and culture is by now well known and widely accepted. Today, there no longer seems to be any need to justify one's concern with urban topographies, the politics of transnational space, or the identity-conflicts of territorial representations when interpreting a literary text's spatial metaphors or tropes.[107]

However, the way spatial representations are analysed can significantly vary according to the respective scholar's historical location, academic discipline, and approach used. In addition, it is important to remind ourselves that thinking (about) space and thinking spatially, just like "space itself[,] has

---

[106] An early proponent and founding figure in the field, who stresses the close relation between the material practice of colonial territorial expansion and the Western literary narratives' worldly referentiality, is, of course, Edward W. Said (*Orientalism* [London: Routledge & Kegan Paul, 1978].). The most influential contribution to the project of theoretically tracing the formation of a third spatiality of ambivalent identification under the conditions of postcoloniality that goes beyond the colonial-racist binary of mutually excluding physical terrains of belonging comes from Homi K. Bhabha (*The Location of Culture*). On the postcolonial concern with discursive transmigrations, with spatial transgressions as conditions of the production and reception of theories, see Nick Perry, "Travelling Theory / Nomadic Theorizing," *Organization* 2.1 (February 1995): 35–54.

[107] See, for example, Chris Prentice, Vijay Devadas & Henry Johnson, "Introduction: Cultural Transformations: Perspectives on Translocation in a Global Age," in *Cultural Transformations: Perspectives on Translocation in a Global Age*, ed. Chris Prentice, Vijay Devadas & Henry Johnson (Cross/Cultures 125; Amsterdam & New York: Rodopi, 2010), which situates its exploration of translocation "at the intersection of postcolonial and global cultural dynamics" (xiii).

a history."[108] As has been demonstrated above, the attempt of understanding the meaning of place and man's motion in space is not at all an innovation of late-twentieth-century theory. Reflections on space and place are much older than the standard references used in today's spatial studies suggest. In addition, it is epistemologically not possible to disregard the close "intersection of time with space."[109]

It is likewise impossible to trace, in this introduction, the long-established, multifaceted, and controversial frequent debates on space–time. Nor is it an easy task to grasp only the latest development of what is variously called the spatial turn, the topographical turn, or the geographical turn. Despite the frequent hype about, and constant reference to, the turn (not accidentally a spatial metaphor) towards space and topography, there are only a few studies that offer precise overviews of how spatial theories and methods are used in a variety of fields within diverse conceptual perspectives and from different geographical positions in francophone and anglophone academia as well as beyond.[110] A closer look at the recent inflation of the use of 'space' as an epistemological metaphor across the disciplines shows that we need to differentiate between many spatial turns and epistemic shifts related to the new spatial thinking if we wish to identify those strands of the international debate that can be followed for conceptualizing postcolonial translocations as (discursive) movements and (representational) spaces which transgress, and at the same time connect, both the inescapable 'locatedness' of places and the static 'placedness' of Cartesian container-space concepts.

6. Decolonization and the Revision of Spatial Knowledge

The spatial turn is not a child of poststructuralism and postmodernism, nor can it simply be understood as a side-effect of the general postcolonial turn of

---

[108] Foucault, "Of Other Spaces," 22.

[109] "Of Other Spaces," 22.

[110] For recent attempts at providing such transdisciplinary overviews on the international debate, see: Bertrand Westphal, *Geocriticism: Real and Fictional Spaces*, tr. Robert T. Tally, Jr. (*La Géocritique*, 2007; New York: Palgrave Macmillan, 2011); *The Spatial Turn*, ed. Barney Warf & Santa Arias (London & New York: Routledge, 2008); *Spatial Turn: Das Raumparadigma in den Kultur- und Sozialwissenschaften*, ed. Jörg Döring & Tristan Thielmann (Bielefeld: transcript, 2008).

the 1980s.[111] Instead, it has its origin in the 'turning' of geographical analysis toward social and historical narratives in the late 1960s. It is usually overlooked that the explosive growth in the human-geography debate which we are confronted with today coincided with the dynamics of political decolonization and the broader social movements of civil rights and anti-war. The necessity of relating space to economics, race, gender, media, and other power-relations did not arise through a strictly inner-academic shift of epistemological paradigms in the Western academy, but is closely related to a conscious politicization of spatial thinking as the precondition for meaningful social action, both in local places and in global spaces.

In the context of this volume, it is therefore of particular importance to remember the specific political events which contributed to revisions of spatial thinking: Under the impression of an ongoing immigration from North Africa to Paris caused by the historic defeat of French colonialism in Algeria, the Marxist urban geographer Henri Lefebvre developed, in 1968, his plea for a new understanding of the (urban) dialectic "of place and non-place (elsewhere)."[112] His conception of space as something that must be seen not as the ontological location of given social events but as the ever-changing product of socio-political processes has now advanced to a standard (sometimes to an instant) reference and starting point for many scholars working in spatial studies. What is, however, rarely addressed is the fact that Lefebvre's seminal *The Production of Space*[113] responds – albeit not exclusively – to a particular historical moment when the principally imperialist divide between centre and periphery, as well as the related dynamics of economic integration and racist segregation, was shifted to the metropolitan urban phenomenon itself. It was after political decolonization and postcolonial migration had become concrete as signs of liminality within the Western nation-space itself that metropolitan intellectuals began to radically question the traditional eurocentric divisions between *here* and *there* as spatial concepts confined by the mutual constitu-

---

[111] But cf. Doris Bachmann–Medick, *Cultural Turns* (Reinbeck: Rowohlt, 2007): 284–90.

[112] Henri Lefebvre, *The Urban Revolution*, tr. Robert Bononno (*La Révolution urbaine*, 1968; Minneapolis: U of Minnesota P, 2003). Here quoted from Henri Lefebvre, "The Urban Revolution" (1970), excerpt in *The Global Cities Reader*, ed. Neil Brenner & Roger Keil (London & New York: Routledge, 2006): 412.

[113] Henri Lefebvre, *The Production of Space*, tr. Donald Nicholson–Smith (*La Production de l'espace*, 1974; Oxford: Blackwell, 1991).

tive strategies of *othering* and *selving*. Adapting a well known and frequently used metaphor of travelling critique coined by Edward Said,[114] one can argue that Frantz Fanon's anticolonial attack on manichaean colonial urban segregation[115] has voyaged into the Western metropolis. Lefebvre's work demonstrates that the physical immigration of postcolonial subjects not only coincides with the local presence of neocolonial spatialities but has also caused a significant decolonization of French spatial reason. This socio-epistemic 'voyage in' can be considered as a major point of departure for the broader decentering of thinking locally and globally as well as questioning the symbolic constructions of Europe's geography.

The ambivalent movement of turning cultural difference "from the boundary 'outside' to its finitude 'within'"[116] – as Homi Bhabha puts it – further sensitized scholars to the general dialectic between spatial isotopy and heterotopia beyond the effects of decolonization. Hence, questioning the semantic coherence of dominant interpretative modes, Lefebvre's reassertion of space can also be understood as related to a broader critical stream of thought within the French structuralism of the 1960s and 1970s. Resisting a hundred years of historicist hegemony and at the same time going "beyond the 'additive' mode that characterizes [...] the effusively geographical historiography of Fernand Braudel and the *Annales* school,"[117] the new generation criticized diachronic developmentalism for discrediting and thus almost excluding space as an analytical category. On the one hand, the notion of place became central to the very definition not only of geography but also of history. On the other, the continuously changing notions of place and location were understood as the result of historically contingent social practices and cultural representations.

---

[114] Said, *Culture and Imperialism*, 216. See also Edward W. Said, "Traveling Theory Reconsidered," in *Reflections on Exile and Other Essays* (Cambridge MA: Harvard UP, 2000): 436–52.

[115] Frantz Fanon, *The Wretched of the Earth*, tr. Richard Philcox (*Les Damnés de la terre*, 1961; New York: Grove, 2004): 3–5. See also Stefan Kipfer, "Fanon and Space: Colonization, Urbanization, and Liberation from the Colonial to the Global City," *Society and Space* 25.4 (January 2007): 701–26.

[116] Homi K. Bhabha, "DissemiNation: Time, Narrative, and the Margins of the Modern Nation" (1990), in Bhabha, *The Location of Culture* (London & New York: Routledge, 1994): 146.

[117] Edward W. Soja, *Thirdspace: Journeys to Los Angeles and Other Real-and-Imagined Places* (Malden MA & Oxford: Blackwell, 1996): 172.

What unifies most proponents of the renewed interest in the representational practice of spacing, in spaces and 'other spaces', or in nomadic movements between places, is the belief that space is not a pre-existing static unit in which history happens and linguistic or cultural meaning appears, but that territorialities are reciprocally constituted by these discursive, psychological, and material events. The works of such diverse intellectuals as Gérard Genette, Julia Kristeva, Michel Foucault, Gilles Deleuze, and Jacques Derrida are symptomatic of this spatial re-conceptualization of theory.[118] Since the 1980s, Edward W. Soja's *Postmodern Geography*, his influential studies on what he calls *Postmetropolis*, and in particular his heterotopological concept of 'thirdspace', have directly drawn on Foucault's provisional geohistory of otherness and Lefebvre's social constructionist theory of space.[119]

7. Social Fabrications and Contested Terrains: Human Geography

It would be reductionist to say that the spatial turn began in Paris and only shifted to Los Angeles much later, because the development of a distinctive programme of spatial research in North America already began as early as the mid-1920s, with the second generation of the Chicago School of urban sociology. Trying to first understand and then to regulate the effects of the intensified population shift from assumedly homogeneous, rural communities to the heterogeneous, industrial American metropolis, their theoretical work in the field of what came to be known as urban ecology proposed to deal with cities as environments which are, similar to natural ecosystems, affected by forces of competition. The publications of Robert E. Park, Ernest W. Burgess, and Roderick D. McKenzie in the field of urban geography,[120] Louis Wirth's studies on immigration and community maintenance,[121] as well as Ellsworth

---

[118] Russell West–Pavlov, *Space in Theory: Kristeva, Foucault, Deleuze* (Amsterdam & New York: Rodopi, 2009).

[119] Edward W. Soja, *Postmodern Geography: The Reassertion of Space in Critical Social Theory* (London: Verso, 1989) and *Postmetropolis: Critical Studies of Cities and Regions* (Malden MA & Oxford: Blackwell, 2000); Michel Foucault, *Utopies et hétérotopies* (Paris: INA, 2004). On Lefebvre, see Soja, *Thirdspace*, 145–83.

[120] Robert E. Park, Ernest W. Burgess & Roderick D. McKenzie, *The City* (Chicago: U of Chicago P, 1925).

[121] Louis Wirth, *The Ghetto* (Chicago: U of Chicago P, 1928).

Faris's contributions to the emerging field of social psychology and urban anthropology[122] prepared the ground for a specific American approach to studying the social fabrication of human communities and urban imageries in metropolitan space.[123] This approach was later taken up by activist scholars such as Jane Jacobs. Jacobs was actively involved in organizing grassroots efforts to block urban-renewal projects in Manhattan that would have destroyed the social life of a vibrant local neighbourhood like Greenwich Village. Her 1961 study *The Death and Life of Great American Cities*[124] provides a powerful critique of urban gentrification in the USA. What matters in our context is that, by doing so, she implicitly stresses the importance of citizens of diverse social and ethnic backgrounds as agents in the making of their own urban surroundings as a lived space.

It is this exchange between research and social activism that informs many early scholarly attempts at opening up the spaces of representation in human geography. At least since the 1980s, the attention to space as a reiterative social practice has gradually turned on the reading of space and place as something struggled over: Geographers concerned with notions of space began to engage with work in social theory and in cultural studies, not only to consider the connections between spatial representation and identification but also to explore the highly politicized relations between power and place. This trend is particularly apparent in studies by John Agnew and James Duncan.[125] Spatial identity in cultural geography came to be a matter of identity-politics and differential access to power in given locales. In addition, as early as 1991, Doreen Massey argued, from a decisive Marxist perspective and with a view

---

[122] Faris contributed some forty articles to various journals. Approximately half of these articles appeared in the *American Journal of Sociology*. One of his most influential essays is "The Nature of Human Nature," *Publications of the American Sociological Society* 20 (1925): 15–29.

[123] See: James F. Short, *The Social Fabric of the Metropolis: Contributions of the Chicago School of Urban Sociology* (Chicago: U of Chicago P, 1971); Anselm L. Strauss, *The American City: A Sourcebook of Urban Imagery* (Chicago: Aldine, 1968); Robert E. Park, *Human Communities: The City and Human Ecology* (Glencoe IL: Free Press, 1952).

[124] Jane Jacobs, *The Death and Life of Great American Cities* (New York: Vintage, 1961).

[125] See John Agnew, *Place and Politics* (Boston MA: Allen & Unwin, 1987), and *The Power of Place*, ed. John Agnew & James Duncan (Boston MA: Unwin Hyman, 1990).

on more distant geographies, for a sense of place which accommodates the cultural dislocations and global networks through which local places are made: "What we need, it seems to me, is a global sense of the local, a global sense of place."[126]

The scholarly concern with spatial constructions of difference with regard to non-Western geographies, the margins within the Western metropolis, and the analysis of those spaces that socio-ethnic exclusion and discriminatory geography make, lies at the heart of many contributions in Michael Keith's and Steve Pile's seminal essay collection *Place and the Politics of Identity*.[127] As Tim Cresswell puts it in *Place: A Short Introduction*, 'place' is understood "through the lens of social and cultural conflict. Issues of race, class, gender, sexuality and a host of other social relations were at the center of this analysis."[128] According to Cresswell, the idea of space and place has been approached in geography on three basic levels: first, the traditional descriptive approach based on "the common-sense idea of the world being a set of places each of which can be studied as a unique and particular entity" (51); secondly, a constructionist approach that treats places "as instances of more general underlying social processes" (51) and emphasizing space as a depersonalized power geometry; and, thirdly, a phenomenological approach concerned with the evidence of human existence as sensing space and being "in-place" (51). Only at first glance do these three approaches correspond to the respective academic disciplines of geography, sociology, and anthropology, or to philosophy. The growing body of work related to the spatial turn is characterized, rather, by decisive interdisciplinarity and the mixing of methods. In fact, under the umbrella term of 'human geography', one can find sociological and anthropological approaches side by side with historical and philosophical approaches. Just as scholars of literary and cultural studies have adapted concepts and categories from critical geographers, human geography in the wake

---

[126] Doreen Massey, "A Global Sense of Place," *Marxism Today* 35.6 (June 1991): 29.

[127] *Place and the Politics of Identity*, ed. Michael Keith & Steve Pile (London & New York: Routledge, 1993). See, in the same volume, Edward Soja & Barbara Hooper, "The Spaces that Difference Makes: Some Notes on the Geographical Margins of the New Cultural Politics," 183–205.

[128] Tim Cresswell, *Place: A Short Introduction* (Malden MA & Oxford: Blackwell, 2004): 29. Further page references are in the main text.

of the spatial turn pays increased attention to representational questions and to the literary and cultural contiguities of reading.[129]

8. Real Places and Other Locations: Sensing Space

The phenomenological approach to space seems to be more concerned with real places than with imaginative spaces or narratives of space. It partly rejects both the idealist conception of space as a static stage set upon which the socio-cultural dramas of history were played out and the constructionist emphasis on space as a trans-individual discursive effect. It is instead characterized by increased attention to place as a lived particularity created by man's being in place. Although Homi Bhabha begins his own theoretical reflections on the postcolonial condition from Martin Heidegger's insight that a "boundary is that from which something *begins its presencing*,"[130] the phenomenological approach to space is rarely practised in literary and cultural studies. For instance, Gaston Bachelard's classic 1957 study *The Poetics of Space*,[131] a phenomenological reflection on the domestic house as a psychological archuniverse and refuge in familiar places and spaces, remains widely neglected by scholars of literature, though the French philosopher draws almost exclusively on poetry and the reception of poetic and literary images to show that "all really inhabited space bears the essence of the notion of home."[132]

The political geographer John Agnew differentiates among three fundamental aspects of place: place as location, place as locale, and the sense of place. The absolute 'location' of a place is defined by the grid references we attach to portions of the earth's surface by conventional latitudinal and longitudinal positioning. By 'locale', Agnew means the material setting for social relations, the actual morphometry of the environments (domestic, daily, and so on) in which people conduct their lives. And 'sense of place' is taken to

---

[129] Westphal, *Geocriticism: Real and Fictional Spaces*.

[130] The German original reads: "die Grenze ist jenes, von woher etwas sein Wesen beginnt." See Martin Heidegger, "Building Dwelling Thinking," in *Martin Heidegger, Poetry, Language, Thought*, tr. & intro. Albert Hofstadter ("Bauen Wohnen Denken," 1952; New York: Harper & Row, 1971): 154. For Bhabha's reading of Heidegger, see *The Location of Culture*, 1, 5.

[131] Gaston Bachelard, *The Poetics of Space*, tr. Maria Jolas (*La Poétique de l'espace*, 1957; Boston MA: Beacon, 1994).

[132] Bachelard, *The Poetics of Space*, 5.

embrace the affective attachment that people have to place.[133] Drawing on this typology, our discussion of postcolonial translocations turns on movements (physical as well as discursive) between locations of different latitude/longitude positions and on how these movements affect concrete locales and people's sense of locales in relation to what might be termed 'translocales'.

In this context, the contributions of geographers, who, already from the mid-1970s onwards, turned to ideas concerning a sensing of place, would appear to be of particular importance. For human geographers such as Yi–Fu Tuan, Anne Buttimer, David Seamon, and Edward Relph, the concept of location does not denote a fractional unit of space, but is approached, rather, as an effect of man's being in the world.[134] Relph explicitly draws on Edmund Husserl's and Martin Heidegger's work to grasp place as a phenomenon directly related to the practice of dwelling: i.e. of placing oneself in space. For Relph, the essence of place "lies in the largely unconscious intentionality that defines places as profound centers of human existence."[135] What does it mean for scholars of postcolonial literatures and cultures when Edward Casey argues that to live as a human is to live locally and to know the place one is in?[136] Appadurai asks: "What can locality mean in a world where spatial localization, quotidian interaction, and social scale are not always isomorphic?"[137] If, indeed, the translocal is more than a non-human or a dehumanized spatiality, what are the knowledges produced by and the emotional responses inherent in that very translocality?[138]

---

[133] Agnew, *Place and Politics*.

[134] See: Yi–Fu Tuan, *Topophilia: A Study of Environmental Perception, Attitudes and Values* (Englewood Cliffs NJ: Prentice–Hall, 1974); Yi–Fu Tuan, *Space and Place: The Perspective of Experience* (Minneapolis: U of Minnesota P, 1977); *The Human Experience of Space and Place*, ed. Anne Buttimer & David Seamon (London: Croom Helm, 1980); Edward Relph, *Place and Placelessness* (London: Pion, 1976).

[135] Relph, *Place and Placelessness*, 43.

[136] Edward Casey, *Getting Back into Place: Toward a Renewed Understanding of the Place-World* (Bloomington: Indiana UP, 1993). See also Edward Casey, *The Fate of Place: A Philosophical History* (Berkeley: U of California P, 1998), and Edward Casey, *Earth-Mapping: Artists Reshaping Landscape* (Minneapolis: U of Minnesota P, 2005).

[137] Appadurai, *Modernity at Large*, 179.

[138] On this question, see Jan Penrose, "Nations, States and Homelands: Territory and Territoriality in Nationalist Thought," *Nations and Nationalism* 8.3 (July 2002): 277–98.

9. Postcolonial Urban Spaces as Translocations

We live in a world of big cities. "Urban contexts often provide privileged spaces for the manifestation of translocality,"[139] as Freitag and von Oppen put it. The postcolonial city is a spatiality in which cultural translocations become particularly visible. It consists of "neighborhoods that belong in one sense to particular nation-states, but that are from another point of view [...] *trans-localities*."[140] Cities, both Western and non-Western, are not only important sites of modernization but also an integral part of the expanding networks of globalization. Hence, the urban experience is increasingly one of global flows and semiotic encounters beyond the boundaries of local belonging. So-called global cities are spaces of exilic or diasporic lives. The notion of the city as "locality [...] is more than ever shot through with contradictions, destabilized by human motion, and displaced by the formation of new kinds of virtual neighborhoods."[141] Global cities are thus not only "'basing points' in the spatial organization and articulation" of the post-imperial world-economy;[142] they are at the same time the locus of long-distance connections and relations between geographically separated individuals and groups. Since movements of postcolonial migration often culminate in, and culturally articulate, metro-politan space, several essays in this volume focus on narratives produced and set in such urban spaces. Gundo Rial y Costas explores the imaginative and real geographies of the Brazilian 'American dream' of New York. Kathy–Ann Tan writes on London's tourist zone of Banglatown, and Jessica Voges discusses the emancipatory strategy of laughter in Bengali London. Markus Schmitz traces the transmigrant crossovers between the Lebanese war-torn capital of Beirut and the American AIDS-torn gay capital of San Francisco. Katharina Rennhak's essay revolves around the translocal poetics of British-Asian London, and Petra Tournay–Theodotou introduces us to Anglo-Cypriot Nottingham. Paloma Fresno–Calleja presents Auckland as a Polynesian city, and Thomas Martinek searches for Nigeria's hidden history in an anonymous city that recalls London.

The variety of contributions demonstrates that the production of city space is not only significantly shaped by narrative representations of the urban, but

---

[139] Freitag & von Oppen, "Introduction: 'Translocality'," 10.

[140] Appadurai, *Modernity at Large*, 192.

[141] *Modernity at Large*, 198.

[142] Anthony D. King, *Global Cities: Postimperialism and the Internationalization of London* (London & New York: Routledge, 1990): 30.

that performative practices also play an important role. They present various ways of exploring the complex nexus of and between city spaces, on the one hand, and translocal narratives, on the other. That the postcolonial metropolis creates new multiple forms of belonging which require the acknowledgement of a post-national understanding of urban citizenship identity has long been acknowledged:

> cosmopolitan centres such as London, New York, Paris and Los Angeles [...] are [...] spaces in which attempts to articulate a global culture are sited. These global cities are, to a large extent, cut off from (or at least have an exceptional relationship with) the nation-states in which they are situated. In many ways [...] they have a distinct identity.[143]

Postcolonial criticism has been slow in penetrating urban and architectural studies. The postcolonial mainstream still focuses on textual discourse, thus deflecting attention from more material ways in which imperial and postcolonial power-relations persist. Until recently, there have been few sustained discussions about what might constitute postcolonial urban studies or postcolonial architectural history.[144] Although the contributions to this volume are mainly concerned with literary representations, they can help to move postcolonial discourse beyond its exclusive preoccupation with text. At the same time, they can challenge the primacy of the visual that still dominates architectural studies, for example.

Over the last two decades, however, architectural critics and scholars in the field of urban studies have begun to trace the interfaces between postcolonial literary studies and their own academic discipline. Slowly, a critical engagement with the field's own theoretical blind spots is developing, not only tracing the history of colonial urbanism and architecture but also seeking to decolonize the academic discipline's knowledge. In our view, scholars of postcolonial literary and cultural studies need to enter cross-disciplinary conversation with scholars working in the field of postcolonial urban and architectural studies. Since colonialism and the struggle over urban geography are intimately linked historically, urban studies should clearly lie at the heart of

---

[143] Sayyid, "Beyond Westphalia," 35.

[144] Two early volumes exploring the connections of postcolonialism, geography, and urban studies are *Postcolonial Space(s)*, ed. Gülsüm B. Nalbantoğlu & Chong T. Wong (New York: Princeton Architectural P, 1997) and *Postcolonial Geographies*, ed. Alison Blunt & Cheryl McEwan (New York & London: Continuum, 2002).

postcolonial endeavours. Thinking about ethnicity and cultural difference in translocal terms encourages a rethinking of the way in which difference and otherness inhabit urban and other spaces. This is also of relevance for studying the representational demands and the spatial politics of colonial cities, as work by Janet Abu-Lughod, David Prochaska, Zeynep Çelik, Vikramaditya Prakash, and others from the early 1980s onwards has shown.[145]

The material effects of colonial urbanism, or the complicity of architects and urban planners in colonial dominion over spaces and societies, is not the primary concern of this volume. Rather, the contributors' readings of postcolonial representations proceed from the assumption that the material effects of colonialism and decolonization, far from being a one-way phenomenon, can be found in both the colony and the metropolis.[146] It becomes clear that there is a particular need to challenge the spatial binary between the Western metropolis and the colonial or formerly colonized city when analysing non-material cultural formations from a postcolonial perspective. If indeed both the metropolis and the colony were deeply altered by colonization,[147] then both of them are also restructured by decolonization and postcolonial translocations. We cannot understand the diverse cultural articulations of intertwined geographies without considering the paradoxical locatedness of discursive translocations within urban space. Discursive space and material spaces of representation coexist in postcolonial translocations, and both determine and translate each other.

---

[145] Janet L. Abu-Lughod, *Rabat: Urban Apartheid in Morocco* (Princeton NJ: Princeton UP, 1980); David Prochaska, *Making Algeria French: Colonialism in Bône, 1870–1920* (Cambridge: Cambridge UP, 1990); Zeynep Çelik, *Urban Forms and Colonial Confrontations: Algiers under French Rule* (Berkeley: U of California P, 1997); and Vikramaditya Prakash, *Chandigarh's Le Corbusier: The Struggle for Modernity in Postcolonial India* (Seattle: U of Washington P, 2002).

[146] Ann Laura Stoler & Frederick Cooper, "Between Metropole and Colony: Rethinking a Research Agenda," in *Tensions of Empire: Colonial Cultures in a Bourgeois World*, ed. Frederick Cooper & Ann Laura Stoler (Berkeley: U of California P, 1997): 1–58. See also *Urbanism: Imported or Exported. Native Aspirations and Foreign Plans*, ed. Joe Nasr & Mercedes Volait (London: Wiley, 2003) and Mark Crinson, *Modern Architecture and the End of Empire* (Aldershot: Ashgate, 2003).

[147] For an early study of the colonial genesis of French modern urbanism, see Paul Rabinow, *French Modern: Norms and Forms of the Social Environment* (Cambridge MA: MIT Press, 1989).

10. Relocating the Global City

In the study of global cities, urban centres like Paris, New York, London, Tokyo, and Hong Kong, which handle a disproportionate share of international financial transactions, have been predominantly analysed from a socio-economic point of view to explain how these cities manage to contain transnational economic spaces for the operation of both domestic and foreign companies. According to Saskia Sassen, the global city is not where the homogenizing effects of globalization can be seen. Rather, it represents the endogenizing dynamics and conditions of the global economy characterized by growing inequality and social segregation. In Sassen's view, the global city is not appropriately conceptualized as a space of ethnic, social, and identitarian flows, but as a place that encapsulates the functions of global networks within the practice of some privileged local actors.[148] In contrast to traditional approaches that have celebrated the success of market-driven globalization, urban studies re-examine the local dynamics of global capitalism and reassert the importance of local politics. Whereas early work in this area inherited its theoretical frame from world-system and modernization theory, today the city is no longer seen exclusively as a site of economic production. Instead of overemphasizing the centrality of footloose capital and treating city inhabitants as labourers and consumers rather than cultural agents within the globalizing city space, recent studies ask which cultural roles local groups might play in a reshaping of global and local dynamics. *Living the Global City*, for example, a collection of critical essays,[149] explores the local within the global. The volume presents case studies on different social and ethnic groups in London who actively participate in the process of urban globalization by formulating new localities in response to global changes. Similarly, Ayşe Öncü and Petra Weyland's *Space, Culture and Power*[150] tries to grasp the transformation of cultural spaces in globalizing cities from a local perspective. Including a number of case studies in non-Western cities and regions, the latter volume at the same time shifts its focus from the old centre to the

---

[148] Saskia Sassen, *The Global City: New York, London, Tokyo* (Princeton NJ: Princeton UP, 2001): 346–50.

[149] *Living the Global City: Globalization as a Local Process*, ed. John Eade (London: Routledge, 1996).

[150] *Space, Culture and Power: New Identities in Globalizing Cities*, ed. Ayşe Öncü & Petra Weyland (London: Zed, 1997).

margin, from the 'first-world city' to 'third-world cities' like Cairo and Beirut.

What becomes obvious in these and more recent studies on the urban spaces of global culture is that cultural articulations of globalization are locally determined by concrete urban spatial configurations and are also transgressive with regard to national and cultural boundaries.[151] Several of the contributions in Öncü and Weyland's collection directly address the question of how distant relations and global discourses are appropriated and negotiated in the everyday struggle of local lives. They suggest that postcolonial urbanity is inevitably characterized by cultural translocation.

11. Disciplinary Translocation / Transdisciplinarity

According to Tim Cresswell, who describes his own critical practice at the intersection of social geography and the humanities as a "geosophical"[152] project, the description and ascription of people, things, and social practices are strongly linked to the disciplinary effects of spatio-ideological modes of value production. Since places and the social practices of locating selves and others within places have a strongly moral component, resistive acts of moral transgression have a spatial dimension, too. When individuals or groups disregard the norms of a certain place – if they do not know their right place within a hierarchically ordered social space or are unwilling to take up their designated positions in that space – they act 'out of place', and hence commit a transgression. This is one of the key arguments of Cresswell's study *In Place / Out of Place*.[153]

---

[151] Anthony D. King, *Spaces of Global Cultures: Architecture, Urbanism, Identity* (London & New York: Routledge, 2004). This is a collection of essays that were originally presented at a symposium on globalization theory. Among its chief contributors are Stuart Hall, Roland Robertson, Immanuel Wallerstein, and Ulf Hannerz. See also *Culture, Globalization and the World-System: Contemporary Conditions for the Representation of Identity*, ed. Anthony D. King (Minneapolis: U of Minnesota P, 1991).

[152] Tim Cresswell, "Race, Mobilities and the Humanities: A Geosophical Approach," in *Envisioning Landscapes, Making Worlds: Geography and the Humanities*, ed. Stephen Daniels, Dydia DeLyser, J. Nicholas Entrikin & Douglas Richardson (London: Routledge, 2011): 74–83.

[153] Tim Cresswell, *In Place / Out of Place* (Minneapolis & London: U of Minnesota P, 1996): 21–30.

Several contributions to the present volume demonstrate that flowing inter-actions and representational references are inherent in the spaces we live in. Just like money, labour, trade or information flows, people can operate, or have an effect, or can imagine themselves to be, in several places (or spaces) at one time. As also noted by Appadurai,

> in today's world [...] primordia (whether of language or skin colour or neighborhood or kinship) have become globalized. That is, sentiments [...which] turn locality into a staging ground for identity, have be-come spread over vast and irregular spaces as groups move yet stay linked to one another [...]. Ethnicity, once a genie contained in the bottle of some sort of locality (however large) has now become a global force, forever slipping in and through the cracks of states and borders.[154]

The global *Geographies of Mobilities*[155] as well as the subjects and cultural practices that are constitutive for these geographies have dramatically increa-sed. Hence the need for a new language to describe the spaces arising between spatial interactions and cultural representations is widely acknowledged. Focusing on filmic representations of so-called illegal immigrants, Lars Eck-stein's contribution to this volume, for example, follows a two-pronged ap-proach; he not only illustrates the predicaments of factually documenting the lives of persons in translocation, but also addresses the strategic questioning of the mimetic capacity associated with the documentary mode. As Eckstein demonstrates, this questioning is achieved by blending the genres of fictional staging (cinematic fiction) and representing real experience (documentary film).

However, there is generally little consensus regarding the appropriate theo-retical approaches and methodological paradigms. While some critics argue for a "mobility turn"[156] from within human geography, others like Bertrand

---

[154] Appadurai, *Modernity at Large*, 41. See also 48–49, 51–52, and similar com-ments on the loosening of connections between territory and nationhood or nation-state (161, 165–66, 172–73, 196) as well as between spatial locality and neighbourhood (178–79, 196).

[155] *Geographies of Mobilities: Practices, Spaces, Subjects*, ed. Tim Cresswell & Peter Merriman (Farnham: Ashgate, 2011).

[156] Tim Cresswell & Peter Merriman, "Introduction: Geographies of Mobilities – Practices, Spaces, Subjects," in *Geographies of Mobilities*, ed. Cresswell & Merriman,

Westphal suggest a geocentred approach to literature and other forms of cultural representations in order to not only produce new narratives of lived spatial transgression but also to grasp the inherent transgressivity of literature itself.[157]

In addition, one needs to consider Philip Ethington's argument that the representation of place and space is always implicitly an intervention "into the (re)telling of the historical constitution of the present."[158] Arguing that historical interpretation is to a certain degree "the act of reading places," he urges historians to critically re-visit the immutable connections between space and time and to engage with the spatial turn in the humanities: "Mapping cartography is vital to my proposal to rethink historical interpretation as a form of mapping."[159] Although spatial analysis has a certain tradition within historical research, there has clearly been a significant rise of interest in this field since the start of the twenty-first century. As Karl Schlögel argues, it is in space that we read time.[160] Thus, it is necessary for scholars of literary and cultural studies to engage in cross-disciplinary dialogues with historians as well.

Geographical sensibility and spatial thinking have not been taken far enough: We need to understand not only how knowledge is produced in individual places and how literatures and other forms of cultural representations are grounded in specific locations, but also how transactions occur between these locations. Spatialization in the context of this volume refers to a particular approach which aims at grasping the translocal process of constructing and deconstructing abstract places of *here* and *there*. It seeks to understand the transformation of spatial practices: something that is regulated by and regulates the cultural representations of our and others' 'being in the world' as being in translocation.

⌘

---

11. Cf. Stephen Greenblatt et al., *Cultural Mobility: A Manifesto* (Cambridge: Cambridge UP, 2010).

[157] Westphal, *Geocriticism*, 41–74.

[158] Philip J. Ethington, "Placing the Past: 'Groundwork' for a Spatial Theory of History," *Rethinking History* 11.4 (December 2007): 465.

[159] Ethington, "Placing the Past," 487.

[160] Karl Schlögel, *Im Raum lesen wir Zeit: Über Zivilisationsgeschichte und Geopolitik* (Frankfurt am Main: Fischer, 2006).

12. Overview of Sections and Essays

The multiple directions postcolonial translocations can take – in space and time as well as beyond both – are reflected by the contributions in this volume. Although the essays deal with a great variety of aspects, there are also shared orientations that underlie the thematic sections that follow. However, unlike a concern with space, place, location, and mobility in English literature,[161] where the texts investigated reflect some kind of teleological development (even if not suggesting "a coherent history of spatial semantics"[162]), this volume represents different cultural and linguistic fields in terms of the choice of writers and artists as well as regarding our contributors' own geographical, cultural, and disciplinary backgrounds.

The material escapes attempts at tracing coherent developments. The diversity of the texts, objects, and events interpreted in this book invites, instead, an arrangement that calls attention to the fact that the topical and methodological similarities emerge, in fact, from difference. The division into six categories is, therefore, based not on genre, chronology, or geography, but on dominant thematic or methodological features shared and complemented by the respective essays. The sections illustrate the arguments made in the theoretical part of this introduction: 'Translocation' is neither a fixed nor a homogeneous concept; there is no consistent and continuous growth of postcolonial translocations. Instead, the directions addressed reflect temporal and spatial, material and intellectual, physical and spiritual mobility – as well as difference, mutability, variety, and controversy.

SECTION I: CONCEPTUAL INTERVENTIONS
AND DISCIPLINARY TRANSGRESSIONS

Although, in this volume, the concern with translocation reflects a certain overbalance of the exploration of literary texts, the interdisciplinary quality of the term 'translocation' itself as well as its path-breaking potential as an interdisciplinary research tool is recalled in three contributions which argue for the necessity of initiating new forms of cultural criticism by going beyond (i.e. transgressing) fixed disciplinary or methodological borders. In this sense, 'intervention' in these essays is to be understood as the interruption of a

---

[161] See, for example, *Spatial Change in English Literature*, ed. Joachim Frenk (Trier: WVT, 2000).

[162] Joachim Frenk, "Introduction" to *Spatial Change in English Literature*, ed. Joachim Frenk (Trier: WVT, 2000): 17.

routine, on the one hand, and as a form of closing a gap between seemingly unconnected, if not contradictory, fields, on the other.

In her essay "'Difficult Forms of Knowing': Enquiry, Injury, and Translocated Relations of Postcolonial Responsibility," Diana Brydon explores what the Australian writer Gail Jones calls 'difficult forms of knowing'. Starting from Homi Bhabha's question of the complex relation between the postcolonial critic's positionality and her or his responsibility, she argues that stories and poems: i.e. fictional imaginings, despite being among the most powerful modes for addressing the challenges now faced by our increasingly interconnected world, cannot stand alone. They need to be placed in dialogue with other socio-political modes of critical inquiry and read as contributing to an emerging global dialogue. Brydon reads two contrasting visual images of charged postcolonial encounters that are currently circulating throughout the global public sphere. Drawing on concepts of planetarity by Gayatri Chakravorty Spivak and Paul Gilroy, her essay interrupts the work of one disciplinary imaginary through another, re-constellating each, and re-thinking notions of autonomy in dialogue with community and suffering in the age of global translocations.

Claudia Perner, in "Dislocating Imagology – And: How Much of It Can (or Should) Be Retrieved?," revisits some basic assumptions of the subfield of literary imagology from a decisive transcultural perspective. Drawing on influential theories of globalization and transculturality that stress the persistent erosion of cultural and national borders, the essay radically questions traditional imagology as a sufficient scholarly tool in postcolonial studies. Perner argues that although recent contributions: i.e. by William L. Chew III, Daniel–Henri Pageaux, and Joep Leerssen, introduced new perspectives and methodological reconceptions which challenge the unquestioned certainties of dominant imagological research practice, the field is still characterized by a focus on national character, a container-model of culture, the synonymous use of image and stereotype, eurocentric bias as well as general conceptual confusion and the absence of self-critical reflections. Perner's critical re-reading thus calls for a radical dislocation of imagology towards an interdisciplinary study of literary stereotypes in relation to non-stereotypical features.

The reading of literary texts in relation to the quest for a non-traditional, non-eurocentric, less idealistic version of cosmopolitanism which is critically aware of the embeddedness of culture in global political and economic realities and inequalities is discussed by Dirk Wiemann. In "Distant Reading: Cosmopolitanism as Unconditional Reception," he postulates an approach of

'distant reading' (as opposed to traditional 'close reading') which thinks beyond the text and beyond (national or international) canons and which is inclusive, non-normative, and non-hierarchical. Wiemann relates literary criticism to social-science and philosophical discourses (especially Kant) and
offers exemplary 'distant readings' of the novella *Pterodactyl, Puran Sahay
and Pirtha* (1993) by the Indian writer Mahasveta Devi.

SECTION II: SPACE, TIME, AND NARRATION

The critical stance of the previous section demanding a revision of the theoretical and disciplinary range of current postcolonial studies is complemented
by this section of five essays focusing on forms of narration. Their shared
concern with the traditional categories of time and space in narrative fiction is
not an illustration of scholarly recession into an exclusively literary debate.
These qualities of translocation are used, instead, for a critical deviation from
canonical literary traditions and for an exploration of the textual, intertextual,
and supratextual potential of texts on new methodological and theoretical
grounds. The composition of this section also demonstrates the productivity
of translocal perspectives: i.e. the juxtaposition of works from different
epochs and cultural traditions for global audiences.

Roland Walter's essay "Transculturation and Narration in the Black Dia-
spora of the Americas" examines the dynamics of diasporic memory and
identification in selected literary representations of pan-American black
writers ranging from Marlene Nourbese Philip and Toni Morrison to Patrick
Chamoiseau and Ana Maria Gonçalves. A special focus is on contemporary
African-Brazilian literature. Drawing on Paul Gilroy's seminal *Black Atlantic*,
Édouard Glissant's notion of violated space–time relations, and Fernando
Ortiz's concept of transculturation, Walter shows how these creative writers
use language, memory, and imagination to transform the experience of
ongoing brutalization into a resistive mnemonic practice of identity-construc-
tion. He categorizes this narrative practice as 'transwriting'.

In "Far Away, So Close: Translocation as Storytelling Principle in Hari
Kunzru's *Transmission*," Lucia Krämer discusses Kunzru's 2004 novel as a
fictiocritical postcolonial narrative that reflects the increasing interconnectedness of cultures and individuals in an age of globalization. Exploring Kunzru's ambivalent representation of translocation as a physical process – "a
simultaneous drawing together and pulling apart" – and translocality as a
structural condition or state, Krämer reads this particular ambivalence as a
meta-fictional comment on the literary politics of storytelling for a global

readership. Consequently, particular emphasis is placed on narrative tech-niques – such as the use of metaphors of noise, intermedial references, or satire – by which Kunzru dismantles the many predicaments of crossing poli-tical, cultural, and psychological boundaries.

Gesa Mackenthun focuses on the historical and cultural context of Herman Melville's *Moby-Dick* as informed by the theoretical/philosophical vantage-point of contemporary debates about cosmopolitanism, global governance, and translocation. In "American Antebellum Cosmopolitanism: Herman Mel-ville's 'Postcolonial' Translocations," Mackenthun explores the gap between an "aesthetic or cultural" and a "political cosmopolitanism." Interpreting *Moby-Dick* as an "allegory of the fate of mankind," she foregrounds the potential of literature for offering views and "solutions" that can "transcend" the limitations of political reasoning.

Lynda Ng's examination of "Translocal Temporalities in Alexis Wright's *Carpentaria*" attempts to take the first step towards bringing together two theoretical approaches. According to Ng, postcolonial studies continues to argue for its continued relevance in a world of increasing globalization and internationalization. She argues that any translocal movement between two spaces cannot be discussed without situating it between two moments in time. As postcolonial translocations demand an engagement with world-literature paradigms such as Franco Moretti's morphology of genres and Pascale Casa-nova's *The World Republic of Letters*, the essay shows how a novel like Alexis Wright's *Carpentaria* consciously operates as a translocal text, both in terms of its influences and in the way it positions the Australian nation within a global context.

In "'We die only once, and for such a long time': Approaching Trauma through Translocation in Chris Abani's *Song for Night*," Daria Tunca ana-lyses Abani's novella, set in Nigeria at the time of the Biafran war, in relation to war literature, trauma studies, and potential processes of healing. 'Trans-location' is here understood in its double sense of, first, a movement between different (physical or abstract) locations, and, secondly, a single location func-tioning as a "site of transition and change." Tunca investigates the interplay of both kinds of translocation in Abani's preoccupation with various kinds of transformation and border-crossing, both physical and non-physical.

SECTION III: TRANSLATION AND CULTURAL REWRITING

The notion of 'translation' as implying different forms of translocation is discussed above. The movements back and forth between two or more languages (switching and code-switching) or the availability of linguistic skills to 'move' texts from one language into another is much more than an automatic process and asks for familiarity with the historical phases and cultural frames of the languages involved. Moreover, when literature is transported from one culture into another or when products and texts from different cultures or epochs are intertextually linked and referred to each other, the resulting tension produces new insights into each of the literary and cultural representations, as three contributions to this volume illustrate.

Sandra Meyer's essay "'The Story that Gave this Land its Life': The Translocation of Rilke's *Duino Elegies* in Amitav Ghosh's *The Hungry Tide*" analyses Ghosh's novel in terms of translation and intertextuality as aspects of dislocation and translocation. Accordingly, many passages of Ghosh's novel could be read as illustrations of the *Duino Elegies*, and vice versa. This translocation also raises the question of whether and, if so, to what extent postcolonial and postmodern literary strategies overlap or differ, and it calls attention to the ways in which postcolonial texts with consistent intertextual references to classic Western texts appeal to implied target audiences in different cultures.

Therese–M. Meyer examines a case of postcolonial (re-)writing in "Reading 'Upstream!': Implications of an Unconsidered Source Text to Julian Barnes' Eighth Chapter of *A History of the World in 10½ Chapters*." Barnes's "Upstream!" (1989) has an intertext not listed in the author's notes: i.e. the *Journal* of Grillet and Bechamel, a travelogue of 1698. Barnes's novella adds a contemporary satirical twist to the expedition of these two Jesuits in Guiana by giving a tragicomic ending to an American film crew's attempt at re-creating their story in the jungles of Venezuela. Jungle rivers on both sides of the Atlantic, as Sir Walter Raleigh, Joseph Conrad, Evelyn Waugh, Redmond O'Hanlon, and Charles Nicholl show, are translocations for a critique of colonialism: They provide unwitting imperialist protagonists with experiences which transcend boundaries of language, culture, self, and space, and which depict the disintegration of Western subjects as an allegory of colonialist crises.

In "Myths of Rebellion: Translocation and (Cultural) Innovation in Mexican-American Literature," Marga Munkelt traces and evaluates formations and transformations of rebellion in texts from the Bible to Mexican-American literature. The investigation assumes the transformation of myths as trans-location in two senses: their transportation into a different historical or cultural context, on the one hand, and their transformation within a different ideological framework, on the other. A fusion of the sins of Lucifer (disobeying God out of pride) and Robin Hood (violating the law in order to implement God's intentions) can be recognized in Mexican-American literature. In the border-*corrido*, for example, the protagonist often becomes an outlaw in order to secure the 'law' for his countrymen. He expresses the need for a Mexican-American identity of self-esteem, for an ethnic or even national identity, and for an escape from disgrace and poverty. In other texts, the protagonists protest against mainstream authorities by emphasizing their otherness.

SECTION IV: DIASPORAS, IDENTIFICATIONS, RESISTANCE

The assertion, re-assertion, and revision of identity becomes a need especially when human beings are removed (forcibly or by consent) from their cultural and/or ethnic contexts, and when another culture threatens their 'heritage' and imaginary homeland. Five essays discuss the ramifications of (multiple) migration and dual (or multiple) cultural affiliation in literary texts. They call attention to the relationship between place and identity as well as between cultural codes and (unknown) environments. And they address the challenge to resist a possible loss of one's human dignity and agency. Characteristics of real or imagined homes and senses of belonging are addressed from various perspectives.

In her essay "Trans/locating Pacific Identities: From the Small Island to the Largest Polynesian City in the World," Paloma Fresno–Calleja discusses how the large Pacific diaspora in New Zealand negotiates identity, belonging, and space 'translocally', at the intersection between real or imaginary 'old homes' in various other Pacific Islands, 'new homes' in New Zealand, and new pan-Pacific affiliations. Translocation is also related to regional concepts of spatial theory, such as the "sea of islands," an "Oceanic imaginary," and "tidalectics." This is illustrated by texts from a range of literary genres.

Thomas Martinek analyses two Nigerian short stories engaged with migration on several levels. The main characters depicted in the stories have "crossed borders" into the UK, but, in contrast to their authors (Segun Afolabi and Ben Okri), they live "on the margins" of modern society. In "Writing (in) the Migrant Space: Discursive Nervousness in Contemporary Nigerian Short Stories," Martinek argues that the stories do not praise hybridity; rather, they reveal the realities of living in exile and contrast the protagonists' position of liminality with the social, political, and cultural mainstream. "Writing the migrant space as short story" thus "lead[s] to the emergence of Bhabha's 'Third Space of enunciation'" and ultimately "challenge[s] structures of authority" and "cosmopolitan complacency."

In "Daljit Nagra's *Look We Have Coming to Dover!* and the Limits of the Translocal," Katharina Rennhak criticizes certain uses of the term 'translocal' which conflate complex and hybrid identities with spatial location (or translocation). She argues that a preoccupation with procedural and ideological readings of location often neglects a more concrete sense of social space for genuinely transcultural interaction and dialogue, and the continuing *scarcity* of such spaces. To illustrate her critique, she analyses how Nagra's poetry depicts Asian-British identities, heterogeneity within the diasporic community, a sense of arrival and of being at home in England, and (nonetheless) the frequent lack of social spaces for true interaction with non-Asian British people which would also entail the latter's acceptance of hybridization as a two-way process.

Petra Tournay–Theodotou's essay "'I love Cyprus but England is my home': Eve Makis' *Eat Drink and Be Married*" introduces Makis's 2004 debut novel as a narrative which gives voice to the experience of Anglo-Greek-Cypriot migrations that, so far, has been conspicuously absent from the map of British multicultural literature. Tournay–Theodotou reads the story of a Greek-Cypriot family in Nottingham at the end of the twentieth century told from the perspective of a young woman caught in-between two cultures as a typical coming-of-age novel that can be read alongside other first novels of minoritarian writers like *Lara* by Bernardine Evaristo or *Anita and Me* by Meera Syal. The essay demonstrates that this particular novel offers an especially compelling discussion of specific Greek-Cypriot cultural configurations regarding gender, spatial differentiation, the importance of food in the process of cultural identification, or the representation of Britishness.

Drawing on relevant theories of laughter, Jessica Voges argues that laughter not only enables the individual to establish group belonging and to transcend cultural barriers but can also counter racist discrimination and alter power-relations. In "Laughter *Movens*: Functions and Effects of Laughter in Black British Literature," she discusses acts of laughter in postcolonial literary texts as performative strategies of translocation. Focusing on the socio-cultural stimuli which evoke laughter, she argues that the black British individual laughing strategically can adapt, mimic, and revise codes and conventions of a dominant group by responding to these specific stimuli. As Voges's reading of selected literary representations such as Andrea Levy's *Small Island* and Zadie Smith's *White Teeth* demonstrates, laughter, as a speech act, has both a resistive capacity and the power of transformative identification.

SECTION V: TRANSMIGRATION: MULTIPLE MIGRATION, AND CULTURAL TRANSGRESSION

There is, at first sight, a narrow margin between the movement from one country or culture to another (possibly even shifting back and forth) and a transgression of (cultural) borders. The concept of (multiple) migration with the possible consequences of relocation is theoretically and practically explored in two essays. The effects of multiple trans- or relocations and transmigration on artistic representations are not the same as on human beings. Both contributors are themselves 'transgressive', in that their examinations of pieces of literature and the visual arts respectively include methods from other disciplines.

Silke Stroh's essay "Theories and Practices of Transmigration: Colonial British Diasporas and the Emergence of Translocal Space" surveys different ways in which the concepts of transmigration and translocation have been used in different fields, and discusses the extent to which these concepts can be applied in postcolonial and transcultural English studies. It also offers a more detailed exploration of the 'transmigration' concept in the particular sense of '*multiple* migration' where people physically relocate to other countries, or even continents, more than once. A case study from the white British colonial settler diaspora of the nineteenth century, through contemporary and modern representations, is used to explore how transmigrants are positioned in relation to their various old and new locations as well as to different local 'branches' of the 'same' transmigrant community. The essay elucidates how these diasporic representations construct identities and (un)belonging across geographical space, and discusses whether at least some discourses of colonial transmigration display features which can be regarded as predecessors of certain forms of deterritorialized identities and translocations, as well as forms of transnational, cosmopolitan, or global consciousness, identified today.

In "Blurring Images: Articulations of Arab-American Crossovers," Markus Schmitz explores selected literary and artistic interventions by Arab-American transmigrants which are decisively influenced by the constant physical and topological-discursive movements between the Middle East and the USA. Scarcely locatable within the binary matrix of ethnicity and stable cultural identity, the works of Rabieh Alameddine, Emily Jacir, and Walid Raad are interpreted as articulations of Arab-American crossovers participating in the formation of a new counter-discursive space of critical correlations. Tracing artistic spheres of resistive performance and literary non-places of narrative identifications to their cross-cultural genesis, Schmitz is particularly concerned with these works' recursive decentering effects. His reading treats representations of Arab-American transmigrancy as cultural documents of the transgressive and transitive act of writing identity and also as epistemic tools for the transgression of our interpretative reference systems in the academic fields of postcolonial studies and comparative cultural criticism. Going beyond inherited notions of world literature or global art, this contribution argues for a critical practice that reveals our provisional sense of (trans-)location in correlation with other spaces and places.

SECTION VI: MEDIA AND PERFORMANCE

The three essays in this section deal with different aspects of performance as translocation and with forms of reception. The frequent cultural translation, in the twentieth century, of printed literature into motion pictures has occluded the awareness that the two forms of reception are based on the traditional rivalry between literature read and literature watched as well as on the genre-characteristic distinguishing literature narrated (novels and stories) from literature performed (plays). This coincidental disappearance of genre distinction is carried further by experiments with films as 'hybrid' genres residing between invention and documentation – types of performance that confuse fiction and life. Like film and TV, the translocation of events or social phenomena into an exhibition of art objects reaches a large number of people and can exert a cultural, political, ideological, and especially commercial influence. It shares with the filmic or theatrical performances its communal characteristic and temporal/transitory quality.

Lars Eckstein's essay "Filming Illegals: Clandestine Translocation and the Representation of Bare Life" revolves around the chances and pitfalls of semi-fictional documentaries of clandestine immigration. Charting some of the ethical and conceptual problems involved in such representational endeavours and drawing on the political philosophy of Giorgio Agamben as well as the media philosophy of Slavoj Žižek, Eckstein offers a comparative reading of two films which have self-reflexively tackled the challenge of representing what Agamben calls 'bare life': These are Sorious Samura's 2006 TV feature *Living with Illegals* and Michael Winterbottom's 2002 film *In This World*.

Both operate strategically with an intricate blending of documentary and fictional modes.

In "Translating the American Dream? A Brazilian Vision of the Promised Land," Gundo Rial y Costas discusses the Brazilian *telenovela* by Gloria Perez, *América* (2005), in terms of Brazil's reputation as 'paradise' and 'promised land' according to the first Portuguese colonizers in the sixteenth century. The *telenovela* questions established categories of homeland and nation-state by using elements of the American Dream (such as the pursuit of happiness and the attempt to realize one's aspirations) and, by incorporating these in a new space, thus dislocating them and constructing a new 'dream narrative', a Brazilian 'American dream'. The argument draws on different cultural translation processes and considers generic connections of *telenovela* and melodrama as well as the dynamic nature of the medium of television.

Kathy–Ann Tan deals with a collaborative intermedia art project titled 'curio' that ran for a period of four weeks from September to October 2002 in London, exactly a year after the 9/11 attacks. The project invited seven artists to respond with site-specific interventions to the nature of the tourist site known as 'Banglatown'. The artists' different cultural backgrounds, perspectives, and approaches resulted in different manifestations of their critical engagement with notions of cultural tourism, stereotypes, authenticity, fantasies of the Other, and terrorism. In "Curio(us) Translocations: Site-Specific Interventions in Banglatown, London," Tan suggests that 'curio' effectively represented a project of temporal and spatial translocation.

In all, the contributions to this volume powerfully demonstrate that space, place, and location have emerged as important epistemological metaphors in postcolonial studies. However, the debate still harbours many traditional metaphysical implications. In literary and cultural studies, place is still taken to be the location (stage-set) of a phenomenon (or plot), a particular positioning with regard to that other larger referent, space. At the same time, it remains a problem that the critical discourse on the spatiality of cultural representations is not always seriously grounded in empirical inquiries, thus not infrequently running the risk of appearing abstract or even abstruse. The simplified notion of place as locality has a long pedigree. In the form of local history, it has provided the paradigmatic and long-unquestioned framework for historical and sociological inquiry. The renewed critical attention to the spatial, to the connections between places, and to transgressions of place, is radically dis-placing our long-standing assumptions about so-called core locations and meanings, opening up new perspectives on both the representations of spatial transgressions and the transgressivity of postcolonial cultural articulations. Drawing on a number of theoretical perspectives and disciplines, and working through diverse genres of cultural articulation, this volume offers a contemporary assessment of the diverse directions that the study of postcolonial translocations can take.

WORKS CITED

Abrams, M.H. *The Mirror and the Lamp: Romantic Theory and the Critical Tradition* (1953; Oxford & New York: Oxford U P, 1971).

Abu-Lughod, Janet L. *Rabat: Urban Apartheid in Morocco* (Princeton N J: Princeton U P, 1980).

Agnew, John. *Place and Politics* (Boston M A: Allen & Unwin, 1987).

——, & James Duncan, ed. *The Power of Place* (Boston M A: Unwin Hyman, 1990).

Anaya, Rudolfo. *Randy Lopez Goes Home: A Novel* (Norman: U of Oklahoma P, 2011).

Anderson, Benedict. *Imagined Communities: Reflections on the Origin and Spread of Nationalism* (London: Verso, 1983).

Anzaldúa, Gloria. *Borderlands/La Frontera: The New Mestiza* (1987; San Francisco: Aunt Lute, 3rd ed. 2007).

Appadurai, Arjun. *Modernity at Large: Cultural Dimensions of Globalization* (Public Worlds 1; Minneapolis & London: U of Minnesota P, 1996).

Ashcroft, Bill, Gareth Griffiths & Helen Tiffin. *Post-Colonial Studies: The Key Concepts* (London & New York: Routledge, 2000).

Auer, Peter. "Introduction: Bilingual Conversation Revisited," in *Code-Switching in Conversation: Language, Interaction and Identity*, ed. Peter Auer (London & New York: Routledge, 1998): 1–24.

Bachelard, Gaston. *The Poetics of Space*, tr. Maria Jolas (*La Poétique de l'espace*, 1957; Boston M A: Beacon, 1994).

Bachmann–Medick, Doris. *Cultural Turns* (Reinbeck: Rowohlt, 2007).

Bailey, Nathan. *An Universal Etymological English Dictionary* (1721; Anglistica & Americana 52; Hildesheim & New York: Georg Olms, 1969).

Bakhtin, Mikhail M. "Forms of Time and of the Chronotope in the Novel: Notes toward a Historical Poetics" (1937–38), tr. Caryl Emerson & Michael Holquist, in *Problems of Literature and Esthetics* (*Voprosy literatury i estetiki*, 1975), repr. in *The Dialogic Imagination: Four Essays by M.M. Bakhtin*, ed. Michael Holquist (U of Texas Slavic Series 1; Austin: U of Texas P, 1981): 84–258.

Basch, Linda, Nina Glick Schiller & Cristina Szanton Blanc. *Nations Unbound: Transnational Projects, Postcolonial Predicaments, and Deterritorialized Nation-States* (Luxemburg: Gordon & Breach, 1994).

Berkeley, George. *A Treatise Concerning the Principles of Human Knowledge* (1710, repr. 1734; Menston: Scolar, 1971).

Bhabha, Homi K. "DissemiNation: Time, Narrative and the Margins of the Modern Nation," in *The Location of Culture*, Homi K. Bhabha (London & New York: Routledge, 1994): 139–70.

——. *The Location of Culture* (London & New York: Routledge, 1994).

Blunt, Alison, & Cheryl McEwan, ed. *Postcolonial Geographies* (New York & London: Continuum, 2002).

Brubaker, Rogers. "The 'Diaspora' Diaspora," *Ethnic and Racial Studies* 28.1 (January 2005): 1–19, http://dx.doi.org/10.1080/0141987042000289997 (accessed 10 November 2011).

Buttimer, Anne, & David Seamon, ed. *The Human Experience of Space and Place* (London: Croom Helm, 1980).

Casey, Edward. *Earth-Mapping: Artists Reshaping Landscape* (Minneapolis: U of Minnesota P, 2005).

——. *The Fate of Place: A Philosophical History* (Berkeley: U of California P, 1998).

——. *Getting Back into Place: Toward a Renewed Understanding of the Place-World* (Bloomington: Indiana U P, 1993).

Çelik, Zeynep. *Urban Forms and Colonial Confrontations: Algiers under French Rule* (Berkeley: U of California P, 1997).

Clifford, James. "Diasporas," *Cultural Anthropology* 9.3 (Summer 1994): 302–38.

Cohen, Robin. *Global Diasporas: An Introduction* (London: Francis & Taylor, 2nd ed. 2008).

Cresswell, Tim. *In Place/Out of Place* (Minneapolis & London: U of Minnesota P, 1996).

——. *Place: A Short Introduction* (Oxford & Malden M A: Blackwell, 2004).

——. "Race, Mobilities and the Humanities: A Geosophical Approach," in *Envisioning Landscapes, Making Worlds: Geography and the Humanities*, ed. Stephen Daniels, Dydia DeLyser, J. Nicholas Entrikin & Douglas Richardson (London & New York: Routledge, 2011): 74–83.

——, & Peter Merriman, ed. *Geographies of Mobilities: Practices, Spaces, Subjects* (Farnham: Ashgate, 2011).

——, & Peter Merriman, "Introduction: Geographies of Mobilities – Practices, Spaces, Subjects," in *Geographies of Mobilities*, ed. Cresswell & Merriman, 1–15.

Crinson, Mark. *Modern Architecture and the End of Empire* (Aldershot: Ashgate, 2003).

Crowther, Paul. *Defining Art, Creating the Canon: Artistic Value in an Era of Doubt* (Oxford: Clarendon, 2007).

Culler, Jonathan. *Literary Theory: A Very Short Introduction* (1997; Oxford: Oxford U P, 2nd ed. 2000).

Curtius, Ernst Robert. *European Literature and the Latin Middle Ages*, tr. Willard R. Trask (*Europäische Literatur und Lateinisches Mittelalter*, 1948; Bollingen Series XXXVI, tr. 1953; Princeton NJ: Princeton UP, 1990).

de Certeau, Michel. *The Practice of Everyday Life,* tr. Steven F. Rendall (*Arts de faire: L'invention du quotidien*, vol. 1, 1980; Berkeley: U of California P, 1984).

Deleuze, Gilles, & Félix Guattari. *A Thousand Plateaus: Capitalism and Schizophrenia,* tr. Brian Massumi (*Capitalisme et schizophrénie 2: Mille plateaux*, 1980; tr. 1988; London & New York: Continuum, 2004).

Descartes, René. *Principles of Philosophy*, tr. Valentine Rodger Miller & Reese P. Miller (*Principia Philosophiae*, 1644; tr. 1983; Dordrecht: Kluwer, 1991).

Döring, Jörg, & Tristan Thielmann, ed. *Spatial Turn: Das Raumparadigma in den Kultur- und Sozialwissenschaften* (Bielefeld: transcript, 2008).

Du Bois, W.E.B. *The Souls of Black Folk* (1903; New York: Vintage, 1990).

Eade, John, ed. *Living the Global City: Globalization as a Local Process* (London: Routledge, 1996).

Eagleton, Terry. *How to Read a Poem* (Malden MA & Oxford: Blackwell, 2007).

Edmond, Jacob. "A Poetics of Translocation: Yang Lian's Auckland and Lyn Hejinian's Leningrad," in *Cultural Transformations*, ed. Prentice, Devadas & Johnson, 105–34.

Erne, Lukas. "Words in Space: The Reproduction of Texts and the Semiotics of the Page," in *The Space of English*, ed. Spurr & Tschichold, 99–118.

Ethington, Philip J. "Placing the Past: 'Groundwork' for a Spatial Theory of History," *Rethinking History* 11.4 (December 2007): 465–93.

Fanon, Frantz. *The Wretched of the Earth*, tr. Richard Philcox (*Les Damnés de la terre*, 1961; New York: Grove, 2004).

Faris, Ellsworth. "The Nature of Human Nature," *Publications of the American Sociological Society* 20 (1925): 15–29.

Foucault, Michel. "Of Other Spaces," tr. Jay Miskowiec ("Des espaces autres," in *Architecture – Mouvement – Continuité*, 1984), *Diacritics* 16.1 (Spring 1986): 22–27.

——. *Utopies et hétérotopies* (Paris: INA, 2004).

Franceschini, Rita. "Code-Switching and the Notion of Code in Linguistics: Proposal for a Dual Focus Model," in *Code-Switching in Conversation: Language, Interaction and Identity*, ed. Peter Auer (London & New York: Routledge, 1998): 51–72.

Freitag, Ulrike, & Achim von Oppen. "Introduction: 'Translocality'," in *Translocality*, ed. Freitag & von Oppen, 1–21.

——, ed. *Translocality – The Study of Globalising Processes from a Southern Perspective* (Studies in Global History 4; Leiden & Boston MA: Brill, 2010).

Frenk, Joachim. "Introduction" to *Spatial Change in English Literature*, ed. Frenk, 9–20.

——, ed. *Spatial Change in English Literature* (Trier: W V T, 2000).

Genette, Gérard. "Time and Narrative in *A la recherche du temps perdu*," tr. Paul de Man, in *Aspects of Narrative: Selected Papers from the English Institute*, ed. J. Hillis Miller (New York & London: Columbia U P, 1971): 93–118.

Gilroy, Paul. "Diaspora," *Paragraph: A Journal of the Modern Critical Theory* 17.1 (March 1994): 207–12.

Greenblatt, Stephen et al. *Cultural Mobility: A Manifesto* (Cambridge: Cambridge U P, 2010).

Gupta, Akhil. "The Song of the Nonaligned World: Transnational Identities and the Reinscription of Space in Late Capitalism," *Current Anthropology* 7.1 (February 1992): 63–77.

Hamid, Mohsin. *The Reluctant Fundamentalist* (London: Hamish Hamilton, 2007).

Hannerz, Ulf. "Transnational Research," in *Handbook of Methods in Cultural Anthropology*, ed. H. Russell Bernard (London & New Delhi: AltaMira, 1998): 235–56.

Heidegger, Martin. "Building Dwelling Thinking," in *Martin Heidegger, Poetry, Language, Thought*, tr. & intro. Albert Hofstadter ("Bauen Wohnen Denken," 1952; New York: Harper & Row, 1971): 143–61.

Hesse, Barnor. "Introduction: Un/Settled Multiculturalisms," in *Un/Settled Multiculturalisms: Diasporas, Entanglements, 'Transruptions'*, ed. Barnor Hesse (London: Zed, 2000): 1–30.

Heuner, Ulf. "Die Wiederentdeckung des Raumes," in *Klassische Texte zum Raum*, ed. Ulf Heuner (Berlin: Parodos, 2008): 7–10.

Hobbes, Thomas. *The English Works of Thomas Hobbes*, ed. William Molesworth (1839–45; London: Scientia Aalen, 1962), vols. 1, 7.

Hoerder, Dirk. "Transcultural States, Nations, and People," in *The Historical Practice of Diversity: Transcultural Interactions from the Early Modern Mediterranean to the Postcolonial World*, ed. Christiane Harzig, Dirk Hoerder & Adrian Shubert (New York & Oxford: Berghahn, 2003): 13–32.

Ikas, Karin. "Interview with Gloria Anzaldúa by Karin Ikas," in *Borderlands/La Frontera: The New Mestiza* (1987; San Francisco: Aunt Lute, 3rd ed. 2007): 227–46.

Jacobs, Jane. *The Death and Life of Great American Cities* (New York: Vintage, 1961).

Kearney, Michael. "Borders and Boundaries of the State and Self at the End of Empire," *Journal of Historical Sociology* 4.1 (March 1991): 52–74.

Keith, Michael, & Steve Pile, ed. *Place and the Politics of Identity* (London & New York: Routledge, 1993).

King, Anthony D. *Culture, Globalization and the World-System: Contemporary Conditions for the Representation of Identity* (Minneapolis: U of Minnesota P, 1991).

——. *Global Cities: Postimperialism and the Internationalization of London* (London & New York: Routledge, 1990).

——. *Spaces of Global Cultures: Architecture, Urbanism, Identity* (London, New York: Routledge, 2004).

Kipfer, Stefan. "Fanon and Space: Colonization, Urbanization, and Liberation from the Colonial to the Global City," *Society and Space* 25.4 (January 2007): 701–26.

Kwei–Armah, Kwame. *Elmina's Kitchen* (London: Methuen, 2003).

Lefebvre, Henri. *The Production of Space*, tr. Donald Nicholson–Smith (*La Production de l'espace*, 1974; Oxford: Blackwell, 1991).

——. *The Urban Revolution*, tr. Robert Bononno (*La Révolution urbaine*, 1968; Minneapolis: U of Minnesota P, 2003).

——. "The Urban Revolution" (1970), excerpt in *The Global Cities Reader*, ed. Neil Brenner & Roger Keil (London & New York: Routledge, 2006): 408–13.

Lennard, John, & Mary Lockhurst. *The Drama Handbook: A Guide to Reading Plays* (Oxford: Oxford UP, 2002).

Locke, John. *An Essay Concerning Human Understanding* (1690), ed. Peter H. Nidditch (Oxford: Clarendon, 1975).

Lord, George de F. "Preface," in Lord, *Homeric Renaissance: The "Odyssey" of George Chapman* (London: Chatto & Windus, 1956): 9–12.

Martindale, Don [Albert], & R[ussell] Galen Hanson. *Small Town and the Nation: The Conflict of Local and Translocal Forces* (Contributions in Sociology 3; Westport CT: Greenwood, 1969).

Massey, Doreen. "A Global Sense of Place," *Marxism Today* 35.6 (June 1991): 24–29.

Mayer, Ruth. *Diaspora: Eine kritische Begriffsbestimmung* (Bielefeld: transcript, 2005).

Melville, Pauline. "The Truth Is in the Clothes," in *Shape-Shifter: Stories* (London: Picador, 1991): 99–112.

Munkelt, Marga. "The Stylistics of Drama: Universal Elements," in *Language and Style: In Honour of Mick Short*, ed. Dan McIntyre & Beatrix Busse (London: Palgrave Macmillan, 2010): 145–61.

Nalbantoğlu, Gülsüm B., & Chong T. Wong, ed. *Postcolonial Space(s)* (New York: Princeton Architectural Press, 1997) .

Nasr, Joe, & Mercedes Volait, ed. *Urbanism: Imported or Exported. Native Aspirations and Foreign Plans* (London: Wiley, 2003).

Nederman, Cary J., & Takashi Shōgimen. *Western Political Thought in Dialogue with Asia* (Lanham MD & Plymouth: Lexington 2009).

Nicoll, Allardyce, ed. *Chapman's Homer: "The Iliad", "The Odyssey" and "The Lesser Homerica"* (London: Routledge & Kegan Paul, 1957).

Nichols, Grace. "Skanking Englishman Between Trains," in *The Fat Black Woman's Poems* (London: Virago, 1984): 33.

Nicolson, Adam. "The Bible of King James," *National Geographic* (December 2011): 36–61.

——. *God's Secretaries: The Making of the King James Bible* (New York: HarperCollins, 2003).

Oakes, Tim, & Louisa Schein. "Translocal China: An Introduction," in *Translocal China: Linkages, Identities, and the Reimagining of Space*, ed. Tim Oakes & Louisa Schein (Routledge Studies on China in Transition; London & New York: Routledge, 2006): 1–35.

Öncü, Ayşe, & Petra Weyland, ed. *Space, Culture and Power: New Identities in Globalizing Cities* (London: Zed, 1997).

The Oxford Dictionary of English Etymology, ed. C.T. Onions et al. (Oxford: Clarendon, 1966).

The Oxford English Dictionary (2nd ed. 1989).

Park, Robert E. *Human Communities: The City and Human Ecology* (Glencoe IL: Free Press, 1952).

——, Ernest W. Burgess & Roderick D. McKenzie. *The City* (Chicago: U of Chicago P, 1925).

Penrose, Jan. "Nations, States and Homelands: Territory and Territoriality in Nationalist Thought," *Nations and Nationalism* 8.3 (July 2002): 277–98.

Perry, Nick. "Travelling Theory/Nomadic Theorizing," *Organization* 2.1 (February 1995): 35–54.

Prakash, Vikramaditya. *Chandigarh's Le Corbusier: The Struggle for Modernity in Postcolonial India* (Seattle: U of Washington P, 2002).

Prentice, Chris, Vijay Devadas & Henry Johnson, ed. *Cultural Transformations: Perspectives on Translocation in a Global Age* (Cross/Cultures 125; Amsterdam & New York: Rodopi, 2010).

——, Henry Johnson & Chris Prentice. "Introduction: Cultural Transformations: Perspectives on Translocation in a Global Age," in *Cultural Transformations*, ed. Prentice, Devadas & Johnson, xi–xxxv.

Pries, Ludger. "The Approach of Transnational Social Spaces: Responding to New Configurations of the Social and the Spatial," in *New Transnational Social Spaces: International Migration and Transnational Companies in the Early Twenty-First Century*, ed. Ludger Pries (Routledge Research in Transnationalism 1; London & New York: Routledge, 2001): 3–33.

Prochaska, David. *Making Algeria French: Colonialism in Bône, 1870–1920* (Cambridge: Cambridge UP, 1990).

Rabinow, Paul. *French Modern: Norms and Forms of the Social Environment* (Cambridge MA: MIT Press, 1989).

Rampton, Ben. "Language Crossing and the Redefinition of Reality," in *Code-Switching in Conversation: Language, Interaction and Identity*, ed. Peter Auer (London & New York: Routledge, 1998): 290–320.

Relph, Edward. *Place and Placelessness* (London: Pion, 1976).

Rouse, Roger. "Making Sense of Settlement: Class Transformation, Cultural Struggle, and Transnationalism Among Mexican Migrants in the United States," in *Towards a Transnational Perspective on Migration: Race, Class, Ethnicity, and Nationalism Reconsidered*, ed. Nina Glick Schiller, Linda Basch & Cristina Blanc–Szanton (New York: New York Academy of Sciences, 1992): 25–52.

——. "Mexican Migration and the Social Space of Postmodernism," *Diaspora* 1.1 (Spring 1991): 8–23.

Russell, D.A., & M. Winterbottom, ed. "Aristotle: Poetics," in *Classical Literary Criticism* (1972; Oxford & New York: Oxford U P, 1989): 51–90.

Safran, William. "Diasporas in Modern Societies: Myths of Homeland and Return," in *Migration, Diasporas and Transnationalism*, ed. Steven Vertovec & Robin Cohen (Cheltenham: Edward Elgar, 1999): 365–80.

Said, Edward W. *Beginnings: Intention and Method* (New York: Basic Books, 1975).

——. *Culture and Imperialism* (1993; New York: Vintage, 1994).

——. "Molestation and Authority in Narrative Fiction," in *Aspects of Narrative: Selected Papers from the English Institute*, ed. J. Hillis Miller (New York & London: Columbia U P, 1971): 47–68.

——. *Orientalism* (London: Routledge & Kegan Paul, 1978).

——. "Reflections on Exile," in *Reflections on Exile and Other Essays* (Cambridge M A: Harvard U P, 2000): 173–86.

——. "Traveling Theory Reconsidered," in *Reflections on Exile and Other Essays* (Cambridge M A: Harvard U P, 2000): 436–52.

Salehi, Hadi. "Translocality and a Duality Principle in Generally Covariant Quantum Field Theory," *Classical and Quantum Gravity* 17.4 (December 2000): 825–34.

Sassen, Saskia. *The Global City: New York, London, Tokyo* (Princeton N J: Princeton U P, 2001).

Sayyid, S[alman]. "Beyond Westphalia: Nations and Diasporas – The Case of the Muslim Umma," in *Un/settled Multiculturalisms: Diasporas, Entanglements, Transruptions*, ed. Barnor Hesse (London: Zed): 33–50.

Schlögel, Karl. *Im Raum lesen wir Zeit: Über Zivilisationsgeschichte und Geopolitik* (Frankfurt am Main: Fischer, 2006).

Schmitz, Markus. *Kulturkritik ohne Zentrum: Edward W. Said und die Kontrapunkte kritischer Dekolonisation* (Bielefeld: transcript, 2008).

Shakespeare, William. "A Midsummer Night's Dream," in *The Riverside Shakespeare*, ed. G. Blakemore Evans et al. (1974; Boston M A: Houghton Mifflin, 2nd ed. 1996): 251–83.

Short, James F. *The Social Fabric of the Metropolis: Contributions of the Chicago School of Urban Sociology* (Chicago: U of Chicago P, 1971).

Sloterdijk, Peter. *Im Weltinnenraum des Kapitals: Für eine philosophische Theorie der Globalisierung* (Frankfurt am Main: Suhrkamp, 2006).

Smith Williams, Henry. "Anthropology," in *The Encyclopaedia Britannica*, 11th ed. vol. 6 (Cambridge: Cambridge UP 1910): 403–10.

Soja, Edward W. *Postmetropolis: Critical Studies of Cities and Regions* (Malden MA & Oxford: Blackwell, 2000).

——. *Postmodern Geography: The Reassertion of Space in Critical Social Theory* (London: Verso, 1989).

——. *Thirdspace: Journeys to Los Angeles and Other Real-and-Imagined Places* (Malden MA & Oxford: Blackwell, 1996).

——, & Barbara Hooper. "The Spaces that Difference Makes: Some Notes on the Geographical Margins of the New Cultural Politics," in *Place and the Politics of Identity*, ed. Michael Keith & Steve Pile (London & New York: Routledge, 1993): 183–205.

Spragens, Thomas A., Jr. *The Politics of Motion: The World of Thomas Hobbes* (London: Croom Helm, 1973).

Spurr, David. "The Study of Space in Literature: Some Paradigms," in *The Space of English*, ed. Spurr & Tschichold, 15–34.

——, & Cornelia Tschichold, ed. *The Space of English* (SPELL: Swiss Papers in English Language and Literature 17; Tübingen: Gunter Narr, 2005).

Stein, Mark. "Translokation und Gedächtnis: *Elmina's Kitchen* von Kwame Kwei–Armah im Kontext des Black Atlantic," in *Literatur und Migration*, ed. Heinz Ludwig Arnold (special issue of *Text + Kritik* 9; Munich: edition text + kritik, 2006): 246–54.

Stoler, Ann Laura, & Frederick Cooper. "Between Metropole and Colony: Rethinking a Research Agenda," in *Tensions of Empire: Colonial Cultures in a Bourgeois World*, ed. Frederick Cooper & Ann Laura Stoler (Berkeley: U of California P, 1997): 1–58.

Strauss, Anselm L. *The American City: A Sourcebook of Urban Imagery* (Chicago IL: Aldine, 1968).

Tuan, Yi–Fu. *Space and Place: The Perspective of Experience* (Minneapolis: U of Minnesota P, 1977).

——. *Topophilia: A Study of Environmental Perception, Attitudes and Values* (Englewood Cliffs NJ: Prentice–Hall, 1974).

Warf, Barney, & Santa Arias, ed. *The Spatial Turn* (London & New York: Routledge, 2008).

West–Pavlov, Russell. *Space in Theory: Kristeva, Foucault, Deleuze* (Amsterdam & New York: Rodopi, 2009).

Westphal, Bertrand. *Geocriticism: Real and Fictional Spaces*, tr. Robert T. Tally, Jr. (*La Géocritique*, 2007; New York: Palgrave Macmillan, 2011).

Wirth, Louis. *The Ghetto* (Chicago: U of Chicago P, 1928).

Worthen, W.B. *Drama: Between Poetry and Performance* (Malden MA & Oxford: Wiley–Blackwell, 2010).

Young, Robert J.C. *Colonial Desire: Hybridity in Theory, Culture and Race* (London & New York: Routledge 1995).

——. *Postcolonialism: A Very Short Introduction* (Oxford & New York: Oxford UP, 2003).

⌘

'Difficult Forms of Knowing'

—Enquiry, Injury, and Translocated Relations of Postcolonial Responsibility

DIANA BRYDON

> Where does the subject of global enquiry and injury stand or speak from? To what does it bear relation, from where does it claim responsibility?[1]

> There is a hush to difficult forms of knowing, an abashment, a sorrow, an inclination towards silence.[2]

T HESE TWO EPIGRAPHS POSE QUESTIONS about translocated relations within postcolonial imaginaries that compel me to ask: what has changed since postcolonial studies first emerged as a field of study and what remains the same? What does it mean to work in the postcolonial field today?[3] If decolonization was one of the major projects of the twentieth

---

[1] Homi K. Bhabha, "Unpacking My Library...Again," in *The Post-Colonial Question: Common Skies Divided Horizons*, ed. Iain Chambers & Lidia Curti (New York: Routledge, 1996): 200. See also Bhabha, "Unsatisfied: Notes on Vernacular Cosmopolitanism," in *Text and Nation: Cross-Disciplinary Essays on Cultural and National Identities*, ed. Laura Garcia–Morena & Peter C. Pfeiffer (Columbia SC: Camden House, 1996): 193.

[2] Gail Jones, *Sorry* (Sydney: Vintage, 2007): 3.

[3] The research for this essay has benefitted from several standard research grants from the Social Sciences and Humanities Research Council in Canada, and was funded, in part, through the Canada Research Chairs programme. I am grateful to Frank Schulze–Engler and to the GNEL/ASNEL conference organizers, especially Mark Stein, for the invitation to think more deeply about Postcolonial Translocations, the theme for their twentieth annual conference, held 21–24 May 2009, in Münster,

century, how has the urgency of that project been re-shaped by the globalizing processes that emerged since the 1980s? In response to Homi Bhabha's question and Gail Jones's caution, this essay reads textual and visual forms of expression to stress the challenges they pose to routine or easy forms of knowing and the assumptions on which they rest.[4] Postcolonial translocations invites us to think about the postcolonial as a disciplinary practice within educational institutional structures and as a subject of study attempting to make sense of colonialism (especially but no longer exclusively European colonialism) and the practices and discourses of Empire in search of better futures.

This is an exciting time for postcolonial studies but also a time for asking whether the postcolonial moment has passed. Breakthroughs seem possible, within global circuits of exchange at the level of geopolitical and economic relations and within educational and research institutions. The ways in which we know and understand the world are being challenged by neoliberal initiatives and by formerly subjugated forms of knowledge construction within revised circuits of power. Bhabha's question, repeated by him in at least two of his essays, asks: "Where does the subject of global enquiry and injury stand or speak from?"[5] This subject is not easily defined. Who is this person, the knower or the known, and what are the conditions giving access to speech? These have been postcolonial questions for some time, but they have changed their shape over the years. How we frame these questions shapes our answers. Postcolonial scholars have no monopoly on the positionality of this potentially global subject but our perspectives are important. According to Boaventura de Sousa Santos et al., "there is no global social justice without global

---

Germany. The research for this essay also benefitted from a workshop session with graduate students at McMaster University in 2009 and a sojourn in early 2010 as a visiting fellow at the Humanities Research Centre at the Australian National University in Canberra. I am grateful to Sandy Annett, my research assistant, for her keen editorial eye and help with the research for this essay.

[4] A limit case for considering Bhabha's question might be the current attempts to rehabilitate torture as a legitimate form of enquiry in certain cases post-9/11. In my view, torture is always wrong, is never acceptable, and is an illegitimate form of enquiry that falls outside the limits I have set myself in this essay.

[5] I address this question from a different angle in "Earth, World, Planet: Where Does the Postcolonial Critic Stand?," in *Cultural Transformations: Perspectives on Translocation in a Global Age*, ed. Chris Prentice, Vijay Devadas & Henry Johnson (Cross/ Cultures 125; Amsterdam & New York: Rodopi, 2010): 3–29.

cognitive justice."[6] This is where injury and enquiry come together and it is important to think the two together. But how?

The epigraph from the Australian Gail Jones's novel *Sorry* advises caution: "There is a hush to difficult forms of knowing."[7] That hush requires respect and understanding. Sometimes that speech will be a stutter or a speaking slant and sometimes it will be silenced altogether. Bhabha's second sentence raises the question of responsibility in a different way: "To what does it [the subject of global enquiry and injury] bear relation, from where does it claim responsibility?"[8] This is a question about location and the potential for accountability in global contexts. For Ngũgĩ wa Thiong'o, the task was to decolonize the mind. For Ulrich Beck, contemplating the risk society of current times, Ngũgĩ's cognitive certainty has yielded to "cognitive uncertainty."[9]

---

[6] Boaventura de Sousa Santos, João Arriscado Nunes & Maria Paula Meneses, "Introduction: Opening up the Canon of Difference," in *Another Knowledge is Possible: Beyond Northern Epistemologies*, ed. Boaventura de Sousa Santos (Reinventing Social Emancipation 3; London: Verso, 2007): xix.

[7] My thanks to Janet Wilson, who alerted me, at the ASNEL conference where this essay was delivered as a keynote address, to the echo here of the opening words of the film *The Piano*, and to Gail Jones's commentary on it. This is an insight into further translocations worth pursuing.

[8] Bhabha, "Unpacking My Library…Again," 1996.

[9] Beck writes:

> What qualifies as causal evidence and as 'proof' under conditions of cognitive uncertainty? Which norms of accountability apply? Who is responsible? Who must carry the costs? As we begin to examine these cognitive power bases of the relations of definition, we gain a deeper insight into the connection between risk and power; we also get some indication of how changes in the power relations of definition – such as redistribution of the burden of proof, or product liability regulations – can influence the political dynamic of risk conflicts.

—Ulrich Beck, *Power in the Global Age: A New Global Political Economy*, tr. Kathleen Cross (*Macht und Gegenmacht im globalen Zeitalter: Neue weltpolitische Ökonomie*, 2002; tr. Cambridge: Polity, 2005): 106.

Such questions are enabling critics to see that "the modern fact" itself has "a history"; Mary Poovey, *A History of the Modern Fact: Problems of Knowledge in the Sciences of Wealth and Society* (Chicago: U of Chicago P, 1998). I am grateful to William D. Coleman for alerting me to Beck's critique of the national outlook as elaborated in *Power in the Global Age*.

We know the damage that has been done but we do not know how to repair it. We are no longer even certain of the identity of this subject, whether it refers to colonized or colonizer or, more likely, to the differentiated responsibilities of both. Changes in what Beck calls "the power relations of definition"[10] are encouraging states and other actors to engage in public acts of apology and remembrance, but in ways that are quickly coming to seem not only routine but also substitutes for more substantive forms of restitution.

Where does postcolonial work stand in relation to the current interest in reconciliation commissions and memorials to the suffering and atrocities of the past? This trend clearly meets some deeply felt needs. Where do postcolonial revaluations of subjugated lives, communities, and knowledges fit within the current ethical and memorializing turns? If the goal is to establish a reciprocal relation of shared enquiry that seeks at minimum to do no harm, to what extent is this direction in the discipline proving helpful? We know that colonialism is not the only disabling inheritance contemporary scholars must confront. How does postcolonial critique connect to other modes of scholarship committed to social justice? How is it relocating itself within the global?

In the title of an earlier essay, I posed the translocational question this way: "Earth, World, Planet: Where Does the Postcolonial Critic Stand?" These resonant nouns conjure up respectively the ecocritical, socio-political, and planetary directions in which postcolonial scholarship is moving. I think it is important to recognize that global theories and theorizations of the global are not identical, nor are all attempts to theorize on this scale necessarily homogenizing or colonizing in their development, although some certainly are.[11] The harder part of thinking on this scale is to rethink the old colonial categories of particular vs universal in new ways, ways that can re-articulate shared values in a language of universality that is not the old, colonizing universality, and that can pay due regard to particularities and differences without subsuming them under blanketing generalities. In this essay, I continue to invoke Gayatri Chakravorty Spivak and Paul Gilroy's alternatively

---

[10] Ulrich Beck, *Power in the Global Age*, 106.

[11] I am responding here to Malini Johar Schueller's article "Decolonizing Global Theories Today," *Interventions* 11.2 (July 2009): 235–54, which makes many excellent points about the need for vigilance in reading some of the new master-narratives offered to make sense of globalization. In identifying problems in some influential theories of globality, she charts a course that requires much closer attention than I can offer here.

based models of planetarity as complementary ways of theorizing postcolonial responsibility, but with some unease. Spivak's turn to the "precapitalist cultures of the world"[12] and Gilroy's to a renewed focus on suffering itself as bases for transforming globality into planetarity may be helpful examples of how to reframe the debates.[13] These theories, too, require, further nuancing and explanation to avoid the traps of falling into frameworks they seek to challenge, such as exotification and compassion fatigue respectively. In crafting this essay, I follow Spivak in modelling interruptions of the logic of one disciplinary imaginary through another, reconstellating each, in an effort to rethink postcolonial translocations in dialogue with revisioned framings of community and suffering.[14] In particular, I ask how Bhabha's question might be read through Ulrich Beck's notion of "zombie categories."[15]

---

[12] Gayatri Chakravorty Spivak, *Death of a Discipline* (New York: Columbia UP, 2003): 101.

[13] In "Storying Home," I write:

Spivak proposes 'the planet to overwrite the globe' (*Death* 72) as a way of bypassing globalization's claims to the tropes and territory of inevitable progress through positing conquering as the only mode of inhabiting the earth. For this reason, she claims that planetarity 'is perhaps best imagined from the precapitalist cultures of the planet' (101), not in a spirit of nostalgia for what has been lost (as in Benjamin's "Storyteller"), but as a way of keeping 'responsibility alive in the reading and teaching of the textual' and a way of inscribing what she cryptically terms 'responsibility as right' (101–102). Spivak seeks a mode of reading that can counter globalization as 'a time and place that has privatized the imagination and pitted it against the political' (*Death* 37–38).

—Diana Brydon, "Storying Home: Power and Truth," in *Tropes and Territories: Short Fiction, Postcolonial Readings, Canadian Writing in Context*, ed. Marta Dvořák & William H. New (Montreal & Kingston, Ontario: McGill–Queen's UP, 2007): 35.

[14] I have approached these questions in different ways in "Metamorphoses of a Discipline: Rethinking Canadian Literature within Institutional Contexts," in *Trans.Can.-Lit: Resituating the Study of Canadian Literature*, ed. Smaro Kamboureli and Roy Miki (Waterloo, Ontario: Wilfrid Laurier UP, 2007): 14–16. See also *Renegotiating Community: Interdisciplinary Perspectives, Global Contexts*, ed. Diana Brydon & William D. Coleman (Vancouver: U of British Columbia P, 2008).

[15] Beck, *Power in the Global Age,* xi. Ben Fine's invocation of the zombie metaphor to define orthodox economics and its malign influence on development economics and other disciplinary modes of thinking, which he terms "zombieconomics," seems compatible with Beck's analysis. See Fine, "Development as Zombieconomics in the Age of Neoliberalism," *Third World Quarterly* 30.5 (2009): 885–904. Like Beck, Fine

Graham Huggan has addressed a tendency in postcolonial thinking to exoticize, fear or romanticize 'Others' seen as divergent from an assumed European norm. Here I follow Jones in asking how such forms of exotification operate within what Jones calls "a kind of terminological Gothicism that has invaded the theorizing of loss and injustice."[16] Whether deliberately or not, Beck's use of "zombie categories" seems a kind of terminological gothicism. In *Democracy and the Foreigner*, Bonnie Honig asks: "What if we read democratic theory gothically instead of romantically?" She favours this shift because gothic modes of reading press us "to attend to the people's perpetual uncertainty about the law and their relation to it."[17] In her view, this uncertainty is better suited than romantic certainties for negotiating democratic politics today. Honig's argument seems potentially comparable to the more fully articulated discussion of related themes in Pheng Cheah's *Spectral Nationality*, but Honig's work stresses the usefulness of "dilemmatic spaces"[18] in contrast to Cheah's investment in the postcolonial nation when read in dialogue with Derridean hauntology.

Cheah begins his book by asking:

---

uses the zombie to suggest something at once enormously powerful and "intellectually dead" (888). While his description of its "increasing appetite for the flesh of other disciplines that it both infects and converts to its own nature" (888) borrows from the vampire, technically a creature distinct from the zombie, the use of this hybrid metaphor is interesting for the insight it provides into the anxieties and conflicts of our present times. Sarah Juliet Lauro and Karen Embry elaborate this conflation of metaphors as the zombie moves from Haitian folk mythology into American cinema and posthuman theorizing in ways that range far more widely than I do here. See Sarah Juliet Lauro & Karen Embry, "A Zombie Manifesto: The Nonhuman Condition in the Era of Advanced Capitalism," *boundary 2* 35.1 (Spring 2008): 85–108. It is interesting to speculate, however, to what extent the zombie category, as Beck employs it, might be seen as continuous with their inspired analysis.

[16] Gail Jones, "Sorry-in-the-Sky: Empathetic Unsettlement, Mourning, and the Stolen Generations," in *Imagining Australia: Literature and Culture in the New New World,* ed. Judith Ryan & Chris Wallace–Crabbe (Cambridge MA: Harvard UP, 2004): 160.

[17] Bonnie Honig, *Democracy and the Foreigner* (Princeton NJ: Princeton UP, 2001): 9.

[18] Bonnie Honig, "Difference, Dilemmas, and the Politics of Home," in *Democracy and Difference: Contesting the Boundaries of the Political*, ed. Seyla Benhabib (Princeton NJ: Princeton UP, 1996): 259.

is organic vitalism an adequate framework for understanding postcolonial nationalism's persistence in the contemporary global order and its
future as an emancipatory project? If not, how should we rethink the
ideas of freedom and emancipation?[19]

Cheah's re-thinking leads him to conclude that "the most apposite metaphor
for freedom today is not the organism but the haunted nation."[20] Cheah sees
the postcolonial nation as a "creature of life-death," but this zombie-like ghost
figures not obsolescence, as in Beck, but a refusal to be exorcised that promises freedom. The difference may lie in Honig's interest in re-thinking
democracy versus Cheah's concern with freedom, particularly in the contexts
of Africa and Asia. Honig's feminism also marks an important difference in
their approaches. Cheah's analysis remains thought-provoking. Nonetheless,
this essay works through some of my uneasiness with Cheah's endorsement
of this particular form of gothic terminology. My emphasis here on the relations between injury, enquiry, and responsibility, rather than on national-
liberation agendas, reflects my divergence from Cheah's project.

   Cheah and Beck each see the nation-state continuing in haunted fashion
but place different valuations on what that means for analysis. Like Honig,
each stresses the cognitive uncertainties of the current moment. Beck uses the
idea of zombie categories to describe how "the categories of state-centred
power, domination and politics, taken as given in the neo-realism of the social
sciences" have survived beyond their usefulness into the global era.[21] In the
postcolonial context, Cheah argues, the categories remain relevant. What is
interesting to me here is the ways in which gothicized metaphor survives in
each, perhaps a legacy from "Hegel's characterization of the state as a spiritual individual," as Cheah suggests.[22] Thought-provoking as it is, I am wondering if it is time to move beyond this terminology.

   Like the re-animated corpse of the zombie, these categories, Beck suggests, have become mindless in the sense that they no longer enable questioning. Like the zombie, they continue to live beyond their death, wreaking
havoc. It's a metaphor that implies the colonial history of these concepts con-

---

[19] Pheng Cheah, *Spectral Nationality: Passages of Freedom from Kant to Postcolonial Literatures of Liberation* (New York: Columbia UP, 2003): 6–7.

[20] Cheah, *Spectral Nationality*, 12.

[21] Beck, *Power in the Global Age*, 63.

[22] Cheah, *Spectral Nationality*, 237.

tinues to haunt them even as conditions of the "second modernity"[23] or globalization are hollowing them out. This is a view that resonates with Sandra
Harding's call for an exorcism. "Western sciences and politics, and their
philosophies," she argues, "need an exorcism if they are to contribute at all to
social progress for the vast majority of the globe's citizens."[24] These are the
very views, in Cheah's analysis, that seek to exorcise the postcolonial nation.
These gothic metaphors, through which Beck sees a haunted structure de-
prived of its spirit and Cheah sees an unquenchable spirit capable of transcending organicism, raise further questions: in particular that of "the genre of
postcoloniality" (explored in an article of that title by Peter Hitchcock) and of
whether or not there could be "a postcolonial aesthetic" and, if there were,
how to describe it (questions raised by Elleke Boehmer).[25] These are questions about the framing of the discipline that require further thinking. I am not
offering the gothic as a postcolonial mode, although I am questioning its
utility for postcolonial analysis, and I think it useful to look more closely at
Beck's candidates for the zombie category and the work they do within the
postcolonial imaginary.

    Sarah Juliet Lauro and Karen Embry's essay, "A Zombie Manifesto: The
Nonhuman Condition in the Era of Advanced Capitalism," proposes that
"reading the zombie as an ontic/hauntic object reveals much about the crisis
of human embodiment, the way power works, and the history of man's sub-
jugation and oppression of its 'Others'."[26] In their discussion of the varied and
widespread appearances of zombies in current times, most salient for my
purposes is the fact that it is "a boundary figure" that "creates a dilemma for
power relations."[27] If the post-Westphalian state has always depended on
clearly delineated boundaries, then to describe it as a zombie category is to

---

[23] Beck, *Power in the Global Age*, xvii, 257.

[24] Sandra Harding, *Sciences from Below: Feminisms, Postcolonialities, and Modernities* (Durham NC & London: Duke UP, 2008): 3.

[25] Peter Hitchcock, "The Genre of Postcoloniality," *New Literary History* 34.2
(Spring 2003): 299–330; Elleke Boehmer, "A Postcolonial Aesthetic: Repeating upon
the Present," in *Rerouting the Postcolonial*, ed. Cristina Şandru & Janet Wilson (London: Routledge, 2009): 170–81.

[26] Sarah Juliet Lauro & Karen Embry, "A Zombie Manifesto," 87.

[27] Lauro & Embry, "A Zombie Manifesto," 90.

suggest not only that it has lost its *raison d'être* but also, perhaps, that it contains the seeds of its own dissolution.[28]

To what extent are state-centred power, domination, and politics (Beck's zombie categories) under-theorized in postcolonial literary and cultural criticism and what alternative views of these categories might we derive from examining the metaphors and genres through which they are engaged in other disciplines? In *The Civil Contract of Photography*, Ariella Azoulay offers a theory of photography "founded on a new ontological-political understanding of photography"[29] that seeks to shift the assumed power-relations involved in the taking and interpreting of the photograph by exploring "The conceptual valences between photography and citizenship."[30] She describes her book as "an attempt to rethink the political space of governed populations and to re-formulate the boundaries of citizenship as distinct from the nation and the market whose dual rationale constantly threatens to subjugate it."[31] The project of her book seems congruent with that advanced by Joseph R. Slaughter, in *Human Rights, Inc.*. Slaughter considers "how norms of legal obviousness manifest in literary forms."[32] He "elaborates the conceptual vocabulary, deep narrative grammar, and humanist social vision that human rights law shares with the *Bildungsroman*."[33] These books exemplify a translocated postcolonialism, which recasts postcolonial problematics as in dialogue with the categories shaping understandings within multiple forms of representation.[34]

---

[28] Not everyone accepts this view of the state under globalization. See Jean–François Bayart, *Global Subjects: A Political Critique of Globalization*, tr. Andrew Brown *(Le Gouvernement du Monde*, 2004; tr. Cambridge: Polity, 2007), for an alternative view. Bayart writes: "The favourite theorem of global studies thus turns out to be erroneous. Not only does globalization neither threaten nor erode the state, it actually produces it, and the transnational aspect is leaven in the dough" (72). My interest here, however, is in pursuing some of the implications of Beck's influential thesis and its metaphors rather than in testing the accuracy of his views.

[29] Ariella Azoulay, *The Civil Contract of Photography* (New York: Zone, 2008): 23.

[30] Azoulay, *The Civil Contract of Photography*, 25.

[31] *The Civil Contract of Photography*, 24

[32] Joseph R. Slaughter, *Human Rights, Inc.: The World Novel, Narrative Form, and International Law* (New York: Fordham U P, 2007): 3.

[33] Slaughter, *Human Rights, Inc.*, 4.

[34] See Slaughter's lengthy discussion of Dangarembga's *Nervous Conditions* on 216–56, especially his point that "The tension between the nationalist, instrumentalist

With Cheah, they ask how categories of governance, citizenship, and human rights shape postcolonial questions and the goals of decolonization. Questions I add to their analysis include: Does every nation automatically require its own state? Are national liberation struggles always to be endorsed? According to what criteria? These are questions that have become urgent for our global era, as indigenous and minority rights gain greater recognition in the international sphere.[35] In accordance with the work of many social scientists, I suggest that autonomy and sovereignty are being reshaped in our global era, yet there is little sustained rethinking of these concepts in the postcolonial field.[36] It may be my Canadian inheritance of values of peace, order, and good government but, from my perspective, these categories are more central to answering Bhabha's question than is the transcendental freedom endorsed by Cheah. There is a tendency in some postcolonial theory to romanticize resistance and liberation struggles and the men who led them.[37] Tsitsi

---

discourse of development and the idealist, transcendental vision of *Bildung* creates some of the conflict that sustains the plot of Dangarembga's *Nervous Conditions*" (216).

[35] See Will Kymlicka, *Multicultural Odysseys: Navigating the New International Politics of Diversity* (Oxford: Oxford UP, 2007), for a thought-provoking elaboration of this argument, which nonetheless relies on assumptions of West-to-East transfer that postcolonial theorists need to address, and see Brydon, "Competing Autonomy Claims and the Changing Grammar of Global Politics," *Globalizations* 6.3 (September 2009): 339–52, for a partial critique of his position.

[36] For exceptions, see Doug Ivison, *Postcolonial Liberalism* (Cambridge: Cambridge UP, 2002), David Scott, *Refashioning Futures: Criticism after Postcoloniality* (Princeton Studies in Culture/Power/History; Princeton NJ & Chichester: Princeton UP, 1999), and David Slater, *Geopolitics and the Post-Colonial* (Oxford: Blackwell, 2004). There is a wider range of texts rethinking the political by putting international relations and development studies in dialogue with the postcolonial. For examples, see April Biccum, *Global Citizenship and the Legacy of Empire: Marketing Development* (London: Routledge, 2009), *Postcolonizing the International: Working to Change the Way We Are*, ed. Philip Darby (Honolulu: U of Hawai'i P, 2006), and *Power, Postcolonialism and International Relations: Reading Race, Gender and Class*, ed. Geeta Chowdhry & Sheila Nair (London: Routledge, 2004). I am also grateful to the ASNEL conference participant who alerted me to Jean–François Bayart's *Global Subjects: A Political Critique of Globalization*, which offers an alternative view of the nation-state under globalization to that provided by Beck.

[37] I am thinking of Robert Young's *Postcolonialism: A Very Short Introduction* (Oxford: Oxford UP, 2003) here, which includes a full page photo of Fanon and ends with

Dangarembga's *The Book of Not* provides an important interruption of such narratives. In her unflinching witnessing to the psychic and physical damages of war, presented without indulging, however, in the usual moves performed by the trauma narrative, she succeeds in disturbing easy ways of knowing both resistance and trauma. In this, she finds her philosophical counterpart in the late Emmanuel Chukwudi Eze's *On Reason: Rationality in a World of Cultural Conflict and Racism*. He refuses what he calls "the revolutionarily or spectacularly moral" because of "a principled reservation against the revolutionary and spectacular as a social or political ideal."[38] Countries suffering from the legacies of colonialism, he argues, have lived through the damages created by such ideals. What they require instead are "the ordinary ideals of citizenship and equality for all."[39] These latter ideals, he implies, may be achieved through continuing to value autonomy, as re-conceived through the expanded understanding of the scope of the rational, as *On Reason*, describes it.

Given this position and pushing Beck's analysis further, I wonder whether there are categories, more specific to the postcolonial field, which function as zombie categories blocking fuller engagement with postcolonial futures. The strength of a zombie category is its invocation of powerful undercurrents of feeling surviving atavistically within supposedly rational constructs. As a coinage, it embodies the challenges postcolonial imaginings continue to pose to European concepts of reason and universality and the ways they have entered postcolonial imaginaries. In her brief but illuminating account of the origin of the term 'zombie' in African and West Indian beliefs subsequently

---

a paean to his "impassioned example" (147) among other accounts of great men and some communal movements. This seems to be an effect of trying to reach a more popular audience, since none of Young's other work employs this strategy. Cheah is far too complex an analyst to adopt this position so baldly, yet his analysis, like Young's, tends implicitly to support it. Equally, I find a dangerous romanticizing of heroic and confrontational posturing in Edward Said's injunction to "speak truth to power." Perhaps it is time to consider other, less heroic, but possibly more effective strategies, such as negotiation across differences, finding some common ground, exploring non-traditional alliances, and generally seeking strategies that can win some gains on an incremental basis.

[38] Emmanuel Chukwudi Eze, *On Reason: Rationality in a World of Cultural Conflict and Racism* (Durham NC: Duke UP, 2008): 252.

[39] Eze, *On Reason*, 252.

disseminated "through the geography of empire,"[40] Marina Warner suggests that as "a living body without a soul" (122), the zombie finds currency today in exemplifying "an anxiety that is not being allayed in this new era" (123). As such, it becomes an appropriate symbol for thinking about relations of enquiry and injury in the global era. Zombies "are annulled; another works their will through them" (124), Warner writes. They are images of servitude who also exert a strange power (159). As unsettling images of metamorphosis, the zombie enfolds "ghosts and spectres of all kinds in its grasp" (128). Along with Cheah's embrace of the ghost, the zombie is part of the lexicon of the current interest in hauntology, which reads capitalism as a haunted world system and advocates "thinking the ghost,"[41] following Marx and Derrida, as a strategy for reanimating materialist critique.[42] Is this one model for what the Australian writer Gail Jones calls "difficult forms of knowing"[43] or is it an example of what she means by the turn to a seductive gothicized vocabulary that does insufficient justice to loss and suffering? I remain undecided, given its potential for both.

Jones's novel *Sorry* begins with these words: "A whisper: ssshh. The thinnest vehicle of breath. / This is a story that can only be told in a whisper. / There is a hush to difficult forms of knowing, an abashment, a sorrow, an inclination toward silence."[44] Decolonization seems an inadequate word to address such difficult forms of knowing, which include remembering much that a society has forgotten – and remembering differently. 'Sorry' as a title when invoked throughout the book defamiliarizes normative understandings of the term by invoking the Australian aboriginal usage of sorry to indicate 'sorry business' or the culturally specific work of mourning associated with cere-

---

[40] Marina Warner, *Fantastic Metamorphoses, Other Worlds: Ways of Telling the Self* (Oxford: Oxford U P, 2002): 124. Further page references are in the main text.

[41] Peter Hitchcock, *Oscillate Wildly: Space, Body, and Spirit of Millennial Materialism* (Minneapolis: U of Minnesota P, 1999): 146.

[42] Cheah's *Spectral Nationality*, for example, concludes by arguing that "The postcolonial nation must be seen as a spectre of global capital [...] But it is also a spectre that haunts global capital and awaits reincarnation, the undecidable neuralgic point that refuses to be exorcised. That is why it is the most apposite figure for freedom today" (395). Such an argument finds hope in the liberating potential of the ghostly postcolonial nation for re-animating the zombie category of the capitalist nation-state, in which the living ghostly nation inhabits the dead body of the capitalist state.

[43] Jones, *Sorry*, 3.

[44] *Sorry*, 3.

monies for the dead. Similarly, elaborating the challenges of remembering differently, Chris Healy's *Forgetting Aborigines* shows the political potential of continued engagement with the field of representation – a cultural exercise the value of which has been questioned in recent years.[45] As an accessible point of entry into difficult forms of knowing, Healy's book may be read in counterpoint to Jones's *Sorry*. These two books translocate decolonizing imperatives into the realm of the everyday.

I have long preferred the language of decolonizing agendas for describing the goals of postcolonial work, given the difficulties the postcolonial causes for so many readers, both lay and academic, but I am now wondering whether decolonization itself as a concept assumes certain frames of understanding that in the changed contexts of the twenty-first century may itself be becoming a zombie category, incapable of addressing what is at stake in changing relations of enquiry, injury, and responsibility. In response to my abstract for the conference presentation of this essay, posted on Facebook, Souroja Moll writes (privately):

> The prefix of (de)colonization has always struck me as impossible: how do I go about reversing that which I am bound to linguistically and historically, and that which is always present even in its absence? How do I undo the familiar? Is the prefix (de) perhaps, a 'zombie category,' a methodology that must engage a ghost, a haunting, a spectre, a trace…

These are the questions Jones addresses indirectly in *Sorry*, a novel that only fitfully engages with conventions of realism in its search for a form adequate to the difficult forms of knowing with which Australians need to engage, once the state has officially apologized for colonialism and recognized some of its injuries. The melodramatic, psychic, and intertextual violences of Jones's novel invoke the various forms of violence enacted and still in force in Australia today.

In addition to physical violence, Couze Venn identifies various forms of violence at the symbolic heart of colonialism, each connecting injury and enquiry in some way:

> epistemic violence, that is, the denial of the authority and validity of the knowledge of the colonized; ontological violence, namely, the refusal to recog-

---

[45] I am thinking here particularly of David Scott's *Refashioning Futures: Criticism after Postcoloniality* (Princeton NJ & Chichester: Princeton UP, 1999).

nize the (non-assimilated) colonized subject as a fellow human being; and symbolic and psychic violence, the silencing of the voice of the colonized, the denial of the latter's ability to tell his or her story.[46]

Each of these forms of violence is present in the novels discussed in this essay, and each is linked to the depictions in these texts of scenes of reading, learning, unlearning, and education.

Fictional imaginings, stories, and poems remain some of the most powerful modes we have for entering and engaging with difficult ways of knowing and thus stretching our imagination in the ways that will be necessary for addressing the challenges now facing our interconnected world with globalization. But they cannot stand alone. They need to be placed in dialogue with other modes of enquiry such as those developed in the civil, social, market, and physical spheres once confined for analysis to the social and natural sciences. Texts once studied within the confines of a national literature need to be read as involved in an emerging global dialogue, but in a manner that bewares of assumptions of easy translatability across different cultural situations. Never must we be more cautious than when the language or genre of expression suggests an "apparent mutual transparency."[47]

So the trilogy of concern I derive from Bhabha's question involves unravelling the tangles of injury, enquiry, and agency formed through colonialism, imperialism, and neoliberalism to find better ways of collectively imagining how to co-create a collective future on this planet. To begin that process, I interpret two contrasting visual images of charged postcolonial encounters that recently circulated through the global public sphere, reading them through Beck's suggestive genre of the zombie category and then setting them in dialogue with fictions produced by the Australian Gail Jones, the Cree-Canadian Tomson Highway, and the Zimbabwean Tsitsi Dangarembga. These particular fictional texts both embody and thematize difficult forms of knowing in colonial situations.

Beck argues that accepting zombie categories, without understanding their new identity as zombies, can cause analysts to fall into the "nationality trap"[48] through which "methodological nationalism" functions as a source of many

---

[46] Couze Venn, *The Postcolonial Challenge: Towards Alternative Worlds* (Thousand Oaks C A & London: Sage, 2006): 11.

[47] Lorraine Code, "How To think Globally: Stretching the Limits of Imagination," *Hypatia* 13.2 (Spring 1998): 82.

[48] Beck, *Power in the Global Age*, 85.

types of error (43). He suggests that "The old concepts of the First, Second and Third World are also turning into zombie categories" (107). Instead, Beck suggests that "the context of globality is now everybody's starting point" (107).

In the version of this essay delivered at the ASNEL/GNEL conference in May 2009, I interpreted an image of the Venezuelan President Hugo Chávez offering US President Barack Obama the gift of a Spanish-language book, Eduardo Galeano's *Open Veins of Latin America*, first published in 1971, which documented the history of the Americas from a postcolonial perspective. The exchange took place during the Summit of the Americas in Trinidad, 18 April 2009.[49] I argued that in this incident the world saw a visual image of continuity and change. I now have in press a lengthier analysis of this photograph, in which I stress the role of the book, the ambiguity of the gift, the re-routed circuits of exchange, and the visual iconography of power-relations marked by this moment between two brown men on the world stage.[50] My reading sees Obama and Chávez as icons of power, representatives of states but also of North and South, Empire and its assumed periphery or backyard. In this exchange, I see the global vocabulary of North and South replacing the postcolonial orientations around West and East and shifting the racialized associations that once underpinned them.

At the time, I was unsure how to interpret the significance of Obama's racial breakthrough and what it might mean for reconstituted racial relations within the USA and globally. Susan Koshy is helpful here, in arguing that scholars in the USA "have no adequate lexicon for dealing with the transformation of racial orders"[51] taking place today. The new conjuncture she sees emerging with the new millennium might be defined, she suggests, "as a shift from *strategic essentialism* to *strategic interracialism*."[52] In her view, Obama's composite identity, in conjoining "blackness, whiteness, and Asianness, immigrant and heartland identities, and mainland and transpacific topographies"

---

[49] For an account of Galeano's work and its importance, see Daniel Fischlin & Martha Nandorfy, *Eduardo Galeano: Through the Looking Glass* (Montreal: Black Rose, 2002).

[50] See Brydon, "Metaphors that Disturb and Inspire."

[51] Susan Koshy, "Why the Humanities Matter for Race Studies Today," *PMLA* 123.5 (October 2008): 1542.

[52] Koshy, "Why the Humanities Matter," 1547.

works to "recast the referentiality of blackness while amplifying the trans-
figurative political power signified by blackness."[53]

The photo of Obama and Chávez together graphically illustrated such
racialized dynamics in a very public scene of postcolonial encounter between
two brown men. The second, contrasting photo discussed was taken a few
days later, on 29 April 2009. This photo functions as much through absence
as through presence. It shows the Canadian First Nations National Chief at the
time, Phil Fontaine, in St. Peter's Square in Vatican City just before his invited private audience with Pope Benedict XVI. No cameras or recorders
were allowed in this meeting. The Vatican requested the meeting, but what
the photo cannot show is the long history of collective activism behind the
scenes on the global stage to get the UN Declaration on the Rights of Indigenous Peoples drafted and passed. This history is recorded in *Indigenous
Diplomacy and the Rights of Peoples: Achieving UN Recognition* by James
(Sa'ke'j) Youngblood Henderson.

In requesting the meeting, Vatican imperialism is changing its techniques,
and, in responding with grace, indigenous politicians employ the stage provided them to get their own message across. While the word 'apology' was
not used, the Pope apparently expressed "sorrow" for the abuse and deplorable treatment that indigenous students suffered at residential schools run by
the Roman Catholic Church. A shift is happening. In early 2009, Fontaine,
himself a residential-school survivor, expressed hope that this meeting would
now "close the book" on the issue of apologies. Now it is time for seeking
legal redress and healing, he said. Fontaine and the Pope are two leaders without states. Indigenous peoples and religion, once relegated to a receding past
within modernity, are assuming an increased importance with globalization.
They have new roles to play within what Beck terms the "second modernity."

These two photos suggest to me that identities still matter politically but
the ways in which they function may be changing. My comments so far have
linked the recent ethical turn in postcolonial studies to the hemispheric turn,
which is reshaping how my own country, Canada, understands its place in the
Americas. Revised understandings of how subjectivity and place are co-con-
structed become translocated when glocalization becomes the new common
sense. How local and global, once opposed, now cross-pollinate and fuse to
produce the glocal is a complicated process that works differently in different
contexts. When the transnational turn mutates into translocation, the spatial

---

[53] Koshy, "Why the Humanities Matter," 1548.

turn is invoked, creating an intensified awareness of how place and space are produced and renewing attention to the situatedness of enquiry, within multiple identity-constructing forces and their identificatory possibilities.

Unpicking those rhizomatically woven connections can be painful as well as challenging. Postcolonial translocations are recalibrating relations of power and shifting understandings of cultural, linguistic, historical, and spatial relations. They direct consideration towards the ways in which postcolonial thinking continues to enter many different locales, changing their modes of endeavour, from the academic to the public sphere beyond the academy. Bhabha's injury and enquiry, Chávez's gift, and Fontaine's reaction to his audience with the Pope each reminds us that postcolonial work always performs its critique in alliance with hope, its history in dialogue with imagining a better future.

Building on my work with the "Globalization and Autonomy" team project, I have become fascinated by the current plethora of nation-based autonomy claims made by collectivities that consider themselves nations but have no nation-state. Canadian First Nations are one such group, but there are many others globally. Their demands are changing the grammar of politics, redefining nation-state autonomy and the meaning of sovereignty.[54] With globalization, as Nancy Fraser argues, "it is not only the substance of justice, but also the frame, which is in dispute."[55] I have joined an international pro-

---

[54] In literary studies, Smaro Kamboureli's TransCanada project combines critical multiculturalism with postcolonial critique in an effort to re-invent Canadian literary studies for global times. Her recent book *Trans.Can.Lit: Resituating the Study of Canadian Literature* (2007), co-edited with Roy Miki, may be seen as a translocating project, which seeks to unravel Canadian literature from its imbrication in a certain view of the nation-state while also transforming postcolonial critique to address specifically Canadian concerns. The tension in the project is how to re-imagine Canada within the logic of the 'trans', which to many expresses a need for more fluid and open borders. The project suggests that formerly nationalist and postcolonial theorists alike need to start thinking within multiscalar modes of location, revising how we understand region, nation, and the globe as constituting multiple forms of belonging and responsibility that can coexist productively. Finally, this thinking of the multiscalar dimensions of engagement needs to attend to the role of institutions and their contexts and to disaggregated forms of citizenship.

[55] Nancy Fraser, "Reframing Justice in a Globalizing World," in *Nationalism and Global Solidarities: Alternative Projections to Neoliberal Globalisation*, ed. James Goodman & Paul James (London: Routledge, 2007): 170. See Diana Brydon, "Com-

ject on "building global democracy"[56] because the deficits our team identifies
in global governance must be addressed if social justice and probably even
human survival are to be achieved. Thinking about global democracy can be
another way to translocate postcolonial critiques and hopes. Our first workshop addressed the question of conceptualizing democracy. In bringing together thinkers from every part of the globe, working within different linguistic, cultural, and political traditions, and in academic, policy, and civil-society
contexts, we began to redefine consensually what global democracy might
involve and how it might work in our global times. I bring postcolonial and
feminist perspectives to these discussions but must engage with colleagues
who come from many different political and belief systems. Perhaps those of
us working in postcolonial studies have spent too much time talking among
ourselves. In thinking about the disputed frames of justice acknowledged by
Fraser, this essay has been concerned with the many ways in which "global
cognitive justice" is linked to "global social justice"[57] in fictional and critical
texts.

   In this respect, *Sorry, The Book of Not*, and *Kiss of the Fur Queen* combine
witnessing and refusal of the falsely redemptive in narratives that embrace
difficult forms of knowing that can re-orient thinking about how Bhabha's
question may be answered. If *Sorry* may be read as taking seriously Spivak's
injunction for white beneficiaries of colonialism to understand our privilege
as our loss, then *The Book of Not* investigates "the things that break and cannot be fixed because the force of wholeness has abdicated."[58] Colonization,
civil war, family dysfunction, white racism, and Western consumer culture
each contributes to this abdication. The challenge of "how to become more of
a person"[59] in such a world proves painfully difficult for the novel's narrator,
Tambu, and full citizenship, even in a free Zimbabwe, eludes her.

---

peting Autonomy Claims and the Changing Grammar of Global Politics," *Globalizations* 6.3 (September 2009) for an analysis of these changing frames.

   [56] *The Building Global Democracy Programme*, http://www.buildingglobaldemo
cracy.org (accessed 14 February 2009).

   [57] See Boaventura de Sousa Santos et al. for an elaboration of these concepts and
how they are interlinked.

   [58] Tsitsi Dangarembga, *The Book of Not* (Banbury: Ayebia Clarke, 2006): 9.

   [59] Dangarembga, *The Book of Not*, 9.

In an essay titled "Sorry-in-the-Sky," Jones assesses "the *traumatic turn* in cultural studies,"[60] suggesting it often carries "a *soteriological drive*, a wish to narrativize injustice in the light of metaphysical redemption."[61] *Sorry* seems to be written explicitly to resist this temptation, creating an "ethical hesitation in reading and addressing witness" while seeking to produce "honourable and careful appraisals of truly traumatic histories."[62] Rosanne Kennedy places Dangarembga's *The Book of Not* within a similar logic of refusal, finding that the novel exemplifies the kind of "empathic unsettlement" which Jones, also citing Dominic LaCapra's first use of this phrase, had called for. Kennedy praises *The Book of Not* for remaining true to its "non-redemptive structure" through to its unresolved ending.[63] *The Book of Not* leads Kennedy to the conclusion that it is difficult "to conceptualize the ongoing psychological damage of racism in terms of a vocabulary of loss and mourning; other concepts are needed."[64] What might those other concepts be?

---

[60] Jones, "Sorry-in-the-Sky," 161.

[61] "Sorry-in-the-Sky," 163.

[62] "Sorry-in-the-Sky," 168.

[63] Rosanne Kennedy, "Mortgaged Futures: Trauma, Subjectivity, and the Legacies of Colonialism in Tsitsi Dangarembga's *The Book of Not*," *Studies in the Novel* 40.1–2 (Spring–Summer 2008): 103. Both authors have been influenced by Dominick LaCapra's *Writing History, Writing Trauma* (Baltimore MD: Johns Hopkins UP, 2001). My thinking about trauma has been deeply influenced by Daniel Coleman's careful engagement with this formation in his article, "Epistemological Cross-Talk: Between Melancholia and Spiritual Cosmology in *Soucouyant* and *Daughters Are Forever*," in *Crosstalk: Canadian and Global Imaginaries in Dialogue*, ed. Diana Brydon & Marta Dvořák (Waterloo, Ontario: Wilfrid Laurier UP, 2012): 53–72.

[64] Kennedy, "Mortgaging Futures," 104. Kennedy argues that in addressing "the ongoing humiliation of racism in everyday colonial life" (94), *The Book of Not* moves beyond the range of trauma theory, demanding a revised, or translocated, form of analysis. Neither notions of a "traumatic event" nor "loss" seem fully adequate to this situation (Kennedy 104). This insight extends the observation on Dangarembga's earlier work, made by Ann Elizabeth Willey and Jeanette Treiber, that this author's "work often challenges our understandings of the common tropes of postcolonial studies" and "invites the reader to rethink categories often used to analyze postcolonial African literature"; "Introduction" to *Negotiating the Postcolonial: Emerging Perspectives on Tsitsi Dangarembga*, ed. Willey & Treiber (Trenton NJ: Africa World Press, 2004): xii. In keeping with this destabilizing function of Dangarembga's writing, *The Book of Not* disturbs many earlier interpretations of *Nervous Conditions*, especially those that see Tambudzai succeeding and Nyasha failing. I am particularly

Highway's *Kiss of the Fur Queen* finds some of those other concepts in the mythologies of the Cree world-system translocated into the structural disciplines of classical music. The Okimasis brothers, like Tambu, struggle to reconcile their residential-school experiences with their lives back home in northern Manitoba, inhabiting Cree language and culture lived according to Cree values. They overhear their ancestral lands described as an uninhabited "last frontier";[65] their language is forbidden; and their names are changed, but, unlike Tambu, they have access to the alternative stories and world-views of the Cree and the languages of music and dance to sustain their creativity in the face of an enforced memorization of another culture's 'facts'. Its dissonant framing between a Cree cosmology and the language of classical music enables Highway's novel to refuse its readers the Christian experience of redemption while celebrating survival. Highways' "productive dissonance," as described by Sarah Wylie Krotz, produces a complex novel exploring both the pain and the potential of transculturality.

The Cree sensibility of Highway's text, with its trickster poetic and bawdy humour, proves especially difficult for students in the classroom who are seeking narratives that enshrine victimization, mourning, and trauma while promising redemption for their white readers. Cree humour that ends a book about horrific child sexual abuse and violent rapes with a wink can be very confusing for students who are willing to acknowledge guilt and sorrow for past wrongs but have more difficulty recognizing the resiliency of a culture that does not share their cosmology. Equally difficult for students who crave cultural authenticity in indigenous figures is the text's use of camp humour, its deployment of the hybrid Fur Queen, and its use of Jeremiah's relationship to classical piano as "an index of the challenges of transculturation."[66] Elsewhere, I have argued that Highway's novel carries a "personal anguish back

---

interested in extending Brendon Nicholls' insight into the ways that Nyasha "is the self-regulating subject *par excellence*" (Nicholls, "Indexing Her Digests: Working through *Nervous Conditions*," in *Negotiating the Postcolonial*, ed. Willey & Treiber, 131) in *Nervous Conditions* to think about the ways in which *The Book of Not* continues Dangarembga's investigation of the self-regulating subject through Tambudzai.

[65] Tomson Highway, *Kiss of the Fur Queen* (1998; Toronto: Anchor Canada, 2005): 141

[66] Sarah Wylie Krotz, "Productive Dissonance: Classical Music in Tomson Highway's *Kiss of the Fur Queen*," *Studies in Canadian Literature / Études en Littérature Canadienne* 34.1 (2009): 183.

into the public sphere to find appropriate forms of redress and progress."[67] Highway uses a persistent strategy of postcolonial translocation to challenge the settler mind-set and destabilize its expectations of what a native text should do. Sam McKegney argues that *Kiss of the Fur Queen* departs from the standard routes taken by residential-school survivor narratives – what he calls *legacy discourse* – by refusing to offer either "closure and healing," on the one hand, or "testimonial evidence," shaped for the purpose of seeking legal redress, on the other.[68] Instead, Highway works toward imagining a new kind of politics in which the spiritual and political are linked. Julia Emberley similarly sees the novel operating "through an ironic de-signification of the Christian myth of origins," contesting "the Christian myth of resurrection," and suggesting the need "to theorize a de-familiar unconscious and perhaps to create an unfamiliar praxis, a network of political kinships strong enough to contest the use of intimate violence to maintain the hegemony of today's global military-communications-industrial complex."[69]

The doubled protagonists of each novel complicate the *Bildung* structure of the traditional novel of education by highlighting the relational autonomy that both links and distinguishes the two non-familial "sisters" in *Sorry*, the two brothers in *Kiss*, and the two cousins in *Not*. Each of these novels contributes to re-thinking the conditions necessary for democratic participation in global times in ways that stress the enabling potential of difficult forms of knowing and relating. Particularly troubling in this respect is Tambu's wrestling with the Shona concept of *unhu* and its refrain, "I am well if you are too"[70] in *The Book of Not*. Tambu can find no way of reconciling her mother's understanding of *unhu*, and her mother's authority within Shona systems of *unhu*, with the alternatively based authority of the Western colonial school. The novel stages these debates to trouble simplified models of understanding that would merely oppose colonized to colonizer, individual to community, in ways that might valorize one above the other. Instead, it shows that reciprocity as a value, while central to survival in certain contexts, can also contain within itself a capacity for encouraging the very kinds of competitions it only appa-

---

[67] Brydon, "Compromising Postcolonialism," 23.

[68] Sam McKegney, *Magic Weapons: Aboriginal Writers Remaking Community after Residential School* (Winnipeg: U of Manitoba P, 2007): 147–48.

[69] Julia Emberley, *Defamiliarizing the Aboriginal: Cultural Practices and Decolonization in Canada* (Toronto: U of Toronto P, 2007): 253–55.

[70] Dangarembga, *The Book of Not*, 65, 123, 145.

rently deplores. *The Book of Not* challenges romanticized notions of indigenous community and the independent individual alike, while dramatizing the
incremental breakdowns in human relations that can lead to what others label
a failed state. Cheah argues that "Culture as freedom is persistently performed
and undone in radical postcolonial nationalist *Bildung*."[71] Is this a helpful way
to describe the undoing of *Bildung* in *The Book of Not*? Or is an alternative
vocabulary required?

These texts pose difficult forms of knowing that challenge readers to move
into spaces of troubling engagement. I have focused on the traumatic turn in
postcolonial studies because of its implications for how postcolonial thinkers
understand the relations that link enquiry, injury, and responsibility in aesthetic structures that function both emotively and politically. It is sobering to
read the complex and principled investigations of Bhabha's question in these
three novels, each engaging the question from a differently situated location
within yet-to-be-decolonized spaces. Through them, I hope to have shown the
value of including attention to settler-colony imaginaries in postcolonial
studies. I have argued for the value of difficult forms of knowing and have
raised questions about the limits of some of the categories through which the
postcolonial has constructed itself and now seeks to renew itself for global
times. Finally, I have suggested that the context of globality disturbs postcolonial certainties, translocating them into new arenas of power where cognitive
and political justice may prove just as elusive but are demanding redirected
investigations into how they might be achieved.

WORKS CITED

Azoulay, Ariella. *The Civil Contract of Photography* (New York: Zone, 2008).
Bayart, Jean–François. *Global Subjects: A Political Critique of Globalization*, tr.
    Andrew Brown (*Le Gouvernement du Monde*, 2004; Cambridge: Polity, 2007).
Beck, Ulrich. *Power in the Global Age: A New Global Political Economy*, tr. Kathleen
    Cross (*Macht und Gegenmacht im globalen Zeitalter: Neue weltpolitische Öko-
    nomie*, 2002; Cambridge: Polity, 2005).
Bhabha, Homi K. "Unpacking My Library… Again," in *The Post-Colonial Question:
    Common Skies Divided Horizons*, ed. Iain Chambers & Lidia Curti (New York:
    Routledge, 1996): 199–211.

---

[71] Cheah, *Spectral Nationality*, 394.

——. "Unsatisfied: Notes on Vernacular Cosmopolitanism," in *Text and Nation: Cross-Disciplinary Essays on Cultural and National Identities*, ed. Laura Garcia–Morena & Peter C. Pfeiffer (Columbia S C : Camden House, 1996): 191–207.

Biccum, April. *Global Citizenship and the Legacy of Empire: Marketing Development* (London: Routledge, 2009).

Boehmer, Elleke. "A Postcolonial Aesthetic: Repeating upon the Present," in *Rerouting the Postcolonial*, ed. Cristina Şandru & Janet Wilson (London: Routledge, 2009): 170–81.

Brydon, Diana. "Competing Autonomy Claims and the Changing Grammar of Global Politics," *Globalizations* 6.3 (September 2009): 339–52.

——. "Compromising Postcolonialism: Tomson Highway's *Kiss of the Fur Queen* and Contemporary Postcolonial Debates," in *Compr(om)ising Post/colonialism(s): Challenging Narratives and Practices*, ed. Greg Ratcliffe & Gerry Turcotte (Sydney: Dangaroo, 2001): 15–29.

——. "Earth, World, Planet: Where does the Postcolonial Critic Stand?" in *Cultural Transformations: Perspectives on Translocation in a Global Age*, ed. Chris Prentice, Vijay Devadas & Henry Johnson (Cross/Cultures 125; Amsterdam & New York: Rodopi, 2010): 3–29.

——. "Metamorphoses of a Discipline: Rethinking Canadian Literature within Institutional Contexts," in *Trans.Can.Lit: Resituating the Study of Canadian Literature*, ed. Smaro Kamboureli & Roy Miki (Waterloo, Ontario: Wilfrid Laurier U P , 2007): 1–16.

——. "Metaphors that disturb and inspire: the challenge of reading across cultures." Forthcoming in *The Edward Baugh Lectures*, ed. Nadi Edwards.

——. "Storying Home: Power and Truth," in *Tropes and Territories: Short Fiction, Postcolonial Readings, Canadian Writing in Context*, ed. Marta Dvořák & William H. New (Montreal & Kingston, Ontario: McGill–Queen's U P , 2007): 33–48.

Brydon, Diana, & William D. Coleman, ed. *Renegotiating Community: Interdisciplinary Perspectives, Global Contexts* (Vancouver: U of British Columbia P , 2008).

The Building Global Democracy Programme, http://www.buildingglobaldemo cracy.org (accessed 14 February 2009).

Cheah, Pheng. *Spectral Nationality: Passages of Freedom from Kant to Postcolonial Literatures of Liberation* (New York: Columbia U P , 2003).

Chowdhry, Geeta, & Sheila Nair, ed. *Power, Postcolonialism and International Relations: Reading Race, Gender and Class* (London: Routledge, 2004).

Code, Lorraine. "How to Think Globally: Stretching the Limits of Imagination," *Hypatia* 13.2 (Spring 1998): 73–85.

Coleman, Daniel. "Epistemological Cross-Talk: Between Melancholia and Spiritual Cosmology in *Soucouyant* and *Daughters Are Forever*," in *Crosstalk: Canadian and Global Imaginaries in Dialogue*, ed. Diana Brydon & Marta Dvořák (Waterloo, Ontario: Wilfrid Laurier U P, 2012): 53–72.

Dangarembga, Tsitsi. *The Book of Not* (Banbury: Ayebia Clarke, 2006).

Darby, Phillip, ed. *Postcolonizing the International: Working to Change the Way We Are* (Honolulu: U of Hawai'i P, 2006).

Emberley, Julia. *Defamiliarizing the Aboriginal: Cultural Practices and Decolonization in Canada* (Toronto: U of Toronto P, 2007).

Eze, Emmanuel Chukwudi. *On Reason: Rationality in a World of Cultural Conflict and Racism* (Durham NC: Duke U P, 2008.)

Fine, Ben. "Development as Zombieconomics in the Age of Neoliberalism," *Third World Quarterly* 30.5 (2009): 885–904.

——. "Zombieconomics: The Living Death of the Dismal Science in the Age of Neo-Liberalism." Paper for ESRC Neoliberalism Seminar (1 April 2008) http://eprints .soas.ac.uk/5621/1/Zombiekean.pdf (accessed 14 February 2009).

Fischlin, Daniel, & Martha Nandorfy. *Eduardo Galeano: Through the Looking Glass* (Montreal: Black Rose, 2002).

Fraser, Nancy. "Reframing Justice in a Globalizing World," in *Nationalism and Global Solidarities: Alternative Projections to Neoliberal Globalisation*, ed. James Goodman & Paul James (London: Routledge, 2007): 168–86.

Gilroy, Paul. "'Where ignorant armies clash by night': Homogeneous Community and the Planetary Aspect," *International Journal of Cultural Studies* 6.3 (2003): 261–76.

Harding, Sandra. *Sciences from Below: Feminisms, Postcolonialities, and Modernities* (Durham NC & London: Duke U P, 2008).

Healy, Chris. *Forgetting Aborigines* (Sydney: U of New South Wales P, 2008).

Henderson, James (Sa'ke'j) Youngblood. *Indigenous Diplomacy and the Rights of Peoples: Achieving U N Recognition* (Saskatoon, Saskatchewan: Purich, 2008).

Highway, Tomson. *Kiss of the Fur Queen* (1998; Toronto: Anchor Canada, 2005).

Hitchcock, Peter. *Oscillate Wildly: Space, Body, and Spirit of Millennial Materialism* (Minneapolis: U of Minnesota P, 1999).

——. "The Genre of Postcoloniality," *New Literary History* 34.2 (Spring 2003): 299–330.

Honig, Bonnie. *Democracy and the Foreigner* (Princeton NJ: Princeton U P, 2001).

——. "Difference, Dilemmas, and the Politics of Home," in *Democracy and Difference: Contesting the Boundaries of the Political*, ed. Seyla Benhabib (Princeton NJ: Princeton U P, 1996): 267–77.

Huggan, Graham. *The Postcolonial Exotic: Marketing the Margins* (London: Routledge, 2001).

Ivison, Doug. *Postcolonial Liberalism* (Cambridge: Cambridge U P, 2002).

Jones, Gail. *Dreams of Speaking* (Sydney: Vintage, 2006).

——. *Sorry* (Sydney: Vintage, 2007).

——. "Sorry-in-the-Sky: Empathetic Unsettlement, Mourning, and the Stolen Generations," in *Imagining Australia: Literature and Culture in the New New World,* ed. Judith Ryan & Chris Wallace–Crabbe (Cambridge MA: Harvard UP, 2004): 159–72.

Kamboureli, Smaro, & Roy Miki, ed. *Trans.Can.Lit: Resituating the Study of Canadian Literature* (Waterloo, Ontario: Wilfrid Laurier UP, 2007)

Kennedy, Rosanne. "Mortgaged Futures: Trauma, Subjectivity, and the Legacies of Colonialism in Tsitsi Dangarembga's *The Book of Not,*" *Studies in the Novel* 40.1–2 (Spring–Summer 2008): 86–107.

Koshy, Susan. "Why the Humanities Matter for Race Studies Today," *PMLA* 123.5 (October 2008): 1542–49.

Krotz, Sarah Wylie. "Productive Dissonance: Classical Music in Tomson Highway's *Kiss of the Fur Queen,*" *Studies in Canadian Literature/Études en Littérature Canadienne* 34.1 (2009): 182–203.

Kymlicka, Will. *Multicultural Odysseys: Navigating the New International Politics of Diversity* (Oxford: Oxford UP, 2007).

LaCapra, Dominick. *Writing History, Writing Trauma* (Baltimore MD: Johns Hopkins UP, 2001)

Lauro, Sarah Juliet, & Karen Embry. "A Zombie Manifesto: The Nonhuman Condition in the Era of Advanced Capitalism," *boundary 2* 35.1 (Spring 2008): 85–108.

McKegney, Sam. *Magic Weapons: Aboriginal Writers Remaking Community after Residential School* (Winnipeg: U of Manitoba P, 2007).

Moll, Sarouja. Facebook commentary. April 29, 2009.

Mustafa, Fawzia. "Reading Development and Writing Africa: UNFPA, *Nervous Conditions,* and *The Book of Not,*" *Comparative Literature Studies* 56.2 (2009): 379–406.

Nicholls, Brendon. "Indexing Her Digests: Working through *Nervous Conditions,*" in *Negotiating the Postcolonial,* ed. Willey & Treiber, 99–134.

Poovey, Mary. *A History of the Modern Fact: Problems of Knowledge in the Sciences of Wealth and Society* (Chicago: U of Chicago P, 1998).

Rooney, Caroline. "Interview with Tsitsi Dangarembga," *Wasafiri* 22.2 (July 2007): 57–62.

Santos, Boaventura de Sousa, João Arrisacado Nunes & Maria Paula Meneses. "Introduction: Opening Up the Canon of Knowledge and Recognition of Difference," in *Another Knowledge is Possible: Beyond Northern Epistemologies,* ed. Boaventura de Sousa Santos (Reinventing Social Emancipation 3; London: Verso, 2007): xix–lxii.

Schueller, Malini Johar. "Decolonizing Global Theories Today: Hardt and Negri, Agamben, Butler," *Interventions* 11.2 (July 2009): 235–54.

Scott, David. *Refashioning Futures: Criticism after Postcoloniality* (Princeton Studies in Culture/Power/History; Princeton NJ & Chichester: Princeton UP, 1999).

Slater, David. *Geopolitics and the Post-Colonial* (Oxford: Blackwell, 2004).

Slaughter, Joseph R. *Human Rights, Inc.: The World Novel, Narrative Form, and International Law* (New York: Fordham UP, 2007).

Söderlind, Sylvia. "Ghost-National Arguments," *University of Toronto Quarterly* 75. 2 (Spring 2006): 673–92.

Spivak, Gayatri Chakravorty. *Death of a Discipline* (New York: Columbia UP, 2003).

Venn, Couze. *The Postcolonial Challenge: Towards Alternative Worlds* (Thousand Oaks CA & London: Sage, 2006).

Warner, Marina. *Fantastic Metamorphoses, Other Worlds: Ways of Telling the Self* (Oxford: Oxford UP, 2002).

Willey, Ann Elizabeth, & Jeanette Treiber. "Introduction" to *Negotiating the Postcolonial: Emerging Perspectives on Tsitsi Dangarembga*, ed. Willey & Treiber (Trenton NJ: Africa World Press, 2004): ix–xix.

Young, Robert J.C. *Postcolonialism: A Very Short Introduction* (Oxford: Oxford UP, 2003).

⌘

Dislocating Imagology
—And: How Much of It Can
(or Should) Be Retrieved?

CLAUDIA PERNER

R EGARDLESS OF HOW ROUTINELY SCHOLARS COMMENT on the erosion of the nation-state and the emergence of hybrid and 'translocal'
spaces,[1] postcolonial studies are among those scholarly fields that
continue to bring about research projects with an imagological scope. Research projects on representations of alterity that rely on a national framework
are likely to pay their dues to the comparative school of literary imagology, in
particular if they originate in a German scholarly background.[2] In the following, I will relate why it may be advantageous to take exception to such a rule,
subjecting the basic assumptions of imagology to a critical re-reading. This, I
claim, has been done to an insufficient extent in the past. Indeed, there have
been few sustained challenges to the validity of imagology as a theoretical

---

[1] See, for instance, Arjun Appadurai, "Sovereignty without Territoriality: Notes for
a Postnational Geography," in *The Anthropology of Space and Place: Locating Culture*, ed. Setha M. Low & Denise Lawrence–Zúñiga (Blackwell Readers in Anthropology 4; Malden MA: Blackwell, 2003): especially 338–39.

[2] Comparative or literary imagology is usually defined as the study of 'the literary
image of the other country'. While the term *imagologie* originally goes back to French
ethnopsychology, the Aachen programme of comparative literary studies around Hugo
Dyserinck began establishing 'literary imagology' in the late 1960s. *Imagologie* remains most widely known and applied in French and German academia. In English
usage, some scholars, such as Joep Leerssen and William L. Chew III, have privileged
the term 'image studies'. However, Leerssen has recently adopted the English term
'imagology', most notably in his co-edited volume *Imagology: The Cultural Construction and Literary Representation of National Characters* (with Manfred Beller).

tool.[3] Following my evaluation of different imagological approaches, I will indicate the potential that the (national) stereotype continues to hold as an analytical category despite the shortcomings of its uses in imagology.

In the present context, it is noteworthy that imagologists have repeatedly declared postcolonial studies a natural sister discipline of their own field. Indeed, some have claimed that postcolonial studies had been 're-inventing' central objectives and insights of imagological research.[4] In opposition to such claims, I argue that most basic assumptions of imagology require a fundamental 'makeover' before they can sensibly be employed in the field of postcolonial studies. Indeed, it may be preferable to choose other theoretical tools at hand rather than to chain oneself to a field riddled with conceptual flaws past and present.

The understanding of imagology current from the late 1960s onwards put emphasis on the political and sociological contextualization of literary texts – an approach that was quite an innovation and hotly debated in comparative literary studies at the time.[5] Hugo Dyserinck has described imagology as a 'concrete form of analysis of the phenomenon of experiencing-the-Other across borders' ["grenzüberschreitende Fremderfahrung"].[6] In reality, imagology has displayed an unfortunate lack of theoretical progress during precisely those decades when research on localities, nationality, and ethnicity was subject to fundamental transformation. Imagology, it appears, has been largely immune even to the draw of globalization. While it is true that there have

---

[3] To my knowledge, Ruth Florack's *Bekannte Fremde: Zu Herkunft und Funktion nationaler Stereotype in der Literatur* (Studien und Texte zur Sozialgeschichte der Literatur 114; Tübingen: Max Niemeyer, 2007) is the most thorough critical effort to date.

[4] See, for instance, Joep Leerssen, "Imagology: History and Method," in *Imagology: The Cultural Construction and Literary Representation of National Characters. A Critical Survey*, ed. Manfred Beller & Joep Leerssen (Studia Imagologica 13; Amsterdam & New York: Rodopi, 2007): 24; Joep Leerssen, "The Rhetoric of National Character: A Programmatic Survey," *Poetics Today* 21.2 (2000): 268–69; see also Angelika Corbineau–Hoffmann, *Einführung in die Komparatistik* (2000; Berlin: Erich Schmidt, 2004): 197.

[5] See Hugo Dyserinck, "Komparatistische Imagologie jenseits von 'Werk-immanenz' und 'Werktranszendenz'," *Synthesis* 9 (1982): 40; see also Manfred S. Fischer, *Nationale Images als Gegenstand Vergleichender Literaturgeschichte* (Aachener Beiträge zur Komparatistik 6; Bonn: Bouvier, 1981): 24.

[6] Dyserinck, "Komparatistische Imagologie," 31. (My tr.)

been certain silent shifts in objective and unannounced reformulations of research focus, these shifts occurred whenever insights from other fields became increasingly hard to ignore. Nevertheless, it is striking how imagological studies still routinely cite a small number of 'founding texts' from the 1970s and early 1980s as their theoretical framework. Beyond that, literary imagology has not produced a sustained theoretical discourse. In addition, the inventory character of many imagological case studies has failed to bring about genuinely new theoretical insights.[7] As a consequence, imagology today faces the same conceptual problems as forty years ago.

1. Scrutinizing Imagology

The first and possibly most fundamental problem is the imagological reliance on national and cultural 'containers' and on the existence of separate 'national literatures'. These 'national literatures' are usually defined by their – supposedly exclusive – use of a distinct national language.[8] Imagology, as developed by Dyserinck, is an examination of the relation between "national entities"[9] and of mutual perceptions across national borders. (This means, for instance, 'The French as seen by the Germans' and 'The Germans as seen by the French.'[10]). Of course, it is one of the commonplaces of imagological research to stress that such cross-national observations and (literary) descriptions tell us more about the observers than about the group that is being

---

[7] Despite the criticism that it has been subjected to, Edward W. Said's *Orientalism* (*Orientalism: Western Conceptions of the Orient* [London: Routledge & Kegan Paul, 1978]) can be counted among the more thought-provoking works with an imagological scope. However, the undeniable qualities of *Orientalism* are hardly based on its conceptual interconnectedness with imagology.

[8] Dyserinck, "Komparatistische Imagologie," 31. In 1990, Karl Ulrich Syndram acknowledged at least that the reliance on national languages as a dividing factor does not solve the conceptual problem. See Syndram, "Das Problem der nationalen Literaturgeschichtsschreibung als Gegenstand der komparatistischen Imagologie," in *Space and Boundaries of Literature / Espace et Frontières de la Littérature: Proceedings of the Twelfth Congress of the International Comparative Literature Association 1988*, ed. Roger Bauer & Douwe Fokkema (Munich: Iudicium, 1990), vol. 4: 37.

[9] Dyserinck, "Komparatistische Imagologie," 34. (My tr.)

[10] Hugo Dyserinck, "Zur Entwicklung der komparatistischen Imagologie," *Colloquium Helveticum* 7 (1988): 23.

observed.[11] As a consequence, imagologists including Dyserinck claim the deconstruction of the concept of 'national character' as one of their prime objectives.[12] What they fail to acknowledge is that their scholarly project at large nevertheless relies on the validity of the very boundaries they claim to deconstruct. More often than not, imagological research continues to be caught up in the implicit validation of national and cultural categories.[13]

A second problem is imagology's eurocentric bias, its largely unquestioned conception of itself as *Europaforschung*.[14] Imagology is still far from having transcended its eurocentric orientation and somehow proceeds on the assumption that a scholarly approach concentrating on Europe can still bring forth results that "ultimately are valuable for humanity as a whole."[15]

One of the most problematical imagological categories – and a surprisingly persistent one at that – is the so-called "supranational standpoint"[16] of the imagologist. Dyserinck's call for an approach that is characterized by "cultural neutrality"[17] has survived through the decades and despite imagology's advances to constructivist theory.[18] Criticism or qualifications of this concept

---

[11] See, for instance, János Riesz, "Einleitung: Zur Omnipräsenz nationaler und ethnischer Stereotype," in *Literarische Imagologie: Formen und Funktionen nationaler Stereotype in der Literatur*, ed. János Riesz (Komparatistische Hefte 2; Bayreuth: Ellwanger, 1980): 4; see also Gonthier–Louis Fink, "Réflexions sur l'imagologie: Stéréotypes et réalités nationales dans une perspective franco-allemande," *Recherches Germaniques* 23 (1993): 21.

[12] Dyserinck, "Zur Entwicklung," 28; Hugo Dyserinck, "Komparatistik als Europaforschung," in *Komparatistik und Europaforschung: Perspektiven vergleichender Literatur- und Kulturwissenschaft*, ed. Hugo Dyserinck & Karl Ulrich Syndram (Aachener Beiträge zur Komparatistik 9; Bonn: Bouvier, 1992): 36.

[13] Cf. Friederike Heitsch, *Imagologie des Islam in der neueren und neuesten spanischen Literatur* (Problemata Literaria 42; Kassel: Reichenberger, 1998): 18.

[14] Dyserinck, "Zur Entwicklung," 39; also Dyserinck, "Komparatistik," 31.

[15] Dyserinck, "Komparatistik," 40. (My tr.)

[16] Dyserinck, "Komparatistische Imagologie," 32 (my tr.); also Dyserinck, "Komparatistik," 37.

[17] Dyserinck, "Zur Entwicklung," 40 (my tr.); also 22–23.

[18] See, for instance, Karl Ulrich Syndram, "The Aesthetics of Alterity: Literature and the Imagological Approach," in *National Identity: Symbol and Representation*, ed. Joep Leerssen & Menno Spiering (Yearbook of European Studies 4; Amsterdam & New York: Rodopi, 1991): 183, and Michail I. Logvinov, "Studia imagologica: zwei methodologische Ansätze zur komparatistischen Imagologie," *Germanistisches Jahr-*

are surprisingly rare, and the 'supranational standpoint' is sometimes still invoked as one of the leading principles of imagology.[19]

Imagologists aim to detect 'images' in texts. The 'image' as a category may be intuitively appealing but loses much of its persuasiveness as soon as one considers its heuristic productivity. While Dyserinck initially claimed indebtedness to Karl Popper's 'World 3',[20] most imagological studies invest little time in the tedious work of conceptual clarification.[21] In 1981, Manfred S. Fischer proclaimed a strict distinction between 'image' and '(national) stereotype'.[22] Nevertheless, the synonymous use of both terms has grown even more commonplace in the meantime.

In 2007, Manfred Beller attempted to provide a more comprehensive characterization of the imagological 'image'. He describes the 'image' as

> the mental silhouette of the other, who appears to be determined by the characteristics of family, group, tribe, people or race. Such an 'image' rules our opinion of others and controls our behavior towards them.[23]

In an attempt to link up with the theoretical jargon of postmodernism, Beller further emphasizes that "we do not know the real thing, but only its simula-

---

buch GUS "Das Wort" (2003): 211. Cf. criticism raised in Heitsch, *Imagologie des Islam*, 20–21.

[19] See, for instance, Logvinov, "Studia imagologica," 215. A rare exception is Jan Nederveen Pieterse's acknowledgement of the fact "that the analysis of representation and otherness itself is historically and culturally determined. There is no Archimedean point, no objective position beyond history from which historical processes of imagining and othering can be monitored and interpreted"; Pieterse, "Image and Power," in *Alterity, Identity, Image: Selves and Others in Society and Scholarship*, ed. Raymond Corbey & Joep Leerssen (Amsterdam Studies on Cultural Identity 1; Amsterdam & New York: Rodopi, 1991): 193.

[20] Dyserinck, "Zur Entwicklung," 29.

[21] One rare attempt is Thomas Bleicher, "Elemente einer komparatistischen Imagologie," in *Literarische Imagologie: Formen und Funktionen nationaler Stereotype in der Literatur*, ed. János Riesz (Komparatistische Hefte 2; Bayreuth: Ellwanger, 1980): 16.

[22] Fischer, *Nationale Images*, 20.

[23] Manfred Beller, "Perception, Image, Imagology," in *Imagology: The Cultural Construction and Literary Representation of National Characters: A Critical Survey*, ed. Manfred Beller & Joep Leerssen (Studia Imagologica 13; Amsterdam & New York: Rodopi, 2007): 4.

crum in the form of mental images."[24] Birgit Neumann, who has proposed a
somewhat updated version of imagology grounded in cultural studies, maintains that the distinction between 'image' and 'stereotype' is valuable.[25] Her
argument rests on the presumably more flexible character of 'images' as
opposed to the 'compressed' nature of stereotypes.[26] Yet she characterizes
stereotyping as a process that does not take place only once but is subject to
ongoing renewal and modification.[27] The 'image' and its difference from the
stereotype remain elusive as ever.

Further conceptual confusion is caused by the assumed relation between
imagological 'image', literary text, and reality. Imagologists often assert that
imagological research is not concerned with the image's claim to reality.[28] On
the other hand, imagology has sometimes been declared to enhance knowledge of reality by literary means.[29] To complicate matters further, some scholars have promoted a 'cultural turn' in imagology, criticizing the prominent
role that literature has ostensibly played so far. I argue that this approach
overlooks the fact that imagology has often all but ignored the specific lite-
rariness of the literary text. Literary texts are frequently read as providing insight into the (collective) perceptions of a nation or a culture. Layers of character representation, narrative voice, authorship, and ostensible national or
cultural 'background' are merged. The result is an analytical maze rather than
a systematic and transparent interpretation of the literary text. Despite this
methodological fuzziness, it is hard to take seriously the claim that imagology
is unconcerned with the relation between literary text and reality. After all,
imagology has often been envisaged as a kind of 'literary diplomacy',[30] its

---

[24] Beller, "Perception," 4.

[25] Birgit Neumann, *Die Rhetorik der Nation in britischer Literatur und anderen
Medien des 18. Jahrhunderts* (ELCH: Studies in English Literary and Cultural History
39; Trier: WVT, 2009): 38. Neumann's approach improves upon some aspects of traditional imagology but suffers from an over-emphasis on clear oppositions of Self/
Other and 'autoimage'/'heteroimage'.

[26] Neumann, *Die Rhetorik der Nation*, 42.

[27] *Die Rhetorik der Nation*, 51.

[28] Dyserinck, "Komparatistische Imagologie," 37. Also Syndram, "The Aesthetics,"
183–84.

[29] Bleicher, "Elemente," 18.

[30] "Elemente," 20. See also Fischer, *Nationale Images*, 17, and Stefanie Stockhorst,
"Was leistet ein cultural turn in der komparatistischen Imagologie? Henry Crabb

aim being to unveil and to fight ideological misconceptions represented in literary texts.[31]

2. Conceptual Reconfigurations: Chew, Pageaux, Leerssen

After having pointed out some of the conceptual challenges that imagology faces, I would like to draw attention to three relatively recent imagological reconceptions.

William L. Chew III, an historian by training, sees imagology as aiming at "creating greater intercultural awareness."[32] As a consequence, Chew argues, imagological research continues to gain topicality in a globalized world:

> Recent international developments, finally, marked by continued regional conflicts and a global terrorism characterised by apparent ethnic and religious incompatibilities [...] has [sic] lent added urgency to the deconstruction of complex stereotypes that seem to obscure and hinder understanding 'the other' rather than provide the true understanding and insight that can lead to a peaceful co-existence, characterised by humanistic values and common respect. If ever a scholarly field had direct relevance to contemporary social issues, it must certainly be imagology.[33]

Chew – like other imagologists before him – conceives of a globalized world as divided into more or less clear-cut entities. Thus he also disregards the fact that imagology depends on a certain amount of transcultural blindness. In the passage I have quoted, Chew refers to *stereotypes* as the central object of imagological research, thereby deviating from Fischer's and Neumann's models.

Robinson als Vermittler deutscher Dichter- und Gelehrtenkultur nach England," *Arcadia* 40.2 (2005): 355.

[31] Dyserinck, "Komparatistische Imagologie," 36.

[32] William L. Chew III, "'Literature, History, and the Social Sciences?': An Historical–Imagological Approach to Franco-American Stereotypes," in *National Stereotypes in Perspective: Americans in France, Frenchmen in America*, ed. William L. Chew III (Studia Imagologica 9; Amsterdam & New York: Rodopi, 2001): 1. Further page references are in the main text.

[33] William L. Chew III, "What's in a National Stereotype? An Introduction to Imagology at the Threshold of the 21st Century," *Language and Intercultural Communication* 6.3–4 (August 2006): 180.

In what he calls his own "pragmatic and functionalist manifesto" (4) for imagology, Chew proposes:

> We are all imagologists, even if we do not realize the fact, and we cannot function socially and politically, in a humane and reasoned fashion, as individuals or groups, without studying the (national) stereotypes so current in our collective memory. For these stereotypes color, to a large extent, not only our self-perception (our 'auto-image'), but determine for better and, regrettably, more often, for worse our behavior toward the other. (3–4)

What Chew suggests here constitutes a serious challenge to *literary* imagology. And, indeed, Chew criticizes a "selective preoccupation with predominantly *fictional* representations of alterity" (8). Instead, he calls for a "total imagology" (8) that incorporates both a history of mentalities approach and methods taken from the social sciences (8–9, 16).

Like Chew, the comparatist Daniel–Henri Pageaux favours an interdisciplinary approach to imagology. In addition, Pageaux offers a sophisticated description of the 'image' and distinguishes between three conceptual levels: The first level, '*le mot*', is the dimension of individual expressions and constitutes what Pageaux calls "a fundamental vocabulary serving representation and communication."[34] On the second level, Pageaux identifies the ruling principle of hierarchical relationships (147) that combine individual expressions into an "anthology of images."[35] Finally, both 'fundamental vocabulary' and 'anthology of images' are integrated into what Pageaux calls an 'image-scenario'. Thus the image constitutes "a more or less complete illustration of a 'dialogue' between two cultures, through a staging [*mise en scène*] of the foreigner that is also an aesthetic and cultural design [*mise en forme*]" (148, my translation).

Pageaux deems it insufficient for the imagologist to merely consider the 'mise-en-text' of the image. Instead, it is equally important to explore its 'mise-en-imaginaire' (155). The imaginary that Pageaux envisages is "the

---

[34] Daniel–Henri Pageaux, "De l'imagerie culturelle à l'imaginaire," in *Précis de littérature comparée*, ed. Pierre Brunel & Yves Chevrel (Paris: Presses Universitaires de France, 1989): 145. (My tr.) Further page references are in the main text.

[35] Daniel–Henri Pageaux, "Image/Imaginaire," in *Europa und das nationale Selbstverständnis. Imagologische Probleme in Literatur, Kunst und Kultur des 19. und 20. Jahrhunderts*, ed. Hugo Dyserinck & Karl Ulrich Syndram (Bonn: Bouvier, 1988): 373. (My tr.)

theatre, the place where the different modes (literature, among others) in which a society sees, defines, dreams itself, express themselves in a pictorial manner [...], that is to say, by means of images, of representations" (135–36, my tr.). It constitutes, in Pageaux's words, 'the library' that includes all images thinkable at a certain time and in a certain place. It is "the reservoir of a collective memory whose contours tend to superimpose on national space."[36] Thus imagological research must inevitably include an inquiry into the history of ideas (136).

Pageaux's theoretical work offers a number of thought-provoking perspectives on the connection between 'image', 'imaginaire', and society. Nevertheless, it is precisely in this respect that Pageaux's approach remains crucially (if elegantly) abstract. The imagological project as Pageaux envisages it is to uncover – through literary texts – the "mental attitudes of an époque, of a society" (141, my tr.). This rather ambitious goal, surely, remains beyond the possibilities of literary research.[37] Hence it is hardly surprising that the two decades since the publication of Pageaux's seminal article "De l'imagerie

---

[36] Pageaux, "Image/Imaginaire," 375. (My tr.)

[37] Literary texts are connected to such mental attitudes, albeit in a more indirect fashion. On the complex interrelatedness of material manifestations of culture (such as the literary text) and the mental dimension of culture, see Ronald Posner, "Kultur als Zeichensystem: Zur semiotischen Explikation kulturwissenschaftlicher Grundbegriffe," in *Kultur als Lebenswelt und Monument*, ed. Aleida Assmann & Dietrich Harth (Frankfurt am Main: Fischer, 1991): 37–74. Posner also stresses that "the boundaries between two societies do not necessarily coincide with the boundaries between two civilizations or two mentalities" (Posner, "Kultur als Zeichensystem," 42; my tr.). See also Ansgar Nünning, "Literatur, Mentalitäten und kulturelles Gedächtnis: Grundriss, Leitbegriffe und Perspektiven einer anglistischen Kulturwissenschaft," in *Literaturwissenschaftliche Theorien, Modelle und Methoden: Eine Einführung*, ed. Ansgar Nünning (Trier: WVT, 1998): 180–81, 184–86. Following Siegfried Schmidt, Nünning claims that culture becomes *beobachtbar* ["observable"] in cultural manifestations such as literature. See Schmidt, "Medien, Kultur, Medienkultur: Ein konstruktivistisches Gesprächsangebot," in *Kognition und Gesellschaft: Der Diskurs des Radikalen Konstruktivismus 2*, ed. Siegfried Schmidt (Suhrkamp-Taschenbuch Wissenschaft 950; Frankfurt am Main: Suhrkamp, 1992): 436). On 'mentality' and 'history of mentalities', see Volker Sellin, "Mentalität und Mentalitätsgeschichte," *Historische Zeitschrift* 241 (1985): 555–98. Sellin stresses that mentality is not merely a type of opinion or idea that could be directly expressed (or not) but an attitude that stands behind a mode of (collective) behaviour (Sellin, "Mentalität," 591).

culturelle à l'imaginaire" have not brought about any convincing application of his theoretical considerations.

Joep Leerssen is currently the most prominent scholar working in the field of imagology. In contrast to Chew and Pageaux, Leerssen promotes a return to a literary focus of imagology. Literature, he argues, is singularly "explicit in reflecting and shaping the awareness of entire societies and [...] often counts as the very formulation of that society's cultural identity."[38] Leerssen defines literary imagology as the study of the "point of intersection between the text's verbal ('poetical') and historical ('ideological') properties, between the text as verbal tissue and the text as social act."[39] Thus imagology is concerned with "representations as textual strategies and as discourse"[40] rather than with cultural or national identity as such. Nevertheless, Leerssen identifies a connection between the imagological 'image' and the construction of national identity:

> Images concerning people, human types or nations have arisen almost out of nothing, from literary commonplaces and intertextual formulae, and have solidified into belief systems and patterns of identification which in turn have given rise to the now-current set of tropes we call 'national identities' – tropes with which many of us, most of the time, actively identify and which thus have become real things in the real world.[41]

Leerssen's research focus is the textual function of stereotypes. Yet 'stereotypical images' in Leerssen's sense are not restricted to the repressive and ideological 'images' of traditional imagology. Quite in agreement with sociological and linguistic findings, Leerssen describes the national stereotype as a

---

[38] Leerssen, "The Rhetoric," 268.

[39] Joep Leerssen, "Echoes and Images: Reflections upon Foreign Space," in *Alterity, Identity, Image: Selves and Others in Society and Scholarship*, ed. Raymond Corbey & Joep Leerssen (Amsterdam Studies on Cultural Identity 1; Amsterdam & New York: Rodopi, 1991): 125–26. See also Joep Leerssen, "L'effet de typique," in *Mœurs et images: Études d'imagologie européenne*, ed. Alain Montandon (Clermont–Ferrand: U Blaise Pascal, 1997): 134.

[40] Leerssen, "Imagology," 27.

[41] Joep Leerssen, "The Downward Pull of Cultural Essentialism," in *Image into Identity: Constructing and Assigning Identity in a Culture of Modernity*, ed. Michael Wintle (Studia Imagologica: Amsterdam Studies on Cultural Identity 11; Amsterdam & New York: Rodopi, 2006): 37.

"shorthand invocation of a highly specific and widely known code of tempe-ramental attributes."[42] National stereotypes are thus part of a "culturally shared set of recognizable literary (as well as social) commonplaces."[43]

It is true that Leerssen's conception of imagology is infinitely more persua-sive than most other approaches. All the more disappointing is the volume that Leerssen co-edited with Manfred Beller in 2007: *Imagology: The Cul-tural Construction and Literary Representation of National Characters*. The book offers a selection of imagological vignettes, once more focusing on Eu-rope and thus reconfirming the geographical bias of traditional imagology. Beller and Leerssen acknowledge this restriction in the introduction but mere-ly voice their hope that postcolonial studies will step in to make up for this deficit.[44] The vignettes featured in the second part of the volume vary in length, supposedly according to the alleged 'importance' of the countries under consideration. Non-European entries include (among a few individual countries) undiversified entities such as 'Africa', 'Arabs', 'Creoles', and 'Latin America' and are considered "only in their impact on European be-holders."[45] Beller and Leerssen point out that the

> European perspective on distant nations and societies is perspectivally and eurocentrically foreshortened, and will reduce real-world com-plexities into simplified clichés even more drastically than is the case in the intra-European process of cross-cultural stereotyping. The edi-tors can only point out this fact, and cannot undo it.[46]

What they fail to acknowledge is that their own descriptions reconstruct both the entities observed *and* the observing entity ('Europe') as largely undiver-sified 'containers'. It is difficult to see the scholarly use of such superficial and often ahistorical inventories of exoticist ideas. If the volume *Imagology* aims to prove the productiveness of current imagological research and to

---

[42] Joep Leerssen, "Mimesis and Stereotype," in *National Identity: Symbol and Re-presentation*, ed. Joep Leerssen & Menno Spiering (Yearbook of European Studies 4; Amsterdam & New York: Rodopi, 1991): 174.

[43] Leerssen, "Mimesis," 174–75. See also Pageaux, "De l'imagerie culturelle," 140.

[44] Manfred Beller & Joep Leerssen, "Foreword," in *Imagology: The Cultural Con-struction and Literary Representation of National Characters: A Critical Survey*, ed. Manfred Beller & Joep Leerssen (Studia Imagologica 13; Amsterdam & New York: Rodopi, 2007): xiv–xv.

[45] Beller & Leerssen, "Foreword," xiv.

[46] "Foreword," xiv.

establish imagology as a theoretical approach fit for the twenty-first century, it surely fails to achieve this.

3. Conclusion

As outlined above, imagologists have increasingly come to claim stereotypes as their main area of research. Pageaux has classified the stereotype as a specific form of image, thus distinguishing it from other, non-stereotypical images.[47] Scholarly usage of both terms today implies quite the reverse: It appears, in reality, that the image is (or has become) a specific subcategory of the stereotype – a type concerned with nationality as opposed to those stereotypes relating to, for instance, social hierarchy, gender, age, or visual characteristics. If this is the case, it seems rather problematical to insist on imagology as a separate scholarly discipline. Research on stereotypes has long become an extremely productive interdisciplinary field and easily accommodates most scholarly projects that otherwise might be labelled 'imagology'.

There is no reason why interdisciplinary research on stereotypes should exclude works that focus on literary texts. Ruth Florack's recent study *Bekannte Fremde* ["familiar strangers"] is a case in point. Ruth Florack provides a persuasive argument against imagology and opts for a more flexible reading of national stereotypes. In keeping with the findings of cognitive psychology, Florack understands the national stereotype as a type of rudimentary cultural knowledge,[48] a repertoire that frequently transcends and thus is shared across national boundaries.[49] Florack examines the productive functions that stereotypes fulfil in literary texts rather than merely assembling thematic inventories. In *Toward a Speech Act Theory of Literary Discourse*, Mary Louise Pratt claims:

> the way people produce and understand literary works depends enormously on an unspoken, culturally-shared knowledge of the rules, conventions, and expectations that are in play when language is used in that context.[50]

---

[47] Pageaux, "De l'imagerie culturelle," 139.

[48] Florack, *Bekannte Fremde*, 39.

[49] *Bekannte Fremde*, 85.

[50] Mary Louise Pratt, *Toward a Speech Act Theory of Literary Discourse* (Bloomington & London: Indiana U P, 1977): 86.

It appears sensible to conceptualize stereotypes as one type of such culturally-shared conventions, a set of conventions that has the potential to serve creative aims.

Along these lines, I argue in favour of an approach that considers the creative potential of national stereotypes in literary texts. As Friederike Heitsch has pointed out, literary scholarship is precisely *not* interested in the ways in which extra-literary reality is represented in literature. Instead, it aims to unveil the ways in which reality is transformed *for* and *through* the literary text.[51]

Interdisciplinary research on stereotypes – rather than imagology – provides insights that are highly valuable to literary scholarship. Literary research can only profit from tearing down artificial divides and considering national and cultural stereotypes side-by-side with stereotypes of class, gender, and age. At the same time, the literary scholar should be prepared and willing to look beyond the stereotypical. Focusing on national stereotypes alone means consciously reading the literary text against the grain and ignoring other central – non-stereotypical – features. It thus seems only sensible to consider stereotypes in their textual relation to and interplay with the non-stereotypical, individualized, and innovative. This holds true in particular for a field like ours where literatures increasingly are shaped by, respond to, and explore transcultural lifeworlds and postcolonial translocations.

Works Cited

Appadurai, Arjun. "Sovereignty without Territoriality: Notes for a Postnational Geography," in *The Anthropology of Space and Place: Locating Culture*, ed. Setha M. Low & Denise Lawrence–Zúñiga (Blackwell Readers in Anthropology 4; Malden MA: Blackwell, 2003): 337–49.

Beller, Manfred. "Perception, Image, Imagology," in *Imagology: The Cultural Construction and Literary Representation of National Characters. A Critical Survey*, ed. Manfred Beller & Joep Leerssen (Studia Imagologica 13; Amsterdam & New York: Rodopi, 2007): 3–16.

——, & Joep Leerssen. "Foreword," in *Imagology: The Cultural Construction and Literary Representation of National Characters. A Critical Survey*, ed. Manfred Beller & Joep Leerssen (Studia Imagologica 13; Amsterdam & New York: Rodopi, 2007): xiiv–xvi.

---

[51] Heitsch, *Imagologie des Islam*, 5.

Bleicher, Thomas. "Elemente einer komparatistischen Imagologie," in *Literarische Imagologie: Formen und Funktionen nationaler Stereotype in der Literatur*, ed. János Riesz (Komparatistische Hefte 2; Bayreuth: Ellwanger, 1980): 12–24.

Chew, William L., III. "'Literature, History, and the Social Sciences?': An Historical–Imagological Approach to Franco-American Stereotypes," in *National Stereotypes in Perspective: Americans in France, Frenchmen in America*, ed. William L. Chew III (Studia Imagologica 9; Amsterdam & New York: Rodopi, 2001): 1–53.

——. "What's in a National Stereotype? An Introduction to Imagology at the Threshold of the 21st Century," *Language and Intercultural Communication* 6.3–4 (August 2006): 179–87.

Corbineau–Hoffmann, Angelika. *Einführung in die Komparatistik* (2000; Berlin: Erich Schmidt, 2004).

Dyserinck, Hugo. "Zur Entwicklung der komparatistischen Imagologie," *Colloquium Helveticum* 7 (1988): 19–42.

——. "Komparatistische Imagologie jenseits von 'Werkimmanenz' und 'Werktranszendenz'," *Synthesis* 9 (1982): 27–40.

——. "Komparatistik als Europaforschung," in *Komparatistik und Europaforschung: Perspektiven vergleichender Literatur- und Kulturwissenschaft*, ed. Hugo Dyserinck & Karl Ulrich Syndram (Aachener Beiträge zur Komparatistik 9; Bonn: Bouvier, 1992): 31–62.

Fink, Gonthier–Louis. "Réflexions sur l'imagologie: Stéréotypes et réalités nationales dans une perspective franco–allemande," *Recherches Germaniques* 23 (1993): 3–31.

Fischer, Manfred S. *Nationale Images als Gegenstand Vergleichender Literaturgeschichte* (Aachener Beiträge zur Komparatistik 6; Bonn: Bouvier, 1981).

Florack, Ruth. *Bekannte Fremde: Zu Herkunft und Funktion nationaler Stereotype in der Literatur* (Studien und Texte zur Sozialgeschichte der Literatur 114; Tübingen: Max Niemeyer, 2007).

Heitsch, Friederike. *Imagologie des Islam in der neueren und neuesten spanischen Literatur* (Problemata Literaria 42; Kassel: Reichenberger, 1998).

Leerssen, Joep. "The Downward Pull of Cultural Essentialism," in *Image into Identity: Constructing and Assigning Identity in a Culture of Modernity*, ed. Michael Wintle (Studia Imagologica: Amsterdam Studies on Cultural Identity 11; Amsterdam & New York: Rodopi, 2006): 31–50.

——. "Echoes and Images: Reflections upon Foreign Space," in *Alterity, Identity, Image: Selves and Others in Society and Scholarship*, ed. Raymond Corbey & Joep Leerssen (Amsterdam Studies on Cultural Identity 1; Amsterdam & New York: Rodopi, 1991): 123–38.

——. "L'effet de typique," in *Mœurs et images: Etudes d'imagologie européenne*, ed. Alain Montandon (Clermont–Ferrand: U Blaise Pascal, 1997): 129–34.

——. "Imagology: History and Method," in *Imagology: The Cultural Construction and Literary Representation of National Characters: A Critical Survey*, ed. Manfred Beller & Joep Leerssen (Studia Imagologica 13; Amsterdam & New York: Rodopi, 2007): 17–32.

——. "Mimesis and Stereotype," in *National Identity: Symbol and Representation*, ed. Joep Leerssen & Menno Spiering (Yearbook of European Studies 4; Amsterdam & New York: Rodopi, 1991): 165–75.

——. "The Rhetoric of National Character: A Programmatic Survey," *Poetics Today* 21.2 (2000): 267–92.

Logvinov, Michail I. "Studia imagologica: zwei methodologische Ansätze zur komparatistischen Imagologie," *Germanistisches Jahrbuch G U S "Das Wort"* (2003): 203–20.

Neumann, Birgit. *Die Rhetorik der Nation in britischer Literatur und anderen Medien des 18. Jahrhunderts* (E L C H : Studies in English Literary and Cultural History 39; Trier: W V T, 2009).

Nünning, Ansgar. "Literatur, Mentalitäten und kulturelles Gedächtnis: Grundriss, Leitbegriffe und Perspektiven einer anglistischen Kulturwissenschaft," in *Literaturwissenschaftliche Theorien, Modelle und Methoden: Eine Einführung*, ed. Ansgar Nünning (Trier: W V T, 1998): 173–98.

Pageaux, Daniel–Henri. "Image / Imaginaire," in *Europa und das nationale Selbstverständnis: Imagologische Probleme in Literatur, Kunst und Kultur des 19. und 20. Jahrhunderts*, ed. Hugo Dyserinck & Karl Ulrich Syndram (Bonn: Bouvier, 1988): 367–79.

——. "De l'imagerie culturelle à l'imaginaire," in *Précis de littérature comparée*, ed. Pierre Brunel & Yves Chevrel (Paris: Presses Universitaires de France, 1989): 133–61.

Pieterse, Jan Nederveen. "Image and Power," in *Alterity, Identity, Image: Selves and Others in Society and Scholarship*, ed. Raymond Corbey & Joep Leerssen (Amsterdam Studies on Cultural Identity 1; Amsterdam & New York: Rodopi, 1991): 191–203.

Posner, Ronald. "Kultur als Zeichensystem. Zur semiotischen Explikation kulturwissenschaftlicher Grundbegriffe," in *Kultur als Lebenswelt und Monument*, ed. Aleida Assmann & Dietrich Harth (Frankfurt am Main: Fischer, 1991): 37–74.

Pratt, Mary Louise. *Toward a Speech Act Theory of Literary Discourse* (Bloomington & London: Indiana U P, 1977).

Riesz, János. "Einleitung: Zur Omnipräsenz nationaler und ethnischer Stereotype," in *Literarische Imagologie: Formen und Funktionen nationaler Stereotype in der Literatur*, ed. János Riesz (Komparatistische Hefte 2; Bayreuth: Ellwanger, 1980): 3–11.

Said, Edward W. *Orientalism: Western Conceptions of the Orient* (London: Routledge & Kegan Paul, 1978).

Schmidt, Siegfried. "Medien, Kultur, Medienkultur: Ein konstruktivistisches Gesprächsangebot," in *Kognition und Gesellschaft: Der Diskurs des Radikalen Konstruktivismus 2*, ed. Siegfried Schmidt (Suhrkamp-Taschenbuch Wissenschaft 950;
Frankfurt am Main: Suhrkamp, 1992): 425–50.

Sellin, Volker. "Mentalität und Mentalitätsgeschichte," *Historische Zeitschrift* 241
(1985): 555–98.

Stockhorst, Stefanie. "Was leistet ein cultural turn in der komparatistischen Imagologie? Henry Crabb Robinson als Vermittler deutscher Dichter- und Gelehrtenkultur nach England," *Arcadia* 40.2 (2005): 354–74.

Syndram, Karl Ulrich. "The Aesthetics of Alterity: Literature and the Imagological
Approach," in *National Identity: Symbol and Representation*, ed. Joep Leerssen &
Menno Spiering (Yearbook of European Studies 4; Amsterdam & New York:
Rodopi, 1991): 176–91.

——. "Das Problem der nationalen Literaturgeschichtsschreibung als Gegenstand der
komparatistischen Imagologie," in *Space and Boundaries of Literature / Espace et
Frontières de la Littérature: Proceedings of the Twelfth Congress of the International Comparative Literature Association 1988*, ed. Roger Bauer & Douwe Fokkema, vol. 4 (Munich: Iudicium, 1990): 36–42.

⌘

Distant Reading

—Cosmopolitanism as Unconditional Reception

DIRK WIEMANN

1. Learning How Not to Read

I
N "LITERATURE AND COSMOPOLITANISM," the American cultural historian Henry Sedgwick claims that "the humanities do render men more humane; literature does fit them to be citizens of the world."[1] If this robust Enlightenment optimism about literature's capacity to further a cosmopolitan humanity seems hopelessly quaint today, it must have appeared outright quixotic on the date of its first publication in August 1915, when the First World War was in full swing. For its contemporary readers, we may assume, Sedgwick's cosmopolitan bugle call for the "international republic of letters"[2] must have rung hollow indeed in the face of the unfolding mass slaughter of the trenches. Almost a century later, cosmopolis has not come any closer. Nor, however, have the catastrophes and crises of the past one hundred years erased the cosmopolitan vision. To the contrary, cosmopolitanism has assumed renewed prominence as a major issue in the social and political sciences, while the question of how literature and cosmopolitan relate has powerfully resurfaced in the recent debate on 'world literature' with its emphasis on how literary texts have the capacity to transgress local, cultural, and temporal demarcations; how literary genres migrate and mingle across spatial and linguistic barriers; how the act of reading occasions encounters with other worlds and thus fosters a translocal imaginary; and how "the literature around

---

[1] Henry Dwight Sedgwick, "Literature and Cosmopolitanism," in Sedgwick, *An Apology for Old Maids and Other Essays* (1916; Freeport NY: Books for Libraries, 1968): 217.

[2] Sedgwick, "Literature and Cosmopolitanism," 203.

us is now unmistakably a planetary system."[3] If all these assumptions were simply true, literature would indeed – in the sense of Sedgwick's cosmopolitanism – anticipate a global cosmopolis waiting to become a socio-political reality. Recent debates on world literature, however, point into a very different direction: Instead of prefiguring some equitably undivided world, literature itself seems to be deeply enmeshed in the power-asymmetries of the globalized present.

Thus, Pascale Casanova deceptively announces a "world republic of letters," only to delineate a highly competitive and hierarchically ordered system. In this "bourse of literary values,"[4] the "great cosmopolitan figures of the world of letters" act as "foreign exchange brokers"[5] who succeed in elevating their literary output to the status of internationally normative validity. Any text's transnational prestige and mobility across "the unequal structure [...] of literary space" depend on its proximity to "what might be called the Greenwich meridian of literature [that] makes it possible to estimate the relative aesthetic distance from the centre of the world of letters."[6] In the same spirit, Franco Moretti describes the global system of literature as an asymmetrical arrangement of centres and margins: a "one-and-unequal literary system" in which peripheral cultures depend on "importing" metropolitan input on "direct and indirect loans."[7] In short, 'world literature' is not based on egalitarian exchange and horizontal cosmopolitanism but on hierarchical stratification and the expansion of norms defined at the central 'Greenwich meridian'.

Yet there is nothing deterministic about this. Indeed, Casanova devotes the second half of her book to the elaboration of writers' strategies for intervening in the given structure by way of "literary revolts and revolutions."[8] Paying attention to the agency of the reader instead of the writer, Moretti urges for an egalitarian reception that would make "the study of world literature [...] a

---

[3] Franco Moretti, "Conjectures on World Literature," in *Debating World Literature*, ed. Christopher Prendergast (London & New York: Verso, 2004): 148. Originally published in *New Left Review*, New Series 1 (January–February 2000): 54–68 (here, 54).

[4] Pascale Casanova, *The World Republic of Letters* (*La République mondiale des lettres*, 1999; Cambridge MA & London: Harvard UP, 2004): 12.

[5] Casanova, *The World Republic of Letters*, 21.

[6] *The World Republic of Letters*, 83; 88.

[7] Moretti, "Conjectures on World Literature," 159; 150.

[8] Casanova, *The World Republic of Letters*, 178.

thorn in the side, a permanent intellectual challenge to national literatures"[9] with their entrenched canons. The punch-line of Moretti's argument is his advocacy of a technique of "distant reading" as opposed to the "theological exercise" of close reading:

> we know how to read texts, now let's learn how not to read them. Distant reading: where distance *is a condition of knowledge*: it allows you to focus on units that are much smaller or much larger than the text: devices, themes, tropes – or genres and systems.[10]

Obviously, then, distant reading is not non-reading but a departure from the paradigms of assiduous textual analysis from the New Criticism to deconstruction, all of which Moretti derides as techniques of "very solemn treatment of very few texts taken very seriously."[11] The main tenet of distant reading is the non-acceptance of the bounded text as its privileged object of affirmation or interrogation. It looks instead for intersections across textual boundaries as well as for the multiple ways in which texts are implicated in the non-literary world at large. Decidedly inclusive and non-selective, distant reading tends towards the virtually unconditional reception of all texts. This emphatically does not imply that all texts are treated as if they had the same value – rather, that literary value itself ceases to function as a viable category, so that every text has the same right to be received in the first place.

If cosmopolitan literature is constituted by cosmopolitan modes of reception, it is no longer grasped as a quality of the individual text or of the literary system at large but relegated to the reader's competence. This concept has at least two advantages: it conveniently conforms to the centrality that most trends in literary studies, over the past thirty years or so, have assigned to the reader; more than that, it allows for legitimate recourse to the arguably most influential reference-point in the debate on cosmopolitanism today: namely, Immanuel Kant's reflections, in *Perpetual Peace*, on the *jus cosmopoliticum* as the right to be received. While it is indeed the aim of this essay to suggest a transfer of the Kantian concept of the cosmopolitan right to the scene of distant reading, this is not meant to imply that the reception of texts is even remotely comparable to the hospitable reception (or hostile rejection) of people. What I am interested in, however, is the similar effect that Moretti's

---

[9] Moretti, "Conjectures on World Literature," 162.

[10] "Conjectures on World Literature," 151.

[11] "Conjectures on World Literature," 151.

distant reading and Kant's cosmopolitan right have on their respective object: namely, to leave it largely unqualified.

2. The Right to Be Received

For Kant, hospitality as the core of the cosmopolitan is "concerned not with philanthropy, but with *right.*" A political (as distinct from an ethical) category, hospitality implies "the right of a stranger not to be treated with hostility when he arrives at someone else's territory."[12] This is not the private affair of a stranger knocking at somebody's door asking to be taken in: The 'someone' at whose territory Kant's outsider arrives is not an individual but the bounded community of an ordered polity, so that the stranger's right implies a collective obligation to hospitality towards the non-member, who "can only be turned away, if this can be done without causing his death" (105–106).

As the general obligation to hospitality, the *jus cosmopoliticum* ensures the right of one who is not included in the *demos*, not affiliated to the polity, not entitled as citizen. It is a human right as distinct from a civic right, and as such it is not derived from the law of the land. As it applies to all human beings as members of a planetary cosmopolitan community, it exceeds the boundaries of any polity, suspends any locally limited perspective, and attains translocal validity. While this inclusive thrust in Kant's argument is hard to reconcile with the racism expressed in some of his other writings,[13] the concept of *jus cosmopoliticum* in *Perpetual Peace* clearly suspends all differentiating categories. However, in proportion to the cosmopolitan right's unlimited extension to everybody, its intension is accordingly limited: it entitles to nothing but survival as such. It is not the stranger's *bios* (good life) but her/his *zoe* (bare life) that is under the cosmopolitan law's protection. Precisely because it entitles to nothing but bare life, this right applies to everyone without any further qualification: The stranger simply has to be taken in without being sub-

---

[12] Immanuel Kant, "Perpetual Peace: A Philosophical Sketch," tr. Hugh Barr Nisbet, in *Kant: Political Writings*, ed. Hans Siegbert Reiss ("Zum ewigen Frieden: ein philosophischer Entwurf," 1795; tr. Cambridge: Cambridge UP, 1991): 105. Further page references are in the main text.

[13] See, for example, Peggy Piesche, "Der 'Fortschritt' der Aufklärung – Kants *race* und die Zentrierung des *weißen* Subjekts," in *Mythen, Masken und Subjekte: Kritische Weißseinsforschung in Deutschland*, ed. Maureen Maisha Eggers et al. (Münster: Unrast, 2005): 30–39.

jected to any act of 'close reading'. Compared to this unconditional reception, recent reformulations of Kant's notion of the cosmopolitan right must appear distinctly restrictive. Thus, for Beck, the cosmopolitan community requires an agreement on "substantive norms,"[14] while for Seyla Behabib strangers have to demonstrate their principal readiness to act "as potential participants in a world republic."[15] As opposed to the Kantian version of reception, these are conditional ones that do not enable "an open futurity dotted by new or emergent rights but a normative validity."[16]

In order to specify why Kant of all thinkers should have arrived at the notion of an unconditional right of reception, it appears necessary to be more precise about the grounds on which this right rests. In Kant, it is based on the assumption of a universal "right to the earth's surface" due to which "all men are entitled to present themselves in the society of others" (106). Everybody's fundamental right to be on earth thus supersedes all exclusive territorial claims upheld by particular communities. Moreover, since terrestrial space is limited, humans cannot avoid contact, hence are compelled to coexistence, as "they cannot disperse over an infinite area but must necessarily tolerate one another's company" (106). With this recourse to the principal scarcity of a resource – space – Kant's argument clearly draws on the traditional cosmopolitan impetus to establish a "relationship between political order and the order found in nature."[17] Obviously, however, Kant does not enlist some natural order as a prescriptive blueprint for a political unit. If he suggests a link "between *cosmos* and *polis*, the Order of Nature and that of Society,"[18] he does so to the opposite effect, through which members and outsiders, recipients, and arrivants alike are reduced to the status of species beings prior to all political entitlements: not citizens of the world in some cosmopolitan utopia but creatures of the planet. The politics of hospitality and the right to be received

[14] Ulrich Beck, *The Cosmopolitan Vision* (Cambridge: Polity, 2006): 49.

[15] Seyla Benhabib, "The Philosophical Foundations of Cosmopolitan Norms," in *Another Cosmopolitanism*, ed. Robert Post (New York & Oxford: Oxford UP, 2008): 22.

[16] Bonnie Honig, "Another Cosmopolitanism? Law and Politics in the New Europe," in *Another Cosmopolitanism*, ed. Robert Post (New York & Oxford: Oxford UP, 2008): 110.

[17] Paul Gilroy, *Postcolonial Melancholia* (New York: Columbia UP, 2005).

[18] Stephen Toulmin, *Cosmopolis: The Hidden Agenda of Modernity* (Chicago: U of Chicago P, 1992): 67.

derive from, or are imposed by, the 'natural' fact of cohabitation on one shared planet and the ensuing dictate to conviviality:

> Since the earth's surface is not infinite but limited by its own config-
> uration, these two concepts [political right and international right]
> taken together necessarily lead to the idea of an *international political*
> *right* (*ius gentium*) or a *cosmopolitan right* (*ius cosmopoliticum*). (137)

Nothing, of course, would be more misleading than to read Kant as a prac- tical advocate of a politics of some global commons: his notion of a general right to the earth's surface "which the human race shares in common" by no means involves an agenda of democratic redistribution but simply an impera- tive to acknowledge the other's presence as a cohabitant of the same empirical given space of the planet to which "no-one originally has any greater right than anyone else." It is only with reference to the *zoe* of the species as a whole that the earth figures as a natural commons – one that then is overwritten, de- marcated, and compartmentalized into so many different and distinct legiti- mate political portions that organize community-specific forms of *bios*. The incoming stranger in Kant's argument has no claim to be admitted to the *polis* he enters – only to a temporary "right of resort" in order to save her/his bare life. Everybody's fundamental and equal shareholding applies to nothing but "soil pure and simple" – not to "what is *erected, constructed, or what sets itself above* the soil: habitat, culture, institution, State, etc. All this [...] must not be unconditionally accessible to all comers."[19] And yet, Kant's receiving community is dependent on the "inclusive exclusion"[20] of the stranger who gives the *polis* occasion to act hospitably: Only through the observation of the cosmopolitan right "can we flatter ourselves that we are continually advan- cing" (108). As bearer of bare life, and reduced to the status of bare life, the stranger thus "has the peculiar privilege of being that whose exclusion [from *bios*] founds the city of man."[21] Even so, it cannot go unnoticed that Kant is arguing to include this very category of *zoe* within the realm of the political by treating it as foundational of the stranger's cosmo*political* right to be

---

[19] Jacques Derrida, *On Cosmopolitanism and Forgiveness*, tr. Mark Dooley & Michael Hughes (*Cosmopolites de tous les pays, encore un effort!*, 1997; London & New York: Routledge, 2001): 21.

[20] Giorgio Agamben, *Homo Sacer: Sovereign Power and Bare Life*, tr. Daniel Heller–Roazen (*Homo Sacer: Il potere soverano e la vita nuda*, 1995; Meridian: Crossing Aesthetics; Stanford CA: Stanford UP, 1998): 8.

[21] Agamben, *Homo Sacer*, 9.

received in the first place. Moreover, the spherical space of the planet figures as a biopolitical category in Kant's argument, one that rhetorically replaces the concept of the qualified citizen with that of the unconditionally human: a figure whose futurity is principally open to a "universal *cosmopolitan existence*" (51).

3. Reading Cosmopolitans Reading

The simple fact of the earth's limitation, the right to be received unconditionally, and the general human condition as planetary creatures: in the following I would like to trace these three aspects of Kant's argument in an attempted transfer to three different distant readings of one exemplary text, Mahasweta Devi's novella *Pterodactyl, Puran Sahay and Pirtha* (1993), which stages its own opacity as an imperative to unconditional reception. In Devi's narrative, Puran, a committed investigative journalist located in Patna, sets out on a research trip to the tribal area of Pirtha in central India in order to cover the outrage of a man-made famine in a naturally fertile region. It is here that he comes across not only the 5,000-years-old civilization of the local indigenous community but, more shockingly, a live pterodactyl – one of those flying dinosaurs that have been extinct for some 75 million years. The narrative gravitates around the problem that Puran and his Adivasi interlocutors have with making sense of this inexplicable heterotopic presence: The pterodactyl's "glance is so prehistoric that Puran's brain cells, spreading a hundred antennae, understand nothing of that glance"; and yet it is stressed time and again that "those eyes have a message for Puran. Puran does not know those eyes' language."[22] This pressing experience of an unbridgeable "communication gap"[23] extends from the intradiegetic world to that of the reader and renders reception itself a serious problem. The appearance of the extinct dinosaur turns this otherwise wryly realist narrative into a properly fantastic text that allows for the co-presence "of events of two orders, those of the natural world and those of the supernatural world"[24] without offering a clue as to which of these orders ultimately prevails. In literary terms, then, Devi's

---

[22] Mahasweta Devi, "Pterodactyl, Puran Sahay, and Pirtha," in *Imaginary Maps: Three Stories*, tr. Gayatri Chakravorty Spivak (Calcutta: Thema, 1993): 151.

[23] Devi, "Pterodactyl, Puran Sahay, and Pirtha," 125.

[24] Tzvetan Todorov, *The Fantastic: A Structural Approach to a Literary Genre*, tr. Richard Howard (Ithaca NY: Cornell UP, 1973): 27.

novella could be neatly classified as a specimen of the fantastic. Yet it is precisely this classificatory gesture that the story denies its reader by virtue of an activist poignancy that makes a merely textual analysis uncomfortably frivolous. After all, this narrative about famine victims and a dying indigenous culture comes, like the opaque pterodactyl at its centre, as a visitation "to give some urgent news"[25] that defies close reading and yet insists on the importance of its undecipherable message. In this respect, Devi's narrative about missing links and communication gaps offers one common ground for characters and readers alike: the urge to acknowledge the presence of that which cannot be deciphered and accommodated – in other words, unconditional reception.

The first of the three announced distant readings of this story comes from Lawrence Buell, who, in his *Writing for an Endangered World* (2001), has a very brief discussion of Devi's 'Pterodactyl' novella. Buell's ecocritical reading of Devi is part of an overarching agenda to analyse literary texts as articulations of "environmentality": i.e. the awareness of the limited spherical character of the earth. As in Kant, therefore, natural space is a limited resource whose scarcity poses, for Buell, the problem of sharing in terms not of cosmopolitan right but of environmental justice. From his readings of literary texts, Buell hopes to gain insight into the explicit and accessible individual or communal "environmental imagination" and, more crucially, into the "environmental unconscious." This latter term, derived from Fredric Jameson's concept of a 'political unconscious', is coined to capture the assumption "that embeddedness in spatio-physical context is [...] intractably constitutive of personal and social identity, and of the way that texts get constructed."[26] Where Jameson, in other words, assumes the ineluctable presence of an ideological subtext structuring every utterance behind the actors' backs, Buell suggests a structurally similar dynamics triggered by any subject's necessary locatedness within, and vis-à-vis, nature.

On this premise, Buell celebrates Devi's text as "one of the most challenging and trenchant fictions of ecological justice ever written."[27] However, while this story of an indigenous community threatened with extinction is, for

---

[25] Devi, "Pterodactyl, Puran Sahay, and Pirtha," 181.

[26] Lawrence Buell, *Writing for an Endangered World: Literature, Culture and the Environment in the U.S. and Beyond* (Cambridge MA & London: Harvard UP, 2001): 27.

[27] Buell, *Writing for an Endangered World*, 230.

Buell, laudably sensitive to the 'environmentality' of the "ecosystem people" it describes, it remains largely specio-centric and thus fails to configure the human catastrophe of famine and extreme destitution with "the plight of the nonhuman environment."[28] In Buell's own scenario, Devi writes in the name of ecological justice but fails to develop a non-anthropocentric ethic. Due to this limited ethical concern, the text marginalizes the suffering of the non-human Other and thus betrays a "tunnel-visioned ferocity." As a consequence, Buell argues, the whole narrative hinges on the notion that 'no communication' can be established between the human and the non-human that, as he sees it, is represented in the inexplicable presence of the palaeontological pterodactyl.

It is precisely at this point that the undeconstructed parochialism of Buell's ecocritical approach becomes apparent: Not only is Devi's text introduced as an anomaly, as a detour from the main path of Euro-American writing that forms the central object of Buell's investigation; furthermore, in Buell's reading Devi's narrative gives expression to an "esoteric cultural particularism"[29] – a give-away formulation that constitutes the text's alterity and implicitly re-asserts a centre–periphery model: All through his book, Buell discusses writers such as Whitman, Thoreau, Dreiser, and Faulkner without ever attesting 'cultural particularism', let alone esoterics. Obviously, "the unsettling implication is that somehow American texts transcend 'cultural particularism' and are always already universalized in ways that postcolonial texts are not."[30] The alterity ascribed to Devi's text highlights its being external to the 'normative' mainstream. The problem is not with alterity here but with the conditional reception that ensues as soon as alterity is derived from the self. In Buell's reading, therefore, the culturally different book requires to be assimilated and familiarized through a denial of unconditional reception. This becomes most obvious in the domesticating treatment of the central figure of the pterodactyl itself, which Buell insistently reads as a figment of (tribal?) imagination, so that, when Puran finally encounters the reptile, "he 'sees' the pterodactyl"[31] in some merely figurative fashion. Above all, the opaque intruder is reduced to a transparent symbol: "The 'pterodactyl' [is] a mythic figure sym-

---

[28] Buell, *Writing for an Endangered World*, 234.

[29] *Writing for an Endangered World*, 230.

[30] Rob Nixon, "Environmentalism and Postcolonialism," in *Postcolonial Studies and Beyond*, ed. Ania Loomba et al. (Durham NC & London: Duke UP, 2005): 245.

[31] Buell, *Writing for an Endangered World*, 232.

bolizing tribal identity (including its imminent extinction)."[32] This rendition of opacity as transparency extends from the figure of the pterodactyl to the narrative as a whole. With his allegorical interpretation, Buell severs the link between characters and reader, as the latter now has privileged access to a 'meaning' that remains hidden from the former. Reception thus becomes conditional on the text's yielding its 'message'.

By contrast, Sara Ahmed approaches Devi's text from a Levinas-inflected poststructuralist feminist platform in an attempt to stage a "generous encounter"[33] between the ('Third-World') text and the (metropolitan) reader. As a formula for "hospitality, *a way of being together with strangers* without assimilating them fully" (150), Ahmed's programme of the generous encounter has clear resonances of Kant's cosmopolitan right to be received unconditionally: "Being hospitable, or generous, is being open to the 'who' I might encounter, but in such a way that this particularity does not hold this 'you' in place" (152). Accordingly, Ahmed's ethic of the generous encounter puts the recipient under the obligation to refrain from arresting the comer in some preconceived identity. This is not simply a stance of tolerance but, rather, a precondition for the fundamental productivity inherent in any encounter as an event that "is ontologically prior to the question of ontology (the question of the being who encounters)" (7). Inasmuch as the encounter does "not necessarily presuppose a meeting between two already constituted beings" (143), it harbours the potential for that 'open futurity' that Bonnie Honig sees in Kant's seminal notion of the cosmopolitan right.

Ahmed conceives of the generous encounter as an instance of unconditional reception that does not identify the Other; all the same, she is cautious of the fact that every encounter necessarily takes place within histories of identification and (mis)recognition that premediate who is and who is not a stranger. "Produced as a category within knowledge," the stranger "is not *any-body* we have failed to recognise but *some-body* that we have already recognised *as* a stranger" (55). This inescapable premediation compels the recipient to a reflexive awareness about the encounter's historical determinants and the asymmetries of power they implement. Only on this condition can the concrete event unfold – not as some impossibly innocent first contact but "as a way of *(re)encountering what is already encountered*" (178). It is in this

---

[32] Buell, *Writing for an Endangered World*, 231.

[33] Sara Ahmed, *Strange Encounters: Embodied Others in Post-Coloniality* (London & New York: Routledge, 2000): 152. Further page references are in the main text.

spirit that Ahmed reflects on her encounter with Devi's text in the form of a letter to the Bengali author. Here Ahmed scrupulously meditates on her own position of a reader striving for the unconditional reception of a culturally different book that, all its alterity notwithstanding, comes in the all-too-familiar form of "this book, this commodity object that moves across the world" (152) labelled as a specimen of postcolonial writing and thus "assimilated [...] into economies of difference" (154). To step out of this premediation requires a subtle shift (which in fact entails a full reversal) of the established configuration: In Ahmed's imaginary letter to Devi, the positions of recipient and incoming stranger begin to interchange, so that Ahmed is no longer only the reader of Devi's narrative, trying to be generous, but simultaneously the writer of an intimate report 'arriving at' the site of the addressee and asking to be generously received in turn. As a result, the cosmopolitan right to be received becomes reciprocal.

> This is how I arrive at you. I want to be generous. And yet when I think of full hands I am sickened. I feel nauseous. This idea of me approaching you with full hands is nauseating. I approach you with hands that have taken, taken from you: my little acts of reading already involve relationships of debt. The reproduction of the economic legacies of colonialism here and now. I cannot simply give. To give in the face of such debts is to forget what has already been taken, including the very names that allow me to pick up this book, to desire to read it, to shelve it, to make it part of 'my collection'. (152)

This restaging of the scene of reception involves more than the transformation of the recipient into an arrivant herself. Unconditional reception is complicated here by the sharp insight into the historical and persistent asymmetries "of the economic legacies of colonialism" that fix the participants in a relation of indebtedness. Since this is not an individual but a systemic debt of the 'First World' to the 'Third', the scripts of hegemonic global financial policy with their mechanisms of foreign debt get inverted here as the former colony figures as the former metropolis's creditor. Moreover, since Ahmed is referring to the appropriative gesture of incorporating the incoming text into "my collection," she alludes to a whole history – still waiting to be retrieved – of Europe's clandestine cultural borrowing from the non-Western world. Given these precautions and provisos, Ahmed is hardly in the same situation as Buell: Instead of measuring the text against a normative standard, her version of distant reading can only reflect on the difficult preconditions under which such a reading occurs. This scrupulous circumspection, however, has the disturbing effect that Ahmed spends pages on her meticulous self-interrogation but has nothing to say about Devi's text itself. Instead of being read at all, then, Devi's narrative is written back to – with the effect of its being silenced by Ahmed's unintentionally solipsistic reflections on the demands of a critical cosmopolitanism that is lucidly aware of "the coloniality of power" but cannot open up to that dialogic co-operativity which would enable a "cosmopolitan project in which everyone participates instead of 'being participated'."[34]

A third distant reading of Devi's narrative can be construed from Gayatri Spivak's scattered remarks on that text. For Spivak, Devi's texts construct scenes of "internal colonization in the name of decolonization,"[35] scenes in which mainstream modern India, complicit with global capital, destroys indigenous India. Like Buell, she thus reads Devi's pterodactyl story as a tale of environmental justice that articulates "the perhaps impossible vision of an ecologically just world."[36] It is important that for Spivak this latter stands in sharp contrast to the powerfully established unified but uneven space of international capital in which "the world is broadly divided simply into North and South [but] the World Bank has no barrier to its division." What the "imaginary mapmaking of the World Bank"[37] produces is "the globe": an abstract figure of the mind that "allows us to think that we can aim to control it."[38] If the 'globe' is thus the name for a manageable world overwritten with vectors, connectors, and barriers of economic and military power, its counterfigure in Spivak's nomenclature – the 'planet' – does not possess any ontological primacy: Unlike Buell, Spivak does not posit an undivided 'natural' space as a given substratum of the differentiated political space of the globe. Instead, the 'planet' remains a project: "that impossible, undivided world of which one must dream, in view of the impossibility of which one must work, obsessively."[39] The first precondition for a planetary instead of a global subjectivity

---

[34] Walter D. Mignolo, "The Many Faces of Cosmo-polis: Border Thinking and Critical Cosmopolitanism," in *Cosmopolitanism*, ed. Carol A. Breckenridge et al. (Durham NC & London: Duke UP, 2002): 182.

[35] Gayatri Chakravorty Spivak, "Appendix," in *Imaginary Maps: Three Stories*, by Mahasweta Devi (Calcutta: Thema, 1993): 209.

[36] Spivak, "Appendix," 203.

[37] "Appendix," 200; 201.

[38] Gayatri Chakravorty Spivak, *Death of a Discipline* (Calcutta: Seagull, 2004): 72.

[39] Gayatri Chakravorty Spivak, *A Critique of Postcolonial Reason: Toward a History of the Vanishing Present* (Cambridge MA & London: Harvard UP, 1999): 382.

is therefore the insight into the unavailability of the Other (emphatically including nature as such) in a relation of "alterity [...] underived from us."[40] Hence the tolerance to opacity with which Spivak, as distinct from Buell, re-states the ambiguity of the central figure of the pterodactyl as well as the coexisting efforts, on the part of the indigenous and mainstream characters, to make sense of its appearance: "The fiction does not judge between the regis-ters of truth and exactitude, simply stages them in separate spaces. [...] The pterodactyl is not a symbol."[41]

Owing to the idea of alterity as 'underived', Spivak is in no position to ap-proach Devi's text with a set of normative standards but, rather, must adopt the ostentatious humility of a reader hoping to "*learn* to learn."[42] Like Ah-med, she offers distant readings that are scrupulously aware of the coloniality of power. Unlike Ahmed, however, she avoids getting self-absorbed in these necessarily reader-centred reflections on global asymmetries and subjec-tivities: Where Ahmed ultimately privatizes the historical determinants of the scene of reception grasped as an individual encounter between reader and text, Spivak conceives of reading as an act "to supplement necessary col-lective efforts to change laws, modes of production, systems of education, and health care."[43] As a consequence, there is a continuity (instead of an opposi-tion) between reading and 'activism', between the responsiveness of the re-cipient of a text and "the structure of responsible (responding and being responded to) resistance"[44] that forms the ethico-political key concept in Spivak's idiosyncratic agenda. From the perspective of responsibility, "life is lived as the call of the wholly other, which must necessarily be answered [...] by accountable reason."[45] This effectively precludes the assimilation of the Other – whether stranger or text – into the precedent normative grid of the re-cipient; rather, it demands a dialogue of responses from both sides. Akin to Ahmed's productive encounter without precedent identities, this dialogue opens a space for "something coming about through the telling, the middle

---

[40] Spivak, *Death of a Discipline*, 73.

[41] Spivak, *Critique of Postcolonial Reason*, 145.

[42] Spivak, "Appendix," 204.

[43] "Appendix," 204–205.

[44] Gayatri Chakravorty Spivak, "Translator's Preface," in *Imaginary Maps: Three Stories*, by Mahasweta Devi (Calcutta: Thema, 1993): xxi.

[45] Spivak, *Critique of Postcolonial Reason*, 427.

voice of *dialegesthai*."[46] The twist through which Spivak exceeds Ahmed's individualism consists precisely in the extension of this basic configuration into the cosmopolitical proper, understood not as an individual or communal "mindset"[47] but as "a catachresis for inscribing collective responsibility as right."[48] While this is a return to Kant's insistence on the politico-juridical kernel of the cosmopolitan, it remains the privilege of literary texts like Devi's to figure "that impossible undivided world" of cosmopolis. Surprisingly, then, Spivak actually offers a highly reflexive deconstructive reclamation of Sedgwick's cosmopolitan and pedagogic optimism according to which "the humanities do render men more humane, and literature does fit them to be citizens of the world." Taking all of Sedgwick's positive terms as catachreses – as figures of speech without reference – Spivak's rephrasing defines "the arena of the humanities as the uncoercive rearrangement of desire [...] to keep responsibility alive in the reading and teaching of the textual."[49]

Spivak's project of viewing alterity as 'underived from us' is clearly closest to the Kantian ideal of unconditional reception; with this latter, however, it also shares its virtual impossibility in the here-and-now, its inapplicability both in the fields of cosmopolitics proper and at the scene of reading: Whether as incoming stranger or as literary text, the Other is always already identified by the recipient, if only *as* an Other. A scenario like Spivak's can therefore not offer a fully realizable programme of cosmopolitanism; it can only insistently point to the fact that distant reading remains to be learned as a future praxis of "democratic indifference."[50]

WORKS CITED

Agamben, Giorgio. *Homo Sacer: Sovereign Power and Bare Life*, tr. Daniel Heller–Roazen (*Homo Sacer: Il potere soverano e la vita nuda*, 1995; Meridian: Crossing Aesthetics; Stanford CA: Stanford UP, 1998).

---

[46] Gayatri Chakravorty Spivak, *Other Asias* (Oxford: Blackwell, 2008): 80.

[47] Spivak, *Other Asias*, 238.

[48] Spivak, *Death of a Discipline*, 102.

[49] *Death of a Discipline*, 101.

[50] Jacques Rancière, *The Politics of Aesthetics: The Distribution of the Sensible*, tr. Gabriel Rockhill (*Le partage du sensible: Esthétique et politique*, 2000; London: Continuum, 2006): 35.

Ahmed, Sara. *Strange Encounters: Embodied Others in Post-Coloniality* (London & New York: Routledge, 2000).

Beck, Ulrich. *The Cosmopolitan Vision* (Cambridge: Polity, 2006).

Benhabib, Seyla. "The Philosophical Foundations of Cosmopolitan Norms," in *Another Cosmopolitanism*, ed. Robert Post (New York & Oxford: Oxford UP, 2008): 13–44.

Buell, Lawrence. *Writing for an Endangered World: Literature, Culture and the Environment in the U.S. and Beyond* (Cambridge MA & London: Harvard UP, 2001).

Casanova, Pascale. *The World Republic of Letters* (*La République mondiale des lettres*, 1999; Cambridge MA & London: Harvard UP, 2004).

Derrida, Jacques. *On Cosmopolitanism and Forgiveness*, tr. Mark Dooley & Michael Hughes (*Cosmopolites de tous les pays, encore un effort!*, 1997; London & New York: Routledge, 2001).

Devi, Mahasweta. "Pterodactyl, Puran Sahay, and Pirtha," in *Imaginary Maps: Three Stories*, tr. & intro. Gayatri Chakravorty Spivak (Calcutta: Thema, 1993): 95–198.

Gilroy, Paul. *Postcolonial Melancholia* (New York: Columbia UP, 2005).

Honig, Bonnie. "Another Cosmopolitanism? Law and Politics in the New Europe," in *Another Cosmopolitanism*, ed. Robert Post (New York & Oxford: Oxford UP, 2008), 102–27.

Kant, Immanuel. "Introduction to the Theory of Right," in *Kant: Polticial Writings*, tr. Hugh Barr Nisbet, ed. Hans Siegbert Reiss (1795; Cambridge: Cambridge UP, 1991): 132–36.

——. "Perpetual Peace: A Philosophical Sketch," in *Kant: Political Writings*, tr. Hugh Barr Nisbet, ed. Hans Siegbert Reiss ("Zum ewigen Frieden: ein philosophischer Entwurf," 1795; Cambridge: Cambridge UP, 1991): 93–130.

Mignolo, Walter D. "The Many Faces of Cosmo-polis: Border Thinking and Critical Cosmopolitanism," in *Cosmopolitanism*, ed. Carol A. Breckenridge et al. (Durham NC & London: Duke UP, 2002): 157–87.

Moretti, Franco. "Conjectures on World Literature," in *Debating World Literature*, ed. Christopher Prendergast (London & New York: Verso, 2004): 148–62. Originally published in *New Left Review*, New Series 1 (January–February 2000): 54–68.

Nixon, Rob. "Environmentalism and Postcolonialism," in *Postcolonial Studies and Beyond*, ed. Ania Loomba et al. (Durham NC & London: Duke UP, 2005): 233–51.

Piesche, Peggy. "Der 'Fortschritt' der Aufklärung – Kants *race* und die Zentrierung des *weißen* Subjekts," in *Mythen, Masken und Subjekte: Kritische Weißseinsforschung in Deutschland*, ed. Maureen Maisha Eggers et al. (Münster: Unrast, 2005): 30–39.

Rancière, Jacques. *The Politics of Aesthetics: The Distribution of the Sensible*, tr. Gabriel Rockhill (*Le partage du sensible: Esthétique et politique*, 2000; London: Continuum, 2006).

Sedgwick, Henry Dwight. "Literature and Cosmopolitanism," in Sedgwick, *An Apology for Old Maids and Other Essays* (1916; Freeport N Y : Books for Libraries P , 1968): 203–21.

Spivak, Gayatri Chakravorty. "Appendix," in *Imaginary Maps: Three Stories*, by Mahasweta Devi (Calcutta: Thema, 1993): 199–210.

——. *A Critique of Postcolonial Reason: Toward a History of the Vanishing Present* (Cambridge M A & London: Harvard U P , 1999).

——. *Death of a Discipline* (Calcutta: Seagull, 2004).

——. *Other Asias* (Oxford: Blackwell, 2008).

——. "Translator's Preface," in *Imaginary Maps: Three Stories*, by Mahasweta Devi (Calcutta: Thema, 1993): xvii–xxvii.

Todorov, Tzvetan. *The Fantastic: A Structural Approach to a Literary Genre*, tr. Richard Howard (Ithaca N Y : Cornell U P , 1973).

Toulmin, Stephen. *Cosmopolis: The Hidden Agenda of Modernity* (Chicago: U of Chicago P , 1992).

⌘

SECTION II

⌘

SPACE, TIME, AND NARRATION

Transculturation and Narration
in the Black Diaspora of the Americas

ROLAND WALTER

A CCORDING TO PAUL GILROY, the black Atlantic is a "transcultural, international formation" characterized by a "rhizomorphic, fractal structure." He furthermore states that critics "specify" the fractally shaped cultural forms through "manifestly inadequate theoretical terms like creolization and syncretism."[1] Taking these statements as a point of departure, this essay examines the term 'New World African diaspora' as an intercultural space of both cultural fusion and cultural fissure characterized by an interstitial belonging, cutting across diverse ethnoracial, gendered, and geographical border(land)s. Constituted by a variety of shifting places, this diasporic space is home to a transcultural consciousness in process that mediates between diverse cultural elements while creating new ones. In the process of examining this consciousness in select works by contemporary Afro-Canadian, Afro-American, Afro-Caribbean, and Afro-Brazilian writers, it addresses the following questions: How is identity constituted, produced, and enacted in a transcultural contact zone nourished by the contradictory complementarities of displacement and relocation, broken origins, and deferred homecomings? Given the heritage of imploded world-views, how do pan-American black writers use memory and imagination to develop conceptions of wholeness and cohesion out of the fragments of cultural and identitarian diasporization? And finally, how do they engage with the inside consciousness of cultural expression in this mnemonic process? Let me begin by juxtaposing the statements of three pan-American black writers.

---

[1] Paul Gilroy, *The Black Atlantic* (Cambridge MA: Harvard UP, 1993): 4, 15.

For Édouard Glissant, two major characteristics of pan-American literature are "a tortured sense of time" and a "violent [...] sense of [...] space."[2] In short, both time and space are suffused with the violence of the past that continues to cast a shadow on the present.

In "América Negra," the Afro-Brazilian poet Élio Ferreira states that in the "Americas / what happened did not pass," but accumulates in social violence, misery, and identity-crisis. Exiled in his country like "a stranger in enemy territory," the poetic voice accuses Brazil of wearing a "white mask" and asks: "when are you paying me your debts?"[3]

Canada, according to the cultural critic Rinaldo Walcott, is home to

> at least three different black configurations [...]: a long black presence dating back to the founding of the colony including slavery and escapes from slavery; a discontinuous and continuous Caribbean presence since the early 1800s; and recent continental African migrations.

One of Walcott's basic arguments is that what links these configurations is a national/cultural un-belonging as "not-quite-citizens": "we are an absented presence always under erasure."[4]

Thus, the brutalization of black people in the Americas is linked to the brutalization of space, and both are rooted in the past: the slave trade, the plantation system, post-slavery racism, and sexism, and their haunting images: "We live in the Diaspora, in the sea in between," writes the Caribbean-Canadian author Dionne Brand. In her critical essays and creative writing, Brand probes this in-betweenness as a consciousness that is haunted by "the spectre of captivity."[5] Whether adrift on a boat, like Adrian, standing in a window in Amsterdam, like Maya, or cracking up in the streets of Toronto, like Verlia, Brand's characters are on schizo-walks through the African diaspora space, one of the postcolonial contact zones par excellence. For Brand and her characters, this transcultural contact zone is a space of ambiguity and

---

[2] Édouard Glissant, *Caribbean Discourse*, sel., tr. & intro. J. Michael Dash (*Le discours antillais*, 1981; tr. Charlottesville: UP of Virginia, 1992): 144–45.

[3] "Américas, / o que passou, não passou"; "estrangeiro em terras inimigas"; "máscara branca"; "quando você me pagará seus débitos?" Elio Ferreira, "América Negra," *Cadernos Negros* 27 (São Paulo: Quilombhoje, 2004): 51, 52, 53.

[4] Rinaldo Walcott, *Black Like Who? Writing Black Canada* (Toronto: Insomniac, 2003): 137, 134, 27.

[5] Dionne Brand, *A Map to the Door of No Return: Notes to Belonging* (Toronto: Vintage, 2002): 20, 29.

incoherence: a heterotopic space of confusion where freedom of choice is forever deferred and in the making. Eula's description of her *Dasein* as a "whole broken-up tragedy, standing in the middle of the world cracking"[6] attests to the fact that what transculturation organizes in this contact zone is cultural fissure, spiralling from one circle of rupture to the next. If New-World African identity has no stable, fixed home, if it drifts in betweenness propelled by a desire for home, then home – the re-creation/re-imagining of one's self and the world through one's own eyes – is one of the key issues in pan-American black literature. In the following, I want to examine diverse attempts at creating this home through discourse, memory, and imagination.

For the Caribbean-Canadian writer Marlene Nourbese Philip, epistemic change that rights the "imbalance of the word / i-mage equation" begins on the level of enunciation. She asserts that this "can only be done by consciously restructuring, reshaping, and, if necessary, destroying the language."[7] In other words, the language of the (neo)colonial oppressor, an alien house, has to be signified upon in order to become a home. Home in language, then, is one of the most crucial means of re-membering and re-creating the broken fragments of an identity violated in the fetid holds of ships, lost in the (in)audible echo of Atlantic waters and (in)visible traces of maroon resistance, shattered by the *hot thing* of the plantation system, the distortions of official discourse, and the various forms of post-abolition racism and sexism. The deconstruction of (neo)colonial discursive practices, then, means hyphenizing signs in order to create a semantic place-as-home. I contend that Philip's poetic resistance in "Discourse on the Logic of Language" is an anthropophagous transwriting embedded in sexuality: "Slip mouth over the syllable; moisten with tongue the word. Suck Slide Play Caress Blow – Love it, but if the word gags, does not nourish, bite it off – at its source – Spit it out Start again."[8] Actually, Philip's discursive blow-job is a signifying that "smash[es] / the in-the-beginning word"[9] by using parts of its signifier/signified and excreting others. This anthropophagous deformation of the sign at the crossroads of intercultural contact, characterized by sexuality and violence embed-

---

[6] Dionne Brand, *At the Full and Change of the Moon* (New York: Grove, 1999): 258.

[7] Marlene Nourbese Philip, *She Tries Her Tongue, Her Silence Softly Breaks* (Charlottetown, PEI: Ragweed, 1996): 21.

[8] Philip, *She Tries Her Tongue, Her Silence Softly Breaks*, 69.

[9] *She Tries Her Tongue, Her Silence Softly Breaks*, 71.

ded in a multi-axial network of power-relations, disrupts as it fuses, links as it separates, imbuing the 'multi-' with the 'trans-': a double writing that links contradictory elements in an uneasy dialogic structure.[10] Thus, Philip supplements both Brand's vision of diasporic in-betweenness as schizo-walks and Radhakrishnan's description of the diasporic location as one of "painful, incommensurable simultaneity [...] that promises neither transcendence nor return," in that she demonstrates through her transwriting how subaltern displacement can be transformed into replacement.[11] Since this move from deterritorialization to reterritorialization is an ongoing process within transculture that transforms identity, space, and place, I want to call it a transplacement that shuttles between a longing to belong, a belonging, and an un-belonging.

Whereas, for many characters in novels by New-World African writers, home seems to vanish on the horizon of their never-ending errantry within and across national racist/sexist borderlands, Toni Morrison describes a "real home" as follows:

> Not some fortress you bought and built up and have to keep everybody
> locked in or out. A real home. Not some place you went to and in-
> vaded and slaughtered people to get. Not some place you claimed,
> snatched because you got the guns. Not some place you stole from the
> people living there, but your own home, where if you go back past
> your great-great-grandparents, past theirs, and theirs, past the whole of
> Western history, past the beginning of organized knowledge, past
> pyramids and poison bows, on back to when rain was new, before
> plants forgot they could sing and birds thought they were fish, back

---

[10] My reading of this passage is inspired by Oswald de Andrade's use of the term 'anthropophagy'. In his *Manifesto antropofágico* (1928), Andrade used the anthropophagous ritual of the Tupinambás – a collective practice of vengeance to maintain the stability of their tribal structure – to redefine Brazil's cultural identity. Throughout the text Andrade argues that the assimilation of the Other, extracting the essence from it while transforming it into something new and different, has always characterized Brazilian culture. His objective, then, was to create an autonomous cultural project through the consumption of the colonizer's legacy.

[11] Rajagopalan Radhakrishnan, *Diasporic Meditations: Between Home and Location* (Minneapolis: U of Minnesota P, 1996): 175. What links Philip and Brand in their difference is a demystification of Canada's multiculturalism. They make cogently clear that otherness, whether cultural, ethnic, or sexual, constitutes the interior alterity that marks the limit of the Canadian multicultural nation-state. Multicultural Canada, in other words, mothers some of her children and orphans others.

> when God said Good! Good! – there, right there where you know your
> own people were born and lived and died. Imagine that [...] place.[12]

Here, home is a *concrete utopia* in the Blochian sense imbued with a transcultural vision: a yearning for a yet-to-come cross-cultural relationship whose
essence is shot through not with racism, sexism, or any other hierarchical
order, but with a collective willingness to accept, respect, and nurture difference as relational diversity of the biota, including human beings. It is a de-
raced "world-as home" where differences are "prized but unprivileged."[13] As
such, it is an example of her transwriting as mediation between cultures, languages, epistemes, and the human and non-human worlds; a mediation in
which the 'trans-' crosses multiculture relating its elements in a continuous
process at the crossroads of diverse intercultural contact zones.

If, according to Fernando Ortiz, who coined the term 'transculturation' in
the 1940s, two-way transcultural interchanges are characterized by "acculturation," "deculturation," and "neoculturation,"[14] then Morrison has not only
shown that these interchanges, which culminate in the creation of new cultural
phenomena, have been a staple of the nation's cultural make-up. Most importantly, she has posited as centrally problematical the fact that the 'new'
culture is never achieved but forever in the making. Her second-latest novel,
A Mercy, delineates the nation-space as a transcultural contact zone inhabited
by characters who long to belong, but whose homecoming is deferred. Set in
the 1680s, the story reveals that throughout the process of colonization the
encounter of people from different cultural backgrounds led to what the narrator describes as "the withering inside that enslaves and opens the door for
what is wild."[15] Forced transculturation, characterized by diverse forms of
domination, resulted in fragmentation and alienation. Europeans, African
Americans, and Native Americans were united in their difference through the
trauma of geographical and/or spiritual dislocation rooted in the colonizers'
aspiration for property:

---

[12] Toni Morrison, *Paradise* (New York: Alfred A. Knopf, 1998): 213.

[13] Toni Morrison, "Home," in *The House That Race Built*, ed. Wahneema Lubiano
(New York: Vintage, 1998): 11, 12.

[14] Fernando Ortiz, *Cuban Counterpoint: Tobacco and* Sugar, tr. Harriet de Onís
(*Contrapunteo cubano del tabaco y el azúcar*, 1940; tr. New York: Alfred A. Knopf,
1947): 102–103.

[15] Toni Morrison, *A Mercy* (New York: Alfred A. Knopf, 2008): 160.

cut loose from the earth's soul, they insisted on purchase of its soil,
and like all orphans they were insatiable. It was their destiny to chew
up the world and spit out a horribleness that would destroy all primary
peoples.[16]

Thus, Morrison's transwriting makes cogently clear that the diverse forms of
violence which brutalized man and space and proliferated in this transcultural
contact zone of colonial domination were interrelated and shaped the national
ethos and world-view.

What I call transwriting is a type of writing that moves through an interstitial space between and within borders, traverses existing territories composed of multiple contact zones, and strives to go beyond, transforming the
ambiguity of cultural in-betweenness into an interior consciousness. Times,
spaces, and identities are fluid, complementary, in process. Western borders
of cultural patterns (identity/alterity; exterior/interior) open up into transcultural borderlands where Western rationalism and African spirituality meet.[17]
We are dealing here with process, passage, traverse, and transition in an interstitial zone of cultural negotiations where remembrance effects alternative/
new visions, structures of authority, and discursive subject-positions – an
interstitial space where transcultural mnemonic and imaginary translations
establish cultural difference as a process of ongoing interrelation. In what
follows, I want to link this temporal, spatial, and identitarian fluidity with the
thematic and structural circularity that expresses afrodiasporic spiritual
knowledge-as-consciousness. In so doing, I will focus on African-Brazilian
literature in an attempt to widen the scope of my comparative analysis.

A *Bildungsroman* by Conceição Evaristo, *Ponciá Vicencio*,[18] delineates an
African-Brazilian woman's identity-crisis resulting from emotional shocks
(the death of her grandfather, father, and seven children; the separation from
her mother and brother) and social factors (poverty, social injustices). What
Ponciá decodes and recodes through memory is the reason for her family's
uprootedness. She describes her errancy between the countryside and the city
as being embedded in the multiple axes of endemic social inequality in Brazil

---

[16] Morrison, *A Mercy*, 54.

[17] For an analysis of this transcultural contact zone in *Tar Baby*, *Beloved*, and *Paradise*, see Roland Walter, *Narrative Identities: (Inter)Cultural In-Betweenness in the
Americas* (Bern & Frankfurt am Main: Peter Lang, 2003).

[18] Conceição Evaristo, *Ponciá Vicencio*, tr. Paloma Martinez–Cruz (*Ponciá Vicêncio*, 2003; tr. New York: Host, 2007).

– race and colour, social class, gender, region, *latifundio* system; that is, as a continuing slave life at the mercy of others. Whenever she writes her name, Ponciá feels the pain of an existential vacuum since her family name was given to her great-grandparents by their owner before abolition. Thus, this name carries the memory of chattel slavery. It turns her into a cipher within an historical process that continues to write endless new chapters of domination and exploitation. African Brazilians, as the novel reveals, stand on the bottom rung on the social scale of the nation's racialized system.

Evaristo points to the collective give-and-take of love and tenderness, memory and artistic creativity as an effective means of consciousness-raising and healing. Ponciá's return to her birthplace to resume her work with clay, which she obtains from the banks of a river and then shapes into figures and sculptures, is deeply embedded in African spirituality. It re-establishes her connection with Oxun, the female *orixá* of freshwater, the luxury of cool, life-giving river water, love and fecundity, and with her dead grandfather. This re-connection with Oxun and her grandfather, which was first established when she was an embryo, consolidated through her childhood and adolescence yet interrupted from the moment she left town to live with her husband, creates a circular life-pattern. Her suffering as a married woman can be seen as an intermediate stage in the process of ritual initiation, a margin or *limen* linking the earlier stage of separation with the later one of re-aggregation. When Ponciá's suffering is channelled through her mnemonic imagination, a ritual healing process takes place which allows her to revise and change her social position and take control of her destiny. The narrative, then, confronts the reader with a multidimensional circularity: the circle of Ponciá's cathartic remembrance; the circle of her artistic work; the circle that links the individual and the collective, the human world and the spirit world, the living and the dead. These circles within circles bespeak a consciousness of cosmic interlock – an interdependence of all things and spheres.

This circularity in the thematic and structural makeup of Evaristo's novel expresses a spiritual knowledge-as-consciousness that characterizes creative works throughout the black diaspora. Whether expressed in poems, music, dance, oral performance, folktales, folksongs, or narrative forms, the cultural significance of the circle in precolonial Africa is endowed with new meaning in the Americas. A symbol of balance, unity, and spiritual continuity, the circle functions as a link between places, times, spheres, and generations.[19] In

---

[19] In this sense, the circle of the Afro-Brazilian Candomblé *terreiro* (yard) sym-

order to further examine the multidimensional significance of the circle, I now want to move to the Caribbean and focus on Patrick Chamoiseau's *Un dimanche au cachot* and *Biblique des derniers gestes*.

In *Un dimanche au cachot*, Chamoiseau establishes a relation between resistance in the past and survival in the present by intertwining two series of events: the story of Oubliée, a slave languishing in a *cachot* (dungeon) of a plantation, and the story of Caroline, a girl who seeks refuge in this same place, which at the beginning of the twenty-first century is a forgotten ruin. In order to heal the girl's trauma, the narrator–author tells her how Oubliée survived her torturous experience in this dungeon. In the process, he transforms this symbol of enslavement, a "mnemonic scab,"[20] into a monument of resistance through his memory – a collective memory nourished by the whispers of the stones, spirit voices, and his personal imagination.

Mnemonic imagination re-creates past violence in order to un-write the official story with its effacements and distortions. Further, and perhaps most importantly, in that it is imbued with the values, visions, and belief-system of those unwritten by the official discourse of History, it incorporates this violence into the present lived experience as a reference. In this sense, words, through memory, recuperate a world of references which contributes to the (re)constitution of identity within an historical process. This superimposition of times and spaces is heightened by an overlap of the characters. In many passages, it is difficult to distinguish between Caroline and Oubliée. Through imagination, the projection of Oubliée's absence-as-presence onto Caroline, Chamoiseau elevates this "impossible memory to the level of testimony."[21] Thus, the terror and violence of the past accumulate in the present not as truth but as an imagined desire. Chamoiseau uses what he believes Oubliée used to survive the dungeon: imagination. Oubliée frees herself by re-imagining reality, the world, the lives of the people she knew, especially the old slave who escaped plantation life.[22] When she encounters the old slave's spirit at the

---

bolizes the re-establishment of the ties with the lost homeland. For an analysis of the circle in African thought, see Sterling Stuckey, *Slave Culture: Nationalist Theory and the Foundations of Black America* (New York & Oxford: Oxford UP, 1987).

[20] "escarre mnésique." Patrick Chamoiseau, *Un dimanche au cachot* (Paris: Gallimard, 2007): 269.

[21] "mémoire impossible au rang de témoignage." *Un dimanche au cachot*, 101.

[22] Patrick Chamoiseau tells the story of the old slave's resistance in *L'esclave vieil homme et le molosse* (Paris: Gallimard, 1997).

humongous stone within which he continues to live, together with all the other forgotten people of the island, she becomes a part of this "*pierre-monde*" – a world of interrelated diversities[23] – and gains energy to resist her enslavers. Freeing oneself, then, means to "turn one's eyes inward"[24] and, in the tradition of the plantation *griots*, to sharpen one's individual imagination through a collective consciousness that includes the entire biota. In order to elaborate this proliferation of the 'I' and briefly outline Chamoiseau's eco-philosophy, let me move to *Biblique des derniers gestes*.

Biblique delineates fragments of the life of Balthazar Bodule–Jules through diverse mnemonic circles. Based on Balthazar's and his friends' interviews, writings, and stories as well as his own imagination triggered by Balthazar's gestures, the narrator–journalist transcribes Balthazar's memories during the last days preceding his death. By revealing Balthazar's trajectory from his birth, childhood, and adolescence in Martinique, his participation as freedom fighter in diverse anticolonial movements to his return and death on the island in the late 1990s within the historical process of the New-World African ex-perience (slavery, plantation system, resistance), Chamoiseau links individual and collective memory in a culturally specific and universal social practice where local Caribbean blackness embraces the world's subaltern *Lumpen-proletariat*. The diverse circles of this mnemonic texture constitute resistance as social practice for two reasons: first, they delineate an alter-version of His-tory by voicing subaltern histories which fill the voids and rectify the distor-tions of the official discourse; second, the revelation and denunciation of the atrocities that were, and continue to be, committed in the name of Western progress and civilization are supplemented by the concrete utopia of an alter-native coexistence of the biota, including human beings.

Chamoiseau seems to agree with Morrison that today's world is a place "where all is known and nothing understood."[25] Therefore it is necessary to "understand the secret meaning of the world" and "reconnect the symbols"[26];

---

[23] This "stone-world" is constituted by the polyrhythm of human and nonhuman relationships. See Patrick Chamoiseau, *Écrire en pays dominé* (Paris: Gallimard, 1997): 281.

[24] "aller en soi." Chamoiseau, *Un dimanche au cachot*, 234.

[25] Toni Morrison, *Love* (New York: Alfred A. Knopf, 2003): 4.

[26] "compren[dre] le sens secret du monde"; "relier les symboles." Patrick Cham-oiseau, *Biblique des derniers gestes* (Paris: Gallimard, 2002): 185, 526.

a process of consciousness-raising and identity (re)construction initiated
through individual and collective imagination, intuition and memory:

> It is necessary to know [...] how to imagine the world, the places,
> invent the histories! [...] Invent this foundational memory that one
> cultivates deep in one's heart and that dictates its principle of openness
> to the powers of this world! Learn how to do this! For each place, each
> hut, each woman imagine their prolongations in the constellations of
> places, huts [...] or perfumes; one calling the other, the other present
> in a thousand others. Proceed like this, wandering from prolongation to
> prolongation until you feel the most human possible![27]

This type of living memory as social practice becomes a means of understanding and actively shaping the past within the present pointing towards the
future. As such, it is a possible site from which to remap the world, or, following Glissant, to free its relational chaos – a translation of cultural difference as separation into cultural diversity as relation that begins with a process
of consciousness-raising and moves outward through imagination. Memory in
Chamoiseau, then, explodes linear monocultural epistemes into fractal transcultural ones, constituting "an open, circular and living organism."[28]

Nature, for Chamoiseau, plays a crucial role in this process: a circle links
the entire biota of different places, spaces, and cultural contexts, but also differences within the species. In *Biblique*, Balthazar is raised by Man L'Oubliée
in the woods. The contact with nature enables Balthazar to survive as a freedom fighter later in his life.[29] Immersed in the world of plants, trees, and
animals, Balthazar learns that all elements of the ecosystem are interrelated in
rhizomic ways through displacement, that is, mobility and transformation.

---

[27] "Il faut savoir [...] imaginer le monde, imaginer les lieux, inventer les histoires!
[...] Inventez-vous cette mémoire fondatrice, que l'on jardine en soi-même et qui dicte
son principe d'ouverture aux puissances de ce monde! Apprenez à faire ça! Imaginez
pour chaque endroit, chaque case, chaque femme, ses prolongements dans des constellations [...] d'endroits, de cases [...] ou de parfums, l'un appelant l'autre, l'autre
présent dans mille autres, allez comme ça, errant de prolongement en prolongement,
jusqu'à vous sentir le plus humain possible!" Chamoiseau, *Biblique des derniers
gestes*, 278–79.

[28] "un organisme ouvert, circulaire et vivant." *Biblique des derniers gestes*, 471.

[29] The mysterious and magic power that Chamoiseau attributes to nature is sym-
bolized by Man L'Oubliée, who, as an ageless healer, cures diseases and surmounts
any difficulty.

In the light of reality-in-process, the act of writing in Chamoiseau cannot possibly translate a stable, fixed truth. Therefore, the aim of storytelling is not to explain something but to illuminate and confirm the impossible, incomprehensible, unthinkable, and unspeakable. It reveals the Other (and the Other within the Self) through possibilities of never-ending displacements, prolongations, and desires. This image of creation as an ongoing search inscribes it in the process of displacement, which explodes systemic limits by working through intercultural fusion and fissure and thereby opening up diverse horizons of free, errant development. Circles of fissure and fusion, rupture and continuity: throughout the Americas, black writers invest the thematic and structural circularity expressing the spiritual knowledge-as-consciousness with an undecidability that locates identity in a fluid time–space continuum.

Creative writing in the black diaspora is a revitalizing salt water of words piling up endings from which new beginnings emerge: a writing which links suffering/death and resistance/life within a circle. Thus, what structures the images in contemporary creative writing throughout the black diaspora is a movement that begins in loss, crosses rupture, fragmentation, and alienation, and continues in an incessant reconstruction whose origin is composed of fractal, fluid roots and whose nature is both rhizomic and circular. As such, it sediments collective memory through diffraction. Glissant has called this movement "a rooted errantry"[30] – a continuing traverse that produces unity in difference. This movement as physical and/or imaginary passage through the *limen* reflects and refracts a collective in-between *Dasein* and marks the transcultural unconscious of pan-American black literature.

Let me further illustrate this by quoting a passage from Ana Maria Gonçalves' recent novel *Um defeito de cor*:

> Sitting in the sand, I was watching the ocean and mourning all those deaths that seemed to be within me. They were occupying so much space that they did not allow me to feel anything else. My eyes stung with salty tears as if they, too, were the sea, and I felt a solitude as immense as the sea.[31]

---

[30] Édouard Glissant, *Poetics of Relation*, tr. & intro. Betsy Wing (*Poétique de la Relation*, 1990; Ann Arbor: U of Michigan P, 1997): 37.

[31] "Sentada na areia, fiquei olhando o mar e chorando todas aquelas mortes que pareciam estar dentro de mim, ocupando tanto espaço que não me deixavam sentir mais nada. Os olhos ardiam com as lágrimas salgadas, como se fossem mar também, e senti uma solidão do tamanho dele." Ana Maria Gonçalves, *Um defeito de cor* (Rio de Janeiro: Record, 2007): 101.

Here, Kehinde alias Luiza Gama, an African woman who survived the Middle Passage and slave life in Brazil, re-creates the limbo of the black diaspora as a collectively inhabited mental and physical place. In this sense, the Atlantic becomes more than a mere individual symbol of traumatic passage. Throughout her life, Luiza Gama, mother of the Brazilian poet Luis Gama, was haunted by the spirits of her grandmother, sister, and all those others she witnessed dying during the passage from Africa to Brazil. In describing Luiza's active role in the Malé uprising in Salvador as well as her journeys in Brazil and to Africa, Gonçalves, somewhat similar to Glissant's images of drowning slaves in *Caribbean Discourse* and *Poetics of Relation*, evokes a circle of endings and beginnings, death and life in which the I and the we are entwined, creating a diasporic network of rhizomic circular times, spaces, and experiences.

This circularity is also stressed in the poem "Mar" by the Afro-Brazilian poet Miriam Alves:

> In the stinking holds of history
> I ate rotten things. I went mad; got sick.
> They threw me into the ocean of oblivion
> I seized the past-present anchors
> rode the waves
>   flowing
>   bound for life.[32]

The sea is a mnemonic monument that does what memory, according to Chamoiseau, should do: namely, "preserve the energy of an indistinct mass fighting for survival."[33] Black diaspora memory is biotic, composed of the intrinsic energy and values of its constitutive elements: a network that sediments knowledge of the entire biota into cultural consciousness, or, as Lissie, the narrator in Alice Walker's *The Temple of My Familiar* puts it: "some people don't understand that it is the nature of the eye to have seen forever, and the nature of the mind to recall anything that was ever known."[34] Thus,

---

[32] "Nos porões fétidos da história / comi podridões. Endoideci. Adoeci. / Atiraram-me ao mar do esquecimento / agarrei-me às âncoras passadas-presentes / cavalguei as ondas / desemboquei / rumo vida." Miriam Alves, "Mar" in *A razão da chama: antologia de poetas negros brasileiros*, ed. Oswald Camargo (São Paulo: GRD, 1986): 94.

[33] "retenir l'énergie d'une masse indistincte en lutte de survie." Chamoiseau, *Écrire en pays dominé*, 144.

[34] Alice Walker, *The Temple of My Familiar* (1989; Harmondsworth: Penguin, 1990): 80.

transwriting as double traverse of the past-present and lost-imposed place/ language redeems the suffering (a fragmented/alienated identity) through identitarian conscientization: a circle that unites in fissure and diasporizes in fusion through discourse, memory, and imagination. As such, New-World African transwriting creates a discursive and epistemic home as "symbolic geography."[35] This geography may be (trans)regional, (trans)national, and (trans)cultural, characterized by rooted and routed citizenship. In this sense, black diaspora writers are transcultural mediators on the hyphen between cultures and epistemes, transwriting the conflicting bonds that hold them in relationship.

In this essay, I have examined the transcultural consciousness of identity (re)construction represented in select works of black writers from Canada, the USA, the Caribbean, and Brazil. In the process of analysing how these writers use language, memory, and imagination to develop conceptions of wholeness and cohesion out of the fragments of cultural and identitarian diasporization, I argued that the brutalization of black people in the Americas is linked to the brutalization of space and both are rooted in a past that is not past but accumulates in the present. In this sense, the slave trade, the plantation system, post-slavery racism, and sexism attest to the fact that what transculturation organizes in this contact zone is cultural fissure, spiralling from one circle of rupture to the next. In an effort to transcend cultural alienation and fragmentation stemming from the colonial past, black authors use writing as a site of memory that recuperates a world of references which contributes to the (re)constitution of identity within an historical process. This transwriting, I contend, moves through an interstitial space between and within borders, traverses existing territories composed of multiple contact zones, and strives to go beyond, transforming the ambiguity of cultural in-betweenness into an inward consciousness. As such, black transwriting sediments collective memory through diffraction with the intention of redeeming suffering through identitarian conscientization.

---

[35] According to Stepto, "a landscape becomes symbolic in literature when it is a region in time and space offering spatial expressions of social structures and ritual grounds on the one hand, and *communitas* and *genius loci* on the other." See Robert Stepto, *From Behind the Veil: A Study of Afro-American Narrative* (Urbana: U of Illinois P, 1991): 67.

WORKS CITED

Alves, Miriam. "Mar," in *A razão da chama: antologia de poetas negros brasileiros*, ed. Oswald Camargo (São Paulo: G R D, 1986): 94.

Andrade, Oswald de. *Manifesto antropofágico*, in *Oswald de Andrade*, ed. Maria Agusta Fonseca (São Paulo: Brasiliense, 1982): 45–54.

Brand, Dionne. *At the Full and Change of the Moon* (New York: Grove, 1999).

——. *In Another Place, Not Here* (New York: Grove, 1996).

——. *A Map to the Door of No Return: Notes to Belonging* (Toronto: Vintage, 2002).

Chamoiseau, Patrick. *Biblique des derniers gestes* (Paris: Gallimard, 2002).

——. *Un dimanche au cachot* (Paris: Gallimard, 2007).

——. *Écrire en pays dominé* (Paris: Gallimard, 1997).

——. *L'esclave vieil homme et le molosse* (Paris: Gallimard, 1997).

Evaristo, Conceição. *Ponciá Vicencio*, tr. Paloma Martinez–Cruz (*Ponciá Vicêncio*, 2003; New York: Host, 2007).

Ferreira, Élio. "América Negra," in *Cadernos Negros* 27 (São Paulo: Quilombhoje, 2004): 50–58.

Gilroy, Paul. *The Black Atlantic* (Cambridge M A : Harvard U P , 1993).

Glissant, Édouard. *Caribbean Discourse*, sel., tr. & intro. J. Michael Dash (*Le discours antillais*, 1981; Charlottesville: U P of Virginia, 1992).

——. *Poetics of Relation*, tr. & intro. Betsy Wing (*Poétique de la Relation*, 1990; Ann Arbor: U of Michigan P , 1997).

Gonçalves, Ana Maria. *Um defeito de cor* (Rio de Janeiro: Record, 2007).

Morrison, Toni. "Home," in *The House That Race Built*, ed. Wahneema Lubiano (New York: Vintage, 1998): 3–12.

——. *Love* (New York: Alfred A. Knopf, 2003).

——. *A Mercy* (New York: Alfred A. Knopf, 2008).

——. *Paradise* (New York: Alfred A. Knopf, 1998).

Ortiz, Fernando. *Cuban Counterpoint: Tobacco and Sugar*, tr. Harriet de Onís (*Contrapunteo cubano del tabaco y el azúcar*, 1940; New York: Alfred A. Knopf, 1947).

Philip, Marlene Nourbese. *She Tries Her Tongue, Her Silence Softly Breaks* (Charlottetown, P E I : Ragweed, 1996).

Radhakrishnan, Rajagopalan. *Diasporic Meditations: Between Home and Location* (Minneapolis: U of Minnesota P , 1996).

Stepto, Robert B. *From Behind the Veil: A Study of Afro-American Narrative* (Urbana: U of Illinois P , 1991).

Stuckey, Sterling. *Slave Culture: Nationalist Theory and the Foundations of Black America* (New York & Oxford: Oxford U P, 1987).

Walcott, Rinaldo. *Black Like Who? Writing Black Canada* (Toronto: Insomniac, 2003).

Walker, Alice. *The Temple of My Familiar* (1989; Harmondsworth: Penguin, 1990).

Walter, Roland. *Narrative Identities: (Inter)Cultural In-Betweenness in the Americas* (Bern & Frankfurt am Main: Peter Lang, 2003).

Far Away, So Close
—Translocation as Storytelling
Principle in Hari Kunzru's *Transmission*

LUCIA KRÄMER

N RECENT YEARS a growing number of novels have addressed and meta-fictionally reflected on the ideological, economic, political, and cultural dimensions of the growing interconnectedness in the current age of glo-balization. This production trend,[1] which we might tentatively term the 'globalization novel', includes books such as Kiran Desai's Booker prize-winning *The Inheritance of Loss*, the celebration of grassroots political activ-ism that is *The Fountain at the Center of the World* (2003) by the comedian and activist Robert Newman, as well as the subject of this essay, Hari Kunzru's *Transmission* (2004). After outlining my understanding of the con-cepts of 'translocation' as a process and of 'translocality' as a condition, I would like to propose a reading of Kunzru's novel here that emphasizes the ambivalence of his depiction of translocation and translocality and interprets this ambivalence as a self-reflexive comment on the topic of the universality of storytelling.

Transmission is full of examples of processes of translocation simulta-neously resulting from and perpetuating the increasingly interconnected nature of today's world. While Kunzru places the transfer of people, signs, and texts in the globalized world at the centre of his novel and emphasizes the

---

[1] Drawing on Rick Altman's theorization of the development processes of (film) genres, I refer to the globalization novel as a production trend in order to indicate that this group of texts has not yet been institutionalized to the degree where it would serve as an established point of reference for writers, distributors, readers, and critics. See Altman, *Film/Genre* (London: BFI, 1999): 38–48.

mechanisms by which they are interlinked, he also insists on the ambivalence of global interconnectedness through his treatment of the metaphor of (noise in) transmission and by providing his characters with a profound sense of isolation, dislocation, and/or alienation. The disjunct cultural flows depicted in *Transmission* thus lead to manifold losses of or inabilities to establish contact: both with oneself and with other people, as well as with both local and translocal culture.

This depiction of translocation on the story level as a simultaneous drawing together and pulling apart is mirrored on the discourse-level by Kunzru's narrative technique. *Transmission* therefore also contains an implicit metafictional reflection on its own status as a cultural product created for a potentially global and transcultural readership.

1. Flows and Nets: Images of Translocation and Translocality

In order to conceptualize globalization processes, theorists of globalization as well as non-specialist language-use have tended to recur to a group of verbal images which may also help us theorize the concepts of 'translocation' and 'translocality'. Apart from images of boundaries and borders, the most prevalent of these metaphors have been those of flows and of networks or webs. Appadurai, for example, has famously theorized the new world order in terms of disjunct global flows of people, media, technologies, capital, and political images, which he designates as 'ethnoscapes', 'mediascapes', 'technoscapes', 'financescapes', and 'ideoscapes'.[2] In his magisterial work on *The Network Society*, Manuel Castells employs the same image to describe the dominant of contemporary life, when he points out that "our society is constructed around flows" of capital, information, technology, organizational interactions, images, sounds, and symbols.[3] One example of how pervasive this trope has meanwhile become is Thussu's attempt to present recent manifestations of media globalization as a sequence of dominant media flows that largely emanate

---

[2] Arjun Appadurai, *Modernity at Large: Cultural Dimensions of Globalization* (Minneapolis & London: U of Minnesota P, 1996): 33.

[3] Manuel Castells, *The Rise of the Network Society* (1996; Oxford & Malden MA: Blackwell, 2000): 442. Vol. 1 of *The Information Age: Economy, Society and Culture*, 3 vols. 1996–98.

from the global North, and so-called 'subaltern flows' originating in the former peripheries of global media industries.[4]

While Castells employs the metaphor of the flow, the key image underlying his work is, as its title indicates, that of the net, which is also contained in the passage in which David Held et al. introduce the parameters by which they analyse the changes and consequent blurring of the boundaries between domestic matters and global affairs in *Global Transformations*:

> a deepening enmeshment of the local and the global such that the
> *impact* of distant events is magnified while even the most local devel-
> opments may come to have enormous global consequences.[5]

Similarly, Hardt and Negri, who repeatedly draw on Deleuze and Guattari's notion of the rhizome, state:

> the general outlines of today's imperial constitution can be conceived
> in the form of a rhizomatic and universal communication network in
> which relations are established to and from all its points and nodes.[6]

Through the terms 'World Wide Web' and 'Internet', which designate what may be the key technical component of globalization processes since the 1990s, the net or web has also become the key image of globalization in general language-use.

The images of both net and flow implicitly emphasize the interconnectedness of the global and the particular. They convey that global processes take shape in particular locations, and that particular processes and actions may have global consequences. Yet the image of the net implies either the infrastructural prerequisite of connecting or a state of interconnectedness, while the image of the flow is more dynamic, hinting at actual processes of exchange, border-crossing, or connecting. In the context of the topic of translocation, the image of the web therefore relates to the state or condition of translocality, while the image of the flow usefully illustrates the processes of

---

[4] Daya Kishan Thussu, "Mapping Global Media Flow and Contra-Flow," in *Media on the Move: Global Flow and Contra-Flow*, ed. Daya Kishan Thussu (London & New York: Routledge, (2007): 11.

[5] David Held et al., *Global Transformations: Politics, Economics and Culture* (Cambridge: Polity, 1999): 15.

[6] Michael Hardt & Antonio Negri, *Empire* (Cambridge MA: Harvard UP, 2001): 319.

translocation – the transposition or movement of, for example, people, information, products, texts, or money.

Translocation in this sense ought not to be conceptualized as a simple removal or displacement, where something simply changes place from one moment to another; a flow is characterized by the fact that the components in flux do not necessarily all move at the same speed or, indeed, change place at the same time. As an example, we might imagine an experiment where water is made to flow from a basin down an incline towards a lower plane. Not all of the liquid will arrive at the lower level at the same time. During a stretch of the experiment, part of the water will instead still be in the original basin, while some of it will be flowing on the incline, and some of it will already be collecting on the lower plane. Rather than occupying an in-between position, entities that are subject to a process of translocation can therefore be simultaneously present in various locations, and these locations may well lie on both sides of a border. The negotiation of borders and boundaries is therefore a major issue connected to many processes of translocation. As we will see, it also plays a major role in Hari Kunzru's novel *Transmission*.

In keeping with this conceptualization of translocation, we can use the term 'translocality' to describe the resulting condition of being in several places at the same time. 'Place' in this context should be interpreted both literally and metaphorically, since the kinds of borders that are crossed in the process of translocation can be multifold, ranging, for example, from national to cultural and ontological boundaries.

2. *Transmission*: Translocation and Translocality on the Story-Level

Although Hari Kunzru's *Transmission*, echoing Bhabha, plays repeatedly with the notions of interstitial spaces and states of in-betweenness,[7] its

---

[7] Hari Kunzru, *Transmission* (Harmondsworth: Penguin, 2005): e.g., 27–28. Further page references are in the main text. This implicit reference to Bhabha forms part of a wider net of covert references to well-known theorists in *Transmission*. Many of them, such as the playful allusions to McLuhan's characterization of the medium as the message (8, 13) or Baudrillard's idea of the simulacrum (e.g., 152, 167), moreover, support the theme of the blurring of (ontological) borders in the novel. See Marshall McLuhan, *Understanding Media: The Extensions of Man* (New York: McGraw–Hill,

depiction of the processes and consequences of globalization mostly functions on the principles of translocation and translocality, which the novel characterizes as a permanent struggle between the opposite impulses of approximation and distancing. On both the story and the discourse-level, a drawing-together is always matched by the opposite movement of pulling apart, and vice versa.

The story revolves around a set of three protagonists who at first glance seem to have little in common, but whose stories are carefully interlinked to create a complex picture of the globalized world and the struggle of individuals to come to grips with it. The first of these three protagonist is Guy Swift, a British marketing executive who finds his life in crisis after several of his international business projects have failed and his relationship with his girl-friend Gabriella Caro is on the verge of breaking apart. Second is Leela Zahir, a young Bollywood star, who is in Britain to shoot a song sequence on the battlements of a Scottish castle for her most recent film. Arjun Mehta, finally, is a young Indian computer specialist and clandestine hacker, who has been hired by an Indian firm and lured to the USA on what another character calls a "slave visa" (64). In fact, Arjun is subject to a new form of indentured labour. Far from being supported by his Indian employer, Arjun has to look for work in the USA himself, and when he finds a job, has to give a considerable amount of his salary to the Indian firm that brought him there in the first place. In this precarious situation, Arjun's life seems to take a turn for the better when he finds employment with a software company specializing in computer viruses.

The lives of the three protagonists, who live and move in completely different places and social spheres, become unexpectedly intertwined when Arjun is made redundant. As a reaction, he launches an extremely complex computer virus, hoping that once computers all around the world have become infected he will be able to provide his employers with the solution to the problem and will regain his job as a reward. The virus is hidden in an email attachment containing a loop of a five-second clip from a dance scene in one of Leela Zahir's films, and various types of the Leela virus, which has the ability to metamorphose, affect computers all over the world, among them the computers in Guy Swift's marketing agency and his notebook. The transmission of the Leela virus thus links all the major characters of the novel as

---

1964): 7, and Jean Baudrillard, *Simulacra and Simulation*, tr. Sheila Faria Glaser (*Simulacres et simulation*, 1985, Ann Arbor: U of Michigan P, 1994).

well as Guy's girlfriend Gabriella, who works for a London PR firm and is called to Scotland to help the Indian film team around Leela deal with the press onslaught that hits the production after the Leela virus is unleashed.

Among the central themes of the novel are the interconnectedness resulting from the transfer of people, signs, texts, and goods in the globalized world as well as the mechanisms and infrastructure behind these translocations. The characters move between various continents and countries, which include India, the US, Mexico, Albania, Australia, and Britain as well as the EU (represented by Brussels) and the Middle East (Dubai). They go there on business or as guest workers, tourists, refugees, or illegal migrants. They continuously use the technical infrastructure of globalization, such as air travel, telephony, and, most importantly, the Internet, which, as the means of spreading the Leela virus around the world, is the most obvious symbol of global interconnectedness in the book. Another, non-technological, one is the very language in which *Transmission* is written: namely the global lingua franca English. Kunzru repeatedly emphasizes this role of English – for example, when his characters mix languages (e.g., Hinglish 25) or when they deviate from British or American standard English through accents or intonational tics (e.g., 72, 113, 121, 150, 249), thus effectively creating alternative standard Englishes (231, 237). Apart from people and signs, the book thematizes travelling goods and their ideological and economic context of consumerism and capitalism (e.g., 8, 14, 23, 212). It especially includes cultural products, such as films, among these travelling goods and hints at their infrastructure of distribution to global audiences (e.g., 18) and the potential economic power of their myth-making qualities (241).

The novel presents various ways in which these processes of translocation lead to a drawing-together of (culturally) disparate elements, not only in the sense that individuals from different countries and cultural backgrounds cross each other's paths and are forced to interact, but also beyond the level of interpersonal contact. One such way is hybridization, which the novel hints at, for example, in references to fusion food (68). Another is the appropriation of foreign cultural elements – for instance, in the case of the Hopi Indian meditation space in the London housing complex where Guy Swift owns an apartment (111). The widespread celebration of particularity in the shape of heritage cultures that the novel repeatedly refers to (95, 126, 152, 225–26) is a further (paradoxical) example of a simultaneous levelling and upholding of (cultural) differences, while the international standardization visible in, among other things, business hotels and golf courses, which the novel de-

scribes as landscape ghosts of Scotland, "an environmental memory abstrac-
ted into universal signs" (165), is a more straightforward case of an erosion of
difference. However, *Transmission* by no means depicts a world where one
world culture has replaced pluriculturality. The world presented in the novel
can instead be characterized as transcultural or even hypercultural.[8] Standardization is, moreover, not represented as a harmonious process, because it is
based on asymmetrical economic power-relationships. Its models tend to be
Western, and it holds dangers of (cultural) identity-loss (e.g., 17–18, 167).

By characterizing Dubai as "some kind of Islamic Las Vegas" (167) and
thus as an imitation of a Western city that is most famous for living on the
reality loss of gamblers and for its simulacrum-like nature, Kunzru introduces
one of many instances in the book where the borders between apparently
separate ontological spheres are blurred. The most obvious of these is the
boundary between dream and reality, since the realities of most characters are
profoundly shaped by their dreams, fantasies, and wishes, which are in turn
informed by a variety of different texts. Yet a blurring of ontological boundaries also occurs, for example, in the novel's motif of humans as machines
(and vice versa 7, 51, 63, 75, 76, 88, 98, 101, 209), or when the chaos created
by the Leela virus "passe[s] effortlessly out of the [computer] networks into
the world of things" (258) and leads to the loss of objects, money, and even
persons. The most obvious instance of this is the episode towards the end of
Transmission in which Guy Swift, due to a computer error caused by the
Leela virus, is mistakenly deported as a *sans-papier* to Albania during a pan-
Europan raid against illegal immigrants. He barely survives an attempt to
return to the EU via a boat run by human traffickers. In this episode, the
chaos caused by Leela crosses the border from computers into real life, and in
its course Guy Swift crosses the borders of various nation-states and interacts
with people from three different continents. It therefore illustrates a compression of spatial distance and the interconnectedness of various ontological
planes.

However, owing to the exclusionary and discriminatory political ideology
behind the raid and the fact that it ultimately causes Guy Swift to cross a psychological threshold that makes him withdraw almost completely from the

---

[8] See Frank Schulze–Engler, "What's the Difference? Notes towards a Dialogue
between Transdifference and Transculturality," *Journal for the Study of British Cultures* 13.2 (2006): 123, 127–29, and Byung–Chul Han, *Hyperkulturalität: Kultur und
Globalisierung* (Berlin: Merve, 2005): 16–17, 22.

world, the episode is also a good example of the fact that the processes of drawing together in *Transmission* are always accompanied by, and even cause counter-processes of pulling apart. Translocation in *Transmission* almost always occurs in combination with manifestations of dislocation and alienation (from oneself and others) and even forms a cause of isolation when the characters fail to connect and consequently retreat from their surroundings, be they culturally familiar or alien. Castells describes this mechanism thus:

> global networks of instrumental exchanges selectively switch on and off individuals, groups, regions, and even countries, according to their relevance in fulfilling the goals processed in the network, in a relentless flow of strategic decisions. It follows a fundamental split between abstract, universal instrumentalism, and historically rooted, particularistic identities. *Our societies are increasingly structured around a bipolar opposition between the Net and the Self.*[9]

This opposition is manifest in all the major characters in *Transmission*, and its resolution generally resists harmonization. At least for the protagonists, the state of translocation therefore presents itself as a state of alienation and isolation. Arjun is not only unable to connect with his co-workers at the software firm and feels profoundly isolated and homesick (203). He is ultimately also forced to flee the USA and go into hiding, basically becoming an outlaw. Leela Zahir not only acts on screen but is forced by her mother to distort herself in oder to keep up her star image; eventually, she, too, runs away and disappears. Guy Swift cultivates irony in his self-image (114), and he is unable to relate to and empathize with others. He thus alienates everybody around him, so that despite his many professional interactions he is a fundamentally lonely character. Fittingly, he ends as a hermit-like figure, pottering on a farm in the North Pennines. And Gabriella Caro, who has no family and has always felt uprooted (70–71), eventually commits suicide and thus effects the most radical retreat from the world represented in *Transmission*.

The reasons for these failures of connection despite constant interaction lie in one of the key notions of Kunzru's book – the noise that impedes the perfect working of transmission processes:

> Perfect information is sometimes defined as a signal transmitted from a sender to a receiver without loss, without the introduction of the smallest uncertainty or confusion. In the real world, however, there is

---

[9] Castells, *The Rise of the Network Society*, 3.

> always noise. [...] Certainty backslides into probability. Information
> transmission, it emerges, is about doing the best you can. (257)

In *Transmission* there are various reasons for the intrusion of noise in the transmission process. Among the most conspicuous is the ambiguity of language, which Kunzru recurs to in a large number of scenes. His characters lie and use metaphors (e.g., 42, 43, 110, 116), and they employ various jargons that disguise and euphemize the real meaning of what they are saying (e.g., 19, 39, 91, 146, 235, 237). This is a problem for Arjun, who longs for a world running on black-and-white binaries and does not like the uncertainties of grey areas. He therefore prefers numbers to words and the world of machines to interacting with people (98–99, 102).

Besides the ambiguity of language, noise in *Transmission* also results from factors regulating the particular character setup of the individual figures. These may include medical conditions, such as Asperger's Syndrome, which a rather large number of Arjun's co-workers seem to suffer from in at least a mild form (54–58), although the novel deliberately refuses to categorize them as either healthy or ill. Some characters are also simply unwilling to engage with others (e.g., 220). More generally, many characters in the book are 'borderline personalities' in the sense that they live in multiple cultural and psychological spaces at the same time, thus mirroring how the migrant experience has become a general feature of transnational citizenship caused by the age of globalization,[10] in which people not only move physically between a large number of disparate spaces but also have a mind-set that may combine a large number of diverse (cultural) influences.

Another important source of noise in *Transmission* is the difference, resulting from the lack of a common code, between the self-image of individuals, nations as well as corporations, and the way they are regarded by others. The most obvious examples of this are the various scenes depicting culture clashes where characters' ideologies, notions of morality, or tastes collide, such as Arjun's discussion with his female colleague Chris about sexuality (74–80), their respective (and very different) interpretations of their sexual encounter (85–88), Guy Swift's disastrous attempt to pitch a marketing concept to a

---

[10] This thought is illustrated by the programmatic subtitle of an article by Jan Nederveen Pieterse, who describes the paradoxical combination of the processes of widening social co-operation and deepening inequalities that are at the heart of *Transmission*. See Pieterse, "Globalization and Human Integration: We Are All Migrants," *Futures* 32.5 (June 2000): 385.

potential client in Dubai (169–73), or Gabriella Caro's futile attempts to collaborate with the Indian film team she is supposed to assist (231).

These examples present the inevitable noise in the transmission process as an important reason for, and effect of, the continuing presence of borders. They illustrate the state of translocality of the migrant or traveller, whose body may have moved across a border to a new state but whose ways of thinking may at least partly remain situated in a fundamentally different cultural zone. *Transmission* shows that the border is very much intact as a separating device, and the alleged dwindling of borders in the globalized world is revealed as a myth. *Transmission* even insists that borders are in effect everywhere, as Guy emphasizes in a selling pitch of an image campaign for the Pan European Border Authority (a fictional version of FRONTEX):

> in the twenty-first century the border is not just a line on the earth any
> more. It's so much more than that. It's about status. It's about opportu-
> nity. Sure, you're either inside or outside, but you can be on the inside
> and still be outside, right? Or on the outside looking in. Anyway, like
> we say in one of our slides, "The border is everywhere." "The border,"
> and this is key, "is in your mind." (238)

Coming from the self-obsessed and rather unsympathetic character of Guy Swift, who displays a firmly eurocentric point of view (e.g., 242–43) and seldom shows insight or understanding of complex issues but prefers to remain on a vacuous surface level (also emotionally), this statement might appear flippant. Yet Kunzru underlines its validity through his depiction of his characters' mostly futile struggles at overcoming cultural and psychological boundaries. He even becomes explicitly political when he describes border control at the US–Mexican border (251) and especially by depicting the above-mentioned coordinated European raid on illegal immigrants (240, 261–69) as a quasi-fascist operation. The most lingering picture of Kunzru's representation of borders thus contains police violence, inhumane deportation conditions, and the ruthlessness of human traffickers. It also underlines the enduring stability, also as an epistemological concept, of the political borders of nation-states. Imitating the news coverage on the development of potential epidemics such as bird flu or swine flu, the spreading of the Leela virus in *Transmission* is therefore represented as the spread of the virus from a place of origin in a specific country via and to other countries (106, 147).

3. Engaging and Distancing on the Discourse-Level: Creating Literary Translocation

The oscillation between approximation and distancing on the story level of *Transmission* is mirrored on the discourse-level. The multiple settings and plot strands are artfully linked, conveying the impression of a compression of world and time. At one point, for example, the novel cuts in an almost cinematic fashion from Leela Zahir rising into the sky in a hot-air balloon during a film shooting, to Arjun Mehta riding on a bus in Delhi and watching the vapour trail of an airplane back into the air, to Guy Swift sitting in the first-class compartment of this very aeroplane (10–11). Yet, despite its largely realistic mode of presentation, the non-linear structure of the story, with repeated flash-forwards and flashbacks and abrupt changes of setting, can also be disorienting for the reader. Kunzru foreshadows this effect in the very first chapter of the book in a passage that interlinks the fates of the yet unknown protagonists, and apparently collapses linearity and causality:

> A chain of cause and effect? Nothing so simple in Leela's summer. It was a time of topological curiosities, loops and knots, never-ending strips of action and inside-out bottles of reaction so thoroughly confused that identifying a point of origin became almost impossible.
> Morning through venetian blinds.
> A cinema crowd watches a tear roll down a giant face.
> The beep of an alarm. Groans and slow disengagement of limbs.
> She shuts down her machine and
> They sit together in a taxi
> A curvature. A stoop.
> swivels her chair towards the window and
> Someone in the stalls makes loud kissing noises
> poor posture
> between the two of them a five-inch gap
> she takes another bite of her sandwich
> laughter
> the posture of a young man standing outside a New Delhi office tower.
> (4–5)

As the reader knows nothing about the characters at this point, the effect of this passage is simultaneously disorienting and intriguing.

Characterization in the novel works in a fashion similar to the structural setup. Kunzru switches between various character focalizers, thus providing the reader with intricate psychological portraits. These are of fundamental importance for the guidance of sympathy in the book. The struggles most of the characters experience and the fact that at least all the major ones are provided with a clear character arc make for engaging drama. Yet at the same time Kunzru continuously distances the reader from the characters and events of the story by means of satire, which frequently serves the themes of difference, isolation, and miscommunication, such as in the description of Arjun's socially dysfunctional colleagues, an exaggerated version of the cliché of computer nerdiness:

> People did their thing and other people left them to get on with it. No one took much notice of Shiro's habit of flapping his arms violently every few minutes or Donny's refusal to allow purple objects into his field of vision. [...] Interaction was via email, even if the participants occupied neighbouring cubicles. [...]
>
> What in-house socializing did exist was largely conducted through the circulation of entertaining data sets. The *joke*, in its classic office form, was popular. [...] Unfortunately jokes seemed to cause confusion for some staff members, often provoking detailed (and even angry) dissections of their semantics. (55–56)

Although the jokes result in an exchange about meaning, the example of the chaotic relations between Arjun and Chris, which start precisely when Arjun contacts her in order to discuss an email of hers, suggests that even such discussions of meaning will ultimately only lead to further misunderstandings, owing to the endless perpetuation of 'noise'.

Another feature of the discourse-level of the novel that causes the reading experience to oscillate between a feeling of distance and proximity is narrative voice. The third-person narrator of the novel seems reliable, yet the narrator does not have all the information about the characters. Frequently his voice resembles that of a reporter or historiographer interested in reconstructing the events surrounding the unleashing of the Leela virus, rather than the authorial narrator of a fictional text. This device contributes to the wry nature of much of the comedy in the book, since the narrator only seems to record the actions of the characters and the situations in which they find themselves without adding his own point of view. It is also one prerequisite of the open ending of the book, where the narrator recapitulates the various theories about the disappearances of Leela Zahir and Arjun Mehta. Kunzru plays with the reader's awareness of narrative conventions and their horizon of expectation here, providing hints that we may construct, for example, into a murder story ending with Arjun's death, or into a romantic happy ending for him and Leela

Zahir. The riddle remains unsolved, however, and leaves the reader wondering what may have been the possible closure of Arjun's and Leela's stories.[11]

Finally, intertextual references, especially those to Bollywood, underline the themes of difference and alienation. Chris's first encounter with Hindi films, for example, leaves her completely baffled (74–75). Yet these references also serve to characterize storytelling in general as a human need. Various characters in the novel, independent of their cultural backgrounds, model their lives in relation to fictional texts and escape into alternate universes. Arjun, for example, tends to think along the line of Hindi film plots (e.g., 93, 138–39), and Leela Zahir's colleague Rajiv Rana presents his rise to stardom as a "classic rags-to-riches tale" (160). The book also describes how players of online role-playing games create new (fictional) life stories for themselves (273), as well as how Arjun Mehta fans construct conspiracy theories around his disappearance. Just as American media and politicians earlier created a specific image of Arjun as a terrorist (146, 201) that forced him into hiding, these fans create their own (changing) versions of Arjun and his history (272–76).

All of the cases in which characters in *Transmission* relate to fictional texts or create stories in this way are presented as attempts to make sense of and impose order and stability onto their world. Together with Kunzru's implicitly metafictional play with the reader's expectations of a resolution to Arjun's and Leela Zahir's stories, these references to storytelling and fabulation underline the role of stories as a means of making meaning as well as providing pleasures and satisfying desires. Kunzru's depiction of the transcultural spreading of stories – for example, in the shape of Bollywood films or online games – underlines, moreover, the nature of stories as a repository of human universals and as a connective device, in which it is precisely the cultural particularities of the stories that paradoxically constitute a significant universal.[12]

Through his self-reflexive references to texts and the nature of stories, Kunzru ultimately also reflects on the politics of storytelling in a globalized world. *Transmission* is an explicitly political book, addressing aspects of neocolonialism and postcoloniality in the framework of its treatment of globalization. It engages, in particular, with the ideological foundations and the effects

---

[11] Similarly, the gaps in the story of Guy Swift's deportation and adventurous return to Britain are never resolved.

[12] See Hardt & Negri's claim that "national particularity is a potent universality" (*Empire*, 105).

of the asymmetrical power-relationships between the economic North and the South on global translocations by depicting, among others, the negative effects of consumerism and the global capitalist system, the abuse and exploitation of (foreign) labour, the criminalization of migrants, and the dangers in the manipulation of political discourse. Kunzru therefore uses his fictional story to impose sense on and interpret the world, and he reinforces this impression through the choice of a realistic mode of presentation and the incorporation of a large number of real-life details into his fictional world.

By representing the growth of consumerism not only in the industrial North but also in emerging markets such as India, which transforms everything into a potential commodity, Kunzru also reflects implicitly on his role and that of his book on the globalized literary market. *Transmission* offers many points of connection to a multitude of readers. Not only is it written in English but it uses human universals in its depiction of characters and themes. The mix of cultures represented and experienced by the characters offers points of entry into the story for readers with a variety of cultural backgrounds.

However, the transmission of signals in the system of literary communication, too, is disturbed by 'noise', and it is precisely the mixture of cultural references and codes typical of globalization novels that may cause disorientation or alienation on the part of the reader. It is not only the characters in *Transmission* who are constantly forced to come to terms with a feeling of being stranded in a psychological and cultural no-man's land or third space, where the differences between self and other become more obvious the closer one gets to one's subject. While providing entertainment, *Transmission* is an uncomfortable text in the sense that it denies readers the fulfilment of their expectations. Unlike most of the Bollywood films *Transmission* references, the novel eschews clear resolution, and instead opts for and insists on the complexities inherent in processes of translocation and transcultural interaction. It forces the reader to negotiate various strategies of creating proximity and distance that transcend the basic negotiation of fiction and real life that all novels demand, and thus to engage with what ultimately constitutes a specific literary form of translocation and translocality.

⌘

WORKS CITED

Altman, Rick. *Film/Genre* (London: BFI, 1999).

Appadurai, Arjun. *Modernity at Large: Cultural Dimensions of Globalization* (Minneapolis & London: U of Minnesota P, 1996).

Baudrillard, Jean. *Simulacra and Simulation*, tr. Sheila Faria Glaser (*Simulacres et simulation*, 1985; Ann Arbor: U of Michigan P, 1994).

Bhabha, Homi K. *The Location of Culture* (1994; London & New York: Routledge, 2004).

Castells, Manuel. *The Rise of the Network Society* (1996; Oxford & Malden MA: Blackwell, 2000), vol. 1 of *The Information Age: Economy, Society and Culture*, 3 vols. 1996–1998.

Desai, Kiran. *The Inheritance of Loss* (Harmondsworth: Penguin, 2006).

Han, Byung–Chul. *Hyperkulturalität: Kultur und Globalisierung* (Berlin: Merve, 2005).

Hardt, Michael & Antonio Negri. *Empire* (Cambridge MA: Harvard UP, 2001).

Held, David, et al. *Global Transformations: Politics, Economics and Culture* (Cambridge: Polity, 1999).

Kunzru, Hari. *Transmission* (Harmondsworth: Penguin, 2005).

Newman, Robert. *The Fountain at the Centre of the World* (London & New York: Verso, 2003).

McLuhan, Marshall. *Understanding Media: The Extensions of Man* (New York: McGraw–Hill, 1964).

Pieterse, Jan Nederveen. "Globalization and Human Integration: We Are All Migrants," *Futures* 32.5 (June 2000): 385–98.

Schulze–Engler, Frank. "What's the Difference? Notes towards a Dialogue between Transdifference and Transculturality," *Journal for the Study of British Cultures* 13:2 (2006): 123–32.

Thussu, Daya Kishan. "Mapping Global Media Flow and Contra-Flow," in *Media on the Move: Global Flow and Contra-Flow*, ed. Daya Kishan Thussu (London & New York: Routledge, 2007): 11–32.

⌘

American Antebellum Cosmopolitanism
—Herman Melville's 'Postcolonial' Translocations

GESA MACKENTHUN

I N RESPONSE TO THE OVERALL TOPIC OF THIS VOLUME, "postcolonial
translocations," and its implications of a possible gap or contrast between 'cultural' and 'literary' or 'new' and 'old' cosmopolitanism, this
essay will look at an 'old' literary manifestation of cosmopolitan thinking –
Herman Melville's novel *Moby-Dick* – and try to relate its translocal and
cosmopolitanist discourse both to political concerns of its own time and to
present discussions on cosmopolitanism. It remains to be seen, by analysing
more recent literary texts, whether the cosmopolitanism of literary discourse,
by being bound to specific cultural–aesthetic registers, is almost inevitably
more idealist (i.e. 'older' and 'unrooted') than a politico-legal cosmopolitanism that tries to come to terms with some of the concrete social problems resulting from migration, translocation, and globalization.

A cursory glance at present discussions of cosmopolitanism suggests a divide between 'universalist' concepts calling for an "allegiance to humanity as
a whole"[1] and a more 'particular' or 'rooted' kind which argues that allegiance to humanity does not necessarily have to exclude allegiance to one's
home country and that patriotism or the love of one's home, family, and
friends might offer a safer grounding for a cosmopolitan consciousness than
high-flying universalist ideals. The former position is most clearly expressed
by Martha Nussbaum, whereas the latter is defended by Kwame Anthony
Appiah. While Nussbaum's notion of cosmopolitanism is based on the mental

---

[1] Bruce Robbins, "Cosmopolitanism: New and Newer," *boundary 2* 34.3 (Fall
2007): 47.

ability to extend one's love to mankind regardless of local affiliations,[2] Appiah argues that a cosmopolitan attitude must be grounded in specific sympathies, that there must be the "grip upon our hearts"[3] in order for a truly cosmopolitan consciousness to evolve. In recent times, as Bruce Robbins shows, types of aesthetic cosmopolitanism have emerged that use the term descriptively for a particular translocal *literary* style, especially the nomadic plot schemes and hybrid character identities of postcolonial and 'global' fiction, rather than, in the Kantian sense, as a normative set of moral rules for regulating international political and legal affairs.[4] But, as Robbins correctly criticizes, these literature-based "celebrations of cosmopolitan diversity have largely been uninterrupted by the issues of economic equality or geopolitical justice."[5] David Harvey, in a recent book,[6] expresses the same apprehension about the reluctance of contemporary theories of cosmopolitanism to address concrete socio-economic aspects. He traces this evasiveness to a curious split in Kant's thinking – between his well-known philosophical theses on cosmopolitan right and the duty of hospitality, on the one hand, and the highly parochial positions expressed in his lesser-known texts on anthropology and geography, on the other.[7]

A glance at the work of Herman Melville may help to illustrate the controversy just sketched. Writing in the 1850s and aesthetically reaching beyond the conventions of Romanticism, Herman Melville is historically positioned somewhere between Kantian idealism and the pragmatic pressures of realpolitik that so much determine discussions of cosmopolitanism in our own time. The composition of Melville's classic texts mentioned in this essay – *Moby-Dick* (1851), "Benito Cereno" (1855), and *The Confidence Man* (1857) – was framed by transformative events within the USA and in the nation's relationship with other countries. Paramount among domestic affairs was the

---

[2] Martha Nussbaum, *Frontiers of Justice: Disability, Nationality, Species Membership* (Cambridge MA: Harvard UP/Belknap Press, 2006); Kwame Anthony Appiah, *Cosmopolitanism: Ethics in a World of Strangers* (New York: W.W. Norton, 2006).

[3] Kwame Anthony Appiah, "Rooted Cosmopolitanism," *The Ethics of Identity* (Princeton NJ: Princeton UP, 2005): 221.

[4] Robbins, "Cosmopolitanism," 51.

[5] "Cosmopolitanism," 51.

[6] David Harvey, *Cosmopolitanism and the Geographies of Freedom* (New York: Columbia UP, 2009).

[7] See Harvey, *Cosmopolitanism,* ch. 1.

passing of the Fugitive Slave Law in 1850, which required all citizens of free states to collaborate with the owners of runaway slaves in handing the latter over to the sheriffs (otherwise they were threatened with high fines and prison terms). The law was a scandalous attack on the principles of the Constitution and on Christian morality. Internationally, the USA was in the middle of its expansionist period, culminating in the annexation of Texas (1845) and the victory over Mexico in the Mexican–American War (1846–48), a gigantic step towards completing its continental empire. As the son of a former merchant who had become aware of cultural differences and even spent a few weeks with the indigenous tribe of the Typee on a Polynesian island, Melville was deeply concerned about these developments. Critics agree that he substantially revised his masterpiece *Moby-Dick* in direct response to the growing racism and the nationalistic parochialism he observed in his country's public discourse. Without doubt, the cosmopolitan vision had been present in the text of *Moby-Dick* from the very beginning, but recent events certainly added an explicitly political twist to Melville's romantic allegory.

Melville's cosmopolitanism is perhaps best expressed in his repeated use of an anecdote from the times of the French Revolution. In various texts, Melville compares the "motley" crew of a ship with an "Anacharsis Clootz deputation from all the isles of the sea," respectively an "Anacharsis Clootz congress of all kinds of that multiform pilgrim species, man," or "an assortment of tribes and complexions as would have well fitted them to be marched up by Anacharsis Cloots before the bar of the first French Assembly as Representatives of the Human Race."[8] Melville refers to an event in 1790 when the Prussian nobleman Anacharsis (né Jean Baptiste du Val de Grâce, Baron) Cloots collected together a group of foreigners in the streets of Paris and marched them to the Revolutionary Assembly in order to express international enthusiasm for the ideas of republicanism and human rights. Here is Thomas Carlyle's account (written almost fifty years later) of the scene:

> the sun's slant rays lighted a spectacle such as our foolish little Planet has not often had to show: Anacharsis Clootz entering the august Salle de Manège, with the Human Species at his heels. Swedes, Spaniards, Polacks; Turks, Chaldeans, Greeks, dwellers in Mesopotamia; behold

---

[8] Herman Melville, *Moby-Dick: or The Whale* (1851; New York: W.W. Norton, 1967): 108; *The Confidence-Man: His Masquerade* (1857; New York: W.W. Norton, 1971): 6; "Billy Budd," in *Billy Budd, Sailor and Other Stories* (Harmondsworth: Penguin, 1970): 321–22.

them all; they have come to claim place in the grand Federation, having an undoubted interest in it. "Our Ambassador titles," said the fervid Clootz, "are not written on parchment, but on the living hearts of all men." These whiskered Polacks, long-flowing turbaned Ishmaelites, astrological Chaldeans, who stand so mute here, let them plead with you, august Senators, more eloquently than eloquence could.[9]

Not much is known about Anarcharsis Cloots. In the *Dictionary of Eighteenth-Century World History* he is dubbed "a wayward itinerant German nobleman with an interest in literature" and "one of the most enthusiastic cosmopolitan supporters of the French Revolution."[10] We know that Cloots was the fourth 'Prussian' besides Alexander von Humboldt, Friedrich Schiller, and Johann Heinrich Pestalozzi (who was actually Swiss) to become a member of the Revolutionary General Assembly (and a French citizen) in 1792 but that he became a victim of Robespierre's terror in 1794.[11] His last words on the steps of the Guillotine were, according to the Durants' anecdotal history, "My friends, don't confuse me with these rascals!"[12]

What is so fascinating for Melville about Anacharsis Cloots's motley delegation of 1790 even sixty years after the event took place? The answer is simply that Melville was a radical cosmopolitan, like Cloots, and wrote his major novels and short stories during one of the intellectually most cosmopolitan periods in world history – a period that Michael Rogin has called the "American 1848"[13] and which saw the first international peace conferences,[14]

---

[9] Thomas Carlyle, *The French Revolution*, vol. 1 (1837; London: Dent, 1908): 273–74.

[10] *A Dictionary of Eighteenth-Century World History*, ed. Jeremy Black & Roy Porter (Oxford: Blackwell, 1994): 161.

[11] Will Durant & Ariel Durant, *The Age of Napoleon: A History of European Civilization from 1789 to 1815* (The Story of Civilization 11; New York: Simon & Schuster, 1975): 43.

[12] Durant & Durant, *The Age of Napoleon*, 76.

[13] Michael Paul Rogin, *Subversive Genealogies: The Politics and Art of Herman Melville* (Berkeley: U of California P, 1979): 120.

[14] The black abolitionist William Wells Brown, for example, was elected as a delegate to attend the International Peace Congress in Paris in August 1849. See Robert S. Levine, "Chronology of Brown's Life and Times," in William Wells Brown, *Clotel, or, The President's Daughter: A Narrative of Slave Life in the United States*, ed. Robert S. Levine (1853; Bedford Cultural Editions; Boston MA: Bedford/St Martin's, 2000): 35.

the emergence of the American women's movement, and an increase in power of the antislavery movement. In view of these international activities – both imperial and anti-imperial – Melville created the symbolically overdetermined figure of Ahab, at once victim and perpetrator of a fatal inhuman force. As Rogin writes, the figure of Ahab

> correctly points to a deeper motive than the rational pursuit of gain, not a higher one. Ahab carries to its extreme the egotistic, bourgeois desire for power, to be alone in the world and to possess it.[15]

Rather than merely implying a critique of the capitalist system, *Moby-Dick* must be seen as an exploration of the philosophical and psychological foundations of Western supremacism – for example, its rootedness in a particular theory of power.

From what we know, Melville's ideas about cosmopolitanism were quite close to those of Kant, who "envisaged a world in which all members of the human race eventually would [become] participants in a civil order and enter into a condition of lawful association with one another."[16] However, according to Seyla Benhabib, one of Kant's best exegetes, with a concern for his contribution to present debates about international justice, Kant distinguishes between the concept of "world government" and that of "world federation."[17] Kant argues that only a federation would be successful and lasting: i.e. each world citizen would at the same time also be a citizen of a particular republic.[18] Thus, Kant himself laid the foundation for the divergent notions of cosmopolitanism that we can encounter today. Melville was fascinated with this distinction between a particular (i.e. national) notion of justice and a universal, even supra-legal, one. Throughout his work we can observe his desire to 'think outside the box', to insinuate himself – often disguised in the mode of satire and burlesque – into the situation of the Other, whether of a Polynesian islander (in *Typee*) or of a religious fanatic (in *Pierre, or, The Ambiguities*). Patriotic 'rootedness' was not one of Melville's priorities; boundless universalism, however, seemed as impractical, bordering on metaphysical speculation. Melville consequently found his position

---

[15] Rogin, *Subversive Genealogies,* 120.

[16] Seyla Benhabib, *Another Cosmopolitanism* (Oxford: Oxford U P, 2006): 24.

[17] Benhabib, *Another Cosmopolitanism,* 24.

[18] See Benhabib, *Another Cosmopolitanism,* 24.

somewhere in between these two extremes – in the aporetic realm of ambiguities.

Carlyle's anecdote, which, having first appeared in 1837, was most likely known to Melville, strikingly resembles Appiah's emphasis, quoted above, on the tangible aspect of a cosmopolitan stance – its rootedness in locally and corporeally experienced reality. Both Appiah and Carlyle actually use the metaphor of the heart ("grip upon our hearts";[19] "titles [...] not written on parchments, but on the living hearts of all men"[20]) to express the physical and emotional power of the cosmopolitan spirit. Yet the great difference lies in Appiah's possessive reductionism ("*our* hearts") against Carlyle's universalism ("hearts of *all* men"). Carlyle conspicuously also mentions the 'muteness' of Cloots's motley crowd, which contrasts sharply with Cloots's own recorded outspokenness. The anecdote can be seen to gesture to a major paradox in many discussions about cosmopolitanism: the uneven global distribution of power, beginning with the power to speak. Arguably, the main representatives of cosmopolitanist thinking were and still are members of social elites, with varying degrees of detachment from the lived experience of past and present motley crowds, whether in the metropolises of the (neo)colonial world or on its geopolitical margins. Melville was very aware of his limited point of view: his novella "Benito Cereno," long regarded as an experiment in narrative perspective, has more recently been seen as a painful dissection of the ideological limits of perspective produced by the colonial world. It ends with the insight that the 'subaltern' cannot speak within the discursive rules of colonialism – quite in concurrence with Gayatri Spivak's famous thesis.[21]

If *Moby-Dick* is seen as Melville's response to national parochialism and anti-enlightenment legislation, the story of the *Pequod*, its multicultural crew, and its vindictive captain may function as a national allegory, a dark prophecy of America's future if the madness of slavery and imperialism were not stopped.[22] But *Moby-Dick* is also an allegory of the fate of mankind as such.

---

[19] Appiah, "Rooted Cosmopolitanism," 221.

[20] Carlyle, *French Revolution*, 273–74.

[21] See Gesa Mackenthun, *Fictions of the Black Atlantic in American Foundational Literature* (London: Routledge, 2004), 125. Routledge Transatlantic Perspectives on American Literature. Further page references to 'postcolonial' readings of "Benito Cereno" are in that chapter.

[22] William Spanos has read *Moby-Dick* as a prophetic allegory of American imperialism, not only of its own time but of the postwar period as well. See his *The*

C.L.R. James argued in 1953 (still under the impression of the Second World War) that the novel amounts to a warning against the seductiveness of totalitarian leaders.[23] Melville's description of the crew as victims of Ahab's charismatic performances supports this argument. In a crucial scene, Ahab unites the pagan harpooneers and mates in a Tarot-inspired ritual, infecting them with the "fiery emotion accumulated within the Leyden jar of his own magnetic life."[24] As a result of this scene and various other shamanistic tricks staged towards the crew (the breaking of the quadrant, the 'taming' of St Elmo's fire [414-17]), the crew of the Pequod seems united by some metaphysical force:

> They were one man, not thirty. For as the one ship that held them all; though it was put together of all contrasting things – oak, and maple, and pine wood; iron, and pitch, and hemp – yet all these ran into each other in the one concrete hull, which shot on its way, both balanced and directed by the long central keel; even so, all the individualities of the crew, this man's valor, that man's fear; guilt and guiltlessness, all varieties were welded into oneness, and were all directed to that fatal goal which Ahab their one lord and keel did point to. (454–55)

This is the allegorical equivalent of the political motto *e pluribus unum* that can be found on every dollar bill. The ethnic and cultural differences between the sailors which Melville emphasizes elsewhere are here abolished. In fact, the novel dramatizes the process of bringing about ideological homogenization by means of charismatic performance. Thus, earlier in the novel, when the crew is introduced, Ishmael notes their aggressive divisiveness, tracing it back to their multicultural composition, as well as the inequalities in power between the men before and those behind the mast (i.e. the officers): "not one of two of the many thousand men before the mast employed in the American whale fishery, are Americans born, though pretty nearly all the officers are" (108). The same, he adds, applies to the American army and merchant navies,

> and the engineering forces employed in the construction of the American Canals and Railroads. The same, I say, because in all these cases

---

Errant Art of "Moby-Dick": The Canon, the Cold War, and the Struggle for American Studies (Durham N C: Duke U P, 1995).

[23] C.L.R. James, *Mariners, Renegades, and Castaways: The Story of Herman Melville and the World We Live In* (1953; Hanover N H: U P of New England, 2001).

[24] Melville, *Moby-Dick*, 145–46. Further page references are in the main text.

the native American liberally provides the brains, the rest of the world
as generously supplying the muscles. (108)

He then tells us how the sailors are hired and fired and that most of them are
born islanders and "isolatoes" who are not

> acknowledging the common continent of men. [...] Yet now, federa-
> ted along one keel, what a set these Isolatoes were! An Anacharsis
> Clootz deputation from all the isles of the sea, and all the ends of the
> earth, accompanying Old Ahab in the Pequod to lay the world's griev-
> ances before that bar from which not very many of them ever came
> back. (108)

In fact, only one of them, the narrator Ishmael, survives the destruction to return and tell the tale.

While formerly locked into global master–servant relationships with clearly defined roles for those providing the "brains" and those providing the
"muscle," the world's "isolatoes" are inseminated with the germ of cosmopolitanism under the influence of Ahab, who functions as their legal representative – significantly, however, not to the bar of earthly justice but to that
of the court of God (or the Devil, as the case may be). As can be seen, the
character of Ahab changes according to the sociality of the sailors. In the
latter passage quoted (108), where the crew is compared to the Cloots deputation, Ahab appears as Cloots himself, presenting the world's complaints at
God's (or Nature's) "bar." Ahab, at first glance, seems to occupy the position
of the leading cosmopolitan, his crew representing all the citizens of the
world. In the former passage quoted (454–55, which comes later in the text,
toward the fatal end), Ahab appears as the totalitarian leader C.L.R. James
read him as (see above). The difference is explained by the implications of
Melville's 'translation' of the Cloots anecdote from a context of international
representation to a struggle against metaphysical power. Pretending that he
leads them on in their quest for human rights and participation in a global
government, Ahab actually hijacks the "isolatoes" for his own megalo-
maniacal purpose. The transformation of the crew implies that the subjection
of individual motives to a collective project, even if not coupled with an
enlightened sense of individual moral responsibility, bears the danger of their
being perverted by totalitarian forces:

> the rushing Pequod, freighted with savages, and laden with fire, and
> burning a corpse, and plunging into that blackness of darkness,

seemed the material counterpart of her monomaniac commander's soul. (353–54)

The ambivalent representation of Ahab is a typical example of the novel's "double talk,"[25] its maddening semantic and symbolic sliding. Yet besides the depiction of Ahab as a cosmopolitan – or, alternatively, an infernal – leader, the novel emphasizes the agency of the unknown mariners; it evokes an untold, and therefore largely unknown, history of common men. The real heroes of the book are the sailors from the New England seaport of Nantucket who, Ishmael claims, explored the ocean's remotest coasts and archipelagoes before the famous explorers Cook and Vancouver came along:

> They may celebrate as they will the heroes of Exploring Expeditions, your Cooks, your Krusensterns; but I say that scores of anonymous Captains have sailed out of Nantucket, that were as great, and greater than your Cook and your Krusenstern. [...] All that is made such a flourish of in the old South Sea Voyages, those things were but the life-time commonplaces of our heroic Nantucketers. Often, adventures which Vancouver dedicates three chapters to, these men accounted unworthy of being set down in the ship's common log. Ah, the world! Oh, the world! (100)

And he adds that it was the whalemen who first broke the Spanish colonial subjection of the South American colonies and contributed to their liberation as well as "the establishment of the eternal democracy in those parts" (100). Here you find Melville writing back to Kant, inscribing the lofty philosophical heights of Kantian theory with the commonplace experience of the true agents of the cosmopolitan transformation – or translocalization – of a formerly localized world. What is more, the whalemen, in this description, play the part of postcolonial agents in helping the Spanish colonies liberate themselves from the fetters of the colonial power. Melville's re-centering of world history on the perspective of the common sailor (whether from Nantucket or elsewhere) amounts to a rewriting of world history as an 'oceanic' history from below.

The cosmopolitan discourse of *Moby-Dick* is probably nowhere better expressed than in the 'bosom friendship' of Ishmael and Queequeg. Although

---

[25] The term is Carolyn Porter's. See her "Call Me Ishmael, or How to Make Double-Talk Speak," in *New Essays on Moby-Dick*, ed. Richard Brodhead (Cambridge: Cambridge UP, 1986): 73–108.

Ishmael is convinced that Queequeg is a cannibal, with a head that, upon phrenological analysis, looks like "George Washington cannibalistically developed" (52), his encounter with the Polynesian native helps him overcome his initial Hobbesian melancholy:

> I felt a melting in me. No more my splintered heart and maddened hand were turned against the wolfish world. This soothing savage had redeemed it. There he sat, his very indifference speaking a nature in which there lurked no civilized hypocrisies and bland deceits. Wild he was; a very sight of sights to see; yet I began to feel myself mysteriously drawn towards him. And those same things that would have repelled most others, they were the very magnets that thus drew me. (53)

It should be noted that Ishmael's affection for Queequeg is the consequence of his disenchantment with his own 'wolfish' world. We do not learn what precisely it is that makes Ishmael lose his cultural moorings, but his own cultural 'rootlessness' is certainly an important precondition for being able to embrace (literally) a 'savage' culture. In the course of the novel, the opposition between 'civilization' and 'savagery' gradually vanishes. This process culminates in a well-known scene in which Ishmael finds himself in a similar mood of cultural relativism as in the passage just quoted. Having caught several sperm whales, the sailors have to squeeze the precious, musky-smelling "sperm"[26] into a fragrant liquid:

> I forgot all about our horrible oath; in that inexpressible sperm, I washed my hands and my heart of it; [...] Squeeze! squeeze! squeeze! all the morning long; I squeezed that sperm till I myself almost melted into it; I squeezed that sperm till a strange sort of insanity came over me; and I found myself unwittingly squeezing my co-laborers' hands in it, mistaking their hands for the gentle globules. Such an abounding, affectionate, friendly, loving feeling did this avocation beget; that at last I was continually squeezing their hands, and looking up into their eyes sentimentally; [...] Come; let us squeeze hands all around; nay, let us all squeeze ourselves into each other; let us squeeze ourselves universally into the very milk and sperm of kindness. (349)

---

[26] That is, 'spermaceti', the waxy liquid contained in a gland in the whale's head and processed into high-quality candles and ointments. 'Sperm' is its commonly used abbreviated form, capitalized on by Melville for humorous effect.

Melville again uses the metaphor of 'melting' to express the collapse of cultural difference. The homoerotic symbolism of this passage finds its counterpart in some of the poems of Walt Whitman whose cosmopolitanism, contrary to Melville's, however, at times slides into imperial jingoism (e.g., in "Passage to India" [27]).

Both passages (*Moby-Dick*, 53, 349) can be related to various aspects of cosmopolitanism. Ishmael's friendship with Queequeg, as well as his loss of his sense of the limits of his own body in relation to those of his companions, abolishes the distinction between 'us' and 'the other' which Ulrich Beck finds so important in Diogenes' definition of cosmopolitanism, while the translocal activities of the Nantucketers, which range below the level of national traffic and discovery, are reminiscent of Diogenes' emphasis on mobility as a precondition for reaching a truly cosmopolitan attitude.[28] While Ishmael's expressions of what might be called cosmic corporeal love can be said to range on a supra-national level (national differences are abolished together with bodily differences), the activities of the Nantucketers range on a level below the official history of nations (sub-national). In their own particular way, the seafaring whalers fulfil what Beck calls the "Sowohl-als-auch-Prinzip"[29] (the 'either–or principle'), which allows one to combine a local identity with a universal one. The hand-squeezing narrator goes one step further by ignoring all distinctions; in his rapture, he seems to enter into what Freud called an 'oceanic' feeling with his companions in which the categories of 'us' and 'them' cease to exist. The example of Ishmael's 'bosom friendship', moreover, contains the important element of a 'dialogic imagination' and what Beck calls the "Anerkennung der Andersheit der Anderen einschließlich des Realismus der damit aufbrechenden Dilemmata und Gewaltpotentiale"[30] ('an acknowledgement of the otherness of others, including both a measure of realism regarding the dilemmas and the potential for violence unleashed by such an acknowledgement').

---

[27] Walt Whitman, "Passage to India," in *Walt Whitman: Complete Poetry and Collected Prose*, ed. Justin Kaplan (New York: Library of America, 1982): 531–40.

[28] Ulrich Beck, *Power in the Global Age: A New Global Political Economy*, tr. Kathleen Cross *(Macht und Gegenmacht im globalen Zeitalter: Neue weltpolitische Ökonomie*, 2002; Cambridge: Polity, 2005): 35–37.

[29] Beck, *Power in the Global Age*, 36.

[30] Beck, *Power in the Global Age*, 37. See also Benhabib, *Another Cosmopolitanism*, 20.

The examples quoted so far testify to a sense of the 'cosmopolitan' that is largely apolitical – as in some recent applications of the term as an aesthetic or merely 'cultural' category. What is missing from most examples (even the Anarcharsis Cloots one) is the important notion of 'planetary justice' that is a crucial aspect of Kant's and the Enlightenment's idea of cosmopolitanism.[31] Melville addresses issues of international rights – for example, in passages that can be read as comments on the Mexican War or the Fugitive Slave Law; in "Benito Cereno" (his novella on a slaveship mutiny), he includes a long section representing a court trial against African rebels, which shows that their right of self-defence is denied them by the colonial legal system. But Melville's texts also seem impeded by the limitations inherent in literary discourse: i.e. in their reluctance to weave the abstract concerns of the 'old' (universal) cosmopolitanism – its notion of universal human rights – into a narrative plot. The ideals of planetary justice and the 'unrooted' love of mankind, because of their abstract nature, do not readily offer themselves for the literary invention of character and place. In the 'global', or translocal, literature of our own time, some efforts in this regard have been made, but frequently with the result that the ideas of planetary justice and cultural difference do not go well together. As Michael Ondaatje implies in *Anil's Ghost* (2000), internationally defined principles of truth and justice frequently collide with local complexities and individual 'rooted' positions whose notions of truth and justice may be incommensurable with international standards and methods. John Le Carré's *The Constant Gardener* (2001), another novel interested in the issue of global justice, can be said to feature a cosmopolitan spatial structure, but the cosmopolitanism of its plot is somewhat modified by the private: i.e. 'rooted' and romanticized, motivation of its protagonist to solve the crime.

The theme of cosmopolitanism seems to offer itself best for a novel of ideas and less for a literary discourse that centres on place and character and ideally includes aspects of semantic and ideological ambivalence. Maybe the greatest potential for infusing novelistic discourse with the theme of cosmopolitanism (instead of somewhat helplessly celebrating cultural heterogeneity in romance-inspired plot structures[32]) lies in a more conscious emphasis on space, place, and region in a global geographical set-up, in engaging in various forms of dialectical heterotoping. Melville himself has made several at-

---

[31] See Robbins, "Cosmopolitanism," 51.

[32] For "helpless heterogeneity," see Robbins, "Cosmopolitanism: New and Newer," 60.

tempts to bring together different socio-political geographies – either by way
of metaphoric troping (as in the case of "Benito Cereno" and its metaphoric
inscription of an historically documented slave revolt on board a Spanish
slaver with the history of American conquest and slave rebellion); or in his
stories "The Paradise of Bachelors and the Tartarus of Maids" (1855) and
"The Poor Man's Pudding and the Rich Man's Crumbs" (1854), both of
which dialectically and translocally relate scenes of poverty and labour exploitation with scenes of gentlemanly opulence in a highly space-conscious
manner (giving descriptions of Dickensian detail of the very *sites* of suffering,
on the one hand, and imperial luxury, on the other).[33] It seems that, in these
stories, Melville has pretty much exhausted the literary means for expressing
his 'old' form of 'unrooted' cosmopolitanism.

On the basis of these textual explorations, a suspicion arises concerning the
'new' cosmopolitanism's promise to close the gap between cultural and literary theory, on the one hand, and political practice, on the other. Certainly, the
gap between the aesthetic and the political cannot be closed by 'grounding'
transnational and transcultural perspectives in such fields as citizenship, civil
society, and human rights. And why should it be closed in the first place? If
literary discourse is to continue fulfilling its cultural function of creatively
testing the potentials and possibilities of human action, the gap ought to be
kept open, in order for literature to articulate alternatives to strictly political
thought and practice.

It seems important to distinguish between an *aesthetic or cultural cosmopolitanism* that might be rhizomorphic and unrooted, hence able to fully sub-
scribe to an ideal notion of universal dialogue and understanding, and a *political cosmopolitanism* that would have to include an aspect of local rootedness.
Political cosmopolitanism has to act within the limits of an incomplete global
legal structure. Literature, by contrast, can imaginatively critique and transcend this order and offer ways of understanding the contradictions and social
inequalities of our times without heeding the pressures of *Realpolitik*. Fictional texts may point their readers towards a clearer view of the global disparities of power and to other solutions than those offered by political practitioners hemmed in by local rules and regulations.

Thus the distinction between 'old' and 'new' cosmopolitanisms may be re-
written as the coterminous existence of two different kinds of cosmopolitan-

---

[33] On Melville's and other writers' art of heterotoping, see Cesare Casarino, *Modernity at Sea: Melville, Marx, Conrad in Crisis* (Minneapolis: Minnesota U P, 2002).

ism, a cultural–aesthetic one (which 'is allowed' to imagine ideal states) and a politico-legal one (which 'has to' respond to particular social and diplomatic needs). The ancient dream of a world united in universal peace and equality is to be pursued in the field of force between these two poles – between demands for (and of) humanity and the pressures of daily political practice.

WORKS CITED

Appiah, Kwame Anthony. *Cosmopolitanism: Ethics in a World of Strangers* (New York: Norton, 2006).

——. "Rooted Cosmopolitanism," in *The Ethics of Identity* (Princeton NJ: Princeton UP, 2005): 213–72.

Beaver, Harold. "Commentary," in Herman Melville, *Moby-Dick*, ed. Harold Beaver (1851; Harmondsworth: Penguin, 1972): 689–967.

Beck, Ulrich. *Power in the Global Age: A New Global Political Economy*, tr. Kathleen Cross *(Macht und Gegenmacht im globalen Zeitalter: Neue weltpolitische Ökonomie*, 2002; Cambridge: Polity, 2005).

Benhabib, Seyla. *Another Cosmopolitanism* (Oxford: Oxford UP, 2006).

Black, Jeremy, & Roy Porter, ed. *A Dictionary of Eighteenth-Century World History* (Oxford: Blackwell, 1994).

Carlyle, Thomas. *The French Revolution*, vol. 1 (1837; London: Dent, 1908).

Casarino, Cesare. *Modernity at Sea: Melville, Marx, Conrad in Crisis* (Minneapolis: Minnesota UP, 2002).

Durant, Will, & Ariel Durant, *The Age of Napoleon: A History of European Civilization from 1789 to 1815* (The Story of Civilization 11; New York: Simon & Schuster, 1975).

James, C.L.R. *Mariners, Renegades, and Castaways: The Story of Herman Melville and the World We Live In* (1953; Hanover NH: UP of New England, 2001).

Le Carré, John. *The Constant Gardener* (New York: Scribner, 2001).

Levine, Robert S. "Chronology of Brown's Life and Times," in William Wells Brown, *Clotel: or The President's Daughter: A Narrative of Slave Life in the United States*, ed. Robert S. Levine (1853; Bedford Cultural Editions; Boston MA: Bedford/St Martin's, 2000).

Mackenthun, Gesa. *Fictions of the Black Atlantic in American Foundational Literature* (London: Routledge, 2004).

Melville, Herman. "Billy Budd," in *Billy Budd, Sailor and Other Stories* (Harmondsworth: Penguin, 1970): 316–409.

——. *Moby-Dick: or The Whale* (1851; New York: Norton, 1967).

——. *The Confidence-Man: His Masquerade* (1857; New York: Norton, 1971).

Nussbaum, Martha. *Frontiers of Justice: Disability, Nationality, Species Membership* (Cambridge M A : Harvard U P / Belknap Press, 2006).

Ondaatje, Michael. *Anil's Ghost* (New York: Alfred A. Knopf, 2000).

Porter, Carolyn. "Call Me Ishmael, or How to Make Double-Talk Speak," in *New Essays on Moby-Dick*, ed. Richard Brodhead (Cambridge: Cambridge U P, 1986): 73–108.

Robbins, Bruce. "Cosmopolitanism: New and Newer," *boundary 2* 34.3 (Fall 2007): 47–60.

Rogin, Michael Paul. *Subversive Genealogies: The Politics and Art of Herman Melville* (Berkeley: U of California P, 1979).

Spanos, William. *The Errant Art of "Moby-Dick": The Canon, the Cold War, and the Struggle for American Studies* (Durham N C : Duke U P, 1995).

Whitman, Walt. "Passage to India," in *Walt Whitman: Complete Poetry and Collected Prose*, ed. Justin Kaplan (New York: Library of America, 1982): 531–40.

⌘

Translocal Temporalities
in Alexis Wright's *Carpentaria*

LYNDA NG

Translocality and Indigeneity

I N HER 2006 NOVEL *CARPENTARIA*, Alexis Wright asserts the importance of local history and traditional customs over the imposed meta-narrative of the nation. Wright begins the novel by stressing the serious consideration that must be given to the unofficial, often unrecorded local narratives which persist and operate below the level of national consciousness. She writes:

> But this was not Vaudeville. Wars were fought here. If you had your patch destroyed you'd be screaming too. The serpent's covenant permeates everything, even the little black girls with hair combed back off their faces and bobby-pinned neatly for church, listening quietly to the nation that claims to know everything except the exact date its world will end.[1]

This is a novel that confronts Western assumptions regarding temporality, history, and indigenous culture, and endeavours to provide a counter-narrative capable of overcoming such deeply inscribed beliefs. It situates itself firmly within the local, relating events which unfold in the fictional town of Desperance, a rural outpost in the far north of Australia. But *Carpentaria* is also concerned with showing the various and cumulative effects that globalization has had on local culture, ultimately describing a translocal space where numerous cultures exist and interact to create a unique milieu. By foregrounding

---

[1] Alexis Wright, *Carpentaria* (Artarmon, NSW: Giramondo, 2006): 11. Further page references are in the main text.

the innately fluid, flexible, and vibrant qualities of indigenous culture, Wright also draws attention to the complex dynamics at work within the translocal.

Given the transformative effects of globalization and the accelerated flows of people, capital, media, and goods across national borders, the translocal has emerged as a more descriptive and useful term for analysing the integration of globalization processes into localized systems. The translocal recognizes the constant movement of people and cultures across national borders, without losing sight of the ways in which objects/subjects embed themselves in local culture and interact with it. As Arif Dirlik has argued, to describe culturally mixed spaces and communities as translocal rather than transnational is to distance oneself from the dominant, and arguably inadequate, frame of the nation. Raising the example of ethnic and diasporic spaces, he writes:

> Translocal [...] is a better term (because it is both more grounded and more flexible) to describe the motions that create these spaces. The move from the transnational to the translocal involves more than choice of vocabulary; it carries us from one conceptual realm – that of nations and civilisations – to another – that of places.[2]

Dirlik rightly draws our attention back to the specificity of place – a move that Wright's novel furthers by insisting on the significance of indigenous culture within specific locales.

Desperance functions as a microcosm of Australian society, illustrating the racial divide through its depiction of the centralized white Uptown folk and the indigenous Pricklebush mob, who live around the perimeter of the official town. There is a clear disparity between the cultures, beliefs, and even language of the two sides of Desperance. The fiery character of Angel Day stands out because, although born and bred within the Pricklebush, she has an innate ability to employ the language of Uptown folk. Watching Angel talk to a delegation from Uptown, her husband, Normal Phantom, observes: "Where did she get it from he wondered? *Itinerants* was not the language of the Pricklebush" (39). But, as Wright takes pains to acknowledge, the Uptown and Pricklebush communities are themselves made up of dissenting individuals and factional disagreements. In an early episode of the novel, an argument between Angel Day and other members of the Pricklebush results in

---

[2] Arif Dirlik, "Performing the World: Reality and Representation in the Making of World Histor(ies)," *Journal of World History* 16.4 (December 2005): 397.

their geographical split into east and west sides. The Uptown folk now find themselves dealing with two separate groups of the Pricklebush mob:

> On the other hand, the townsfolk of Desperance could not make heads or tails out of why they were being sandwiched between Aboriginal people, not only living on either side of them now, but setting up two camps without even saying a word to anybody what they were doing. (31–32)

Even within the context of a small town we can observe that communities can be plagued by deep rifts and internal divisions.

Translocations contain an imbricated time with their memory of a past location and their situatedness within a present one. By recognizing the distinct histories generated by different cultures, the translocal conjures up a palimpsest of temporal layers. As Roy Sommer points out, unlike the permutations examined in travelling theory, translocations have no sense of return.[3] The addition of a new culture has transformative effects upon the existing one. In this manner, Wright recognizes the permanent and indelible effects that white settler culture has had upon the originary indigenous culture. It is important to note that Wright's assertion of the indigenous is not an exclusionist strategy to label the white mainstream culture 'foreign' in the same way that the pioneer families try to exclude the Aborigines from the town. Instead, she argues that recognition of the indigenous is an important means for a nation to learn how to operate productively in a globalized context. Elsewhere, Wright has written:

> Perhaps the way for Australia to create credible relationships worldwide will be through the development of a literature that understands not only how Aboriginal people think, along with the cultural matrices of the foundation myths that Australians of immigrant backgrounds cling to.[4]

Carpentaria is an attempt at synthesizing these two viewpoints. It is told predominantly from the perspective of Aboriginal characters, using a unique

---

[3] Roy Sommer, "No Size Fits All: Postcolonial Ways of Seeing in the 21st Century" (paper presented at the Postcolonial Translocations: Twentieth Annual GNEL/ASNEL Conference, University of Münster, 23 May 2009).

[4] Alexis Wright, "On the Question of Fear," in Gideon Haigh, Cristos Tsiolkas & Alexis Wright, *Tolerance, Prejudice and Fear: Sydney Pen Voices, the 3 Writers Project* (Crows Nest, Victoria: Allen & Unwin, 2008): 138.

idiom that draws on indigenous folklore. But it also presents a flexible cultural framework that is capable of integrating with belief-systems from other cultures.

Rather than viewing the translocal as a recent development of globalization, Wright encourages us to see it as a form of cultural interaction that has been occurring for many centuries. In *Carpentaria*, a translocation is not necessarily a movement between a home locale and a foreign destination, but a movement between two points equally weighted with the connotations of the familiar and the exotic. Her depiction of contemporary Australia through an indigenous voice immediately problematizes the common association of white, mainstream Australian culture as the local and authentic culture of home. While white mainstream Australian culture has traditionally been concerned with cultural invasion from 'foreign' countries overseas, Wright's novel rightly points out the 'foreignness' of white mainstream Australian culture itself. Setting the scene for the events which unfold in Desperance, Wright's narrator observes that "the descendants of the pioneer families, who claimed ownership of the town, said *the Aboriginal was really not part of the town at all*" (4). But she immediately counters this position put forward by the white pioneers:

> No, the Pricklebush was from the time before the motor car, when goods and chattels came up by camel train until Abdul and Abdullah, the old Afghan brothers, disappeared along the track called the 'life-line', connecting north to south. (4)

This interrogation of what constitutes an authorial and originary 'home' culture reflects the dilemma which the frequency and volume of contemporary translocations pose to former conceptions of home and nation.

Wright's work addresses a lacuna within the Australian national policy of multiculturalism that has been in effect since the 1980s. Multiculturalism was instituted as an effort to distance contemporary Australian society from the blatantly racist, non-white immigration policies, better known under the umbrella term 'White Australia Policy', which officially ended in 1973. It was an attempt to broaden the parameters of Australian nationality and to recognize the cultural heterogeneity that was becoming increasingly difficult to ignore. However, as pointed out by critics such as Ghassan Hage and Sneja Gunew, discourses of multiculturalism often continued to function in a similar manner to previous white Australian discourses, with the end result being the marginalization of minority views and the elision of indigenous culture in debates regarding Australian nationality.[5] While the novel's main focus is on the interaction between the Pricklebush and the dominant white Uptown folk, references to other cultures can be found throughout Wright's work. Her acknowledgement of "Abdul and Abdullah, the old Afghan brothers" as two of the initial settlers who had early contact with the indigenous inhabitants of Desperance is but one example.

The relegation of indigenous culture to the margins, or its complete omission from our descriptions of contemporary globalized society, can be seen as the extension of a colonial bias that regards indigenous culture as primitive and static, in contrast to the progressive and dynamic aspects of modern civilization. One of the dangers of the macro-perspective demanded by globalization is, as Timothy Brennan points out, the assumption of homogeneity within our models. Brennan writes that current globalization theory "does not merely claim that economic or cultural integration is occurring on a global scale. [...] The intended point is rather that the world is being reconstituted *as a single social space*."[6] The unfortunate corollary of the simplifying tendencies of globalization theories is often an erasure of the notion of the indigenous. As Brennan notes, this fusion of the world into a "single social space" leads to an unsettling similarity between globalization and former processes of colonization.[7] The rhetoric of globalization tends to construct a cosmopolitan citizen with severed national ties, a world where exile and displacement have no countervailing localizing force. This has led Mieke Bal to conclude that "in today's global culture, it is no longer possible to posit the idea of 'native.' Plurality, change, and displacement make any fixed position hard to sustain."[8] Wright's novel, however, exposes the utopian underpinnings of such a claim. Characters such as Normal Phantom have a connection to the land which undeniably marks them as 'native' in a manner that the Uptown folk cannot be.

---

[5] See Sneja Gunew, *Haunted Nations: The Colonial Dimensions of Multiculturalisms* (London: Routledge, 2004), and Ghassan Hage, *White Nation: Fantasies of White Supremacy in a Multicultural Society* (Sydney: Pluto, 1998).

[6] Timothy Brennan, "From Development to Globalisation: Postcolonial Studies and Globalisation Theory," in *The Cambridge Companion to Postcolonial Literary Studies*, ed. Neil Lazarus (Cambridge & New York: Cambridge U P, 2004): 123.

[7] Brennan, "From Development to Globalisation: Postcolonial Studies and Globalisation Theory," 137.

[8] Mieke Bal, *Travelling Concepts in the Humanities: A Rough Guide* (Toronto: U of Toronto P, 2002): 19.

In *Carpentaria*, the intimate knowledge that certain characters have of the land confers them with special powers. For instance, Normal Phantom's knowledge of the sea makes him appear superhuman. His affinity with water gives him a deep connection to the past and his ancestors. We are told: "The Pricklebush mob say that Normal Phantom could grab hold of the river in his mind and live with it as his father's fathers did before him" (6). His ability to survive situations in which most people would perish makes it almost believable that he is not beholden to the same rules of physics as other men. The prospect that Normal might be immortal is raised at the beginning of the novel when the unidentified narrator writes: "The old people say the groper lives for hundreds of years and maybe Normal would too" (6). Later, when we follow Normal on one of his sea journeys, his physical stamina is apparently inexhaustible:

> Very different indeed for Norm rowing over the shadowy surface where sleeping men sunk into deadly illusions. Not him though. He could last forty days and nights without a wink of sleep. (503)

However, Normal's talents for reading the land and surviving upon it have only a limited use in the modern context. His wisdom and status as a powerful elder is recognized by the Uptown folk, but he has no real power to effect changes in Desperance, nor does he seem to have much of a desire to (37). His understanding of the land does not help him prevent a transnational mining company from causing great environmental damage, nor does it enable him to deflect a devastating cyclone that eventually wipes out the town. Normal remains a depository of information that is ignored and under-utilized by the people and political powers of Uptown.

The Frontier

Carpentaria, with its name, epic scope, and broad social concerns, immediately brings to mind Xavier Herbert's 1938 novel *Capricornia*.[9] Both novels are set in the Gulf of Carpentaria, a remote location that allows both authors to examine the importance of the frontier for Australian national identity. Away from the urban environment of the city, the land assumes greater importance, becoming a matter of survival for the people living on it. Paul

---

[9] Xavier Herbert, *Capricornia*, intro. Mudrooroo Nyoongah (1938; Imprint Classics 1; North Ryde, N S W: Angus & Robertson, 1990).

Sharrad notes that Wright's novel follows in the tradition of "leftist realist-romancers," and identifies the key precedents of this sub-genre as Xavier Herbert or Katharine Susannah Prichard.[10] These novels situate their stories in rural outposts of Australia, reinforcing notions of 'authentic' Australian national identity as being tied to a romanticized view of frontier culture.

Where Wright's novel differs from those of her predecessors, however, is in her representation of the frontier from an indigenous perspective. This re-orientation presents us with frontier country not as a hostile land, but as one that immigrants have failed to take the time to understand. While the Australian frontier is often depicted as a harsh and unforgiving environment where man must battle against the land for survival,[11] Wright's novel shows a land that can be fertile and giving for those who understand how to work with it. The unpredictable force of natural disasters can be neutralized if one acknowledges the dynamism of the land from the start. The land is not a static entity that is simply settled on, either as a place of origin or as place of destination – it moves and changes, a protean quality indicated in the opening pages of the novel:

> In one moment, during a Wet season early in the last century, the town
> lost its harbour waters when the river simply decided to change course,
> to bypass it by several kilometres. (3)

This leaves Desperance a "waterless port" (3). The town becomes a relic of a past incarnation of the landscape. The refusal of the townsfolk to relocate Desperance emphasizes the rigid strictures of Western thought.

Wright presents aspects of indigenous culture and ontology as a viable strategy for reconceptualizing notions of community, identity, and the trans-local within the dynamic flows of globalization. In her novel, Mozzie Fishman leads a convoy of men on a continual spiritual pilgrimage, retracing the path of the Dreaming across their country. We are told:

> The spiritual Dreaming track of the ceremony in which they were all
> involved, moved along the most isolated back roads, across the
> landscape, through almost every desert in the continent. (124)

---

[10] Paul Sharrad, "Beyond Capricornia: Ambiguous Promise in Alexis Wright," *Australian Literary Studies* 24.1 (April 2009): 52–65.

[11] For instance, this passage from Herbert's *Capricornia*: "Nature was against it. The wholesale planting was begun at the end of the Wet Season in 1916. The following Wet was the heaviest for many a year. Every plantation was washed bare" (93).

Mozzie's convoy fulfils an ancient function, but this does not mean that they have retreated into the past. The convoy travels in cars, and their journey not only links them with their ancestors but also connects them with the rest of their community, for they are performing a ceremony which is necessary to maintain the Law in the land:

> They were totally responsible for keeping the one Law strong by performing this one ceremony from thousands of creation stories for the guardians of Gondwanaland. (124)

Although constantly in motion, Mozzie Fishman and his convoy avoid the disenchantment and feeling of exile that plagues many deracinated modernist writers. Their journey fosters within them a strong sense of belonging to the land. Through their nomadism, Wright shows how peregrinations have long been a constitutive part of indigeneity.

The frontier is a natural place to examine the translocal, for it is where cultures inevitably collide. The tense inter-racial relations that characterize novels set in the frontier are still present in *Carpentaria*. Anne Brewster has argued that this unflinching depiction of the divided racial relations in Australia serves as a reminder of the deep scars of racism that still blot Australia's multicultural landscape: "[Wright] describes the indigenous population of Desperance as 'the edge mob' [62] – geographically, economically and racially located at the periphery of the white nation."[12] But while Wright's novel depicts a clear binary between white and black Australia, she makes it clear that she sees indigenous culture as one capable of embracing new immigrants and integrating with other cultures. Her criticism is levelled at the failure of white culture to do the same. The downfall of Desperance comes from the unwillingness of the town planners to accept and learn from the knowledge of its indigenous inhabitants. As Gelder and Salzman note,

> There are accordingly two 'histories' in the novel: a teleological settler history that seems irresistible, and an ancient indigenous history that will not be suppressed. Wright's most searching examination of this issue occurs late in the novel when a cyclone literally blows away the town of Desperance, pushing the landscape back into a version of its pre-colonial shape.[13]

---

[12] Anne Brewster, "Indigenous Sovereignty and the Crisis of Whiteness in Alexis Wright's *Carpentaria,*" *Australian Literary Studies* 25.4 (November 2010): 85.

[13] Kenneth Gelder & Paul Salzman, *After the Celebration: Australian Fiction 1989–2007* (Carlton, Victoria: Melbourne U P, 2009): 92.

By seeing the land as a fixed locality, rather than as part of a dynamic trans-local process, the white governance of the town of Desperance has doomed itself to such disasters.

Carpentaria looks to the overwhelming force and power of the environment as a potential source for unification between different communities. In the final chapter, the town is united as both white and black people flee from the ravaging effects of the cyclone. When faced with an emergency, Western science and indigenous ontology find themselves in accord: "The Bureau of Meteorology had called and translated the message from the ancestral spirits" (466). Wright here alludes to an integration that has occurred between the two cultures, for the majority of the Pricklebush evacuate the town alongside the white Uptown folk. She therefore suggests that only certain elders have maintained a connection with the land and an understanding of its movements, and that indigenous Australians are no less susceptible to the alienating distractions of modern life. Many in the Pricklebush depend on the information provided by Uptown, rather than having the ability to independently assess the situation themselves. This is illustrated by the refusal of a minor character, Moochie, to panic during the evacuation. He says: "It is going to go around the town like the last time they got us evacuating for nothing and we should have stayed there if you ask me" (468). This stands in contrast to the wisdom espoused by the elder, Joseph Midnight. When asked how long it will take before the cyclone arrives, Midnight says: "Listen to the ocean. Soon. *Warawara yanja ngawu ninya lajib*" (470).

The insertion of minor characters such as Moochie is important, for it guards against an over-exoticization of the indigenous figure into an all-knowing, magical being. The knowledge held by the elders is exceptional, to both white and black sides of Desperance. While Adam Shoemaker has rightly determined that Wright's novel and non-fictional work show an "ultimate transformational positivism,"[14] it is on the level of the secondary and often walk-in characters that we glimpse the possibility of eventual reconciliation between the two sides. Wright shows the border between white and black Australia to be porous, capable of generating its own fusion of cultural traits. The frontier in her novel is not simply a space of conflict between two irreconcilable cultures, but a place of creative possibility where modern tech-

---

[14] Adam Shoemaker, "Hard Dreams and Indigenous Worlds in Australia's North," *Hecate* 34.1 (2008): 60.

nology integrates itself into traditional indigenous life-styles, and where indigenous culture can diffuse into and inform the science of the West.

Translocality and the Dreaming

The translocations that occur in localized systems over time can be seen by a very simple example – Wright's explicit use of the term 'the Dreaming' in her novel. Describing Mozzie Fishman's convoy of pilgrims, she writes:

> The spiritual Dreaming track of the ceremony in which they were all involved, moved along the most isolated back roads, across the landscape, through almost every desert in the continent. (124)

Wright uses 'the Dreaming' to conjure up a sense of the ancient folklore and traditions which permeate the land. By following the Dreaming, Mozzie and his men are given access to a primordial sense of community that pre-dates white settlement and the modern Australian nation. However, upon closer examination the use of this term to refer to an indigenous concept reveals the shadowy borders of identity-politics.

First of all, the term itself is a mistranslation. The difficulties of the phrase 'the Dreaming' and its translation into English both as a concept and as a collective term were examined in detail by Patrick Wolfe in a 1991 essay.[15] Wolfe traces the genealogy of this term back to the English anthropologists who initially wrote about Aboriginal tribes in Australia. He writes:

> That the Dreaming complex was an invention of the anthropologists' own culture can be seen from the extraordinary success it enjoyed once it had been coined in the ethnography of Frank Gillen. Indeed, before Gillen's phrase was even introduced, it had been advertised in advance by an Englishman, Baldwin Spencer, who spoke no Koori language, as "aptly" and "appropriately" rendered from the aboriginal. (199)

The metaphor of 'the Dreaming' to refer to Aboriginal ontology was therefore coined with an inherently eurocentric bias. Its initial conception betrayed a dismissive attitude towards indigenous beliefs, relegating their very specific philosophy and conception of the world into the nebulous world of dreams.

---

[15] Patrick Wolfe, "On Being Woken Up: The Dreamtime in Anthropology and in Australian Settler Culture," *Comparative Studies in Society and History* 33.2 (April 1991): 197–224.

Secondly, the concept of 'the Dreaming' is a difficult one to grasp in English. This is a result of its mistranslation as a catch-all phrase that attempts to convey many different aspects of indigenous cultural practice. The Dreaming is supposed to encapsulate an indigenous world-view regarding our relationship with time, history, and religion. Trying to describe the Dreaming, the writer Robyn Davidson says:

> No matter how much I read about the Dreaming, the confidence that I understand it never quite takes root in my mind. To me it is on a par with, say, quantum mechanics, or string theory – ideas you think you grasp until you have to explain them… One could say that the Dreaming is a spiritual realm which saturates the visible world with meaning; that it is the matrix of being; that it was the time of creation; that it is a parallel universe which may be contacted via the ritual performance of song, dance and painting; that it is a network of stories of mythological heroes – the forerunners and creators of contemporary man.[16]

Here we come up against the limitations of language and its cultural specificity. The English language does not yet have the vocabulary to describe the complex ontological concepts that shape the Dreaming.

Thirdly, and finally, the metaphor of 'the Dreaming' has been reclaimed by indigenous Australians and has coalesced into a legitimate term, used to celebrate their unique culture. While discussing her motivations for writing *Carpentaria*, Wright has said:

> I wanted to examine how memory is being recreated to challenge the warped creativity of negativity, and somehow becomes a contemporary continuation of the Dreaming story.[17]

The Dreaming pervades Wright's novel. She opens with the focus not on any human character but on the Rainbow Serpent, a spiritual ancestor whose initial journey across the land explains the geographical topography that we see today (1). Because of their knowledge of the stories of the Dreaming, indigenous characters are sensitive to the past and history in a manner that others, such as the Uptown folk, are not. We are told:

> In these times it was assumed that any outsider to these dreams would never see the stones of Desperance, if he carried a different under-

[16] Robyn Davidson, *No Fixed Address: Nomads and the Fate of the Planet* (Melbourne: Black, 2006): 14.

[17] Alexis Wright, "On Writing *Carpentaria*," *Heat* 13 (Autumn 2007): 82.

standing of worldly matters originating from ancient times elsewhere. The outsider to these dreams saw only open spaces and flat lands. (59)

While the Uptown folk sees the land as an inert object, ready for appropriation and development, the Pricklebush perceive it as a living creature that changes, adapts, and grows along with the men who live upon it.

Wright's decision to call the path that Mozzie's convoy follows 'the spiritual Dreaming track' is a re-appropriation of what was, initially, a foreign term to indigenous Australians. It reveals an awareness of her audience and of the need to use terms familiar to them in order to educate them in the ways of indigenous culture. But Wright's use of the Dreaming also serves as a reminder of the integration that occurs between cultures within the translocal. She speaks not only as an indigenous Australian but also an English-speaking Australian and the inheritor of both the indigenous and the white-settler culture that has formed the Australian nation. As Wolfe has noted,

> Kooris' submission to anthropological language was the result of invasion rather than of cultural selection. With the spread of settlement, settler, and Koori discourses merged. (216)

His criticism of the use of the phrase 'the Dreaming' is directed at the amorphous and indefinite nature of the term. As he puts it,

> The claim that the Dreaming expressed the sacred was a contradiction in terms: Rather than a way of talking about the sacred, the Dreaming provided a way of *not* talking about it. (218)

In Wright's novel, the Dreaming is depicted as the ontological fabric which textures all events, from both Uptown and the Pricklebush. Wright seizes the opportunity to define the Dreaming for her audience, and demonstrate the many ways in which it can operate.

Wright proposes the Dreaming as a means by which to recognize and manage the paradoxes created by globalization. Contained in the Dreaming is an acknowledgement of motion and change, of the importance of networks and of interconnectedness between people. The amorphousness of the term, which made it ineffective as a means of accurately describing indigenous culture in the past, now makes it useful as a means of showing the relevance of indigenous culture to the present. Wright shows us how the Dreaming has the flexibility to incorporate the histories and narratives of non-indigenous cultures when the foreigner, Elias Smith, arrives in Desperance. Elias emerges from the sea, an amnesiac with no recollection of his actual identity or of how he came to be in the water (75). Described variously as "a very strange white man" (77), a "white-haired man" (80), and having "ironic Slavic eyes" (63), Elias is a blank slate on which the inhabitants of Desperance can project their greatest hopes and fears. Despite his overt status as a foreigner, his story is incorporated easily into the Dreaming. The narrator tells us:

> This was the story about Elias Smith which was later put alongside the Dreamtime by the keepers of the Law to explain what happened once upon a time with those dry claypans sitting quietly out yonder there for anybody to look at, and wonder about what was happening to the world, and to be happy knowing at least this was paradise on earth, and why would anyone want to live anywhere else. (54–55)

As the accelerated processes of globalization continue to reveal the limitations of the nation and nationalism, Wright suggests the Dreaming may be a flexible framework that is capable of incorporating various discourses of identity and belonging. It shows us how the translocal can absorb foreign influences and reconceptualize them to assert the cultural specificity of a distinctive locale.

Collapsed Time, Translocality, Transnational Style

Alexis Wright has said that she wanted to show 'collapsed time' in *Carpentaria*.[18] She associates a *longue dureé* or deep-time perspective with the indigenous people of Australia, arguing that their oral culture and the continuing importance of myths and traditions in their lives provides an important counterpoint to the presentism of the contemporary world. This collapse of time can be seen as a defiant critique of the Darwinian-influenced belief that indigenous cultures were at more primitive stages of development than European cultures. A popular Victorian myth was the belief that indigenous Australians represented an earlier form of mankind, a myth that continues to influence the contemporary framing of indigenous culture. This attitude is perhaps best summed up by the anthropologist Sir Baldwin Spencer's preface to his 1927 book *The Arunta*. Not only was the tagline for his book 'The Stone Age People' but he opened it by saying:

---

[18] Alexis Wright & Kerry O'Brien, "Extended Interview with Miles Franklin Winner Alexis Wright," Australian Broadcasting Corporation (21 June 2007).

> Australia is the present home and refuge of creatures, often crude and
> quaint, that have elsewhere passed away and given place to higher
> forms. [...] It has been possible to study in Australia human beings
> that still remain on the culture level of men of the Stone Age.[19]

Wright's stated purpose in depicting a collapsed time is to re-insert an indigenous temporality into Australian history. The artificial severing of Australia's
history is particularly evident from the way in which the initial British settlers
described Australia as a *terra nullius*, an empty land. As Maureen Perkins has
observed, nineteenth-century representations of indigenous peoples perpetuated the myth that Indigenous culture had no temporal awareness or vocabulary to describe time.[20] Their supposed ignorance of temporality was given
as a further example of the primitive beliefs and underdeveloped culture of
Australia's indigenous inhabitants. Perkins also notes: "Time was a means of
imposing order on 'disorder', and the colonial experience involved temporal
domination as much as territorial control."[21] Wright's novel shatters these
myths by constantly drawing our attention to the way in which members of
the Pricklebush are capable of relating present-day events to deeper layers of
temporality and history.

Wright acknowledges the importance of oral culture and suggests that it
may be inherently more suited to conceptualizing the cumulative transformations that occur within the translocal. When Normal Phantom sets out to return the body of his friend Elias to the home of the gropers, a spiritual location, we are told that: "Norm would start rowing again in the middle of the
night, navigating by his memorised map, following the star of the fish" (241).
Normal's knowledge is memorized rather than written down. His act of recollection immediately collapses the time between the past and present, for
Normal's ancient knowledge does not exist as an artefact or historical remnant separate from him, but must emerge from him in a visceral manner.

The primary difference between a written culture and an oral culture is that
the act of writing something down fixes it immediately in a certain period and
place. The method of transmitting knowledge in an oral culture, that of one
person re-telling a story to another one, allows the information to be per-

---

[19] Sir Baldwin Spencer & Francis James Gillen, *The Arunta: A Study of a Stone Age
People* (London: Macmillan, 1927): vii.

[20] Maureen Perkins, "Timeless Cultures: The 'Dreamtime' as Colonial Discourse,"
Time & Society 7.2–3 (September 1998): 335–51.

[21] Perkins, "Timeless Cultures: The 'Dreamtime' as Colonial Discourse," 349.

sonalized, adapted, and made relevant to the time in which it is being re-told. We see the importance of this oral transmission when Normal's son, Will Phantom, sets off on his own sea journey to rescue his wife and child. Joseph Midnight knows that they have been taken to a secret island by the transnational mining company. He teaches Will a song which contains the directions to the island, but this knowledge seems to emerge spontaneously from Midnight:

> Old man Midnight remembered a ceremony he had never performed in his life before, and now, to his utter astonishment, he passed it on to Will. (375)

It is suggested that this knowledge is encoded in his body, vibrant and relevant in a manner that knowledge preserved in ancient texts is not:

> He went on and on, fully believing he was singing in the right sequence hundreds of places in a journey to a place at least a thousand kilometres away. (375)

Within the collapsed time of the novel, Wright seeks to create "a novel capable of embracing all times."[22] This concept of 'all times' recognizes the heterogeneity of Australia's multicultural composition and the fact that different ethnic or cultural groups in Australia have different versions of history. With the concept of 'all times', Wright in effect splinters the unitary, linear time-line of history preferred by nations. In the case of Australia, this is the narrative of white settlement on an empty and untamed continent. Indeed, the epigraph of her novel opens with the line: "A nation chants, *but we know your story already*" (1). But the first chapter quickly dispels the notion that the real stories have been told. We are told:

> after the mining stopped, neither Normal Phantom and his family, nor his family's relations, past or present, rated a mention in the official version of the region's history. There was no tangible evidence of their existence. (10)

Carpentaria is one version of a previously unwritten and unrecorded history, but it gestures towards other narratives that are out there, waiting to be incorporated into the official body of Australian national discourse.

Wright expands the concept of Australian nationality, not only by giving indigenous culture a primacy often denied it by white Australian discourse,

---

[22] Wright, "On Writing *Carpentaria*," 81.

but by integrating techniques garnered from Latin American writers. In order
to represent collapsed time, Wright looks beyond the canon of Australian literature and turns to the techniques of a well-documented transnational genre –
magical realism. The latter is a genre (or, rather, mode) that has been changed
dramatically through translocations. In its initial translocation it moved from
being a German art movement in the 1920s to a Latin American literary
movement in the 1960s. In its latest incarnation it has become a popular mode
in English literature. Wright's use of magical realism gives indigenous Australians the potential for greater political agency by aligning them with indigenous people worldwide. Tellingly, Wright has written that "the stories of
Aboriginal people are similar to those of South America, Europe, Africa,
Asia, or India."[23] By emphasizing the affinities that indigenous Australian
culture shares with other traditional cultures across the globe, Wright suggests
that an indigenous world-view, encapsulated here by the Dreaming, may be a
useful means of reconciling our present life with past cultures.

As Graham Huggan reminds us, translocality is also a relocalization:

> The focus on the translocal or, perhaps better, the *relocalized* represen-
> tational and administrative mechanisms of Orientalism have produced
> some powerful anti-authoritarian scholarship: in Japan and Latin
> America, for instance, and in many regions of the formerly colonised
> world.[24]

Carpentaria re-localizes us by re-imagining Australia within the wider world.
It re-inserts indigenous culture into the narrative of modern Australia, showing us how we continue to perpetuate Western colonial stereotypes by asso-
ciating indigenous culture with past times. It reminds us that, although we
struggle with how to deal with the paradoxes of the modern world, the modernist break with the past is only one of a series of major cultural shifts that
have occurred throughout world history. The world-view posited by Wright in
this novel accords with that of world-literature theorists such as Wai Chee
Dimock, who writes that,

> finally, the concept of a global civil society, by its very nature, invites
> us to think of the planet as a plausible whole, a whole that, I suggest,
> needs to be mapped along the temporal axis as well as the spatial, its

---

[23] Wright, "On Writing *Carpentaria*," 88.

[24] Graham Huggan, "(Not) Reading Orientalism," *Research in African Literatures*
36.3 (Fall 2005): 126.

membership open not only to contemporaries but also to those centuries apart.[25]

The constant change demanded by modern life is a huge break from the routines and rhythms of settled, agrarian cultures. But it was an accepted way of life for nomadic people in various cultural contexts. Recognizing translocations provide us with an opportunity to find deeper connections between the past and present, and to recognize the parallels that can be drawn between our contemporary lives and those of different cultures across the globe.

WORKS CITED

Bal, Mieke. *Travelling Concepts in the Humanities: A Rough Guide* (Toronto: U of Toronto P, 2002).

Brennan, Timothy. "From Development to Globalisation: Postcolonial Studies and Globalisation Theory," in *The Cambridge Companion to Postcolonial Literary Studies*, ed. Neil Lazarus (Cambridge & New York: Cambridge UP, 2004): 120–38.

Brewster, Anne. "Indigenous Sovereignty and the Crisis of Whiteness in Alexis Wright's *Carpentaria*," *Australian Literary Studies* 25.4 (November 2010): 85–100.

Davidson, Robyn. *No Fixed Address: Nomads and the Fate of the Planet* (Melbourne: Black, 2006).

Dimock, Wai Chee. *Through Other Continents: American Literature across Deep Time* (Princeton NJ: Princeton UP, 2006).

Dirlik, Arif. "Performing the World: Reality and Representation in the Making of World Histor(ies)," *Journal of World History* 16.4 (December 2005): 391–410.

Gelder, Kenneth, & Paul Salzman. *After the Celebration: Australian Fiction 1989–2007* (Carlton, Victoria: Melbourne UP, 2009).

Gunew, Sneja. *Haunted Nations: The Colonial Dimensions of Multiculturalisms* (London: Routledge, 2004).

Hage, Ghassan. *White Nation: Fantasies of White Supremacy in a Multicultural Society* (Sydney: Pluto, 1998).

Herbert, Xavier. *Capricornia*, intro. Mudrooroo Nyoongah (1938; Imprint Classics 1; North Ryde, NSW: Angus & Robertson, 1990).

Huggan, Graham. "(Not) Reading Orientalism," *Research in African Literatures* 36.3 (Fall 2005): 124–37.

---

[25] Wai Chee Dimock, *Through Other Continents: American Literature across Deep Time* (Princeton NJ: Princeton UP, 2006): 5.

Perkins, Maureen. "Timeless Cultures: The 'Dreamtime' as Colonial Discourse," *Time & Society* 7.2–3 (September 1998): 335–51.

Sharrad, Paul. "Beyond Capricornia: Ambiguous Promise in Alexis Wright," *Australian Literary Studies* 24.1 (April 2009): 52–65.

Shoemaker, Adam. "Hard Dreams and Indigenous Worlds in Australia's North," *Hecate* 34.1 (2008): 55–64.

Sommer, Roy. "No Size Fits All: Postcolonial Ways of Seeing in the 21st Century," paper presented at the Postcolonial Translocations: Twentieth Annual GNEL/ASNEL Conference, University of Münster, 23 May 2009.

Spencer, Sir Baldwin, & Francis James Gillen. *The Arunta: A Study of a Stone Age People* (London: Macmillan, 1927).

Wolfe, Patrick. "On Being Woken Up: The Dreamtime in Anthropology and in Australian Settler Culture," *Comparative Studies in Society and History* 33.2 (April 1991): 197–224.

Wright, Alexis. *Carpentaria* (Artarmon, NSW: Giramondo, 2006).

——. "On the Question of Fear," in *Tolerance, Prejudice and Fear: Sydney Pen Voices, the 3 Writers Project*, Gideon Haigh, Cristos Tsiolkas & Alexis Wright (Crows Nest, Victoria: Allen & Unwin, 2008).

——. "On Writing *Carpentaria*," *Heat* 13 (Autumn 2007): 79–95.

——, & Kerry O'Brien. "Extended Interview with Miles Franklin Winner Alexis Wright," Australian Broadcasting Corporation (21 June 2007), http://www.abc.net.au/7.30/content/2007/s1958553.htm (accessed 8 February 2009).

⌘

"We die only once, and for such a long time"

—Approaching Trauma through Translocation
in Chris Abani's *Song for Night*[1]

DARIA TUNCA

I don't know how long I die. But I think I die for very very long time.[2]

M
ANY SCHOLARS IN THE FIELD OF POSTCOLONIAL STUDIES are
familiar with the work of Chris Abani, an author of Nigerian and
English parentage now living in the USA. Even though his
poetic writing style and emotional subtlety enjoy wide recognition, in-depth
analyses of his texts are still relatively few. This can, of course, partly be explained by the fact that his major novels and collections of poetry have only
been published recently. However, it seems that this scarcity of critical studies
can also be traced to the elusiveness of Abani's art, by which I mean that his
works strongly resist textbook postcolonial approaches – theories which, despite their limitations, still offer interpretative avenues into much contemporary African literature of the diaspora. This is not to say that the author's
books do not provide reflections on the postcolonial condition and its inherent
hybridity or, in the current context of globalization, on adjacent themes such
as metropolitan cosmopolitanism. These cross-cultural currents arguably form

---

[1] I would like to express my gratitude to Prof. Bénédicte Ledent for her invaluable
guidance and support through the multiple drafts of this article. I also wish to extend
my appreciation to the participants in the "Translation and Translocation" session held
at the ASNEL conference in Münster in May 2009, during which this article was first
delivered – several of the panellists' helpful suggestions have found their way into the
final version of this essay.
[2] Ken Saro–Wiwa, *Sozaboy* (1985; New York: Longman, 1994): 113.

the background to his prose and poetry, and their role has been cogently underlined in existing examinations of his writing. However, while Abani himself has respectfully acknowledged the usefulness of such culturally oriented approaches, he has also stated that the principal focus of his works – his novels in particular – lies elsewhere: namely, in their exploration of "transformation."[3]

The entire body of Abani's fiction is indeed informed by changes in physical and emotional states, and, more generally, his texts are replete with crossings of concrete and abstract frontiers of all kinds. It therefore comes as no surprise that an array of concepts beginning with the prefix 'trans-' could be used to capture the gist of his narratives and, in some cases, offer interpretative leads. For instance, 'transgendering' provides one of the main motifs in *The Virgin of Flames*,[4] which features a cross-dressing artist living in Los Angeles; 'transgression' perhaps best characterizes the protagonists' overstepping of moral boundaries in *Becoming Abigail*,[5] the account of an adolescent Nigerian girl forced to emigrate to London; and 'translocation', as I will argue in the course of this essay, constitutes a pivotal paradigm in *Song For Night*,[6] the story of a child soldier, set during the final days of the Biafran war, the civil conflict that divided Nigeria between 1967 and 1970.

The prefix 'trans-' evidently finds its roots in Latin, and etymologically means 'across', 'over', or 'through'. Interestingly, an analogous notion occupies a central position in the broader theoretical framework in which I wish to situate my examination of Abani's war novella: that of trauma studies, an area of investigation which has, among other things, dissected the mechanisms of working *through* – that is, of progressively, and often only partially, overcoming terrifying ordeals such as genocide. In its early stages, this critical movement mainly concerned itself with the repercussions and representations of the Holocaust, but in recent years its methods have been repeatedly applied to postcolonial sources.[7] This encounter has encouraged scholars to develop a

---

[3] Chris Abani, reading held in the context of the "Incroci di Civiltà" series, Libreria Mondadori, Venice, Italy (29 March 2008).

[4] Chris Abani, *The Virgin of Flames* (New York: Penguin, 2007).

[5] Chris Abani, *Becoming Abigail* (New York: Akashic, 2006).

[6] Chris Abani, *Song for Night* (New York: Akashic, 2007). All page references will be given in the text.

[7] The problems that may potentially arise from the application of a set of theories with a largely 'Western' cultural anchorage to postcolonial texts have been debated

hermeneutics better suited to the exploration of psychologically devastating experiences occurring either across civilizations or in non-Western cultural contexts.

A methodology inspired by trauma studies seems particularly relevant to the analysis of Abani's *Song for Night*, if only because the experiences recounted by the main character and narrator of the novella, a fifteen-year-old boy called My Luck, may be called 'traumatic' in the most widely accepted sense of the term. The many atrocities that he, both a victim and a perpetrator, either witnesses or participates in, include the murder of his Igbo mother at the hands of Hausa soldiers, his accidental shooting of a seven-year-old girl, and his frenzied killing of a group of old women about to eat a dead baby. These accumulated scenes of intense violence overpower the reader and have caused some discomfort in reviewers,[8] but Abani's hyperbolic strategy is by no means gratuitous, as it serves the ultimate purpose of his novella: exploring man's capacity to cross moral boundaries in extreme situations. For the writer, facing the unbearable, including taboo subjects such as cannibalism, is necessary to initiate a communal healing process, whether in Nigeria or elsewhere. The emphasis placed on the moral aspects of human experience clearly appears in the following extract from an interview, in which the author is asked to comment on the effects of the Biafran war:

---

within the new movement of 'postcolonial trauma studies' itself – see, for example, Stef Craps & Gert Buelens, "Introduction: Postcolonial Trauma Novels," *Studies in the Novel* 40.1–2 (Spring–Summer 2008): 2–3, and Michael Rothberg, "Decolonizing Trauma Studies: A Response," *Studies in the Novel* 40.1–2 (Spring–Summer 2008): 227–29. While one should heed cultural generalizations, I concur with Michael Rothberg that a "tendency toward hyper-particularism" ("Decolonizing Trauma Studies," 228) whereby the application of theoretical models would be restricted to their contexts of origin may be equally counterproductive.

[8] For instance, Malcolm Knox lists some of the traumatizing occurrences recounted in the opening pages of the book and notes:

> Such horrors have certainly befallen young soldiers in African wars, though it is unlikely that they have all happened to one. It is, of course, the novelist's liberty to concentrate many events into one life but I couldn't help asking why. Why is Abani piling all the horrors of several lives into one? What is the desired effect?

—Knox, "Haunted by the Ghosts in a Child Soldier's Life," *Sydney Morning Herald* (8 November 2008), www.smh.com.au/articles/2008/11/07/1225561105879.html (accessed 5 April 2010).

> In every war there is cannibalism, and nobody talks about it. One of
> the most amazing things that has emerged recently is tales of the con-
> centration camps in Germany, and of how people would eat each other
> and not talk about it afterwards.
>
> For me there is no subject, if we are to regain any kind of internal
> moral landscape, there can be nothing that is not [to] be confronted.[9]

This mention of the horrors of Nazi Germany in the context of a discussion of
the Biafran war is not unique, but the parallel is nonetheless striking.[10] Such
pronouncements undeniably testify to the cross-cultural, or indeed universalist, nature of Abani's writerly commitment[11] – a humanistic world-view
which aligns him with followers of postcolonial trauma theory, and perhaps
indicates that he may share more concerns with this movement than African
authors such as Chinua Achebe or Chimamanda Ngozi Adichie, who place
greater emphasis on the divisive character of individual and collective geo-
cultural specificities.

Above all, Abani's statement reminds us that literature has an important
role to play in addressing the subject of trauma. Keenly aware of this, the
writer has stated that one of his main preoccupations since his incarceration as
a political prisoner in Nigeria – a harrowing experience recorded in his collection of poetry *Kalakuta Republic*[12] – has been to "[rebuild] the language
that one can use to approach trauma."[13] For him, the act of working through is

---

[9] Chris Abani, "The Model of African Wars," *Voices Education Project* (nd), http:
//voicesinwartime.org/content/chris-abani (accessed 5 April 2010).

[10] A reference to Nazi Germany is also contained in *Song for Night*, in which the
young protagonist encounters an old man playing a gramophone record of a German
song that the man finds "beautiful" but which is in fact "a long slow lament for the
Aryan race." See Abani, *Song for Night*, 124, 125. Such passages contribute to the
writer's exploration of the concepts of beauty and ugliness – a recurrent topic in
Abani's fiction that would deserve to be examined in more detail.

[11] For a reflection on the link between the Holocaust and the "universality of the
human experience" in Abani's work, see Francesca Giommi, "Negotiating Freedom on
Scarred Bodies: Chris Abani's Novellas," in *Experiences of Freedom in Postcolonial
Literatures and Cultures*, ed. Annalisa Oboe & Shaul Bassi (Abingdon & New York:
Routledge, 2011): 180.

[12] Abani, *Kalakuta Republic* (London: Saqi, 2000).

[13] Chris Abani, in Kevin Rabalais, "The Clarity of Distance," *Australian* (30 August
2008),   www.theaustralian.com.au/news/arts/the-clarity-of-distance/story-e6frg8n6-
1111117306592 (accessed 5 April 2010).

closely connected to that of searching for words to depict the suffering inflicted by man on his own kind. His artistic challenge therefore resides in finding the narrative and stylistic techniques best suited to broaching the delicate issue of trauma, for, as the author himself has said, "The art is never about what you write about. The art is about how you write about what you write about."[14]

Whether there are appropriate ways of writing about the 'unspeakable' has been a subject of contention since at least the Second World War and Theodor Adorno's famous statement that "to write poetry after Auschwitz is barbaric."[15] More recently, practitioners of trauma studies have turned their attention to the ethical challenges posed to writers, filmmakers, and historians engaged in describing the atrocities endured by others. The work of Dominick LaCapra, in particular, provides an illuminating examination of the potential difficulties faced by "secondary witnesses" in their documentation of "limit events." In his seminal book *Writing History, Writing Trauma*, LaCapra argues that one's response to another person's or people's traumatic experience should be marked by a form of "empathic unsettlement."[16] Empathy, the author insists, "should not be conflated with unchecked identification, vicarious experience, and unchecked victimage,"[17] but "should rather be understood in terms of an affective relation, rapport, or bond with the other recognized and respected as other."[18] LaCapra thereby denounces the appropriation of traumatic experiences by those recording them; further, he is adamant that the accounts of extreme events and their aftermath should not serve as excuses to

---

[14] Chris Abani, Interview by Carlye Archibeque, *Poetix* (2005), http://poetix.net /abani.htm (accessed 5 April 2010).

[15] Theodor Adorno, "Cultural Criticism and Society," in Adorno, *Prisms*, tr. Samuel Weber & Shierry Weber ("Kulturkritik und Gesellschaft," 1951; Cambridge MA: MIT Press, 1981): 34. However, Adorno later acknowledged that "perennial suffering has as much right to expression as the tortured have to scream." Adorno, *Negative Dialectics*, tr. E.B. Ashton (*Negative Dialektik*, 1966; New York: Continuum, 1973): 362.

[16] Dominick LaCapra, *Writing History, Writing Trauma* (Baltimore MD: Johns Hopkins UP, 2001). The phrases 'secondary witnesses', 'limit events', and 'empathic unsettlement' are used throughout the study.

[17] LaCapra, *Writing History, Writing Trauma*, 40.

[18] *Writing History, Writing Trauma*, 212–13.

reinforce the readers' or viewers' sense of security. Thus, he maintains, narratives of trauma should remain unsettling to the very end.[19]

In spite of potentially normative undertones, LaCapra's theory provides valuable guiding principles. In the present essay, I will use the concept of 'empathic unsettlement' as a critical instrument to assess Abani's *Song for Night* and suggest that the novella can be termed a successful exploration of trauma from beginning to end. Crucially, the ways in which the writer achieves this are subtle and thus easily missed, for Abani *does* employ a number of techniques traditionally associated with "surrogate victimage"[20] or pathos, such as first-person interior monologue or the appeal to readers' emotions. Nevertheless, the originality of his writing largely resides in his unpredictable use of these elements to introduce provocative questionings and to present an original artistic vision. I will be arguing that, in *Song for Night*, one such element used creatively is the concept of translocation, which not only refers to a movement from one place – whether abstract or concrete – to another, but may simultaneously denote a single site of transition and change: i.e. a 'trans-location'.[21] In other words, my main argument will rely on the idea that the interplay between these two meanings of 'translocation' can help us understand Abani's fictional strategy, more particularly as it relates to the exploration of the protagonist's trauma.

In what follows, I will first of all underline the thematic ubiquity of translocation in the novella, and then endeavour to show how the book, by revealing the character's apparent movement in space to have been a 'trans-location' all along, achieves 'empathic unsettlement'. More precisely, I will try to demonstrate that Abani's substitution of one understanding of translocation

---

[19] LaCapra is critical of what he perceives as the impropriety of "harmonizing narratives that provid[e] the reader or viewer with an unwarranted sense of spiritual lift" (*Writing History, Writing Trauma*, 14). In his discussion, the author suggests, for instance, that the ending of Steven Spielberg's *Schindler's List* turns the film into such a "harmonizing" or "redemptive" narrative.

[20] *Writing History, Writing Trauma*, 40.

[21] I owe this distinction to the editors of the present volume, who suggested a somewhat similar double definition in the call for papers for the 2009 ASNEL conference. For the purpose of clarity, my use of 'translocation' will henceforth refer to the term in its double meaning; 'translocation as a single site' will be rendered with the hyphenated spelling 'trans-location', while translocation as the transfer from one locale to the next will be designated by the terms 'translocation-as-movement' or 'translocation-as-journey'.

for the other acts as a distancing device, either to prevent "unchecked identification" with the hero on the reader's part or to bypass the danger of providing a "harmonizing narrative." The writer's skilful and versatile use of translocation allows him to lay the foundation for his examination of the same concept in another, more abstract form: the passage from traumatic experience to language, a link touched upon earlier in this essay in relation to Abani's conception of writing as a way of articulating trauma. By way of conclusion, I will briefly comment on how the author's representation of trauma in *Song for Night* may be understood in the context of his entire artistic project.

Translocation is a pervasive motif in Abani's novella, starting with its two epigraphs. Taking as a point of departure a narrower, culturally related avatar of the concept (arguably the default mode in postcolonial studies), one may rapidly conclude that *Song for Night*'s paratextual elements situate this work at a cross-cultural crossroads. Indeed, while the story is that of a young soldier during the Biafran war, neither of the introductory quotations belongs to the African literary tradition. Interestingly, however, neither of the epigraphs is borrowed from the canon of the former British imperial centre, either, since the first is from a work by the seventeenth-century French playwright Molière, while the second comes from a book by the controversial twentieth-century US-Peruvian author Carlos Castaneda.[22] This eclectic literary genealogy may leave postcolonial critics somewhat puzzled, which only emphasizes the need for them to discard traditional counter-discursive approaches – or even temporarily leave aside political and cultural considerations altogether – and envisage a more open reading of these excerpts and of the novel at large.

---

[22] The extract is part of an epigraph cited by Castaneda (in both Spanish and English) in one of his works, and attributed to the Amerindian shaman Don Juan Matus. See Carlos Castaneda, *The Teachings of Don Juan: A Yaqui Way of Knowledge* (1969; Berkeley & Los Angeles: U of California P, 1998): xx. It is now widely accepted that Don Juan was in fact a fictional figure created by Castaneda in his 1969 book. The questions surrounding the frontier between fact and fiction raised in the figure of Don Juan may partly have motivated Abani's choice of this quotation for, as will shortly become apparent, the blurring between the realms of reality and illusion plays a central role in *Song for Night*. For an overview of the controversy surrounding Castaneda and his work, see, for example, Robert Marshall, "The Dark Legacy of Carlos Castaneda," *salon.com* (4 April 2007), www.salon.com/books/feature/2007/04/12/castaneda (accessed 5 April 2010).

A brief examination of the quotations' metaphoric qualities reveals that both passages deal with travelling.[23] The extract from Castaneda's work reads "on any path that may have heart. There I travel," while the passage from Molière, borrowed for the title of this essay, reflects on the ultimate journey: i.e. death. Importantly, the English version of Molière's statement, unlike the French original,[24] is ambiguous, since dying 'for a long time' can mean either that the state of death is eternal (the French playwright's actual suggestion) or that the process of dying is very slow.[25] This possible 'misreading' of Molière's assertion provides one of the keys to the interpretation of Abani's novella, for, as I will now briefly show, the book's narrative strategy rests largely on the idea that death can be regarded as a long journey.

Song for Night opens as My Luck, who has been working as a mine diffuser for three years, regains consciousness after an explosion and is unable to locate his fighting unit. The narrative proceeds as follows:

> The rule of thumb is that if you hear the explosion, you survived the blast. [...] I heard the click and I heard the explosion even though I was lifted into the air. [...] When I came to, everyone was gone. They must have thought I was dead and so set off without me [...]. Stupid fools. Wait until I catch up with them. (22)

The average reader is unlikely to question the narrator's statement, and will most probably assume that, since My Luck has "hear[d] the explosion," he has really "survived the blast." A greater level of attentiveness is required to notice that the logic of this argument is fundamentally flawed, for the young soldiers cannot possibly know whether those who died did not hear the explosion too. And, indeed, as the story progresses and one strange occurrence follows on from another, the suspicion gradually dawns that My Luck might

---

[23] Proponents of culturally based approaches may legitimately argue that diasporic authors are more likely than other writers to use the theme of travelling as a metaphor, considering that displacement is at the heart of their condition. However, my suggestion will be that the notion of travelling as it appears here seems to have more markedly metaphysical undertones than it does in most diasporic writing.

[24] "On ne meurt qu'une fois, et c'est pour si longtemps !" See Molière, *Le Dépit amoureux* (1656), *Œuvres de Molière* 1, ed. Eugène Despois (Paris: Hachette, 1873): Act V, Scene 4.

[25] This interpretation may be assigned to my epigraph from Saro–Wiwa's *Sozaboy*. It should nevertheless be noted that, in Saro–Wiwa's novel, the narrator is not literally dying but falling asleep while wounded.

be hallucinating and, at the very end of the novella, the reader acquires the certainty that the narrator's search for his lost comrades, depicted throughout the story, was in fact an imaginary march towards death. Of course, the use of the journey to conceptualize the passage into death is not unique to Abani. It brings to mind sources as varied as the river Styx in Greek mythology,[26] the Bible's twenty-third psalm, and the hero's trip to "Deads' Town" in Amos Tutuola's *The Palm-Wine Drinkard*.[27] At this point, one might easily dismiss Abani's narrative as yet another variation on a well-known trope, if not for the fact that the writer defies expectations by narrating a journey which unsuspecting readers do not straight away identify as being anything but physical. What one initially assumes to be a movement in space turns out to be an experience situated at a single 'trans-location': the boundary between life and death. In other words, Abani's novella problematizes the concept of translocation-as-journey in order to explore the many forces at work in the transitions between different realms.

One such transition treated in *Song for Night* is the transposition of reality into language. As will gradually become apparent, this transfer may, in a manner similar to death, be perceived both as a figurative translocation-as-movement and as a trans-location: on the one hand, the linguistic articulation of events involves a progressive passage from experience to expression; on the other, the only empirically observable trace of this process is the trans-location in which it is recorded: i.e. the site of language itself. At first glance, the protagonist's journey towards death and his attempt to relate his painful experiences under the author's guiding hand may appear only tenuously linked, but they are in fact two sides of the same coin, for both can be considered as steps in the character's slow coming to terms with trauma. If the former type of translocation – the apparent movement in space – effects My Luck's gradual reconciliation with death,[28] the latter – the articulation of his

---

[26] Significantly, My Luck also encounters a river towards the end of the story. That "the river slowly takes on the metaphorical weight of the Styx" was remarked upon by Nicole Gluckstern ("Shorts," *San Francisco Bay Guardian Online* [25 September 2007], www.sfbg.com/2007/09/25/shorts (accessed 5 April 2010)).

[27] Amos Tutuola, *The Palm-Wine Drinkard* (London: Faber & Faber, 1952).

[28] According to Abani, the narrator eventually "ma[kes] peace with death." See Chris Abani, "Ethics and Narrative: The Human and Other," *Witness* 22 (2009), http://witness.blackmountaininstitute.org/archive/xxii/Witness_XXII-Abani.pdf (accessed 5 April 2010): 172.

ordeal – helps him to probe his psychological wounds. Importantly, however, the novella does not draw a simplistic equation between the victim-cum-perpetrator's voicing of trauma and the act of working through, as might be the case in a "harmonizing narrative" providing a reassuring sense of closure. One way in which the text avoids this pitfall is by means of self-reflexive narrative gestures.

Indeed, from the very beginning, the book draws attention to its own fictional quality. The powerful opening sentences of the novella are a case in point, as they establish that My Luck is mute, and therefore technically unable to address the reader orally as he does: "What you hear is not my voice. I have not spoken in three years" (19). Readers are asked to believe that the words they are 'hearing' are the narrator's 'thoughts', which are further identified as renditions in English of his mental reflections in his Igbo mother tongue: "You are in fact hearing my thoughts in Igbo" (21). Addressees are thus forced to suspend their disbelief and adhere to a parallel reality that does not obey the laws of the 'real' world. The immersion in this alternative universe only reinforces the sense of shock experienced when the reason behind My Luck's muteness is revealed. He reports that, when he was in boot camp, a doctor "severed" his and his comrades' "vocal chords," so that, if one of the young soldiers should be "blown up by a mine," the others would not be scared by their friend's "death screams" (35). But this brutal silencing has not had the intended effect, since the narrator adds that "in the silence of our heads, the screams of those dying around us were louder than if they still had their voices" (35). From the onset, then, the text establishes the existence of two levels of reality: one is an 'objective', outside realm in which the mute hero and his friends cannot communicate verbally with each other and with the world; the other is an inner, imaginary sphere in which My Luck tells his story and can hear his friends' thoughts and feelings. This step back from mimetic realism certainly acts as a safeguard against any 'unchecked identification' on the part of the reader; put differently, one of the ways in which the beginning of the novella achieves 'empathic unsettlement' is by forcing readers to engage with the mechanisms of fictional representation.

In addition to this key metafictional function, the protagonist's inability to speak has deep symbolic significance, too, as it may be said to stand for the metaphorical voicelessness of all casualties of history. Figurative speechlessness is a well-known symbol for political and social oppression in postcolonial studies – as suggested by the famous example of Gayatri Chakravorty

Spivak's "Can the Subaltern Speak?"[29] – but once again Abani's use of a familiar trope goes well beyond the received acceptation of the notion by postcolonial scholars, for his hero's muteness may be perceived as a compelling questioning of the ability assigned to conventional language to express human experience. More than once, My Luck's words fall short of being able to convey the horror of the situation which he vividly summons in his memory. For instance, during the ethnic troubles that lead to the war, he witnesses the brutal killing of his mother while he is hiding in a narrow space in the ceiling, and reports the events – or, rather, fails to describe them – in the following words:

> Below me it happens, it happens that night bright as day, but I cannot name it, those things that happened while I watched, and I cannot speak something that was never in words, speak of things I cannot imagine, could never have seen even as I saw it. (43)

My Luck is unable to appropriately translate into words the traumatic occurrences that his imagination is unable to grasp. The limits of verbal communication are similarly emphasized when the narrator attends to his dying girlfriend Ijeoma after she has been severely mutilated by an explosion:

> She [...] wasn't much more than a bloody torso, lacerated by shrapnel, body parts scattered *in a way that cannot be explained or described.* Instead I read her mind, or her eyes, or something, and understood everything – what she wanted, what she regretted – all of it. (54, my emphasis)

For My Luck, Ijeoma's suffering is unspeakable – he can neither find words to describe her physical state nor communicate with her using the allegedly "crude" (130) sign language that the young soldiers have developed to compensate for their muteness. The only medium that seems capable of connecting the two characters and of leading to some form of comprehension is a spiritual link based on visual contact. This imaginary translation of trauma into impalpable units of meaning involves another (figurative) form of translocation-as-movement, from the visual to the mental realm, and epitomizes the character's constant struggle with language.

---

[29] Gayatri Chakravorty Spivak, "Can the Subaltern Speak?," in *Marxism and the Interpretation of Culture*, ed. Cary Nelson & Lawrence Grossberg (Urbana & Chicago: U of Illinois P, 1988): 271–313.

That My Luck should be unable to capture his experience using traditional
language even in his imaginary narration has wide-ranging ramifications.
While I agree with Francesca Giommi that Abani depicts war as "an experience which [...] can hardly be described or grasped in any human language,"[30] I would also contend that the writer uses My Luck's struggle with
the linguistic medium as a metaphor for the character's vulnerability. Abani,
once asked how his writing had helped him to reconfigure the idea of home,
replied: "For me, home has always existed in language."[31] The fact that the
author expressly denies his hero the privilege of this comfort zone may point
to his wish to emphasize the distress of those who, unlike the artist, cannot
find refuge in words and are forced to wander, fumble in the dark, in search of
other ways of articulating their experience. In *Song for Night*, My Luck's
quest for his lost companions may be viewed as an apt symbol of his sense of
disorientation and of his difficult pursuit of alternative means of expression.
Ironically, while the narrator finds no solace in language, the unspoken modes
of communication that he develops to establish contact with Ijeoma and exchange information with his comrades are transient and destined to disappear,
and they can only be retrieved by readers through the words on the page. This
seems to suggest that, paradoxically, the only hope we have of transcending
the limitations of language lies in language itself, and in its recording in the
literary form. While literature is inherently flawed because it owes its very
existence to the linguistic medium, it is nevertheless an interface – a translocation – that can gesture towards an understanding of the complex, figurative translocation-as-movement that is the transition from reality to language.

The telepathic medium that My Luck shares with Ijeoma is not his only
alternative means of communication. He develops another surrogate language
of sorts, which serves his urge for recovering his traumatic past. This code,
likened to "Braille" (26), takes the form of small crosses that the protagonist
carves on his left forearm to represent all the loved ones that he has lost and,
more disturbingly, all the people that he has enjoyed killing – a collection of
scars that he calls the "map of [his] consciousness" (25). Thus, the narrator's

---

[30] Giommi, "Negotiating Freedom on Scarred Bodies," 181. This article briefly discusses the importance of language in *Song for Night* and in Abani's entire "artistic
enterprise" (181).

[31] Abani made this comment at the EACLALS conference "Try Freedom: Rewriting Rights in/through Postcolonial Cultures."

body is presented as a site of remembrance,[32] but the emphasis on the character's pleasure during some of his own murderous acts prevents any romanticized interpretation of memory. In other words, My Luck's "own personal cemetery" (38) is neither exclusively a record of unjust acts committed against innocent human beings by immoral ones, nor a reminder of the triumph of the virtuous over the despicable. By blurring the lines between innocence and guilt, the author rejects any manichaean approach to his protagonist's personality and, by extension, to the Biafran war, even if the conflict was triggered by the mass killing of Igbos by Hausas. This nuanced position is forcefully illustrated by the rhetorical question that My Luck asks toward the end of the novella: "If we are the great innocents in this war, then where did we learn all the evil we practice?" (143). Abani's thought-provoking treatment of innocence and guilt arguably exposes the flawed nature of all clear-cut judgments and, in doing so, rejects any sentimental approach to the trauma of war.

The subtlety with which the writer invites readers to reflect on his character's response to the harrowing experience of the Biafran conflict has been praised by other critics – among them Louise Bernard, who has saluted the novella's "commit[ment] to an engaged empathy." However, according to Bernard, Abani's narrative "gives way to sentimentality at the very end,"[33] when My Luck is reunited with his dead mother and his voice returns. Even though the conclusion to the novella may indeed elicit an emotional response, an interpretation which reduces the ending to a ploy to bring forth unrestrained empathy on the part of the reader would overlook one of the work's most profound insights. Such an insight, I believe, arises partly from the unexpected clash between the different levels of reality established at the beginning of the narrative. As the story draws to an end and it is unambiguously revealed that the narrator has been dead all along, readers are compelled to realize that the hero's search for his platoon, a quest which they had (at least to some extent) assumed to be a translocation-as-movement situated on the 'objective' level, in fact entirely took place in an imaginary trans-location. Once again, this obligation to re-assign the events recounted in the narrative to the realm of fantasy encourages readers to approach the text critically, as it forces them to

---

[32] See also Giommi, "Negotiating Freedom on Scarred Bodies," 181.

[33] Louise Bernard, "Silent Warrior," *Washington Post* (2 September 2007), www .washingtonpost.com/wp-dyn/content/article/2007/08/30/AR2007083001619.html (accessed 5 April 2010).

acknowledge the deception upon which their emotional involvement with the character has been based.

For those more closely acquainted with Nigerian literature, the sense of distance thereby established may be reinforced by the realization that the ending of the novella reverses the scenario found in the conclusion to Ken Saro–Wiwa's novel *Sozaboy*, in which the hero is mistaken for a ghost by the inhabitants of his village even though he is well and truly alive. Such possible signs of intertextuality, as Stef Craps has argued in another context, may be used by a writer to "signal his historical [...] remove from, and his inevitably mediated mode of access to, the reality he represents."[34] Admittedly, Abani does not explicitly show any willingness to subvert (or even directly address) *Sozaboy*, and it might be further objected that the protagonist of *Song for Night* is nowhere as naive as Mene, the narrator of Saro–Wiwa's tragicomic tale. However, the connections that may be established between the books' inverse narrative patterns inevitably make *Song for Night* enter into dialogue with *Sozaboy*. This comparison is also supported by the eerie echoes between the Molière quotation that opens Abani's novella, and the passage from Saro–Wiwa's text that I have used as my own epigraph. These potential intertextual links may encourage the reader to temporarily disengage from My Luck's personal story and more carefully consider some of the common reflections featured in the two narratives, including the chain of events that led to the devastation of countless young lives during the Biafran war.

Eschewing unrestrained sentimentality, Abani offers his character a poignant but highly ambiguous reunion with his mother. At the end of the journey that has allowed My Luck to "relive and release [his] darkness" (104), his mother hugs him and says: "You are home" (167), upon which the boy's voice returns. The association between the protagonist's homecoming and his symbolic recovery of language seems to be charged with meaning, but it does not lend itself to easy interpretation. On the one hand, the combination may be an indication of the redemptive possibilities of literature: the end of My Luck's story coincides with the end of his wandering, which may suggest that Abani's book has helped the narrator to find a home *through* language, and that the protagonist may now find a sense of belonging *in* language, as the author always has. On the other hand, My Luck's redemption of sorts, his sec-

---

[34] Stef Craps, "Linking Legacies of Loss: Traumatic Histories and Cross-Cultural Empathy in Caryl Phillips's *Higher Ground* and *The Nature of Blood*," *Studies in the Novel* 40.1–2 (Spring–Summer 2008): 200.

ond chance at happiness, as it were, only occurs at the moment that seals his death – which, of course, does not offer a viable solution for the human race.[35] Ultimately, *Song for Night* is perhaps not so much about redemption as it is about "becoming"[36] – that is, about a process which, one day, might allow human beings to become reconciled with, and perhaps move beyond, their own contradictions.

In this essay, I have attempted to unravel the literary strategies that lie at the core of Abani's humanistic project. I have examined various incarnations of translocation in *Song for Night*, particularly those relating to the metaphoric representation of death and to the transposition of reality into language; further, I have tried to underline the pivotal role played by these instances of translocation in the novella's development of distancing devices. What has been holding these diverse interpretative threads together is the concept of, and methodological framework around, trauma, and more specifically the belief that, despite appearances, Abani's narrative maintains a constant equilibrium between eliciting emotional involvement and triggering critical reactions – a balance characteristic of works that encourage 'empathic unsettlement'. The writer's response to the ethical challenge posed to 'secondary witnesses' of trauma is similarly discernible in the novella's ending, which promotes ambiguity rather than closure. Abani's cautious evocation of the possibility of redemption indicates that his vision is "open to the challenge of utopian aspiration," yet arguably resists "the enigmatic call of an open or empty utopia."[37] Indulging neither in euphoria nor in despair, Abani's art maintains a glimmer of hope in the bleakest of circumstances, a position perhaps most fittingly summarized in the writer's own words:

> One of my earliest spiritual advisers told me that to be human is to accept that there will never be world peace, but to live life as though it

---

[35] The concept of redemption, which recurs in Abani's work, is to be understood "not in a spiritual sense, but in the sense of becoming fully human." According to the writer, reflecting on the possibility of redemption consists in examining "how far into darkness […] a being [can] go and still find their way back to light." See Chris Abani, "The Truthdig Interview," by Zuade Kaufman, *Truthdig* (18 April 2006), www .truthdig.com/report/item/20060418_chris_abani_truthdig_interview/?/interview/item/ 20060418_chris_abani_truthdig_interview (accessed 5 April 2010).

[36] This is another central notion in Abani's imagination, as suggested for instance by the title of his novella *Becoming Abigail*.

[37] LaCapra, *Writing History, Writing Trauma*, 42, 197.

is possible. This is the core of my aesthetic: belief in a deeper human-
ness that is beyond race, class, gender, and power, even as I know that
it is not possible. And yet I strive for it in every way, even when I fail.
In the end, we may never know. Perhaps it is enough […] to know that
it will always be hard. May we cry, but may we never die of heart-
break.[38]

WORKS CITED

Abani, Chris. *Becoming Abigail* (New York: Akashic, 2006).
——. "Ethics and Narrative: The Human and Other," *Witness* 22 (2009), http:
//witness.blackmountaininstitute.org/archive/xxii/Witness_XXII-Abani.pdf (acces-
sed 5 April 2010): 167–73.
——. Interview by Carlye Archibeque, *Poetix* (2005), http://poetix.net/abani.htm (ac-
cessed 5 April 2010).
——. *Kalakuta Republic* (London: Saqi, 2000).
——. "The Model of African Wars," *Voices Education Project* (nd), http://voices
inwartime.org/content/chris-abani (accessed 5 April 2010).
——. *Song for Night* (New York: Akashic, 2007).
——. "The Truthdig Interview," by Zuade Kaufman, *Truthdig* (18 April 2006), www
.truthdig.com/report/item/20060418_chris_abani_truthdig_interview/?/interview/it
em/20060418_chris_abani_truthdig_interview (accessed 5 April 2010).
——. *The Virgin of Flames* (New York: Penguin, 2007).
Adorno, Theodor. "Cultural Criticism and Society," *Prisms*, tr. Samuel Weber &
Shierry Weber ("Kulturkritik und Gesellschaft," 1951; Cambridge MA: MIT Press,
1981): 17–34.
——. *Negative Dialectics*, tr. E.B. Ashton (*Negative Dialektik*, 1966; New York: Con-
tinuum, 1973).
Bernard, Louise. "Silent Warrior," *Washington Post* (2 September 2007), www
.washingtonpost.com/wp-dyn/content/article/2007/08/30/AR2007083001619
.html (accessed 5 April 2010).
Castaneda, Carlos. *The Teachings of Don Juan: A Yaqui Way of Knowledge* (1969;
Berkeley & Los Angeles: U of California P, 1998).
Craps, Stef. "Linking Legacies of Loss: Traumatic Histories and Cross-Cultural Em-
pathy in Caryl Phillips's *Higher Ground* and *The Nature of Blood*," *Studies in the
Novel* 40.1–2 (Spring–Summer 2008): 191–202.
——, & Gert Buelens. "Introduction: Postcolonial Trauma Novels," *Studies in the
Novel* 40.1–2 (Spring–Summer 2008): 1–12.

---

[38] Abani, "Ethics and Narrative," 173.

Giommi, Francesca. "Negotiating Freedom on Scarred Bodies," *Experiences of Freedom in Postcolonial Literatures and Cultures*, ed. Annalisa Oboe & Shaul Bassi (Abingdon & New York: Routledge, 2011): 176–184.

Gluckstern, Nicole. "Shorts," *San Francisco Bay Guardian Online* (25 September 2007), www.sfbg.com/2007/09/25/shorts (accessed 5 April 2010).

Knox, Malcolm. "Haunted by the Ghosts in a Child Soldier's Life," *Sydney Morning Herald* (8 November 2008), www.smh.com.au/articles/2008/11/07/1225561105 879.html (accessed 5 April 2010).

LaCapra, Dominick. *Writing History, Writing Trauma* (Baltimore MD: Johns Hopkins UP, 2001).

Marshall, Robert. "The Dark Legacy of Carlos Castaneda," *salon.com* (4 April 2007), www.salon.com/books/feature/2007/04/12/castaneda (accessed 5 April 2010).

Molière. *Le Dépit amoureux* (1656), *Œuvres de Molière* 1, ed. Eugène Despois (Paris: Hachette, 1873).

Rabalais, Kevin. "The Clarity of Distance," *Australian* (30 August 2008), www.the australian.com.au/news/arts/the-clarity-of-distance/story-e6frg8n6-1111117306592 (accessed 5 April 2010).

Rothberg, Michael. "Decolonizing Trauma Studies: A Response," *Studies in the Novel* 40.1–2 (2008): 224–34.

Saro–Wiwa, Ken. *Sozaboy* (1985; New York: Longman, 1994).

Schindler's List, dir. Steven Spielberg. Universal, 1993.

Spivak, Gayatri Chakravorty. "Can the Subaltern Speak?" *Marxism and the Interpretation of Culture*, ed. Cary Nelson & Lawrence Grossberg (Urbana & Chicago: U of Illinois P, 1988): 271–313.

Tutuola, Amos. *The Palm-Wine Drinkard* (London: Faber & Faber, 1952).

⌘

SECTION III

⌘

TRANSLATION AND CULTURAL REWRITING

"The Story that gave this Land its Life"[1]
—The Translocation of Rilke's *Duino Elegies* in Amitav Ghosh's *The Hungry Tide*

SANDRA MEYER

MITAV GHOSH'S NOVEL *THE HUNGRY TIDE* is set in the Sundarbans, a part of the world's largest delta formed by the rivers Ganges, Brahmaputra, and Meghna. The novel, which was published in 2004, is a highly intertextual and meta-narrative one, profoundly concerned with the necessity as well as the problem of translation in a hybrid society. This is first and foremost illustrated by the protagonist Kanai, who is a translator and interpreter by profession and works as a mediator between different characters as well as between narrator and reader. In addition to this, there are two key intertexts which reappear throughout the novel and which are both presented in translated versions to the characters as well as to the readers. The first text is the local story "The Glory of Bon Bibi," a Hindu–Muslim story[2] about an island goddess who rescues the boy Dukhey when he is threatened by the tiger-demon Dokkhin Rai (246). This story has been primarily passed on orally from one generation to the next. In contrast to this, the second central intertext is a piece of canonical poetry: namely, Rainer Maria Rilke's *Duino Elegies*. This famous piece of poetry, originally written in German, is dislocated and integrated – translocated – into a postcolonial novel dealing with India's past and present and possibly also her future.

---

[1] Amitav Ghosh, *The Hungry Tide* (London: HarperCollins, 2005): 354. Further page references are in the main text.

[2] That it is a Hindu–Muslim story can, of course, also be regarded as significant, because it marks the text as a hybrid one.

This essay will try to show that the translocation of Rilke's *Duino Elegies* intensifies the tone[3] and adds to the multiple levels of meaning in Ghosh's novel. Many passages of *The Hungry Tide* can, in fact, be read as illustrations of the key notions in Rilke's poem[4] and vice versa. The intertextual references thus have various connected and mutually reinforcing functions. This is achieved, for instance, by connecting certain quotations with specific characters to illustrate further the difficult situations they find themselves in. In addition, as other critics have pointed out before, *The Hungry Tide* is structured by means of binary oppositions such as land and water or ebb and flood.[5] At first sight, the *Duino Elegies* appear to fit seamlessly into this meta-narrative structure of the novel, as they seem to be diametrically opposed to the other major intertext, the local story of Bon Bibi. However, this binary opposition, though it appears to be so obvious at first, is somewhat resolved in the ending of the novel. This dissolution of the diametrical structure suggests a reading of *The Hungry Tide* as a novel indicating the need for syncretism in postcolonial societies.

'Intertextuality' is, of course, a term frequently used but hardly ever clearly defined. As Heinrich Plett notes, "everybody who uses it understands it somewhat differently."[6] Thus, it seems necessary to briefly explain the underlying assumption of this essay in relation to existing theories and types of intertextuality. When referring to the fact that *The Hungry Tide* uses Rilke's *Duino Elegies* as an intertext, intertextuality is here to be understood in the sense of

---

[3] 'Tone' here refers to the emotional attitude expressed in a text. In *The Hungry Tide*, the tone is one of loss, homelessness, and alienation from the self. However, towards the close of the novel, the tone changes, when one of the main characters, Piya, who is formally depicted as feeling homeless, settles down to make plans for the future. This is comparable to the change of tone in Rilke's *Duino Elegies*.

[4] Critics agree that Rilke's *Duino Elegies* express the overwhelming experience of pain, alienation, transience, and the craving of human beings for sense, a coherent identity and intimacy. See, for instance, Manfred Engel, *Rainer Maria Rilkes „Duineser Elegien" und die moderne deutsche Lyrik: Zwischen Jahrhundertwende und Avantgarde* (Germanistische Abhandlungen 58; Stuttgart: Metzler 1986): 124.

[5] See Jens Martin Gurr, "Emplotting an Ecosystem: Amitav Ghosh's *The Hungry Tide* as an Eco-Narrative," in *Local Natures, Global Responsibilities: Ecocritical Perspectives on the New English Literatures*, ed. Laurenz Volkmann, Nancy Grimm & Ines Detmers (Cross/Cultures 121, ASNEL Papers 15; Amsterdam & New York: Rodopi, 2010): 75–76.

[6] Heinrich F. Plett, *Intertextuality*, ed. Plett (Berlin & New York: de Gruyter, 1991): 3.

Genette's "cinq types de relations transtextuelles."[7] In the first category of his system he defines intertextuality as a form of transtextuality which is characterized by the "explicit summoning up of a text that is both presented and distanced by quotation marks,"[8] as opposed to paratextuality, metatextuality, hypertextuality, and architextuality. This is precisely how the various quotations of the *Duino Elegies* are presented to the reader: namely, as straightforward statements with quotation marks.[9] Furthermore, an underlying assumption of this essay is that there is a "triangular interaction of reader–writer–text"[10] which somewhat rejects the "New Criticism's notion of the autonomy of the text."[11] Monica Loeb talks about the fact that a writer who includes intertextual references in his writings is first of all a reader who then makes use of what he or she read earlier and integrates it into his or her own writing. I would even prefer to speak of a process consisting of four points of interaction rather than three, as there is not only the writer who used to be a reader, but also a reader who notices the intertextual references and sees them as signs adding to his understanding of the text. This is of importance, as the aim of this essay is to figure out why a text with a Western cultural background can be meaningful to a postcolonial readership, assuming it is absolutely no coincidence that the *Duino Elegies* were chosen as an intertext, but that there are in fact several reasons for this choice. As the essay will try to show, one reason for choosing the *Duino Elegies* is to be found in the content of this cycle of poetry which aims at symbolically overcoming feelings of alienation after the devastating experience of the First World War. In addition, there is a parallel to be found between the biography of Rainer Maria Rilke

---

[7] Gérard Genette, *Palimpsestes* (Paris: Seuil, 1982): 8.

[8] Gérard Genette, *Paratexts: Thresholds of Interpretation*, tr. Jane E. Lewin, foreword by Richard Macksey (*Seuils*, 1987; tr. 1997; Cambridge, New York & Melbourne: Cambridge U P, 2001): xviii.

[9] Because the quotations from the *Duino Elegies* are presented in quotation marks and Rilke is explicitly mentioned, it does not need a particularly well-read and attentive reader to detect the references in the novel.

[10] 'Text' in this essay is to be understood in Barthes' and Kristeva's sense as a "mosaic" of other texts. See Monica Loeb, *Literary Marriages: A Study of Intertextuality in a Series of Short Stories by Joyce Carol Oates* (Berlin: Peter Lang, 2002), 46. Ghosh integrates the *Duino Elegies* – and also the Hindu–Muslim story of Bon Bibi – into his own writing and thus creates a new, hybrid piece of writing which appears to appeal to several target audiences at the same time.

[11] Loeb, *Literary Marriages*, 46.

and that of Nirmal, the character in *The Hungry Tide* who quotes from the Elegies.

The Hungry Tide deals with a young cetologist called Piya, who grew up in the USA but is of Indian origin. However, she is rather ignorant of her Indian heritage and speaks no Bangla, nor does she know much about the country itself. In the novel, she travels to the Sundarbans, also known as the 'Tide Country', in order to do research on dolphins, and she finds herself torn between two men who represent wholly opposed life-styles. On the one side, there is Kanai, a well-educated and urbane translator and interpreter who lives in New Delhi. On the other, there is Fokir, an illiterate fisherman who lives on Lusibari, one of the tiny islands in the Tide Country. He does not speak any English at all. The topic of translation and the difficulties arising when translating from one language and/or culture into another are thus deeply embedded in the narrative.[12] This is not only apparent with regard to the characters of Kanai, Fokir, and Piya; there are, in fact, numerous passages which reflect extensively on the nature of language, as when Fokir's wife Moyna states that "words are just air [...]. When the wind blows on the water, you see ripples and waves, but the real river lies beneath, unseen and unheard" (258).

As an intertext, Rilke's elegies, originally written in German, are doubly mediated, as they are read by Kanai in a Bangla translation and presented to the reader in English. Kanai's role as a translator is thus not restricted to mediating between Fokir and Piya; he also mediates between the writings of his uncle Nirmal, which contain references to the elegies in Bangla, and the reader, who depends on the English translation.

Even though critics such as Christopher Rollason have noted the intertextual references to Rilke's *Duino Elegies*, they have failed to recognize that the expressiveness of the latter goes far beyond the fact that the poems derive from a different linguistic background.[13] It is certainly significant that a piece of poetry originally written in German is part of an anglophone novel so deeply concerned with the various shortcomings of language and translation. However interesting this observation on the level of form may be, it by no means exhausts the intertextual significance. It is not only the level of form

---

[12] It is made clear throughout the text that translation always includes interpretation and that problems of hermeneutics are part of every act of translation.

[13] Christopher Rollason, "'In Our Translated World': Transcultural Communication in Amitav Ghosh's *The Hungry Tide*," *Atlantic Literary Review* 6.1–2 (January–June 2005): 86–107.

but also the level of content, that appears to be meaningful in connection with the story told in Ghosh's novel.

The elegies, published in 1922, the *annus mirabilis* of modernist writing, are generally perceived as rather complex pieces of literary achievement and not easily accessible. There is, however, a recurrent theme in the text: namely, that of alienation and deprivation. These major feelings underlying human existence seem to dominate the first half of the elegies.[14] This becomes apparent in the opening lines of the first elegy:

> And if I cried, who'd listen to me in those angelic orders?
> Even if one of them suddenly held me
> to his heart, I'd vanish in his overwhelming presence. Because
> beauty's nothing
> but the start of terror we can hardly bear,
> and we adore it because of the serene scorn
> it could kill us with. Every angel's terrifying.
> So I control myself and choke back the lure
> of my dark cry. Ah, who can we turn to,
> then? Neither angels nor men
> and *the animals already know by instinct*
> *we're not comfortably at home in our translated world.*[15]

The last part of the above passage with its idea that the animals are aware of people's discomfort in the translated world re-appears frequently throughout the novel. Even though other passages of the elegies are referred to in the

---

[14] Engel, *Rainer Maria Rilkes "Duineser Elegien,"* 123–24. See also Peter Krumme, *Eines Augenblickes Zeichnung: Zur Temporalität des Bewusstseins in Rilkes Duineser Elegien* (Würzburg: Königshausen & Neumann, 1988): 27. The elegies are very much in line with other poetic cycles of this time such as T.S. Eliot's *The Waste Land* (New York: Boni & Liveright, 1922). As Rilke himself said, modernist poetry written in a time in which traumatizing events like the First World War influenced people's way of looking at the world and their own existence, attempts at coming to terms with this new and devastating inhuman spectacle. These cycles can thus be read as attempts to overcome the traumatized status quo – if not in reality, then at least on a fictional level. See Engel, *Rainer Maria Rilkes "Duineser Elegien"*, 123.

[15] Rainer Maria Rilke, *Duino Elegies and The Sonnets to Orpheus,* tr. A. Poulin, Jr. (*Sämtliche Werke,* vol. 1, 1955; tr. 1975; New York: Houghton Mifflin, 2005): 195. This is the translation used by Ghosh.

novel as well,[16] these lines can be regarded as the major statement setting the tone. They are the only lines mentioned more than once in *The Hungry Tide*. Just like all the other references to Rilke's elegies, they are first and foremost quoted and referred to in the diary of Kanai's uncle Nirmal, who adores Rilke's poetry so much that he treats the elegies as a kind of prophecy. Whereas the quotations from the *Duino Elegies* in Nirmal's diary are given in verse, the two lines mentioned above are also indirectly referred to outside the diary and in prose when Kanai wonders "why people who lived in close proximity with tigers so often regarded them as being something more than just animals" (328) and comes to the conclusion that maybe "the tiger was the only animal that forgave you for being so ill at ease in your translated world" (328). This indirect intertextual reference once again emphasizes the significance and importance of Rilke's elegies for *The Hungry Tide*. They are so much in line with the tone of the novel that they not only appear as direct quotations but even merge with the thoughts of characters. Kanai, who has read the direct quotation before, now integrates it subconsciously into his own reflections. That the narrative connects him, of all the characters, with the *Duino Elegies* and particularly with the excerpt quoted above is not surprising at all if one takes into account the fact that he works as a professional translator and interpreter. Hence, he is very much aware of the difficulties involved when translating from one language and its cultural context into another. The narrative connection between Rilke's poetry and Kanai thus seems to emphasize one of the key notions of the novel: namely, the problem of linguistic transfer.[17]

However, Kanai is not the only one who is associated with the conspicuous repetition of and allusion to the quotation from Rilke's first elegy. The character who presumably best illustrates a being ill at ease in the translated world is the cetologist Piya. Even though she is regarded as "the American" who does not speak any Bangla and depends on a translator as well as on someone

---

[16] For reasons of space, it is impossible to analyse the significance of all the other passages from the *Duino Elegies* that are referred to in *The Hungry Tide*. As the passage quoted above is the only one referred to more than once, it seems justifiable to focus on it in my analysis.

[17] Numerous passages in the novel stress the fact that linguistic transfer always includes difficulties and that one cannot easily translate from one language to the other. Apart from general questions of hermeneutics, it is the cultural context that can be decisive. This is best illustrated by Kanai's difficulties when he tries to translate the local story of Bob Bibi for Piya (see 309).

to inform her about the country's environment and customs, she is of Indian origin. This Indian part of her identity does not, however, necessarily have a positive connotation for her. It seems to be there on a subliminal level as part of her childhood, but even with regard to the past it is only marginal, and those aspects which do play a role bear rather negative associations for her. Piya remembers Bangla to be the language which "was an angry flood trying to break down her door" (93), because her parents' "accumulated resentments of their life were always phrased in that language" (93) during their numerous quarrels. At university, she is referred to as "the little East Indian girl" (74) owing to her outward appearance. But her origin is neither the only nor the most important aspect labelling Piya as a character who has no idea "of what her own place was in the great scheme of things" (35). It becomes clear that she does not feel at home anywhere at all, and one occasionally has the feeling that she uses tactics of avoidance so as not to admit her inner emptiness (see, for instance, 126, 302, and 314). In addition to this, she has obviously not come to terms with one or the other aspect of her past, such as her childhood, which used to be affected by her mother's depressions (see 94–95). Furthermore, Piya thinks that doing research on dolphins, even though it "would not revolutionize the sciences, or even a minor branch of them" (126), is nevertheless something that serves well enough "as an alibi for life" (127). This again shows that she is rather restless and that she is not all too sure about the meaning of her existence. Even though this uncertainty may be fundamental to all human life, it becomes apparent that Piya suffers from it as she perceives it as problematical with regard to her own mode of existence.

While one would tend to associate Kanai with the *Duino Elegies* on the level of form because of his role as a translator, Piya could be read as an illustration of the quotation from the first elegy on the level of content: she has not really settled down and thus often seems to be at odds with her life. In addition to this, she perceives human communication, including translation, as a failure (159), as she often seems to prefer animals to human beings, or at least thinks of them as being more honest and more social beings (159). Interestingly enough, she is fascinated by dolphins. These animals are known for living together in social, family-like groups, which is something Piya has not yet achieved. She even doubts that this will ever happen, as she cannot really trust people. What is more, dolphins use an elaborate system of communication which consists of various distinct sounds. To Piya, this way of communicating is more natural and honest than human speech, which – according to her – is only "a bag of tricks that fooled you into believing that you could see through the eyes of another being" (159). Of all the characters in *The Hungry Tide*, Piya seems to be the one who struggles most with developing stability and coherence in her life. She thus appears to be an illustration of the emptiness of human existence as expressed in the *Duino Elegies*. That she is also the one who utterly depends on translation during her visit to the Sundarbans and has a strong interest in a rather intelligent kind of animal strengthens the connection between Rilke's quotation about the animals' awareness of our unease in the world and the character of Piya.[18]

The translocation of Rilke's *Duino Elegies* has the function of setting the tone of the novel. By connecting the character of Piya with a quotation from the first elegy, the alienation and deprivation described by Rilke also become apparent in *The Hungry Tide*. More than any other character in the novel, it is Piya who feels that language is a failure. This not only leads to a somewhat distrustful attitude towards other people, but, of course, also to isolation and alienation as described in the opening lines of the *Duino Elegies*. Furthermore, the opening lines of Rilke's poem are also connected with Kanai, which underlines the problem of translation and interpretation.

Interestingly enough, a particular translation of the *Duino Elegies* was chosen to serve as a meta-commentary in *The Hungry Tide*.[19] In this version by A. Poulin, Jr., the decisive passage quoted above reads "we're not comfortably at home in our *translated* world."[20] Compared to this, there are other translations (for instance, those of Stephen Mitchell) which render Rilke's

---

[18] In addition to Piya's illustrating topics of the *Duino Elegies* such as alienation and the shortcomings of human communication, she is also connected to the theme of love and intimacy, another major aspect of the elegies. Piya is torn between two men, Fokir and Kanai, and this experience changes her attitude towards life at the close of the novel.

[19] For further analysis of the translation of Rilke's works into English, see Roy Woods, *Rilke Through a Glass Darkly: The Poetry of R.M. Rilke and its English Translations. A Critial Comparison* (Trier: WVT, 1996). For the function of intertextuality as a meta-commentary in fictional works, see Bruno Zerweck, *Die Synthese aus Realismus und Experiment: Der englische Roman der 1980er und 1990er Jahre aus erzähltheoretischer und kulturwissenschaftlicher Sicht* (Trier: WVT, 2001): 99.

[20] Rilke, *Duino Elegies and The Sonnets to Orpheus,* 5 (my emphasis). See also *Rilke's Duino Elegies: Cambridge Readings*, ed. Roger Paulin & Peter Hutchinson (London: Duckworth, 1996): 5.

original verse as "we're not comfortably at home in our *interpreted* world."[21]
This translation even seems to be more suitable and true to Rilke's original
version,[22] as a native speaker of German would certainly translate Rilke's
phrase *in der gedeuteten Welt* as "in the interpreted world," which would give
a semantic emphasis different from and richer than the Poulin translation.
Interpreting always implies more than mere linguistic transfer, since the one
who interprets also has the power to recode the message and filter it.[23] This
problem of recoding and filtering information while translating is foregrounded in the novel: namely, when Fokir's wife Moyna asks Kanai to interpret
between her husband and Piya. As she is afraid that Piya might feel attracted
to her husband, she asks Kanai to filter Piya's and Fokir's messages:

> It's you who stands between them: whatever they say to each other
> will go through your ears and your lips. But for you neither of them
> will know what is in the mind of the other. Their words will be in your
> hands and you can make them mean what you will. (257)

Thus, the problems of translation, on the one hand, and of interpretation in
both its meanings, on the other, already become apparent on the story level of
the novel. That the novel uses the Poulin translation of the *Duino Elegies* is
arguably more appropriate in a narrative which is set in such a multilingual
country as India and in which one of the protagonists, Piya, is wholly dependent on translation. As 'interpretation' has more than one meaning, the choice
of Poulin's translation appropriately enhances the thematic connection between being confronted with an unknown language and being ill at ease in the
world.

As mentioned above, the Rilke elegies are doubly mediated, as Kanai reads
them in his uncle Nirmal's diary in Bangla but presents them to the reader in
English. Apart from this being important with regard to the problem of translation and interpretation, it also seems to be significant that Nirmal, a dreamy
leftist intellectual "in love with the idea of revolution" (119), chose Rilke of
all poets. If one takes a closer look at Rilke's biography, it becomes clear that

---

[21] *The Selected Poetry of Rainer Maria Rilke*, ed. & tr. Stephen Mitchell (London:
Vintage, 1989): 151 (my emphasis).

[22] Rainer Maria Rilke, *Duineser Elegien* (1922; Frankfurt am Main: Suhrkamp,
2003).

[23] As mentioned earlier, the novel stresses the fact that translation includes more
than mere linguistic transfer.

he has been strongly criticizing the zeitgeist ever since his traumatizing experiences in Paris in 1902.[24] Great parts of his works, such as the *Duino
Elegies* and *The Sonnets to Orpheus*, can be seen as attempts to create new
approaches to life,[25] in that they describe a status quo of society in a cycle of
poetry and then try to overcome this status quo in precisely this poetry cycle.
Thus, poetry is regarded as a means of overcoming current problems of society and showing ways out of a devastating situation – at least on a symbolic
level.[26] As Manfred Engel notes, the *Duino Elegies* ask their readers to think
actively, to get involved, and to act.[27] Even though Engel here primarily refers
to the contumacy of the elegies, which asks for a dedicated and concentrated
reader, they may also be understood as an appeal to the reader to find new
forms of living in a time shaken by unrest.[28] This is exactly what Nirmal asks
of his nephew Kanai:

> I will hand it [the diary] to Horen in the hope it finds its way to you,
> Kanai. I feel certain you will have a greater claim to the world's ear
> than I ever had. Maybe you will know what to do with it. I have
> always trusted the young. Your generation will, I know, be richer in
> ideals, less cynical, less selfish than mine. (278)

Nirmal thus hopes that later generations will benefit from his report of what
happened during the Morichjhāpi massacre and that they will feel the need for

---

[24] See *Rilke Handbuch: Leben – Werk – Wirkung*, ed. Manfred Engel (Stuttgart &
Weimar: Metzler, 2004): 368.

[25] See Hans Dieter Zimmermann, *Der Wahnsinn des Jahrhunderts: Die Verantwortung der Schriftsteller in der Politik* (Stuttgart, Berlin & Cologne: W. Kohlhammer, 1992): 164.

[26] This is, of course, evocative of Karlheinz Stierle's idea of fictional texts as a
laboratory in which the reader can encounter ideas and try out concepts he could not
play around with in reality. See Stierle, "Die Fiktion als Vorstellung, als Werk und als
Schema," in *Funktionen des Fiktiven*, ed. Dieter Henrich & Wolfgang Iser (Poetik und
Hermeneutik 10; Munich: Wilhelm Fink, 1983): 173–82, 176.

[27] See Engel, *Rilke Handbuch*, 369.

[28] See, for instance, Zimmermann, *Der Wahnsinn des Jahrhunderts,* 157. Zimmermann talks about the fact that writers such as Rilke were regarded solely as artists.
Their political attitudes or ideas concerning new forms of living were consequently
hardly ever taken seriously – were thought to be the daydreams of some crazy artist.
Nevertheless, Zimmermann expresses the conviction that Rilke promoted an attitude
against the zeitgeist in his poetry (165).

change. It is through writing that Nirmal hopes to make people aware of what is going on and show them ways out of the current situation.[29] This is presumably what makes the *Duino Elegies* so attractive for a writer like Ghosh: in the same way as Rilke's *Duino Elegies* can be seen as describing a state of affairs and then delineating a symbolic overcoming of this, *The Hungry Tide* offers a way out of the problems of postcolonial societies like India when it supports a reading in terms of syncretism as a solution.

As mentioned earlier, Ghosh's novel is almost obtrusively structured by means of binary oppositions. At first sight, the two major intertexts, Rilke's *Duino Elegies* and the local story of "The Glory of Bon Bibi," seem to be diametrically opposed as well. Whereas Rilke's text is internationally acclaimed and has been translated into various languages, the local story is primarily passed on orally from one generation to the other. Therefore, one would associate the oral, local text with the illiterate fisherman Fokir, while one would connect the *Duino Elegies* with the sophisticated Kanai. First of all, this is due to their different cultural and educational backgrounds. Kanai and Fokir seem as diametrically opposed as the two intertexts themselves. However, it becomes clear at the close of the novel that this clear distinction between the two intertexts is no longer valid. Kanai, for instance, who is usually praised for his language abilities, initially has to admit that he cannot translate the local legend, as it is beyond his power (309). This is not the first and only time this local and at first glance naive legend puts Kanai in his place: when he tells Kusum, a childhood friend in Lusibari, that he does not know the story, she asks him who he calls on when in trouble (101). This forthright question engrosses Kanai's thoughts for quite some time, which is a rather unexpected reaction from an otherwise so self-assured person. He has to realize that religious belief, however simple and naive it may seem, can offer people some stability in an otherwise chaotic existence. Additionally, he cannot resist the fascination of the story when watching a performance of the legend, even though he initially doubts whether it will be capable of impressing him (105). However, he is not the only one riveted by the local legend. Piya is also fascinated by it, and it is thus no great surprise that Kanai should finally prepare a translation of the story for her as a token of his love. Accordingly, the two outsiders – in Kanai's case possibly only a semi-outsider – of the

---

[29] Nirmal treats the *Duino Elegies* as if they were prophecies. According to Nirmal, acting like Rilke, as suggested in the elegies, appears to be a way out of the problematical situation.

Sundarbans society are both affected by a story they would formerly not have recognized for what it is: "the story that gave this land its life" (354). It becomes obvious that a local story can influence people from distinct cultural contexts, but the translocation of the Western *Duino Elegies* also shows that such a text can be meaningful to various societies. Apart from underlining people's deprivation in contemporary society in general, their use also points to the necessity of constantly renegotiating collective as well as individual identities. One of Nirmal's diary entries ends with a quotation from Rilke's seventh elegy, which states that "life is lived in transformation" (225). First of all, this shows that the fundamental aspect of life in the Sundarbans – namely the constant reshaping of the islands through the ecological conditions of ebb and flood – can be aptly delineated with the help of verses from a different cultural context. Furthermore, it also indicates that not only the land is reshaped and thus transformed, but that people, too, need to transform themselves and adapt to new conditions. This indication may imply a need for syncretism in postcolonial societies. The fact that, on the one hand, the local legend influences the 'westernized' characters Piya and Kanai, while, on the other, the Western text written by Rilke appears to be quite meaningful to Nirmal and other people of the Tide Country community, shows that hybridity does not threaten contemporary society. Instead, the different cultural achievements can be fruitfully combined into something new.

The novel thus presents a way out of the difficulties of postcolonial societies and presents syncretism as a solution for the future. Both works, Rilke's *Duino Elegies* and Ghosh's *Hungry Tide*, describe a traumatizing and devastating present situation and then attempt to overcome this situation in writing. As with Rilke, who, as it seems, was not listened to much during his lifetime,[30] Nirmal is regarded as merely a dreamy intellectual. But there is hope that future generations will be able to see and turn the symbolic overcoming of oppositions into reality. This is presumably why the elegies appeal to Ghosh's target audience. In his combination of a local legend with a Western text, Ghosh offers a hopeful perspective on the future of postcolonial societies.

In short, it can be maintained that the translocation of Rilke's *Duino Elegies* into Ghosh's *The Hungry Tide* has different functions on various levels. First of all, it is a meta-commentary which emphasizes the alienation and powerlessness of the human being in a world in which the arbitrary system of

---

[30] See Zimmermann, *Der Wahnsinn des Jahrhunderts,* 157.

language is the only tool of communication available. Further, the translocation also enhances the perception of the *The Hungry Tide* as a hybrid text,
particularly in connection with the second major intertext, "The Glory of Bon
Bibi." Whereas the translocated verses of the *Duino Elegies* help to emphasize several major topics in the novel, the story of Bon Bibi fascinates Piya
and Kanai, who, at first, both reject the rural part of India and its culture, but
who are made by this local story, which, in its printed form, "looked like
prose and read like verse" (247),[31] to perceive the beauty and fascination of
the Sundarbans. Although the narrator claims that the story of Bob Bibi is
"the story that gave this land its life," a close look at the translocation of Rilke
and its effect on the story as well as its characters invites the conclusion that it
is, rather, the hybrid combination of the oral local story and the internationally
acclaimed piece of poetry that "gives this land its life," particularly with regard to the life which is still to come, the future.

The dissolution of the binary opposition between the originally Indian and
the translocated European text thus supports a reading of *The Hungry Tide* as
a novel indicating the need for syncretism in a postcolonial society. This conclusion is designated not only by the form of the novel, which combines two
culturally different texts of distinct genres, but also by the protagonist Piya,
who is – in a sense just like the *Duino Elegies* – doubly translocated. Her first
translocation takes place when she moves from India to the USA at an early
age, while the second translocation is her return to India. Just as the poems by
Rilke, at first glance, seem to be out of place in the Indian context and its culture, so, too, is Piya, as she does not speak the language and is not really interested in the country. But, as mentioned above, it becomes fairly obvious after
some time that the *Duino Elegies*, by definition a classic Western text, can
very well appeal to target audiences in different cultures and that this poetry is
by no means opposed to the local stories found in the Sundarbans. In fact, the
two different and in themselves hybrid texts can easily coexist and enrich
each other in a syncretic way. Comparable to this is the situation of Piya, who
also perceives herself as a hybrid character: when she is in the USA, she is
referred to as the "Indian girl," and when she finally returns to India, she is
"the American." Her being perceived as "the American" is mainly due to her
reluctance and, arguably, even her fear of learning more about her origins and
the country she left at an early age. But after a certain time and with the help
of a mediator, the urbane translator Kanai, who not only knows both Bangla

---

[31] This inherently hybrid mode is itself highly suggestive, of course.

and English but also the different cultural contexts, Piya starts to assimilate
and discovers that India can after all offer her a new perspective on life, if
only she allows this to happen. Thus, one could argue that the hybrid combination of different genres and texts from distinct cultural contexts on the
level of form reinforces what is happening on the story level. Hence, the
translocation of Rilke's *Duino Elegies* not only adds enormously to the tone
of *The Hungry Tide*, but also suggests the need for syncretism in postcolonial
societies. This is further stressed by Nirmal, the character who treats the
elegies as a prophecy. Just as the poetic cycle depicts the difficult situation of
life in modernist times and tries to illustrate a way out of this, Nirmal's
writing addresses not only the hardship society has to face but also expresses
his hope that people will find a solution and put his ideas into practice.

WORKS CITED

Eliot, T.S. *The Waste Land* (New York: Boni & Liveright, 1922).

Engel, Manfred. *Rainer Maria Rilkes "Duineser Elegien" und die moderne deutsche
     Lyrik: Zwischen Jahrhundertwende und Avantgarde* (Germanistische Abhand-
     lungen 58; Stuttgart: Metzler 1986).

——, ed. *Rilke Handbuch: Leben – Werk – Wirkung* (Stuttgart & Weimar: Metzler,
     2004)

Genette, Gérard. *Palimpsestes* (Paris: Seuil, 1982).

——. *Paratexts: Thresholds of Interpretation*, tr. Jane E. Lewin, foreword by Richard
     Macksey (*Seuils*, 1987; tr. 1997; Cambridge, New York & Melbourne: Cambridge
     UP, 2001).

Ghosh, Amitav. *The Hungry Tide* (London: HarperCollins, 2005).

Gurr, Jens Martin. "Emplotting an Ecosystem: Amitav Ghosh's *The Hungry Tide* as an
     Eco-Narrative," in *Local Natures, Global Responsibilities: Ecocritical Perspectives
     on the New English Literatures*, ed. Laurenz Volkmann, Nancy Grimm & Ines
     Detmers (Cross/Cultures 121, ASNEL Papers 15; Amsterdam & New York:
     Rodopi, 2010): 69–80.

Krumme, Peter. *Eines Augenblickes Zeichnung: Zur Temporalität des Bewusstseins in
     Rilkes Duineser Elegien* (Würzburg: Königshausen & Neumann, 1988).

Loeb, Monica. *Literary Marriages: A Study of Intertextuality in a Series of Short
     Stories by Joyce Carol Oates* (Berlin & New York: Peter Lang, 2002).

Paulin, Roger, & Peter Hutchinson, ed. *Rilke's Duino Elegies: Cambridge Readings*
     (London: Duckworth, 1996).

Plett, Heinrich F., ed. *Intertextuality* (Berlin & New York: de Gruyter, 1991).

Rilke, Rainer Maria. *Duineser Elegien* (1922; Frankfurt am Main: Suhrkamp, 2003).

———. *Duino Elegies and The Sonnets to Orpheus,* tr. A. Poulin, Jr. (*Sämtliche Werke,* vol. 1, 1955; tr. 1975; New York: Houghton Mifflin, 2005).

———. *The Selected Poetry of Rainer Maria Rilke,* ed. & tr. Stephen Mitchell (London: Vintage, 1989).

Rollason, Christopher. "'In Our Translated World': Transcultural Communication in Amitav Ghosh's *The Hungry Tide,*" *Atlantic Literary Review* 6.1–2 (January–June 2005): 86–107.

Stierle, Karlheinz. "Die Fiktion als Vorstellung, als Werk und als Schema," in *Funktionen des Fiktiven,* ed. Dieter Henrich & Wolfgang Iser (Poetik und Hermeneutik 10; Munich: Wilhelm Fink, 1983): 173–82.

Woods, Roy, *Rilke Through a Glass Darkly: The Poetry of R.M. Rilke and its English Translations. A Critial Comparison* (Trier: W V T, 1996).

Zerweck, Bruno. *Die Synthese aus Realismus und Experiment: Der englische Roman der 1980er und 1990er Jahre aus erzähltheoretischer und kulturwissenschaftlicher Sicht* (Trier: W V T, 2001).

Zimmermann, Hans Dieter. *Der Wahnsinn des Jahrhunderts: Die Verantwortung der Schriftsteller in der Politik* (Stuttgart, Berlin & Cologne: W. Kohlhammer, 1992).

⌘

Reading "Upstream!"
—Implications of an Unconsidered Source Text to Julian Barnes' Eighth Chapter of *A History of the World in 10½ Chapters*

THERESE–M. MEYER

J ULIAN BARNES' POSTMODERN NOVEL *A History of the World in 10½ Chapters*[1] is an interrelated collection of ten short stories and an essay (the eponymous half chapter of the title). The author carefully traces historical sources in an author's note at the end of the book. He lists them chapter by chapter and ends with some additional, personal thanks. No source is listed for chapter eight, "Upstream!," an epistolary narrative in which Charlie, a satirically two-dimensional London actor, writes to Pippa, his girl-friend, about his experiences filming a river journey in the jungles of Vene-zuela. In *cinéma verité* fashion, the Hollywood crew has been brought to a nameless river where a native tribe has agreed to pole the two actors across white water in their re-enactment of a Jesuit mission. As Fred Botting sums it up, this journey

> draws on the *Bildungsroman* and the colonial narrative, the river itself raising the spectre of *Heart of Darkness*, to present and dissolve char-acter in a process of self-discovery and critical cultural reflection. [...] Commenting on modes of representation, moreover, the story's gene-ric assemblage discloses a reflexive space which ironises and exposes the limits of western assumptions, language, projections and mean-ings.[2]

---

[1] Julian Barnes, *A History of the World in 10½ Chapters* (New York: Vintage, 1990). Further page references are in the main text.

[2] Fred Botting, *Sex, Machines and Navels: Fiction, Fantasy and History in the Future Present* (Manchester: Manchester UP, 1999): 75.

Although this summary is to the point, Botting's reading ignores the issue of historiography[3] crucial to Barnes' novel: the question of the native Americans' oral histories of the mission behind this river journey. What and whose history is the film going to reproduce? To use Charlie's less lofty phrases,

> Do they have ballads about transporting the two white men dressed as women up to the great watery Anaconda to the south, or however they might put it? Or did the white men vanish from the tribe's memory as completely as the tribe vanished for the white man? (201)

Modes of representation are indeed pertinent to questions of historiography, yet they are a concern shared by the actors of historical drama. Keeping in mind Schiller's statement that "all dramatic forms make the past something present"[4] and function as translocations of events across time and space, Charlie's ample if somewhat confused reflections on acting, lying, and the opacity of semiotic signs across cultures acquire renewed urgency, as does his insistence on the blend of history and the present in his film crew's visit to the Venezuelan jungles. To address these questions, it will be necessary to read the "Upstream!" chapter against the background of its – as yet – unknown historical source-text, a Jesuit missionary account of an exploration of 1674 into the jungles of the Orinoco–Amazon basin. In turn, this method necessitates scrutiny of the generic features of tropical river journeys, which will be seen to illuminate larger issues pertinent to Barnes' chapter, particularly the binaries of historiography vs legend and science vs theology that provide the thematic unity to his novel. In the epistolary narrative of Charlie, these issues become embodied in the *candirú* fish (legend vs science) and its relation to the chapter title, which emerges as deliberately misleading. While the excessive diversity of form and content of the other chapters makes it impossible to

---

[3] On historiography as central to the novel and various critical readings of Barnes' employment of it, see Vanessa Guignery, *The Fiction of Julian Barnes: A Reader's Guide to Essential Criticism* (London: Palgrave Macmillan, 2006): 6. Botting traces chapter references to *The Mission*, a 1986 movie, which in one episode shows Jeremy Irons as a Jesuit missionary scaling the Iguaçú Falls between Argentina and Brazil and about to start yet another 'reduction' (Botting, *Sex, Machines and Navels*, 75). He will be joined by Robert de Niro in the role of Captain Mendoza, who turns Jesuit as well. Here the similarity ends.

[4] Friedrich Schiller, "On the Art of Tragedy" (1792), in *Essays*, tr. Daniel O. Dahlstrom, ed. Walter Hinderer & Daniel O. Dahlstrom (*Schillers Werke*, ed. Benno von Wiese, 1962; 1993; New York: Continuum, 2005): 16.

consider Barnes' novel in its entirety, a few thoughts on the possible implications of the eighth chapter for the novel's rewriting of colonial history will
conclude this essay.

There is, to begin, the journal record of an historical expedition, in which
two Jesuits, Jean Grillet and Francois Bechamel (John and Francis in the
English edition of 1698), penetrate the Guiana hinterland too deeply for their
own good. Setting out in Cayenne, Grillet and Bechamel appear to have
crossed all of the Early Modern Guianas, judging by the length of their journey (thirty-six days on the move, using various rivers and overland, and
thirty-three days for the return) and their claim to have reached "Acoqua"
territory (the contemporary Achagua people live in eastern Columbia on the
borders of Venezuela). Sick and with nearly no resources left, they are forced
to rely on indifferent native helpers to reach the coast again.[5] They, too, are
poled by natives across white water, capsizing several times, yet in contrast to
the events at the end of Barnes' chapter, in which the American actor Matt
drowns, both missionaries make it out of the jungle, if only just alive. They
are dumped by their native guides on the beaches opposite Cayenne and left
there to fend for themselves. The missionary exploration is altogether a barely
disguised failure;[6] Grillet can report only one possible placement for a missionary outpost and no conversions. Contrary to Sesto's assumption, Barnes'
two actors thus do not "impersonate figures whose own historicity, though

---

[5] See, for example, John Grillet & Francis Bechamel, *A Journal of the Travels of
John Grillet and Francis Bechamel into Guiana, in the Year, 1674* (London: Samuel
Buckley, 1698): 36, 40. Unless otherwise indicated, further page references are in the
main text.

[6] The French branch of the Jesuit order attempted the establishment of 'reductions'
by missions from their outpost at Cayenne, following the model of Paraguay. Ten
years before the worldwide banning of the order in 1773, Cayenne outlawed the Jesuits
and transferred their reductions to Franciscan friars, whose initial complaints concerned their inefficiency, particularly their lack of converts. See Philip P. Boucher,
France and the American Tropics to 1700: Tropics of Discontent? (Baltimore MD:
Johns Hopkins UP, 2008): 77, 212, and Jesuit Presbytery Guyana, "Guyana Early
History," *The Jesuits in Guyana*, http://www.guyanajesuits.org/page.asp?PageID=318
(accessed 12 June 2009). Histories favouring the Jesuit position attempt to put up a
smokescreen by praising individual missionaries' short-term successes in the Guianas;
for a striking example, see Barbara Neive, *The Jesuits: Their Foundation and History*,
vol 1 (New York: Benzinger Brothers, 1879): 152. Grillet and Bechamel have trouble
rhetorically concealing the abysmal extent of their failure.

purportedly real, is just as fictitious as that of the 'actors' who portray them in the film."[7] Although the two Jesuits in the novel are called Firmin and Antonio, the historical missionaries behind them are easily identified. The alias used for Charlie's role, Firmin, additionally blends echoes of Philip Firmin, the Surinam botanist and doctor,[8] with puns on *firm* and *vermin*. What, then, is the link between Charlie's letters and telegrams from the jungles of the Guianas[9] and this Jesuit missionary account, the unnamed historical background to Barnes' eighth chapter?

Necessarily, the generic features of tropical river journeys in a colonial setting are the starting point of such an enquiry, which will enable a focus on the peculiarities of these two specific river journeys. After a brief discussion of these generic features, I will first apply them to Barnes and then move into a consideration of his historical intertext. Looking at two crucial episodes of Grillet's account, my analysis next addresses how these illuminate and possibly contextualize Charlie's 'mystery' in the chapter, the death of Matt, and Charlie's reflections about the relationship between dramatic action and history, legend, and scientific truth.

Allegorically, since Antiquity, river journeys have depicted the passage of time, and the rivers themselves have provided emblems of human life, from the purity and passion of fountain and white water to the meandering slowness and depth of old age. In contrast to Bakhtin's chronotope of roads and passageways, travelogues of tropical river journeys, however, do not provide epiphanies or even circular character development[10] though they make use of

---

[7] Bruce Sesto, *Language, History, and Metanarrative in the Fiction of Julian Barnes* (New York: Peter Lang, 2001): 100.

[8] Fermin is also the author of *Nieuwe algemeene beschryving van de colonie van Surinam: Behelzende al het merkwaardige van dezelve, met betrekkinge tot de historie, aardryks en natuurkunde* (Harlingen: V. van der Plaats jr., 1770), a publication that describes the *candirú* fish (see below).

[9] 'Guianas' is here used in its geographical sense to indicate the land-mass of the so-called Guiana shield and the corresponding northern Amazon–Orinoco river system, which encompass parts of Venezuela, Guyana, Surinam, La Guyane Française, and border areas of Brazil and Columbia.

[10] See Mikhail M. Bakhtin, "Forms of Time and of the Chronotope in the Novel: Notes toward a Historical Poetics" (1937–38), tr. Caryl Emerson & Michael Holquist, in *Problems of Literature and Esthetics* (*Voprosy literatury i estetiki*, 1975) repr. in Bakhtin, *The Dialogic Imagination: Four Essays by M.M. Bakhtin*, ed. Michael Holquist (U of Texas Slavic Series 1; Austin: U of Texas P, 1981): 98–99, 243.

a dissolution of time and place for the protagonist identified as peculiar to the adventure chronotope.[11]

As exploratory travel accounts from the Early Modern period until the eighteenth century were (of financial necessity) less private than public ventures, a journey upstream would allegorically become representable as moving into the common prehistoric past of author and reader of exploratory literature, taking 'prehistoric' in its first sense recorded by the *OED* to mean "before the existence of written historiographic records." This in consequence connects, for example, the Orinoco in Columbus's account with an expectation of earthly paradise,[12] making his journey one into an antediluvian age. More apocalyptically and in far greater detail in Ralegh, the anticipation of the earthly equivalent of Jerusalem the Golden – Manoa, the city of El Dorado – evokes the eschatological dissolution of history.[13] There is, to complement Johannes Fabian's analysis in *Time and the Other* (1983), a decisively Christian allegorical tradition of representing tropical river journeys that considerably predates the nineteenth century's colonial practice, and operates with its own notions of the prehistoric. Following this earlier tradition, Fabian's understanding of evolutionist time (nineteenth- and early twentieth-century texts defining such journeys as palaeolithic and the human inhabitants of such

---

[11] Bakhtin, "Forms of Time and of the Chronotope in the Novel," 87–110. See, for an early example, Sir Walter Ralegh:

> We might haue wandred a whole yeere in that laborinth of riuers, ere we had found any way, either out or in, especially after we were past the ebbing and flowing, which was in fower daies: for I know all the aerth doth not yeeld the like confluence of streames and branches, the one crossing the other so many times, and all so faire and large, and so like one to another, as no man can tell which to take: and if we went by the Sun or compasse hoping thereby to go directly one way or other, yet that way we were also carried in a circle amongst multitudes of Ilands, and euery Illand so bordered with high trees, as no man could see any further than the bredth of the riuer, or length of the breach.

—Ralegh, *Discoverie of Guiana*, ed. Joyce Lorimer (London: Hakluyt Society, 2006): 95.

[12] José Rabasa, *Inventing America: Spanish Historiography and the Formation of Eurocentrism* (Norman & London: U of Oklahoma P, 1993): 77.

[13] On Manoa as Jerusalem the Golden, see Mary B. Campbell, *The Witness and the Other World: Exotic European Travel Writing, 400–1600* (Ithaca NY: Cornell UP, 1988): 251.

spaces as Stone-Age people) can be seen as a literary adjustment of earlier
Christian allegory to the new demands of a developing (post-Darwinian) evo-
lutionary notion of history vs prehistory. To name but the two novels most
pertinent to such an evolutionist concept of time: in an echo of Conrad's
Heart of Darkness,[14] Evelyn Waugh's novel of a river journey in British
Guiana leads his protagonist into a no-place, feverishly out of all time. In *A
Handful of Dust*, palaeolithic Guianese natives are led and controlled by a
psychotic old man with a surreal obsession with Charles Dickens.[15] Similarly,
Arthur Conan Doyle's protagonists in*The Lost World* (1912) give a scientific
twist to the old adage of "there be dragons" by their discovery of dinosaurs in
the Guianese highlands. Yet, besides offering the possibility of such an evolutionist time, tropical river journeys in a colonial setting still employ their
earlier, allegorical features, leading to atopic, anachronistic dissolution.

The maze of jungle rivers in the Amazon–Orinoco basin, as even a modern
travel account like Charles Nicholl's re-enactment of Ralegh's journey[16] indicates, obviously lends itself to such a representation. The crucial consequence (and one anticipated by Bakhtin's subjectivity of the chronotope in
quest adventures,[17] if taken to extremes) is the subsequent dissolution of the
explorer's experiencing self. Out of time and out of place, the experiencing
subject dissolves.[18] Nicholl, in consequence, prefaces part II of the account of

---

[14] Joseph Conrad, *Heart of Darkness*, ed. Robert Hampson (1902; Harmondsworth:
Penguin, 1995). Peter Firchow considers the similarities to be accidental, as the differences are alienating; Firchow, "In Search of *A Handful of Dust*: The Literary Background of Evelyn Waugh's Novel (1972)," in *Reluctant Modernists: Aldous Huxley
and Some Contemporaries*, ed. Evelyn Firchow & Bernfried Nugel (Münster: LIT,
2003): 117. He sees horror as the only common feature of both texts. His arguments
are somewhat weak, considering that a *response* to Conrad is not necessarily an
imitation either of his plot or of his characters. Cf., for a different view, Jerome
Meckier, "Why the Man Who Liked Dickens Read Dickens Instead of Conrad:
Waugh's *Handful of Dust*," *Novel* 13.2 (Winter 1980): 171.

[15] Interestingly, Waugh had originally intended a religious maniac but settled instead
for a "wholly secular lunatic." David Wykes, *Evelyn Waugh: A Literary Life* (London:
Palgrave Macmillan, 1999): 105.

[16] Charles Nicholl, *The Creature in the Map: A Journey to El Dorado* (Chicago: U
of Chicago P, 1995).

[17] Bakhtin, "Forms of Time and of the Chronotope in the Novel," 130.

[18] See Ralegh's account quoted in footnote 11 above. For similar depictions, see
Nicholl, *The Creature in the Map*, 116, and Redmond O'Hanlon, *In Trouble Again: A*

his travel on the Orinoco whimsically with a "Venezuelan Boatsong": "Who travels on the Orinoco / either dies or goes mad,"[19] which nicely lays out the only two options available to subjects exploring a tropical river.

The rivers themselves enforce an episodic structure to such a degree that landfall at various points of the journey disrupts the monotony of no-place and no-time. Events and experiences there are disjointed from former or later stations, obstructing and often threatening in ways that could not have been anticipated. The plot is consequently one of climax from station to station, in which disorientation leads to increasing fear, and finally peaks in an existential threat. Either (predictably) provisions run out, or (less predictably and more shockingly) death and/or madness strike/s in some form. This is a generic constant of tropical river journeys that even shows in texts in which such journeys are mere episodes. John Gabriel Stedman's comparatively brief posting on the Cottica river in Surinam provides a good example. In the last weeks he sees his crew of forty-five men dwindle, first, to fifteen men, then to seven. His daily reports of further burials create a vivid impression of impending annihilation, with the narrator himself being, burial-spade in hand, at last "between the fits of the fever" and "in a pitiful condition."[20] The striking mortality rates of the Guianese environment up to the nineteenth century supplies the mimetic condition of such a trope.[21]

The quest plot which often underlies exploratory accounts is naturally doomed in this setting, and retrospective travel accounts of the Guianas acquire a certain degree of apologetic rhetoric when faced with the inevitable failure of an attempt at imperialist supremacy over such a *u-topos*. Homodiegetic narrators provide closure of tropical river narratives in their own, narrow escapes, their bodies wrecked by fever and accidents, their minds harrowed by past experiences, but alive. You cannot step into the same river

---

Journey Between the Orinoco and the Amazon (London: Hamish Hamilton, 1988): 113.

[19] "Quien se va a Orinoco / O se muere o vuelve loco," *The Creature in the Map*, 147. (My tr.)

[20] John Gabriel Stedman, *Narrative of a Five Years Expedition against the Revolted Negroes of Surinam*, ed. Richard Price & Sally Price (1796; Baltimore MD: Johns Hopkins UP, 1988): 140.

[21] See the chapter on "The Caribbean Disease Environment" in Jan Rogozinski, *A Brief History of the Caribbean: From the Arawak and Carib to the Present* (New York: Plume, 1999): 17.

twice: a cyclical return to a former self-assurance is impossible.[22] In this respect, too, tropical river journeys generically break with the Bakhtian chronotopes.

In its employment of the epistolary present tense, Barnes' chapter "Upstream!" exemplifies these features of river-journey narratives. The epistolary form increases the disjointed immediacy of a river-journey plot, making most retrospective inspection and causal manipulation impossible – with the notable exception of Letter 12, already from Caracas, in which Charlie struggles with various retrospective explanations for his experiences (213). On the other hand, the whirlpool of stagnant correspondence in "Upstream!" exemplifies anachronism to perfection. Several days' experiences flow into one letter (e.g., 202) or several letters gush over one day's experience (212). Yet all remain ultimately contained in a postbag nicknamed "Our Lady of Communications" (193) until the next helicopter arrives to lift them out into another time and place where they can fulfil their communicative function.

As befits a postmodern novel, Barnes puts such communicative and semantic crises to direct, metafictional use. The reader is left to question his or her own (largely condescending) understanding of Charlie, whose torrential stream of writing and meandering, inconclusive narrative is left precariously balanced on the brink of textual performance. This chapter, after all, immediately precedes the "Parenthesis" chapter of essayistic direct address to the reader.

An as yet unconsidered essential characteristic of "Upstream!" is the fact that the film crew's river journey is meant to be a re-enactment of a missionary exploration, in which, to the narrator, Father Firmin's and Father Antonio's

---

[22] Botting fails to consider Charlie's being an actor in his reading of the final telegram's assumption of icy disdain (*Sex, Machines and Navels*, 220). Seeing instead a psychological subject, Botting diagnoses Charlie thus: "The reduction of his sense of relationship to a mirror that reflects his own self-image takes the form of a 'dual simplification' and a repudiation of the Other, symptoms, for Lacan, of psychosis. The subject is returned to where he always has been, but this time he is without the support of other or Other" (79). Charlie can thus experience a positive "process of self-transformation" (75) and become "the person [sic] who identifies most with their [native American] culture" (78). Kenneth C. Pellow, by contrast, notes that "they [Charlie's letters] alternate between degrading the native people who assist the film crew and aggrandizing them in a most patronizing manner." Pellow, "Braithwaite's Rules and Barnes's Reversals," *Notes & Queries* 55.4 (December 2008): 508. For a very similar evaluation, see Merritt Moseley, *Understanding Julian Barnes* (Columbia: U of South Carolina P, 1997): 118.

exchange of arguments over native baptism figures largely as a possible explanation for Father Antonio/Matt's death. Theology and religion-in-history
is a crucial thematic strand uniting the chapters of Barnes' novel, including
Grillet's and Bechamel's Guianese river journey.

Characteristically, their account is one of temporal and spatial dissolution
as well. Against missionary custom,[23] Grillet and Bechamel do not re-name
their stations according to the saints in the church calendar, which makes reconstructing their passage in time as difficult as pinning it down spatially.
Grillet reports expecting a ten-day trip one way (3), which then turns into a
half-year journey.[24] Landfalls at native settlements prove to be hold-ups between one river episode and the next. There is further dramatic irony in Grillet's apologetic complaints of unreliable native timing leading to "often Three
Months in doing what they might perform in the space of Ten Days" (12).
Whatever delays may have plagued them, he implies, were due to their de-
pendence on such inferior native support. Yet he is forced to admit having
slowed down their native guides on walks overland (10). Distances are also
unreliable. Grillet claims to have traversed 240 French leagues (43). With the
league a variable measurement, this would translate into something between
780 and 1123 km: vague enough already. Even so, the leagues he does account for are only approximations and do not add up.[25]

Information on space thus relies largely on names of rivers and people and
latitude measurements, longitude being indeterminate. Yet names for people
and landmarks are ambiguous and sometimes openly manipulated:

> The Principal [native] of 'em whose Name was *Paratou*, told us, for
> our comfort, that in the place where we now were, which they call
> *Caraoribo*, from the Name of a little River that passes by it, we should
> find a great many *Paratous*, he meant a great many *Nouragues*, as
> good humor'd as himself. (11)[26]

---

[23] See Luke Clossey, *Salvation and Globalization in the Early Jesuit Missions* (New
York: Cambridge UP, 2008): 92.

[24] They leave Cayenne on 25 January and return on 27 June 1673.

[25] At the very beginning of the account, for instance, Grillet reports twelve plus two
(6), then "near Fifty" (7) and next twenty-four (8) leagues, the last overland, and ends
by stating they were now eighty leagues from Cayenne (11). Yet he only starts measuring one full day's journey from the settlement (4).

[26] Another example is the identity of one of the guides, identified as Morou ("the
name of an Indian Nation," 22), and "whome we then took to be a *Nourague*" (22).

Does this make "Paratou" a generic or an individual designation?[27] And why does Grillet call the river close by "Aproage" (18) instead of "Caraoribo"? Is it perhaps the same river in another language – and if so, which one? As in Barnes, communication errors and troubles with translator figures[28] haunt Grillet's account. Yet while Charlie seems mainly concerned with various sublunar matters, modes of narration and representation take on necessarily metaphysical dimensions with Grillet and Bechamel.

> Father Bechamel immediately began to apply himself to the study of this [Nourague] Language; and I made so much advantage of his Labour in which he succeeded to admiration, that by means of the *Galibis* Language[29] I made a small Discourse of the Creation of the World; to make these [Nourague] people know something of their Creator. *Imanon* the Master of this Hut was the first that took delight in hearing this Discourse, and after him the Chief himself; and Five or Six others, as they were working would repeat in that very indifferent Galibis I could speak, these Words; God made the Heavens, God made the Earth, &c. (13)

Grillet seems blithely unfazed by the Nourague parroting of his own "indifferent" (i.e. faulty) Galibi. He also has been forced to admit a little earlier that there is no linguistic similarity between the Nourague and the Galibi languages.[30] Optimistically, he reads the passage as an agreement with the theological content of the paraphrase of Genesis 1:1 he hopes to have produced. The possibility of parody in his audience's response does not enter into his account, and the additional possibility of his own distortions of the divine

---

[27] In O'Hanlon, *In Trouble Again*, 123, a native boatman's name is Culimacaré. Culimacaré's village is also called Culimacaré.

[28] For a discussion of the practical joke played on Charlie by his native (female) translator, see Botting, *Sex, Machines and Navels*, 78.

[29] *Galibi* is the term given by the French to mainland Carib people, to distinguish them from the island 'Caraïbes'. Neil Whitehead, *Lords of the Tiger Spirit: A History of the Caribs in Colonial Venezuela and Guyana, 1498–1820* (Dordrecht: Foris, 1988): 96.

[30] "This *Nouragues* tongue is not of an easie and soft Pronunciation like that of the *Galibis*, but has a great number of Words that must be pronounc'd with very rough Aspirations, others of 'em can't be pronounced without shutting the Teeth; at another time one must speak through the Nose; and sometimes these Three difficulties all occur in the same Word" (13).

message he means to convey remains just visible under the surface of his rendition. The mirror of the Other here simply serves as projection. Simultaneously, however, the missionary endeavour of the two Jesuits is reduced to farce.

In the absence of linguistic common ground, assumptions of understanding largely rest on interpreting body-language and guessing motivation behind observed behaviour. Truth – and in the passage quoted above, divine truth as well – thus falls prey to the semantic ambiguity of reality. In this respect, too, Grillet's experience shares features with Barnes' narrator-figure Charlie and touches on issues central to *A History of the World* as a whole. Two of Grillet's episodes can be seen to prefigure Charlie's attempts at guessing reasons, and trying to come to terms with harrowing experiences. The first episode has Grillet come face to face with infanticide:

> I had before Baptiz'd a little Girl in the Cottage of this *Imanon* immediately after it was born, because the Mother of it when she brought it into the world had left it in the Dirt, from whence they would not take it up for a long time, being told of this disorder, and finding they would put nothing under the Infant to keep it from the coldness of the Mud, and of the Night I baptiz'd it. (19)

Customarily, Grillet and Bechamel only baptize dying native Americans they encounter on their expedition, and, though not explicitly stated here, Grillet's curt and uncommented closing phrase indicates his conviction that the newborn rejected by its mother (why? how could Grillet tell?) and unprotected by the community (why again?) is dying and that his enquiring after it does not change the situation. Interestingly, Grillet does not intervene beyond calming his own conscience by an emergency baptism. Yet this is behaviour exhibited by the same Imanon's hut community, which just a few pages before gives Grillet a blissful illusion of shared understanding. In the next sentence, Grillet reports leaving Imanon's hut just as abruptly as he reports the episode of the rejected newborn. The reader is left with no explanation for the mother's refusal to accept her child or the hut members' communal refusal to take over responsibility from her.

The second disconcerting situation is a confrontation with cannibalism:

> and besides, one of the People of the Cottage having set before us the Jaw of a young man [killed and eaten]; we told 'em, This was not well done, and that God forbids us to kill an Enemy, when we take him

> Prisoner, and to eat him afterwards: At this they look'd down very
> much without giving one word of reply. (26)

Classically, apart from this metonymic manifestation of the jaw-bone, cannibalism remains a report only in other episodes,[31] yet one that Grillet credits
with truth.[32] The jaw-bone represents not only the supposed reality of cannibalism but in contemporary emblematic usage metonymically encloses the
pagan fierceness and vengefulness[33] variously associated by Grillet with the
Nourague tribe. The silent response is read by Grillet as shame – once again a
projection, based on assuming a shared body-language.[34] Ultimately, though,
the Nourague response remains a cipher, as do the actual identity and purpose
of the jaw-bone placed before Grillet and Bechamel.

Similarly, in Julian Barnes' novel, Charlie's first realization of the ultimate
Otherness of native culture comes with his trouble accounting for the native
lack of response to the drowning of one of the rafters (203). Charlie, like Grillet in the episode of the newborn, comes up against what appears to him to be
callous indifference:

> I half expected that when we pitched camp for the night there'd be
> some sort of ceremony – I don't know, burning a bundle of clothes or
> whatever. Not so. Same old jolly camp-fire life went on as per usual.
> (203)

---

[31] On the discussion surrounding the credibility of such reports and eye-witness
accounts, see Philip P. Boucher, *Cannibal Encounters: Europeans and Island Caribs,
1492–1763* (Baltimore MD: Johns Hopkins UP, 1992): 6.

[32] For example: "The Fourteenth we left this Hutt, and presently enter'd into the River
of *Tenaporibo*, which is very deep and rapid, tho' it winds much; we were not the first
French-Men that had been upon this River; and we have been inform'd that Three
English-Men were kill'd and Eaten there some Years ago by the *Nouragues*" (19).

[33] *Emblemata: Handbuch zur Sinnbildkunst des XVI. und XVII. Jahrhunderts*, ed.
Arthur Henkel & Albrecht Schöne (Stuttgart: Metzler, 1996): 1849. Relating the jaw-
bone of an ass to that of a young native is easily possible emblematically, though it
may appear obscure to modern readers, as the ass is the Christian emblem of the to-be-
converted pagan. The ox and ass in the manger at Bethlehem, for example, were seen
as emblems of the Christian (ox = obedience) and pagan (ass = stubbornness) presence
respectively. On long-term vengefulness among the Nourague, see Grillet, 22.

[34] Native 'shame' can then be employed by Grillet as an indication that "it seems, by
what I have been relating, to be no difficult matter to restrain 'em from this Savage
Practice of killing and eating their Enemies" (27).

The second episode is the crucial event of the American actor's death by drowning. Charlie lists oddities in the behaviour of the native American rafters, and reports the disappearance of their camp as well as the vanishing of the rope supposed to have held the raft to prevent capsizing.[35] The foregone conclusion for Charlie is that the above is not merely a list of observations but a trail of evidence. What he thought was a "post-acting civilization" (203) has staged the 'accidental' capsize of the raft. The need to explain these events gains existential momentum from Charlie's egoism. He sees himself and his Jesuit persona as the original target of this plot (217). Matt's death, by comparison, could only be a coincidental outcome: "My line held, Matt's line broke. That's how it was. That's my luck" (215).

Trail of evidence – or red herring? Assuming that we take at face value Charlie's assertions based in part on the translator Miguel's assertions (215), are we to conclude that the rafters' poling the broken-adrift raft straight into white water indicates murderous intent?[36] One clue, surprisingly, lies buried in the missionary travelogue of Grillet and Bechamel:

> 'Tis abundantly more dangerous to go down these Falls, than to get up
> 'em; because they chose those places where the Water runs less viol-
> ently to get the Canoo up with main Strength, whereas in going down
> 'em they take the swiftest Part of the Stream, so that one runs a greater
> Hazard of one's life, than can easily be express'd. (33)

Despite the chapter's title,[37] the raft on which Charlie and Matt are acting two Jesuits cannot drift upstream at all. They are drifting downstream, and poling

---

[35] "Instead of a dozen Indians on the raft there were only two, each with just a pole at the back of the raft. [...] Then at the end of the scene we noticed the Indians weren't doing what they normally did which was stick their poles in to stop the raft. They were just poling away [...] the Indians were heading us – straight into a pile of rocks and foaming water – " (214). "Then we went to see what had happened to the rope round the tree and there wasn't anything left, it had just gone. Which was pretty odd as it was fixed with one of those fancy knots which simply can't pull out" (215).

[36] Sesto falls unwittingly prey to this textual strategy: "The final shock to Charles comes when he learns that the natives, whom he suddenly refers to as 'those fucking Indians' in one of his letters, have not only caused Matt's death but also stolen food, clothing, and much of the crew's film equipment" (*Language, History and Meta-narrative*, 100).

[37] Sesto, for one, takes the title explicitly at face value (*Language, History and Metanarrative*, 104).

into the white-water current is precisely what the two rafters are doing once the rope is torn. Regardless of Charlie's foregone conclusion about a native fabrication of deadly events, the tribe's actions remain entirely opaque. In fact, to return to the full implication of the chapter's title, "upstream" as indication of an overall direction is worthless in the context of the Amazon–Orinoco water basin. Redmond O'Hanlon, to exemplify this, quotes at length from Alexander Humboldt's travel account,[38] and it is worth recalling at this point that Barnes' author note thanks O'Hanlon for his assistance (308).

Only one being in Barnes' eighth chapter clearly goes upstream, the *candirú* fish. Charlie reports, incredulously at first (195) and then convinced by native corroboration (202), the hearsay that men peeing into the river fall prey to an obscene attack: a local fish is said to swim up its victim's urine and bury itself in the urethra.[39] Here, too, motivation in Charlie's letters remains unaccountable (194). Why the fish would act this way is beyond any reasonable understanding to Charlie. As the existence of the woodworm problematizes accounts of Noah's Arc in the first chapter ("The Stowaway"),[40] the legendary mention of the *candirú* problematizes evolution in "Upstream!" Its behaviour is a case of parasitic over-specialization; human victims are accidental hosts.

Following the trail of ammonia into a bigger fish's gills to lodge itself there and, for a few minutes, feed on its victim's blood is normal *candirú* behaviour. Upstream, then, the *candirú* instinctively follows a trail of ammonia so intense that it points to a feeding paradise, an illusion bound to end with the *candirú*'s death – though, in the case of its accidental host, not quite with the emasculation dreaded by Charlie.[41] The legend embedded in the chapter so far seems scientifically correct. Yet, ironically, oral history has blended a multitude of different parasitic catfish species into one *candirú* (among them *Tridensimilis brevis*, and two groups of *Vandelliinae* – especially *Vandellia*

---

[38] "I have collected on one plate of my atlas several examples of these ramifications with counter-currents, those apparent movements against the general slope, these bifurcations of rivers, the knowledge of which is interesting to hydrographic engineers" (O'Hanlon, *In Trouble Again*, 33).

[39] This piece of local knowledge, incidentally (or perhaps not), is recounted in a gleefully dramatic description by O'Hanlon.

[40] See Daniel Candel, "Julian Barnes' *A History of Science in 10½ Chapters*," *English Studies* 82.3 (August 2001): 253.

[41] Botting once again assumes Charlie's reliability here and sees this as an instance of phallocentric dismemberment (*Sex, Machines and Navels*, 78).

cirrhosa – and *Stegophilinae*).[42] The "little fish" of Charlie's letters denotes a whole mass of different haematophagous parasitic fish. Charlie's assumption of a more truthful (since more empirical) knowledge on behalf of his native informants is thus as much empirical as it is scientifically erroneous. Similarly erroneous is the reader's assumption of the validity of Charlie's supposedly authentic clues explaining the events, or, indeed, on a metafictional level, as erroneous as it would be to assume that the title of the chapter (with its exclamation-mark promising big-screen fictional drama) may be indicative of the story's and the jungle journey's linear progression. As the novel's various chapters insist, historiography, scientific truth, religious myth, and oral traditions are interwoven in circular, repetitive relations akin to a symphony,[43] in which one truth and one account mirrors another. According to a statement in the chapter immediately before "Upstream!,"

> the point is this: not that myth refers us back to some original event which has been fancifully transcribed as it passed through the collective memory; but that it refers us forward to something that will happen, that must happen. Myth will become reality, however sceptical we might be (181).

Even though Charlie's capsizing on the river is somehow related to the events during the unnamed historical journey of Grillet and Bechamel, whose own upstream journey tried to lodge the *candirú* of Christianity – at the risk of being blasphemously offensive – terminally among the tribes of the Guiana hinterland, his experience is not the main point. Instead, in "Upstream!" Barnes shows acting (as a form of translocation) as transforming a missionary past into a contemporary present, mutating oral history as well as historiographic past into reality. In the sense of the well-known Marxist phrase, Charlie's postcolonial farce and its evolutionist concepts repeat the colonial tragedy of missionary exploration. That the postcolonial tragedy of Father Antonio's downstream drowning, propelled by misunderstandings and a capitalist movie-making venture, in turn echoes the colonial farce of Grillet and Bechamel's ultimate missionary failure is Barnes' postmodern up-ending of intertextual reality.

---

[42] See Dominique Adriaens, "Evolutionary morphology in trichomycterid catfishes: structural and functional adaptations in haematophagous vertebrates," *Evolutionary Morphology of Vertebrates* (University of Ghent), http://www.fun-morph.ugent.be /Projects/Trichomycterids/Trichomycterids.htm (accessed 12 June 2009).

[43] See Moseley, *Understanding Julian Barnes*, 115.

WORKS CITED

Adriaens, Dominique. "Evolutionary morphology in trichomycterid catfishes: structural and functional adaptations in haematophagous vertebrates," *Evolutionary Morphology of Vertebrates* (University of Ghent), http://www.funmorph.ugent.be/Projects/Trichomycterids/Trichomycterids.htm (accessed 12 June 2009).

Bakhtin, Mikhail M. "Forms of Time and of the Chronotope in the Novel: Notes toward a Historical Poetics" (1937–38), tr. Caryl Emerson & Michael Holquist, in *Problems of Literature and Esthetics* (*Voprosy literatury i estetiki*, 1975), repr. in *The Dialogic Imagination: Four Essays by M.M. Bakhtin*, ed. Michael Holquist (U of Texas Slavic Series 1; Austin: U of Texas P, 1981): 84–258.

Barnes, Julian. *A History of the World in 10½ Chapters* (New York: Vintage, 1990).

Botting, Fred. *Sex, Machines and Navels: Fiction, Fantasy and History in the Future Present* (Manchester: Manchester UP, 1999).

Boucher, Philip P. *Cannibal Encounters: Europeans and Island Caribs, 1492–1763* (Baltimore MD: Johns Hopkins UP, 1992).

——. *France and the American Tropics to 1700: Tropics of Discontent* (Baltimore MD: Johns Hopkins UP, 2008).

Campbell, Mary B. *The Witness and the Other World: Exotic European Travel Writing, 400–1600* (Ithaca NY: Cornell UP, 1988).

Candel, Daniel. "Julian Barnes' *A History of Science in 10½ Chapters*," *English Studies* 82.3 (August 2001): 253–261.

Clossey, Luke. *Salvation and Globalization in the Early Jesuit Missions* (New York: Cambridge UP, 2008).

Conrad, Joseph. *Heart of Darkness*, ed. Robert Hampson (1902; Harmondsworth: Penguin, 1995).

Fabian, Johannes. *Time and the Other: How Anthropology Makes Its Object* (New York: Columbia UP, 1983).

Fermin, Philip. *Nieuwe algemeene beschryving van de colonie van Surinam: Behelzende al het merkwaardige van dezelve, met betrekkinge tot de historie, aardryks en natuurkunde* (Harlingen: V. van der Plaats jr., 1770).

Firchow, Peter. "In Search of *A Handful of Dust*: The Literary Background of Evelyn Waugh's Novel (1972)," in *Reluctant Modernists: Aldous Huxley and Some Contemporaries*, ed. Evelyn Firchow & Bernfried Nugel (Münster: LIT, 2003): 103–18.

Grillet, John, & Francis Bechamel. *A Journal of the Travels of John Grillet and Francis Bechamel into Guiana, in the Year, 1674* (London: Samuel Buckley, 1698).

Guignery, Vanessa. *The Fiction of Julian Barnes: A Reader's Guide to Essential Criticism* (London: Palgrave Macmillan, 2006).

Henkel, Arthur, & Albrecht Schöne, ed. *Emblemata: Handbuch zur Sinnbildkunst des XVI. und XVII. Jahrhunderts* (Stuttgart: Metzler, rev. ed. 1996).

Jesuit Presbytery Guyana, "Guyana Early History," *The Jesuits in Guyana*, http://www
.guyanajesuits.org/page.asp?PageID=318 (accessed 12 June 2009)

Meckier, Jerome. "Why the Man Who Liked Dickens Read Dickens Instead of Conrad: Waugh's *Handful of Dust*," *Novel* 13.2 (Winter 1980): 171–187.

Moseley, Merritt. *Understanding Julian Barnes* (Columbia: U of South Carolina P,
1997).

Neive, Barbara. *The Jesuits: Their Foundation and History*, 2 vols (New York: Benzinger Brothers, 1879).

Nicholl, Charles. *The Creature in the Map: A Journey to El Dorado* (Chicago: U of
Chicago P, 1995).

O'Hanlon, Redmond. *In Trouble Again: A Journey Between the Orinoco and the Amazon* (London: Hamish Hamilton, 1988).

Pellow, Kenneth C. "Braithwaite's Rules and Barnes's Reversals," *Notes & Queries*
55.4 (December 2008): 507–10.

Rabasa, José. *Inventing America: Spanish Historiography and the Formation of Eurocentrism* (Norman: U of Oklahoma P, 1993).

Ralegh, Sir Walter. *Discoverie of Guiana*, ed. Joyce Lorimer (London: Hakluyt
Society, 2006).

Rogozinski, Jan. *A Brief History of the Caribbean: From the Arawak and Carib to the
Present* (New York: Plume, 1999).

Schiller, Friedrich. "On the Art of Tragedy" (1792), in *Essays*, tr. Daniel O. Dahlstrom,
ed. Walter Hinderer & Daniel O. Dahlstrom (*Schillers Werke*, ed. Benno von
Wiese, 1962; tr. 1993; New York: Continuum, 2005): 1–21.

Sesto, Bruce. *Language, History, and Metanarrative in the Fiction of Julian Barnes*
(New York: Peter Lang, 2001).

Stedman, John Gabriel. *Narrative of a Five Years Expedition against the Revolted
Negroes of Surinam*, ed. Richard Price & Sally Price (1796; Baltimore MD: Johns
Hopkins UP, 1988).

Waugh, Evelyn. *A Handful of Dust*, ed. Robert Murray Davies (1934; Harmondsworth:
Penguin, 2000).

Whitehead, Neil. *Lords of the Tiger Spirit: A History of the Caribs in Colonial Venezuela and Guyana, 1498–1820* (Dordrecht: Foris, 1988).

Wykes, David. *Evelyn Waugh: A Literary Life* (London: Palgrave Macmillan, 1999).

⌘

Myths of Rebellion
—Translocation and (Cultural) Innovation in Mexican-American[1] Literature

MARGA MUNKELT

1. Introduction: *Ur*-Rebels

IN WESTERN CULTURE, it is generally believed and maintained (for example, in proverbs or sententious sayings) that pride is a sin and that it invariably entails one's fall. According to the Christian tradition, it is Lucifer who is the first to compete with God and thereby to commit the sin that causes his fall,[2] and in Greek mythology it is Icarus whose ambition to fly as high as possible causes his fall.[3] Lucifer's sin of pride results in his loss of God's grace and, physically, in his expulsion from Heaven to Hell: i.e. in his fall from high to low.[4] This movement also represents the basic tragic experience according to Chaucer's definition of 'tragedy' in "The Monk's Tale" as man's life beginning "in prosperity" but ending in "misery."[5] Chaucer's

---

[1] This essay does not transform 'Mexican Americans' into 'compound' Americans but hyphenates 'Mexican-American' only when it is used attributively. Also within the framework of this essay, 'Mexican American' and 'Chicano/a' are used interchangeably.

[2] *The Bible: Authorized King James Version with Apocrypha*, ed. & intro. Robert Carroll & Stephen Prickett (Oxford: Oxford UP, 1997): 778 (Isaiah 14:12–14).

[3] Literature and painting illustrate this myth, such as W.H. Auden's poem "Musée des Beaux Arts" (1938), which focuses on Brueghel's painting "Icarus" in the Museum of Fine Arts in Brussels. See Auden, "Musée des Beaux Arts," in *The Norton Anthology of Poetry*, ed. Margaret Ferguson et al. (New York: W.W. Norton, 1996): 1367.

[4] *The Bible*, 309 (Revelation 12:9–10).

[5] Geoffrey Chaucer, "The Prologue of the Monk's Tale," in *The Riverside Chaucer*,

Monk does not specify the misery – which can be the loss of possessions, of love, of everything one esteems dear, and, of course, one's life.

Since Lucifer, the vow *non serviam* ("I will not serve") has been identified as not only inherently Satanic but also as a synonym for protest, rebellion, and resistance, and the archetypal quest for self-assertion. Numerous literary examples illustrate this thesis, among them James Joyce's Stephen Dedalus in *A Portrait of the Artist as a Young Man*, where the protagonist's "I will not serve"[6] marks his decision against priesthood and in favour of becoming an artist. This decision is not only marked as a direct reference to Lucifer (Stephen's friend Cranly reminds him that "that remark was made before"[7]) but also implies most of the aspects associated with rebellion, such as deviating from the rules of society; deviating from the rules of the Church; deviating from one's education; and claiming the right to one's assertion as an individual: "I was not myself as I am now, as I had to become," says Stephen.[8]

A combination of pride and protest is also used by Shakespeare to characterize some of his villains. When Richard Gloucester (the future King Richard III) is "determined to prove a villain"[9] and Iago holds that "'tis in ourselves that we are thus, or thus: our bodies are gardens, to the which our wills are gardeners,"[10] both, like Lucifer and Satan together, redefine their originally subordinate roles as positions of independence and autonomy.

The *ur*-rebel Lucifer is punished by being cast down below the earth into Hell, where he changes his identity and becomes Satan, the devil, no longer associated with light[11] but with darkness. Milton's *Paradise Lost* charac-

---

ed. F.N. Robinson (Boston MA: Houghton Mifflin, 1987): 241 (ll. 1973–77). Chaucer's definition of 'tragedy' is simultaneously the first occurrence of this term in the English language.

[6] James Joyce, *A Portrait of the Artist as a Young Man*, ed. & intro. Jeri Johnson (1914–15; Oxford: Oxford UP, 2000): 201.

[7] Joyce, *Portrait*, 201.

[8] *Portrait*, 202.

[9] William Shakespeare, "The Tragedy of Richard the Third," in *The Riverside Shakespeare*, ed. G. Blakemore Evans et al. (1974; Boston MA: Houghton Mifflin, 2nd ed. 1997): 753 (I.i.30).

[10] William Shakespeare, "The Tragedy of Othello, the Moor of Venice," in *The Riverside Shakespeare*, ed. G. Blakemore Evans et al. (1974; Boston MA: Houghton Mifflin, 2nd ed. 1997): 1258 (I.iii.319–21).

[11] Lucifer, i.e. the 'light-bearer', is one of the angels who belongs to God's inner circle.

terizes Satan not only as unwilling to accept this fall but also as someone who rebels a second time by not accepting his punishment as a loss. Instead, he redefines God's banishment as a gain and as a chance, when he protests that it is "Better to reign in Hell, then [sic] serve in Heav'n."[12] In order to be able to rise again, Satan disguises himself and applies devices of hypocrisy and deception.[13] In Book 5 of *Paradise Lost*, Satan is repeatedly qualified as "counterfe[i]ted truth."[14] His various disguises culminate in his assuming a serpent's shape – in itself a lowering of his physiognomy and a form of self-denigration[15] – but thereby covering up his intellectual superiority. This aspect of masquerading also plays an important role for Shakespeare's two satanic protagonists, Richard III and Iago. Their numerous soliloquies reveal to the spectator almost from the beginnings of both plays that they are not as they present themselves to the other characters.[16]

The principles of protest and rebellion find yet another expression in those mythical characters who are not self-centred like those in the tradition of Lucifer but whose rebellion has altruistic, if not socio-utopian, motivations. The Robin-Hood figure, for example, does not try to rival God or to upset the hierarchy of the universe; rather, he intends to implement God's intentions. This kind of rebel violates the rules of society in order to correct them.[17] Thus, the sense of superiority shared by the *ur*-rebels Lucifer and Robin Hood has different sources: Whereas Lucifer's sin is rooted in envy and pride, Robin Hood's offences are initiated by contempt for those in possession of wealth and by his compassion with the common man. Rebellion can thus result in a satisfaction of internal independence and sense of identity as much as in an external confrontation with power-structures.

---

[12] John Milton, "Paradise Lost," in *The Riverside Milton*, ed. Roy Flannagan (Boston MA: Houghton Mifflin, 1998): 362 (Book 1, l. 263).

[13] See Milton, "Paradise Lost," esp. Books 3 and 4.

[14] "Paradise Lost," 500 (Book 5, l. 771).

[15] "Paradise Lost," Book 9.

[16] Both are traditionally classified as intellectual or Machiavellian villains.

[17] This myth has survived, although a branch of recent scholarship doubts the altruistic motives of the historical Robin Hood. Mike Dixon–Kennedy, for example, identifies him as a man "who was forced to take to the forests" as well as one "who fought the wrongs done to him" and concludes that he "did not rob from the rich to give to the poor, he robbed from the rich and kept it." See *The Robin Hood Handbook: The Outlaw in History, Myth and Legend* (Stroud: Sutton, 2006): 415.

These types of rebellion can be considered to be the predecessors of and models for Mexican-American resistance to the claim of Anglo-American superiority and political authority. In the phase of territorial competition between Mexico and the USA in the nineteenth century and again in the early stages of the Chicano Movement, the 1970s, variants of the Lucifer/Satan/Robin-Hood characters or their fusion are used to formulate the need for a Mexican-American identity of self-esteem and for an escape from oppression, poverty, and disgrace. The earliest expressions of rebellion appear in nineteenth-century Mexican ballads (*corridos*) and are concerned mostly with life in the borderland. This form of rebellion is often represented by the so-called *bandido*. Another form of protest is directed against Anglo-American authorities with an emphasis on one's otherness – often by means of visible ethnic attributes or exaggerated signs of affiliation with ethnic, political, or criminal organizations as well as by clothes. This form of rebellion is represented by the *pachuco* (a term which implies foreignness). Both types of rebels are established as protagonists in Mexican-American drama as well.

This essay assumes the transformation of myths as translocation in two senses: its transportation into a different historical or cultural context, on the one hand, and its transformation within a different ideological framework, on the other. No attempt is made to trace and document the precise itinerary and transmission of the myths. The tacit assumption is that they have moved in time and space into the culture of the Mexican-American borderland by way of both Americas – as a product of the Spanish conquerors in the sixteenth century and as a tradition of the New England colonizers in the seventeenth century.

2. Bandidos

The Spanish word for 'rebel' used in the Mexican-American literature under investigation is *bandido* with the English senses "bandit, robber; criminal, outlaw."[18] However, the nouns *bandido* and 'bandit' are derived from the past participle of Latin *bannire* (meaning "proclaim, proscribe, BANISH"[19]). The basic condition of being a *bandido*, is, accordingly, one's being excluded from the confines of society and the law; in this sense, a *bandido* is a 'bandit'

---

[18] Rubén Cobos, *Dictionary of New Mexico and Southern Colorado Spanish* (Santa Fe: Museum of New Mexico P): 17, s.v. 'bándido'.

[19] *The Oxford English Dictionary* (2nd ed. 1989), s.v. 'Bandit'.

or 'outlaw'. Using the political potential of lyric poetry, the *corrido,* a "narrative musico-literary genre, the Mexican ballad,"[20] calls attention to the fact that, in the borderland, not all human beings have equal access to the law. It not only expresses "a form of cultural resistance"[21] but also "transcends class difference and involves the total ethnic group,"[22] although there is unanimous agreement that *corridos* are usually more concerned with local and regional aspects of communal life than with world-shaking political events. Its similarity to its ancestor, the Scottish border ballad, is obvious: the people living in the "rectangle with corners at Newcastle, Penrith, Dumfries and Edinburgh [...] were Borderers before they were either Scots or English,"[23] and it is significant that the 'Borders' is "not a line but an area, in many respects historically and traditionally almost an independent region."[24] According to Gloria Anzaldúa, a "borderland [in contrast to a border line] is a vague and undetermined place created by the emotional residue of an unnatural boundary."[25] In

---

[20] Manuel Peña, "Foreword" (1994), *A Texas-Mexican Cancionero: Folksongs of the Lower Border* by Américo Paredes (Austin: U of Texas P, 1976): xxv. The *corrido* of border-conflict flourished between 1836 and 1930. See Américo Paredes, *With His Pistol in His Hand: A Border Ballad and Its Hero* (1958; Austin: U of Texas P, 2003): 132. But the *corrido* has survived into the present with new themes addressing contemporary social problems such as unemployment and drug addiction. There are various theories accounting for its origin and development. See María Herrera–Sobek, *Northward Bound: The Mexican Immigrant Experience in Ballad and Song* (Bloomington: Indiana UP, 1993), and José E. Limón, *Mexican Ballads, Chicano Poems: History and Influence in Mexican-American Social Poetry* (Berkeley & Los Angeles: U of California P, 1992). The standard assumption is that the Spanish *conquistadores* brought their traditional epics (for example, *El Cid*) to Mexico, and the indigenous peoples developed stories about "their own heroes and their own historical events" according to this model. See Américo Paredes, *A Texas-Mexican Cancionero: Folksongs of the Lower Border*, ed. Paredes (Austin: U of Texas P, 1976): 5. For details on the form and music of the *corrido*, see John Donald Robb, *Hispanic Folk Songs of New Mexico*, ed. Robb (1954; Albuquerque: U of New Mexico P, 2008): 1–9.

[21] Peña, "Foreword," xxviii.

[22] "Foreword," xxix.

[23] James Reed, *The Border Ballads* (London: Athlone, 1973): 10. See also Américo Paredes, *With His Pistol in His Hand: A Border Ballad and Its Hero* (1958; Austin: U of Texas P, 2003): 243–44.

[24] Reed, *Border Ballads*, 10.

[25] Gloria Anzaldúa, *Borderland/La Frontera: The New Mestiza* (1987; San Francisco: Aunt Lute, 3rd ed. 2007): 25.

this sense, the "frontier community"[26] from the Middle Ages to the early seventeenth century resembles the condition of Mexican Americans, most of whom neither emigrated nor immigrated in the second half of the nineteenth century but became Americans because the borders between Mexico and America were changed; hence the designation "foreigners in their native land."[27] Those Mexicans and Americans who lived in the border area between Mexico and the USA were subjected to multiple territorial changes and to shifting political affiliations to Mexico or America. In 1848, the Treaty of Guadalupe Hidalgo concluded the Mexican–American War and endowed those Mexicans who had become Americans with American civil rights. But ignorance of the language of their new country and racial prejudice prevented their feeling or being accepted as 'real' Americans.[28] The "civil wars among the Rio Grande people"[29] and the "kinds of indignities" experienced by the newly created Mexican Americans[30] became a dominant topic in the border-*corrido*.

As a Mexican American, the *bandido* is a passive 'outlaw' without the same access to the law as his Anglo-American fellow citizens, but in his "protest against exploitation and injustice"[31] he becomes an active 'outlaw', trying to secure 'the law' for himself and his fellow countrymen. The "[Corrido de] Gregorio Cortez"[32] is the "prototype of the *corrido* of border conflict"[33] and

---

[26] Reed, *Border Ballads*, 10.

[27] See *Foreigners in Their Native Land*, ed. David J. Weber (1973; Albuquerque: U of New Mexico P, 2003).

[28] F. Arturo Rosales, *Chicano!: The History of the Mexican American Civil Rights Movement* (Houston TX: Arte Público, 1997): xxi-xxii.

[29] Américo Paredes, *A Texas-Mexican Cancionero: Folksongs of the Lower Border*, ed. Paredes (Austin: U of Texas P, 1976): 21.

[30] Paredes, *Cancionero*, 22.

[31] *Cancionero*, 27.

[32] "[El Corrido de] Gregorio Cortez," in *With His Pistol in His Hand: A Border Ballad and Its Hero*, ed. Américo Paredes (1958; Austin: U of Texas P, 2003): 151–74. An exact dating of this and the other *corridos* discussed in this essay is not possible. But the assumption is that "Gregorio Cortez" was composed after 1901 (Paredes, "Last Word," in *With His Pistol*, 241–47). — Popular history recounts that, in 1901, in Karnes County, Cortez shot Sheriff Brack Morris, who had shortly before killed Cortez's brother while trying to arrest him for a crime which the brother had not committed. Cortez did not even try to legally claim his right but fled, killing at least another sheriff in self-defence before finally being captured (*With His Pistol*, 52–54).

[33] Paredes, *With His Pistol*, 241.

deals with the motivations for a murder and its consequences. This *corrido* is probably the most famous historical and literary example of the fight against injustice, as Cortez's "case united Mexican-Americans in a common cause, and […] the *corrido* about him [is] a milestone in the Mexican-American's emerging group consciousness."[34] The ballad builds up the protagonist as a kind of scapegoat-figure in an environment of inequality and injustice, and a sense of uncontrollability is evoked by the unitedness of those pursuing Gregorio Cortez for murdering the sheriff. Thus, the speaker summarizes that they "succeeded in surrounding him, / Quite a few more than three hundred."[35]

The first four stanzas describe the process of creating an 'outlaw', incriminating Gregorio Cortez with the unsolved death of a sheriff (and possibly of other victims) but without uncovering his motivations:

> Now they have *outlawed* Cortez,
> Throughout the whole state
> Let him be taken dead or alive;
> He has killed several men. (154, stanza 4; emphasis added)

The ultimately successful chase of the alleged murderer reveals the Americans' fear and their impression that "trying to overtake Cortez / Was like following a star" (155, stanza 9). A possible sense of 'outlaw' as being "above the law" is suggested when Cortez escapes twice by leaping out of the "corral" (155–56, stanzas 11–12), and, even more so, when he ultimately arranges his own capture in order to prevent further murders (157, stanzas 20–21):

> When they surrounded the house,
> Cortez suddenly appeared before them,
> "You will take me if I'm willing,
> But not any other way." (175, stanza 23)

---

[34] See Paredes, *Cancionero*, 31.

[35] Variant X of "Gregorio Cortez," in *With His Pistol in His Hand: A Border Ballad and Its Hero* (1958; Austin: U of Texas P, 2003): 155 (stanza 11). Further references are in the main text. — This *corrido* exists in numerous variant English versions which have been collected and described by Américo Paredes. See "Variants of Gregorio Cortez," in *With His Pistol*, 151–74. Variant versions A, B, C, D, E, F, G, H, and I are "collected from traditional sources" and all but Variant A "now are part of the Texas Folklore Archive at the University of Texas" (Paredes, *With His Pistol*, 177). Unless otherwise mentioned, this essay quotes from Variant X.

This fact alone ridicules the Americans' demonstration of power through numbers, and Cortez himself puts the key message into words that imply his contempt as well as his recognition of their fear of the unknown, of the Other:

> Then said Gregorio Cortez,
> With his pistol in his hand,
> "Don't run, you cowardly rangers,
> From just one Mexican." (156, stanza 13)[36]

In addition to dissociating the meanings of 'majority' and 'minority' from their respective connotations of power and weakness, this *corrido* points a finger at the majority's interest in the pursuit of gain under the cover of implementing the law. The speaker explains that "they wanted to get / The thousand dollars they were offered" (157, stanza 22).

The characteristics assigned to the protagonist go beyond the description of purely human qualities. The sheriff's murder, called a "misfortune" in several of the variant versions[37] or described as having "happened,"[38] is not unequivocally made Gregorio Cortez's deed. Also, the details about the 'historical' Cortez are omitted, as if the speaker wants to keep him innocent. These and other details in the ballad recall archetypal elements of a scapegoat hunt rather than a legal pursuit. The defendant, however, transforms himself from someone hunted into a hunter. Cortez's own sense of unimpeachability is illustrated by his demonstration of pride, as he enlists a fellow Mexican's assistance:

> Now he has met a Mexican;
> He says to him haughtily,
> "Tell me the news;
> I am Gregorio Cortez." (156–57, stanza 19)

Cortez's escape by leaping out of their "corral" (155, 156, stanzas 11 and 12)[39] means that he is separating himself from his followers and leaving man-made boundaries behind. His repeated refusal to abandon his weapon to the Amer-

---

[36] A shortened version of this *corrido* runs: "Ah, so many mounted Rangers / Just to take one Mexican!" See Paredes, *With His Pistol*, 3 (stanza 8).

[37] See, for example, Variants B, C, D, G, and H in Paredes, *With His Pistol*, 161, 164, 166, 171, 172 (stanza 1).

[38] As in Variants X, A, and E in *With His Pistol*, 154, 158, 168 (stanza 1).

[39] In accordance with the rural framework as a genre element of the *corrido*, the language of resistance is taken from contexts like regional farming, livestock production, and horse-breeding.

ican authorities (127–28, stanzas 25–26) marks the killing tool as part of himself: only when they manage to put him in prison will he abandon his pistol. The myth of Lucifer's fall and resistance is varied in the figure of Gregorio Cortez when he makes the pending punishment (imprisonment as well as probable death) his choice. By making these decisions his own, he demonstrates his pride, as he, the 'minority', faces so many opponents, the 'majority'.

The comparison of Gregorio Cortez's chase with "following a star" (155, stanza 9) recalls the fall of Lucifer (the light-bearer that will fall) as well as the hope of a new leader (not unlike the birth of Jesus, announced by a star) and also the metaphoric 'star', a famous person. Although Gregorio Cortez does not literally transform loss into gain, he resists defeat. The *bandido's* pending death can likewise be transformed: It can turn out, as is suggested, not to be the tragedy of Cortez but, instead, that of the sheriff, who, by having to kill Cortez in order to lay hands on him, would become a murderer himself and, additionally, would transform the *bandido* into a hero or martyr.[40]

The criticism in "Gregorio Cortez," that xenophobia entails injustice, is more indirectly expressed in "[El Corrido de] Joaquín Murieta."[41] Its embeddedness in the territorial and gubernatorial shifts in the borderland enhances the aspect of 'homelessness' caused by the *bandido's* being a 'foreigner in his native land'. As a Mexican American in the borderland, Murieta is uncertain about where he belongs, and this marks him as feeling excluded by both countries, his native land and his new 'nation'. In the *corrido* of "Joaquín Murieta," the *bandido's* goal of revenge implicitly refers to the historical Murieta's enumeration of wrongs done to him by Americans: His original admiration for Americans (the reason for his immigration) turned into the contrary when, instead of improvement and liberation, he experienced deni-

---

[40] Américo Paredes finds that Variant X of Gregorio Cortez, in this sense, is "typical of the Border heroic corrido" (*With His Pistol*, 187).

[41] This famous *corrido* is likewise based on semi-historical reports. Joaquin Murieta (also spelled Murrieta) has been called the "Robin Hood of El Dorado," because his heroism is based on social protest. See Walter Noble Burns, *The Robin Hood of El Dorado* (New York: Coward McCann, 1932). The historical Murieta, a young *vaquero* (i.e. 'cowboy') from Alamos in Sonora (Mexico), became the leader of a rebellion of Sonoran miners who, after Mexico's defeat in 1848, rebelled against having been driven from their claims. As a result, he "rode into defeat and history to become a folk hero." See Arnold R. Rojas, "Joaquin Murrieta," in *Aztlán: An Anthology of Mexican American Literature*, ed. Luis Valdez & Stan Steiner (New York: Alfred A. Knopf, 1972): 105.

gration and exploitation – an example of which is "his gold mine claim being stolen and his wife and brother being killed by the claim jumpers."[42] In the *corrido*, the speaker, Murieta himself, expresses his goal "to kill Americans" as an extended revenge:

> Now I go out onto the roads
> To kill Americans
> You were the cause
> Of my *brother's* death
> You took him defenseless
> You disgraceful American.[43]

Although 'brother' may refer to the historical Murieta's sibling, it is more likely an echo of biblical style, with 'brother' meaning "fellow human being," or of political discourse with 'brother' as "fellow countryman" – both picking up the idea of "civil wars among the Rio Grande people" mentioned above.[44] At the same time, Murieta verbally echoes Lucifer, although his is not an autonomous revolt but a reaction against collective suppression, when he vows:

> I will not submit tamely to outrage any longer. I have killed many; I have robbed many; and many more will suffer in the same way. I will continue to the end of my life to take vengeance on the race that has wronged me so shamefully.[45]

---

[42] Rosales, *Chicano*, 7. Another source specifies that the womanizer Murieta had finally found the love of his life and, in 1849, moved with his bride to the gold-fields of California. One day she was raped by thirteen gringos and ultimately killed. Murieta himself fought and tried in vain to save her. He survived and, after that, revenge became his only goal. See Arnold R. Rojas, "Joaquin Murrieta," in *Aztlán: An Anthology of Mexican American Literature*, ed. Valdez & Steiner, 107–108, and Anon., "Love Secrets of Joaquin Murrieta," in *Aztlán*, 109–10.

[43] "[El Corrido de] Joaquín Murieta," in F. Arturo Rosales, *Chicano!: The History of the Mexican American Civil Rights Movement* (Houston TX: Arte Público, 1997): 7 (stanza 1; emphasis added). Further references are in the main text.

[44] Note that Shakespeare defines 'civil war' as "Make war upon themselves, brother to brother / Blood to blood, self against self," in "The Tragedy of Richard the Third," in *The Riverside Shakespeare*, 728 (II.iii.62–63).

[45] Joaquín Murrieta, "I Will Not Submit," in *Aztlán: An Anthology of Mexican American Literature*, ed. Valdez & Steiner, 106–107.

The refusal to 'submit' is transformed into a decision to take revenge on the American majority. In "From the rich and avaricious / I took their money" (stanza 2) and "Oh, what unjust laws / I'm going to become a bandit" (stanza 2) Murieta voices his only chance for personal, social, and political independence. The wilful *bandido* confirms his isolation and in return banishes those to whom he does not (and does not wish to) belong. The territorial 'homelessness' in the borderlands is not a defeat but becomes a moral accusation.

Quite differently, the borderland experience results in the protagonist's self-inflicted 'exile' in the *corrido* of "Rito García."[46] In this ballad, García is criminalized because he "react[s] violently to what would now be termed [Anglo-American] 'police brutality'"[47] against a family member. When he calls upon the Mexican authorities (although he is a citizen of Texas, but still thinks of himself as *mexicano*), he is treated like a foreigner as they hand him over to American (i.e. Texan) legal institutions: i.e. to his 'new' country:[48]

> My own land was cruel to me, because they gave me no shelter,
> and though I was a Mexican I did not find a friend.[49]

Rito García, thus, suffers from being 'outlawed' by both countries in the borderland. The *corrido* presents a protagonist who does not persist in his rebellion but who confirms his 'homelessness' by leaving the borderland. This *bandido* does not transform defeat into victory; rather, he accepts his loss:

> Farewell, my beloved country, farewell, all my friends;
> farewell, my dear family, I am leaving you forever. (59, stanza 17)

His solitude is not that of a rebel who asserts himself but that of a tragic hero who "ends in misery," as Chaucer's Monk says. Rito García's suffering is that of a tragic hero in the medieval sense of 'tragedy'.

In contrast to Rito García, Joaquín Murieta echoes the double banishment (or double rebellion, for that matter) of Lucifer and is transformed from victim or scapegoat into avenger. The *bandido* assumes the role of judge, as he feels he has the right to punish others. The roles of Satan and Robin Hood are

---

[46] "[El Corrido de] Rito García," in *A Texas-Mexican Cancionero: Folksongs of the Lower Border*, ed. Américo Paredes (Austin: U of Texas P, 1976): 57–59.

[47] Paredes, *Cancionero*, 27.

[48] *Cancionero*, 28, 58–59.

[49] "Rito García," in *A Texas-Mexican Cancionero: Folksongs of the Lower Border*, ed. Paredes, 59 (stanza 9). Further references are in the main text.

merged. Stealing from the rich and, as implied, giving to the poor (stanza 2), is not caused by compassion with the poor but by hate and envy of the rich. By the decision to act as both judge and executioner the rebel chooses solitude over communal life.

3. Pachucos

Whereas the stories of the borderland rebels are invariably embedded in or conditioned by a rural environment, the so-called *pachuco*-character is the product of life in the city; he illustrates yet another translocation of the myths of rebellion, becoming the "urban prototype of Chicano defiance."[50] The *pachuco*-style is a life-style created and developed in the 1940s in connection with the so-called Zoot-Suit Riots after the 'Sleepy Lagoon Murder Trial' of 1942, in which a group of young Mexican Americans were accused of and ultimately indicted for murder. The trials revealed stereotypical generalizations based on racist attitudes and were conducted with highly questionable methods.[51] The so-called zoot suit[52] was an outfit chosen by the criminalized young adults as a form of protest against being stereotyped. There was, accordingly, a *pachuco* movement associated with the trials, and this was revived in the 1970s as part of the Chicano Movement.[53]

According to Octavio Paz, *pachucos* are "instinctive rebels," their only goal being "not to be like those around them."[54] Adopting a *pachuco* life-style

---

[50] Marcos Sanchez–Tranquilino & John Tagg, "The Pachuco's Flayed Hide: Mobility, Identity, and Buenas Garras," in *Cultural Studies*, ed. Lawrence Grossberg, Cary Nelson & Paula A. Treichler (London & New York: Routledge, 1992): 569.

[51] See Jorge Huerta, "Introduction" to Luis Valdez, *"Zoot Suit" and Other Plays* (Houston TX: Arte Público, 1992): 13–16, and Rosales, *Chicano!*, 102–103.

[52] The 'zoot suit' is "a flashy suit of extreme cut typically consisting of a thigh-length jacket with wide padded shoulders and peg-top trousers tapering to narrow cuffs." See *Webster's Third New International Dictionary of the English Language* and *The Random House Dictionary of the English Language*, which latter adds that 'zoot suit' is a "rhyming compound based on 'suit'."

[53] See Huerta, "Introduction," 13–16.

[54] Octavio Paz, "The Pachuco and Other Extremes," in Paz, *The Labyrinth of Solitude and Other Writings*, tr. Lysander Kemp et al. (*El laberinto de la soledad*, 1950, 1961 & 1972; tr. New York: Grove, 1985): 14. Further page references are in the main text.

is thus a strategy against invisibility and assimilation. The *pachuco* "does not want to become a Mexican again; at the same time he does not want to blend into the life of North America" (14). Paz's thesis that the *pachuco's* "whole being is sheer negative impulse" (14) and "anarchic behavior" (14) is not unequivocally applicable, however, as the *pachuco* creates new strategies of identification as well as a visible boundary through an emphasis on the language of clothes.

Octavio Paz's opinion that the *pachuco's* attitude is an attempt to "demonstrate his personal will to remain different" (15) coincides with Alison Lurie's classification according to which "social protest and social disaffection both tend to adopt some characteristic costume"[55] and intend "alienation from mainstream values."[56] However, in the original situation, the zoot suit becomes an instrument of opinion and distinction, because the *pachuco* or zoot-suiter is denied a form of 'true' belonging as well as a personal identity. Instead of having a proper name, his designation is determined by the place where he lives (*el pachuco* means "the man from El Paso, Texas"[57]). Unlike the *bandido*, who either fights against an Anglo-American majority or fights for those with whom he shares the condition of being excluded, the *pachuco* creates – with and for those with whom he shares the outlaw-situation – a new community, although it is not territorially defined. Whereas one type of *bandido* seems to be a successor to Robin Hood in his fighting for others, the *pachuco*, or zoot-suiter by definition, seems to be chiefly motivated by vanity in his wish to create a personal reputation. Paradoxically, his identification with a racial stereotype allows him to feel that he belongs, but his simultaneous desire for individualism and self-assertion entails the tendency to exaggerate – belonging to a group but also being special. As Alison Lurie stresses, "the expression of national origin and ethnic identity through dress is often a matter of *personal* pride."[58]

The Mexican Americans' quest for a distinctive personal identity in their ethnic community is articulated in their most famous piece of poetry, Rodolfo

---

[55] Alison Lurie, *The Language of Clothes* (1981; New York: Random House, 1983): 161.

[56] Lurie, *The Language of Clothes*, 162.

[57] See Cobos, *Dictionary of New Mexico and Southern Colorado Spanish*, 124, s.v. 'pachuco, -ca'.

[58] Lurie, *The Language of Clothes*, 93 (emphasis added).

"Corky" Gonzales's epic poem "I Am Joaquín."[59] This poem assumes a voice
for all Mexican Americans and confirms their wish to belong – but even more
so the claim to a homeland as well as the wish for a distinctive personal identity. The first name, Joaquín, identical with that of Joaquín Murieta, is not a
random choice but intentionally calls attention to and refers to the *corrido*-
hero as model for this quest: "I, / of the same name, / Joaquín. / In a country
that has wiped out / all my history, / stifled all my pride."[60] As has been
shown, Gregorio Cortez, too, uses the 'I am' formula (157, stanza 12).

From merely using characteristics of the *pachuco* for the translocation of a
type of rebel into Mexican-American culture, Luis Valdez goes a step further
in his play *Zoot Suit*[61] and creates a character whose name is El Pachuco.
Exploiting the potential inherent in the genre of drama, Valdez crosses the
boundaries of historical narrative or documentation and transforms El Pachuco
into an allegorical figure (thus echoing the medieval morality play)[62] as well
as a multifunctional character. In the play, El Pachuco is one of the zoot-
suiters in the Sleepy Lagoon Murder Trial, but every now and then he steps
out of his character – as is typical of the epic theatre à la Bertolt Brecht – and
becomes commentator, theatrical director, and alter ego of the play's protagonist, Henry Reyna. This element of assuming different roles is, of course,
reminiscent of Satan himself in his various disguises as well as of Richard
III's and Iago's diabolic role-playing. Although the *pachuco* thus "represents
the defiance against the system that identifies and determines the pachuco
character,"[63] the multifunctional character El Pachuco in *Zoot Suit* transcends
the boundaries of time and place to also represent the Mexican Americans'
Aztec past.[64] Interestingly, Valdez's El Pachuco often speaks in verse and
uses speech-forms reminiscent of those *corridos* in which the hero's voice

---

[59] Rodolfo "Corky" Gonzales, "I Am Joaquín: an Epic Poem, 1967," in *Message to
Aztlán and Selected Writings*, ed. Antonio Esquibel (Houston TX: Arte Público,
2001): 1–29. This poem was originally composed in English and translated by the poet
himself into Spanish as "Yo soy Joaquín, un poema épico" (2000). See Rodolfo
"Corky" Gonzales, "Preface," in *Message to Aztlán*, ix–x.

[60] Gonzales, "I Am Joaquín," in *Message to Aztlán*, 17.

[61] Luis Valdez, "Zoot Suit," in Luis Valdez,*"Zoot Suit" and Other Plays* (Houston
TX: Arte Público, 1992): 21–94.

[62] Jorge Huerta, "Introduction" to Valdez, *"Zoot Suit" and Other Plays*, 15.

[63] Huerta, "Introduction," 15.

[64] "Introduction," 15.

(rather than that of a narrator) outlines the events (as in "Joaquín Murieta" and "Rito García").

Another play by Luis Valdez, *Bandido!*,[65] forms a bridge between the two mythic representations under discussion: i.e. *corrido*-hero and zoot-suiter, *bandido* and *pachuco*. The protagonist of *Bandido!*, Tiburcio Vásquez, was the last man "publicly hanged in California"[66] (in 1875), and his reputation rests to a large extent on his sense of theatricality, noticeable in the attention he pays to his costumes and staged public appearances as well to his sex appeal. In Valdez's play, Vásquez is "a social bandit, a gentleman who never killed anyone but who was forced into a life of crime by the Anglo invaders of his homeland."[67]

Tiburcio Vásquez shares with the rebellion of Shakespeare's Richard III and Iago the quality of entertainment and humour. Pride and protest are combined with vanity and the enjoyment of role-playing and show. Rebelling against the system of power is not an exclusively serious matter: after being banished from paradise, one has nothing to lose and might as well enjoy one's life without boundaries but also without bonds. The sin of pride is complemented by vanity, and the rebels enjoy the certainty of their intellectual superiority. This combination of sins can be enjoyed privately, as in Iago's case, or displayed publicly in pomp, as by Richard III as king. Being a rebel can add humour and enjoyment to one's life unbound by the fear of punishment, because one is already 'outlawed'. Humour as a quality of the *pachuco* and *bandido* is much more pronounced in drama than in lyric poetry.

4. Conclusion: Myths in Motion

Both the *bandido* and the *pachuco* are recognizably indebted to their Western predecessors, but they have become key representations of Mexican-American resistance and rebellion. Their translocation in time, space, and culture not only transforms but also transcends their sources. Lucifer's original rebellion persists in his continued strategy of deception. Robin Hood's violation of the law contributes to his reputation and makes him famous. Lucifer wants to become more powerful than he is, as does Shakespeare's Richard III,

---

[65] Luis Valdez, "Bandido!," in Valdez, *"Zoot Suit" and Other Plays* (Houston TX: Arte Público, 1992): 95–153.

[66] Huerta, "Introduction," 16.

[67] "Introduction," 17.

whereas Iago does not want others to know who he is and how powerful he is. In his strategies of deception and hypocrisy, Iago disguises himself in modesty while he rivals even God himself: His confession "I am not what I am"[68] echoes and reverses God's assertion "I am that I am"[69] – a statement of unquestioned identity, reliability, and stability – but also contrasts sharply with the straightforward pride of self as expressed in "I Am Joaquín." Obviously, one aspect inherent in the refusal to serve touches on the question of one's identity – whether it is given, chosen, or wished-for, and whether it is displayed or concealed.

The *pachuco*, seemingly identified as a group member, paradoxically, is deceptive in his affiliation because he also seeks personal recognition. By contrast, the *bandido's* refusal 'to serve' implies his rejection of, if not revenge on, his oppressors, on the one hand, and his possible attention to those who are 'outlaws' like himself, on the other. In other words, whereas the *bandido's* rebellion consists in the substitution of one type of service for another, the "*pachuco* does not defend anything except his exasperated will-not-to-be. [...] The *pachuco* is the prey of society, but instead of hiding he adorns himself to attract the hunter's attention."[70] In order to be recognized as an individual, he becomes a group member. Thus, the *pachuco* fights against solitude rather than against inferiority like the *bandido*.[71]

The transformations, in Chicano culture and literature, of the myths of Lucifer and his successors function in two different and simultaneously paradoxical ways: the *bandido's* achievement is praised in a narrative poem that emphasizes his historical fame, usually based on one event. But, whereas Robin Hood secures his own fame by protesting against the existing laws in order to help the poor, the *bandido*, by helping a disadvantaged group, fosters a sense of ethnicity and communal belonging and simultaneously, since he is part of that group, contributes to his own assertion. He resists disappearance within the stereotypical group by using his name and stressing his personal achievement and sacrifice. Robin Hood and the *bandido* alike follow "the medieval hero's custom of shouting his name in battle," indicating "pride in a name that has been earned through deeds and not through birth or wealth."[72]

---

[68] Shakespeare, "Othello," in *The Riverside Shakespeare*, 1252 (I.i.65).

[69] *The Bible*, 68 (Exodus 3:14).

[70] Paz, "Pachuco," 17.

[71] "Pachuco," 27.

[72] Paredes, *With His Pistol*, 236.

The *pachuco* likewise refuses to accept his assigned position as member of a denigrated minority. In a rebellious counter-movement, he stresses his otherness by the exaggerated use of outside characteristics of ethnicity. This seems, at first sight, to entail his dissolution as an individual by his merging with a chosen group. However, the *pachuco's* continued emphasis on his cultural difference resembles Satan's re-interpretation of his loss as gain when he assembles his followers in Hell. *Non serviam* turns out to be less an absolute refusal 'to serve' than a change of 'master'. Moreover, as Lucifer does not confirm Chaucer's definition of 'fall' as inherently tragic, the *pachuco* counterbalances his possible fall with vanity. The *bandidos*, however, are split: some of them fall and die and become tragic heroes, whereas, for others, fusing the figures of Satan and Robin Hood, the fall motivates further action – revenge or compassionate activities – on behalf of the *bandidos'* community.[73]

WORKS CITED

Anon. "Love Secrets of Joaquín Murrieta," in *Aztlán: An Anthology of Mexican American Literature*, ed. Valdez & Steiner, 109–10.

Anzaldúa, Gloria. *Borderland/La Frontera: The New Mestiza* (1987; San Francisco: Aunt Lute, 3rd ed. 2007).

Auden, W.H. "Musée des Beaux Arts," in *The Norton Anthology of Poetry*, ed. Margaret Ferguson et al. (New York: W.W. Norton, 1996): 1367.

The Bible: Authorized King James Version with Apocrypha, ed. & intro. Robert Carroll & Stephen Prickett (Oxford: Oxford UP, 1997).

Chaucer, Geoffrey. "The Prologue of the Monk's Tale," in *The Riverside Chaucer*, ed. F.N. Robinson (Boston MA: Houghton Mifflin, 1987): 240–41.

Cobos, Rubén. *Dictionary of New Mexico and Southern Colorado Spanish* (Santa Fe: Museum of New Mexico P, 1983).

"[El Corrido de] Gregorio Cortez," in *A Texas-Mexican Cancionero*, ed. Paredes, 64–67.

"[El Corrido de] Joaquin Murieta," in *Chicano!: The History of the Mexican American Civil Rights Movement* by Rosales, F. Arturo (Houston TX: Arte Público, 1997): 7.

---

[73] This result is also reflected in the popular reception of the *bandidos*. An example is the famous mural painting at Stanford University, "Last Supper of Chicano Heroes" (1985–94), by José Antonio Burciaga and students, in which both Joaquín Murieta and Tiburcio Vásquez are immortalized together with important mythic and political figures of Mexican-American history.

"[El Corrido de] Rito García," in *A Texas-Mexican Cancionero*, ed. Paredes, 57–59.

[Cortina, Juan Nepomuceno]. "Suffer the Death of Martyrs: Proclamation of Juan Nepomuceno Cortina" (1859), in *Aztlán: An Anthology of Mexican American Literature*, ed. Valdez & Steiner, 111–16.

Dixon–Kennedy, Mike. *The Robin Hood Handbook: The Outlaw in History, Myth and Legend* (Stroud: Sutton, 2006).

Gonzales, Rodolfo "Corky." "I Am Joaquín: an Epic Poem," in *Message to Aztlán and Selected Writings*, ed. Antonio Esquibel (Houston TX: Arte Público, 2001): 1–29.

Heide, Markus. *Grenzüberschreibungen: Chicano–Erzählliteratur und die Inszenierung von Kulturkontakt* (Heidelberg: Winter, 2004).

Herrera–Sobek, María. *Northward Bound: The Mexican Immigrant Experience in Ballad and Song* (Bloomington: Indiana UP, 1993).

Huerta, Jorge. "Introduction" to Luis Valdez, *"Zoot Suit" and Other Plays* (Houston TX: Arte Público, 1992): 7–20.

Joyce, James. *A Portrait of the Artist as a Young Man*, ed. & intro. Jeri Johnson (1914–16; Oxford: Oxford UP, 2000).

Limón, José E. *Mexican Ballads, Chicano Poems: History and Influence in Mexican-American Social Poetry* (Berkeley & Los Angeles: U of California P, 1992).

Lurie, Alison. *The Language of Clothes* (1981; New York: Random House, 1983).

Milton, John. "Paradise Lost," in *The Riverside Milton*, ed. Roy Flannagan (Boston MA: Houghton Mifflin, 1998): 297-710.

Murieta, Joaquín. "I Will Not Submit," in *Aztlán: An Anthology of Mexican American Literature*, ed. Valdez & Steiner, 106–107.

Noble Burns, Walter. *The Robin Hood of El Dorado* (New York: Coward McCann, 1932).

The Oxford English Dictionary (2nd. ed. 1989).

Paredes, Américo. *With His Pistol in His Hand: A Border Ballad and Its Hero* (1958; Austin: U of Texas P, 2003).

——, ed. *A Texas-Mexican Cancionero: Folksongs of the Lower Border* (Austin: U of Texas P, 1976).

Paz, Octavio."The Pachuco and Other Extremes," in *The Labyrinth of Solitude and Other Writings*, tr. Lysander Kemp et al. (*El laberinto de la soledad*, 1950, 1961 & 1972; New York: Grove, 1985): 9–28.

Peña, Manuel. "Foreword" (1994), in *A Texas-Mexican Cancionero*, ed. Paredes, xxv–xxxi.

The Random House Dictionary of the English Language (1971).

Reed, James. *The Border Ballads* (London: Athlone, 1973).

Robb, John Donald, ed. *Hispanic Folk Songs of New Mexico* (1954; Albuquerque: U of New Mexico P, 2008).

Rojas, Arnold R. "The Vaquero," in *Aztlán: An Anthology of Mexican American Literature*, ed. Valdez & Steiner, 50–53.

Rojas, Arnold R. "Joaquin Murrieta," in *Aztlan: An Anthology of Mexican American Literature,* ed. Valdez & Steiner, 107–108.

Rosales, F. Arturo. *Chicano!: The History of the Mexican American Civil Rights Movement* (Houston T X: Arte Público, 1997).

Sanchez–Tranquilino, Marcos, & John Tagg. "The Pachuco's Flayed Hide: Mobility, Identity, and Buenas Garras," in *Cultural Studies*, ed. Lawrence Grossberg, Cary Nelson & Paula A. Treichler (London & New York: Routledge, 1992): 556–70.

Shakespeare, William. "The Tragedy of Othello, the Moor of Venice," in *The Riverside Shakespeare*, ed. G. Blakemore Evans et al. (1974; Boston M A: Houghton Mifflin, 2nd ed. 1997): 1246–96.

——. "The Tragedy of Richard the Third, in *The Riverside Shakespeare*, ed. G. Blakemore Evans et al. (1974; Boston M A: Houghton Mifflin, 2nd ed. 1997): 748–808.

Webster's Third New International Dictionary of the English Language (2nd ed. 1981).

Valdez, Luis. "Bandido!," in Valdez, *"Zoot Suit" and Other Plays* (Houston T X: Arte Público, 1992): 95–153.

——. "Zoot Suit," in Valdez, *"Zoot Suit" and Other Plays* (Houston T X: Arte Público, 1992): 21–94.

——, & Stan Steiner, ed. *Aztlán: An Anthology of Mexican American Literature* (New York: Alfred A. Knopf, 1972).

⌘

Trans/locating Pacific Identities
—From the Small Island to the Largest Polynesian City in the World

PALOMA FRESNO–CALLEJA

> What keeps us here?
> Islands in an ocean.
> What makes us leave?
> Islands in an ocean.
> What calls us back?
> Islands in an ocean.[1]

N THESE LINES, THE KIRIBATIAN POET TERESIA TEAIWA calls attention to the material and cultural contingencies which have historically
forced Pacific peoples out of their home islands but also to a more
mythic dimension of the island as a territory which has kept luring travellers,
migrants, and their descendants back. The history of the Pacific region has
always been determined by multiple trans/locations and diverse patterns of
mobility and exchange: from precolonial inter-island voyages and colonial
encounters on the beach to postcolonial negotiations in urban diasporic
centres. This essay focuses on how the New Zealand Pacific community articulates its identity across this range of fractured but interconnected locations,
combining varying degrees of allegiance to their real or imaginary homelands
with new pan-Pacific formulas resulting from the combination of global
trends and reformulated local traditions. This is in fact a complex process
which, as James Clifford reminds us, cannot be simply considered as an historical progression in which village life gives way to cosmopolitan modernity

---

[1] Teresia Teaiwa, "No One is an Island," in *Searching for Nei Nim'anoa* (Suva: Mana, 1995): 16.

or indigenous roots are replaced by diasporic routes. Instead, he insists, "we are left with a spectrum of attachments to land and place – articulated, old and new traditions of indigenous dwelling and travelling"[2] which continue to evolve and re-define communities across Pacific shores. In this essay, I employ the term 'trans/location' to refer to this complex and ever-changing 'spectrum of attachments' to place, as well as to the mechanisms devised by the New Zealand Pacific community to handle their diverse degrees of be/longing. As opposed to terms like 'relocation' – which suggests the un-problematical replacement of the old with the new – or 'dislocation' – which emphasizes the disruptive effects of the migratory process – the word 'trans/location' suggests a fluidity – between past and present, the small island and the big city – which acknowledges and engages critically with the complex and ambivalent dimensions of the diasporic condition.

The Pacific community is the fastest-growing ethnic group in an increasingly multicultural Aotearoa New Zealand. According to recent data, it amounts to 6.9 percent of the population, but it is estimated that, due to the high birth rates and the continuous migration flows, it will reach 12 percent by the year 2051. More than 90 percent of its members now live in urban areas, mainly in the Auckland region, and in some of the city's southern suburbs, such as Otara, Mangere, or Manukau, the percentage of Pacific peoples reaches 25 percent. The effects that this rapid growth has had on some Pacific nations is evident; at the moment, for example, there are more people from nations like the Cook Islands, Niue, or Tokelau living in New Zealand than in their own home countries, and six out of ten children of Pacific descent are already born in New Zealand.[3] This has resulted in the formation of what Spoonley, McPherson, and Anae call "transnational corporations of kin" or "transnational island societies":[4] i.e. communities whose members might have never visited their islands or, conversely, never been out of them, but who nevertheless remain interconnected through material dependencies (remit-

---

[2] James Clifford, "Indigenous Articulations," *The Contemporary Pacific* 13.2 (Fall 2001): 477.

[3] Gilbert Wong, "Pride of the Pacific," *Metro* 256 (October 2002): 104. See also *Statistics New Zealand, Tatauranga Aotearoa*, www.stats.govt.nz (accessed 10 May 2009).

[4] *Tangata o Te Moana Nui: The Evolving Identities of Pacific Peoples in Aotearoa/ New Zealand*, ed. Melani Anae, Cluny Macpherson & Paul Spoonley (Palmerston North: Dunmore, 2001): 13.

tances, education, employment, and sponsoring networks) or less tangible though equally powerful ties (memories, nostalgia, familial obligations, or moral attachments).

The literature produced by the youngest members of the Pacific community has reflected these transnational dis/connections, and has grown to illustrate the transition from the displacement and alienation experienced by the first migrants to the gradual accommodation and sense of belonging achieved by those who have made New Zealand their home.[5] This transition can also be read in the light of evolving notions of space and its effects on the formation of identity. From the last quarter of the twentieth century, spatial theorists have discarded the notion of space as neutral and static, considering it instead as a social product[6] which both constructs and is constructed in diverse relational social practices.[7] Using examples from recent literary works, I would like to consider these diverse formations of be/longing as directly related to spatial notions, in particular to how these authors discard Western assumptions about their islander status and inscribe their voices as urban dwellers, emphasizing ideas of citizenship and urban belonging, without renouncing their transoceanic heritage.

1. Destination Niu Sila:[8] From Island to I-Land

In his article "Pacific Writing and the Diminishing Islands," Chris Tiffin argues that, despite the centrality of the island trope in Western and colonial texts, modern Pacific writers have "largely repudiated" this motif, showing that "the condition of insularity has more to do with residual European desire than with [their own] experiences."[9] The rejection of the island trope does not entail a simple denial of colonial representations, which invariably present

---

[5] Michelle Keown, *Pacific Islands Writing: The Postcolonial Literatures of Aotearoa/New Zealand and Oceania* (Auckland & Oxford: Oxford UP, 2007): 193.

[6] Henri Lefebvre, *The Production of Space*, tr. Donald Nicholson–Smith (*La Production de l'espace*, 1974; Oxford: Blackwell, 1991): 26.

[7] Doreen B. Massey, *Space, Place and Gender* (Minneapolis: U of Minnesota P, 1994).

[8] Transliteration of 'New Zealand' common to several Pacific languages.

[9] Chris Tiffin, "Pacific Writing and the Diminishing Islands," in *A Talent(ed) Digger: Creation, Cameos and Essays in Honour of Anna Rutherford*, ed. Gordon Collier, Geoffrey V. Davis & Hena Maes–Jelinek (Cross/Cultures 20; Amsterdam & Atlanta GA: Rodopi, 1996): 429.

islands as secluded and isolated spaces demanding continuous visitation and control;[10] I would suggest that this dismissal is also a reaction against the persistence of Orientalist perceptions which continue to gain strength under the power dynamics of neo-imperialism and globalization. In the context of diaspora, for example, this discursive regime of "islandism"[11] is stamped on their passports upon arrival, and consistently sustained in diverse spatial and social practices which work as an efficient form of control by reiterating the migrants' condition as islanders.

This is seen, for example, in Tusiata Avia's "Ode to da Life," a poem in-cluded in her first collection *Wild Dogs Under My Skirt* (2004), in which Niu Sila is depicted as a paradise where "da life is happy an perfek / Everybodys smile, everybodys laugh."[12] New Zealand is presented as a cross between an Antipodean Arcadia and a modern arcade-land, where happiness is measured by the amount of material possessions one can accumulate and, more impor-tantly, send back home. The enumeration of Western commodities and cul-tural referents (McDonald's, beer, TV programmes) allows Avia's poem to reflect critically on the perpetuation of neocolonial dependencies and the reinforcement of belittled conceptions of the home islands as places where these goods are unavailable. The mythologizing of Niu Sila as the "land of milk and h(m)oney,"[13] of ice cream and fast food in this case, constitutes an ironic reversal of well-known representations of the colonial Pacific. Here, the native Palagi welcome newcomers with open arms and the promise that they will be "jus happy an laughing evry time," a happiness which, among other things, will allow girls to ignore moral and familial impositions prevalent in the home islands. In Niu Sila, the female speaker insists, they can do "any-fing, even in front your fadda / An never ever get da hiding" (25). This truly appears as a brave new world in which the moral codes are transcended and restrictions apparently suspended, as they move from island to I-land, over-

---

[10] Elizabeth DeLoughrey, "'The Litany of Islands, the Rosary of Archipelagos': Caribbean and Pacific Archipelagraphy," *ARIEL: A Review of International English Literature* 32.1 (January 2001): 26.

[11] Elizabeth DeLoughrey, *Routes and Roots: Navigating Caribbean and Pacific Island Literatures* (Honolulu: U of Hawai'i P, 2007).

[12] Tusiata Avia, *Wild Dogs under My Skirt* (Wellington: Victoria UP, 2004): 25.

[13] Melani Anae, "From Kava to Coffee: The 'browning' of Auckland," in *Almighty Auckland*, ed. Ian Carter, David Craig & Steve Matthewman (Palmerston North: Dun-more, 2004): 96.

coming community impositions and theoretically enjoying greater individual freedom. Yet Avia's poem can be read as a problematical revision of the triumphant narratives of migration, because, although in this new paradise the roles of traveller and natives are reversed, she suggests that the power dynamics are eventually reinforced. In fact, the naive voice in Avia's poem echoes stereotyped views of Pacific peoples in the early migration period, the happy-go-lucky islander or the gullible migrant lost in the big city – reflected in pejorative terms like "fresh off the boat," "fob," "freshies," or "coconuts" – and defined essentially according to their status as islanders. This perspective reiterates notions of a backward native subject who "continues to be ideologically 'incarcerated' in a homogeneous, atemporal, space [and who] is rarely associated with modernity."[14]

A more painful example of how this constructed insularity is imposed on the first migrants can be found in John Pule's novel *The Shark that Ate the Sun* (1992), a portrait of Niuean migration to New Zealand in the 1950s, very much in the light of the bleak portrait of Māori urban culture offered by Alan Duff in *Once Were Warriors* (1990).[15] When the family arrives in Auckland, they settle in Karagahape Road, a popular Pacific enclave at the time, as their daily activities are soon restricted to a few streets, a small urban island in which similar notions of seclusion are perpetuated:

> On Karangahape Road, little Polynesian street, that's where the Niueans drink, at the infamous Family and Naval and the Rising Sun, where men get drunk and shuffle from one tavern to another; where bloody fights paint the walls red and men are thrown into police wagons while two hundred yards away there you were at the Central Police Station on Ponsonby Road. Walking distance to Symonds Street at the Edinburgh Castle, where the working man starts the evening, great crowds of sweating men, guzzling pint after pint until their pockets empty and the jugs are full of air, they stagger home, baptise the sidewalks with several hours of heavy boozing, and the fights with the police, and the next day another day, forget Niue, forget home, forget the dusty roads, forget the plantation, the melon fields, the coconuts, the crabs, the fish and the church, the church that sucks money from the poor, forget everything from the past.[16]

---

[14] DeLoughrey, *Routes and Roots*, 197.

[15] Alan Duff, *Once Were Warriors* (Auckland: Tandem, 1990).

[16] John Pule, *The Shark that Ate the Sun* (Auckland & Harmondsworth: Penguin, 1992): 55–56. Further page references are in the main text.

As Dolores Hayden reminds us, "one of the consistent ways to limit the economic and political rights of groups has been to constrain social reproduction
by limiting access to space."[17] The novel demonstrates the limiting effect of
such spatial practices, as the conflicts experienced by the newly arrived migrants unfold in a number of enclosed spaces (blocks of state houses, shops,
pubs, prisons) where they are kept at bay. The protagonists are displaced from
one state house to another, from the inner city area to the southern suburbs, a
sort of urban "island hopping," which culminates with their settlement in
Otara:

> The sons and daughters of Polynesia were labelled the forgotten child-
> ren. If we were forgotten it was because of the policy at the time to
> push the labourers, low income earners, back, back to the south, back
> south land is cleared of bush, farmhouses, and in its place houses,
> block boxes, cheap, ugly. So there we were, Polynesian, outcasts,
> living in a state house, with others like ourselves. [...] The rest of the
> nation saw Otara as the Bronx of the South Pacific: social outcasts;
> islanders who hardly spoke a word of English. (183)

The abyss between the islands and the host country seems unbridgeable, not
only due to social or economic differences, but because the ocean does not
seem to work as a connecting space, except when it comes to the shipping of
goods or the journeys of new migrants. As the narrator explains, upon arrival
"the Polynesian always found his way to the sea, to see it and feel the water"
but gradually "the excursions to the sea were replaced slowly by going to
these shops" (63), shops in which "Polynesians gather around the [...] mus-
sels, fish, oysters, fish heads, octopus [which] shine like sparkling waters
under the fluorescent light" (125).

The novel documents the gradual, although quite problematical, transition
from estrangement to belonging, a shift which occurs when the youngest
members of the family gradually find their place in the city, transcending the
spatial limitations imposed on them and rejecting official views of these migrant enclaves as capable of containing difference. In fact, these areas work as
what Macpherson calls "potential sites for accelerated change,"[18] social

---

[17] Dolores Hayden, *The Power of Place: Urban Landscapes as Public History*
(Cambridge MA: MIT Press, 1995): 22.

[18] Cluny Macpherson, "One Trunk Sends out Many Branches: Pacific Cultures and
Cultural Identities," in *Tangata o Te Moana Nui*, ed. Melani Anae, Cluny McPherson
& Paul Spoonley (Palmerston North: Dunmore, 2001): 72.

laboratories, whose demographic and cultural fabric harbingers wider social transformations within and outside the limits of the suburb. The New Zealand-born protagonist of the novel experiences these multiple attachments, the neighbourhood is no longer the artificially created island it was for his parents. As in Donne's dictum, in his Otara "no man is an island":

> In this life, in this Otara, there is no such thing as solitude, you became part of a life that is stormy, happy people, languages of ancient migration, mingling in the adopted soil, footsteps upon the labourer's sweat. [...] Otara is a survivor. [...] As far as I was concerned Otara was brand new. Houses were built in a week and by the following week a family moved in. Kids shily staking out the area, and the buses, yellow longboats we called them, were the noisiest in the world, and in these machines the many languages of Otara flew like birds down the aisle. [...] On Sundays the church people, dressed immaculately in white, filled the seats and gave the bus and Otara a sense of pride and harmony. (194)

The reference to "the church people" attests to the role of religion in the maintenance of cultural cohesion in diaspora and, implicitly, points at the church building as a central meeting point. Congregational membership acted in the early migration period as a form of "social location"[19] and the church functioned like "a Pacific 'village' for Pacific peoples throughout Auckland,"[20] since it was precisely the location of these buildings that determined the choice and further settlement of the area. The notion of the village, rather than the island, seems a more appropriate way of articulating their identity, since migrants often saw themselves as "members of families and villages rather than members of a coherent migrant community";[21] these 'villages' allowed for the replication of kinship ties, bypassing connotations of isolation and seclusion associated with the Western notion of the island and allowing for the regeneration and transformation of traditional cultural practices. This permits a revision of the notion of the island as a static piece of land (or concrete), detached from its surroundings and uncontaminated by outside contact. Significantly, Pule presents the migrants' daily incursions into the city centre

---

[19] Cluny Macpherson, "From Moral Community to Moral Communities: The Foundations of Migrant Social Solidarity among Samoans in Urban Aotearoa/New Zealand," *Pacific Studies* 25.1–2 (March–June 2002): 73.

[20] Anae, "From Kava to Coffee," 90.

[21] Macpherson, "One Trunk Sends Out Many Branches," 71.

(in the yellow longboats) or the children's exploration of neighbouring suburbs by drawing on voyaging metaphors, which are, of course, ubiquitous in
postcolonial Pacific writing, and placing the emphasis on movement and
interdependence rather than on stasis.

This shift has also informed the most relevant spatial theories by critics of
the region. The Tongan critic Epeli Hau'ofa, for instance, has rejected the
prevalent Orientalist discourse of islandism which continues to define Pacific
nations as "islands in a far sea," in favour of a more holistic perception of
inter-island and transoceanic connections in what he calls the "sea of islands."[22] Similarly, Subramani has talked about "a sea of artists and writers"
working on an "Oceanic imaginary,"[23] in which the Pacific serves as a fluid
medium accounting both for inter-island commonalities and the shifting boundaries of cultures and identities in the diaspora. Elizabeth DeLoughrey has
proposed a critical framework of "tidalectics," to explore the complex relationships between sea and land, in an attempt to complicate "the notion of
static roots and offering a fluid paradigm of migratory routes,"[24] thus dissolv-
ing national boundaries in favour of transnational connections and favouring
native epistemologies over Western notions of space.

2. Navigating the City: Auckland's Pacific Cartographies

The extent to which this transoceanic dimension has provided the Pacific
community with renewed tools for identity-formation is seen, for example, in
the way pejorative terms like 'Pacific Islander', which capitalized on notions
of remoteness and insularity, have been replaced by self-definitions such as
'Pacific peoples', 'Pacificans', or 'Tagata Pasifika'. While implicitly acknowledging the indigenous status of the Māori people as *tangata whenua*
('people of the land'), this last definition replicates a sense of belonging
which depends on their new urban location but underlines their specific connections with the ocean. These pan-Pacific denominations also reinforce inter-
island commonalities ignored or suppressed in colonial mappings of the
region and serve to articulate a group identity, through which national boun-

---

[22] Epeli Hau'ofa, "Our Sea of Islands," *Asia/Pacific as Space of Cultural Production*, ed. Arif Dirlik & Rob Wilson (Durham NC: Duke UP, 1995): 86–98.

[23] Subramani, "The Oceanic Imaginary," *SPAN* 48–49 (April–October 1999): 1–13.

[24] DeLoughrey, *Routes and Roots*, 23.

daries are redefined and insular restrictions transcended, without necessarily renouncing their Samoan, Tongan, or Fijian origins.

In fact, the youngest members of the community have embraced pan-Pacific labels in combination with more specific denominations, like 'NZ borns', 'Fa'a Niu Sila', or 'Fa'a Aukilani' (which function as substitutes of the label "fa'a Samoan" – the Samoan way).[25] In this way, they call attention to the fact that the negotiation of their translocal cultural affiliations pivots around their status as New Zealand citizens and, more specifically, as Aucklanders. These terminological readjustments can be framed within the larger process of what the sociologist Melani Anae calls the "browning of Auckland":

> Pacific peoples [...] are from their sea of islands, continuing the voyages of their ancestors across time and space and taking breathers along the way. Auckland is one of these breather sites.[26]

Anae conceives of this "browning," which she explains via the oceanic metaphor, as determined by three interrelated phenomena:

> the consolidation of a strong Pacific identity, the growth of a Pacific 'middle class' and the infiltration of Pacific identity [...] on New Zealand's infrastructure at national and community levels.[27]

Upward social mobility has allowed the youngest generations to gain access to multicultural capital which they have invested in the articulation of new Pacific ethnicities, in Hall's understanding of the term,[28] and has granted them the chance to revise not only the homeland narratives inherited from their parents but also those imposed on them in the host country.

Part of this process has consisted in reassessing the implications of deeming Auckland 'the largest Polynesian city in the world', a celebratory label which overshadows renewed forms of social or economic segregation. In their article "'Welcome to Auckland': A City Bus Tour," Claudia Bell and John Lyall analyse how the city-tourist narratives are constructed to explicitly

---

[25] Augie Fleras & Paul Spoonley, *Recalling Aotearoa: Indigenous Politics and Ethnic Relations in New Zealand* (Auckland & Oxford: Oxford UP, 1999): 212.

[26] Anae, "From Kava to Coffee," 92.

[27] "From Kava to Coffee," 92.

[28] Stuart Hall, "Old and New Identities, Old and New Ethnicities," in *Culture, Globalization and the World-System: Contemporary Conditions for the Representation of Identity*, ed. Anthony D. King (1991; Minneapolis: U of Minnesota P, 1997): 41–68.

ignore the Pacific heritage of the city. For example, although the bus goes through areas like Ponsonby, a key site for understanding the early period of Pacific migration, the guide makes no reference to the Pacific population.[29] Despite its emphasis on Auckland's internationally well-known maritime profile as 'City of Sails', the tour resoundingly ignores the Polynesian voyaging legacy and its contemporary replication in recent migration routes. Granting that a tour like this cannot engage in political or sociological analysis,[30] the authors nevertheless note the significance of these gaps in the narrative of a city which has simultaneously been marketed as Polynesian. A number of recent works have explored these alternative cartographies of the city, hoping to transcend Orientalist visions of the island and previous representations of the urban centres as spaces of limited availability to the community, and claiming access to new ways of representing and inhabiting hegemonic spaces which are now redefined in fluid terms, in agreement with the position of the youngest generation of New Zealand-born Pacific peoples.

A case in point is the play *N2*, in which Toa Fraser, of Fijian and British descent, narrates a family gathering in the neighbourhood of Mount Roskill. In the preface to the play, Fraser makes a point of mentioning the importance of this location while he was growing up in England:

> for as long as I remember Mt Roskill has been a romantic, mythical place [...] one part Mt Olympus, and one part Big Whiskey: a place where powerful, immortal figures sat around their ambrosia, a place where passions ran wild and whisky was poured, not sipped.[31]

In acknowledging the influence of Mt Roskill and Auckland as shapers of his urban and ancestral mythologies, Fraser accounts for a basic shift which is dominating the lives of the new generations. The significance of these multiple cultural referents has also been noted by Patrick Evans in talking of John Pule,

> who writes of his native Niue as a paradise he can return to and write about, but whose childhood state house in South Auckland meant enough to him that he claims to have tried to fund its detachment from

---

[29] Claudia Bell & John Lyall, "'Welcome to Auckland': A City Bus Tour," in *Almighty Auckland*, ed. Ian Carter, David Craig & Steve Matthewman (Palmerston North: Dunmore, 2004): 213.

[30] Bell & Lyall, "'Welcome to Auckland'," 214.

[31] Toa Fraser, *Two Plays* (Wellington: Playmarket, 2007): 51.

the connected house next door and transportation across the Tasman as a cultural artefact for exhibition.[32]

The childhood house in its suburban enclave becomes here an alternative standpoint from which to explore one's ancestral background; this spatial shift demonstrates the gradual change in previous hegemonic cartographies both of the city as an alien and menacing place and the island as a primitive and re-mote location.

A similar perception of the neighbourhood as a sort of archipelago where previously undocumented interconnections and exchanges are made visible can be found in *Niu Sila*, a play co-written by Oscar Kightley and Dave Arm-strong.[33] Through the portrayal of the friendship between a Samoan boy, Ioane, and his Palagi neighbour, Peter, in 1970s Ponsonby, we witness how the cultural distance between the boys and their families diminishes each time they cross the boundaries of each other's driveways. The play shows that cul-tural struggles are to a great extent struggles over space and its representation. For example, when the boys first meet, Ioane tells Peter that he has been living in "the reservation," a Pacific enclave he describes as "the best part of town [...] 'cos we live there" (15), a naive assumption which bypasses prac-tices of urban segregation imposed on the early migrants. The play trans-gresses against these spatial restrictions temporarily, by allowing the children to erase the real and imaginary frontiers which mark different cultural prac-tices and separate their communities; for instance, Peter's parents take Ioane to his first concert, and Ioane's family invite Peter to church and other family gatherings. The negotiation of cultural difference which occurs in the specific locations of the house, the classroom, or the neighbourhood serves as a meto-nym of wider social negotiations; but, although racial tensions are temporarily suspended through a friendship which announces a possible horizon of inter-cultural understanding, the play ends on a bitter note with Ioane's death after he returns to his home island. As an adult, Peter also shows the persistence of these barriers, by referring to renewed practices of spatial segregation as when he mentions that Ponsonby has changed into "a trendy part of town, [with] no Islanders around. The only tapa cloth in the street is at the local café – which does a lovely flat white. In fact, he says, the whole neighbourhood's flat and

---

[32] Patrick Evans, *The Long Forgetting: Post-Colonial Literary Culture in New Zealand* (Christchurch: Canterbury U P, 2007): 203.

[33] Dave Armstrong & Oscar Kightley, *Niu Sila* (Wellington: Playmarket, 2009). Further page references are in the main text.

white… almost" (79). Peter describes the erasing of Pacific elements from an
area which has been shaped into "apartment city, yuppie heaven, café and
restaurant mile,"[34] the tapa cloth on the wall being the residual and exotic
symbol which has replaced the presence of Ioane and his family. The play
concludes, however, with a significant twist, when a Chinese kid comes to
play with Peter's son twenty years after Ioane first visited Peter, a suggestion
that there are many ethnic groups simultaneously claiming visibility and space
and that reading Auckland as a Polynesian city does not preclude other multiple readings and projections.

A more optimistic view of the multi-ethnic city can be found in the poem
"Octopus Auckland: Eight suburbs" by Karlo Mila (of Tongan, Samoan, and
Palagi descent).[35] The poem takes the reader on an alternative poetic tour
around Auckland, each stanza reflecting critically on the gaps implicit in
traditional hegemonic representations of the city. Similarly to *Niu Sila*, in this
poem Ponsonby is described as a place where "the flat white crowd / sips long
blacks for breakfast"; the speaker thus condemns official projections of the
city designed for local taste, with Pacific ingredients being displaced or isolated into ethnic compartments, a "boutique multiculturalism"[36] through which
the multi-ethnic fabric of the city is celebrated without compromising the
official bicultural narratives or granting these communities real power and
visibility. In Grey Lynn, she digs out the archaeological evidence of this Pacific presence when contemplating the old villas which she insists must still
"remember back thirty years / to the slap of jandals" (39). In Mount Eden, she
complains that the doctor who sees her still feels the need to ask "in perfect
earl grey english / where I came from / originally?" (41). By not specifying
where she comes from and replying instead that she does not come from
Auckland, the speaker shifts the emphasis from roots to routes, rejecting the
fiction of pure identities and pointing at the hybrid configurations and the new
intercultural mixtures which define the city. This is also seen in Mangere
Bridge, where she refers to a group of Tongan boys who speak Samoan, as
they fish stingrays from an ocean which connects them with their ancestors
and their myths; or in Hillsborough, where she observes the Indian dairy

---

[34] Anae, "From Kava to Coffee," 91.

[35] Karlo Mila, *Dream Fish Floating* (Wellington: Huia, 2005): 38–42. Further page
references are in the main text.

[36] Stanley Fish, "Boutique Multiculturalism, or Why Liberals Are Incapable of
Thinking about Hate Speech," *Critical Inquiry* 23.2 (Winter 1997): 378–95.

owner wondering when "he made the choice / that brought him here / sitting behind chocolate bars / bordered by boxes of cigarettes / pornography above his head" (41). Mila has talked of Auckland as "everyone's first stop"[37] – a "breather site," going back to Anae's term – but not necessarily your final destination, a city "which changes faster than the rest of the country"[38] and where almost everybody comes from somewhere else:

> an unusual combination of migrants, water, markets and motorway. Auckland, for me, has always made most sense by the suburb [...]. Combined, the cities of Auckland are unwieldy, sprawling and un- manageable. But suburb, by suburb [...] it somehow seemed possible to make sense of the sprawl and find comfort even, in the small plea- sures of familiarity.[39]

Mila's poem thus goes one step further: it not only focuses on the private space of the house and the limited space of the neighbourhood but also claims access to possible alternative representations of the public space of the city. The poem transcends both the fearful and idealized assumptions of 'the big city' as expressed by early migrants, it reacts against the spatial seclusion imposed on newcomers, it leaves behind the timid incursions of the yellow longboats into the city centre narrated by Pule and enlarges the possibilities presented by Fraser or Kightley in their plays. The poem becomes a mediated and mediating re/vision which might well appear as a poetic reworking of Hau'ofa's notion of the 'sea of islands'. In re-imagining the city as a sprawl- ing and interconnected archipelago of different suburbs which she has man- aged to navigate while negotiating the cultural distances between each area, Mila offers a more fluid notion of Auckland as *feke* ('octopus'), a living entity, an ever-changing sea of suburbs which, as she suggests in the final lines of the poem, is "wrapping your tentacles around me / clinging to my skin / sticking to my surfaces" (42). The reference to the octopus, whose arms embrace the newcomers, leaving "welts and bites," problematizes earlier accounts of Niu Sila as a friendly host land and points to a more realistic experience of the city, as a place which leaves its marks on its peoples, a

---

[37] "Poet Karlo Mila to Visit Christchurch," *Christchurch City Libraries*, http: //christchurchcitylibraries.com/Literature/People/M/MilaKarlo/ (accessed 10 May 2009).

[38] "Poet Karlo Mila to Visit Christchurch," *Christchurch City Libraries.*

[39] "Karlo Mila," *Huia Publishers*, www.huia.co.nz/from-the-night-kitchen-%E2% 80%9Cback-to-palmy%E2%80%9D/ (accessed 10 May 2009).

living organism in constant transformation and negotiation, a place which can be welcoming and hostile at the same time. The notion of the city transmitted in this poem agrees with the conception of space "as always in process, as never a closed system,"[40] and therefore opens up new possibilities for the revision of what it means to be a New Zealander of Pacific descent living in contemporary Auckland. This revision overcomes spatial conceptions of seclusion and isolation and acknowledges the compatibility of transcultural and transoceanic connections which can hopefully give way to alternative and fairer social practices and renewed conceptions of identity for the New Zealand Pacific community.

WORKS CITED

Anae, Melani. "From Kava to Coffee: The 'browning' of Auckland," in *Almighty Auckland*, ed. Ian Carter, David Craig & Steve Matthewman (Palmerston North: Dunmore, 2004): 89–106.

Anae, Melani, Cluny Macpherson & Paul Spoonley, ed. *Tangata o Te Moana Nui: The Evolving Identities of Pacific Peoples in Aotearoa/New Zealand* (Palmerston North: Dunmore, 2001).

Armstrong, Dave, & Oscar Kightley. *Niu Sila* (Wellington: Playmarket, 2009).

Avia, Tusiata. *Wild Dogs under my Skirt* (Wellington: Victoria U P, 2004).

Bell, Claudia, & John Lyall. "'Welcome to Auckland': A City Bus Tour," in *Almighty Auckland*, ed. Ian Carter, David Craig & Steve Matthewman (Palmerston North: Dunmore, 2004): 210–24.

Clifford, James. "Indigenous Articulations," *The Contemporary Pacific* 13.2 (Fall 2001): 468–90.

DeLoughrey, Elizabeth. "'The Litany of Islands, the Rosary of Archipelagos': Caribbean and Pacific Archipelagraphy," *ARIEL: A Review of International English Literature* 32.1 (January 2001): 21–51.

——. *Routes and Roots: Navigating Caribbean and Pacific Island Literatures* (Honolulu: U of Hawai'i P, 2007).

Duff, Alan. *Once Were Warriors* (Auckland: Tandem, 1990).

Evans, Patrick. *The Long Forgetting: Post-Colonial Literary Culture in New Zealand* (Christchurch: Canterbury U P, 2007).

Fish, Stanley. "Boutique Multiculturalism, or Why Liberals Are Incapable of Thinking about Hate Speech," *Critical Inquiry* 23.2 (Winter 1997): 378–95.

---

[40] Doreen Massey, *For Space* (Thousand Oaks C A & London: Sage, 2005): 11.

Fleras, Augie, & Paul Spoonley. *Recalling Aotearoa: Indigenous Politics and Ethnic Relations in New Zealand* (Auckland & Oxford: Oxford UP, 1999).

Fraser, Toa. *Two Plays* (Wellington: Playmarket, 2007).

Hall, Stuart. "Old and New Identities, Old and New Ethnicities," *Culture, Globalization and the World-System: Contemporary Conditions for the Representation of Identity*, ed. Anthony D. King (1991; Minneapolis: U of Minnesota P, 1997): 41–68.

Hau'ofa, Epeli. "Our Sea of Islands," *Asia/Pacific as Space of Cultural Production*, ed. Arif Dirlik & Rob Wilson (Durham NC: Duke UP, 1995): 86–98.

"Karlo Mila," *Huia Publishers*, www.huia.co.nz/from-the-night-kitchen-%E2%80%9Cback-to-palmy%E2%80%9D/ (accessed 10 May 2009).

Keown, Michelle. *Pacific Islands Writing: The Postcolonial Literatures of Aotearoa/New Zealand and Oceania* (Auckland & Oxford: Oxford UP, 2007).

Lefebvre, Henri. *The Production of Space*, tr. Donald Nicholson–Smith (*La Production de l'espace*, 1974; Oxford: Blackwell, 1991).

Macpherson, Cluny. "From Moral Community to Moral Communities: The Foundations of Migrant Social Solidarity among Samoans in Urban Aotearoa/New Zealand," *Pacific Studies* 25.1–2 (March–June 2002): 71–93.

——. "One Trunk Sends out Many Branches: Pacific Cultures and Cultural Identities," in *Tangata o Te Moana Nui*, ed. Melani Anae, Cluny McPherson & Paul Spoonley (Palmerston North: Dunmore, 2001): 63–80.

Massey, Doreen B. *For Space* (Thousand Oaks CA & London: Sage, 2005).

——. *Space, Place and Gender* (Minneapolis: U of Minnesota P, 1994).

Mila, Karlo. *Dream Fish Floating* (Wellington: Huia, 2005).

"Poet Karlo Mila to Visit Christchurch," *Christchurch City Libraries*, http://christchurchcitylibraries.com/Literature/People/M/MilaKarlo/ (accessed 10 May 2009).

Pule, John. *The Shark that Ate the Sun* (Auckland & Harmondsworth: Penguin, 1992).

Statistics New Zealand. Tatauranga Aotearoa, www.stats.govt.nz (accessed 10 May 2009).

Subramani. "The Oceanic Imaginary," *SPAN* 48–49 (April–October 1999): 1–13.

Teaiwa, Teresia. *Searching for Nei Nim'anoa* (Suva: Mana, 1995).

Tiffin, Chris. "Pacific Writing and the Diminishing Islands," in *A Talent(ed) Digger: Creation, Cameos and Essays in Honour of Anna Rutherford*, ed. Gordon Collier, Geoffrey V. Davis & Hena Maes–Jelinek (Cross/Cultures 20; Amsterdam & Atlanta GA: Rodopi, 1996): 423–29.

Wong, Gilbert. "Pride of the Pacific," *Metro* 256 (October 2002): 102–107.

⌘

Writing (in) the Migrant Space

—Discursive Nervousness in Contemporary Nigerian Short Stories

THOMAS MARTINEK

W E LIVE IN A PERIOD OF MASS MIGRATION, much of contemporary Western culture is the work of exiles, and displacement has
been transformed into one of the most potent motifs in postcolonial writing. In the words of Salman Rushdie, the migrant has come to be
"the archetypal figure of our age."[1]

At the same time, a fierce debate has been raging for years now about
sharply contrasting artistic and scholarly evaluations of migrancy. Salman
Rushdie and Homi Bhabha are in the vanguard of a group of thinkers who
construe the conditions of exile as artistically and politically radical, for they
destabilize essentialist categories and force individuals to constantly (re)nego-
tiate personal, social, and cultural identities.[2] Other commentators, most famously Aijaz Ahmad and Arif Dirlik,[3] have scathingly criticized what they
think is a celebratory interpretation of migrancy privileging experiences of
postcolonial intellectuals, cosmopolitan escapism, and apolitical aestheticism.
Tobias Wachinger is exceptionally fierce in his denigration of what he terms

---

[1] Salman Rushdie, *Step Across this Line* (London: Jonathan Cape, 2002): 415.

[2] See Graham Huggan, *The Post-Colonial Exotic: Marketing the Margins* (London:
Routledge, 2001): 21; Andrew Smith, "Migrancy, Hybridity, and Postcolonial Literary
Studies," in *The Cambridge Companion to Postcolonial Literary Studies*, ed. Neil
Lazarus (Cambridge: Cambridge U P, 2004): 252.

[3] See Arif Dirlik, "The Postcolonial Aura: Third World Criticism in the Age of
Global Capitalism," *Critical Inquiry* 20.2 (Winter 1994): 328–56; Aijaz Ahmad, "The
Politics of Literary Postcoloniality," *Race and Class* 36.3 (January 1995): 1–20.

the 'posing in-between' of postcolonial intellectuals writing (in) the migrant space and suggests that artists and thinkers turn away from "the clichéd terms and programmatic writing that [...] dominated postcolonial discourse throughout the last decade of the twentieth century."[4] Robert Young perfectly summarizes the concerns of this group of critics in one sentence: "How can a migratory identity be celebrated in the refugee camps of Qetta, Jalozai, and elsewhere in Pakistan, [...] in the West Bank, in the former Sangatte camp in France?"[5]

However, as my discussion of contemporary Nigerian short stories will show, writing on migration can be more than an apolitical celebration of "hybridity that is merely skin deep and a mere effect."[6] The two short stories under consideration were written by the Booker Prize-winner Ben Okri and Segun Afolabi, winner of the Caine Prize for African Writing. These two writers are renowned representatives of post-Achebe generations of Nigerian authors, whose members, among others Helon Habila, Chimamanda Ngozi Adichie, Zaynab Alkali, Biyi Bandele, and Sola Osofisan, have published, since the mid-1980s, ground-breaking works of short fiction which revisit many of the classic themes of (West) African and postcolonial literatures while departing from the aesthetic preoccupations of their predecessors through radical innovation and experimentation in the fields of narrative technique, structure, and language.

Ben Okri and Segun Afolabi engage with the theme of migration on several levels. First, both authors were born in Nigeria and have relocated to the metropolis. Second, the main characters depicted in their stories, in Okri's "A Hidden History" and Afolabi's "Moses," have similarly crossed borders into the UK but, quite in contrast to the writers, are condemned to what Bhabha calls "a life lived on the cultural margins of modern society."[7] Third, a major thematic preoccupation in the stories is the negotiation between the protagonists' position of liminality and the social, political, and cultural mainstream.

---

[4] Tobias A. Wachinger, *Posing In-between: Postcolonial Englishness and the Commodification of Hybridity* (Frankfurt am Main: Peter Lang, 2003): 204.

[5] Robert J.C. Young, *Postcolonialism: A Very Short Introduction* (Oxford: Oxford UP, 2004): 53.

[6] Rajagopalan Radhakrishnan, "Adjudicating Hybridity, Co-ordinating Betweenness," *Jouvert* 5.1 (2000), http://english.chass.ncsu.edu/jouvert/v5i1/radha.htm (accessed 17 October 2010): para 8.

[7] Homi K. Bhabha, "At the Limits," *Artforum* 27 (May 1989): 12.

This essay will argue that these texts create moments of radical "textual indeterminacy":[8] rhetorical and symbolic ambiguity, structural discontinuity, and outright gaps in the narratives repeatedly deflate readers' expectations and complicate interpretation. The resulting "discursive nervousness"[9] is heightened by the very form of the short story – a genre that has often been conceived of as 'recalcitrant', 'liminal', or 'difficult'. I would like to show how writing the migrant space as short story can thus lead to the emergence of Bhabha's "Third Space of enunciation"[10] and challenge structures of authority, received wisdom, and cosmopolitan complacency.

Ben Okri's "A Hidden History" is set in a contemporary Western city which is supposedly London even though it is never explicitly named. Immigrants from West Africa populate a street on the outskirts of the city. Soon, they are faced with the threat of annihilation as the government attempts to demolish the area. The immigrants are additionally threatened by mobs of unemployed racist thugs from the adjacent tower blocks and begin to vacate the street, leaving only the narrator of the story behind. The street is turned into a rubbish dump and the houses begin to fall apart. One night, a supposed madman, called the "List-maker," arrives to settle in the ruins of one of the houses and is repeatedly harassed by the thugs. Finally, the remnants of the decrepit buildings along the street are demolished and a green lake takes their place.

"A Hidden History" is told by a first-person, homodiegetic narrator, whose unity as a narrating subject crumbles while his or her identity remains stubbornly obscure until the very end of the story. This results in radical indeterminacy at the very heart of the story's discursive universe. The story becomes, in Fanon's words, "a zone of occult instability."[11] One of the first indicators of a loss of stability is the late revelation that the narrator is, in fact, a character in the story. After almost two pages, the narrator suddenly uses the pronoun 'I' to intrude on what initially seemed to be a third-person omniscient narrative. From then on, nagging questions about the narrator's identity

---

[8] Homi K. Bhabha, *The Location of Culture* (1994; New York: Routledge, 2004): 248.

[9] Ato Quayson, "Looking Awry: Tropes of Disability in Post-Colonial Writing," in *An Introduction to Contemporary Fiction*, ed. Rod Mengham (Cambridge: Polity, 1999): 63.

[10] Bhabha, *The Location of Culture*, 54.

[11] Frantz Fanon, *The Wretched of the Earth*, preface by Jean–Paul Sartre, tr. Constance Farrington (*Les Damnés de la terre*, 1961; New York: Grove, 1963): 227.

haunt the story while the narration oscillates between a detached, seemingly third-person point of view and a more involved first-person perspective. The ending apparently discloses parts of the narrator's identity; but in fact, it abounds with ambiguity:

> afterwards they came and demolished what was left standing of the crumbled houses. It was all so much that, with all my burden, I asked for a clear sky and a warm little sun like a golden eye always seeing. I slept. It rained a thousand times and sunned a thousand others in the long spaces of that sleep. I awoke as black an angel as I've always been, my wings heavy and black like all the sin they make me carry in their language.[12]

The paragraph adds strong allegorical overtones to the story, as it seems to transfer the narrator to a mythical realm. This technique is typical of Okri's later works, above all the novel *The Famished Road,* in which the narrator is an *abiku*, a spirit-child from Yoruba mythology. It is thus tempting to read the narrator in "A Hidden History" in similar fashion as a mythical figure (indeed, a black angel with black wings), the embodiment of the fates of all colonized, oppressed, and black people. But this would be in stark contrast to most other parts of the story, which largely pursue a paradigm of realism and do not hint at the existence of any supernatural elements or prototypical Okrian spirit-worlds at all. In addition, the narrator is obviously *not* a member of the immigrant community, for other inhabitants of the street are scared of him or her. In fact, we have no choice but to accept the elusiveness and liminality of the narrator: his or her identity remains, to use the words from the story's title, a 'hidden history'. This is deeply unsettling, as we have to rely on the narrator's consciousness to describe and interpret events for us. To borrow a formulation from Ato Quayson, the entire discursive universe is produced through a 'trope of liminality';[13] the story evolves as a 'nervous' tale, "a discourse that is *somehow beyond control*,"[14] beyond our everyday understanding of the world.

Okri's handling of style further increases the textual nervousness. With the exception of the last two paragraphs, Okri mainly resorts to a realist, mimetic mode of representation. As Robert Fraser points out, the story "stare[s] ugli-

---

[12] Ben Okri, "A Hidden History," in *Incidents at the Shrine* (1985; London: Vintage, 1993): 90. Further page references are in the main text.

[13] See Quayson, "Looking Awry," 65.

[14] Bhabha, *The Location of Culture,* 18.

ness in the face,"[15] describing the at times disturbing events in the minutest detail so that the depicted objects, characters, and events acquire a (photo) graphic, hyper-realist, almost painful quality. In the fine arts, hyper-realists have experimented with the effects of magnifying seemingly unimportant details in portraiture since the 1960s. In Chuck Close's oversized self-portraits or his colossal *Nat*, for instance, details of the human body which often go unnoticed in our conventional perception of people, such as pores or facial hair, gain such prominence that the people depicted seem freakishly distorted and, paradoxically, almost unreal. Okri applies a similar technique in the most violent scene of "A Hidden History," when the thugs from the tower blocks present the insane List-maker with a black woman's mutilated body:

> they [i.e. the thugs] held their breath as they watched him going up and down, circling inevitably towards the rubbish bin lining. He got to the lining and opened it and dipped his hand in. His eyes twitched. He brought out a bloodied leg: its toes were big and blue-black with a strange rot of the feet. He brought out a hand that was gnarled and withered like a twig. He brought out an arm chopped off at the shoulder, dangling a sticky mess of blood vessels and nerves. Then he brought out the head of a black woman, roughly hacked, the eyes open and bloated, the nose cut like a harelip that had repeated itself. He brought them out, smelling, listening, thorough in his investigation. He was drawn by the temptation to list. [...] the List-maker fixedly examined the parts of the woman's body. He tried to fit them into a coherent picture, a thing, and it seemed his memory utterly failed him. (89)

Here, the hyper-realistic depiction of the dead body is taken to such extremes that the gory details – blue-black toes, blood vessels, nerves, or bloated eyes – acquire a surreal quality. At the very moment when the images become almost unbearable for the reader, however, realism trips over into hyperbole, and the thugs, watching the scene from a distance, begin to vomit exaggeratedly:

> suddenly one of his [i.e. the List-maker's] antagonists on the refuse threw up. Another one threw up as well, convulsively. Then they all fell to vomiting. They scrambled down the refuse and they were throwing up and choking all the way into the distance. (89–90)

---

[15] Robert Fraser, *Ben Okri: Towards the Invisible City* (Tavistock: Northcote House, 2002): 49.

This hyper-realism, pushed to and beyond the limits, the tension between a detailed realistic description of the dead body and the exaggerated non-realistic vomiting – all this self-consciously interrogates aesthetic categories and probes into the capability of art to represent atrociously violent histories, such as those of colonialism, racism, or xenophobia.

These aesthetic preoccupations partly mirror one of the major themes in the story: the relationship between experiences of migration, memory, and the writing of history. The government tries to erase from national memory the street, the immigrants, and the legacy of colonialism that they represent. It does so quite literally, by sending demolition hulks to tear down the houses. Even though it seems to succeed by creating a green lake in lieu of the street, the narrator reminds us that "nothing can be pushed beneath the surface of memory" (90). The fate of the street and its former immigrant inhabitants may be 'hidden' from the annals of the nation, but it can never be wiped from the narrator's mind. It returns to haunt us in the form of a truly 'uncanny' tale. In Freud's and Bhabha's understanding of the term, the uncanny "is the name for everything that ought to have remained [...] secret and hidden but has come to light."[16] The inscrutable gaps and ambivalences of Okri's "A Hidden History" are "an uncanny echo"[17] of the migrant histories at the margins of the metropolis that the mainstream has been trying hard to repress, a "past which is always about to break through into the present."[18]

Segun Afolabi's "Moses" is an equally uncanny tale, although it resorts to different means in order to achieve this effect. The events that take place during the roughly twenty-four hours depicted in the story can be summarized very briefly. On a Friday morning, the male protagonist, who is an immigrant but never named, visits the grave of his dead son Moses on the outskirts of London. He takes a train back to the town centre; goes to work; has a drink at a pub after work; goes home to the apartment he shares with his British lover; has sex and dinner with her; goes out to a club to dance with her; returns home; is too drunk to have sex again; urinates on the floor before going to sleep; cleans up the mess the next morning; and prepares breakfast. This brief synopsis, however, is entirely inadequate to capture the nuances and subtleties in Afolabi's story.

---

[16] Sigmund Freud, quoted in Bhabha, *The Location of Culture,* 14–15.

[17] Robert Fraser, *Ben Okri: Towards the Invisible City,* 78.

[18] David Huddart, *Homi K. Bhabha* (London: Routledge, 2006): 82.

Despite the relative economic security that the protagonist enjoys, a deep melancholia and a constant threat of instability pervade the story. This is created by a minimalist handling of style and narrative technique. Minimalism, according to Ewing Campbell, "suggests density that encompasses more than is obvious, the evidence of things present but unseen or things seen but not there, the universe in a grain of sand."[19] Technically speaking, minimalism resorts to surface description and ellipsis in its portrayal of characters and depiction of events, creating "empty spaces"[20] and relying on the reader to 'fill in'. The careful arrangement of seemingly insignificant details, repetition, parallelism, and opposition can help the reader to supply missing information and 'complete' the story.[21]

There is an abundance of 'empty spaces' in Afolabi's story. For instance, the third-person narrator seems to stay out of the characters' affairs almost deliberately,[22] relying heavily on external descriptions of people and actions while the inner emotional life of characters, above all that of the male protagonist, is not commented on. A good example of this is the opening scene, which shows the protagonist at his son's graveside:

> The man knelt at the edge of the grave. He dusted away the leaves and the muck with his clean, bare hands. Even though it was warm he had worn his wool blazer. It seemed to wheeze as he moved his arms, his shoulders; he had put on weight since the boy died and now all his clothes complained. A film of perspiration coated his face and neck. His skin sizzled in the unceasing stare of the sun. [...] He snatched a fistful of dead grass and leaves and wilted flowers and stuffed them into his jacket pocket; he could find no other container for these things. [...] When he had arranged everything so that there was no more he could achieve, he lowered his knee in genuflection. No thoughts came to him. A train hurtled by and when peace descended again he could

---

[19] Ewing Campbell, "How Minimal Is Minimalism," in *The Tales We Tell: Perspectives on the Short Story*, ed. Barbara Lounsberry et al. (Contributions to the Study of World Literature 88; Westport C T & London: Greenwood, 1998): 15.

[20] Campbell, "How Minimal Is Minimalism," 15.

[21] See "How Minimal Is Minimalism," 15; Hilary Siebert, "Social Critique and Story Technique in the Fiction of Raymond Carver," in *The Tales We Tell: Perspectives on the Short Story*, ed. Barbara Lounsberry et al. (Westport C T London: Greenwood, 1998): 22.

[22] See Siebert, "Social Critique and Story Technique in the Fiction of Raymond Carver," 23.

make out the sounds of things; the cadence of birdsong, the mischievous whispering of leaves, the crunch of gravel beneath the feet of the
few other people in the cemetery as they attended to their own. When
he could not remember how long he had remained without a single
thought, he opened his eyes, placed a fist on the freshly cut grass and
pushed himself up. His bones cracked.[23]

While there is not a single reference to the man's emotional response to his
son's death in this passage, inanimate objects are personified and seem to be
invested with emotional life: clothes *complain*, the sun *stares*, leaves whisper
mischievously. It almost seems as if everyday objects and actions were endowed with mysterious power. Raymond Carver, one of the masters of the
minimalist short story, explains that this has to do with the use of commonplace but

> clear and specific language, language used so as to bring to life the
> details that will light up the story for the reader. [...] The words can be
> so precise they may even sound flat, but they can still carry; if used
> right, they can hit all the notes.[24]

I would argue that all the "notes" are indeed hit in this first passage. We almost feel the skin sizzle in the sun, sense the touch of the freshly-cut grass on
our skin, hear our bones crack as we get up. The evocation of these sensory
images in precise language and fine detail has the potential to trigger an emotional response in the reader.

This emotional response, however, can only be ambivalent. From the very
first paragraphs of the story, we have a sense of the importance of the things
that are unsaid. The story of the protagonist's dead son becomes a "second
story."[25] The second story is carefully embedded in the first, an "undercurrent
of suggested meaning [that is] necessary to the intelligibility of the first
[story],"[26] the visible action. But as the second story in "Moses" can never be
unravelled, the first story cannot be interpreted unambiguously. The second
story becomes an *uncanny* and *haunting* undercurrent, looming under the

---

[23] Segun Afolabi, "Moses," *A Life Elsewhere* (2004; London: Vintage, 2007): 127–
28. Further page references are in the main text.

[24] Raymond Carver, "On Writing," in *The New Short Story Theories*, ed. Charles E.
May (Athens: Ohio U P, 1994): 277.

[25] Armine K. Mortimer, "Second Stories," in *Short Story Theory at a Crossroads*,
ed. Susan Lohafer & Jo E. Clarey (Baton Rouge: Louisiana State U P, 1989): 276.

[26] Mortimer, "Second Stories," 276.

"surface of things,"[27] a constant threat of instability that increases the tension in the story to an almost unbearable extent.

We finally get to the point where the second story breaks through the surface, where suppressed memories seem to hit the protagonist with full force. This happens at the dance club, where the man suddenly has to think of his dead son:

> The man was first to drain his glass. As he waited for the others he thrust his hands into his jacket pockets. There were the leaves and the dead flowers and the dirt, the soiled handkerchief, either side of him. He had forgotten to empty his pockets all day. He thought of the boy then, in the middle of the spirited club. He leaned heavily against the edge of the bar. His legs were trembling. (137–38)

The man's emotional reaction is again absent from the text, but it must be violent because only a short time later, we witness the following scene in the couple's bedroom:

> Finally he sat on the edge of the bed and then stood and swayed and fell to the bed again.
> "What the fuck are you doing?" the woman continued to laugh. "You're on top form tonight." She heard a stream of liquid running to the floor. She turned to him as if for the first time. He was beyond himself now, there was no control, the body not doing what the mind required. The urine washed against the side of the bed, spilling onto the wooden floor. For a time that was the only sound they listened to. Then she was up, pushing him off the bed, screaming. It was always like this: the drinking, the fighting, the release of held tensions. She stood over him as he sat on the floor, barely conscious. (138–39)

The second story has finally overpowered the protagonist, and we are confronted with a taboo, an almost unthinkable loss of control: the profoundly disturbing image of a grown-up urinating on the bedroom floor. We can speculate as to the reasons for this; but the story remains uncomfortably silent.

There is only one sentence in "Moses" that explicitly refers to the characters' emotions. It occurs in the very last paragraphs of the story, which shift the point of view to the woman for the first time:

> Mid-morning when the woman woke, the man had already cleaned the room. She could hear him moving about the flat, humming to a tune on

---

[27] Carver, "On Writing," 277.

the radio. [...] She turned in the bed to face the chestnut tree, its leaves
fluttering quietly in the still of the morning. The blue sky gave off an
intense heat. The curtains lapped at the edge of the window, but the
breeze was hardly felt.

They would eat the meal the man prepared as they did every Saturday afternoon. They would begin to speak, moving warily around each
other. *The only force keeping them together was their terror of being
alone.* (139–40; my emphasis)

Being the only sentence that comes close to internal focalization, it perfectly
represents, in only twelve words, the entire emotional 'universe' of the story,
a universe pervaded with loss, longing, loneliness, and alienation – experiences that are ubiquitous in the migrant space.

To sum up, the two short stories trace radically different fates of migrants
in stylistically and technically disparate literary forms. They do not homo-
genize experiences of migration, do not shy away from a representation of the
harsh realities of living in exile, and never romanticize the 'outsider' position
of their protagonists or narrators.

In addition, the stories challenge the status quo by countering conventional
perceptions of the migrant space, by destabilizing their own narrative worlds,
by wholeheartedly embracing textual nervousness and indeterminacy. In
doing so, they create the discursive conditions necessary for the emergence of
Homi Bhabha's "Third Space of enunciation."[28] In my tentative interpretation
of Bhabha's concept, the Third Space is a performative reading and writing
strategy that attempts to challenge manichaean conceptions of the world,
received wisdom, and restrictive notions of what Bhabha calls primordial
unity, fixity, or homogeneity of cultures and their symbols.[29] In Bhabha's analyses, the Third Space almost always arises from gaps in colonial and postcolonial discourses, from "an ambivalence in the act of interpretation,"[30] "cultural uncertainty and [...] significatory or representational undecidability"[31] –
in short, from indeterminacy of the kind I have traced in Okri's and Afolabi's
short stories. Because these gaps cannot be filled in, ambivalences not resolved and uncertainties not reduced, they are subversive. They make multiple
readings of discourses possible and ensure that the two narratives under

---

[28] Bhabha, *The Location of Culture,* 54.

[29] See *The Location of Culture,* 53–55.

[30] *The Location of Culture,* 53.

[31] *The Location of Culture,* 51.

consideration have to be "[re-]appropriated, translated, rehistoricized and read anew"[32] each time we confront them, which may ultimately lead to so far unrecognizable positions[33] and new ways of perceiving the world.

I will, finally, argue that the short story is the perfect aesthetic medium for writing (in) the migrant space and evoking the Third Space. A plethora of commentators,[34] above all Frank O'Connor in his classic *The Lonely Voice*, have stressed that the short story is characterized by its preference for portraying liminal characters on the margins, "the submerged population group,"[35] to which migrants undoubtedly belong:

> Always in the short story there is this sense of outlawed figures wandering about the fringes of society [...]. As a result there is in the short story at its most characteristic something we do not often find in the novel – an intense awareness of human loneliness.[36]

While I feel that this is too sweeping a generalization, it is definitely true of the two short stories discussed in this essay and the migrants depicted in them: the List-maker and the narrator in Okri's story are isolated in their "prison of a street,"[37] cast out by both the immigrant communities and the inhabitants of the approaching tower blocks; and the protagonist in Afolabi's story is a solitary figure among the crowd in the club where the traumatic memory of his dead son hits him so unexpectedly.

Not only that, it seems to me that the genre of the short story is essentially 'indeterminate': the ongoing debate on providing generic definitions shows that the form stubbornly refuses to be pinned down. The short-fiction writer and Stanford professor Elizabeth Tallent goes even further and propounds that the short story is a potentially subversive genre:

> The short story's first line often signals, subtly or confrontationally, *Be careful what you trust*. Time and again, in that very first line, the literary story hints at *subversion*. Counter to convention of one kind or

---

[32] Bhabha, *The Location of Culture*, 55.

[33] See Bhabha, "The Third Space," 211.

[34] See Mary Louise Pratt, "The Short Story: The Long and the Short of It," in *The New Short Story Theories*, ed. Charles E. May (Athens: Ohio UP, 1994): 91–103.

[35] Frank O'Connor, *The Lonely Voice: A Sketch of the Short Story* (Cleveland OH: World Publishing Company, 1962): 51.

[36] O'Connor, *The Lonely Voice*, 19, 21.

[37] Okri, "A Hidden History," 89.

> another, *disruptive* of its own literary culture – making a break for it.
> Short stories are always breaking something. This is the *least trust-*
> *worthy* of literary forms. A form that likes to waylay complacency and
> to do it fast. [...] So this [...] protean form sets out to deconstruct
> romanticism, fracture realism, *wreak havoc* with chronology, portray
> violent death and complex love and transformed perception: and to do
> it between the time a reader sits down with the book and the time she
> gets up.[38]

We have seen how the narrator's evasiveness in Okri's "A Hidden History"
makes us uncertain about *what and whom to trust* and how the hyper-realist
depiction of violence *disrupts* the story's aesthetic. The minimalism in Afolabi's "Moses" may be more subtle, but its gaps hint at the uncanny undercurrent of the second story that is always just about to *wreak havoc*, to *subvert*
the first story, and to overpower its protagonist.

Finally, we should not underestimate the sheer physical impact of short
stories. As Poe and Tallent point out, the brevity of the short story makes it
possible to read it at one sitting,[39] to take in the work of art in its entirety. This
enables us to see connections among images more clearly and to attend to fine
linguistic detail more carefully. As a result, we may be affected more directly
by mounting tensions or gory violence; and we will be troubled more deeply
by the threat of instability and discursive nervousness – the preconditions, as I
have argued, for the emergence of the Third Space.

Okri's and Afolabi's decision to write the migrant space as short story is,
thus, ultimately a political act. It ensures that histories of migrancy cannot be
consumed as an exotic commodity or as an exclusively pleasurable reading
experience. The uncanny gaps and ambivalences in the idiosyncratic migrant
(hi)stories "A Hidden History" and "Moses" may return to haunt us, forcing
us to confront the migrants' "perplexity of living in the liminal spaces"[40] of
Western societies again and again.

⌘

---

[38] Elizabeth Tallent, unpublished lecture notes for "Development of the Short Story:
Continuity and Innovation" (lecture, Stanford University, April 2009), my emphasis.

[39] Edgar Allan Poe, "Review of [Hawthorne's] *Twice-Told Tales*" (May 1842), in
The New Short Story Theories, ed. Charles E. May (Athens: Ohio UP, 1994): 60.

[40] Bhabha, *The Location of Culture*, 232.

WORKS CITED

Afolabi, Segun. "Moses," in *A Life Elsewhere* (2004; London: Vintage, 2007): 127–40.

Ahmad, Aijaz. "The Politics of Literary Postcoloniality," *Race and Class* 36.3 (January 1995): 1–20.

Bhabha, Homi K. "At the Limits," *Artforum* 27 (May 1989): 11–12.

——. *The Location of Culture* (1994; New York: Routledge, 2004).

——. "The Third Space," in *Identity: Community, Culture, Difference,* ed. Jonathan Rutherford (London: Lawrence & Wishart, 1990): 207–21.

Campbell, Ewing. "How Minimal Is Minimalism," in *The Tales We Tell: Perspectives on the Short Story,* ed. Barbara Lounsberry et al. (Contributions to the Study of World Literature 88; Westport CT & London: Greenwood, 1998): 14–19.

Carver, Raymond. "On Writing," in *The New Short Story Theories,* ed. Charles E. May (Athens: Ohio UP, 1994): 273–77.

Dirlik, Arif. "The Postcolonial Aura: Third World Criticism in the Age of Global Capitalism," *Critical Inquiry* 20.2 (Winter 1994): 328–56.

Fanon, Frantz. *The Wretched of the Earth*, preface by Jean–Paul Sartre, tr. Constance Farrington (*Les Damnés de la terre*, 1961; New York: Grove, 1963).

Fraser, Robert. *Ben Okri: Towards the Invisible City* (Tavistock: Northcote House, 2002).

Huddart, David. *Homi K. Bhabha* (London: Routledge, 2006).

Huggan, Graham. *The Post-Colonial Exotic: Marketing the Margins* (London: Routledge, 2001).

Mortimer, Armine K. "Second Stories," in *Short Story Theory at a Crossroads*, ed. Susan Lohafer & Jo E. Clarey (Baton Rouge: Louisiana State UP, 1989): 276–98.

O'Connor, Frank. *The Lonely Voice: A Study of the Short Story* (Cleveland OH: The World Publishing Company, 1962).

Okri, Ben. "A Hidden History," in *Incidents at the Shrine* (1985; London: Vintage, 1993): 81–90.

Poe, Edgar Allan. "Review of *Twice-Told Tales*," in *The New Short Story Theories,* ed. Charles E. May (Athens: Ohio UP, 1994): 59–72. Originally published in *Graham's Magazine* (May 1842): 298–300.

Pratt, Mary Louise. "The Short Story: The Long and the Short of It," in *The New Short Story Theories*, ed. Charles E. May (Athens: Ohio UP, 1994): 91–103.

Quayson, Ato. "Looking Awry: Tropes of Disability in Post-Colonial Writing," in *An Introduction to Contemporary Fiction,* ed. Rod Mengham (Cambridge: Polity, 1999): 53–68.

Radhakrishnan, Rajagopalan. "Adjudicating Hybridity, Co-ordinating Betweenness," *Jouvert* 5.1 (2000), http://english.chass.ncsu.edu/jouvert/v5i1/radha.htm (accessed 17 October 2010).

Rushdie, Salman. *Step Across this Line* (London: Jonathan Cape, 2002).

Siebert, Hilary. "Social Critique and Story Technique in the Fiction of Raymond Carver," in *The Tales We Tell: Perspectives on the Short Story*, ed. Barbara Lounsberry et al. (Westport CT & London: Greenwood, 1998): 21–28.

Smith, Andrew. "Migrancy, Hybridity, and Postcolonial Literary Studies," in *The Cambridge Companion to Postcolonial Literary Studies*, ed. Neil Lazarus (Cambridge: Cambridge UP, 2004): 241–61.

Tallent, Elizabeth. "Development of the Short Story: Continuity and Innovation" (lecture, Stanford University, April 2009).

Wachinger, Tobias A. *Posing In-between: Postcolonial Englishness and the Commodification of Hybridity* (Frankfurt am Main: Peter Lang, 2003).

Young, Robert J.C. *Postcolonialism: A Very Short Introduction* (Oxford: Oxford UP, 2004).

⌘

Daljit Nagra's *Look We Have Coming to Dover!* and the Limits of the Translocal

KATHARINA RENNHAK

1. Introduction: On the Relationship of 'Trans-' and 'Location'

A DISCUSSION OF 'THE LIMITS OF THE TRANSLOCAL' must base its argument on a precise definition of the conceptual implications of the terms 'local' and 'translocal', particularly since 'limits' in the title of this article affect the *term* 'translocal' rather than its referent (if such a referent exists). To begin with the prefix 'trans-': In his introduction to *Postcolonial Literatures in English*, Tobias Döring stresses that "in the field" of postcolonial studies "the prefix 'trans-'," which modifies so many different terms "like 'transnational' and 'transcultural'," refers to a "kind of foreignizing dynamics."[1] Terms with the prefix 'trans-', Döring goes on to explain,

> differ from the previously established terms 'international' and 'intercultural': they do not focus on the links between two given entities – nations, cultures – assuming that these entities essentially remain the same; they rather presuppose border transgressions and constitutive transformations to take place all along and they explore the productive instabilities, fluidities and conflicts *within* such entities – nations, cultures – which render all political attempts to draw a rigid boundary around them questionable.[2]

My reading of the poetry in Daljit Nagra's acclaimed debut collection *Look We Have Coming to Dover!* (2007) will point to the dangers inherent in the prevalent practice of simply conflating this idea of a "foreignizing dynamics"

---

[1] Tobias Döring, *Postcolonial Literatures in English* (Stuttgart: Klett, 2008): 30.

[2] Döring, *Postcolonial Literatures in English*, 30.

with the spatial concept of the 'local' in the use of the term 'translocal.' Such
a conflation of concepts can be found, for example, in an article by Jahan
Ramazani[3] which draws on Stuart Hall's notion of 'diaspora identities'. Quoting from Hall's influential article "Cultural Identity and Diaspora,"[4] he states
that the poems of black British poets are defined "by the recognition of a
necessary heterogeneity and diversity; by a conception of 'identity' which
lives with and through, not despite, difference; by *hybridity*."[5] What I find
problematical about Ramazani's approach is not, of course, that he draws on
Hall's concept of an internally differentiated and dynamic identity as such,
but the fact that he – like quite a number of other critics – equates this idea
with the spatial aspect of the 'translocal'. A passage where this equation of
the hybrid with the spatial is particularly obvious reads:

> [Black British writers'] poems are 'translocal', in that they see the
> metropolis afresh [...] and shuttle across and unsettle imperial hier-
> archies of centre and periphery, motherland and colonial offspring,
> North and South. In short, they dislocate the local into translocation.[6]

In Ramazani's definition of the term, 'translocation' becomes a rather abstract
quality. His use of 'translocation' activates only the first sense of 'location' as
defined by the *OED*: "the *action* of placing; the fact or condition of *being*
placed."[7] By focusing on the important dynamic and procedural aspect of
'(trans)location', Ramazani loses sight of the second, no less important,
meaning of 'location': "the fact or condition of *occupying* a particular place;
local position, situation."[8] This is the meaning also covered by the term

---

[3] Jahan Ramazani, "Black British Poetry and the Translocal," in *The Cambridge
Companion to Twentieth-Century English Poetry*, ed. Neil Corcoran (Cambridge:
Cambridge UP, 2007): 200–14.

[4] Stuart Hall, "Cultural Identity and Diaspora," in *Identity, Community, Culture,
Difference*, ed. Jonathan Rutherford (London: Lawrence & Wishart, 1990): 222–37,
repr. in *Theorizing Diaspora: A Reader*, ed. Jana Evans Braziel & Anita Mannur (Malden MA: Blackwell, 2003): 233–46.

[5] Ramazani, "Black British Poetry and the Translocal," 202. Ramazani cites Hall,
"Cultural Identity and Diaspora," 244.

[6] Ramazani, "Black British Poetry and the Translocal," 202.

[7] My emphasis.

[8] 'location, n.', *Oxford English Dictionary Online,* November 2010, Oxford UP,
www.oed.com:80/Entry/109574 (accessed 27 February 2011), my emphasis.

'locality', which unambiguously refers to the static "fact or quality of having a place, that is, of having position in space."[9]

In other words, when the ideas of the 'hybrid' and the 'spatial' are conflated in 'trans-location' the more concrete aspect of the term 'location' all too often seems to get completely lost, and with it the specific conceptual power which the term 'translocation' – unlike, for example, 'translation', 'transgression' or 'transition' – can unfold, if one takes seriously its capacity to point at attempts to 'ground' and stabilize in a "position in space" the foreignizing dynamic encapsulated in the prefix 'trans-'. To put it differently again, what is lost in Ramazani's and other critics' exclusive concentration on the procedural dynamic of 'translocation' is the *social* space.[10] In what follows, I will analyse Nagra's poetry in order to demonstrate that it is worthwhile in some contexts to keep apart the idea of the dynamic and hybrid, on the one hand, and that of the local or spatial, on the other. To put this more positively once again: the special value of the term 'translocation' which distinguishes it from terms like 'translation' or 'transgression' seems to me to lie in the way it persistently points to the concrete, social aspect of 'location' and its resistance to monopolizing abstract theories.

Recent cultural and postcolonial theories that "yearn for the cessation of aggressive [post 9/11] binary discourse,"[11] like Kwame Anthony Appiah's reconceptualization of 'cosmopolitanism' in his *Cosmopolitanism: Ethics in a World of Strangers* (2006) or Paul Gilroy's reflections on the future of multiculturalism and his notion of 'conviviality' in *After Empire* (2004), emphasize the importance of the ordinary, daily social praxis of multicultural coexistence "in Britain's urban areas and in postcolonial cities elsewhere."[12]

---

[9] 'locality, n.', *Oxford English Dictionary Online*, my emphasis.

[10] It would be unfair to claim that, in Ramazani's and similarly abstract uses of the term 'translocation', 'trans-' must – in the process of its being 'de-spatialized' – *inevitably* accrue the meaning of a transcendental beyond. I would argue, however, that this danger is always lurking as soon as one conflates the dynamic foreignizing power of the hybrid with the 'local' in 'translocation'.

[11] Yasmin Alibhai–Brown, "Common People: *Cosmopolitanism: Ethics in a World of Strangers* by Kwame Anthony Appiah," review, *The Independent* (4 August 2006), www.independent.co.uk/arts-entertainment/books/reviews/cosmopolitanism-ethics-in-a-world-of-strangers-by-kwame-anthony-appiah-410408.html (accessed 28 September 2010).

[12] Paul Gilroy, *After Empire: Melancholia or Convivial Culture?* (London: Routledge, 2004): xi.

Appiah even asserts "the primacy of practice" for his model of cosmopolitan conversation: "When the issue is what to do, differences in what we think and feel can fall away," he suggests, and goes on to claim that "our political co-existence, as subjects or citizens, depends on being able to agree about practices while disagreeing about their justification."[13] The hope invested by Gilroy in "processes of [multicultural] cohabitation and interaction" and Appiah's "primacy of practice" take it for granted that the different cultures that live in our globalized world's postcolonial cities do indeed interact and converse in certain social places and spaces. My analysis of Nagra's poetry in *Look We Have Coming to Dover!* is set in this larger theoretical context.

Nagra's volume of poetry, I will argue, problematizes certain fashionable notions of the translocal and of Britain as an 'open' multicultural society. Certainly agreeing in principle with the main aspects of Appiah's and Gilroy's theories, Nagra points to the desperate need for a social locale where ethnically different Londoners meet. Much more sceptical than the two cultural critics, however, Nagra also exposes a lamentable lack of such a 'locality': i.e. the absence of a concrete place or space where the dynamizing and foreignizing effects, which are typical of the various cross-cultural translations of the Asian-British speakers of Nagra's poetry, reach the non-Asian British.[14] Before I can substantiate my main thesis in the fourth section of this essay, I

---

[13] Kwame Anthony Appiah, *Cosmopolitanism: Ethics in a World of Strangers* (New York: W.W. Norton, 2006): 69–70.

[14] In what follows, I prefer the terminology that draws on geographical or national signifiers (e.g., 'Asian-British'), because it can serve much more obviously as a simple heuristic tool with which to conceptualize identities (which is all it is for me) than the currently more fashionable biological (and therefore more dangerously essentializing?) terms 'black British' or 'white British'. I also gratefully take up my peer reviewer's hint that "Anglo-Saxons have a hyphen, too!" – although, crucially, these 'traditional British' identities are often *perceived* as *un*hyphenated and non-hybrid, and thus wrongly placed *in opposition* to the Asian-British and other diasporic identities, whose hyphenated and hybrid character is often more readily acknowledged. A particularly differentiated discussion of the problem of hyphenated identities can be found in Radhakrishnan's influential article "Ethnicity in an Age of Diaspora," *Transition* 54 (1991): 104–15, repr. in *Theorizing Diaspora*, ed. Braziel & Mannur, 119–31. Also see Vijay Mishra, "The Diasporic Imaginary: Theorizing the Indian Diaspora," *Textual Practice* 10.3 (Winter 1996): 421–47, and, on hyphenated identities in Nagra's poetry, Dave Gunning, "Daljit Nagra, Faber Poet: Burdens of Representation and Anxieties of Influence," *Journal of Commonwealth Literature* 43.3 (2008): 99–100.

must elaborate on two preconditions in the following two sections, which demonstrate that Nagra's yearning for a common and concrete 'location' where all Londoners meet is built a) on the by now familiar concept of the internal differentiation of ethnic communities, which problematizes simplistic binary oppositions, and b) on the equally received notion that the Asian community have found their place in Britain.

2. *Look We Have Coming to Dover!* and the Representation of an Internally Differentiated Asian-British Community

Daljit Nagra was born and raised in West London and Sheffield. His poetry reflects the experience of a second-generation British Asian, and, thus, a subject who has not actually been 'translocated': i.e. who has not been removed from one place to another, but lives, and has always lived, in the place where he was born, in England. Still, in England (and I am tempted to write 'in this locality') he is part of a diasporic community that is, as a whole, partly defined by its past in a different place. Written by a hyphenated Asian-British subject, the poems in *Look We Have Coming To Dover!* certainly partake of two cultures.

Dave Gunning has convincingly shown how Nagra's verse is consistently marked by anxiety about his right to represent 'his people' and how his "depiction of the heterogeneity of the community flows out from his image of his self as protean."[15] In other words, it has already been demonstrated by Gunning (and I can take for granted in what follows) that what Stuart Hall says of "the diaspora experience" also correctly describes Nagra's second-generation Asian-British experience, which, as already quoted, "is defined, not by essence or purity, but by the recognition of a necessary heterogeneity and diversity; by a conception of 'identity' which lives with and through, not despite, difference; by *hybridity*."[16] It is often forgotten that in "Cultural Identity and Diaspora" Hall does not conceive of diasporic identity as primarily a hybrid that contains elements of all the cultures, places, and histories which the diasporic community partakes of but, rather, as an identity which is characterized by a differentiating dynamic *within* the diasporic community. He himself places emphasis on this:

---

[15] Dave Gunning, "Daljit Nagra, Faber Poet," 103.

[16] Hall, "Cultural Identity and Diaspora," 244.

> Visiting the French Caribbean for the first time, I also saw at once how
> different Martinique is from, say, Jamaica: and this is no mere diffe-
> rence of topography or climate. It is a profound difference of culture
> and history.[17]

For my argument it is important to realize that it is such a 'hybridity within',
in Nagra's case a hybridity within the Asian-British community, which the
poems in *Look We Have Coming to Dover!* point to and unfold.

A number of poems highlight "the class divisions within British Asian
communities,"[18] as Gunning has already shown. In "The Furtherance of Mr
Bulram's Education," for example – in which the eponymous character, an
Asian-British schoolteacher, finds himself in disagreement with his new-
immigrant neighbours – illustrates how class differences are reflected in and
entail different senses of the aesthetic (or, rather, Western aesthetic): While
Bulram loves "the neatness of his decorative garden," his neighbours dig up
"their English gardens to plant foodstuffs."[19] In addition, Bulram and the
lower-class Asian British are contrasted by their "different attitudes to language," as the new immigrant has no ear for the beauty of the English tongue,
but only "wishes Bulram to teach him pragmatic '*quick "shop-keeper" English*'."[20]

Like this particular poem, Nagra's collection as a whole contains different
languages. Dramatic monologues in Punglish can be found alongside confes-
sional or self-reflective lyrical poetry written sometimes in a colloquial, and
sometimes in a decidedly literary, English. What is true of "The Furtherance
of Mr Bulram's Education" also holds for the whole of *Look We Have
Coming to Dover!*: the enormous variety in "our lingoes" (32), to use an expression from the eponymous poem of the collection, always points to a
difference *within* the Asian-British community rather than to a difference between the Asian British and the non-Asian British.

The diasporic community is internally differentiated by more than class
differences, different aesthetics, and different attitudes to the English language. In the present context, I can only briefly mention some other factors
which are also shown to dynamize and problematize the processes of personal

---

[17] Hall, "Cultural Identity and Diaspora," 238.

[18] Gunning, "Daljit Nagra, Faber Poet," 104.

[19] "Daljit Nagra, Faber Poet," 104.

[20] "Daljit Nagra, Faber Poet," 104, quoting Nagra, *Look We Have Coming to
Dover!*, 38.

and communal identity-construction of British Asians, such as, most importantly, religion,[21] gender, and, again and again, generational differences. Gender and generation, it can be noted, often intersect insofar as it is repeatedly
the first-generation immigrant mother who complains about the westerniza-
tion of the next generation. In "Bibi & the Street Car Wife!," for example, a
widowed mother complains to her son about how much her daughter-in-law
has changed

> Ever since we loosened our village acres
> for this flighty mix-up country, like moody
> actress she buy herself a Datsun, with legs
> of K F C microphoning her mouth
> (ladies of temple giddily tell me her tale):
> she manicured waves men, or honking horn
> to unbutton her hair she dirty winking:
> *Come on friend, I like it letting you in!* (16; my emphasis)

In "In a White Town," to point to a second example, the second-generation
Asian-British speaker remembers how his mother was the greatest obstacle to
his many attempts to forget his Asian-British background and assimilate:

> I would have felt more at home had she hidden
> that illiterate body, bumping noisily into women
> at the market, bulging into its drama'd gossip,
>
> for homework – in the public library with my mates,
> she'd call, scratching on the windows. (18)

Again, it is the mother who wishes to keep the Asian-British and the non-
Asian-British world apart and hopes to maintain the South Asian tradition by
her son's marriage to a good Indian girl:

> laughing, she'd say I was a gora, I'd only be freed
> by a bride from India who would double as her saathi. (19)

However, it is not my chief aim simply to demonstrate that Nagra depicts the
Asian-British community as heterogeneous and dynamic – even though the
observation that he does so is very important for my argument. What I want to

---

[21] With regard to this aspect, I can only refer the reader to "Our Town with the
Whole of India!" in Daljit Nagra, *Look We Have Coming to Dover!* (London: Faber &
Faber, 2007): 12–13. See also the discussion of the same poem in a different context
below. Further page references are in the main text.

emphasize is, rather, that, on the one hand, in *Look We Have Coming to Dover!* this internally differentiated community is shown to have arrived in England. The Asian British have made themselves at home in the UK, and Nagra has found in London a position or locality from which to speak and from which to represent his and his community's heterogeneous, hybrid, and dynamic identity. This is why the collection – published by one of the most renowned British publishers (Faber & Faber) – is entitled *Look We Have Coming to Dover!* On the other hand, the problem that Nagra presents as yet unresolved is encapsulated in the first word of the title, in the urgent invitation to "Look!"[22] The non-Asian British have not noticed the Asian British as a community which has something to offer and which wants to make contact. Nagra's collection repeatedly points to the problem that there is no common ground, no location, from which the Asian British and the non-Asian British could begin to develop a sense of community, a new and common cultural identity which, for the lack of a better term, one may provisionally designate as 'British-Asian-British'. The following textual analyses will develop this claim step by step.

3. *Look We Have Coming to Dover!*: Locating the Asian-British Community in Britain

One of the poems which portray a very lively, heterogeneous Asian-British community that has settled and found a home in England is "Our Town with the Whole of India!":

> Our town in England with the whole of India sundering
> out of its temples, mandirs and mosques for the customised
> streets. Our parade, clad in cloak-orange with banners
> and tridents, chanting from station to station for Vasaikhi
> over Easter. Our full-moon madness for Eidh with free
> pavement tandooris and legless dancing to boostered
> cars. (12)

---

[22] The continuous form of the verb 'coming' in the title cannot go unmentioned here. In my reading it points to the inevitably procedural and dynamic process of all kinds of identity-formation rather than to a specific problem of the diasporic community.

Here the communal spirit is invoked by a speaker who opens not only every stanza of the poem, but also every sentence of the first stanza with a communal "our." It is significant that the speaker uses and almost obsessively repeats the *possessive* pronoun 'our' and not just the personal pronoun 'we', as the former indicates that the Asian-British community has clearly taken possession of a British locality. The ending of the first stanza shows particularly well how the various Indian traditions connect with Western traditions and myths, and points to the 'foreignizing dynamic' encapsulated in the prefix 'trans-' which constructs a hybrid Asian-British identity.

> [...] Our Guy Fawkes' Diwali – a kingdom of rockets
> for the Odysseus-trials of Rama who arrowed the jungle
> foe to re-palace the Penelope-faith of his Sita. (12)

The strange verb 're-palace' is particularly interesting in the present context. First, this neologism emphasizes that the South Asian traditions are precisely *not* 'replaced' by something else, but reorganized or hybridized as a consequence of their relocation. Secondly, the unusual and unexpected verb "re-palace" revitalizes the spatial aspect which tends to be overheard in our everyday use of the (more often than not abstract) term 'to replace'. Thus, it is by means of revitalizing a dead metaphor that Nagra here emphasizes his focus on concrete social places (like palaces) which are the precondition for any unfolding of a 'foreignizing dynamic'.

The two dramatic monologues which begin and end the collection, entitled "Darling & Me" and "Singh Song!" respectively, open the view into the more private realm of the Asian-British home in England. Here male second-generation Asian-British speakers celebrate their recent love marriages. In "Singh Song!," in particular, the English home of the newly-weds is shown to be firmly anchored in the Asian-British community as the speaker's neighbours and customers complain that the newly-wed neglects his shop:

> *Hey Singh, ver yoo bin?*
> *Yor lemons are limes*
> *yor bananas are plantain,*
> *dis dirty little floor need a little bit of mop*
> *in di worst Indian shop*
> *on di whole Indian road –* (51)[23]

---

[23] Italics in the original.

The domestic idyll depicted in "Singh Song!" is thus not the kind of Holly-wood "'masala' resolution"[24] that Radhakrishnan criticizes. Nagra's version does not imply that the two second-generation "hybrids" simply "walk out of their 'prehistories' into the innocence of physical, heterosexual love."[25] Rather, their private home is shown to be firmly anchored in a lively British-Asian community in England.

Another poem which points to the fact that the Asian British have formed a new community and one that is firmly located in Britain is "For the Wealth of India," which expresses an unadorned and quite unflattering view of some Asian British. It depicts a young Asian-British woman and her mother on a shopping tour at an Indian bazaar in Jullunder, India. Belonging to those who profit from capitalist globalization, these two women have

> […] Aeroflot[ed] the savage miles
> in a moment, tucking under
> continents to clip the distance,
> zoomed to our ancestral homeland
> so we ransack the bazaar tracks
> of back-alley bounteous Jullunder. (8)

While mother and daughter clearly define their British-Asian identities by berating, patronizing, and exoticizing their Asian Others, they are also shown to bond with other Asian-British visitors to India, who have also profited socially and financially from their having settled in Britain:

> The pongy tailors run like flies
> now that time is against them
> as we debate with the queue of Englanders
> the top-carat beauty of exotic
> things. (9)

Once they are done with their shopping, the two women only want to get away from the mud and the flies and the dirt, and it becomes very clear where their home is located:

> […] we lap up our
> suits, shoes and bags
> of bangles and cheapo knickers

---

[24] Radhakrishnan, "Ethnicity in an Age of Diaspora," 124.

[25] "Ethnicity in an Age of Diaspora," 124–25.

> tossing them at the slouched driver
> of the flimsy rickshaw to shout,
> *Jaldi! Jaldi! Back to Britain!*
> *Get us out of here!* [...] (9)

It could hardly be more obvious that Nagra's collection presents the Asian British as having found a place in Britain. The foreignizing dynamic associated with the prefix 'trans-' is present in a firmly grounded and socially specific location. What remains to be demonstrated is that *Look We Have Coming to Dover!* also addresses the problem that, despite the fact that the Asian-British community has made itself, and feels, at home in Britain, this has not enabled them to enter into a productive dialogue with the non-Asian British. Nagra's collection exposes the lack of a location where the Asian British and the non-Asian British interact or converse (i.e. as cosmopolitans in Appiah's sense).

4. *Look We Have Coming to Dover!* and the Lack of a Location Where the Asian British and the Non-Asian British Meet

In his poetry-collection, Nagra not only depicts the dynamic processes involved in constructing a heterogeneous hyphenated cultural identity that is firmly situated in Britain, but also claims that this same process does not affect the cultural identity of the non-Asian British. There are many poems in *Look We Have Coming to Dover!* which suggest that this is the case – there is simply no location, neither a literal place nor a metaphorical space, where the Asian British and the non-Asian British come into a form of contact which would allow them to develop a sense of community. There are, of course, 'contact zones' in Mary Louise Pratt's sense of the term – "social spaces where disparate cultures meet, clash, and grapple with each other"[26] – in contemporary London. But Nagra's poetry does not depict a single zone which allows for any kind of rewarding or fruitful interaction between the Asian British and the non-Asian British. On the contrary, in a number of dramatic monologues and pieces of expressive lyrical poetry *Look We Have Coming to Dover!* stages, as it were, the deplorable absence of such a location. Reformulating a question posed by Radhakrishnan, who is concerned with Asian-American diasporic identities, Nagra seems to ask: "If the Asian is to be

---

[26] Mary Louise Pratt, *Imperial Eyes: Travel Writing and Transculturation* (London: Routledge, 1992): 4.

[Anglicised], will the [British] submit to Asianisation? Will there be a reciprocity of influence whereby [British] identity itself will be seen as a form
of openness to the many ingredients that constitute it?"[27] It is beyond doubt
that in Nagra's poetry the 'British' in the hyphenated adjective 'Asian-British'
has been reconstituted; it remains doubtful, however, to say the least, whether
the usually unhyphenated non-Asian-British subject will ever partake of and
participate in this new British identity.

The poems in *Look We Have Coming to Dover!* that envisage contact
zones and portray encounters between the Asian British and the non-Asian
British can be roughly divided into three categories: 1) 'poems of assimilation', which feature Asian-British subjects who try to totally assimilate into
the British community; 2) 'poems of separation' or 'gap poems', which delineate the borderlines that divide England into an Asian-British sphere and a
non-Asian-British sphere; and 3) 'poems of failed communication', which test
the extent to which metaphorical spaces – such as 'love' or 'poetry' – can
serve as contact zones that stimulate fruitful interaction between Asian-British
and non-Asian British processes of identity-construction.

Of the two most important locations of assimilation, the first is, predictably, the global market economy. In "Bibi & and the Street Car Wife!," a
'poem of assimilation' which has already come into view in a different context above, a widowed mother deplores the drifting-away of her daughter-in-
law into a foreign Western world of undifferentiated market-place pluralism.
A second domain which is shown to invite and foster (rather painful and
traumatic) processes of assimilation contains, perhaps more surprisingly, the
school and the public library. In "In a White Town," it becomes quite clear in
lines like

> never confessing my parents' weird names
> or the code of our address when I was licked
> by Skinheads (by a toilet seat)
> desperate to flush out the enemy within (18)

that the young Asian-British speaker's wish to assimilate is, ultimately, an
attempt to evade different kinds of racially violent practices and situations
rather than a true desire to re-negotiate his personal and cultural identity.

Nagra's 'poems of separation' or 'gap poems' depict contact zones which
eventually only widen the seemingly unbridgeable gap between the Asian
British and the non-Asian British. Such a zone is the pub in "Darling & Me,"

---

[27] Radhakrishnan, "Ethnicity in an Age of Diaspora," 127.

where the speaker has a drink with his English mates from work. In the pub, however, even though he tries to socialize, he only ever seems to notice the differences between himself and his non-Asian-British colleagues. Ultimately, this first poem in the volume, while it situates the speaker right at the heart of one of the most British of institutions, is – as the title clearly indicates – a dramatic monologue about the speaker's perfect marriage. Rather than being a poem about a potential 'Asian-British–non-Asian-British' contact zone, it is driven by the speaker's impatience to be able to leave the pub and go home to his beloved Asian-British wife. The very first line in Nagra's collection, "Di barman's bell done dinging" (3), thus emphasizes the impatiently awaited ending of contact with the non-Asian-British rather than the cultural contact itself.

The speaker of another pub-poem, "The Man Who Would be English!," tells of his attempt to socialize with the non-Asian British while they all watch a football match:

> [...] I shouldered the bulk
> as they broadened like brick houses to broadly take me in,
> we plundered up gulps of golden rounds for the great game,
> united at our local, we booed at the mounted screen –
> at the face of the anthem'd foreigner when we were at home. (15)

Here again, a process of assimilation, rather than an integration which triggers the foreignizing dynamic of the 'trans-', is set in "our local," *the* British contact zone. This experience is again depicted by an Asian-British speaker as being rather menacing and imprisoning ("they broadened like brick houses to broadly take me in") right from the beginning. Again, a British locale is shown to be a contact zone which allows no mutual cultural exchange, even though an Asian-British person is, seemingly, welcomed 'with broad shoulders', if not open arms: "I was one of us, at ease, so long as I passed / my voice into theirs" (15). And again, the Asian-British speaker also ultimately withdraws from this cultural encounter into a – this time almost nightmarish – daydream. "At an own goal," he begins to fantasize about how his mother as goal-keeper is responsible for this catastrophe; and when he comes home, his wife reminds him of the racism they constantly suffer from, admonishing him to "*Lookk lookk ju nott British ju rrr blackkk ... !!!!*" (15).

Other contact zones which only serve to define and widen the gap between the Asian British and the non-Asian British are "the communal / sweat of a Saturday tube home" in the poem "Yobbos!" where the Asian-British speaker is reading the poet Paul Muldoon when "some scruffy looking git pipes to his crew – / *Some Paki shit, like, / eee's lookin into!*" (11), or, as in "Parade's End," a store. "Parade's End" shows how racist hatred culminates in an act of vandalism, when non-Asian-British locals pour acid over the newly sprayed car belonging to the Asian-British shopkeepers. The "Sheffield store" is clearly demarcated as yet another location which could bring the Asian British and the non-Asian British into some kind of non-antagonistic contact. When the speaker depicts the daily routine of barricading their shop, however, it becomes quite obvious that it does not actually provide such a space:

> At nine, we left the emptied till open,
> clicked the dials of the safe. Bolted
> two metal bars across the back door
> (with a new lock). Spread trolleys
> at ends of the darkened aisles. Then we pressed
> the code for the caged alarm and rushed
> the precinct to check it was throbbing red.
>
> Thundering down the graffiti of shutters
> against the valley of high-rise flats. (22)

The focus here is clearly on demarcating one's territory. The Asian British are confronted with a degree of violence that forces them to shut themselves off against aggressive intruders rather than encourage them to open up a space for a non-violent encounter.

But *Look We Have Coming to Dover!* does not only depict violence, racism, and more or less forced attempts at assimilation. There are also poems that portray attempts to communicate and come together peacefully, such as "Karela!," in which a male Asian-British speaker addresses Katherine, his non-Asian-British lover, and explains his hope that her eating karela, "This dish from my past" (34), will help her share his experiences. As an extended metaphor, eating karela[28] encapsulates the experiences and feelings of some-body who must straddle two cultures, whose past within the Asian-British family is so different from the present with the "English lover," and who yearns for both worlds to be somehow united.

---

[28] Karela (one of many names for the cucumber- or okra-like bitter gourd or bitter melon) is widespread throughout Asia, the Indian Ocean, and (via indenture) Trinidad. In India, the plant's extreme bitterness is commonly offset or weakened in cooking by mixing karela with 'sweetening' spices, sugar, caramelized onions and the like. The resulting broad range of delicious dishes clearly connotes, in the context of the poem, the experience of a 'marriage' or 'cultural synthesis' of extreme contrasts.

> [...] my body craves
> taste of home but is scolded
> by shame of blood-desertion
> (that simmers in me unspoken),
> save that we are in love –

the speaker explains, and hopes

> that you bite as well your mind
> with karela-curses, requited
> knowledge before our seed
> can truly bloom [...] (35)

Whether this adjustment of desires and experiences is, indeed, possible, whether the sexual encounter of lovers provides a space where Asian-British and non-Asian-British people can meet in love and mingle, remains open. They do not even begin to do so in Nagra's "Karela!," however. The poem clearly depicts a love that does not "truly bloom" (as yet?); the lyric situation of utterance, while certainly representing an attempt at communication, is ultimately not dialogic or conversational (as yet?), either. Katherine remains silent.

"Booking Khan Singh Kumar," another 'failed communication poem', is the most rigorously metapoetical piece in the collection, and runs counter to the expectation that literature in general or the poetry of Daljit Nagra in particular[29] could provide the location creating a space that can serve as common ground on which the community-building of the Asian British and the non-Asian British might begin. The idea that you book a poet, as expressed in the title and realized in the situation of utterance projected by the poem, points to the fact that the market ideology which has been shown above to be detrimental to any kind of healthy contact between different cultures also pre-structures the encounter between the Asian-British poet and his non-Asian-British customers.

> Did *you* make me for the gap in the market
> Did *I* make me for the gap in the market (6)

runs the refrain of the poem. Gunning finds "the italicization of the pronouns interesting in that it [...] remains unsure as to whom the agency involved in

---

[29] Khan Singh Kumar is the pseudonym under which Nagra published his first poems.

[the] creation [of the poetic persona] belongs."[30] I would put the emphasis differently and suggest that, whatever the influence or agency that the individual
'you' or 'I' can claim, the objectified poet's voice, the 'me', only ever becomes relevant as a commodity. Whatever the agency of the individual party,
the market is the force that governs the agency of the 'you' and the 'I' in this
encounter at a poetry reading (and in Nagra's poem as a whole).

The contact zone which the literary market provides is a location that either
enables the passive consumption and exoticization of the British-Asian's representation of his dynamic and heterogeneous cultural identity or initiates an
aggressive antagonism invoked in lines like the following:

> Will I flame on the tree that your canon has stoked
> Will I thistle at the bole where a bull-dog cocked (6)

Neither the direct encounter of the poet with his audience at a poetry reading
nor the production or consumption of poetry is shown to trigger any kind of
interaction which could lead to dialogue between the Asian British and the
non-Asian British and could thus affect the latter's identity with the foreignizing dynamic that governs the identity-construction of the Asian-British poet,
who has "worn a sari bride and an English Rose" (7) and who has various
Eastern and Western poetic discourses at his disposal. According to "Booking
Khan Singh Kumar," not even poetry provides a location, a literal place or
metaphorical space, where the Asian British and the non-Asian British enter
into a mutual and common process of identity-construction. This is also made
clear by the fact that all of the lines in "Booking Khan Singh Kumar" are syn-
tactically formulated as questions but never end with a question mark. These
questions are not just rhetorical. The missing question marks, I suggest, demonstrate that these rhetorical questions float free of any real dialogic situation. Nagra's own reading of the poem, which produces these pseudo-ques-
tions as so many accusations or, rather, spits them out at the audience, makes
this all too obvious.[31] In short, even a poetry reading does not bridge the gap.
Rather than filling a cultural gap, Asian-British poetry falls into "the gap in
the market."

Look We Have Coming to Dover! has been celebrated for the way in which
Daljit Nagra represents the Asian-British community as heterogeneous by

---

[30] Gunning, "Daljit Nagra, Faber Poet," 101.

[31] Daljit Nagra, *Look We Have Coming to Dover! Read by The Author*, Audio CD
(London: Faber Audio, 2008): track 3.

giving the different voices in the community "room to speak" and by "incor-porat[ing] voices of conflict within British-Asian communities."[32] This is certainly just praise. What must also be emphasized, however, is that Nagra's collection, in general, and "Booking Khan Singh Kumar," a poem which re-flects these strategies on a meta-poetic level, in particular, also demonstrate that this "placing of [the Asian-British speaker] in multiple positions"[33] (not only that of Khan, Singh, and Kumar, but also among many others that of a London "ghetto poet" [6] and a lover of "an English Rose" [7]) does not ne-cessarily open up a dialogue with a non-Asian-British audience or readership. Susheila Nasta shows that this strategy of adopting multiple positions has a long tradition:

> [Such] strategies for survival in Britain [were] employed even by an eighteenth-century writer like Sake Dean Mahomet in his negotiation of a number of different cultural and racial roles – whether assimila-tive, subversive or simply exploitative of the populist economy of orientalism. [...] [Mahomet] managed both in *The Travels of Dean Mahomet* and *Shampooing* to construct himself within a range of dif-ferently inflected positions. He thus *avoided marking out* an insupport-able *territory* of conflict between East and West, colonizers and colonized.[34]

Nagra's poetry demonstrates that this avoidance of 'marking out a territory of conflict' also forecloses any real dialogue. To put it differently again, even the Asian-British poet's writing as such does not serve as a contact zone for the Asian-British and the non-Asian British, because the Asian-British poet can only speak for himself and – under certain circumstances – for his commu-nity. In doing so, not only can he represent this community but he can also show that all – hyphenated and usually unhyphenated – personal and cultural identities are dynamic. What his poetry is shown to be unable to provide, however, is a space in and from which he can speak for or with the non-Asian-British Other. Thus, not even his poetry can serve as a true transloca-tion, as a space where the foreignizing dynamic referred to by the 'trans-' can

---

[32] Gunning, "Daljit Nagra, Faber Poet," 104.

[33] "Daljit Nagra, Faber Poet," 104.

[34] Susheila Nasta, *Home Truths: Fictions of the South Asian Diaspora in Britain* (Basingstoke: Palgrave Macmillan, 2002): 17 (my emphasis). This passage is also quoted in Gunning, "Daljit Nagra, Faber Poet" (103–104), where it is simply used to show that Daljit Nagra's strategy is not new.

unfold. Not even his poetry can serve as the common ground from and on which a common 'Asian-British–non-Asian-British' identity can be built.

5. Conclusion: Nagra's Poetry and the Relation of the Terms 'Trans-' and 'Location'

To conclude: with regard to the question of 'location', Nagra's poetry shows some of the ways in which the Asian-British community has taken possession of some London ground and has thus found a position from which to speak and represent their own heterogeneous and dynamic cultural identity. However, it also reveals the lack of common ground, the absence of a location where the Asian British and the non-Asian British meet and interact or converse. What I find striking is that this lack is a very real and concrete one in Nagra's collection. There simply is no contact zone which enables multicultural communication to 'take place' on an equal footing. There simply is no place or space in Nagra's London where the non-Asian-British culture openmindedly meets the Asian-British. As a consequence, it cannot be affected by and profit from processes of Asian-British identity-construction that go on right inside England. It is in this particular context that I do not find helpful those concepts of 'translocation' which conflate the 'foreignizing dynamic' of the 'trans-' with (usually rather abstract notions of) the spatial. What the future of multiculturalism requires (according to Nagra and before him Gilroy and Appiah, to name but three) is not 'a place beyond' or 'a place elsewhere', neither in a literal nor in a metaphorical sense. Nagra's poetry demonstrates that so far there is only "a gap" wherever the Asian British and the non-Asian British meet – not even literature and "the [literary] market" (6), to quote again from "Booking Khan Singh Kumar," can provide such a realm. Nagra's poems in *Look We Have Coming to Dover!* neither represent nor even inveigh, but desperately yearn for a very real and concrete meeting place, a location where the foreignizing dynamic of the 'trans-' may unfold to enfold everybody.

⌘

Works Cited

Alibhai–Brown, Yasmin. "Common People: [Rev. of] *Cosmopolitanism: Ethics in a World of Strangers* by Kwame Anthony Appiah," *The Independent* (4 August 2006), www.independent.co.uk/arts-entertainment/books/reviews/cosmopolitanism -ethics-in-a-world-of-strangers-by-kwame-anthony-appiah-410408.html (accessed 28 September 2010).

Appiah, Kwame Anthony. *Cosmopolitanism: Ethics in a World of Strangers* (New York: W.W. Norton, 2006).

Döring, Tobias. *Postcolonial Literatures in English* (Stuttgart: Klett, 2008).

Gilroy, Paul. *After Empire: Melancholia or Convivial Culture?* (London: Routledge, 2004).

Gunning, Dave. "Daljit Nagra, Faber Poet: Burdens of Representation and Anxieties of Influence," *Journal of Commonwealth Literature* 43.3 (2008): 95–108.

Hall, Stuart. "Cultural Identity and Diaspora," in *Identity, Community, Culture, Difference*, ed. Jonathan Rutherford (London: Lawrence & Wishart, 1990): 222–37, repr. in *Theorizing Diaspora: A Reader*, ed. Jana Evans Braziel & Anita Mannur (Malden MA: Blackwell, 2003): 233–46.

Nagra, Daljit. *Look We Have Coming to Dover!* (London: Faber & Faber, 2007).

——. *Look We Have Coming to Dover! Read by The Author* (audio CD; London: Faber Audio, 2008).

Mishra, Vijay. "The Diasporic Imaginary: Theorizing the Indian Diaspora," *Textual Practice* 10.3 (Winter 1996): 421–47.

Nasta, Susheila. *Home Truths: Fictions of the South Asian Diaspora in Britain* (Basingstoke: Palgrave Macmillan, 2002).

Oxford English Dictionary Online, November 2010, Oxford University Press, www .oed.com:80/Entry/109574 (accessed 27 February 2011).

Pratt, Mary Louise. *Imperial Eyes: Travel Writing and Transculturation* (London: Routledge, 1992).

Radhakrishnan, R. "Ethnicity in an Age of Diaspora," *Transition* 54 (1991): 104–15, repr. in *Theorizing Diaspora: A Reader*, ed. Jana Evans Braziel & Anita Mannur (Malden MA: Blackwell, 2003): 119–31.

Ramazani, Jahan. "Black British Poetry and the Translocal," in *The Cambridge Companion to Twentieth-Century English Poetry*, ed. Neil Corcoran (Cambridge: Cambridge UP, 2007): 200–14.

⌘

"I love Cyprus but England is my home"
—Eve Makis' *Eat Drink and Be Married*

P ETRA T OURNAY—T HEODOTOU

1. Introduction

I N HER FIRST NOVEL, *Eat, Drink and Be Married* (2004), Eve Makis explores the lives and mores of an Anglo-Cypriot family in Nottingham at the end of the twentieth century. In many respects this is a typical coming-of-age novel told from the perspective of a young Greek-Cypriot woman caught in-between two cultures, the one "I hail from" and the one that "I was brought up in,"[1] and can thus be read alongside first novels such as *Lara* by Bernardine Evaristo, *Anita and Me* by Meera Syal, and *Every Light in the House Burning* by Andrea Levy.

In the light of the lively literary production by members of other immigrant communities in Britain, Cypriot voices have to date been few and far between, and it is thanks to Eve Makis that Cyprus and its specific diasporic narrative has finally been placed firmly on the literary map. As the only full-length novel describing the Cypriot diaspora experience in Britain, *Eat Drink and Be Married* can almost inevitably only be received as a novel that speaks as 'representative' of that experience. Despite the problems surrounding the issue of the 'burden of representation' that results for minoritarian writers who are faced with the expectation that they "'speak for' the marginalized communities from which they come,"[2] Eve Makis willingly and consciously wants to meet these expectations. As she explained in an interview,

---

[1] Eve Makis, *Eat, Drink and Be Married* (London: Black Swan, 2004): 216. Further page references are in the main text.

[2] Kobena Mercer, *Welcome to the Jungle: New Positions in Black Cultural Studies* (New York: Routledge, 1994): 235.

> I wanted to write something that honestly reflected the lives of Greek-
> Cypriots. [...] It might not be everyone's personal experience, but 99
> percent of the families I knew had left Cyprus in the 1960's, having
> lived through the time when it finally became independent from colo-
> nial rule. I felt that it hadn't been dealt with before in mainstream lite-
> rature."[3]

Deplorably, though, to my knowledge *Eat, Drink and Be Married* has not received any critical attention in academic circles so far, even after it was voted
the Young Booksellers International Book of the Year 2005.[4] Given Cyprus's
colonial history and the large number of Cypriots who emigrated, mainly to
the UK, it is indeed surprising that up to now there has been virtually no fictional representation of that particular experience. In academia, there has been
equally little interest in exploring the admittedly modest production of Cypriot diaspora literature written in English.[5] Even though John McLeod calls
for a consideration of the differences between the fortunes of the diverse immigrant communities, he does not include Cypriots in his otherwise very
useful observation:

> The cultural representations [...] refer [...] to a number of historical
> trajectories that cannot be readily totalized into a common story of
> arrival and settlement. The factors which affected the arrival and
> fortunes of Caribbeans in London is not necessarily commensurate
> with that of South Africans, Australians or South Asians" [or Cypriots
> for that matter].[6]

Taking McLeod's comment as a point of departure, in this essay I wish to explore the specificities of an Anglo-Cypriot diasporic voice and narrative in the
context of British multicultural literary production addressing issues such as

---

[3] David Baldwin, "World of Literature," Metro Life, in *Metro* (8 July 2005): 33.

[4] Even though Eve Makis's voice is not the only one coming out of the Greek-
Cypriot diaspora, it is the only one that has dealt with the specific Greek-Cypriot diaspora experience in a full-length novel. Both Andreas Koumi's novel *The Cypriot*
(2006) and Andriana Ieridiakonou's novels *Margarita's Husband* (2007) and *Avraam
Salih* (forthcoming) are set in Cyprus.

[5] Among the more notable Cypriot authors writing in English, there are also two
Turkish-Cypriot writers, the poet Alev Adil and the short-story writer Aydin Mehmet
Ali.

[6] John McLeod, *Postcolonial London: Rewriting the Metropolis* (New York & London: Routledge, 2004): 22.

cultural and gender identity, hybridity, memory and the past, the politics of food, the representation of Britishness, and the relationship to the homeland.

Eat, Drink and Be Married is a first-person narrative told from the perspective of Anna, a young Anglo Greek-Cypriot woman, who, while dreaming of a university career, works long hours in her parents' fish and chip shop located on a British council estate in Nottingham. This dream, "Anna's dream" clashes with the "Anna dream" (18) held by Tina, Anna's mother, who cannot wait to see her daughter married to a "good boy" – meaning "anyone Greek, with a sensible haircut and a well-paid job" (219). While the promiscuous life-style of Anna's brother Andy is regarded as a "natural part of a young man's life before he settles down" (17), Anna is confined to a life of subservient domesticity. The book is populated not only with Cypriot characters, including Yiayia, Anna's maternal grandmother, and two aunts, one of whom is married to an Englishman, and their children, but also with a variety of native British characters who enable Makis to explore the many facets of Britishness.

2. Generational Differences and Identity-Formation
Anna finds herself in an in-between situation typical of second-generation immigrants trying to negotiate their own desires with their parents' values and expectations. The novel thus oscillates between the two opposing forces of hybridity (as represented by the second-generation Anna and Andy), on the one hand, and a crippling and oppressive cultural nationalism represented predominantly by their mother Tina, on the other.

Tina essentializes her cultural identity and constantly affirms the purity of the separate and distinct culture of the diaspora as a ghetto culture. She strongly opposes assimilation to the dominant society and advocates purity, integrity, and monoculturality. What she fears most is that

> I [Anna] will fraternize with English people and forget my Greekness,
> that I will meet a pale man with blond hair, a kastrishi, and shatter the
> dreams that are her life force. (74)

At the same time, she asserts the obligation one has to one's family – and, by extension, one's community – over one's personal wishes and aspirations: "We are not individuals but members of a family… we must draw together or else we will be pulled apart" (74).

In the few glimpses the novel allows of Tina's initial experience upon her arrival in England, the reader learns about her feelings of "fear and lone-liness" (195) and her dislike of the weather. In an ironic reversal of the well-known phrase that the sun never sets on the Empire, Tina felt "oppressed by the greyness, the dank air [...] in a country where the sun never seemed to rise" (195). Tina's most traumatic experience, however, was the tragic loss of her first child shortly before birth. This loss, for which she blames England (197), serves as the most concise and powerful symbol for the bitter resent-ment she harbours towards the country she has come to.

Interestingly, though, despite all her monocultural fervour, Tina is much more implicated in British culture than she realizes. Not only does she run a fish and chip shop, which in itself is a prime marker of British (food) culture, but she also has two close English friends: Doreen, who works in the shop, and Mrs Collins, a regular at the shop and a confidante who has gained Tina's "whole-hearted admiration" (22) for being an accomplished housewife. Nevertheless, despite the different cultural locations held by Anna and her mother, as John McLeod argues,

> These *generational differences* are not absolute. Migrants can share both similarities and differences with their descendants, and the rela-tionship between generations can be complex and overlapping, rather than forming a neat contrast.[7]

In fact, to a large extent Anna tries to integrate her Cypriot heritage with the English culture she has grown up in, in an attempt to replace monocul-turalism with multiculturalism. In her acceptance and appreciation of many aspects of her heritage culture as a healthy basis for successful acculturation, she aims for a balance between locations and cultural expressions. For ex-ample, while Anna's best friend Heather – who later in the novel is also re-vealed to be her brother's fiancée – is English, it is through her close rela-tionship with her grandmother that she is introduced to her homeland's pain-ful history and initiated into the Cypriot magical art of coffee-cup readings. Anna is thus not disoriented by a loss of her heritage culture; on the contrary, she accepts and celebrates elements of her Cypriot background as an impor-tant part of her identity, but she also claims the liberties and freedom that

---

[7] John McLeod, *Beginning Postcolonialism* (Manchester: Manchester UP, 2000): 213.

English society has to offer her on her way to full integration and self-realization.

3. The *Bildungsroman* and Cultural Difference

In this sense, *Eat, Drink and Be Married* conforms to the convention of the *Bildungsroman*, in that it traces the central character's quest for her own identity or, more precisely, young womanhood. If the *Bildungsroman* has been defined as a form that "has often been adopted by feminist writers, as a narrative of emancipation or growing consciousness,"[8] Anna's experience stands side by side with a vast number of female protagonists in British immigrant literature.[9] In order to cope with her unrelenting mother, who looks at her as if she is "somehow dysfunctional" (72) and "too clever for a woman" (73), Anna turns to books to escape her dire reality: "Reading is my balm, my comfort, a consolation for having no life" (72). Interestingly, the brief description of the contents of an otherwise unidentified book she reaches for suggests that she is reading Charlotte Brontë's *Jane Eyre*, the exemplary nineteenth-century female *Bildungsroman* about a young woman trying to attain personal and intellectual fulfilment. Anna identifies completely with the novel's protagonist – the "sceptical protagonist['s] [...] sense of 'absolute stagnation' seems to mirror my own" (72). Amplifying her comparison, she describes the protagonist as a "woman agitated by 'restlessness',," who suffers from "a wicked aunt and an oppressive institution" (72).[10] The fact that Anna reaches for a nineteenth-century text powerfully suggests Anna's need for escape to a remote elsewhere; more importantly, and at the same time, it reflects the hope-

---

[8] Marion Wynne–Davies, *The Bloomsbury Dictionary of English Literature* (London: Bloomsbury, rev. ed. 1997): 63.

[9] To name just a few: Irie Jones in Zadie Smith's *White Teeth* (2000), Lara in Bernardine Evaristo's *Lara* (1999), Hyacinth in Joan Riley's *The Unbelonging* (1985), Angela in Andrea Levy's *Every Light in the House Burnin'* (1994).

[10] Some passages taken from the influential definition of the *Bildungsroman* by Jerome Buckley also seem to be immediately relevant to Anna's situation – for example, when he says that the child "finds constraints, social and intellectual, placed upon the free imagination" or that the "family proves doggedly hostile to his [the child's] creative instincts or flights of fancy, antagonistic to his ambitions." Buckley, *Season of Youth: The Bildungsroman from Dickens to Golding* (Cambridge MA: Harvard UP, 1974): 17.

less anachronism of her condition which leads this young Greek-Cypriot twentieth-century woman to identify with the predicaments of a very *English* nineteenth-century heroine.[11]

Another typical feature of the *Bildungsroman*, especially of the female immigrant tradition, is the heroine's dissatisfaction with her body, her physical appearance, a feeling that Anna shares with many other female protagonists in immigrant British fiction (e.g., Irie in Zadie Smith's *White Teeth* or Lara in Bernardine Evaristo's eponymous novel) who compare themselves to the standards of beauty in their 'host' country and inevitably fall short of these expectations. Typically, as also in Anna's case, the physical features that single her out negatively are her "unruly" hair (34) which, using a Greek metaphor as a cultural definer, she refers to as "the head of a Medusa" (34) and the shape of her body:

> I am too tall and ungainly to prance about in skimpy tops and skirts above the knee. I have bits that rub together when I walk, that gently concertina when I sit down, that quiver when I run. I hover on the brink of acceptable largeness. (16)

For her mother, on the other hand, she has "the curves of a 'real woman'" (30), her shape according with Tina's Mediterranean ideal of the female body. The body as a stigmatizing feature hence serves as another marker of cultural differentiation. Not only is Anna made to feel her difference in comparison to her half-English cousin Athena, "a Pre-Raphaelite Ophelia" (71), but she is firmly put in her place and reminded of her *embodied* cultural difference when one of the council estate's worst thugs, Kevin, calls her a "fat cow" (156) while accusing her of having short-changed him.

> The words 'fat cow' hissed with such vitriol start swimming around my head. "Fat cow," a throwaway phrase, used to describe a range of body shapes, a casual expression that can pulverize a fragile ego in a split second. I feel wretched and unsightly. (157)

I would contest that this epithet not only shatters Anna's fragile adolescent ego but that, ironically in this encounter, the English thug Kevin, himself hovering on the margins of society, is elevated to the position of guardian of

---

[11] Anna's need for escapist flights of the imagination is also manifested in several dream passages in the novel, which testify to her desire for freedom and emancipation from the fetters of her mother's cultural purism and gender oppression (125, 157–58).

Britishness who operates by way of exclusion and decides who belongs and who does not.

In another key scene following a terrible fight between Andy and Kevin, his mother Irene – equally without prospects – is assigned the same guardian function when she shouts "This lot, they think they can come to our country and behave like they own the place" (267). What exacerbates the pain caused by this racist attack is that many of the customers seem to agree with Irene:

> Among the sniggers and shouts of 'shut up, Irene' there are those who listen and nod their heads in agreement. I know their faces. I've been serving them for years, week in week out, with a 'yes please sir' and 'thank you madam'. (268)

Anna's reaction is one of acute hurt and anger, which she bottles up inside:

> Somehow, I get through the night without crying, internalizing my anger, compressing it into a small hard ball that sits heavily in my grinding stomach. [...] I am a pressure valve ready to blow, straddling belligerence and tears. (269)

4. Space as a Marker of Differentiation

At first sight, Anna's quest for her own identity seems to be a predominantly private struggle that takes place within the domestic sphere rather than the public. There are no descriptions of negative public experiences such as bullying at school or misrepresentations by politicians so typical of other immigrant writing. However, as the above scenes testify, negative public encounters are by no means absent from the novel; on the contrary, they are very much present, played out in the microcosm of the family's fish and chip shop.

There is only one episode in which the Papamichael family suffers from what could be described as a form of institutional racism, more specifically through misrepresentation by the media, which is, however, immediately triggered by an event that takes place in the shop. This occurs when Kevin's mother Irene makes the wrongful accusation of finding a slug in her fish and chips – which she had strategically placed there herself previously. Following this allegation, the local newspaper publishes an article entitled: "Tony's Fish Bar – Pukka Pies" (129) and continues to offer a list of unappetizing 'discoveries' made in other ethnic restaurants (Chinese and Indian), thus capitalizing on the racist prejudice about the unhygienic conditions prevailing in multicultural food establishments (130). This case shows clearly that the

Greek-Cypriot family is as vulnerable to racist denunciations as are the members of any other immigrant community. When the allegation is later followed by a visit from the local health inspector, the family come under public scrutiny as their 'otherness' requires close surveillance in order to secure the health and well-being of their English clientele.[12]

Given that all the decisive public encounters – all the 'culture-clashes' – are set in the clearly circumscribed 'contact zone' of the fish and chip shop, it seems worthwhile to take a brief look at the ways in which Makis explores the significance of space as a marker of differentiation. Throughout the novel she makes interesting suggestions about space as a means of demarcating and enforcing ethnic and class boundaries. Although the Papamichael family does not live on the council estate but in a middle-class neighbourhood – which testifies to their financial success – their business, which provides them with their livelihood, is located on a dismal council estate. This in turn confirms afresh their chronic social marginalization. Their being consigned to the inferior location of the Fairfield estate – a name which is itself highly ironic, as the place is anything but fair – suggests that the upward social mobility granted to the ethnic Other is restricted and that it is only among the lower classes, the socially excluded, that they are allowed a space. But even here – or, rather, especially here – they are only just tolerated, as the abundance of scenes depicting violent confrontations in the novel demonstrates. If, as I suggested above, the fish and chip shop can be read as a prime signifier of British food culture – where it is precisely not souvlaki or gyros that is being served but the quintessentially English diet of fish and chips – the Greek-Cypriot family, the 'Other', has paradoxically appropriated a symbolically charged British space, thus subtly undermining or at least challenging the notion of belonging. Conversely, on the one occasion on which Malcolm, Anna's patronizing English uncle, enters the shop he does so "with the air of a man surrounded by Lilliputians" (133), displaying the attitude of the cultural and social superior looking down on an establishment that is run by a cultural 'Other' and mainly frequented by members of the lower classes. His brief visit to the shop thus constitutes a strong comment on the significance of space as a means of social and cultural differentiation.

---

[12] The health inspector's worst fears are indeed confirmed when he encounters a raw goat's head, a Greek delicacy, in the shop's refrigerator (132). Rendering this encounter in a very humorous fashion, Makis manages to strike a balance with the racist slandering that precedes it.

Within the confines of the shop, another spatial signifier that acquires prime importance is the counter, the "stainless steel divide" (133) which comes to serve as both a powerful spatial and socio-cultural boundary. The counter clearly divides the small universe of the Papamichael family between the public 'English' space in front of the counter and the private 'Cypriot' space behind it. It is "behind the counter" (270) that the family members spend most of their time, keep forbidden Greek delicacies like a raw goat's head (132); it is here that food and hard-earned cash to pay protection-money is handed "over the counter" (258). Objects are thrown "across the counter" (267), and Tina is described as a "slave to the counter" (27). It is also interesting to note who is invited behind the counter: namely, Heather and Doreen, the family's two close female English friends, who thus cross the divide and enter the zone of the 'Other'. This further suggests that close relationships and solidarity are only possible with members of other social minority groups: i.e. women (or between men and women, considering Andy's later engagement to Heather) or with a socially ostracized male character like Elvin, a former patient in a psychiatric hospital and a regular at the fish and chip shop.[13]

5. The Politics of Race

If, according to John McLeod, "one of the most persistent issues which emerges across a number of different postcolonial [...] texts is race,"[14] the factor of phenotype seems, in comparison with other novels written by ex-colonial subjects, to be somewhat underdeveloped in *Eat, Drink and Be Married*, since, as a Mediterranean, the Cypriot ranges somewhere in the middle of the colour spectrum. Nevertheless, in several key passages it is precisely 'skin' that serves as "the locus of social differentiation."[15] In another scene involving Kevin, the "disaffected youth" (81), this differentiation is captured as follows:

---

[13] Anna's solidarity with the socially marginalized further manifests itself in her dismay at and bitter criticism of the opposition raised by the council-estate dwellers against the mental hospital's open-door policy (108). Makis further exposes the bigotry of the protesters by ironically giving the acronym POOF (Patients Out Of Fairfield) to the protest group (109).

[14] John McLeod, *Postcolonial London*, 22.

[15] Sara Ahmed, *Strange Encounters: Embodied Others in Post-Coloniality* (London & New York: Routledge, 2000): 155.

> Kevin claims Doreen as one of his own. He thinks she has no place
> fraternizing with the likes of us. Them and us: the served and the
> servile; insiders and outsiders; white skin and brown with a hint of
> olive; the have and the have-nots, throwing the natural order. (81)

Anna's choice of words reveals that she has internalized the various binary
oppositions, including skin pigmentation, along which an exclusionary nationalistic discourse operates. In another instance, when Anna visits her friend
Heather's house and Heather's father is "taciturn to the point of rudeness,"
she conveys her strong sense of otherness in racial terms, contrasting her
darker Mediterranean complexion with the white English skin colour by
taking recourse to food similes: "I felt like a dark shiny aubergine set among
Granny Smiths" (88).

   If Anna, the female, experiences her slightly darker colour as an exclusionary presence, the male case is more complex, in that it is represented in
terms of the well-known ambivalence of provoking simultaneously female desire and male rejection. Her brother Andy's darker colour turns him into an
object of desire, more specifically into the sexually alluring 'latin lover'.
When this male is described as "dark enough to be exotic and light enough to
be acceptable" (17), an ambivalent blurring of boundaries takes place that
allows for this subject to be at once excluded and included. In other words, a
conflict of identity plays itself out epidermally. One can therefore conclude
that, despite their relative racial proximity to the English as immigrants and
former colonial subjects, the Greek-Cypriot family is perceived and made to
feel as an ethnic and racial 'Other', hence subjected to the same racist prejudice, verbal abuse, and physical violence as that faced by members of other
immigrant communities. Just like attacks on members of other ethnic groups,
the racist attacks suffered by this family include damage to their property, and
verbal and physical abuse.

   Apart from the instance referred to above in which the fish and chip shop
was mentioned indiscriminately along with other ethnic food places in the
newspaper article, the term 'Paki' seems to serve as the great leveller for all
immigrant groups. The generic racist term 'Paki' is employed twice in the
novel; once clearly with the intention to insult: "'f'ing Paki' [...] 'I am Greek
Cypriot,' Tony called out [...] giving them an impromptu lesson in ethnicity"
(90), while it is used a second time in seemingly complete ignorance of its
abusive force when, at the sight of Andy's car, a customer says: "You Pakis
are doin allright for yourselves" (153), making the term's racism even more
acutely felt.

It is not surprising that it is frequently Kevin and his buddy who hurl verbal and physical abuse; "racial violence is often the rage of those who fail or are falling, a way of asserting masculinity when in other ways deballed."[16] This need for masculine self-assertion becomes particularly obvious when Kevin and his buddy urinate on the bonnet of Andy's Capri (80). Here, and in the above example, the car serves simultaneously as a prime phallic signifier and a symbol of the economic success of the 'Other' and must as such pose a major provocation and threat to the bleak existence of the socially doomed English estate-dwellers. This frustration also finds frequent expression in the detailed descriptions the novel provides of alarmingly violent assaults directed predominantly at the male members of the Papamichael family.[17] In fact, the depiction of the drab and dangerous existence on a council estate offers a depressing revaluation of Britishness. In a form of cultural reversal, the novel exposes the allegedly civilized British nationals as its exact opposite, as savagely violent and uncivilized.[18]

However, Makis does not exclude criticism of Cypriot racism towards the 'darker' races when she has one of the detestable Greek-Cypriot characters utter his disgust at a young Cypriot man who "set up home with a black woman, subsequently fathered two mixed-race children and was 'naturally' ostracized by his parents and his community as a whole" (188).

⌘

---

[16] Bruce King, "Mike Phillips and the Making of Black British Literature," in *Bridges Across Chasms: Towards a Transcultural Future in Caribbean Literature,* ed. Bénédicte Ledent (Liège: University of Liège, 2004): 142.

[17] See, for example, the descriptions of two violent confrontations between Andy and a customer (203–204) and Andy and Kevin (240–42), but also Anna's injury (268).

[18] For full discussion of the state of Britain around the turn of the millennium as a result of the perceived threat of the nation's seeming disintegration, see, for example: David Cannadine, *Class in Britain* (Harmondsworth: Penguin, 1998); Jeremy Paxman, *The English: A Portrait of a People* (Harmondsworth: Penguin, 1999); Robert Colls, *Identity of England* (Oxford: Oxford U P, 2002); Peter Clarke, *Hope and Glory: Britain 1900–2000* (Harmondsworth: Penguin, 2004); Arthur Aughey, *The Politics of Englishness* (Manchester: Manchester U P, 2007).

6. History and Memories of the Past

For Anna to gain access to her culture of origin, Makis does not explore the classical journey home (even though Anna does travel to Cyprus for short family visits on a few occasions) but has her protagonist make her encounters with her culture of origin predominantly on British soil. The protagonist's engagement with the cultural markers of her heritage such as food, language, family traditions, music and dance, rites, hidden histories, and the violent politics of the past is captured through a lived diasporic community culture.

As far as the island's history and memories of the past are concerned, it is through the stories and songs of her grandmother, Yiayia, that Anna is initiated into the personal memories and collective traumata of her heritage culture. According to seminal anthropological work carried out by Floya Anthias and Nira Yuval–Davis,[19] this is in fact the typical way of passing on knowledge from one generation to the other, as it has always been the women's role to transmit the national culture and heritage and thus function as cultural carriers for the ethnic group.[20] In the great number of passages in which Eve Makis has Yiayia recall personal memories connected with her husband Andreas, she covers the events of the independence struggle from British colonial rule in the late 1950s and the Turkish invasion following the Greek military coup against President Makarios in the summer of 1974 which led to the eventual partition of the island. Even though key dates are maintained, the events Yiayia recounts are not immediately factual but recall similar incidents and thus reflect an inner truth. In an interview, Eve Makis describes her novel as a work of "faction – a mixture of fact and fiction, with the line between the two very blurred."[21] This being the case, Makis subscribes to the postcolonial project of keeping the memories alive by imaginatively "retelling the past."[22] More urgently, however, she seems to wish to remind her implied British readership of the extent of British involvement in the events in Cyprus. Written in English and directed at a predominantly British readership, *Eat, Drink*

---

[19] See Floya Anthias & Nira Yuval–Davis, *Woman – Nation – State* (London: Macmillan, 1989).

[20] In Bernardine Evaristo's novel *Lara,* for example, it is also Lara's grandmother Zenobia who reveals the story of her ancestors to her.

[21] Kyriakou Bookshop, Flyer (Limassol, Cyprus).

[22] Stuart Hall, "Cultural Identity and Diaspora" (1990), in *Colonial Discourse and Post-Colonial Theory: A Reader*, ed. Patrick Williams & Laura Chrisman (New York & London: Harvester, 1994): 393.

and Be Married presents a powerfully imagined intervention into British memory politics. The novel provides a scathing critique of British colonial rule in Cyprus and presents British readers with knowledge of the inglorious aspects of the British Empire.

Eat, Drink and Be Married offers a revision, a lesson in British colonial history in Cyprus, a chapter hitherto not explored to this extent by other English writers.[23] More specifically, the narrative resurrects the memory of a silenced past of curfews, lock-ins, imprisonment without trial, and executions. For example, for his support of the independence movement EOKA, Anna's grandfather subsequently spent two years in a detention camp (174–77).

Makis speaks most unequivocally to a British audience when Anna recalls the involvement of Malcolm's father, an ex-army officer who served in Cyprus during the EOKA conflict, in the hanging of a youth whom he suspected of inflicting a flesh wound on him. Despite the fact that the boys' parents appealed for clemency to him personally and that he couldn't be sure that the right person had been apprehended, his "only consolation was watching the suspect swing from the gallows" (52). Upon his return to Britain, Mr Jameson "put the sordid episode behind him and lived quite happily in his glass house until Miriam appeared on the scene, like a curse" (52). In this episode, Makis provides the most scathing indictment of British political indifference towards its colonial presence in Cyprus, exacerbated by the manner in which Malcolm "tells his father's story with thick-skinned jocularity" (53).

But it is not only British implication in the colonial history of Cyprus that Makis restores to memory but also the more recent events surrounding the Turkish military intervention in 1974 which led to the division of the island, "a land of incongruous bedfellows [...] and barbed-wire partitions" (15). Here, it is the bitterness at the idleness of the guarantor powers Greece and England, who "did nothing to protect us. [...] They sat and watched us burn" (282). The reader learns that, after the landing of Turkish troops, thousands became refugees, while mostly men and boys were captured and shot or sent to Turkish mainland prisons, from which the majority never returned and

---

[23] When the British presence in Cyprus is explored by English writers, as by Lawrence Durrell in his famous travelogue *Bitter Lemons* (1959), the struggle for independence is presented from the biased perspective of the British colonial implicated in and threatened by the events, who identified increasingly with British colonial interests as the troubles intensified.

went missing, as was the case of Anna's grandfather, Papou Andreas, "whose fate is classified as 'unknown'" (283).

With all due respect for a writer's freedom, I feel constrained to observe that in her re-writing of the turbulent history of Cyprus, Eve Makis has in my view regrettably opted to exclude the Turkish-Cypriots from the narrative in favour of presenting an exclusively Greek-Cypriot perspective, when it would have been desirable and possibly more accurate to mention the peaceful co-existence and eventual strife between the two communities leading up to the tragic events in 1974. To be fair, she 'makes up' for this 'omission' in her second novel, *The Mother-in-Law* (2006), in which she creates a Turkish-Cypriot childhood friend, Oya, for the female Greek-Cypriot protagonist Elektra, with whom she meets up again twenty-nine years after the island's division following the opening of the border in 2003.

In *Eat, Drink and Be Married*, Makis also informs her British readers of one of the painful aftermaths of the island's partition (an issue which she again explores more fully in her second novel), and this is the issue of Greek-Cypriot property having been sold illegally to foreign investors (a hot potato in the current negotiations about possible reunification of the island). In the novel, Yiayia fears that in her home in the occupied North "there may be foreign holidaymakers, squatting without conscience or decency" (284). This information serves as a bitter reminder that it is predominantly English and German citizens who have profited by acquiring cheap holiday homes.

Even if at times the historical passages smack of an overly didactic zeal, *Eat, Drink and Be Married* offers a powerfully imagined intervention into British memory-politics. As a *Bildungsroman* – or, to use Mark Stein's term, 'novel of transformation' – the book accords with the assumption that such novels are "nearer to 'testimonio' than others"[24] and are therefore inevitably to a large extent instructive and didactic. It is, however, precisely the im-migrant *Bildungsroman* that outlines remembrance-learning, and, as such, *Eat, Drink and Be Married* obliges its British readership to take responsibility for its past and present involvement in the fate of Cyprus.

⌘

---

[24] Mark Stein, *Black British Literature: Novels of Transformation* (Columbus: Ohio State UP, 2004): 53.

7. The Politics of Food

As the novel's title, the inclusion of several recipes, and the frequent references to food and eating throughout the novel suggest, food is a central issue. Given its generally accepted significance in postcolonial literary texts, these references are much more than a simple means of creating verisimilitude in the literary work. Food and cooking are major markers of a local culture and identity and are, as such, intimately associated with cultural roots and cultural expression[25] – "the cooking of a society is a language in which it unconsciously translates its structure."[26]

In the novel, food discourse is primarily employed to highlight the opposition between two worlds, England and Cyprus, played out most prominently in the contrast between Tina and her sister Miriam together with her English husband Malcolm. When the Papamichael family is invited to the Jameson house for a Sunday lunch, Miriam has prepared a typical English meal consisting of "Yorkshire puddings, roast potatoes, boiled cabbage, garden peas and gravy" (44). The "modesty of Miriam's Sunday lunch" (44) is contrasted with the embellishments that a roast dinner receives in Tina's house. In highlighting Miriam's dissociation from her culture of origin and her full assimilation to English culture, food serves as a signifier to differentiate English restraint from Cypriot excess and self-indulgence. This opposition is also revealed in the amount of food consumed: "Miriam eats to live while we live to eat" (45) and, further, in differences in table manners:

> The roast beef is handed out *refectory style*, two *wafer-thin* slices to a plate. There is no noisy free for all, no collective scramble for food. The distribution of portions is *serenely orchestrated*, serving dishes *circumnavigate* the table in a *tidy procession* like *synchronized swimmers*. (44–45; my emphases)

In the diction employed in this passage, one cannot help but notice the irony of constructing Englishness as well-organized but somehow stale, lacking in vitality and passion.

---

[25] For references to various types of foods and dishes, see, for example, pp. 19 and 139. On one occasion, Makis establishes the abundance of food as an ancient Greek-Cypriot custom passed down through the ages by referring to the ancient kings of Salamis and to Zeus, the God of Hospitality (120–21).

[26] Claude Lévi–Strauss, "The Culinary Triangle" (1965), tr. Peter Brooks, *Partisan Review* 33.4 (Fall 1966): 595.

The way in which the preparation of food differs may, furthermore, convey how food chauvinism parallels cultural and class chauvinism. This dynamic becomes apparent when Tina complains that "the meat is no cook" and Malcolm replies "It's rare, Constantina" in a "haughty, didactic voice" (45), and Yiayia in her turn comments that "Bloody beef is not part of our culinary tradition" (45). Even though the grandmother's retort could also be viewed as a form of cultural chauvinism, the fact that she finds herself on the defensive suggests a different reading.

If, as Brinda Mehta argues, food can be used "to transcend feelings of immigrant powerlessness,"[27] in Yiayia's response food serves precisely this purpose, in that it functions as a means of a subaltern's cultural self-affirmation in the face of the culturally supremacist attitude of a member of the dominant majority. In this brief exchange between Malcolm and his two Cypriot relatives, food is thus used as a marker of difference operating along the well-known binaries of inclusion vs exclusion, rational vs irrational, civilized vs savage.

The preparation of food may also sometimes symbolize love. In the novel this is certainly true for Tina, who regards food as a panacea for all problems, personal or marital. For example, when Anna is in a state of shock following hospitalization of Elvin, a regular at the fish and chip shop, Tina's reaction is that her daughter has probably not had enough breakfast – which prompts Anna to say: "As usual, every dilemma has food as its root cause" (205); or, when Miriam is heart-broken over her husband's cheating, Tina suggests having a raspberry pavlova, "offering her own brand of food-centered marriage guidance, her super-sweet cure for a broken heart" (264). Even though Anna is ironical about her mother's culinary offers of love, ultimately she prefers precisely this offer and the comfort it provides to the staleness of the Jameson household: "the Jameson house has no warm, beating heart. It feels cold and sanitary in comparison to Tina's homely womb of sweet smells and creature comforts" (71). If one considers the offering of food as a typically maternal way of showing one's love, Anna's concise summary confirms Anne Goldman's proposition that "The culinary metaphor is distinctly feminine [...]. The reproductive model of cultural development and identity is specifically

---

[27] Brinda J. Mehta, "Creativity, Identity and Culinary Agency," in *Diasporic (Dis) locations: Indo-Caribbean Women Writers Negotiate the Kala Pani* (Kingston, Jamaica: U of the West Indies P, 2004): 111.

maternal."[28] This notion is also clearly illustrated when, during a visit to her best friend Heather's house, Heather's mother "cooked a runny Bolognese, served with overcooked spaghetti and I [Anna] found myself, though I knew it was very wrong, judging the poor woman on her cooking skills" (88). This passage highlights how Anna is trying to negotiate her cultural position between her mother's cultural patriotism, which she has partly internalized, and the loyalty she feels towards her friend and her mother, who, by extension, represent yet another synecdoche of Englishness. In the novel, drink, more specifically the consumption of tea, also serves as an index of acculturation and assimilation. Considering that tea can be regarded as a sign of quintessential Englishness, it is striking to note that it is particularly Tina who, at moments of crisis, demands a cup of tea. For example, when the family is being blackmailed, it is she who says "I need a cup of tea" (271). The tea-drinking ritual, an integral part of English daily life, has significantly become a part of the immigrant's everyday life; moreover, it serves as a source of comfort and well-being. Hence, far from merely providing the narrative with local colour, the centrality given to food images reveals the vast complexity of underlying social and cultural ideologies connected to the representation of food and drink.

8. The Return to the Homeland

As in most returnee narratives, Anna's return journeys to Cyprus are characterized by ambivalent feelings. On the one hand, she experiences the beauties of her native island intensely, as in a childhood memory of a holiday spent on the island in 1973, a year prior to the war (37–39); on the other, she is also painfully aware of her difference when she describes the rejection and exclusion that she as a 'Charlie' (106), the nickname for English Cypriots, is subjected to by the local population.

> I don't feel at one with the country that purports to be my own. I feel like an outsider, an interloper, an unwelcome guest. An undercurrent of animosity exists between the indigenous population and those who left for foreign shores. Between 'them' and 'us'." (106–107)

---

[28] Anne Goldman, "I Yam What I Yam: Cooking, Culture and Colonialism," in *De/Colonizing the Subject: The Politics of Gender in Women and Autobiography*, ed. Sidonie Smith & Julia Watson (Minneapolis: U of Minnesota P, 1992): 191.

This interplay of belonging and difference – with the sense of difference out-
weighing the feeling of sameness – operates within diasporic subjects, resulting in their split or hybrid identity, which then determines the perception and
representation of the people and the place they return to. Even though Anna is
quite caustic about local nepotism and arrogance,[29] she is equally critical of
the snobbishness and the superior attitude of the nouveau riche equipped with
'imperial eyes' – to quote the title of Mary Pratt's seminal study – adopted by
the Anglo-Cypriot expatriates:

> When I look at 'us' from afar I want to cringe. At the conspicuousness
> of the parental generation and the hybrids they have raised. We visit
> 'our' country and extol the virtues of England. [...] We are Greek
> when it suits us and English when it doesn't. We flash our money, ...
> and walk with our pseudo-European noses in the air. We gatecrash a
> house that we abandoned long ago and behave like we own the place,
> boasting of our riches, when riches are all we have to show. (107)

As in her depiction of likeable and despicable English as well as Cypriot characters, in yet another attempt at striking a balance Eve Makis assigns equal
responsibility for the culture-clash between the natives and the expatriates.

For many returnees, nostalgia for home reifies into a problematical experience, as is illustrated by a family friend who, after trying to realize his "Cyprus dream [in which] life is a veritable utopia" (103), returns to England
three years after his failed attempt at repatriation, realizing that "I love
Cyprus, but England is my home" (106). In other words, he acknowledges
that even against his will he has become acculturated, that "Over time a culture diffuses into your fabric, however much you fight it" (106).

As Stuart Hall reminds us, the return to the homeland is therefore never "a
simple return to the past which is not re-experienced through the categories of
the present."[30] There is no simple recovery that is not "transformed by the
identit[y] of the present."[31]

However, the conundrum of occupying an in-between space, of trying to
negotiate between two homelands, remains unresolved. In the end, the decision of which place to make one's home is left up to the individual. Whereas

---

[29] See, for example, the encounter in a bank with a "Barbie aspirant, an artificial of-
fence to womanhood" (103), who accuses Tony of presenting a fake passport.

[30] Stuart Hall, "New Ethnicities," in *Critical Dialogues in Cultural Studies*, ed.
David Morley & Kuan–Hsing Chen (London & New York: Routledge, 1996): 448.

[31] Hall, "New Ethnicities," 448.

Anna never even considers the possibility of returning to Cyprus, her cousin Maria, who suffered the negative consequences of an arranged marriage, asserts: "This place is my home. I never would have left if it wasn't for the war" (315).

9. Conclusion

By the end of the novel, it is not only the female protagonist but also (indeed, especially) her mother who has undergone development. Shocked by the disastrous results of her niece Maria's arranged marriage into recognition that she may have to change her ways, Tina develops a more accepting stance which leads her to be "secretly elated" (295) by the engagement between Andy and "my Heatha" (297) and to proudly announce that "my daughter is going to university. Marriage can wait" (316).

The novel, in fact, ends on a general note of reconciliation and acceptance. Anna's aunt Roulla finally approves of the union between her son Petros – whom she had disowned for years – and his English wife Melissa when she meets her little grand-daughter for the first time. Here the child can not only be read as the symbolic 'fruit' of a successful intercultural relationship but also as a symbol of rebirth and, as such, as a provider of hope for a more conciliatory future. As this chance encounter, significantly, takes place at grandmother Yiayia's funeral in Cyprus, the suggestion seems to be that it is the grandmother's spirit and the spirit of the place that finally bring the family together, heal wounds, and open up a space for the future.

The very last scene sums up Anna's change and newly acquired sense of empowerment when, significantly, she reads her mother's coffee cup "with a newfound eloquence and a captivating aura" (316). At the end of the narrative, Anna is finally allowed to combine her heritage culture with the opportunities offered by her host culture in order to develop a coherent identity.

By way of conclusion: *Eat Drink and Be Married* explores the tensions experienced by an oppressed Cypriot female growing up in England in the 1980s and struggling to escape the stranglehold of family and tradition while trying to find a space in her host country. In addressing issues such as identity-formation, generational conflicts, cultural difference, and other markers of differentiation, the novel fits the established pattern of the coming-of-age novel of the female immigrant pattern, but deals with these issues as they are specific to the Cypriot diaspora experience (e.g., the mother's consumer dream vs the daughter's dream of going to university, running a fish and chip shop, Cypriot social gatherings, gender codes of conduct, the magic of the coffee-cup readings). Taking Eve Makis's debut novel as its point of entry, this essay has attempted to fill the gap of representing the fortunes of a small, relatively invisible community – possibly with fewer pressing social issues to contend with – and bringing its specific diasporic narrative to the attention of a wider audience / readership.

WORKS CITED

Ahmed, Sara. *Strange Encounters: Embodied Others in Post-Coloniality* (London & New York: Routledge, 2000).

Anthias, Floya, & Nira Yuval–Davis. *Woman – Nation – State* (London: Macmillan, 1989).

Aughey, Arthur. *The Politics of Englishness* (Manchester: Manchester UP, 2007).

Baldwin, David. "World of Literature," *Metro* (8 July 2005), Metro Life: 33.

Buckley, Jerome Hamilton. *Season of Youth: The Bildungsroman from Dickens to Golding* (Cambridge, MA: Harvard UP, 1974).

Cannadine, David. *Class in Britain* (Harmondsworth: Penguin, 1998).

Clarke, Peter. *Hope and Glory: Britain 1900–2000* (Harmondsworth: Penguin, 2004).

Colls, Robert. *Identity of England* (Oxford: Oxford UP, 2002).

Goldman, Anne. "I Yam What I Yam: Cooking, Culture and Colonialism," in *De/Colonizing the Subject: The Politics of Gender in Women and Autobiography*, ed. Sidonie Smith & Julia Watson (Minneapolis: U of Minnesota P, 1992): 169–95.

Hall, Stuart. "Cultural Identity and Diaspora," in *Colonial Discourse and Post-Colonial Theory: A Reader*, ed. Patrick Williams & Laura Chrisman (New York & London: Harvester, 1994): 392–403. Originally in *Identity: Community, Culture, Difference*, ed. Jonathan Rutherford (London: Lawrence & Wishart, 1990): 222–37.

——. "New Ethnicities," in *Critical Dialogues in Cultural Studies*, ed. David Morley & Kuan–Hsing Chen (London & New York: Routledge, 1996): 441–49.

King, Bruce. "Mike Phillips and the Making of Black British Literature," in *Bridges Across Chasms: Towards a Transcultural Future in Caribbean Literature*, ed. Bénédicte Ledent (Liège: University of Liège, 2004): 139–46.

Kyriakou Bookshop. Flyer (Limassol, Cyprus).

Lévi–Strauss, Claude. "The Culinary Triangle," tr. Peter Brooks, *Partisan Review* 33.4 (Fall 1966): 589–95. Originally published as "Le triangle culinaire," *L'Arc* 25 (1965): 19–29.

McLeod, John. *Beginning Postcolonialism* (Manchester: Manchester UP, 2000).

——. *Postcolonial London: Rewriting the Metropolis* (New York & London: Routledge, 2004).

Makis, Eve. *Eat Drink and Be Married* (London: Black Swan, 2004).

Mehta, Brinda J. "Creativity, Identity and Culinary Agency," in *Diasporic (Dis)locations: Indo-Caribbean Women Writers Negotiate the Kala Pani* (Kingston, Jamaica: U of the West Indies P, 2004): 106–25.

Mercer, Kobena. *Welcome to the Jungle: New Positions in Black Cultural Studies* (New York: Routledge, 1994).

Paxman, Jeremy. *The English: A Portrait of a People* (Harmondsworth: Penguin, 1999).

Stein, Mark. *Black British Literature: Novels of Transformation* (Columbus: The Ohio State UP, 2004).

Wynne–Davies, Marion. *The Bloomsbury Dictionary of English Literature* (London: Bloomsbury, rev. ed. 1997).

⌘

Laughter *Movens*

—Functions and Effects of Laughter in Black British Literature

JESSICA VOGES

AT THE VERY LEAST SINCE ANTIQUITY, laughter has been considered a social phenomenon.[1] One assumption that most of the corresponding theories agree on is that laughter can be seen as a specifically human attribute. Not only Aristotle underlined this aspect when he claimed that the human is the only animal that laughs; the philosopher Henri Bergson also came to this conclusion: "The comic does not exist outside the pale of what is strictly *human.*"[2] Although we can 'laugh' at ourselves (inwardly rather than through physiological release) and at something humorous that we perceive and decode intellectually on a textual or visual level (here, more usually signalled by physiological release of tension after problem-solving), most laughter is relational in the sense of being interpersonal and social.

One central aspect of laughter in social domains that I am particularly interested in concerns intercultural encounter (and even confrontation) in the context of Caribbean–British relations, and in the representation of such encounters in fiction. Here is an example – a passage, taken from Andrea Levy's novel *Small Island*, which describes the first meeting of two of the main characters, Queenie and Hortense. The excerpt is set in 1948 and describes Hor-

---

[1] See, for example, Plato, *Laws*, tr. Robert Mayhew (Oxford & New York: Clarendon, 2008): 816d–17a.

[2] Bergson, *Laughter: An Essay on the Meaning of the Comic*, tr. Cloudesley Brereton & Fred Rothwell (London: Macmillan, 1911): 10. "Il n'y a pas de comique en dehors de ce qui est proprement *humain*"; Henri Bergson, *Le rire: Essai sur la signification du comique* (1900; Paris: Librairie Félix Alcan, 1928): 3.

tense's arrival in England, where she wants to meet up again with her husband Gilbert. Queenie, an Englishwoman, rents rooms to immigrants, which often enough causes trouble with her neighbours, who consider the presence of black people as a threat to their 'good' neighbourhood.

> 'Is this the household of Mr Gilbert Joseph?'
> 'I beg your pardon?'
> 'Gilbert Joseph?' I said, a little slower.
> 'Oh Gilbert. Who are you?' She pronounced Gilbert so strangely that for a moment I was anxious that I would be delivered to the wrong man.
> 'Mr Gilbert Joseph is my husband – I am his wife.'
> The woman's face looked puzzled and pleased all at one time. She looked back into the house, lifting her head as she did. Then she turned to me and said, 'Didn't he come to meet you?'
> 'I have not seen Gilbert', I told her, then went on to ask, 'but this is perchance where he is abiding?'
> At which this Englishwoman said, 'What?' She frowned and looked over my shoulder at the trunk, which was resting by the kerbside where it had been placed by the driver of the taxi vehicle.
> 'Is that yours?' she enquired.
> 'It is.'
> 'It's the size of the Isle of Wight. How did you get it there?' She laughed a little. A gentle giggle that played round her eyes and mouth.
> I laughed too, so as not to give her the notion that I did not know what she was talking about as regards this 'white island'.[3]

The concluding sentence here demonstrates laughter's performative force. The first-person narrator explains that Hortense actively chose to laugh in order to make Queenie believe that she understood the joke. She tries to become part of Queenie's in-group by adapting her codes and conventions. In this context, 'in-group' refers to the group that is considered as one's own and as more favourable than other groups (out-groups). This process of categorization offers the individual a high degree of identification with the group. In-group members thus often stereotype out-group members.[4]

I shall be returning to this passage in due course. In the meantime, and as indicated above, emphasis in the following will be placed on those qualities of

---

[3] Andrea Levy, *Small Island* (London: Review, 2004): 13.

[4] Perry R. Hinton, *Stereotypes, Cognition and Culture* (Sussex: Psychology, 2000): 113–14.

laughter that can be interpreted as a performative act in literary texts. Laughter, as consciously applied on the story level, constitutes the focus of attention. It will be argued that laughing partners: i.e. the characters involved in the laughing situation, can become part of a laughing community if the laughter is employed as a strategic instrument. The characters have the opportunity to perform a shift in social status by laughing intentionally, even complicitly, in specific situations. They acquire the qualities of a laughing community. In this community, group-constitutive qualities that form the basis for a sense of belonging can be identified. The characters perform an act and react to a stimulus for laughter that is not physical but, rather, socio-cultural in origin. In the examples analysed here, it will be shown that laughter can have an intentional function and can act as a social practice.

Black British literature is a fitting object of investigation for laughter as a performative act, as it often deals with such topics as assimilation, hybridity, and group belonging. These issues are mostly expressed in the context of conflicting groups of different cultural or social origin. Racism and diverse social statuses can be reasons for stereotypes and prejudice that are dealt with in such literature. The fictional descriptions aim to present these conflicts from opposing perspectives to give the intended reader the opportunity to identify with characters who have a different world-view from his or her own. Black British literature can have a didactic function, enabling the reader to overcome possible prejudices through newly acquired views.

Laughter acts in a similar way: as it is an anthropological constant, laughter can be identified by everyone, irrespective of his or her origin or social status. Yet the connotations laughter can have are both various and innumerable. Laughter is first and foremost the expression of lively amusement. In the present analysis, however, laughter will be considered as a meaningful performative act. In order to understand its meaning, laughter has to be interpreted and decoded by the recipient in the respective context. In order to employ laughter as a communicative device, partners in such interchanges have to share similar cultural, social, and educational backgrounds. Otherwise laughter might be misinterpreted; to laugh at the same jokes means to belong to the same laughing community and thus to share the same codes. As a communicative device, laughter provides an opportunity for potential outsiders to gain group access. In literary texts, the possibility is given to identify the trigger for laughter. If it is indicated that characters laugh in order to reach a certain goal, the reader can follow the reasons for laughter and may come to understand that laughter might not always be simply an expression of amusement. Rather, laughter can be a significant means of communication in everyday conversation. Thus, laughter in literary texts, too, can have a didactic effect on readers, as its potential intentionality and effects are made obvious.

The broader and equally fruitful domain of intra-cultural laughter is not part of my brief here. In the anglophone Caribbean itself, as well as in much Caribbean fiction written by authors located outside the region, the social consensus underlying laughter involves tensions that may be inter-ethnic (as in Trinidad and Guyana) or even communal (e.g., Caribbean and African migrants coexisting in the UK), but the patterns of humour and laughter, and of conflict-resolution, clearly operate within a different forcefield. In this forcefield, theorists frequently adduce explanations (the plantation past; conventions of humorous world-view encoded in and brought across from African folkways; disparities in social and sociolinguistic status; the creole continuum and code-switching; 'laughing to keep from crying') that have less bearing on inter-ethnic situations as represented in black British fiction, but which are no less complex.[5]

In the following, a brief overview of theories on laughter will be provided. After this, the concept of laughter as a performative act will be demonstrated by means of two examples taken from the area of black British literature.

1. Laughing Matters

When considering laughter in connection with societies and interpersonal interaction, it becomes clear that the three main theoretical approaches – relief, incongruity, superiority – focus on laughter's social function as well as on its effect in social environments.

Ideas and concepts that can be assigned to the relief theory understand laughter as a mechanical response, mostly to jokes. Laughter is seen not sole-

---

[5] For an especially fruitful example of engagement with laughter in the work of Trevor Rhone, Derek Walcott, Meryl Hodge, Samuel Selvon and others, see the essays in the proceedings of the Ninth Conference on West Indian Literature (Cave Hill, Barbados), *The Comic Vision in West Indian Literature*, ed. & intro. Roydon Salick (Marabella, Trinidad: Printex Converters, 1994), and, more generally, *Cheeky Fictions: Laughter and the Postcolonial*, ed. Susanne Reichl & Mark Stein (IFAVL 91; Amsterdam & New York : Rodopi, 2005), esp. Ulrike Erichsen, "Smiling in the Face of Adversity: How to Use Humour to Defuse Cultural Conflict" (27–41), and Susanne Mühleisen, "What Makes an Accent Funny, and Why? Black British Englishes and Humour Televised" (225–43).

ly as an autonomous human expression but, rather, as a means of discharging tension and excess energy that has hitherto been suppressed. Freud's work on jokes and the unconscious, for example, is often counted among the relief theories.[6]

Incongruity theories, by contrast, consider the structure of comic and humorous communication. The comic is, in this context, explained as the consequence of two incompatible frames of reference that are perceived in common situations.[7] This formal object of amusement is equated with the incongruous. It is assumed that we are amused by contradiction: i.e. we laugh as a sign of release from a situation of unfulfilled expectations that, paradoxically, find resolution in the solving of a hermeneutic crux.[8]

Superiority theories, again, act on the assumption that laughter is a means of expressing dominance. Here the focus lies on 'laughing at'. Well into the eighteenth century, most theories in the West adhered to a specifically Christian tradition that proclaimed a dismissive attitude towards laughter.[9] This assumption was supported by the Bible, in which ridicule and laughter were described as something that had to be avoided, as in: "Woe to you who laugh now, for you will mourn and weep" (Luke 6:25). As a consequence, in this tradition laughter is associated with folly and sinfulness.

So, even though laughter was, and still is, assumed to be a human quality, it has overwhelmingly harboured negative connotations. This applies not only to 'laughing at' someone or something, but also to the physicality of laughter in general. Aristotle's ideas can generally be assigned to the superiority theory, in which negative perception of laughter becomes evident:

> Those then who go to excess in ridicule are thought to be buffoons and
> vulgar fellows, who itch to have their joke at all costs, and are more

---

[6] Carl Pietzcker, "Sigmund Freud: Der Witz und seine Beziehung zum Unbewussten," in *Lachen*, ed. Wolfram Mauser & Joachim Pfeiffer (Freiburger Literaturpsychologische Gespräche 25; Würzburg: Königshausen & Neumann, 2006): 21.

[7] Ulrike Erichsen, "Smiling in the Face of Adversity: How to Use Humour to Defuse Cultural Conlficts," in *Cheeky Fictions*, ed. Reichl & Stein, 29.

[8] John Morreall, *The Philosophy of Laughter and Humor*, ed. Morreall (Albany: State U of New York P, 1987): 5. See also Arthur Koestler, "Laughter and Emotion," in Koestler, *The Act of Creation* (1964; London: Hutchinson, 2nd ed. 1976): 51–63.

[9] Ernst Robert Curtius, *European Literature and the Latin Middle Ages*, tr. Willard R. Trask (*Europäische Literatur und Lateinisches Mittelalter*, 1948; Bollingen Series XXXVI, tr. 1953; Princeton NJ: Princeton UP, 1990): 418.

concerned to raise a laugh than to keep within the bounds of decorum
and avoid giving pain to the object of their raillery.[10]

Even though this seems to be a restrictive view on laughter, this approach,
too, demonstrates its social significance.

Almost 2,000 years later, Thomas Hobbes followed a similar approach to
laughter.[11] In his view, human beings constantly struggle with one another for
power, particularly for its effects:

> The passion of laughter is nothing else but sudden glory arising from
> sudden conception of some eminency in ourselves, by comparison
> with the infirmity of others, or with our own formerly.[12]

With this assumption Hobbes underlined his theory of the human as a social
being. Yet for him, too, laughter was the ridiculing of others and their failures.
The laughing individual can gain power at the expense of the ridiculed.[13]

Henri Bergson worked with this very assumption. At the beginning of the
twentieth century, he developed a theory that focuses on laughter's social and
cultural functions. In the context of his work, laughter is always associated
with a group and can only be analysed in its natural environment, which is
society – and only within society can laughter serve a useful (i.e. social) function.[14] Apart from its social significance, laughter for Bergson had a more
general symbolic meaning, that of a normative instrument. It is first and foremost a means of correction, a gesture of 'laughing at' that considers social
blunders to constitute a symbolic threat. Bergson claimed that the actual trigger for laughter would be the mechanical, a socio-physical defect that occurs
in case of unfulfilled expectations and is embodied by automated rigidity.[15]
This rigidity is seen by the laughing individual as an abnormality, and is thus
socially suspect. Hence, laughter acts as a response to deviant behaviour – not

---

[10] Aristotle, *The Nicomachean Ethics* (London: Heinemann, 1968): 245.

[11] Cited in Stefanie Köhler, *Differentes Lachen: Funktion, Präsentation und Genderspezifik der Ridicula im zeitgenössischen Englischen Roman* (Tübingen: Stauffenburg, 1997): 25, with reference to Hobbes's doctrine of emotions in *De homine* (1658).

[12] Thomas Hobbes, "Human Nature, or the Fundamental Elements of Policy"
(1650), in *The English Works of Thomas Hobbes*, vol. 4, ed. William Molesworth
(London: Bohn, 1840): 46.

[13] Thomas Hobbes, *Leviathan*, ed. & intro. Crawford Brough MacPherson (1651;
1968; Penguin Classics; Harmondsworth: Penguin, 1974): 125.

[14] Bergson, *Laughter*, 13–15; *Le rire*, 6–8.

[15] Bergson, *Laughter*, 17; *Le rire*, 10.

merely as punishment (as Aristotle would have it) but also as a corrective –
even, for Bergson, a humiliation – that enables the individual to re-enter society.[16] The 'laughing at' is also an opportunity for the individual to be recognized by the social group he or she wants to belong to, hence to become part
of it once more. In this context, laughter becomes a social practice that works
to guide the individual's social behaviour. This superiority-based approach
will be of interest in the following analyses with respect to the marginalization of individuals through laughter.

What is clear from the theoretical consideration of laughter is not only that
the diversity of approaches needs to be acknowledged, but also that such concepts as humour, laughter, and the comic have to be clearly differentiated.

In general, laughter is an ambiguous concept, its multiple character making
it resistant to categorization and clear definition. The subjective factor seems
to be the only constant. The same conclusions apply to humour, which, in a
semiotic approach, can be defined as "any message – transmitted in action,
speech, writing, images or music – intended to produce a smile or a laugh."[17]
Here, it is not the question of who *laughs* when, where, and how that is important but who transmits *what kind of humour* where, when, and to whom.
Further, laughter may be an overt indication of a humorous experience, but, in
contrast to humour, laughter is an anatomically and physiologically observable and evident activity.[18] Humour and laughter are both culturally determined and can thus be employed to gain insights into cultural systems.
"Humor is culture based in the sense that individual cultural systems significantly influence the mechanism that triggers the humor experience."[19] Thus,
humour can be a trigger for laughter, but the terms describe different concepts.

Laughter is, rather, part of a set of communicative practices. First and foremost, laughter is the expression of a certain emotion. Yet, as outlined above, it
can also express derision, threat, liberation, or other forms of interaction. If
one acts on the assumption that laughter is the response to a certain stimulus

---

[16] On this, see also Köhler, *Differentes Lachen*, 28.

[17] Jan Bremmer & Herman Roodenburg, "Introduction: Humour and History," in
A Cultural History of Humour, ed. Bremmer & Roodenburg (Cambridge: Polity,
1997): 1.

[18] Mahadev L. Apte, *Humor and Laughter: An Anthropological Approach* (Ithaca
NY & London: Cornell UP, 1985): 14.

[19] Apte, *Humor and Laughter*, 16.

that is mostly, but not necessarily humorous, it becomes clear that even though the response remains the same, the stimuli can vary enormously. As social and cultural ambiguities can act as ways of eliciting laughter, one can point to the distinction between interpersonal and socio-cultural stimuli, on the one hand, and physical stimuli, on the other. This distinction can perhaps be compared to the famous example of the twinkle in Clifford Geertz's *Thick Description*: to twinkle with the eye might just be a physical reflex, but it could also be an intended act in order to communicate with another person. It is the recipient's task to analyse and understand the twinkle or, in this case, the laughter, in order to create and interpret its connotations in the respective context.[20]

Laughter is here considered as a performative act: i.e. the realization of a performative adaptation of cultural codes. This means that, comparable to a speech act, something is done by laughing.[21] Here, it is not speech that initiates a process, but laughter. The laughing individual performs a shift in order to become part of the laughing community that embodies desired values. By consciously choosing to laugh, the individual can imitate social conventions that might not correspond to his or her own. Laughing is then not only the response to a natural trigger but a decision, a strategically placed act. Laughter thus has a perlocutionary (effective) force that represents its performative character.

It is this performative approach that focuses on the interpretation of laughter's connotations and functions. Hence, performative laughter functions in this context as a communicative device with the potential to, on the one hand, enable social integration, avoid conflict, and cross cultural borders and, on the other, to act as an exclusionary and offensive signal. Performative laughter initiates a movement that has the potential to change an individual's social status. The individual is translocated to the laughing community.

⌘

---

[20] Clifford Geertz, "Thick Description: Toward an Interpretative Theory of Culture," in Geertz, *The Interpretation of Cultures: Selected Essays* (New York: Basic Books, 1973): 6–7.

[21] Uwe Wirth, "Der Performanzbegriff im Spannungsfeld von Illokution, Iteration und Indexikalität," in *Performanz: Zwischen Sprachphilosophie und Kulturwissenschaften*, ed. Uwe Wirth (Frankfurt am Main: Suhrkamp, 2002): 11–12.

2. How to Do Things with Laughter

Let us look more closely at the passage from *Small Island* introduced at the outset of this essay. Since the first-person narrator implies what would be the result of failing to join in the laughter: namely, showing that she does not share the same geographical knowledge and thus revealing that there is a difference between the two characters, it could be concluded that this is an iterative procedure performed by Hortense. She seems to know from experience that laughter has a performative force and enables a form of disguise. Drawing on this experience, she acts accordingly, and laughs along with her interlocutor.

From Hortense's perspective, Queenie's laughter about her trunk, and the associated comparison, excludes her from Queenie's in-group. Although it might not be done on purpose, Queenie in effect positions herself as superior to Hortense because her joke involves knowledge not shared by Hortense. Queenie's laughter about her own joke opens up a gap between the two characters. Yet this gap is only recognizable from the viewpoint of the first-person narrator. It would arguably be difficult for Queenie to identify Hortense's ploy. But the reader is able to see through it. From Hortense's perspective, an asymmetrical speaking situation is established, requiring a reaction from her.

One can, then, conclude that Queenie's comment about the trunk provokes laughter. By comparing Hortense's trunk with the Isle of Wight, Queenie mixes two different frames of reference. The humorous effect results from this unexpected and hyperbolic comparison. However, this effect is only achieved on the part of the joke-teller, as is underlined by the first-person narrator. According to Freud's theory of jokes, Queenie's humorous comment does not fulfil the conditions for successfully telling a joke. Freud worked on humour and the comic in connection with his assumption that the psyche is an apparatus that has to keep the circulating energy in the human organism on a relatively low level. Laughter, for Freud, was the consequence of humour and not central to his investigations.[22] He compared his work on wit with dream work. In both cases, the unconscious is transported past a censor, and thus suppressed and hidden feelings of aggression are expressed.[23] If an individual tells a joke, the producer of the joke has to overcome his or her own con-

---

[22] Pietzcker, "Sigmund Freud," 21.

[23] Sigmund Freud, "Wit and its Relation to the Unconcious (Der Witz und seine Beziehung zum Unbewussten)" (1905), in *The Basic Writings of Sigmund Freud*, tr., ed. & intr. A.A. Brill (New York: Random House, 1938): 754–59.

straints and would therefore need to expend psychic energy. At the same time, the individual must always be afraid of overstepping the boundaries of the forbidden and consequently being excluded from the community. The producer of the joke needs the approval of an audience, as embodied by laughter, on the one hand, in order to realize that his fear was unreasonable, and thus to 'laugh it off', and, on the other hand, to gain acceptance and reassurance. The recipient's laughter completes his own. In this sense, every culture has its own laughing culture, and that has its own history.[24] Similar to the assumptions of the superiority theory, laughter is here again conceptualized as an indicator of social acceptance and integration, on the one hand, and exclusion from the community, on the other.

On a formal level, Hortense laughs in response to Queenie's joke. And her laughter helps the joke to appear successful. But as is indicated by the first-person narrator, Hortense does not laugh for the right reasons – she only pretends to have understood the joke. Hortense's laughter response demonstrates a perlocutionary force because it enables her to become part of Queenie's in-group. By laughing she actively performs a shift: Right from the beginning of the conversation there is an imbalance between the two speakers. This is made clear, for example, by Hortense's use of language. The Englishwoman Queenie has difficulty understanding the school-teacher Hortense, since the latter speaks in a somewhat dated and very formal register and in a Jamaican inflection. Hortense's language choice can be considered an attempt to set herself apart from, and at the same time fit into, English society. To admit that she does not know what Queenie is talking about would strip away the façade of being a 'superior' person that she wants to embody. On the other hand, it is Queenie's joke and the subsequent laughter that re-introduces an imbalance between the characters, now putting Queenie in the superior position. The difference lies in the respective reactions to these asymmetrical situations: Queenie ignores Hortense's language and ridicules her with regard to the trunk. Hortense, conversely, laughs along with her in order to hide her own insecurity. Thus, Hortense's laughter translocates her to Queenie's sphere: i.e. laughter becomes a performative act that makes the two characters members of a laughing community. During the laughing situation, this community, in which similar codes and values are shared, lasts for the duration of the laughter. The partners in laughter belong to the same group as they (seemingly) laugh for the same reasons. Hortense responds to a laughter stimulus that is

---

[24] Pietzcker, "Sigmund Freud," 26–27.

triggered because she wants to cover up her ignorance of the Isle of Wight and not because of any physical stimulus. Wishing to be acknowledged as a respected person on the same level as the English, she complies with the expectations insinuated by Queenie's laughter.

In the above passage, the first-person narrator is the indicator for the performative act. This device establishes a close relationship between reader and text and also affords insight into the character's thoughts and feelings. It is only through the first-person narrator that the reader learns about Hortense's motive for laughing. Additionally, internal focalization is used to express Hortense's feelings. This device enables the representation of internal thought processes (impressions, emotions, and thoughts) by the character concerned.[25] The focalizer influences the reader's view of the characters.[26] In the passage taken from *Small Island*, internal focalization is applied to enable a high degree of identification with Hortense's point of view. By becoming a focalizer she provides emotions that evoke sympathy on the part of the reader. The same applies to Hortense's character. The reader only learns through her perspective that she actively chooses to laugh in order to avoid the awkward situation of not being able to respond appropriately to Queenie's joke. She feels she has mastered the situation by responding with laughter. Internal focalization enables the reader to comprehend her behaviour. Thus a close reader–text relationship is established.

However, the use of the first-person narrator and internal focalization also present a very restricted and subjective point of view. As far as Hortense is concerned, the reader must assume that he or she can trust the statements. The description of Queenie's behaviour, however, is highly subjective and influenced by Hortense's expectations. She believes that Queenie's house would be her own and is therefore all the more surprised to see her at all. This is reflected in her dismissive characterization of Queenie as "this Englishwoman." The reader is offered a manipulated view of Queenie that alters in the course of the novel only when the story is told from a different point of view. Thus, in this passage, it is not entirely clear to the reader what motivates Queenie to make the joke. Yet Hortense's reaction can considered a performative act, as

---

[25] Angela Walz, *Erzählstimmen verstehen: Narrative Subjektivität im Spannungsfeld von Trans/Differenz am Beispiel zeitgenössischer britischer Schriftstellerinnen* (Münster: LIT, 2005): 31.

[26] Mieke Bal, "The Narrating and the Focalizing: A Theory of the Agents in Narrative," *Style* 17.2 (Spring 1983): 244.

she actively joins in the laughter so that she can become part of the laughing community.

The second example is taken from Zadie Smith's *White Teeth*.[27] Here, laughter has an exclusionary effect, as the laughing community is established at the expense of the character Joshua Chalfen:

> 'She's got a dark complexion which she's trying to lighten by means of make-up, artifice. The Elizabethans were very keen on a pale skin.'
>
> 'They would have loved you, then,' sneered Millat, for Joshua was pasty, practically anaemic, curly-haired and chubby, 'you would have been Tom bloody Cruise.'
>
> Laughter. Not because it was funny, but because it was Millat putting a nerd where a nerd should be. In his place. (271)

In this quotation, the focus shall be on the functions and effects of laughter provoked by Millat – one of the central characters in the novel, he is a second-generation immigrant of Bengali origin who grew up in London. Joshua, whose family members are proud of their strict, conservative traditions, is his antagonist in this situation.

Here, laughter acts a mechanism of superiority that stabilizes social groups. By ridiculing Joshua, Millat puts "a nerd where a nerd should be. In his place." He provokes laughter in order to set Joshua apart from the rest of the class. At the same time, the class responds to this provocation with laughter, thereby actively excluding Joshua. Millat's joke has perlocutionary force – a certain effect is expected. As in the example above, it is not the joke that evokes the laughter. In this situation, the reader has to rely on the omniscient narrator, who indicates that the laughter is not a natural or intuitive response to the joke but instead a reaction to Millat's behaviour. In this case, the class is expected to laugh. It is Millat who provides the trigger. The general laughter not only excludes Joshua from the majority of the class, but it also reinforces Millat's standing in the group. In the novel, he is characterized as strong and convincing; that is why he can establish himself as a leading figure – a position is backed up by the class, who respond as expected. Millat has gained standing within the group that allows him to control the others, as, afraid of becoming his victim, they are eager to express their solidarity. So, even though the rest of the class might not wholly agree with Millat, they

---

[27] Zadie Smith, *White Teeth* (Harmondsworth: Penguin, 2000).

respond with laughter. They assign themselves to the laughing community that is established by Millat.

Through their performative laughter, the class position themselves on Millat's side and consequently becomes part of his in-group; they can thus share the characteristics he represents, such as his reputation. Hence, the laughter in this specific context can be interpreted as a reaction, partly out of fear of being neglected by Millat and partly out of admiration. He sets the standards that are shared during the laughing situation. At the same time, those who respond with laughter consider themselves to be on the same level with him.

As it is not clearly pointed out who laughs, but, rather, that general laughter is indicated, it can be assumed that most of the class members respond with laughter. This underlines the scope and the force laughter has in this situation. As an effect, Joshua, who is characterized as a nerd, represents all outsiders and is again marginalized through the laughter; he becomes a member of the out-group. The passage points to the stabilizing characteristics of laughter. On the one hand, it secures and stabilizes Millat's in-group; on the other, the laughter translocates Joshua from the class and the laughing community. Translocation refers in this context to the shifting of social or cultural status through outside influences (such as laughter). In his joke, Millat focuses on idiosyncrasies that would not be seen as positive by schoolchildren, as is indicated by the omniscient narrator. Joshua is represented as a typical outsider. By comparing Joshua to a famous movie star, Millat simultaneously exaggerates and underlines the absurdity of the possible resemblance. Besides, Millat is throughout the novel described as the good-looking character who is aware of his qualities. Thus, Millat is the opposite of Joshua, possessing the self-confidence and, consequently, the more advantageous position necessary for humiliating the latter. The joke is thus also an expression of superiority.

Apart from generating group belonging, laughter as a performative act also has a productive potential as a liberating reaction to traditions. In the present context, this turns on the subversion of the idea of Englishness: Millat, as a second-generation immigrant, ridicules Joshua by comparing him to an Elizabethan ideal of Englishness based on cosmetic artifice. It is the character with an immigrant background who laughs about the English cultural heritage and at the same time succeeds in animating the whole class to join in. This guidance that Millat represents can work on the reader–text level as well. In a literary text, laughter can direct readers' sympathies and perspectives. At the same time, it has the potential to break with expected reactions. In the passage quoted, it is the notional 'outsider' (the second-generation immigrant) who controls the class; he has the power to decide who is to be ridiculed. This might not correspond to the intuitive expectations of those reading this text. Even though concepts like multiculturalism have become part of everyday life, the attitude of an intended reader could well be to expect the character with immigrant background to be marginalized, rather than the white boy. Yet, as Millat is assigned a strong position by the omniscient narrator, he is given a certain agency. The reader tends to follow his perspective even though it might not fulfil his or her previous expectations; consequently, an intuitive reading is disrupted. This catches the reader unawares and might well make him or her alert to more differentiated perceptions of social groups.

In contrast to the first example, the story is here told by an omniscient narrator. This might be an instance that creates a distance between reader and text; yet, as the omniscient narrator is at this point not objective, which can be underlined by the description of Joshua, the reader is led to agree with Millat's opinion and his joke. Millat is made more sympathetic, whereas Joshua's character would be pitied. Thus, the omniscient narrator influences the reader by using laughter as a socially regulatory instrument. The purist description of the laughter stands in contrast to the depiction of the effect that laughter has in this passage: namely, that 'a nerd' is put in his place. Here, the hierarchies in the group are made clear by using laughter as a distinguishing mechanism. Only within the laughing community that is established by Millat are the differences dispersed. For Joshua, it represents the Other. By laughing along, the class actively takes part in the laughing situation and opts for Millat and against Joshua. The omniscient narrator here becomes an advocate of the laughing community.

3. Conclusion

It has been indicated that laughter is the response to an interpersonal or socio-cultural stimulus that, as a performative act, can establish laughing communities, thereby enabling the characters to perform a social shift from one level to another. When considering the question who laughs, it is notable that in *White Teeth* it is the character with an immigrant background who provides the trigger for laughter and who excludes the white boy from the rest of the group. In the excerpt from *Small Island*, conversely, it is Hortense who performs the shift through her laughing along. It is the immigrant character who adapts codes and conventions of the white Englishwoman, who, in this case, determines what is to be laughed about. Hence, the positions of dictating what is to be laughed about are inverted.

My interpretations of laughter as a performative act are readings which consider laughter as a social practice. With regard to postcolonial translocations, it has been shown that laughter as a performative act has a transformative power that enables individuals to perform a socio-cultural shift by adapting codes and conventions of a different group. Laughter criticism tends to focus on its social function: laughter can be excluding, can act as a corrective, and can even re-integrate an excluded individual into society. In a broader context, there are, among other things, issues of identity-construction, hybridity, and group belonging which are of significance for black British literature. Here, the protagonist often has to cope with different, sometimes even clashing, cultures, or with questions of how or whether to adapt different cultural codes of conduct, or to become part of the dominant group, in order not to violate given norms. In both cases, laughter is the social practice that, in the sense of a lingua franca, not only enables communication on a non-verbal level but involves a performativity that has both exclusionary and integrating qualities. It is within the laughing community that the partners of the laughing situations can establish a sense of belonging to the same social and cultural group. Thus, the laughing community provides identity-constitutive qualities that stabilize the members of the laughing communities for the duration of the laughing situation.

The interpretations offered in this essay also show how laughter is used on the reader–text level. Laughter can guide the reader in identifying with uncommon situations. At the same time, laughter enables intuitive reading expectations to be overcome, leading to a revision of fixed prejudices on the part of the reader as the counter-intuitive narrative opens new ways of thinking. Laughter on the story level provides guiding concepts that may change the reader's approach to stereotyped situations. Consequently, the didactic function of literature can be underlined, with the help of laughter as a performative act. Laughter can move not only the characters but also the reader.

⌘

WORKS CITED

Apte, Mahadev L. *Humor and Laughter: An Anthropological Approach* (Ithaca N Y & London: Cornell U P, 1985).

Aristotle. *The Nicomachean Ethics* (London: Heinemann, 1968).

Bal, Mieke. "The Narrating and the Focalizing: A Theory of the Agents in Narrative," *Style* 17.2 (Spring 1983): 234–69.

Bergson, Henri. *Le rire: Essai sur la signification du comique* (1900; Paris: Librairie Félix Alcan, 1928). Tr. by Cloudesley Brereton & Fred Rothwell as *Laughter: An Essay on the Meaning of the Comic* (London: Macmillan, 1911).

Bremmer, Jan, & Herman Roodenburg. "Introduction: Humour and History," in *A Cultural History of Humour*, ed. Jan Bremmer & Herman Roodenburg (Cambridge: Polity, 1997): 1–10.

Curtius, Ernst Robert. *European Literature and the Latin Middle Ages*, tr. Willard R. Trask (*Europäische Literatur und Lateinisches Mittelalter*, 1948; Bollingen Series X X X V I, tr. 1953; Princeton N J : Princeton U P, 1990).

Erichsen, Ulrike. "Smiling in the Face of Adversity: How to Use Humour to Defuse Cultural Conflicts," in *Cheeky Fictions*, ed. Reichl & Stein, 27–41.

Freud, Sigmund. "Wit and its Relation to the Unconcious (Der Witz und seine Beziehung zum Unbewussten," 1905), in *The Basic Writings of Sigmund Freud*, tr., ed. & intro. A.A. Brill (New York: Random House, 1938): 631–804.

Geertz, Clifford. "Thick Description: Toward an Interpretative Theory of Culture," in Geertz, *The Interpretation of Cultures: Selected Essays* (New York: Basic Books, 1973): 3–30.

Hinton, Perry R. *Stereotypes, Cognition and Culture* (Sussex: Psychology, 2000).

Hobbes, Thomas. "Human Nature, or the Fundamental Elements of Policy" (1650), in *The English Works of Thomas Hobbes*, vol. 4, ed. William Molesworth (London: Bohn, 1840): 1–77.

——. *Leviathan*, ed. & intro. Crawford Brough MacPherson (1651; 1968; Penguin Classics; Harmondsworth: Penguin, 1974).

Köhler, Stefanie. *Differentes Lachen: Funktion, Präsentation und Genderspezifik der Ridicula im zeitgenössischen Englischen Roman* (Tübingen: Stauffenburg, 1997).

Levy, Andrea. *Small Island* (London: Review, 2004).

Koestler, Arthur. "Laughter and Emotion," in Koestler, *The Act of Creation* (1964; London: Hutchinson, 2nd ed. 1976): 51–63.

Morreall, John, ed. *The Philosophy of Laughter and Humor* (Albany: State U of New York P, 1987).

Mühleisen, Susanne. "What Makes an Accent Funny, and Why? Black British Englishes and Humour Televised," in *Cheeky Fictions*, ed. Reichl & Stein, 225–43.

Pietzcker, Carl. "Sigmund Freud: Der Witz und seine Beziehung zum Unbewussten," in *Lachen*, ed. Wolfram Mauser & Joachim Pfeiffer (Freiburger Literaturpsychologische Gespräche 25; Würzburg: Königshausen & Neumann, 2006): 19–29.

Plato. *Laws*, tr. Robert Mayhew (Oxford & New York: Clarendon, 2008).

Reichl, Susanne, & Mark Stein, ed. *Cheeky Fictions: Laughter and the Postcolonial* (IF A V L 91; Amsterdam: Rodopi, 2005).

Salick, Roydon, ed. & intro. *The Comic Vision in West Indian Literature* (Marabella, Trinidad: Printex Converters, 1994)

Smith, Zadie. *White Teeth* (Harmondsworth: Penguin, 2000).

Walz, Angela. *Erzählstimmen verstehen: Narrative Subjektivität im Spannungsfeld von Trans/Differenz am Beispiel zeitgenössischer britischer Schriftstellerinnen* (Münster: L I T, 2005).

Wirth, Uwe. "Der Performanzbegriff im Spannungsfeld von Illokution, Iteration und Indexikalität," in *Performanz: Zwischen Sprachphilosophie und Kulturwissenschaften*, ed. Uwe Wirth (Frankfurt am Main: Suhrkamp, 2002): 9–63.

⌘

Theories and Practices of Transmigration
—Colonial British Diasporas and the Emergence of Translocal Space

SILKE STROH

FOR SEVERAL YEARS, the field of postcolonial studies has increasingly paid attention to concepts and phenomena of transnationalism and transculturalism.[1] While the implications of these terms, and their distinction from more traditional terms beginning with 'inter-' (internationalism, interculturalism), can now be regarded as well-established and widely accepted, the fashionableness of the 'trans-' prefix has prompted scholars to introduce further 'trans-' terms into the postcolonial field, such as 'transmigration' and 'translocation'.[2] In certain cases, one might be tempted to ask whether this proliferation of 'trans-' terms really produces any worthwhile innovation on the conceptual and content levels, or whether the innovation is only semantic – old concepts and themes wrapped in new words, or spruced up with new prefixes, to give a semblance of innovation for tactical purposes of (self-)marketing, career-boosting, and funding applications. Are 'translocation' and 'transmigration' merely the latest newcomers in a large pool of

---

[1] See the end of this essay for a list of references at *.

[2] For transmigration, see, for example, the essay by Markus Schmitz in the present volume. Concerning translocation, see, for example, Jahan Ramazani, "Black British Poetry and the Translocal," in *The Cambridge Companion to Twentieth-Century English Poetry*, ed. Neil Corcoran (Cambridge: Cambridge UP, 2007): 200–14, and *Cultural Transformations: Perspectives on Translocation in a Global Age*, ed. Chris Prentice, Vijay Devadas & Henry Johnson (Cross/Cultures 125; Amsterdam & New York: Rodopi 2010), which situates itself "at the intersection of postcolonial and global cultural dynamics" (Prentice, Devadas & Johnson, "Introduction" to *Cultural Transformations*, xiii).

pretentious and superfluous terms of little analytical value whose main purpose it is to serve as an exclusive badge of belonging to an in-group of academic theorists? Is this just another instance of the inflationary jargon for which postcolonial theory is so often criticized? Or do some of the new concepts really have implications that differ significantly from others which have been used more widely, and for a longer time (at least in the postcolonial field)? How does transmigration differ from other forms of migration; and how does translocation differ from dislocation or relocation?

This essay explores these questions mainly with regard to the concept of transmigration, but partly also with reference to translocation. I will sketch important ways in which these concepts have been used before, and discuss the extent to which they might be fruitfully applied in postcolonial and transcultural English studies. This will be followed by a slightly more detailed exploration of one particular way in which the term 'transmigration' has been used: i.e. that of '*multiple* migration', where people physically relocate to other countries, or even continents, more than once. These theoretical considerations will be discussed by means of a case study of a nineteenth-century transmigrant British colonial settler community and the ways in which their experiences have been textualized over time. I will elucidate how these representations of transmigration construct identities and belonging (or unbelonging) in relation to *different* geographical spaces that the community has inhabited; but partly also *across* geographical space, thus creating de-territorialized trans-locations which anticipate certain contemporary forms of deterritorialized identities and/or transnational consciousness.

1. Different Uses of the Terms
'Translocation' and 'Transmigration'

The oldest uses of 'translocation' and 'transmigration' given in the OED^3 date from the early modern period. They have often been used as fairly general terms for movement from one place to another; and 'dislocation' and 'displacement' are listed as synonymous in certain circumstances. 'Transmigration' could, for instance, refer to people changing countries, to immaterial things (souls of the dead passing into new bodies, 'mental' locations), or the movement of cells within organisms. In neither of these senses is it clearly

---

[3] Oxford: Oxford UP, 2nd ed. 1989, http://dictionary.oed.com (accessed 15 January 2010).

distinguishable from the term 'migration'. 'Translocation' can, for example, refer to movement of animals between habitats, of chemical substances within plants, or (more recently) of chromosome sections. Current interest in these terms in the social sciences, anthropology, as well as literary and cultural studies, is intricately bound up with an ever-increasing interest in human migration, diaspora studies, transnationalism, and globalization.[4] However, the precise ways in which 'transmigration' and 'translocation' have been used in these contexts vary considerably. Both terms remain insufficiently defined and seriously under-theorized. There is no established consensus about their exact implications, usage, and relationship to other similar terms.

For instance, the editors of *Cultural Transformations: Perspectives on Translocation in a Global Age*[5] do not explore the implications of 'translocation' in any depth. There is no exploration of the term's etymology, and not even a partial survey of the ways in which it is used by other scholars. Even the editors' own understanding of the concept is explained only in a very brief, vague, and somewhat piecemeal fashion. These explanations associate translocation with translation, both between languages and between other spheres (e.g., cultural, medial, disciplinary), a "carry[ing] across" boundaries. It is also associated with questioning and undermining the very integrity of these boundaries through liminality, ambivalence, hybridity, and migration. The intensification of these processes is attributed to recent technological innovations and globalization, with its impact on population flows and the media (xi–xiv, xix–xxi, direct quotation from xi). Rather sweepingly, the editors summarize the term's implications as "encounter, exchange, and transformation, disruption, and renewal, revision and the emergence of the totally new" (xix). The almost synonymous relationship which Prentice et al. see between translocation and translation is reflected in the phrase "translation in – and as – translocation" (xix), and in their use of the spelling "transl(oc)ation" or "transl(oc)ational" (xii–xiii). This vague use of translocation as a mere synonym for any kind of translation, border-crossing, or border-deconstruction begs the question of whether 'translocation' *used in this sense* offers any

---

[4] See the end of this essay for a list of references at **.

[5] Chris Prentice, Vijay Devadas & Henry Johnson, "Introduction" to *Cultural Transformations: Perspectives on Translocation in a Global Age*, ed. Prentice, Devadas & Johnson (Cross/Cultures 125; Amsterdam & New York: Rodopi 2010): xi–xxxv. Further page references are in the main text.

added value as a new theoretical term: i.e. any added conceptual and descriptive precision.

Elsewhere in the same volume, Jacob Edmond's "A Poetics of Transloca-tion"[6] suffers from similar vagueness. Again, translocation is associated with various kinds of border-crossing, in-betweenness, and translation (on the latter, see 107, 120, 123, 127). More especially, Edmond uses it as a synonym or abbreviation for 'transculturality combined with dislocation', speaking of a "transcultural vision based on aesthetic and lived dislocation, which I [...] term *translocation*" (105; see also 123–24), of "a poetics of translocation, which combines transcultural engagement with an aesthetic of [...] disloca-tion" (131), and of certain writers' attempts "to explore the intersection be-tween dislocation and transcultural avant-garde poetic strategies – in short, to create a poetics of translocation" (112). The locations and dislocations he en-visages can be spatial and physical, as in situations of travel and exile, or of a more metaphorical nature – for instance, referring to international cultural interests, to the position of intellectuals in society, to the unstable relationship between "word and world," or to the deconstruction of categories (106–107, 109–10, 118–25; direct quotation from 110). While the use of 'translocation' as a synonym for 'dislocation' is arguably in line with some traditional uses of the term, in social and cultural theory such synonymous usage might not be easily recognizable, thus creating conceptual confusion among readers who assume that some terminological distinction is implied, and who thus look for added meaning in the increasingly fashionable 'trans-' term.

Further imprecision stems from the fact that 'translocation', 'transcultural-ism', and 'transnationalism' are more or less equated. For instance, the title of Edmond's essay, which privileges the term "poetics of translocation," is closely followed by a sub-section heading that speaks instead of "transcultural poetics" and "dislocation." The first sentence of this sub-section speaks of both transculturalism and transnationalism:

> The search for a poetics that *traverses the boundaries of nation and culture* has been a major driver of avant-garde poetries for the past one hundred years, creating a powerful if ill-defined imagined *trans-national* poetic community whose shared sense of location is based,

---

[6] Edmond, "A Poetics of Translocation: Yang Lian's Auckland and Lyn Hejinian's Leningrad," in *Cultural Transformations*, ed. Prentice et al., 105–34. Further page references are in the main text.

> paradoxically, on its very valorization of *dislocation*. (105, my empha-
> sis; see also 106, 109, 111)

Ill-defined indeed. Edmond's own use of terminology does little to remedy
this. Although translocation, transculturalism, and transnationalism are closely connected in many circumstances, they are not *always* related, and are not
entirely the same, so that Edmond's failure to clearly distinguish between
them weakens the conceptual usefulness of his essay.

Nonetheless, there are some aspects of Edmond's use of 'translocation'
which can be made fruitful for a further, more specific development of the
concept. He implies (as in the passage quoted above) that a sense of shared
location (in the metaphorical sense) and community does not necessarily require physical proximity, the occupation of the same local or national territory, or even *any* feeling of territorial rootedness (whether shared or not).
Instead, a sense of 'shared location', community, or (perhaps more loosely)
commonality can be based on similarities in outlook and experience, even
across different physical locations. It is also important that such translocal
connections need not elide all the disjunctures that arise from different spatial
or cultural locations, but can expressly foreground differences and commonalities at the same time (106–107, 110–11, 119, 123–25, 129, 131). A third useful
aspect of Edmond's treatment of translocation is the possibility of occupying
two or more different cultural locations at once – for instance, where diasporic
writing forms part of different national literary traditions (121, also see 122–
23). That is, 'trans-locations' can be seen as connected spaces which are distant and different, yet also mutually connected. Fourthly, translocation as
understood by Edmonds (as well as Ramazani) can also mean that two physically distinct locations can, in the imagination and in representations, be
conjoined and merge with each other, again with diasporic writing as an example. The latter sense of 'translocation' also reappears in Chris Prentice's
essay on "Integral Culture."[7] Here, the idea of translocation as a collapse of
several geographically distinct locations into one and the same representational space is applied to a cultural theme park on Pacific island cultures
which purports to "'featur[e] all of Polynesia in one place' – truly a trans-

---

[7] Chris Prentice, "Integral Culture: Agora-Phobia at the Polynesian Cultural Centre,"
in *Cultural Transformations: Perspectives on Translocation in a Global Age*, ed.
Prentice, Devadas & Johnson (Cross/Cultures 125; Amsterdam & New York: Rodopi
2010): 239–74.

location!"[8] These more specific ways of understanding translocation are also relevant in the transmigrant contexts examined below. There as well, social spaces span national borders and geographical distances; and de-territorialized identities play a crucial part.

The term 'transmigration' has likewise been put to a range of different uses by recent scholars of transnational, migration, and diaspora studies. Some employ it in the sense of physical multiple migration, either as movement back and forth between only two locations, or as an 'onward' movement that involves at least a third location.[9] In some cases, the transmigrants' multiple movements are so frequent and regular, and their existence is so much across and between locations, that transmigration is not only associated with notions of settlement (however transitory and multiple) but also requires a strong emphasis on the movement itself as a way of life.[10]

Alternatively, and more vaguely, transmigration and transmigrancy are sometimes understood in a sense which does not necessarily require repeated physical movement, as the movement between (or simultaneous existence in) different locations can also be merely intellectual or emotional, as when migrants maintain strong and regular contacts with their 'old home' through correspondence, media consumption, diasporic (trans)cultural practices and performances in their 'new homes', the retention of old national or ethnic loyalties, etc. Where the term 'transmigration' is used in this more general sense without being tied to multiple physical migration, it is little more than shorthand for 'transnational migration' – just as 'translocation' is occasionally used as shorthand for 'transnational dis- and re-location.'[11] Even more vaguely, 'transmigration' is sometimes used as a synonym for 'transnationalism' in general, where the concept encompasses not only movements of people but also movements of commodities and capital.[12] Several scholars con-

---

[8] Prentice, "Integral Culture," 254; see also 267.

[9] For instance, both of these usages can be found in Ludger Pries, *Internationale Migration*, 49.

[10] For example, *Internationale Migration*, 5–6, 8–9, 49–51, 53, 60.

[11] For an instance of the latter, see Pnina Werbner, "The Translocation of Culture: 'Community Cohesion' and the Force of Multiculturalism in History," *Sociological Review* 53.4 (November 2005): 745.

[12] Generalized applications of the concept of 'transmigration' in connection with 'transnationalism' can be found in, for instance: Basch et al., "Towards a Definition of Transnationalism," ix, xii–xiii, and *Nations Unbound*, 7, 16, 18, 22–24, 29, 75–76, 102–105, 119, 126–28, 130, 134–40, 143, 147–48, 171, 174, 183, 203, 206, 228, 236–

sider transmigration as synonymous with transnational or translocal social spaces. This frequent vagueness is another commonality between the concepts of 'transmigration' and 'translocation'; it reveals that these concepts are still in need of much more systematic theorization and interrogation, to ascertain whether, and how far, they can lead to new insights and play a useful role in literary and cultural studies.

The present essay aims to make a contribution to such interrogations by exploring 'transmigration' in what at present seems its most precise sense: i.e. '*multiple* migration' where individuals and communities physically relocate to different countries not only once, but repeatedly, involving at least a third location. This kind of transmigration can occur within the same generation or individual biography: i.e. where a single person completes more than one long-distance migratory relocation. In other cases, transmigration takes places across several generations – for instance, when people complete one 'leg' of the transmigrant journey by migrating once and raising children in their new location, before these children – already diasporically 'once removed' from their family's place of origin – transmigrate onwards to a third location. These children (and their own descendants) can be understood as 'transmigrants' inasmuch as they still retain an identity which considers the previous, ancestral migration/s (and locations of ancestral settlement) as a significant component of their own identity. Transmigration in what is here regarded as its primary sense (the physical one) also entails a second kind of transmigration: i.e. transmigrations of the mind, where transmigrant communities and individuals have evolved forms of consciousness, life practices, and representations which consciously position these people as belonging to more than one location and/or to more than one 'imagined community'.[13]

Such a plurality of belonging is also frequently associated with people and communities who only look back to one physical migration. Thus, those cases of multiple physical migration which already occupy a prominent position in postcolonial and transcultural English studies have not always been explicitly

---

38, 241, 259–62, 267–68, 271–72; Feldman–Bianco, "Multiple Layers of Time and Space," 170; Jones, "Which Migrant?"; Avtar Brah, *Cartographies of Diaspora: Contesting Identities* (London & New York: Routledge, 1996): 242–44; Goldring, "Disaggregating Transnational Social Spaces," e.g., 73.

[13] A main source for the concept of 'imagined communities' is, of course, Benedict Anderson, *Imagined Communities: Reflections on the Origin and Spread of Nationalism* (1983; London & New York: Verso, 2006).

distinguished terminologically from 'single' migrations and 'singly diasporic' predicaments. In other disciplines (anthropology and the social sciences), the term 'transmigration' is used more frequently to make such distinctions. If a *quantitative* difference in the number of migrations (multiple versus single migration) also involves a *qualitative* difference in the way in which migrants and diasporas conceptualize their identities, then the terminological distinction between 'migration' and 'transmigration' might also be useful in the field of postcolonial and transcultural English studies. However, the question of whether such a qualitative difference really exists is still open to further investigation. Do transmigrants textualize their experiences and identities by means of concepts and metaphors which are significantly different from the concepts and metaphors used by 'once-migrants' who have only performed a single long-distance migration? Are transmigrant diasporas imagined differently from 'once-migrant' diasporas? Much-discussed areas in postcolonial and transcultural studies which might be fruitfully related to an investigation of the 'transmigration' concept include the 'Black Atlantic'[14] and parts of the South Asian diaspora (e.g., where family histories span India, East Africa, and the UK).[15] Another area of postcolonial enquiry where concepts of transmigration might be useful concerns the British colonial settler diasporas, where further interesting cases of multiple transcontinental migration can be found.

These British colonial diasporas are also interesting beyond the more specific context of transmigration: namely, with regard to postcolonial diaspora studies in general. Although settler cultures and their relationship to the 'mother country' have long been an object of postcolonial enquiry, recent postcolonial diaspora studies have shown comparatively little interest in ap-

---

[14] The term is most famously used in Paul Gilroy's book *The Black Atlantic: Modernity and Double Consciousness* (Cambridge MA: Harvard UP, 1993), where it refers not only to the transatlantic mobility of people but also to that of ideas and cultural forms. However, it also includes instances of what I would call transmigration, e.g., the migration of African Americans to Europe.

[15] See, for example, Vijay Mishra, *The Literature of the Indian Diaspora: Theorizing the Diasporic Imaginary* (London & New York: Routledge, 2007): 154–72. Briefly, the importance of what I would call transmigration as a phenomenon which can entail qualitative differences in South Asian diasporic identities was also already discussed by Makarand Paranjape in "Displaced Relations: Diasporas, Empires, Homelands," *CRNLE Journal* (2000), special issue: *Sri Lankan and Indian Diasporic Writing*, ed. Chandani Lokuge & Dianne Schwerdt, 71.

plying diaspora theory to the European colonizers and their post-colonial descendants. Instead, the main focus currently seems to be directed at non-white diasporas, both in colonial contexts (e.g., slavery and Indian indentured labour) and in the context of post-colonial migrations to the metropoles of the West and North (e.g., concerning post-World War Two immigration from Africa, the Caribbean, or South Asia to Britain or Canada). While these are obviously crucial fields of enquiry, extending the perspective of postcolonial diaspora studies to include the diasporas of the colonizer will also yield interesting insights. While such an extension of perspectives jars with the still widespread tendency to strongly associate 'diaspora' with victimization and trauma, the concept has also been used in a more inclusive sense (e.g., by sociologists and anthropologists), with 'victim diasporas' as only one sub-category among others. Other sub-categories, such as Appadurai's "diasporas of hope" or Cohen's "imperial diasporas," can be based on less dire circumstances of migration, a stronger element of choice, and even (e.g., imperial) hegemony.[16] Such a more inclusive use of the diaspora concept also ties in with established research interests in colonial history, where at least certain segments of the white British colonial settler population have long been textualized as diasporas, perhaps especially in the case of the Irish and Scottish diasporas. Here as well, certain claims of victimization (e.g., by famine or English hegemony) have been made, but the 'victim' narrative is not always dominant, as there is also a strong sense of initiative, empowerment, and imperial success. In various respects, the study of British colonial migrants can thus offer useful comparative perspectives to postcolonial diaspora studies – both in general terms and with regard to the more specific topic of transmigration.

In the remainder of this essay, I would like to illustrate this by drawing on a case study of one particular group of British colonial transmigrants which is commonly referred to as 'Normanists' or 'Waipu community'.[17] The focus

---

[16] See, for example, Arjun Appadurai, *Modernity at Large: Cultural Dimensions of Globalization* (Public Worlds series 1; Minneapolis & London: U of Minnesota P, 1996): 6; and Robin Cohen, *Global Diasporas: An Introduction* (1997; London & New York: Routledge, 2nd ed. 2008), as well as his "Diasporas, the Nation-State, and Globalisation," in *Global History and Migrations*, ed. Wang Gungwu (Global History series 1; Boulder CO & Oxford: Westview, 1997): 117–43.

[17] The examples cited here are drawn from a larger ongoing research project I am currently undertaking. The results of this research will be published as a monograph.

will be on the way in which narratives by and about this community have portrayed the experience of transmigration and multi-sited (and at times trans-local) diasporic space.

2. A Case Study of Colonial Transmigration: The 'Waipu Community'

At the centre of the community and its transmigrations stood Norman McLeod (1780–1866), a fundamentalist Scottish Calvinist preacher at odds with the 'laxity' of the mainstream churches. In search of a better livelihood and greater freedom for their religious aims, he and his growing following (who came to be dubbed 'Normanists') emigrated from Scotland to the mainland of Nova Scotia (in today's Canada) between 1817 and 1820. Dissatisfied with social and moral conditions there, they briefly considered transmigration to the USA, but then settled instead in a rural district on Nova Scotia's Cape Breton Island and (largely) prospered until the 1840s, when a series of crop failures and particularly hard winters induced many of them to wish for re-settlement in warmer climes. From 1851 onwards, part of the community re-located, on a few successive ships, to the Southern Hemisphere. Here, the initial destination was Australia, but the transmigrants were dissatisfied with with the 'immorality' of local society – apparently much exacerbated by the gold rush – and unable to obtain suitable land. Thus, in 1853 they began to move to New Zealand. When land acquisition there, again, turned out to be problematical, this time owing to bureaucratic and legal difficulties, the community began to make formal arrangements for resettlement in South Africa, which, however, proved unnecessary, as inter-colonial competition for well-organized, capable, and 'respectable' pioneers pressurized New Zealand authorities to conclude their land-grant allocation to the Normanists in a manner that satisfied the community and induced them to stay. By 1860, the main part of the community – over 800 men, women, and children – had arrived in the east-coast district of Waipu in New Zealand's Northland, though contacts with the remaining community in North America, as well as individuals and smaller groups that had stayed in Scotland and Australia, have been maintained up to the present.[18]

---

[18] On the history of the Waipu community, see Neil Robinson, *Lion of Scotland* (1952; Edinburgh: Birlinn, 1999), and *To the Ends of the Earth: Norman McLeod and the Highlanders' Migration to Nova Scotia and New Zealand* (Auckland: HarperCollins,

The ways in which transmigrant and translocal identities complicate conventional notions of group identities (even diasporic ones) is already evident in the difficulty of finding an appropriate label for this transmigrant group. 'Waipu community' seems a convenient shorthand, but it problematically privileges one particular settlement location, the New Zealand 'end point' of the group journeys. For a discussion of the community in terms of transmigration, multi-sitedness, and deterritorialized identities, this privileging of one place is problematical. It might be more acceptable as a label for the New Zealand 'branch' because previous stages of their journeys are at least implied in its prior history, but it is a tricky label for those parts of the community whose journey 'ended' elsewhere – for instance, those who remained in Canada. 'St Ann's – Waipu community' would at least imply a plurality of locations by metonymically invoking the two most distinctive and lasting settlements, but would be rather unwieldy. The label 'Normanists' has the advantage of being independent of territory but, strictly speaking, it should only be used in a religious sense to denote those community members who identified with McLeod's brand of Calvinism. But various community members did not (or not always) belong to the 'inner circle' of devoted religious followers; rather, they entered (or stayed in) the group for other reasons, such as family connections or economic motives. Many of these people would still have attended church and broadly adhered to McLeod's rules (if only to avoid trouble), but there were also some who openly expressed disagreement with his tenets. Moreover, the community lost its religious distinctiveness over time. Nonetheless, few would have doubted the central role of this preacher and his ideas in the life, migrations, identity, and historical memory of this group, so that, for the purposes of this essay, it seems justified to use 'Normanist' as a more general label for the community as a whole, particularly in view of the fact that available alternative labels are similarly troublesome. Along with 'Normanists', this essay will also use the label 'Waipu community' as another convenient (albeit metonymic) shorthand term for this translocal group, again for want of better terminology. However, this should not imply lack of awareness of the various problems that these terms entail. Such problems of naming are in themselves indicative of how pervasive territorially based identity-concepts are, and how they can complicate the

---

1997), as well as Flora McPherson, *Watchman against the World: The Remarkable Journey of Norman McLeod & His People from Scotland to Cape Breton Island to New Zealand* (1962; Wreck Cove, Nova Scotia: Breton, 1993).

development of alternative concepts and representations. They are also indicative of how easily alternative group-identities: i.e. those based on common
values rather than territories, can obscure internal dissent. Both of these problems are frequently reflected in the numerous texts that have attempted to
recount the story of the Normanist/Waipu transmigrants.

In this and many other respects, the Waipu community offers a great deal
of material for the study of different ways in which transmigrant identities
have been constructed, preserved, and re-invented through everyday practices,
writing, reading, commemoration, and performance. These various cultural
expressions offer interesting reflections on the somewhat oxymoronic status
of these people as 'transmigrant settlers'. Whereas conventional notions of
'settlement', whether in colonial or non-colonial contexts, tend to connote a
sense of arrival and homing, the essence of 'transmigration' is mobility.
Nonetheless, the history and the narratives of the Normanists embody precisely this oxymoronic experience. Moreover, this community's relationship
to, and constructions of, space might be fruitfully related to certain concepts
of translocation.

Unlike many representations of 'singly diasporic' communities, the textual-
ization of Normanist transmigrants does not privilege a single place of origin.[19]
Speaking of 'the Irish diaspora', 'the Indian diaspora', and so forth implicitly
stresses and privileges Irishness, Indianness, etc., as a defining basis of identity. Images of Normanist identity, by contrast, often show no hierarchization
between places of origin and those subsequently reached. Partly, this is related
to the fact that there are multiple countries and even continents of origin: old
community members might have gone all the way from the U K to New Zea-

---

[19] These traditional 'roots-based' implications of the concept have so far not been
entirely relativized, despite many recent problematizations and re-conceptualizings of
'diaspora' that have posited a more 'routes'-based approach. Prominent examples of
such reconceptualizings are Stuart Hall, "Cultural Identity and Diaspora," in *Identity,
Community, Culture, Difference*, ed. Jonathan Rutherford (London: Lawrence & Wishart, 1990): 222–37, repr. in *Colonial Discourse and Post-Colonial Theory: A Reader*,
ed. Laura Chrisman & Patrick Williams (New York: Harvester Wheatsheaf, 1994):
esp. 401–402; Gilroy, *The Black Atlantic*, 117, 133; James Clifford, "Diasporas," *Cultural Anthropology* 9.3 (1994; special issue *Further Inflections: Toward Ethnographies of the Future*): 308; and Rogers Brubaker, "The 'Diaspora' Diaspora," *Ethnic
and Racial Studies* 28.1 (January 2005): 6, 11. Transmigration may be said to take one
step further the idea that migrant and diasporic identities are not so much 'rooted' as
'en route'.

land, while younger ones might only have completed one or two 'legs' of the journey. Since this multiplicity is linked to a nonetheless strong sense of a unified community, there is frequent confusion about ethnic, national, or regional group labels. Relatedly, there are frequent shifts between labels: even within the same text, the same people are in turn marked as 'Highlanders' or 'Scots', 'Nova Scotians' or 'Canadians', and 'Waipu settlers'/'New Zealanders' – for instance, in the history book *Lion of Scotland*, by Neil Robinson, himself a descendant of Waipu transmigrants. This slippage between categories is symptomatic of the complex identities, and the complex relationship to space, that transmigration entails. The multiplicity of places of origin, attachment, and belonging, and the lack of hierarchization between them, seems to go against more simplistic, traditional concepts of diasporicity which tend to assume, and privilege, a single place of origin.

Nonetheless, more traditional concepts of 'diasporicity' are not *entirely* abandoned – quite the contrary. In fact, there are frequent alignments between the Normanists and the most archetypal diaspora: i.e. the Hebrew/Jewish one, where diasporicity is likewise tied to *multiple* relocations and a religiously based identity. Thus, at least two history books, Robinson's *Lion of Scotland* and the Canadian author Flora McPherson's *Watchman against the World*, depict Normanists as resembling a "chosen people"[20] in search of a "Promised Land."[21] Norman McLeod as the spiritual and secular leader of this people is expressly compared to Moses.[22] McPherson also makes connections to the Book of Ezekiel, which is likewise concerned with diaspora and the Promised Land. An important difference between textualizations of Israelite and Normanist diasporic experiences is that, in accounts of the latter, it is not the homeland but the diaspora itself that becomes a 'Promised Land' where a better life is possible, so that a permanent return to the 'old country' is not envisaged.[23] Thus, the transmigrant diasporicity of the Normanists is less

---

[20] For example, McPherson, *Watchman against the World*, 54.

[21] For example, Neil Robinson, *Lion of Scotland*, Chapter 4: "In Search for the Promised Land," 68–80.

[22] On the back cover of *Lion of Scotland*, for example.

[23] Other groups of modern European colonizers who have been textually remodelled in the Jewish image as an elect people conquering a Promised Land include the Boers in South Africa and the English Puritans in New England. William B. Nelson, Jr., "Promised Land," in *The Oxford Guide to People and Places of the Bible*, ed. Michael D. Coogan & Bruce M. Metzger (Oxford: Oxford UP, 2001), www.oxfordreference.com [accessed 14 January 2010]).

strongly linked to loss, victimhood, and oppression (as well as, in many cases, resistance to such odds and oppression) than that of Israelites and Jews, Indian indentured labourers and their descendants, or the African diasporas of the Black Atlantic. For instance, Itala Vivan has commented on the Black Atlantic as follows:

> The African diaspora, with its repeated transatlantic crossings, its voyages out and back, its impossible returns to a home elsewhere, generates a geography of its own and marks our globe with a crisscross of scars inscribed on land and water. New and multiple identities were and still are born and reborn in the process, and their marks can be traced in the tormented visions of many artists.[24]

Here, (trans)migration is largely regarded as a story of scars, whereas the story of the white transmigrants of the Waipu community is more usually told in a way that celebrates the migrants' (eventual) success as colonizers. The fact that the Normanists were white British colonizers of course has a significant impact on the way in which their transmigration and diasporicity have been experienced and represented: narratives of loss, oppression, and anti-hegemonic resistance are partly superseded by triumphalist narratives of pioneer achievement and imperial(ist) success.[25] Nonetheless, narratives of victimhood and loss can be present in white British colonial settler discourses as well – for example, in representations of oppressive Highland landlords as a motivating (and in some cases directly coercive) force in the emigration of Scottish people to the colonies. This dimension is also present in narratives about the Scottish emigrants who were led by Norman McLeod.[26]

Another interesting feature of the Normanist transmigrants is that they sometimes appear less as part of a larger British or Scottish diaspora than as a small translocal ethnic community of their own, described as a 'clan' or 'tribe' and united not by allegiance to a specific territory or homeland but by shared religious and moral values as well as close interpersonal relations. Identity is thus predicated on factors which can be, and in this case clearly are,

---

[24] Itala Vivan, "The Iconic Ship in the Atlantic Dialogue of Black Britain," in *Re-charting the Black Atlantic: Modern Cultures, Local Communities, Global Connections*, ed. Annalisa Oboe & Anna Scacchi (New York & London: Routledge, 2008): 233.

[25] This is evident in, for instance, the cover blurb of the 1993 edition of McPherson's *Watchman against the World*.

[26] See, for example, Robinson, *Lion of Scotland*, 33–40.

deterritorialized and 'portable'. Another deterritorialized aspect of Normanist group-identity is the formative experience of transmigration itself.[27] The survivors of the New Zealand voyage called themselves 'sea-birds'.[28] This is also the title of a novel about their experiences, written by the Canadian author Marsha Boulton, though this book is as yet unpublished and apparently still unfinished.[29] Many human group-identities are strongly tied to land and territory, clearly demarcated borders, or the common metaphor of 'putting down roots' where the plant image requires a soil. The Waipu transmigrants, by contrast, chose a metaphor for their self-image which requires no ties to land, territory, and borders. The association of sea-birds with flight, air, and water makes them a metaphor for connections between even the most distant territories, and for transmigrant identities moving through vast and supposedly borderless spaces. The title 'sea-birds' locates these people's 'home' and entire mode of existence in the air and on the ocean: i.e. in spaces which exist between or above bordered territories, and thus transcend the borders.

The sea is not *really* a borderless space, at least not if we understand 'border' in the sense of 'state border': states have not only land borders but also maritime borders and territorial waters, and imperial powers often also try to extend their naval influence far beyond their own territorial waters. Nonetheless, the sea is often *imagined* as a borderless space, or at least as a space where border transgression is easier than on land. Moreover, the symbolic power of the sea as an image of mobility and border-crossing relates not only to the borders of states and nations but also to the borders of land-masses such as islands and continents. The oceans of the world surround our land-

---

[27] The importance of distinct community rules and the prolonged migration experience for the formation of a new group-identity may again be linked to Moses' Israelites: "Israel's theology located the giving of the Law and the formation of the national life outside the land it occupied and thus considered the wilderness period as its constitutional time" (John H. Hayes, "Moses," in *The Oxford Guide to People and Places of the Bible*, ed. Coogan & Metzger).

[28] McPherson, *Watchman against the World*, unpaginated illustration page opposite p. 86.

[29] Pre-publication entry, Canadian National Catalogue, http://amicus.collections canada.gc.ca (accessed 14 January 2010); Hilary Stead, "Author Wants Seized Computer Back," *Guelph Mercury* (10 October 2003): A5, http://pqasb.pgarchiver.com /guelphmercury/access/640760751.html (accessed 30 January 2010); Boulton, *Wally's World: Life with Wally the Wonder Dog* (2006; New York: Thomas Dunne, 2008): 148, 212–13, 228, 257–59; www.marshaboulton.com (accessed 30 January 2010).

masses and limit them; but at the same time these waters form a geographical continuum which *connects* the land-masses – sailing across them makes it possible to travel from one continent to another. It is the latter connotation of linkage and mobility, rather than that of water as a barrier, that often informs symbolic readings of the sea. This is also the case in Normanist contexts.[30]

The self-alignment of these transmigrants with birds claims an ability to cross borders with ease – borders of territories but also, by extension, borders of regional or national human identities. The Normanists' self-portrayal as 'sea-birds' might thus be seen as an early expression of deterritorialized identity. As with the sea, the appropriateness of birds as a symbol of border-crossing is not entirely unproblematical. On the one hand, their ability to fly has made them a basic symbol of freedom in the human imagination. But the ability to fly does not necessarily entail a complete loosening of territorial ties. Such an association is understandable with regard to migratory birds, but there are also sedentary species – even among the sea-birds. With regard to the latter, one could also distinguish between coastal ones that stay close to the shore and pelagic ones that roam the open seas.[31] Normanist uses of bird imagery seem to rely primarily on an association with migratory birds. Their specific preference for *sea*-birds is apparently based mainly on an image of *pelagic* sea-birds as long-distance travellers of the high seas. This is suggested by an early use of the epithet 'sea-birds' to refer specifically to those people who had participated in the sea voyage from Canada to the Southern Hemisphere.[32] The specific choice of *sea*-birds, rather than any other kind of bird, as a metaphor for *human* migration seems particularly apt in a nineteenth-century context, when humans could only perform their long-distance journeys in ocean-going ships rather than in today's aeroplanes. Although sea-birds, like other birds, travel by flight rather than by swimming, their association with water might have facilitated metaphoric associations

---

[30] In a different framework, the symbolic power of the sea (and, relatedly, ships) as an image of border transgression, cross-border connection, and in-betweenness also features prominently in Gilroy's *The Black Atlantic* (see esp. 4).

[31] See, for example, the information on birds in the articles "migration" and "Arctic," *Encyclopædia Britannica*, Online Academic Edition (Encyclopædia Britannica Inc., 2011], www.britannica.com/EBchecked/topic/381854/migration and www .britannica.com /EBchecked/topic/33100/Arctic (accessed 25 November 2011).

[32] Quoted in McPherson, *Watchman against the World,* unpaginated illustration page opposite p. 86.

with human sea-travel. Nonetheless, although pelagic sea-birds seem to have been the main source of the Normanist 'sea-bird' metaphor, a secondary association with coastal sea-birds may also occasionally come into play, as the choice of lands for settlement was significantly influenced by the desire to stay close to the coast. It may, further, be argued that the *combination* of the metaphoric fields 'sea' and 'bird', each of which is already widely associated with borderlessness even when taken separately, further intensifies the association with deterritorialization.

The sea-bird metaphor is not the only expression of deterritorialized identity in Normanist contexts. Another example is the general emphasis on the sea, rather than the land, as the main focus of the transmigrants' activities and 'homing' in the seventh chapter of Robinson's *Lion of Scotland*, which is entitled "Seamen on many Oceans."[33]

As *state* borders were not yet crossed by migrations within the British Empire, they cannot be called fully transnational in a modern sense. Nonetheless, there was already a clear awareness of the differences between the colonies, which can be regarded as a nucleus of the separate national identities which were to evolve later. It has long been recognized that national identities do not always require a fully formed modern nation-state. The same could be said of trans-national identities; a transmigrant diasporic awareness which bridges both the geographical and the already recognized socio-cultural distances between different colonies can be regarded as transnationalism *avant la lettre*. Subsequently, in the post-colonial period when these colonies had transformed into nation-states proper, the ocean-spanning 'sea-bird' identities of the surviving transmigrants and their descendants can be regarded as evidence of a more fully transnational mind-set.

Some accounts also stress a *permanency* of migration as part of the community's life – for instance, with regard to the onward movement of many individuals as sailors to the Pacific Islands and further afield. Examples can not only be found in McPherson's history *Watchman against the World* (e.g., 177, 179) but also in Robinson's *The River of No Return*. In this novel, water clearly functions as a leitmotif for the transmigrant experience and as a focus of transmigrant identity which is more important than land and territory.[34]

---

[33] Neil Robinson, *Lion of Scotland*, 111–26.

[34] Robinson, *The River of No Return* (written mid-twentieth century; Auckland: Samahani, 2002): e.g., 1, 6.

Deterritorialized transmigrant identities are also manifest in a transcontinental discourse of memory where historians, creative writers, public figures,
and organizations from Britain, Canada, and New Zealand consciously engage with each other in the writing of what is perceived as a shared story.[35]
This is, for instance, reflected in another novel by a New Zealand author,
Fiona Kidman's *The Book of Secrets*, a fictional family story divided into
three main parts centering on three female protagonists on three continents in
different phases of the Normanist transmigrations and their aftermath. The
youngest, the New Zealand-born protagonist Maria, lays claim to her transmigrant ancestry and its different locations through active imaginative engagement. This connection is reinforced by the novel's circular construction,
which emphatically likens her to her British-born grandmother who was already on the first migratory journey, and whose diaries assist Maria in engaging with with her community's past.[36] This suggests a unity and community which stretch not only across time but also across space.

In social reality, twentieth-century improved travel and communications
facilities have also resulted in the renewal of family connections and transoceanic visits on public occasions of commemoration. A village-twinning
society, corresponding memorials, and, in two cases, corresponding museums,
to be found in Scotland, Canada, and New Zealand emblematize tricontinental
connections and offer 'windows' on the respective other locations. At times, it
almost seems as if the three distant but intimately connected locations were
being collapsed into one, or as though they co-inhabited a single translocal
space, a trans-location. Confronted with a palimpsest of spaces, we focus on
one of the three and see the others 'shine through'.[37]

---

[35] For example, McPherson, *Watchman against the World*, ix–x, 1, 29, 47, 151; Norman MacAskill, "Introduction" to the 1999 edition of Robinson's *Lion of Scotland*, v–
vi, viii; Robinson, *To the Ends of the Earth*, 210–28.

[36] Kidman, *The Book of Secrets* (1987; Auckland: Vintage, 1994): e.g., 1, 10–11.

[37] To some extent, the function of these museums as translocal exhibition spaces is
comparable to the other kind of translocal exhibition space analysed in Prentice's
aforementioned essay on a cultural theme-park about the Pacific Islands. However,
there are also important differences. For instance, the case criticized by Prentice is
problematical owing to a quasi-imperialist commodification of indigenous cultures for
the tourist economy and an undue homogenization of differences. The Normanist
museums are less problematical in this respect, as they follow different trajectories.

3. Conclusion

As a preliminary conclusion, one might say that cultural representations of the Waipu transmigrants, both by themselves and by outsiders, indeed display several features which suggest that multiple migration can produce specific concepts of identity that differ from the identity-concepts typically associated with 'single' migration and traditional ideas of diasporicity. There seems, namely, to be a greater readiness to dissociate identity from 'homeland', or from territory in general, and thus a greater tendency towards deterritorialized constructs of culture and belonging. It is widely recognized that modern European overseas colonialism, that of the UK included, played an important role in establishing and expanding transcontinental connections which helped pave the way for the even greater globalization of the twentieth and twenty-first centuries. Relatedly, certain constructions of colonial transmigrant identities might be regarded as comparatively early instances of deterritorialized, trans-local identities that provide interesting points of comparison with the more recent forms of deterritorialized identity which are of such great interest to postcolonial and globalization scholars today. This is also one of the reasons why, despite the recent focus of postcolonial studies on the contemporary, the colonial era continues to deserve attention in this field. More specifically, it would also be interesting to compare the Normanist case with other instances of colonial transmigration and deterritorialized life-styles – not only with regard to other groups of multiply diasporic settlers, but also with regard to the colonial civil service, the military, and the merchant navy.

If the study of deterritorialized social spaces is extended to earlier periods which precede contemporary transnational frameworks, 'translocation' also becomes a particularly useful terminological alternative to 'transnationalism'. As the latter is tied to the nation-state and to the crossing of state borders, it is problematical in contexts where deterritorialized spaces arise within one and the same state. This is, for instance, the case in the colonial frameworks explored here: the Normanist transmigrations took place within the borders of the British empire; and the deterritorialized spaces which they created in the colonial period can thus not properly be called 'transnational' in the narrow sense, although these spaces might share many features with transnational ones, and might be regarded as embryonic forms of the latter. A more fully 'transnational' situation only arises later, with regard to the more recent social and cultural activities of the Normanists' descendants in modern Britain, and in the by now independent states of Canada, Australia, and New Zealand. By contrast, the term 'translocal' refers more generally to a linking of localities which may lie either in different states or in the same state. It can also be understood to refer to very specific links between smaller geographical and social entities, such as particular villages and cities, whereas 'transnationalism' can be used more vaguely to imply links between much larger geographical entities (i.e. entire states) and between very large and heterogeneous national collectivities. The deterritorialized social spaces created by the Normanists and their descendants are centred on connections between very specific villages and small-scale rural areas; the connections are thus translocal rather than transnational. 'Translocation' can thus be a useful term for historical phenomena which are in many ways similar to transnationalism, but take place in pre-nation-state historical contexts, or in a contemporary but nonetheless non-nation-state-related framework: i.e. in the sense 'from local to local'.[38]

Thus, despite certain problems related to the vagueness with which terms such as 'transmigration' and 'translocation' are often used, they deserve further exploration, as they have the potential to become useful concepts for specific forms of migration and diasporicity – for instance, those related to multiple migration – and for specific forms of deterritorialized social space. As deterritorialized social spaces are often (though not always) connected to migration and diasporicity, it can also be profitable to investigate transmigration and translocation together. However, it is also clear that more precise definitions, and a critical and detailed investigation of these theoretical concepts in relation to a greater number of specific case studies, are necessary.

⌘

*The turn towards the transcultural is reflected in various recent developments and publications in postcolonial studies. Sometimes the concepts of the postcolonial and the transcultural are used simultaneously or even synonymously, whereas other treatments envisage a shift from one to the other: i.e., the notion that the concept of the transcultural should, or does, replace the postcolonial. The question of whether these developments are beneficial or problematical has also been the subject of critical debate. See: Frank Schulze–Engler, "Theoretical Approaches: Commonwealth Literature – New Literatures in English – Postcolonial Literature," in *Postcolonial Theory:*

---

[38] For instance, this is the sense in which the term is used by Guarnizo and Smith in "The Locations of Transnationalism," 13; see also 6–7, 12, 14–15, 21, 26.

The Emergence of a Critical Discourse: A Selected and Annotated Bibliography, ed. Dieter Riemenschneider (ZAA Studies 17; Tübingen: Stauffenburg, 2004): 10–11, and his "Introduction" to *Transcultural English Studies*, ed. Sissy Helff & Frank Schulze–Engler (Cross/Cultures 102, ASNEL Papers 12; Amsterdam & New York: Rodopi 2009): ix–xvi, esp. xi–xiii, xvi; *Detective Fiction in a Postcolonial and Transnational World*, ed. Nels Pearson & Marc Singer (Farnham & Burlington VT: Ashgate, 2009); Graham Huggan, "Derailing the 'trans'? Postcolonial Studies and the Negative Effects of Speed," in *Inter- und transkulturelle Studien: Theoretische Grundlagen und interdisziplinäre Praxis*, ed. Heinz Antor (Heidelberg: Winter, 2000): 55–61; and *English Literatures across the Globe: A Companion*, ed. Lars Eckstein (UTB 8345; Paderborn: Wilhelm Fink 2007) – in the latter, see, for example, the editor's "Introduction" (13–19) and Frank Schulze–Engler's chapter "Theoretical Perspectives: From Postcolonial to Transcultural World Literature" (20–32). Within GNEL/ASNEL, the 'transcultural turn' is reflected in the fact that its conference themes did not feature the term 'transcultural' at all between 1979 and 1994; it then appeared for the first time in "Intertextuality and Transcultural Communication" (1995), and has already featured twice in the new millennium: namely, in "Towards a Transcultural Future: Literature and Society in a 'Post'-Colonial World" (2000; proceedings published as *Towards a Transcultural Future: Literature and Human Rights in a 'Post'-Colonial World*," ed. Geoffrey V. Davis & Peter H. Marsden, 2004, and *Towards a Transcultural Future: Literature and Society in a 'Post'-Colonial World*, ed. Davis et al., 2 vols. (all in the Cross/Cultures series, 76, 77 & 79, ASNEL Papers 8, 9.1 & 9.2; Amsterdam & New York: Rodopi, 2004–2005) and "Transcultural English Studies" (2004, proceedings published under the same title, see above). Postcolonial and transcultural studies have increasingly been mentioned in the same breath – for instance, in the name of the Institute for Postcolonial and Transcultural Studies (INPUTS) at Bremen University (Germany), founded in 2002. A Google search for the phrase 'postcolonial and transcultural' on 2 November 2011 produced a staggering 22,300 hits. It is also possible to list book titles such as *Postcolonial Postmortems: Crime Fiction from a Transcultural Perspective* (ed. Christine Matzke & Susanne Mühleisen [Internationale Forschungen zur Allgemeinen & Vergleichenden Literaturwissenschaft; Amsterdam & New York: Rodopi, 2006]).

The connection between postcolonial/transcultural studies and transnationalism is reflected in: Hena Maes–Jelinek, "Postcolonial Criticism at the Crossroads: Subjective Questionings of an Old-Timer," in *Towards a Transcultural Future: Literature and Society in a 'Post'-Colonial World* vol. 1, ed. Davis et al., 4; Frank Schulze–Engler, "From Postcolonial to Preglobal: Transnational Culture and the Resurgent Project of Modernity," in *Towards a Transcultural Future: Literature and Society in a 'Post'-Colonial World*, vol. 1, ed. Davis et al., esp. 49, 58–59, 62, "Theoretical Perspectives," 22–23, 28–30, and "Introduction" to *Transcultural English Studies*, xi–xiii, xvi; as well as in the article on "Transnational Literatures" added to the second edition of Bill

Ashcroft, Gareth Griffiths & Helen Tiffin's *Post-Colonial Studies: The Key Concepts* (2000; London & New York: Routledge, 2007): 214–15. Since 2006, Münster University has preferred to refer to this research field as 'Postcolonial, Transnational and Transcultural Studies'.

**With regard to translocation, this is evident in, for instance: Luis Eduardo Guarnizo & Michael Peter Smith, "The Locations of Transnationalism," in *Transnationalism from Below*, ed. Guarnizo & Smith (Comparative Urban & Community Research 6; New Brunswick NJ & London: Transaction, 1998): 6–7, 12–15, 21, 26; Pnina Werbner, "The Translocation of Culture: 'Community Cohesion' and the Force of Multiculturalism in History," *Sociological Review* 53.4 (November 2005): 745–68; Ramazani, "Black British Poetry and the Translocal"; Anja Peleikis, "Heritage and the Making of (Trans-)Local Identities: A Case Study from the Curonian Spit (Lithuania)," in *Translocality: The Study of Globalising Processes from a Southern Perspective*, ed. Ulrike Freitag & Achim von Oppen (Studies in Global History 4; Leiden & Boston MA: Brill, 2010): 232; as well as the volume on *Cultural Transformations* edited by Chris Prentice et al. For further information on the etymology and previous usages of the concept of translocation, see the "Introduction" to the present volume.

For examples of relevant scholarship on transmigration, see Linda Basch, Cristina Blanc–Szanton & Nina Glick Schiller, "Towards a Definition of Transnationalism: Introductory Remarks and Research Questions," in *Towards a Transnational Perspective on Migration: Race, Class, Ethnicity, and Nationalism Reconsidered*, ed. Basch, Blanc–Szanton & Glick Schiller (New York: New York Academy of Sciences, 1992): ix–x, xii–xiii, and *Nations Unbound: Transnational Projects, Postcolonial Predicaments, and Deterritorialized Nation-States* (1994; Amsterdam: Gordon & Breach, 1997): e.g., 7; Bela Feldman–Bianco, "Multiple Layers of Time and Space: The Construction of Class, Ethnicity, and Nationalism among Portuguese Immigrants," in *Towards a Transnational Perspective on Migration*, ed. Basch et al., 146, 170; Delmos Jones, "Which Migrant? Temporary or Permanent?", in *Towards a Transnational Perspective on Migration*, ed. Basch et al., e.g., 219, 223; Ludger Pries, *Internationale Migration* (Bielefeld: transcript, 2001): 49–53; Luin Goldring, "Disaggregating Transnational Social Spaces: Gender, Place and Citizenship in Mexico–US Transnational Spaces," in *New Transnational Social Spaces: International Migration and Transnational Companies in the Early Twenty-First Century*, ed. Ludger Pries (London & New York: Routledge, 2001): 59–76; Fernando Herrera Lima, "Transnational Families: Institutions of Transnational Social Space," in *New Transnational Social Spaces: International Migration and Transnational Companies in the Early Twenty-First Century*, ed. Pries, e.g., 81, 83.

WORKS CITED

Anderson, Benedict. *Imagined Communities: Reflections on the Origin and Spread of Nationalism* (1983; London & New York: Verso, 2006).

Appadurai, Arjun. *Modernity at Large: Cultural Dimensions of Globalization* (Public Worlds 1; Minneapolis & London: U of Minnesota P, 1996).

Ashcroft, Bill, Gareth Griffiths & Helen Tiffin. *Post-Colonial Studies: The Key Concepts* (2000; London & New York: Routledge, 2nd ed. 2007).

Basch, Linda, Cristina Szanton Blanc & Nina Glick Schiller. *Nations Unbound: Transnational Projects, Postcolonial Predicaments, and Deterritorialized Nation-states* (1994; Amsterdam: Gordon & Breach, 1997).

——, ed. *Towards a Transnational Perspective on Migration: Race, Class, Ethnicity, and Nationalism Reconsidered* (New York: New York Academy of Sciences, 1992).

——. "Towards a Definition of Transnationalism: Introductory Remarks and Research Questions," in *Towards a Transnational Perspective on Migration: Race, Class, Ethnicity, and Nationalism Reconsidered*, ed. Linda Basch, Cristina Blanc–Szanton & Nina Glick Schiller (New York: New York Academy of Sciences, 1992): ix–xiv.

Boulton, Marsha. *Wally's World: Life with Wally the Wonder Dog* (2006; New York: Thomas Dunne, 2008).

——. Personal website. http://www.marshaboulton.com (accessed 30 January 2010).

Brah, Avtar. *Cartographies of Diaspora: Contesting Identities* (London & New York: Routledge, 1996).

Brubaker, Rogers. "The 'Diaspora' Diaspora," *Ethnic and Racial Studies* 28.1 (January 2005): 1–19.

Clifford, James. "Diasporas," *Cultural Anthropology* 9.3 (1994), special issue: *Further Inflections: Toward Ethnographies of the Future*: 302–38.

Cohen, Robin. "Diasporas, the Nation-State, and Globalisation," in *Global History and Migrations*, ed. Wang Gungwu (Global History series 1; Boulder CO & Oxford: Westview, 1997): 117–43.

——. *Global Diasporas: An Introduction* (1997; London & New York: Routledge, 2nd ed. 2008).

Coogan, Michael D., & Bruce M. Metzger, ed. *The Oxford Guide to People and Places of the Bible* (Oxford et al.: Oxford UP, 2001). http://www.oxfordreference .com (accessed 14 January 2010).

Davis, Geoffrey V., & Peter H. Marsden, ed. *Towards a Transcultural Future: Literature and Human Rights in a 'Post'-Colonial World* (Cross/Cultures 76, ASNEL Papers 8; Amsterdam & New York: Rodopi, 2004).

——, et al., ed. *Towards a Transcultural Future: Literature and Society in a 'Post'-Colonial World*, 2 vols. (Cross/Cultures 77 & 79, ASNEL Papers 9.1 & 9.2; Amsterdam & New York: Rodopi, 2004–2005).

Eckstein, Lars, ed. *English Literatures across the Globe: A Companion* (UTB 8345; Paderborn: Wilhelm Fink, 2007).

——. "Introduction" to *English Literatures across the Globe: A Companion*, ed. Eckstein, 13–19.

Edmond, Jacob. "A Poetics of Translocation: Yang Lian's Auckland and Lyn Hejinian's Leningrad," in *Cultural Transformations*, ed. Prentice, Devadas & Johnson, 105–34.

Encyclopædia Britannica. *Encyclopædia Britannica, Online Academic Edition* (Encyclopædia Britannica Inc., 2011), http://www.britannica.com (accessed 25 November 2011).

Feldman–Bianco, Bela. "Multiple Layers of Time and Space: The Construction of Class, Ethnicity, and Nationalism among Portuguese Immigrants," in *Towards a Transnational Perspective on Migration: Race, Class, Ethnicity, and Nationalism Reconsidered*, ed. Linda Basch, Cristina Blanc–Szanton & Nina Glick Schiller (New York: New York Academy of Sciences, 1992): 145–74.

Gilroy, Paul. *The Black Atlantic: Modernity and Double Consciousness* (Cambridge MA: Harvard UP, 1993).

Goldring, Luin. "Disaggregating Transnational Social Spaces: Gender, Place and Citizenship in Mexico–US Transnational Spaces," in *New Transnational Social Spaces: International Migration and Transnational Companies in the Early Twenty-First Century*, ed. Ludger Pries (London & New York: Routledge, 2001): 59–76.

Guarnizo, Luis Eduardo, & Michael Peter Smith. "The Locations of Transnationalism," in *Transnationalism from Below,* ed. Guarnizo & Smith (Comparative Urban & Community Research 6; New Brunswick NJ & London: Transaction, 1998): 3–34.

Hall, Stuart. "Cultural Identity and Diaspora," in *Identity, Community, Culture, Difference*, ed. Jonathan Rutherford (London: Lawrence & Wishart, 1990): 222–37, repr. in *Colonial Discourse and Post-Colonial Theory: A Reader*, ed. Laura Chrisman & Patrick Williams (New York: Harvester Wheatsheaf, 1994): 392–403.

Hayes, John H. "Moses," in *The Oxford Guide to People and Places of the Bible*, ed. Michael D. Coogan & Bruce M. Metzger (Oxford: Oxford UP, 2001), http://www.oxfordreference.com (accessed 14 January 2010).

Huggan, Graham. "Derailing the 'trans'? Postcolonial Studies and the Negative Effects of Speed," in *Inter- und transkulturelle Studien: Theoretische Grundlagen und interdisziplinäre Praxis*, ed. Heinz Antor (Heidelberg: Winter, 2000): 55–61.

Jones, Delmos. "Which Migrant? Temporary or Permanent?" in *Towards a Transnational Perspective on Migration: Race, Class, Ethnicity, and Nationalism Reconsidered*, ed. Linda Basch, Cristina Blanc–Szanton & Nina Glick Schiller (New York: New York Academy of Sciences, 1992): 217–24.

Kidman, Fiona. *The Book of Secrets* (1987; Auckland: Vintage, 1994).

Lima, Fernando Herrera. "Transnational Families: Institutions of Transnational Social Space," in *New Transnational Social Spaces: International Migration and Transnational Companies in the Early Twenty-First Century*, ed. Ludger Pries (London & New York: Routledge, 2001): 77–93.

MacAskill, Norman. "Introduction," in *Lion of Scotland*, Neil Robinson (1952; Edinburgh: Birlinn, 1999): v–ix.

Maes–Jelinek, Hena. "Postcolonial Criticism at the Crossroads: Subjective Questionings of an Old-Timer," in *Towards a Transcultural Future: Literature and Society in a 'Post'-Colonial World*, ed. Geoffrey V. Davis et al. (Cross/Cultures 77 & 79, ASNEL Papers 9.1 & 9.2; Amsterdam & New York: Rodopi, 2004–2005), vol. 1 (2004): 1–20.

Matzke, Christine, & Susanne Mühleisen, ed. *Postcolonial Postmortems: Crime Fiction from a Transcultural Perspective* (Internationale Forschungen zur Allgemeinen & Vergleichenden Literaturwissenschaft; Amsterdam & New York: Rodopi, 2006).

McPherson, Flora. *Watchman against the World: The Remarkable Journey of Norman McLeod & His People from Scotland to Cape Breton Island to New Zealand* (1962; Wreck Cove, Nova Scotia: Breton, 1993).

Mishra, Vijay. *The Literature of the Indian Diaspora: Theorizing the Diasporic Imaginary* (London & New York: Routledge, 2007).

Nelson, William B., Jr. "Promised Land," in *The Oxford Guide to People and Places of the Bible*, ed. Michael D. Coogan & Bruce M. Metzger (Oxford: Oxford UP, 2001). http://www.oxfordreference.com (accessed 14 January 2010)

Oxford English Dictionary (Oxford: Oxford UP, 2nd ed. 1989), http://dictionary.oed .com (accessed 15 January 2010).

Paranjape, Makarand. "Displaced Relations: Diasporas, Empires, Homelands," *CRNLE Journal* (2000), special issue: *Sri Lankan and Indian Diasporic Writing*, ed. Chandani Lokuge & Dianne Schwerdt, 64–72.

Pearson, Nels, & Marc Singer, ed. *Detective Fiction in a Postcolonial and Transnational World* (Farnham & Burlington VT: Ashgate, 2009).

Peleikis, Anja. "Heritage and the Making of (Trans-)Local Identities: A Case Study from the Curonian Spit (Lithuania)," in *Translocality: The Study of Globalising Processes from a Southern Perspective*, ed. Ulrike Freitag & Achim von Oppen (Studies in Global History 4; Leiden & Boston MA: Brill, 2010): 229–47.

Prentice, Chris. "Integral Culture: Agora-Phobia at the Polynesian Cultural Centre," in *Cultural Transformations*, ed. Prentice, Devadas & Johnson, 239–74.

——, Vijay Devadas & Henry Johnson, ed. *Cultural Transformations: Perspectives on Translocation in a Global Age* (Cross/Cultures 125; Amsterdam & New York: Rodopi, 2010).

——. "Introduction: Cultural Transformations: Perspectives on Translocation in a Global Age," in *Cultural Transformations*, ed. Prentice, Devadas & Johnson, xi–xxxv.

Pries, Ludger. *Internationale Migration* (Bielefeld: transcript, 2001).

——, ed. *New Transnational Social Spaces: International Migration and Transnational Companies in the Early Twenty-First Century* (London & New York: Routledge, 2001).

Ramazani, Jahan. "Black British Poetry and the Translocal," in *The Cambridge Companion to Twentieth-Century English Poetry*, ed. Neil Corcoran (Cambridge: Cambridge UP, 2007): 200–14.

Robinson, Neil. *Lion of Scotland* (1952; Edinburgh: Birlinn, 1999).

——. *The River of No Return* (Auckland: Samahani, 2002).

——. *To the Ends of the Earth: Norman McLeod and the Highlanders' Migration to Nova Scotia and New Zealand* (Auckland: HarperCollins, 1997).

Schulze–Engler, Frank. "From Postcolonial to Preglobal: Transnational Culture and the Resurgent Project of Modernity," in *Towards a Transcultural Future: Literature and Society in a 'Post'-Colonial World*, ed. Geoffrey V. Davis et al., 2 vols. (Cross/Cultures 77 & 79, ASNEL Papers 9.1 & 9.2; Amsterdam & New York: Rodopi, 2004–2005), vol. 1 (2004): 49–64.

——. "Introduction" to *Transcultural English Studies*, ed. Sissy Helff & Frank Schulze–Engler (Cross/Cultures 102, ASNEL Papers 12; Amsterdam & New York: Rodopi, 2009): ix–xvi.

——. "Theoretical Approaches: Commonwealth Literature – New Literatures in English – Postcolonial Literature," in *Postcolonial Theory: The Emergence of a Critical Discourse. A Selected and Annotated Bibliography*, ed. Dieter Riemenschneider (ZAA Studies 17; Tübingen: Stauffenburg, 2004): 1–14.

——. "Theoretical Perspectives: From Postcolonial to Transcultural World Literature," in *English Literatures across the Globe*, ed. Eckstein, 20–32.

Stead, Hilary. "Author Wants Seized Computer Back." *Guelph Mercury* (10 October 2003): A5, http://pqasb.pgarchiver.com/guelphmercury/access/640760751.html (accessed 30 January 2010).

Vivan, Itala. "The Iconic Ship in the Atlantic Dialogue of Black Britain" in *Recharting the Black Atlantic: Modern Cultures, Local Communities, Global Connections*, ed. Annalisa Oboe & Anna Scacchi (New York & London: Routledge, 2008): 225–37.

Werbner, Pnina. "The Translocation of Culture: 'Community Cohesion' and the Force of Multiculturalism in History," *Sociological Review* 53.4 (November 2005): 745–68.

⌘

Blurring Images
—Articulations of Arab–American Crossovers

MARKUS SCHMITZ

> We'll speak their language without either a sense of guilt or a sense of
> gratitude. [...] And if we are lies we shall be lies of our own making.[1]

FIRST PUBLISHED IN ENGLISH TRANSLATION in 1969, Tayeb Salih's
novel *Season of Migration to the North* has long been incorporated
into the canon of postcolonial literature. Since Edward W. Said's
contrapuntal interpretation of this prose narrative as a resistant mimetic recip-
rocation of Joseph Conrad's classic *Heart of Darkness*[2] (1899/1902), it has
become a paradigmatic example of what has been variously termed 'writing
back'[3] or 'voyage in'.[4] Although originally composed in Arabic, the well-
known piece of postcolonial fiction in translation can be interpreted as "an
important intertext for our reading of later Anglophone writing by Arabs."[5]
However, the contours of the complex discursive sphere were sketched out
long before Salih sent his Sudanese hero Mustapha Said to London into a
deadly love–hate relationship of mutual exoticist desire and desperate revenge. What has been regularly overlooked in the recent controversy about

---

[1] Tayeb Salih, *Season of Migration to the North*, tr. Denys Johnson–Davies
(*Mausim al-hijra ila-sh-shamal,* 1967; tr. 1969; London: Heinemann, 2010): 49–50.

[2] Edward W. Said, *Culture and Imperialism* (1993; New York: Vintage, 1994):
210–39.

[3] Bill Ashcroft, Gareth Griffiths & Helen Tiffin, *The Empire Writes Back: Theory
and Practice in Post-Colonial Literatures* (London & New York: Routledge, 1989).

[4] Said, *Culture and Imperialism*, 216.

[5] Geoffrey Nash, *The Anglo-Arab Encounter: Fiction and Autobiography by Arab
Writers in English* (Bern & New York: Peter Lang, 2007): 62.

the future presence of Muslims in Lower Manhattan is that, already at the beginning of the twentieth century, the area near the World Trade Center Site had become the cultural centre of Arab immigration to the USA.[6]

The year 2011 brought the centennial anniversary of the first publication of a very early anglophone novel by a native Arabic speaker which allows us to revisit precisely this forgotten immigrant neighbourhood once known as 'Little Syria'. Ameen Fares Rihani's *The Book of Khalid* is the first anglophone Arab novel ever.[7] The novel is much more than an auto-fictional piece of Arabic immigrant literature. Presenting itself to the reader as an edited composition of dubious Arabic and French sources in translation, it is about two young Arab men, Khalid and his friend Shakib, who immigrate to New York City at the turn of the century. The story both ambitiously and ironically confronts issues that still confound the complex relations between Americans and Arabs. When Khalid first enters into a liaison with a white American bohemian woman, she is drawn to his exotic background, and soon "his dark eyes and her eyes of blue" seem to "flow and fuse" (49). In the course of an extended "tête-à-tête [...] the stranger is made a member of the Spiritual Household" (49) and "she, in an effort to seem Oriental, calls the Dervish, 'My Syrian Rose,' 'My Desert Flower,' 'My Beduin Boy' [...] always closing her message with either a strip of Syrian sky or a camel load of the narcissus" (51). The anonymous editor–narrator, however, warns: "Ah, but not thus, will the play close" (51). The Arab-American anti-hero gets into another erotic relationship with a female writer, "a huntress of male curiosities, orginales" (50) who "only skims the surface of things" (50). After "a hectic uprush about pearly breasts, and honey-sources, and musk-scented arbours" (52), she "withdraws from the foreigner her favour" (52), then narratively exhibiting him in the "magazine supplement of one of the Sunday newspapers" (52). There, the immigrant Khalid is made into a stereotypical Orientalist copy, "thrown into the cauldron along with the magic herbs. Bubble-bubble" (52). The following question posed by the narrator anticipates, in many ways, the ambivalence of strategic self-orientalization and omnipotently resistive Occidentalism that is narrativized so powerfully in

---

[6] Anon., "When an Arab Enclave Thrived Downtown," *New York Times* (25 August 2010): A16, New York edition.

[7] Ameen Fares Rihani, *The Book of Khalid* (New York: Dodd, Mead, 1911). Further page references are in the main text.

Tayeb Saleh's literary voyage in: "The fire-eating Dervish, how can he now swallow this double-tongued flame of hate and love?" (52).

Rihani (1876–1940), a late-nineteenth-century Lebanese-Maronite immigrant to the USA, was one of the leading anglophone Arab writers of his time and a founding member of *Al-Rabita al-Qalamiya* ["The Pen League"], a diasporic literary organization established in 1920 in New York City by the poet and painter Gibran Kahlil Gibran (1883–1931) with other writers of Arab descent. Already by the 1910s, several Arab-American literary societies and journals had come into existence. These authors, who wrote in Arabic as well as in English, produced what is known in the Arab world as *Adab al-Mahjar*, the émigré school of Arab-American writing.[8] Although, to this day, Rihani's early literary articulation of Arab-American crossovers has remained neglected in the intellectual history of both the Arab world and North America, a re-reading of *The Book of Khalid* can help us to grasp the cross-cultural dynamics between the USA and the Middle East in our own times. The largest part of the novel tells the story of two Arab peddlers in turn-of-the-century Manhattan. In this regard, it provides the classical immigrant narrative of coming to America and becoming an American. In addition, it is a story of emigration from and re-migration to the Arab world. By not only providing an account of the immigrants' travails but also beginning and ending with a Syro-Lebanese setting, it touches the core of Arab-American transmigrant experiences. After the main protagonists' attempt to adapt to the new political, cultural, and ethnic environment tragically fails, the remaining part of the novel accounts for the subsequent return to their old and suddenly strange homeland. America proves to be a humiliating experience, and Khalid retreats to the Lebanese forest like an ascetic mystic or hidden Shiite Mahdi, before emerging again in order to preach socio-political and spiritual reform in the Arab world. Instead of relating his protagonists to the material actuality of Arabic-Islamic cultures, Rihani, like other Mahjar writers, stresses his Christian-Oriental spirituality. At first glance, the narrative seems to engage American readers in familiarizing the exotic, thus representing a unidirectional project of cultural translation, of bridging the East–West binary and bringing about a civilizational synthesis between two cultures of intrinsic

---

[8] Nash, *The Anglo-Arab Encounter,* 32–47. *Adab* is the Arabic word for 'literature'; *Mahjar* translates as 'place of immigration or exile'.

difference.[9] However, the seemingly naive endeavour to envisage a universal humanity free from religious, racial, and cultural chauvinism[10] willingly clashes with dominant American perceptions of the Middle East and Middle Easterners. Against the historical background of an increasing and expanding struggle in the Middle East for Arab independence from both the Ottoman Empire and European colonialism, the ambitious literary project is deeply grounded in the experience with and anticipation of West–Eastern misrepresentations. Rihani knows that addressing a Western readership requires more than the ability to write in English. Comparable to Khalid and Shakib, who are forced to live in a damp cellar and to sell trinkets that they claim are relicts from the holy land while exploiting their exotic attraction to American women "with all the rude simplicity and frankness of the Arabian Nights,"[11] early anglophone Arab writers of the 1910s and 1920s had to situate their work in relation to a powerful discourse through which their readers had already formed their perception of a distant culture: "The first generation of Arab-American writers [...] dressed carefully for their encounter with the American public, putting on the guise of prophet, preacher, or man of letters."[12] Instead of simply conforming to mainstream American expectations, Rihani's narrative exaggerates the Orientalness of its title character to the point of caricature – a caricature that existed in Western representations of Arabs long beyond the early-twentieth century. Hence, *The Book of Khalid* not only fictionalizes a failed attempt to bridge worlds by way of a self-orientalizing assimilation but also constitutes an early expression of the Arab-American anxiety of mutual Orientalist–Occidentalist misrepresentations.

⌘

---

[9] Waïl S. Hassan, "The Rise of Arab-American Literature: Orientalism and Cultural Translation in the Work of Ameen Rihani," *American Literary History* 20.1–2 (Spring–Summer 2008): 245–75.

[10] See Naji Queijan, "The Formation of the Universal Self," in *Ameen Rihani: Bridging East and West. A Pioneering Call for Arab-American Understanding*, ed. Nathan C. Funk & Betty J. Sitka (Lanham MD: UP of America, 2004): 83–92.

[11] Rihani, *The Book of Khalid,* 49.

[12] Evelyn Shaki, "Arab American Literature," in *New Immigrant Literatures in the United States: A Sourcebook to Our Multicultural Heritage*, ed. Alpana Sharma Knippling (Westport CT: Greenwood, 1996): 6. See also Hassan, "The Rise of Arab-American Literature."

1. Cultural Articulations in Transmigration

> Can there be any *here*? No. She understands *there*.[13]

This essay seeks to demonstrate that a one-way integration and a defensive assertion of foreign-born whiteness are no longer seen by contemporary Arab-American intellectuals as an adequate response to collective criminalization, individual discrimination, institutionalized islamophobia, and everyday political racism. It argues that their cultural articulations have not only moved from a self-orientalizing defensiveness to a form of critical self-assertion, but clearly also demonstrate a willingness to gain emancipation from both Orientalist and Occidentalist representations of selves and others. Once the assimilationist instrument of cultural translation affirming the dominant split version of East versus West, Arab-American writing and art have developed a narrative counter-strategy that calls for political liberation on the global level and for individual emancipation in specific, local contexts. In the following, I shall explore selected literary and audiovisual non-places of narrative identifications produced by Walid Raad (1967), Larissa Sansour (1973), Emily Jacir (1970), and Rabieh Aalameddine (1959). The biographies of these intellectuals are decisively influenced by constant physical and topological-discursive movements between the Middle East and the USA. By taking the audiovisual arts and travelling literature as the subject-matter of cross-cultural analysis, this essay intentionally goes beyond an exclusive interest in the ethnic situation of the USA as well as the predominant focus on works of literature in the still emerging field of Arab-American studies. At least two possible objections to my argument have to be considered. One is related to the sheer claim of an Arab-American cultural sphere. The other arises from the concept of transmigration itself. The assertion of an Arab-American hyphenated identity today – maybe more than ever – is seen as an oxymoron. At first glance, this seems to be mostly due to ongoing ideological, political, and military conflicts in the wake of 11 September 2001. Epistemologically, however, it underlines the continuing neglect of overlaps between two seemingly mutually exclusive cultural spheres – overlaps whose position is scarcely fixable within the old and still dominant binary of the Euro-American West and the Arab-Islamic East. It is precisely this imagined cultural geography and the inherent claim of

---

[13] Rabih Alameddine, *I, the Divine: A Novel in First Chapters* (New York: W.W. Norton, 2001): 99.

authentic places of origin or of destinations of assimilation that are in many ways blurred by the historical movement, explanatory concept, and cultural articulations of transmigration. While Arab Americans as an ethnic-minority group have long been largely invisible (at least when they were not being demonized and targeted as enemies within), their cultural articulations have been doubly invisible. Arab-American writing has only recently begun to be recognized as part of the ethnic landscape of American literature. The events of 9/11 and their aftermath have clearly drawn new attention to the Arab-American cultural sphere. Although the national security apparatus still covers this particular immigrant community as a veiled pool of potential terrorist sleepers, new public interest has led to a shift in academic and curatorial focus as well as in publishing practice. The last decade, in fact, has seen a dramatic increase in production by Arab-American artists, critics, and writers. Their works reflect both the shifting social and political contexts that have created new urgencies of expression and the emergence of new platforms for these forms of expression.

My location of the Arab-American cultural sphere intentionally goes beyond a dual understanding that either sees it as a transplanted culture characterized by specific anthropological markers and social practices related to language, cuisine, religion, and gender relations or as a quintessentially American immigrant culture emerging from and articulated in what is celebrated as US multiculture. I do not believe that Arab-American cultural productions, in order to deserve that designation, must be about specifically ethnic Arab and/or national American topics. Nor must it feature authentic baklava and belly dancing or place itself within the nation's multiethnic scene, severed from the socio-political realities in the Middle East. It can be argued, instead, that, at least since the late 1960s, for many Arab-American intellectuals, a dissident relationship to US Middle-East policy has been foundational to their critical interventions. The close engagement with cultural, political, and military events within the Arab world and dissent from American interventionist foreign policy seems, indeed, to have played a more prominent role in the work of many Arab-American writers, artists, and critics than the long history of everyday racism and legal discrimination.

The Arab-American cultural sphere explored in the present discussion is a culture of decisively transnational and transmigrant identifications rather than a hyphenated immigrant culture. Contrary to received ideal types of international migration, such as immigration, re-migration, and diasporic migration, the transmigration approach shall be used as in the social sciences, in particular in international and transnational migration studies, to interpret cultural works that travel across multiple national and cultural borders. Transmigrants are defined by the social anthropologists Linda Basch, Christina Szanton Blanc, and Nina Glick Schiller as migrants whose continuing migratory movements transcend the boundaries of nation-states and whose complex socio-economic relationships challenge the traditional isomorphism of people, territory, and belonging.[14] While the dominant focus in transmigration research on the social and economic dimensions of the globalization of capital fails to grasp its effects on the reformulation or transformation of cultural articulation, my analysis is concerned with the literary and artistic practice of transmigrants. It utilizes the paradigm of transmigration as an open explanatory model that allows the cultural works of Arab-American transmigrants to be illuminated without screening out the material clashes between specific frequently polarized mono-localities. Thus, the phenomenon of Arab-American transmigration is addressed as a process, topos, idea, and ideology, while Arab-American transmigrants can be grasped as actors and objects of socio-political actions and cultural representations or misrepresentations. Paying particular attention to strategies and effects of critical revisions and artistic or literary re-significations under the conditions of postcolonial migration and a globalized cultural industry, I will argue that the Arab-American articulations selected for this essay have a particular decentering quality. Although their genesis is directly tied to the minoritary experience of a stigmatized diasporic group, they cannot be grasped simply as acts of translation between different cultures. These works transgress both the dominant image-repertoire of the Western archives and the leading representational modes of Arab culture. Instead, they represent the recursive blurring effects of continuous crossovers.

⌘

---

[14] The concept of transmigration was first employed in the mid-1990s by Basch et al. to provide an analytical point of entry to the examination of key processes in a world that is increasingly restructured by economic globalization and transnational migration. Nina Glick Schiller, Linda Basch & Cristina Szanton Blanc, "From Immigrant to Transmigrant: Theorizing Transnational Migration," *Anthropological Quarterly* 68.1 (January 1995): 48–63.

2. Sex and Death Between Worlds

> I know your stories [...] and I can tell you my stories. If you want.[15]

The novel *Koolaids* was first published in 1998. It is about the AIDS epidemic in the USA, the civil war in Beirut, death, sex, and the meaning of life between worlds. Competing first-person narrators provide a polyphonic mosaic of diary entries, memories and hallucinations, news reports, and hilarious short plays. The novelist Rabieh Alameddine grew up in Lebanon, attended secondary school in England, and has academic degrees from UCLA and the University of San Francisco. He divides his time between San Francisco and Beirut. The novel was quite successful in the USA and became a best-seller in Beirut in 2001, too. However, its translation into Arabic fell victim to Lebanese censorship. While the literary figures in *Koolaids* fit into America without belonging there, they do belong in Lebanon without fitting into Lebanese society. This uneasy fact of their always being somehow out of place constantly forces the protagonists to situate their own displaced subjectivities in relation to dominant fixations of identity and culture, thus questioning habitual representations of the Arab world and the West in both the USA and Lebanon itself. This happens, for instance, when one of the main characters wants to write a piece of pulp fiction:

> I want to write a book [...]. A stunningly beautiful American woman with perky breasts is sold as a slave to an Arab prince. He, on the other hand is an incredibly successful American corporate executive pretending to be an Arab prince, for what Americans fantasize about being seduced by an Arab.[16]

The first-person narrator, Mohammad, clearly locates himself outside ethnic and national units of belonging and of filiation (243). Distancing himself from "naïve and dumb" (243) Americans as well as from "arrogant" Lebanese who are "too busy judging everybody else's life to live their own" (243), he can, however, not escape being perceived by others through the essentialist parameters of mutually excluding cultures. The Arab-American artist does not manage to get rid of those reductive stereotypes that recognize him as someone he is not or does not want to be:

---

[15] Rabih Alameddine, *The Hakawati* (New York: Alfred A. Knopf, 2008).

[16] Rabih Alameddine, *Koolaids: The Art of War* (London: Abacus, 1998): 117. Further page references are in the main text.

> The happiest day in my life was when I got my American citizenship
> and was able to tear up my Lebanese passport. That was great. Then I
> got to hate the Americans. And I really do. [...] I tried so hard to rid
> myself of anything Lebanese. [...] The harder I tried, the more it
> showed up in the unlikeliest places. Would people think of me as a
> painter or as a Lebanese painter? (244)

In 2008 Alameddine published his third novel, *The Hakawati*. It opens with
the following address: "Listen! Allow me to be your god. Let me take you on
a journey beyond imagining. Let me tell you a story."[17] At the heart of Alameddine's saga of four generations of a Lebanese family is a storyteller of
such dubious origins – a bastard Armenian whose father was an American
missionary and who escaped the 1915 genocide in Turkey – that his employer
and patron, a Lebanese nobleman, gives him his surname al-Kharrat, the liar.
Within one generation, the storyteller's oral profession is replaced by mun-
dane commerce and a family empire is spawned. The only one to continue the
grandfather's survival strategy of spinning tales within tales is the first-person
narrator of the frame-story and main protagonist, the hakawati's grandson
Osama, who returns to his country from California for his own father's death
bed as a family outsider: "I was a tourist in a bizarre land. I was home."[18] *The
Hakawati* is simultaneously a book about an American Lebanese's coming
home, about the modern history of Beirut, and also a metafiction about storytelling – a fictionalized narrative that reflects on the conditions for the
(im)possibility of telling stories. By adapting the polyphonic structure of the
Arabian Nights[19] it addresses both the tropes and the images of classical
Arabic narratives and the stereotypical representations of the Western Orientalist archive. Reflecting these formerly separated and now interwoven representational modes in the broken mirror of our postcolonial present, the novel
at the same time explores the complex narrative precedents of cross-cultural
understanding.[20]

---

[17] Alameddine, *The Hakawati*, 5.

[18] *The Hakawati*, 7.

[19] Ferial J. Ghazoul, *Nocturnal Poetics: The Arabian Nights in Comparative Context*
(Cairo: American U in Cairo P, 1996).

[20] Elias Khoury, "Ar-riwaya wa miraya al-waqi' al-maksur" ("The Novel and the
Broken Mirror of Reality"), *Al-Mulhaq ath-Thaqafi/An-Nahar* (25 May 1996): 18–19
& (1 June 1996): 18–19.

The main subject of the *The Hakawati* is already announced in the Amer-
ican-Arab hybrid title. The reader learns that a *hakawati* is a professional
storyteller. And in case one loses the novel's narratological focus, each of its
four sub-books opens with a series of epigraphs testifying to the power of
storytelling, from sources as diverse as the Koran, Hannah Arendt's *The
Human Condition* (1958), or literary works by Fernando Pessoa and Emile
Habibi. While the ever-shifting narrative does not allow the reader to immediately form a strong attachment to any of the characters of the many subplots,
each individual story sets its hook, giving him or her just enough of a death-
bed scene, piece of family history, or fantastic tale to draw him/her further in.
Thousands of Arabian desert miles are travelled in a sentence, historic battles
are fought in a paragraph, and an encounter with jinns ["ghosts"] receives
only a minimalist description. This illustrative bareness, on the one hand,
explores and thereby exposes the limits of what needs to be given to the
readers to keep them hooked into the frame story. On the other hand, the
multiplying dissection of the Kharrat's family story at the same time provides
a template for the *The Hakawati*'s larger experiment, to question the ways we
understand ourselves and our worlds. Mythic stories of the heroic Islamic
Sultan Baybars who is fighting the European crusaders are interposed with
stories of Osama's personal history and the stories of his family. The readers
learn about the mythic twinned lovers Shams and Layla against pieces from
Osama's intoxicant undergraduate years in California or his grandfather's
birth. In other sections we find references to Western and Middle-Eastern
mass media. Each of the narrative fragments participates in building Osama's
self, whether by illuminating his family's complex genealogy or his personal
cross-cultural past. For this novelistic process of narrative identification, the
story of how his grandparents first met is as important as the story of a jinn
having sex with a human being.

   The individual ego that the novel narrates is made up of many intertwined
stories, canonized representations of pivotal historical moments, and fleeting
personal experiences. As Osama's grandfather explains, each story's power
comes not from any causal importance or intrinsic logic, but from its being
told: "Events matter little, only stories of these events affect us."[21] It is this
insight that guides the novel's narrative structure. Coherent historical events
or linear biographical strands are as irrelevant as authentic authorship or
narrative originality. Instead, *The Hakawati* focuses on the selective proce-

---

[21] Alameddine, *The Hakawati*, 450.

dure of making meaning and listening. None of the many narrators has the authority of an historical chronist: "Never trust the teller [...]. Trust the tale."[22] Most of Osama's stories are of other people and also told by other people. However, these are the stories that make up Osama's self because they prefigure how other people perceive him. In cross-cultural perspective, the transmigrant Osama's intimate reflection on his difficult personal relation to his dying father in the final section of the novel can also be read as an allegorical comment on the mutual ignorance between the West and the so-called Arab world. In this reading, the personal relation symbolizes the collective history of Orientalist and Occidentalist (mis)representations:

> What happens is of little significance compared with the stories we tell
> ourselves about what happens. [...] My father and I may have shared
> numerous experiences, but, as I was constantly finding out, we rarely
> shared their stories.[23]

3. The Power to Affirm

More than other cultural sectors in the Middle East, concept and performance arts have been significantly influenced by Arab-American transmigrants, who directly participate in the formation of local independent projects, galleries, and festivals, which, at least since the end of the 1990s, have offered new platforms beyond the state-controlled cultural spaces of phobocratic censorship. At the same time, these concept and performance artists are increasingly present(ed) at international art shows in Venice, Kassel, New York, or Abu Dhabi.[24]

A significant example of the artistic practice of calling into question stories and histories from an Arab-American point of view is Walid Raad's brain-

---

[22] Alameddine, *The Hakawati*, 206. Alameddine here refers to D.H. Lawrence's famous 1923 essay "The Spirit of Place." The original phrase is "Never trust the artist. Trust the tale." In his essay, Lawrence argues that the proper function of a literary critic "is to save the tale from the artist who created it." D.H. Lawrence, "The Spirit of Place," in *Studies in Classic American Literature*, ed. Ezra Greenspan, Lindeth Vasey & John Worthen (Cambridge: Cambridge U P, 2003): 14.

[23] *The Hakawati*, 450.

[24] Kaelen Wilson–Goldie, "Off the Map: Contemporary Art in the Middle East," in *The Future of Tradition – The Tradition of Future*, ed. Chris Dercon, León Krempel & Avinoam Shalem (Munich: Haus der Kunst, 2010): 62–63.

child *The Atlas Group Project*. Founded in 1999, it forms the constant basis
for Raad's multi-media performances. The pseudo-scientific laboratory
mimics and thereby exposes the mechanisms of the archive as a place where
the production of historical knowledge happens.[25] When the *Atlas Group* first
appeared on the Lebanese art scene, it immediately afforded a space in high-
profile international venues such as Documenta, the Whitney Biennale, and
the Venice Biennale. The artist and Cooper Union School of Arts teacher
Raad is based between Brooklyn and Beirut. He is particularly concerned
with selections and representations of knowledge of the Middle East. His
specific approach to the accumulation of documents related to Lebanon's
recent history, therefore, has all the trappings of the documentary genre. A
typical *Atlas Group* production involves press photographs, news clippings,
interview transcripts, video footage, graphics, elements of collage, and video
art – all rolled up in the framework of the artist's talk or lecture.

The Atlas archives file with the title *Missing Lebanese Wars* contains a
richly illustrated notebook by Dr Fadl Fakhoury (see Fig. 1 below). It is about
historians who spend their wartime gambling at Beirut's horse-race track.
These historians do not, however, bet – as one might expect – on the winning
horse, but on the distance between the winning horse and the finish line as to
be reconstructed in the published photo-finish photograph. Against the background of competing versions of the so-called civil war and roles or responsibilities along the lines of different sectarian and political groups, this work
can be interpreted as a direct comment on the unresolved inner-Lebanese
struggle over historical representation (for instance, in schoolbooks) and
reconciliation. At the same time, it can be read as a translocal metaphor for
the production and control of historical evidence through acts of deferment
and extension of meaning. These acts or counter-acts of controlling the distance between a signified thing or event (here the winning horse's running-in)
and its signification (the published photo) are at the core of Walid Raad's
artistic practice.

[25] See Regina Göckede, "Zweifelhafte Dokumente – Die zeitgenössische arabische
Kunst, Walid Raad und die Frage der Re-Präsentation," in *Der Orient, die Fremde:
Positionen zeitgenössischer Kunst und Literatur*, ed. Regina Göckede & Alexandra
Karentzos (Bielefeld: Transcript, 2006): 185–203, and Sarah Rogers, "Forging His-
tory, Performing Memory: Walid Raad's The Atlas Project," *Parachute (Bey-
routh_Beirut)* 108 (2002): 68–79.

The cross-cultural implications of this counter-archival approach become obvious when watching the so-called *Bachar Tapes*. The fifty-three video-tapes form another file of the *Atlas Group* archives. They serve as a testimony to the experiences of Soheil Bachar, a Lebanese man claiming to be a sixth hostage held in captivity with five American men in Lebanon during the so-called Iran hostage crisis of the late 1970s and early 1980s.

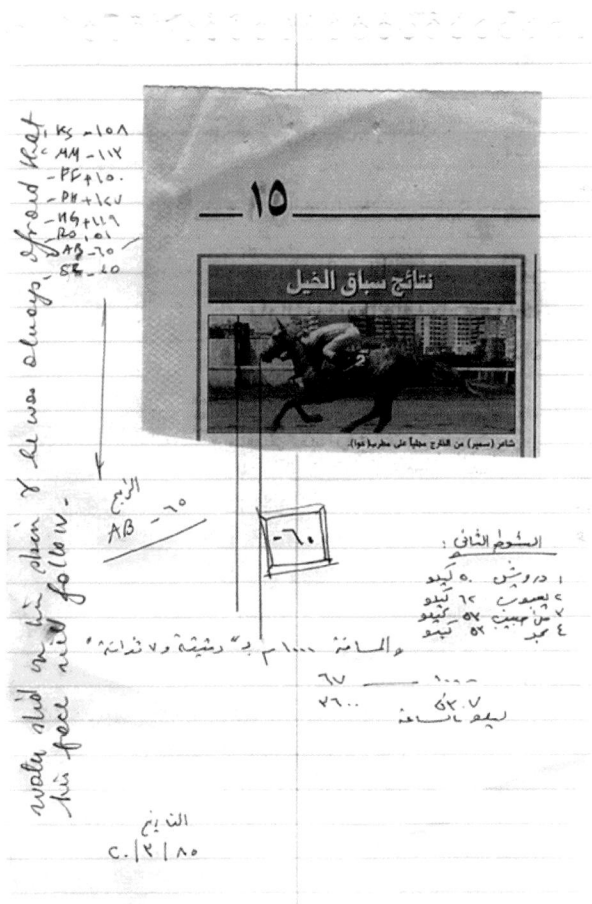

Fig. 1: Walid Raad/The Atlas Group, from "Notebook Volume 72:
Missing Lebanese Wars" (1999), in *The truth will be known when the last
witness is dead*, ed. Hélène Chouteau & François Piron
(Paris: La Galerie de Noisy-le-Sec, Cologne: Walther König, 2004): 46.
Reproduced by kind permission of Walid Raad.

Fig. 2: Walid Raad/The Atlas Group, video still from "Hostage: The Bachar
Tapes (English Version)," 4:3, 16.17 min (2001).
Reproduced by kind permission of Walid Raad.

Fig. 3: Walid Raad/The Atlas Group, video still from "Hostage: The Bachar
Tapes (English Version)," 4:3, 16.17 min (2001).
Reproduced by kind permission of Walid Raad.

Whereas the captivity memoirs written by American ex-hostages[26] primarily represent the experience of captivity as a completely depoliticized individual phenomenon without prequel, Bachar insists on laying bare the concrete pretexts and contexts of the American presence in the Middle East as well as the motives of the hostage-takers. He wants to demonstrate that these backgrounds, such as the Reagan administration's military support of the Israeli army during its occupation of Lebanon, are systematically displaced in Western representations. He explains his approach of using the gaps and blind spots of Western narratives as starting points to set off his own counter-narrative as follows:

> My interest today is how this kind of experience can be documented and represented. I am convinced that the Americans have failed miserably in this regard but that in their failure they have revealed much to us about the possibilities and limits of representing the experience of captivity.[27]

Raad's documents do not function as scraps of historical evidence. The faked documents are presented as 'art-facts' rather than as 'artefacts'. Functioning as artistic traces between what is known to be true and what has to be believed from a certain political, ideological, or cultural point of view, these projects expose the performative genesis of (cross-cultural) meaning. In recent years, Raad's art practice has expanded upon this research-based methodology of the *Atlas Group*. The project *Scratching on Things I Could Disavow* (2007, ongoing) radically questions the current modes of representation and perception of art in and from the Arab world. In particular, the project explores the ideological, economic, and political dimensions of the global art-market phenomenon, asking whether and how the recent hype around and commodification of Arab art can really help to establish representational spaces that are defined by Arab artists and not by its Western consumers. Hence, his virtual micro-expositions perform as model platforms for future

---

[26] Two well-known classics of this genre are Terry A. Anderson, *Den of Lions* (New York: Ballantine, 1994), and Tom Sutherland, *At Your Own Risk: An American Chronicle of Crisis and Capitivity in the Middle East* (Golden CO: Fulcrum, 1996).

[27] The Atlas Group / Walid Raad, "Civilizationally, We Do Not Dig Holes To Bury Ourselves," in *Tamáss: Contemporary Arab Representations Beirut / Lebanon 1*, ed. Catherine David (Barcelona: Fundació Antoni Tàpies, 2002): 163.

art-shows. These platforms are explained by Raad himself as "stage-sets from a forthcoming play about the history of art in Beirut."[28]

4. The First Palestinian on the Moon

Larissa Sansour's 2009 mixed-media installation *A Space Exodus* from the outset eludes the 'fact-question' of whether there has ever been or will be a Palestinian on the moon. Born in Jerusalem in 1973 to a Russian mother and a Palestinian father and educated in New York, Sansour lived in Copenhagen for ten years and is now based in London and regularly works in Bethlehem. The activist–artist grew up well aware of the reductive meaning of truth when it comes to the representations and misrepresentations of the Palestinian people and of the 'peace process' in international mass media. Her installation combines a video clip, still photos from the video, and sculptures of little Palestinian astronauts taking over the installation's space. The audiovisual work presents an impossible alternative (or anti-alternative) to both, the one-state and the two-state solution. It does so at a particular historical moment after extended interim periods and multiple interrupted roadmaps which have manifested a final status of continuing occupation and expanding settlements – a moment when many Palestinians, in Palestine as well as in exile, have given up waiting for a just solution between equals, although the international community is still talking about the need for mutual compromises.

Sansour's extraterrestrial dystopian solution to the Palestinian question is as charmingly mischievous as it is despairing. The 5:25 minute experimental video shows the artist herself as a Palestinian astronaut landing on the moon and establishing a Palestinian exile-colony. While *Space Exodus* is shot and choreographed with state-of-the-art special effects, it explicitly does not look real. The video, which had its world premiere in 2008 at the Dubai festival's short-film competition, opens with a close-up of female fingers running over the controls of a space ship. "Jerusalem, we have a problem," a woman's voice says. But there is no response from the Holy City on earth. After an uncanny moment of deafening silence, a woman dressed in a space-suit plants her foot in the moon-dust as she proclaims: "One small step for a Palestinian, one giant leap for mankind." This proclamation directly refers to the first US

---

[28] Anon, "Walid Ra'ad – Scratching on Things I Could Disavow," *Kunstaspekte*, http://www.kunstaspekte.de/index.php?action=termin&tid=52070 (accessed 22 September 2011).

moon landing. The soundtrack – an arabesque variation of Richard Strauss's musical interpretation of Nietzsche's late-romantic critique of European morality *Also sprach Zarathustra* (1885) – as well as the following scenes recall Stanley Kubrick's famous 1968 movie *2001: A Space Odyssey*.

Fig. 4: Larissa Sansour, video still from "A Space Exodus," 5.24 min (2009). Reproduced by kind permission of Larissa Sansour.

Fig. 5: Larissa Sansour, "Space Earth," 45 x 80 cm, C-Print (2009), edition of 10. Reproduced by kind permission of Larissa Sansour.

In fact, the video sometimes appears like a very brief remake of a few key images from Kubrick's science-fiction classic on the pitfalls of human evolution. In Sansour's *Space Exodus*, the Palestinian flag is prominently featured (see Fig. 4 above), as is her Palestinian space-suit and the uniquely designed orientalized space-shoes. But it is the twinkling stars and the earth in the distance as well as her low-gravity gliding across the image that evoke some transcendent freedom, far from the political 'facts on the ground' – far from the continuing occupation of the Palestinian ground. The film takes a paradigmatic narrative of extreme technological progress and transposes it onto a situation in which a population is bound, constrained, and denied the most rudimentary rights of movement. In the final scene, the female palestinaut waves to Planet Earth (see Fig. 5 above). The camera focuses on her boots bouncing on the surface of the moon, and eventually pans out as she fades away into outer space.

Larissa Sansour's work leaves us grasping for meaning. Mankind's dream of extraterrestrial discoveries has become a nightmare in which the moon functions as a false promise of a better future for Palestinians. The non-planet, hostile to life, is imagined as a land without a people for a people increasingly without land. Without using a single image of an Israeli soldier, a checkpoint, a wall, or a refugee camp, *A Space Exodus* emphasizes the traumatically exilic condition of the Palestinian people, unheard by the international community and threatened to fade into nothingness. At first glance, the work seems to exclusively portray Palestinian de-territorialization and loss in outer space. By doing so, however, it directs our attention to a very real and earthly struggle: the unfinished struggle for self-determination and for a just solution in today's geographical Palestine. Hence, the audiovisual exodus narrative does not represent Palestinian pain and trauma as an end in itself; Sansour's project needs, rather, to be seen as an artistic act of *sumud*: a powerful alternative to the armed struggle.[29] It is at the same time a non-violent and translocal strate-

---

[29] Derived from the verbal form '*samada*' (Arabic for 'to proudly raise one's head'), the Palestinian term *sumud* translates as 'steadfastness'. It was introduced into Palestinian national discourse in the late 1960s to designate a non-violent strategy of resisting occupation that goes beyond passive subordination to oppression and armed struggle by staying in Palestine and keeping daily life going, thus physically and morally affirming the collective Palestinian presence. In the realms of cultural representation and education, it refers to the relentless persistence of narrating the Palestinian experience, preserving Palestinian heritage, and struggling for human dignity and justice by means of art and literature. See Raja Shehadeh, *The Third Way: A*

gy of cultural resistance. By taking the local struggle for dignity into the global art market, it voices the Palestinian demand to overcome ignorance and almost unconditional acceptance of military occupation and settlements that are blatant violations of international law. In this view, the work can be interpreted as a metaphoric encouragement of moral and practical solidarity with those who cannot emigrate to the moon.

5. (Hi)Stories Not Yet Told

Emily Jacir was born in 1970 in Bethlehem, in the occupied territories. She grew up in Saudi Arabia, Italy, and the USA. Today she divides her time between New York City und Ramallah, Palestine. The dilemma of mutually excluding systems of evidence so powerfully addressed in Raad's and Sansour's work is an important point of departure for her concept art as well. The insights gained from the study of the cross-cultural dissemination of meaning are directly incorporated into her own mode of artistic production.

Jacir first caused a stir on the New York art scene when, in 2000, she placed Christmas postcards in Manhattan's small grocery and stationery stores (see Fig. 6 below). Reciprocating the traditional Orientalist iconography of Western Christmas aesthetics, her postcard project smuggles the continuing actuality of military occupation and repression into the representational spaces of the US Christmas industry.

Since 2005, Jacir has worked on the long-term project *Material for a Film*. The multimedia work is dedicated to the remembrance of the Palestinian activist, writer, and translator Wael Zuaiter, who was killed at the age of 38 by Mossad agents in Rome on 16 October 1972. While the PLO representative himself had always renounced political violence against civilians, he was suspected of being a member of the militant Black September group responsible for the massacre of Israeli athletes during the 1972 Summer Olympics. His murder marks the beginning of series of secret retaliation attacks and assassinations perpetrated by Israeli intelligence against Palestinian activist–intellectuals in the diaspora. The details of what really happened in Rome have never been clarified. To this day, the Israeli government has denied any involvement and responsibility.

Journal of Life in the West Bank (London: Quartet, 1982), and Edward W. Said, "Permission to Narrate," *Journal of Palestine Studies* 13.3 (1984): 27–48.

Fig. 6: Emily Jacir, "Christmas 2000," 10.26 x 15.24 cm, C-Print (2000), in
Jenny Gheith, "Exhibiting Politics: Palestinian-American Artist Emily Jacir
Talks About her Work," *The Electronic Intifada* (4 November 2004), http:
//electronicintifada.net/content/exhibiting-politics-palestinian-american-artist-
emily-jacir-talks-about-her-work/5295 (accessed 19 May 2012).

It is not the fictional visualization of Zuaiter's murder in Steven Spielberg's 2005 film *Munich* that spurred Jacir to present a Palestinian counter-
narrative but, rather, this filmic depiction's lack of detail and background regarding Zuaiter's and other Palestinian lives. The most important conceptual

starting point of her documentary allegory is *Per un Palestinese,* an anthology of tribute essays, poems, memoirs, and drawings edited in 1979 by Janet Venn–Brown.[30] In one of the book's chapters, the neorealist film director Elio Petri and the famous novelist and screenplay writer Ugo Pirro elaborate on their plan of producing a documentary about Zuaiter's life. Under the title *Material for a Film,* the two Italian intellectuals present the scripts of conversations and interviews with persons who knew Zuaiter in Rome.[31] Pirro's premature death brought the project to an end. The film was never realized. In 2007, almost thirty years later, coinciding with the thirty-fifth commemoration of Zuaiter's assassination, a Palestinian American investigation that takes up Pirro's idea of shedding light on the lost and obscured fragments of Zuaiter's life was awarded the Venice Biennale's prestigious Golden Lion. Jacir's ongoing artistic research project collects and exhibits historical documents with the aim of narrating an individual life story that has not been told. At the same time, Zuaiter's personal history stands for the marginalized experiences of numerous Palestinians. Thus, *Material for a Film* is as much about the Palestinian people as about one man.

Each of Jacir's performances and multimedia installations sheds light on another biographical fragment or contextual aspect, as in 2006, when Jacir was invited to the Sydney Biennale: When Zuaiter was assassinated in Rome he was carrying with him the second volume of an old Arab edition of the *Arabian Nights.* Since all available Italian editions were translations from European versions, the Palestinian intellectual was working on a direct Italian translation of the Arabic classic. According to the artist, Zuaiter's Arabic copy was perforated by a 22-bore bullet. *Material for a Film* picks up this deadly end to a failed cross-cultural transfer of a text which has influenced Western perceptions of the Arab-Islamic world more than any other narrative. In her Sydney performance, Jacir fires a gun at a thousand blank-paged books. In the installation that follows, she exhibits these perforated empty carriers of meaning together with the single pages ripped out of Zuaiter's copy. Going beyond the particular tragedy of Zuaiter's murder, *Material for a Film* visualizes the dense relation between physical power and cultural validity in the Palestinian–Israeli conflict and at the same time dismantles the violent adjustment of cross-cultural representations.

---

[30] *For a Palestinian: A Memorial to Wael Zuaiter*, ed. & tr. Janet Venn–Brown (*Per un Palestinese*, 1979; tr. London & Boston: Kegan Paul International, 1984).

[31] *For a Palestinian*, ed. & tr. Venn–Brown, 75–116.

Roma 16 ottobre 1972

Fig. 7: Emily Jacir, Detail from "Material for a Film" (2005 ongoing), in
Emily Jacir, ed. Roland Wäspe & Andreas Baur
(Nuremberg: Verlag für moderne Kunst, 2008): 71.

Fig. 8: Emily Jacir, Detail from "Material for a Film" (2005 ongoing), in
Emily Jacir, ed. Roland Wäspe & Andreas Baur
(Nuremberg: Verlag für moderne Kunst, 2008): 73.

Fig. 9: Emily Jacir, "Material for a Film," Performance, Sydney 2006, in
Emily Jacir, ed. Roland Wäspe & Andreas Baur
(Nuremberg: Verlag für moderne Kunst, 2008): 68–69.

Fig. 10: Emily Jacir, Detail from "Material for a Film" (2005 ongoing), in
Emily Jacir, ed. Roland Wäspe & Andreas Baur
(Nuremberg: Verlag für moderne Kunst, 2008): 65.

6. Dialogic Imagination and Critical Correlation – In Lieu of a Conclusion

How to interpretatively grasp these counter-representations of Arab-American histories and present-day realities? Characterized by a particular translocal and decentering quality, these works cannot be safely placed in the traditional matrix of ethnicity and cultural identity. They demonstrate both the diversity of the Arab cultural backgrounds on which they draw and the diverse ways in which these backgrounds play out, or are played out, in the US context and the Middle East. Whereas, for some, Arab-American art and literature must always narrate the story of leaving behind one's original identity and acquiring a new American one as a component of a worldwide Arab cultural diaspora, the works discussed in this essay choose, rather, to articulate the ambivalent experience of continuing cross-overs without final resolution. As acts of artistic research, the stories and visual works produced by Jacir, Sansour, Raad, and Alameddine implicitly contribute to the exploration of alternative epistemologies and research directions in transnational art and literatures and comparative cultural criticism.

These Arab Americans provide alternative ways of seeing, hearing, reading, and thinking that enable the remaking of the many worlds they live in simultaneously from within and against each other. To grasp their works theoretically, one first needs to view them as socio-cultural articulations shaped by and requiring the representational norms that they anticipate, local as well as global. Secondly, it is important to realize that these works are not only directed at the dominant Western discourse: They aim at the same time at, and critically question, the very mass-produced images of and from the Arab world by which they are determined. These transmigrant works powerfully illustrate how a cultural signifier does not necessarily carry a stable signified, a specific essence that it claims to encapsulate. They must therefore make a double effort when travelling from the Arab world to the West and back. On the one hand, they address a web of hegemonic Western ideas about what the 'East' is about, what it should be, and what it is expected to say. On the other hand, they confront dominant Arab discourses, which not only carry a lot of intellectual freight about the West that need to be shed but also participate in the local hegemonization of Orientalizing images. The artist and critic Jayce Salloum puts this productive dilemma as follows:

> How do you represent the unrepresentable – unrepresentable due to
> overexposure or lack of exposure? [...] When the Arab subject speaks,
> who listens and with what preconceived notions constricting the inter-
> pretation of these words and images? We do not perceive without a
> massive amount of baggage informing or misinforming us.[32]

Of course, one needs to revisit Michel Foucault's notion of the archive[33] as
well as his celebration of modern literature and art as counter-discourse[34] to
understand the particular cross-cultural practice at work here. One is also
tempted to resort to Mikhail Bakhtin, who, in his 1975 essay "Discourse in the
Novel," argues that "every word is directed toward an *answer* and cannot
escape the profound influence of the answering word it anticipates."[35] In the
context of this essay, Foucault's sceptical archaeology of the production and
dissemination of meaning and Bakhtin's argument about the dialogic principle of novel-writing bring up two important issues: the overlapping of the
abstract formal and the socio-political and ideological in the artistic and
literary production of Arab-American transmigrants and its potential recipients. In these works, the gaze of the anticipated watcher/listener rather than
the genesis, functioning, and effects of aesthetic forms or images advances to
the main subject-matter. Contemporary literary and artistic production by
Arab Americans is more preoccupied with the seductiveness of critical practices than with the creation of new (aesthetic) forms.

The cultural articulations discussed not only speak against dominant narratives – Western and non-Western alike. They are also speaking from specific
histories – American histories and Arab histories. They are not articulations of
some abstract national or ethnic identity or of an unknown hidden Oriental

---

[32] Jayce Salloum, "History of Our Present: New Arab Film and Video," *Rouge* 1
(2003), http://www.rouge.com.au/1/arab.html (accessed 25 June 2011).

[33] Michel Foucault, *Archeology of Knowledge*, tr. A.M. Sheridan Smith (*L'Archéologie du savoir*, 1969; tr. 1972, London & New York: Routledge, 2002): 142–50.

[34] Michel Foucault, *The Order of Things: Archaeology of the Human Sciences* (*Les
Mots et les choses: Une archéologie des sciences humaines*, 1966; tr. 1970; London,
New York: Routledge, 2002): 48.

[35] Mikhail M. Bakhtin, "Discourse in the Novel," tr. Caryl Emerson & Michael Holquist, in *Problems of Literature and Esthetics* (*Voprosy literatury i estetiki*, 1975), repr.
in *The Dialogic Imagination: Four Essays by M.M. Bakhtin*, ed. Michael Holquist (U
of Texas Slavic Series 1; Austin: U of Texas P, 1981): 280.

world but semi-documentary expressions within something.[36] "Forming itself in an atmosphere of the already spoken"[37] and using "that which has not yet been said"[38] as a starting point, these works perform acute expressions within a concrete historical moment under the global condition of decreasing Western cultural hegemony and postcolonial migrations. They thus need to be seen as a social phenomenon rather than an aesthetic display. Arab-American transmigrant writers and artists are speaking to their own realities and charting a space for their own voices. What is highlighted is the act of speaking or narrating and the dialectical relationship between the speaker and those spoken to. Speech itself is laid bare and layered between (hi)stories, between the fields of competing prefigured images, and between competing frames of reference. Hence, we are dealing with statements that explicitly reflect the intertextualities and interpictoralities in which they are grounded. These ficto-critical articulations make an argument while telling stories and producing images.[39]

However, the critical inquiries and heterodox provocations at stake do not just counter what passes for representation by Westerners, but also produce stories and images that challenge Occidentalist perceptions.[40] Claiming and reconstructing an agency that is as self-questioning as self-determining, the works of Sansour, Jacir, Alameddine, and Raad have the potential to blur mutually excluding essentialist identity constructions – the potential for what the Lebanese writer and critic Elias Khoury calls "identification through correlation."[41] In my view, these works can be grasped as expressions of a new postcolonial didactics (and maybe a decolonized future epistemology) of cross-cultural correlation. I read them as literary and artistic articulations of the critical project of linking the universalist Western conceptions of alterity and the diverse and often marginalized experiences of other(ed) people within

---

[36] Wilson–Goldie, "Off the Map," 65.

[37] Bakhtin, "Discourse in the Novel," 280.

[38] "Discourse in the Novel," 280.

[39] See Stephen Muecke, "The Fall: Fictocritical Writing," *Parallax* 8.4 (2002): 108–12.

[40] Sadik Al-Azm, "Orientalism, Occidentalism, and Islamism," *Comparative Studies of South Asia, Africa and the Middle East* 30.1 (2010): 6–13.

[41] Elias Khoury, "Reading Arabic," in *DisOrientation: Contemporary Arab Artists from the Middle East / Zeitgenössische arabische Künstler aus dem Nahen Osten* (Berlin: Haus der Kulturen der Welt, 2003): 12.

other worlds. To evaluate this particular quality, the research focus must be on the specific conditions determining the emergence and acceptance of Arab-American transmigrant works – including resistance and revisions instead of ex-ante synthesizing and dismissing them into a depoliticized sphere of theoretical transculturality. They need to be evaluated against those situations in which they themselves are playing a role in their own worldliness.

There is no definite conclusion to this ongoing project. Provisional insights are usually better had from literature than from scholarship. The following words are those of Mohammad, the main narrator and anti-hero in Rabieh Alameddine's novel *Koolaids*. While dying from AIDS in San Francisco, he remembers a skyjacking scene from the famous 1986 Hollywood action movie *Delta Force*. The passage not only addresses the dominant Arab screen image of the hostage-taking terrorist,[42] but at the same time criticizes the common (neo)colonial conceptualization of the Arab world as an exterritorial playground and world-historical stage of Western civilization; a perception that reduces cities like Cairo and Beirut to being mere copies, extensions, or appendices of the Western metropolis.[43]

> One of the hijackers in the movie tells the hostages that the *New Jersey* bombed Lebanon. The priest, one of the hostages, denies it. He says Americans never bombed Beirut. There is no rebuttal. When the hijacked plane lands in Beirut, one of the passengers said this used to be a wonderful city. You could do whatever you want. I couldn't believe what he said next. Beirut used to be the Las Vegas of the Middle East. Now that's fucking insulting.[44]

Eroding the referential system by which we are used to position ourselves against others, contemporary articulations of Arab-American transmigration unsettle our convictions regarding our own cultural and epistemic location. These works do not claim to be located in a fixed place that is defined by static referential entities of belonging; rather, they represent the dynamic experience of translocal conjunctions between the referential virtuality and material power of circulating cultural signs. Sensitizing us to our provisional

---

[42] Jack G. Shaheen, *Reel Bad Arabs: How Hollywood Vilifies a People* (New York & Northampton MA: Olive Branch, 2001).

[43] Cairo in the early-twentieth century has been described as Paris on the Nile. Beirut was known as the Paris of the Middle East. Before the so-called civil war, Lebanon was represented in Western debates as the Switzerland of the Arab world.

[44] Alameddine, *Koolaids*, 244.

location in correlation with other spaces and places, they can trigger critical reflection on the performative and narrative process of identification as a process of identifying other locations.[45] Demonstrating that we always speak, write, and act within concrete political or cultural relations, these works not only prompt a critical rethinking of the global circulation of cultural representations, but also an understanding of their ambiguities and collisions. The transmigrant artist and writers discussed in this essay thus intervene in both the imagined exceptionality of the local and the all too often overestimated continuity of the global.

In lieu of deliberatively presenting a well-balanced coda or offering a one-sided conclusion, I finish up this essay with another literary disorientation. Intending to provoke (a continuing conversation), I quote from the opening of Rihani's *Book of Khalid*. Here the anonymous editor–transcriber, who presents his English text as a translation based on the Arabic manuscript of Khalid's neo-Byronic autobiography and the French *histoire intime* written by his Sancho Panza-like companion Shakib, radically questions the possibility of assigning the Arab-American narrative's final cultural location. Weakening the readers' Orientalist orientation, he asks us to question our own subject-position as well as that of our formerly silent object:

> For we are all tourists, in a certain sense, and this world is the most ancient of monuments. We go through life as those pugreed-solar-hatted-Europeans go through Egypt. We are pestered and plagued with guides and dragomans of every rank and shade; [...]. And there thou art left in perpetual confusion and despair. Where wilt thou go? Whom wilt thou follow? [...] No; travel not on a Cook's ticket; avoid the guides.[46]

WORKS CITED

Anon. "When an Arab Enclave Thrived Downtown," *The New York Times* (25 August 2010): A16, New York edition.

Anon. "Walid Ra'ad – Scratching on Things I Could Disavow," *Kunstaspekte*, http://www.kunstaspekte.de/index.php?action=termin&tid=52070 (accessed 22 September 2011).

---

[45] Irit Rogoff, "The Where of Now," *Kein.org* (8 April 2006), http://www.kein.org /node/64 (accessed 24 September 2011).

[46] Rihani, *The Book of Khalid*, 5.

Alameddine, Rabih. *I, the Divine: A Novel in First Chapters* (New York: W.W. Norton, 2001).

——. *The Hakawati* (New York: Alfred A. Knopf, 2008).

——. *Koolaids: The Art of War* (London: Abacus, 1998).

Al-Azm, Sadik. "Orientalism, Occidentalism, and Islamism," *Comparative Studies of South Asia, Africa and the Middle East* 30.1 (2010): 6–13.

Anderson, Terry A. *Den of Lions* (New York: Ballantine, 1994).

Ashcroft, Bill, Gareth Griffiths & Helen Tiffin. *The Empire Writes Back: Theory and Practice in Post-Colonial Literatures* (London & New York: Routledge, 1989).

The Atlas Group / Walid Raad. "Civilizationally, We Do Not Dig Holes To Bury Ourselves," in *Tamáss: Contemporary Arab Representations Beirut / Lebanon 1*, ed. Catherine David (Barcelona: Fundació Antoni Tàpies, 2002): 122–37.

Bakhtin, Mikhail M. "Discourse in the Novel," tr. Caryl Emerson & Michael Holquist, in *Problems of Literature and Esthetics* (*Voprosy literatury i estetiki*, 1975), repr. in *The Dialogic Imagination: Four Essays by M.M. Bakhtin*, ed. Michael Holquist (U of Texas Slavic Series 1; Austin: U of Texas P, 1981): 259–422.

Foucault, Michel. *Archeology of Knowledge*, tr. A.M. Sheridan Smith (*L'Archéologie du savoir*, 1969; tr. 1972; London & New York: Routledge, 2002).

——. *The Order of Things: Archaeology of the Human Sciences* (*Les Mots et les choses: Une archéologie des sciences humaines*, 1966; tr. 1970, London & New York: Routledge, 2002).

Ghazoul, Ferial J. *Nocturnal Poetics: The Arabian Nights in Comparative Context* (Cairo: American U in Cairo P, 1996).

Glick Schiller, Nina, Linda Basch & Cristina Szanton Blanc. "From Immigrant to Transmigrant: Theorizing Transnational Migration," *Anthropological Quarterly* 68.1 (January 1995): 48–63.

Göckede, Regina. "Zweifelhafte Dokumente – Die zeitgenössische arabische Kunst, Walid Raad und die Frage der Re-Präsentation," in *Der Orient, die Fremde: Positionen zeitgenössischer Kunst und Literatur*, ed. Regina Göckede & Alexandra Karentzos (Bielefeld: transcript, 2006): 185–203.

Hassan, Waïl S. "The Rise of Arab-American Literature: Orientalism and Cultural Translation in the Work of Ameen Rihani," *American Literary History* 20.1–2 (Spring–Summer 2008): 245–75.

Khoury, Elias. "Ar-riwaya wa miraya al-waqi' al-maksur" ("The Novel and the Broken Mirror of Reality"), *Al-Mulhaq ath-Thaqafi / An-Nahar* (25 May 1996): 18–19; (1 June 1996): 18–19.

——. "Reading Arabic," in *DisOrientation: Contemporary Arab Artists from the Middle East / Zeitgenössische arabische Künstler aus dem Nahen Osten* (Berlin: Haus der Kulturen der Welt, 2003): 10–13.

Lawrence, D.H. "The Spirit of Place" (1923), in *Studies in Classic American Literature*, ed. Ezra Greenspan, Lindeth Vasey & John Worthen (Cambridge: Cambridge UP, 2003): 13–19. Original version in the *English Review* 27 (1918): 319–31.

Muecke, Stephen. "The Fall: Fictocritical Writing," *Parallax* 8.4 (2002): 108–112.

Nash, Geoffrey. *The Anglo-Arab Encounter: Fiction and Autobiography by Arab Writers in English* (Bern & New York: Lang, 2007).

Queijan, Naji. "The Formation of the Universal Self," in *Ameen Rihani: Bridging East and West. A Pioneering Call for Arab–American Understanding*, ed. Nathan C. Funk & Betty J. Sitka (Lanham MD: UP of America, 2004): 83–92.

Rihani, Ameen Fares. *The Book of Khalid* (New York: Dodd, Mead & Company, 1911).

Rogers, Sarah. "Forging History, Performing Memory: Walid Raad's The Atlas Project," *Parachute (Beyrouth_Beirut)* 108 (2002): 68–79.

Rogoff, Irit. "The Where of Now," *Kein.org* (8 April 2006), http://www.kein.org/node/64 (accessed 24 September 2011).

Said, Edward W. *Culture and Imperialism* (1993; New York: Vintage, 1994).

——. "Permission to Narrate," *Journal of Palestine Studies* 13.3 (1984): 27–48.

Salih, Tayeb. *Season of Migration to the North*, tr. Denys Johnson–Davies (*Mausim al-hijra ila-sh-shamal,* 1967; tr. 1969; London: Heinemann, 2010).

Salloum, Jayce. "History of Our Present: New Arab Film and Video," *Rouge* 1 (2003), http://www.rouge.com.au/1/arab.html (accessed 25 June 2011).

Shaheen, Jack G. *Reel Bad Arabs: How Hollywood Vilifies a People* (New York & Northampton MA: Olive Branch P, 2001).

Shaki, Evelyn. "Arab American Literature," in *New Immigrant Literatures in the United States: A Sourcebook to Our Multicultural Heritage*, ed. Alpana Sharma Knippling (Westport CT: Greenwood, 1996): 3–18.

——. "Politics and Exclusion: The Arab American Experience," *Journal of Palestine Studies* 16.2 (1987): 11–28.

Shehadeh, Raja. *The Third Way: A Journal of Life in the West Bank* (London: Quartet, 1982).

Sutherland, Tom. *At Your Own Risk: An American Chronicle of Crisis and Capitivity in the Middle East* (Golden CO: Fulcrum, 1996).

Venn–Brown, Janet, ed. & tr. *For a Palestinian: A Memorial to Wael Zuaiter* (*Per un Palestinese,* 1979; London & Boston MA: Kegan Paul International, 1984).

Wilson–Goldie, Kaelen. "Off the Map: Contemporary Art in the Middle East," in *Future of Tradition, the Tradition of Future: 100 Jahre nach der Ausstellung Meisterwerke muhammedanischer Kunst in München*, ed. Chris Dercon, León Krempel & Avinoam Shalem (Munich: Haus der Kunst, 2010): 60–67.

SECTION VI

⌘

MEDIA AND PERFORMANCE

Filming Illegals

—Clandestine Translocation and the Representation of Bare Life

LARS ECKSTEIN

1. Introduction

N THIS ESSAY, I DISCUSS the problematic of representing 'illegal' immigrants by investigating two very different attempts at capturing their predicament in British film. Human 'illegality' is not a marginal phenomenon; in summer 2005, the British government estimated that around 430,000 people lived in Britain entirely off the records, while the number of registered asylum seekers was put at roughly another 750,000.[1] Building on these figures, the London School of Economics estimated in 2009 that Britain hosts around 750,000 'illegals'.[2] Despite the fact that Britain and other European powers have rigorously stepped up measures over the last two decades to deter clandestine migration while encouraging so-called 'managed' immigration of non-Western elites, these figures indicate that people will continue to live 'illegally' in Britain (and throughout the West). A great number of illegals do not enter Europe in the back of a lorry or on fishing boats as the media often suggest, but overstay a regular visa or enter with forged documents. But, clearly, clandestine migration, too, is very unlikely to decrease anytime soon under the current economic world system and its reverberations

---

[1] See "430,000 illegal immigrants in UK," *The Guardian* (30 June 2005), www
.guardian.co.uk

[2] The London School of Economics suggests that an amnesty of illegal immigrants would lead to a benefit of up to three billion pounds for the British economy. See "UK immigrant amnesty 'worth £3bn'," *BBC News* (16 June 2009), http://news.bbc.co.uk /2/hi/uk_news/england/london/8102056.stm

for societies and ecologies in the South. According to several estimates, already more than 100,000 people try to enter the European Union clandestinely every year via the Mediterranean Sea alone, often by hazardous boat voyages which many do not survive.[3] Obviously, ever-new measures of force and fortification have had little effect on those desperate enough to risk imminent deportation and, ultimately, death.[4]

Illegal immigration into Europe and Britain is hardly a new phenomenon, yet in postwar Europe, when immigrant labour was in demand and few refugees reached European shores, they still had a relatively secure standing.[5] This changed quite dramatically with the establishment of a new world order after 1989 (and particularly with the ensuing Balkan crisis) which, together with the effects of (neoliberal) globalization, led to a sharp increase in clandestine migration and asylum claims. The legitimacy of political asylum has been systematically discredited in most western European countries ever since, and the chances of obtaining asylum began to be effectively minimalized. In this increasingly hostile context, the year 2001 marked another significant caesura in the British discourse on illegality. In the run-up to the general election in June, the issue of immigration and asylum for the first time became a central weapon in the campaigning of all political parties, but most notably of Labour, who denounced it as one of Britain's main economic problems. Such populism followed one of the most widely publicized tragedies of illegal people smuggling, when in summer 2000 fifty-eight Chinese immigrants were found suffocated in a sealed container in the port of Dover. But, of course, it was especially the events of September 11 that added a new dimension to the perception of illegals. Detailing "the impact of anti-terrorism measures on refugees and asylum seekers in Britain" in 2007, the Refugee Council UK not only confirmed the construction of an immediate link between asylum and terrorism in political debates and media reports in the wake

---

[3] James Kirkup, "EU plans flights to deport illegal immigrants," *The Telegraph* (29 October 2009), www.telegraph.co.uk (accessed 3 April 2010).

[4] A 2009 *Telegraph* report claims that the number of illegal migrants detected in lorries on British soil more than doubled over a recent two-year period. See David Barret, "Rise in illegal immigrants entering Britain," *The Telegraph* (7 February 2009) www.telegraph.co.uk (accessed 3 April 2010).

[5] Didier Fassin, "Compassion and Repression: The Moral Economy of Immigration Policies in France," in *The Anthropology of Globalization: A Reader*, ed. Jonathan Xavier Inda & Renato Rosaldo (Oxford, Malden MA & Carlton, Victoria: Blackwell, 2008): 212–33.

of 9/11, but also testified to the rather draconian effects of the ensuing anti-terrorism legislation on refugees – such as extended stop-and-search rights, detention rights, and ludicrously accelerated asylum procedures.[6]

It is probably no coincidence, therefore, that the illegal migrant took hold in British literature and film as a veritable icon at the beginning of the twenty-first century, between 2001 and 2002. It is remarkable, at least, that it is precisely this period which saw the publication of widely reviewed novels about illegals by Abdulrazak Gurnah (*By the Sea*, 2001), Benjamin Zephania (*Refugee Boy*, 2001), and, slightly later, Caryl Phillips (*A Distant Shore*, 2003), and of films by directors as notable as Stephen Frears (*Dirty Pretty Things*, 2002) and Michael Winterbottom (*In This World*, 2002). Apart from the latter example, all these texts and films present fully fictional versions of illegality which have served to counter and complicate the medial demonization of clandestine existence in post-9/11 Britain. What I am interested in here, however, is less centrally fictional presentations than representations that purport to more or less *factually document* the lives of those who live among us "visible but unseen," as Salman Rushdie famously put it in *The Satanic Verses*. My assumption is that the task of documenting the 'unseen' presence of illegals presents a particular challenge from two intersecting angles: one *political* and mostly familiar from the field of postcolonial studies; the other *conceptual* and rather familiar from the field of media studies, as I will outline in the following. I will then proceed to discuss two filmic representations in order to illustrate some of the opportunities and discontents involved in recent documentary approaches to illegal existence.

2. Documentary Representation and its Discontents

Let me begin, then, by briefly outlining some of the fundamental difficulties involved in the task of representing, or documenting, the existence of those who, on paper, do not exist. It is useful in this context to draw on Georgio Agamben's work in *Homo Sacer* (1998) and, more recently, its part-sequel *State of Exception* (2005),[7] the former of which, in retrospect, uncannily pro-

---

[6] Anja Rudiger, *Prisoners of Terrorism?: The Impact of Anti-Terrorism Measures on Refugees and Asylum Seekers in Britain*, Refuge Council research report. *Oxfam* (February 2007), http://repository.forcedmigration.org/show_metadata.jsp?pid=fmo :5440 (accessed 3 April 2010).

[7] Giorgio Agamben, *Homo Sacer: Sovereign Power and Bare Life*, tr. Daniel Heller-Roazen (*Homo Sacer: Il potere soverano e la vita nuda*, 1995; Meridian:

phesied, for instance, Silvio Berlusconi's declaration of a nation-wide state of emergency over the arrival of more than 10,000 boat people on Italian shores in the first half of 2008. Agamben's political philosophy is built around a distinction between what he calls "bare life" (pure biological existence or *zoé*) and "qualified life" (socially and politically involved and sanctioned existence or *bios*), which he traces from Aristotle's *Politics* to notorious biopolitical practices in the twentieth century. Crucially, Agamben sees "bare" and "qualified" life as interlinked in a genealogical dialectic, whereby sovereign power constantly needs to define itself against "bare life," and thus relies on the possibility of exposing subjects to it as an act of self-definition. "The production of a biopolitical body," Agamben famously argues with reference to Foucault, "is the original activity of sovereign power."[8] Without being able to do justice to the complexity of Agamben's argument, it should suffice to note that the qualification of 'bare life' (and its politicization in modern discourses) largely applies to the figure of the 'illegal' migrant. Once illegals have managed to slip into Europe and destroyed their documents of identification, as most illegal migrants do in order to delay deportation upon detection, they are indeed reduced to "bare life." They are persons living among us from whom civil liberties are withheld, and who have no agency to inscribe themselves in the discourse-formations of the social and political.

This, of course, has profound consequences for any project trying to document the lives of illegals. Without access to discursive power and in constant danger of discovery and deportation, illegal subalterns 'cannot speak' or represent themselves, but will necessarily be represented by others, if at all. This, as I will try to show in relation to documentary film in particular, puts a huge burden of responsibility on those who mediate the experiences of 'bare life' to predominantly Western audiences, and calls for creative strategies which acknowledge the viable role of the mediator. The problem of representation, here, applies in the sense of 'stepping in for' or 'speaking for' (as in the German *Vertretung*), in a situation where the documented subject is almost entirely at the mercy of the filmmaker and his or her crew. As I will argue in the following, filmmakers increasingly deal with this problem by reflexively questioning the mimetic principle of documentarism itself: i.e. by

---

Crossing Aesthetics; Stanford CA: Stanford UP, 1998), and *State of Exception*, tr. Kevin Attell (*Stato di eccezione* = *Homo sacer* II.1, 2003; Chicago & London: U of Chicago P, 2005).

[8] Giorgio Agamben, *Homo Sacer*, 6.

exposing the fictional elements and their own mediating position in the documentary process.

In this way, of course, they simultaneously respond to an intricately related and much larger problematic which has haunted cultural and media studies more generally: namely, the problem of representation as 'mediatizing' or 'staging' (very much in the sense of the German *Abbildung*). The familiar argument here is that the pretension of the documentary mode: namely, to represent the thing *as it is* without medial distortions, is a fallacy in the first place. There is no such thing as the innocent gaze; what is more, in the thoroughly mediatized world of the twenty-first century, our perception of the 'real' is by definition always prefigured by previous medial discourses. The precarious 'reality' of illegals is thus not exclusively challenged by their biopolitical exclusion in Agamben's sense, but is further complicated by the fundamental problem of deferral by mediatization.

Let me briefly turn to Slavoj Žižek and his famous post-9/11 piece "Welcome to the Desert of the Real" to elaborate on this dilemma.[9] Žižek proceeds from Alain Badiou's (debatable) observation that the   twentieth century is characterized by a "passion for the real."[10] This passion is "strictly correlative to the virtualization of our environs," as Žižek puts it, and has resulted in compensatory excesses of physical destruction, read by Badiou and Žižek as acts in pursuit of the bare "Real" which is increasingly lost in an everyday world of simulations. Žižek famously goes so far as to proclaim that "one can effectively perceive the collapse of the W T C towers as the climactic conclusion of the 20th century art's 'passion for the real'."[11] Personally, I find this type of pyschological rather than sociological argument slightly simplistic, not least in its glossing over concrete political and material processes. What I do find useful in Žižek's analysis, though, is the reflection upon how material

---

[9] Slavoj Žižek, "Welcome to the Desert of the Real," *The Symptom* 2 (Spring 2002), http://www.lacan.com/desertsymf.htm For Žižek's ambivalent reading of Agamben, see his "From *Homo sucker* to *Homo sacer*," in Žižek, *Welcome to the Desert of the Real* (London: Verso, 2002): 83–110.

[10] Alan Badiou, *The Century*, tr. Alberto Toscano (New York: Polity, 2007): 115. I find slightly dubious the postulation that the excessive violence of the twenty-first century directly correlates with a progressive virtualization of one's environs and is thus a compensatory phenomenon, not least because it seems to ignore the colonial difference (Mignolo) and the excessive, often genocidal historical violence outside of Europe.

[11] Žižek, "Welcome to the Desert of the Real."

and political processes are overwritten by mediatized images in such a way that our perception of them is inevitably refracted. Žižek's core argument in this context is precisely that 9/11 shattered not the West's fantasies about itself but, rather, its fantasies about the rest of the world. He writes:

> it is prior to the WTC collapse that we lived in our reality, perceiving the Third World horrors as something which is not part of our social reality, as something that exists (for us) as a spectral apparition on the (TV) screen – and what happened on September 11 is that this *screen fantasmatic apparition entered our reality.*[12]

In the age of post-9/11 anxiety, this implies, more generally, that there has been a tendency in Western medial discourse to acknowledge the clandestine global flows of human beings as a precarious reality whose "visible but unseen" presence in the West is of consequential – and at times only too real – effect. Žižek's "desire for the real," I would therefore argue, is also a desire to eventually get to 'really know' those spectres, those *homine sacri* haunting the affluent West.

Not only, then, do documentary projects which give in to this desire and attempt to document illegals bear the ethical weight of having to speak for a voiceless Other, but they are simultaneously confronted with the refracting quality and distancing thrust of medial representation itself, in an overall medial context that is already fraught with the distortions of sensationalism and paranoia. My central thesis is again that the documentary genre can only confront this situation by admitting to, and indeed manifestly capitalizing on, its own medial constructedness in various ways. I will in the following investigate two examples of 'new documentary' approaches to filming illegals and try to showcase their potentials and limitations.[13] The first is Sorious Samura's TV feature *Living with Illegals*, shot and first screened in 2006.

3. Sorious Samura, *Living With Illegals* (2006)

Sorious Samura came to Britain himself as a refugee from Sierra Leone in the late-1990s, and, living and working in London for the past ten years, now holds a British passport. He made his breakthrough as one of the most celebrated documentary film makers of our time with his coverage of the brutal

---

[12] "Welcome to the Desert of the Real."

[13] *Constructing Media Reality: The New Documentarism*, ed. Eckart Voigts–Virchow & Christiane Schlote, special issue of *ZAA* 56.2 (2008).

climax of the Sierra Leonean civil war in January 1999, staying behind as the last remaining journalist in Freetown filming the unspeakable atrocities committed by RUF rebels whilst capturing the capital city. The CNN-produced *Cry Freetown* won him, among other prizes, an Emmy Award and a George Foster Peabody Award in 2001,[14] yet perhaps more importantly, it is said to have led to the establishment of a UN peace-keeping mission in Sierra Leone. Samura has been an established presence on CNN international and Channel 4 ever since as a senior spokesperson for the plight of Africa and the Third World. The feature which I discuss in the following is part of his documentary series "Living with." As the press release claims, this series establishes

> a new kind of journalism which not many others can do. It's 'real' reality TV – stories that offer a unique perspective into the lives of people facing terrible situations.[15]

The underlying concept is that Samura, for one month, lives the lives of the people he documents; thus, he assumes the identity of a refugee in Darfur in *Living with Refugees*, that of a starving Ethiopian villager in *Living with Hunger*, or of an orderly in a Zambian hospital in *Living with AIDS*. In *Living with Illegals*, he accordingly lives the life of an illegal immigrant for one month.

The DVD blurb text gives a rough idea of the content of Samura's feature, yet it already also highlights a peculiar conceptual blurring of the boundaries between fictional staging and 'real' experience on the level of story:

> In "Living with Illegals" award winning journalist Sorious Samura *becomes* an illegal immigrant trying to break into 'Fortress Europe'. He undertakes an epic journey, travelling with other immigrants from Africa through to Spain and France and finally crosses the Channel to Britain. He lives *in exactly the same conditions* as they do and smuggles himself illegally across borders. [...] Once Samura reaches 'dreamland Europe', he is surprised to find living conditions and scenes of desperation as bad as those in Morocco. He learns the 'tricks of trade' required to survive, he begs, he sleeps rough, sells cheap

---

[14] "Awards 1999–2006," *Insight TV News*, http://www.insightnewstv.com/awards (accessed 3 April 2010).

[15] Claudio von Planta & Simon Atkins, dir., "Living with Refugees (Surviving Sudan)," *Insight News TV* (4 December 2009), http://www.insightnewstv.com/refugees/ (accessed 3 April 2010).

goods on the streets and has to deal with unscrupulous smugglers to reach his destination.[16]

On the level of filmic discourse, the blending of fictional and documentary strategies is even more pronounced. Much of the material is shot with hand-held digital camera, or, alternatively, undercover filming gear installed by Samura himself, clearly aiming at an aesthetic of the clandestine and authentic. Other sequences, however, unmistakably imply the presence of a camera team filming Samura on his journey, ultimately providing the external perspective that is indispensable to the 'Living with'-concept, which, after all, requires that the documentary filmmaker Samura be portrayed as the protagonist of his own feature. Claims to authenticity are thus constantly paired with acknowledgments of the constructedness of the story. Even if one never sees a camera as wielded by a film crew, Samura repeatedly mentions the latter in his voice-over narrative (as in such remarks as "now my crew more or less waved good bye, they gave me 10 Euros and I am hoping to beg around and see how much I can raise").

The result of this is a stunning double movement. One the one hand, *Living with Illegals* stubbornly stakes its claims to the real: Samura "becomes an illegal immigrant," experiencing "exactly the same conditions" and is thus able to truthfully document what 'bare life' is like. On the other hand, the setup is also evidently fictional, with celebrity auteur Sorious Samura, once a refugee but now a British national leading, in Agamben's terms, a fully 'qualified life', in the undisputed lead role. One scene that illustrates well this strange oscillation between faction and fiction is this: picture Samura in a French train to Calais without a ticket, locking himself in the toilet. Hear Samura's voice speaking to the microphone of a secretly installed camera, on diegetic sound – the experiencing I, if you like – whispering:

> Someone has tried to open the door. I do not know who the hell it is. Every time the door goes, this scares me. It is like your heartbeat misses a beat.

Once Samura is found by the ticket inspector, listen to his voice-over comment, or narrating I, matter-of-factly explaining:

> I just got caught without a ticket a third of the ways to Calais. The crew had to buy my ticket for the rest of the journey. But it is feasible an illegal immigrant would have to jump many trains to get here.

---

[16] Sorious Samura, dir., *Living with Refugees*, Insight News TV (2006), DVD, blurb, my emphases.

Like so many others, this scene shows that, first, much of the 'reality' documented in *Living with Illegals* is a carefully staged one, second, that Samura
readily acknowledges this in the filmic discourse, and third, that the film
nevertheless steadfastly insists that this staged reality is as authentic as it gets.

What, then, is the rational behind this slightly twisted logic? If we believe,
as I do, that Samura has a genuine agenda and is ultimately interested less in
his own medial presence than in the concerns of actual illegal immigrants, it
must be this: Following Žižek's observation that Western audiences are prone
to simply shrug off the fates of the Third-World poor as "a spectral apparition
on the (TV) screen," Samura seems to believe that by representing his own
self-aware simulation of the real thing, as a celebrity mediator between First
and Third World, he will provoke a more empathetic response than by merely
representing the thing itself. This logic is in many ways nothing less than an
inversion of Baudrilliard: for Samura, the simulation of a simulation apparently does not lead to infinite deferral but ultimately provides the necessary
bridge to the original model.

4. Michael Winterbottom, *In this World* (2002)

Unlike Samura's *Living with Illegals*, Michael Winterbottom's highly acclaimed feature film *In this World*, winner of the Golden Bear at the Berlinale
in 2003, is not officially labelled a documentary, but falls within the genre of
cinematic fiction. It tells the story of two Afghan cousins, Jamal and Enyatullah, who embark on an epic overland journey from Peshawar on the Afghan–Pakistani border to Europe. The basic plot is that Enyatullah is sent to
London at considerable cost to help provide for his extended family in Peshawar. As he speaks no English, his orphaned younger cousin Jamal, who lives
in the refugee camp of Shamshatoo, accompanies him as an interpreter. Their
odyssey leads them through Pakistan and Iran to Turkey, from where they are
shipped in a sealed container to Italy. Only Jamal is shown as surviving this
leg of the journey, in a filmic sequence that must count among the most harrowing ever shot. He then continues on to Sangatte in the north of France, and
finally crosses the English Channel in the chassis of a truck. The story closes
with Jamal calling Enyatullah's uncle from a London café where he found
work as a dishwasher, telling him that his nephew did not make it and is "no
longer in this world."

In this World is in this sense much more self-consciously fictional than
Samura's documentary allows itself to be, as all the cast in the film are acting,

whereas in *Living with Illegals*, only Samura really does, and probably would not even quite call it that himself. Nevertheless, Winterbottom's film stakes its claims to the real almost as rigorously, and in a not entirely dissimilar fashion. Concomitant strategies of authentification can be traced both on the level of story and on the level of discourse. On the story level, Winterbottom and his scriptwriter Tony Grisoni adamantly tried to 'keep it real'; the opening sentence of the DVD's 'making of' feature accordingly states: "I think it is worth saying that we did not make anything up for the film."[17] Based on the information gathered from Afghan refugees living in Britain, Grisoni and Winterbottom embarked upon a research trip from Peshawar to Istanbul in October 2001, travelling, not unlike Samura, as refugees would, on lorries and pick-ups with the help of fixers and smugglers, meeting most of the people who would later play themselves in the film. Two months later, they returned to Pakistan with a minimal film crew, cast their lead actors Jamal and Enyatullah among the thousands of Afghan refugees in Shamshatoo camp and the town of Peshawar, and retraced their earlier trip with them, shooting the film with the actual fixers, police officials, café owners etc. they had met before. Winterbottom comments on the resulting layering of fiction and reality:

> The first person we met was Imran, a travel agent from Peshawar, and he became our fixer for the research trip and then again the fixer when we were filming. And he also acted the fixer in the film. I guess that is the relationship between fiction and reality we tended to forge: It is not a documentary; it is a fiction; people are acting; but generally, we found people who play themselves in the film.[18]

On the level of discourse, the film's anchorage in reality is strategically supported by a number of further techniques. This concerns, again, the use of digital video to create an aesthetic of the raw and authentic. The most ingenious twist, however, is the creation of opening and closing sequences which self-consciously establish a documentary frame of reference. Thus, *In this World* opens with coverage of the Shamshatoo refugee camp, using voice-over narration which crops up again some twelve minutes into the film, and then disappears. The factual tone and text clearly nod to the documentary genre:

---

[17] Tony Grisoni, in "The Making of," *In this World*, dir. Michael Winterbottom, The Film Consortium (2002), DVD.

[18] Michael Winterbottom, in "The Making of."

> 53,000 Afghan refugees live in Shamshatoo camp in the city of Peshawar in Pakistan. The first arrived in 1979 fleeing the Soviet invasion of their country. The most recent came to escape the US-led bombing campaign which began on October 7, 2001. Many of these children were born here, like Jamal ...[19]

This type of narrative is set to frames which crucially show children who directly interact with the camera, something that is absolutely taboo in traditional cinematography, which insists on the invisibility of the filming process. One way of reading this type of framing device is to follow Winterbottom himself, who remarks:

> it is easy to forget that Afghan refugees are just as interested in us as we are in them. [...] And so the idea of us being present and making a film was something we tried to include in the film itself.[20]

However, given that the camera, after the opening sequence, is 'invisible' again until the very final shots taking us back to Shamshatoo, the full effect is slightly more complex. What the sequence clearly also does surreptitiously is to condition the viewer to also perceive Jamal and Enyatullah's subsequent odyssey in the documentary mode initially established, even if the film does little to hide the fact that this journey is in reality a fictional simulation.

This strategic blurring of faction and fiction, again, should not be read as a playful device of defamiliarization or deferral; like Samura, Winterbottom makes use of his strategies to paradoxically both admit to the vanities of documentary realism *and* to insist on the representationality of his film. The fact that he triumphantly succeeded in the eyes of his critics and the wider public, however, ironically has to do with a final twist that did not lie in the filmmaker's own hands. In a curious case of life imitating art, Winterbottom's fictional protagonist Jamal decided to use the earnings he made with the film to retrace his trip to London shortly after the shooting ended and he was returned to Pakistan. Back in Britain, he immediately appealed for asylum (which he was denied by the British government, yet given permission to stay until his eighteenth birthday). Much more convincingly than Samura, who claims to have 'become' an illegal migrant, Jamal thus literally 'became' in many ways the illegal he acted in the film.[21]

---

[19] Winterbottom, *In this World.*

[20] Michael Winterbottom in "The Making of."

[21] That fact, that this twist was turned into one of the film's main marketing coups, ultimately vouching for its 'realness', should give us pause. But there is also something

5. Conclusion: The Politics of Representing Bare Life

What is my verdict, then, about the two approaches to filming illegals by Winterbottom and Samura? In order to come to some sort of conclusion, let me return to my earlier remarks about the twofold problematic of representation. My point was, first, that there is a prevailing desire to know the Other living in our midst in the age of post 9/11 anxiety, but that catering to what Žižek calls the "desire for the real" is inevitably complicated by the fact that any medial representation is just a simulation, a screen apparition, that may lead us away from the real thing, rather than closer to it. Both Samura and Winterbottom have clearly reacted to this challenge by disrupting the naive identification of the filmic image with reality, and by employing, in Brechtian terms, alienation techniques which in different ways admit to the construc-tedness and fictional elements of the documentary process. In Samura's case, this mainly concerns the semi-fictional doubling-up of the filmmaker himself as an illegal migrant to bridge the chasm between Western audiences and the screen apparition of 'real' illegals. In Winterbottom's case, we have an even more self-conscious and elaborate layering of fiction and faction on the story level, and a highly intricate blending of documentary and fictional modes on the level of discourse. In both cases, the 'desire for the real' on the part of the audience is thus not easily gratified, but instead, in a first instance, disrupted, complicated, and returned to the viewer. Both filmmakers seem to assume that this type of bouncing back of the 'desire for the real' encourages and helps Western audiences to see through the medial construction to the realities of 'bare life'. Ultimately, though, I believe that Winterbottom is much more successful in this vein.

This finally has to do with the second aspect of representation concerning the political dimension of documenting those who, as non-persons, have little or no authorial agency themselves. The major difference between Samura and Winterbottom here is that Winterbottom facilitated a film that admits to the presence of a Western film crew, but still primarily attempts to let the illegal migrants speak for themselves. Even if these migrants merely *act* their own lives as *potential* immigrants into Europe, the underlying impression, at least

---

genuinely affecting about the reciprocity between reality and fiction here. As Winter-bottom recounts, when Jamal, to their great surprise, joined him and his crew in the post-production process, it was almost uncanny to observe Jamal watching himself playing himself leaving behind at Shamshatoo camp his little brother, whom he had in the meantime left for good in real life.

for me, is still that the film is mainly in their own voice. In contrast, Samura's choice of doing the acting himself runs the danger of drowning, rather than amplifying, the voices of the 'real' illegals he films. Or, to put it more sceptically: whether through him his audiences perceive the realities of illegal immigration, as Samura hopes, or whether reception habits work rather more along the line of reality TV-shows such as *I'm a Celebrity – Get Me Out of Here*, based on the comic sensation of First-World celebrities volunteering to 'go native', is a difficult question to answer.

But these may be merely academic qualms. Surely, there are few others who, like Samura, reach as many viewers (including policy-makers) via his broad exposure on Channel 4 and particularly CNN International, whose journalistic conventions in many ways structurally prefigure his films. While I hold Winterbottom's take to be the aesthetically and conceptually more successful attempt at representing bare life, it is difficult to say which film has done more to eventually help those who are represented. Given the current political climate throughout a Europe still shaken by ongoing economic 'crises', there is little evidence that either (self-reflexive) art or political journalism has had much impact on the continuing biopolitical production of bare life in our midst. Still, should such an impact be at all possible, it seems that it is precisely through a creative marriage of the two that it may be brought about.

WORKS CITED

Agamben, Giorgio. *Homo Sacer: Sovereign Power and Bare Life*, tr. Daniel Heller–Roazen (*Homo Sacer: Il potere soverano e la vita nuda* = *Homo sacer* I, 1995; Meridian: Crossing Aesthetics; Stanford CA: Stanford UP, 1998).

——. *State of Exception*, tr. Kevin Attell (*Stato di eccezione* = *Homo sacer* II.1, 2003; Chicago & London: U of Chicago P, 2005).

"Awards 1999–2006," *Insight TV News*, http://www.insightnewstv.com/awards

Badiou, Alain. *The Century*, tr. Alberto Toscano (*Le Siècle*, 2005; New York: Polity, 2007).

Barret, David. "Rise in illegal immigrants entering Britain," *The Telegraph* (7 February 2009), www.telegraph.co.uk (accessed 3 April 2010).

Fassin, Didier. "Compassion and Repression: The Moral Economy of Immigration Policies in France," in *The Anthropology of Globalization: A Reader*, ed. Jonathan Xavier Inda & Renato Rosaldo (Oxford, Malden MA & Carlton, Victoria: Blackwell, 2008): 212–33.

"430,000 illegal immigrants in U K ," *The Guardian* (30 June 2005), www.guardian
    .co.uk (accessed 3 April 2010).

Kirkup, James. "EU plans flights to deport illegal immigrants," *The Telegraph* (29
    October 2009), www.telegraph.co.uk (accessed 3 April 2010).

Planta, Claudio von & Simon Atkins, dir. "Living with Refugees (Surviving Sudan),"
    Insight News T V (4 December 2009), http://www.insightnewstv.com/refugees/
    (accessed 3 April 2010).

Rudiger, Anja. *Prisoners of Terrorism?: The Impact of Anti-Terrorism Measures on
    Refugees and Asylum Seekers in Britain.* Refuge Council research report. *Oxfam*
    (February   2007),   http://repository.forcedmigration.org/show_metadata.jsp?pid
    =fmo:5440 (accessed 3 April 2010).

Samura, Sorious, dir. *Living with Refugees*, Insight News T V (2006), D V D .

"U K immigrant amnesty 'worth £3bn'," *B B C News* (16 June 2009), http://news.bbc
    .co.uk/2/hi/uk_news/england/london/8102056.stm (accessed 3 April 2010).

Voigts–Virchow, Eckart, & Christiane Schlote, ed. *Constructing Media Reality: The
    New Documentarism*, special issue of *Z A A* 56.2 (2008).

Winterbottom, Michael, dir. *In this World*, D V D , The Film Consortium (2002).

Žižek, Slavoj. "From *Homo sucker* to *Homo sacer*," in Žižek, *Welcome to the Desert
    of the Real* (London: Verso, 2002): 83–110.

——. "Welcome to the Desert of the Real," *The Symptom* 2 (Spring 2002), http:
    //www.lacan.com/desertsymf.htm (accessed 3 April 2010).

⌘

Translating the American Dream?
—A Brazilian Vision of the Promised Land

GUNDO RIAL Y COSTAS

1. Introduction

I N ANY POLYPHONIC TEXT, and particularly in a postcolonial sphere, overlapping meaning-constructions can be detected, and the ever-growing simultaneous flow of images and narratives[1] in a globalizing world adds further dimensions to this fact. This is, for example, the case with the over-determination of iconic representations without clearly defined referents. When meanings are stripped off their original contexts, historical connotations or rhetorical devices (like parody) may get lost in translation, and hermeneutic breakdowns can be triggered by the attempt to translate conflated cultural codes. In some cases, however, this loss may have the performative potential for doing it differently.[2]

The following essay singles out one concrete aspect in which the above-mentioned hermeneutic breakdowns become obvious. It tackles the ambivalence evoked by negotiations between the levels of words and images as well as their contexts and cultural conventions in order to uncover the tension between semantics, pragmatics, and iconic representation. The performative power of translation is exemplified by a recent Brazilian *telenovela* called *América*. For this migration saga, the scriptwriter literally and audiovisually translated 'American Dream' as "Sonho Americano" in Brazilian Portuguese.

---

[1] Arjun Appadurai, *Modernity at Large: Cultural Dimensions of Globalization* (Minneapolis: U of Minnesota P, 1996): 13; Scott Lash & Celia Lury, *Global Culture Industry* (Cambridge & Malden MA : Polity, 2007): 19.

[2] See Homi K. Bhabha, *The Location of Culture* (New York & London: Routledge, 1994): 175–98.

Equality of opportunity, economic success, and the idea of migration to the USA are all aspects of the hegemonically established signifieds inscribed into its signifier in American English: i.e. 'American Dream'. Nonetheless, by describing the migration of Brazilians to the USA, the author 'cannibalizes' the original ideas and reconfigures them in an audiovisual representation. Hence, the vector of the original meaning is shifted from the implication of historical European migration processes to the USA to those of Brazilians in the present time. Yet one of the underlying latent signifieds of 'American Dream' – economic success – has been preserved. One may ask, as a consequence, how far these overdetermined linguistic and cultural translations produce ambiguity, based as they are on similarities between the grand narrative of the American Dream and the more recent discourse of the 'Sonho Americano'. Against this background, theoretical approaches of cultural translation shall be used to contextualize the idiosyncrasies of the object of study, Brazilian *telenovelas*.

2. Translating Concepts and Cultures

This discussion is embedded theoretically in an argument concerned with the relationship between cultural concepts and translation. First, on a synchronic level, 'translation' will be regarded as the general principle of any form of (cultural) communication: i.e. of one linguistic element transported into another language by taking into account the cultural context. Secondly, on a diachronic and conceptual level, the historical formations and often heterogeneous genealogies[3] of meaning-construction shall be considered. Thirdly, going beyond the mere transportation of genealogical formations and concepts, Homi Bhabha's postcolonial sense of "cultural translation"[4] shall be taken as the basis for the analysis, as it describes the "interstitial"[5] processes of cultural difference inscribed in the "in-between" of translations.[6] In this context, the latter is of particular relevance for the (post)colonial situation in Brazil and the Americas generally. This can be attributed to the fact that the

---

[3] Michel Foucault, "Nietzsche, Genealogy, History," tr. Donald F. Bouchard & Sherry Simon, in *Language, Counter-Memory, Practice: Selected Essays and Interviews*, ed. Donald F. Bouchard ("Nietzsche, La Généalogie, L'Histoire," in *Hommage à Jean Hyppolite*, 1971; tr. New York: Cornell UP, 1977): 162.

[4] See Homi Bhabha, *Location of Culture*, 303–37.

[5] Bhabha, *Location of Culture*, 310.

[6] *Location of Culture*, 310.

very first encounters of the indigenous people with their European conquerors were frequently based on errors of translation[7] and can therefore be regarded as a specific type of hermeneutic breakdown. As a consequence, new terms had to be imagined or invented, often directly translated and imposed from the 'hegemonic' memories (mental references brought from Spain) of the matrix language.[8] Fourthly, one should bear in mind that all translation processes, even if ironically subverted or parodied, still share a degree of similarity with the matrix text.[9] Finally, although a translation may represent a transformation or a renovation of the source text, Walter Benjamin's insistence remains relevant – that the 'spirit' of the original has to be maintained.[10] The latter is further echoed by current globalization theory as elucidated by Arjun Appadurai's emphasis on the necessity of careful translations from context to context that consider the varying contextual conventions.[11]

3. Media, Messages, and Mediations

(Cultural) translation as a basis for communication and the performative potential of historical formation, both of which aim at similarity while leaving room for reconfigurations, constitute the above-mentioned theoretical principles which shall now be consolidated with the object of study, Brazilian *telenovelas*. The title of this section may therefore be read as an allusion to

---

[7] Tzvetan Todorov, *The Conquest of America: The Question of the Other*, tr. Richard Howard (*Conquête de l'Amérique*, 1982; New York: Harper & Row, 1984): 36.

[8] An example is Columbus's constant references to the existence of mosques on the subcontinent, evoking those in the South of Spain. Florian Borchmeyer, *Die Ordnung des Unbekannten* (Berlin: Matthes & Seitz, 2009): 372.

[9] Dorothy Kenny, "Equivalence," in *Routledge Encyclopedia of Translation Studies*, ed. Mona Baker & Gabriela Saldanha (1978; New York & London: Routledge, 2008): 97.

[10] Walter Benjamin, "The Task of the Translator: An Introduction to the Translation of Baudelaire's *Tableaux Parisien*," tr. Harry Zohn, in *The Translation Studies Reader*, ed. Lawrence Venuti ("Die Aufgabe des Übersetzers," in *Sprache und Geschichte*, 1927; tr. 1969; London: Routledge, 2000): 76.

[11] Arjun Appadurai, "Disjuncture and Difference in the Global Economy," in *The Anthropology of Globalization: A Reader*, ed. Jonathan Xavier Inda & Renato Rosaldo (Oxford, Malden MA & Carlton, Victoria: Blackwell, 2003): 52.

Marshall McLuhan's seminal idea that "the medium is the message"[12] and to the central concern, "from media to mediation," of the media philosopher Jesús Martín–Barbero.[13] In other words, the basic principles for the translation of cultures and their concepts also matter for the special dynamic of the processes of mediation involved in *telenovelas*.

Brazilian *telenovelas* are particularly grounded in the genre of melodrama. Unlike the rather traditional Hispano-American versions with their tendency to omit the integration of 'real' elements, they are audiovisual narratives which often incorporate fragments of TV news or amateur film footage while covering a wide range of current social or political issues. They have been produced for more than forty years as the most successful format of TV broadcasting in that country. This can be seen on an international level in the way in which *telenovelas* have been successfully exported to almost a hundred countries, including a large number with no similar cultural matrices.[14] Further evidence of this global media phenomenon is offered by its transmission slot: the main *telenovelas* are always aired at prime time, with more than half of the country's TV sets switched on to watch.

A look back in history may help us understand this phenomenon. First, a transition from a first to a secondary orality[15] can be observed in Brazil. Because the introduction of radio followed by TV had occurred before nation-wide literacy had been established, television assumed relatively uncontested importance. Secondly, because of great poverty in many regions together with high asymmetry in the distribution of wealth, *telenovelas* have become, for many, the only form of entertainment to which they have access. Thirdly, the constant modernization of their format has turned *telenovelas* into a market kaleidoscope in which commodities, (fashion) trends, and debates are depicted, yet in a specific aesthetic with mostly light-skinned actors (belying the country's ethnic reality).

---

[12] See his visionary work *Understanding Media: The Extensions of Man* (New York: McGraw–Hill, 1964) as well as Marshall McLuhan et al., *The Medium is the Message: An Inventory of Effects* (New York: Bantam, 1967).

[13] See Jesús Martín–Barbero, *De los medios a las mediaciones: Comunicación, cultura y hegemonía* (Mexico City: Gustavo Gili, 1987).

[14] Immacolata Vasallo Lopes, *Telenovela, internacionalização e interculturalidade* (2002; São Paulo: Loyola, 2004): 13.

[15] Sérgio Costa, "Der Kampf um Öffentlichkeit: Begriffe, Akteure, politische Dynamiken," in *Jahrbuch Lateinamerika: Analysen und Berichte: Medien und ihre Mittel*, vol. 28, ed. Wolfgang Gabbert et al. (Münster: Westfälisches Dampfboot, 2004): 28.

The latter can be further sustained by arguments regarding the indebtedness of the *telenovela* to the origin of the genre as well as its dynamic in society: unlike the frequently open-ended US series, Brazilian *telenovelas* have a closed structure and usually last about eight months, before they are replaced by the next one. During the screening time, a parallel kind of dramaturgy is created by a system of frequent advertising spots with the aim of enhancing the viewers' expectations regarding the main narrative. Furthermore, and following the tradition of their European precursor, the serialized novel, they are parcelled-out. Each chapter is subdivided into four parts. They are interrupted by 'cliff-hangers' in order to increase the tension, then continued after the commercial breaks or the following day.[16] The time-lags between the broadcasts of the narratives serve as vital vehicles for the transportation of the represented on-screen discussions from the narrative level to a discursive one. These viewing practices are continued in Brazil's living rooms, office parlours, waiting-rooms, and school-yards.

Consequently, it comes as no surprise that reception studies like that of Vasallo Lopes[17] should stress the narratives' potential to shape public opinion. According to this research, *telenovelas* also serve as a basis for both individual and collective identity-construction. They penetrate all layers of the population, all age groups, and both sexes, and they are transmitted to the most remote regions of the country. On the level of reception, many of the gestures or linguistic expressions depicted in these series will be imitated or parodied, frequently creating new fashion styles of talking.[18]

In this context, one also has to bear in mind the rather negative sides of the Brazilian culture industry: lacking an influential public TV system, the biggest private channel, TV Globo – which also produces *América* – holds the lion's share of audiences. As part of one of the largest media conglomerates in the world, Globo also owns other television stations, several radio stations, and newspapers. Thanks to this hegemonic constellation with a strong focus on its best-selling product, the *telenovela*, a complicated hierarchical scheme

---

[16] Roberta Manuela Barros de Andrade, *O Fascinio de Scherazade* (São Paulo: Annablume, 2003): 77.

[17] Immacolata Vasallo Lopes, *Vivendo com a telenovela: Mediações, recepção, teleficionalidade* (São Paulo: Summus, 2002).

[18] Vanessa Ferreira Costa & Marluce Zacariotti, "Telenovela e Merchandising Social: Ficção e Realidade," in *UNIrevista* 1.3 (2006): 1.

is at work.[19] Because of the large investment in this product, a high number of spectators is required, this being frequently connected to a formula for success that consists of re-adapting already aired narratives. One might assume, therefore, that the creative liberty of the screenwriters will be somewhat limited. This argument seems to be supported by the fact that the narrative must initially conform to general social norms, a generic expectation that is weakened by the obvious possibility, if the product is successful, for scriptwriters and directors to integrate such hotly debated topics as human cloning, interracial marriage, or undocumented migration processes into the narrative: Commercial success allows the author's imagination to run to the inclusion of controversial issues.[20]

4. Initial Dimension of Similarity:
Historical Narratives of Exceptionalism

The national narratives of both the USA and Brazil are based on biblical themes. This representation of the respective countries as promised lands can be traced back to the first colonial contacts. These originary topoi contribute to the construction of national narratives in which the USA has, since the nineteenth century at the latest, openly laid claim to a certain exceptionalism.[21] In Brazil, such a linkage occurred at a considerably later stage and to a smaller extent.[22] Brazil and the parts of the Americas that were 'discovered' first were not acknowledged as such until Amerigo Vespucci's letter from the New World initiated awareness about the 'new' continent.[23] Still, no single

---

[19] Mauro Alencar, *A Hollywood Brasileira: Panorama da Telenovela no Brasil* (Rio de Janeiro: Senac, 2002): 71–73.

[20] Ester Hamburger, *O Brasil antenado: A sociedade da telenovela* (São Paulo: Jorge Zahar, 2005): 163.

[21] George M. Frederickson, "Models of American Ethnic Relations: A Historical Perspective," in *Cultural Divides: Understanding and Overcoming Group Conflicts*, ed. Deborah A. Prentice (New York: Russell Sage Foundation, 1999): 25.

[22] Mary Del Priore & Lucy Murray, "A América no Teatro do Mundo: Uma Cartografia de Imagens," in *América Latina: Imagens, imaginação e imaginário*, ed. Bessone Tavares, Maria Tánia & Tereza Aline P. Queiroz (São Paulo: EDUSP, 1997): 502.

[23] Stefan Rinke, "25.4.1507: Tauftag Amerikas: Die Prägkraft einer Namensgebung," in *Amerika – Amerikas: Zur Geschichte eines Namens von 1507 bis zur*

signifier for the 'discovered' territory was in constant use, as indicated by the parallel synonymous usage of the notions of 'New World', 'Terra Brasilis', 'Terra Incognita', or 'America'.[24]

Whereas in the New World the territories held by the Portuguese remained more or less homogeneous,[25] the Spanish territories were fragmented over the centuries. A change could be observed in the nineteenth century with the initiation of the independence movements in Latin America. They were based on the dream of a single Hispano-American country[26] echoed by a philosophy of 'Nuestra América'.[27] Brazil was not included in this debate because of its conservative continuation as a monarchy. Yet, economic success gradually granted the country a privileged status in the region, expressed by a narrative that shifted from marginalization to exceptionalism.[28] The latter is also manifested in the attempts of Brazil to "latinize Monroism"[29] by allusions to the US doctrine.

Passing thus from a country described "as the land of the future"[30] due to its supposedly rather unused – exceptional – potential, Brazil, in recent decades, has played a vital role in South America, and its leadership has been recognized along with a corresponding narrative of a certain exceptionalism. Unlike this, in the USA, one specific narrative, that of the Pilgrim Fathers, eclipsed all others during the era of colonization and was instrumentalized as

---

Gegenwart, ed. Ursula Lehmkuhl & Stefan Rinke (Stuttgart: Akademischer Verlag 2008): 22.

[24] James Dunkerley, *The United States and Latin America: The New Agenda* (London: Institute of Latin American Studies, 1999): 14.

[25] Disputes about territory have existed since the 'discovery', as manifested, for example, by the *bandeirantes*, pioneers who would often invade the land of the Spanish colonies.

[26] Simón Bolívar, "Carta desde Jamaica," in *Ideas en torno de Latinoamérica*, ed. Leopoldo Zea (1814; Mexico City: Universidad Nacional Autónoma de México, 1986), vol. 1: 19.

[27] José Martí, *Nuestra América* (1891; Guadalajara: Centro de Estudios Martianos, 2002): 189.

[28] James Dunkerley, *The United States and Latin America*, 7.

[29] Oliveira Lima, *Pan-Americanismo: Monroe – Bolívar – Roosevelt* (Rio de Janeiro: H. Garnier, 1907): 6.

[30] See Stefan Zweig, *Brazil: A Land of the Future*, tr. Lowell A. Bangerter (*Brasilien: Ein Land der Zukunft*, 1941; tr. 1942; Riverside CA: Ariadne, 2000).

the blueprint for the imagination of a homogenizing national identity.[31] This is why the respective historical narratives placed such a strong accent on the idea of a new pilgrimage to the New World in order to build a "new Jerusalem."[32]

Despite this national construction by means of an imagined historical narrative, even in North America, an onomastic confusion long predominated. Several names were applied to the newly founded nation-state, such as "United Colonies of America" or "North America" or "Columbia."[33] With the entry of some of the basic principles of national identity-construction into the Constitution together with its economic rise, the USA, in the nineteenth century, consolidated itself as the world leader. Economic expansion was accompanied by a territorial one through the acquisition and invasion of territories, along with a linguistic phenomenon that reflected these processes by using the *totum pro parte* 'America' with an exclusive reference to the USA.[34] The latter was complemented by the development of the idea of pan-Americanism,[35] the expansion of US influence within the Americas. One should add, though, that, particularly since 9/11, US hegemony has entered a severe crisis. Comparing the two narratives of exceptionalism, one perceives a certain similarity, particularly expressed by the linkage between economic success and dominance.

⌘

[31] Lisbeth Fuisz, "We are the People: The U.S. Government's Recent Recruitment of Literature for Nation Building," in *Moment to Monument*, ed. Andrea Ochsner et al. (Bielefeld: transcript, 2009): 116.

[32] Peter Freese, *The American Dream and the American Nightmare* (Paderborn: Universitätsverlag, 1987): 15.

[33] Dagmar Bechtloff, "Imago Mundi Cartographica: Frühneuzeitliche Vor- und Darstellungen der Neuen Welt in Europa und Amerika," in *Amerika – Amerikas: Zur Geschichte eines Namens von 1507 bis zur Gegenwart*, ed. Ursula Lehmkuhl & Stefan Rinke (Stuttgart: Akademischer Verlag, 2008): 99.

[34] Stefan Rinke, "25.4.1507: Tauftag Amerikas," 8.

[35] Marat Antiásov, *Panamericanismo: Doctrinas y hechos* (Moscow: Progreso, 1986): 11.

5. Second Dimension of Similarity: Concepts of Dreams and Migrations

Fazer a América, is a direct translation from Italian (*fare l'America*) into Portuguese and means "to make America,"[36] referring to the mass migrations from Europe to Brazil at the end of the nineteenth century. Originally, it was an immigrants' narrative created by the arriving multitudes and, instead of entailing a national consolidation, it emphasized prosperity as well as the passing of the ocean. This is probably due to the fact that the groups of European immigrants came to only a few regions in Brazil and would often return to their homeland. This may also be the reason why, in the course of the twentieth century, the Italian contribution to the construction of a Brazilian nation-state became vital for the collective memory in addition to the linguistic expression: *Fazer a América* may be described as a 'secondary narrative', in that it dissolved in the official foundational myth of Brazil called *mestiçagem*, the supposed mixture of indigeneous people, Europeans and blacks, that resulted in the invention of the Brazilian nation.[37]

The concept of 'making America' was based on a mythic narrativization of some selected aspects of historical processes while negating or suppressing others. Today, the term has undergone a substantial resignification,[38] as it also refers to the emigration of Brazilians to the USA. Thus, the old idea of consolidating the nation-state, if only on a secondary level, has found a new dynamic which reverses the signified. Now it even contributes to questioning the nation-state by describing the movement of people leaving their country.

As regards the USA, the 'American Dream', too, has become a somewhat diffuse term, subjected to several reformulations, expansions, parodies, and rejections. The original idea behind it, "Life, Liberty and the Pursuit of Happiness,"[39] as expressed in the First Amendment to the US Constitution, refers to equality of opportunity and the belief in the achievement of prosperity. This

---

[36] Mary Del Priore & Carla Beozzo Bassanezi, *História das mulheres no Brasil* (São Paulo: Contexto, 1997): 11.

[37] See Gilberto Freyre, *Casa Grande e Senzala* (1933; Rio de Janeiro: Record, 1998).

[38] See, for example, Gundo Rial y Costas, "The (Trans)migrant in the Spotlight: Space and Movement in Brazilian Telenovelas," in *Aesthetic Practices and Politics in Media, Music and Art: Performing Migration*, ed. Davis Rocío, Dorothea Fischer & Joana Kardux (New York: Routledge, 2010).

[39] Lisbeth Fuisz, "We are the People," 111.

concept echoes the first ideas of the Pilgrims in connection with their plan to build a city on the hill.[40] During the process of European immigration in the late-nineteenth century, the notion of the American Dream was stressed as economic success by mixing hope with utopia. Since then, the idea has undergone many modifications owing to constantly growing claims for the inclusion of minority groups such as African Americans, Chicanos, Hispano-Americans, and Asian Americans. The increasing global political and economic presence of countries from other world regions has contributed to a reformulation of the American Dream. One of the major consequences is the newly contested role of the USA, whose exceptional position is currently becoming more and more vulnerable.

A comparison of the two narratives, American vs Brazilian, makes obvious that the case of Brazil represents a rather limited and more recent form of exceptionalism, with the idea of *fazer a América* as a secondary narrative. It concerns only one group of immigrants in some areas, from where it has evolved into the main foundation of *mestiçagem*. By contrast, in the USA one can observe a long, if debated, history of exceptionalism, with the American Dream, as one of its major expressions, entering a state of crisis in the last century. Nevertheless, one can also observe similarities between the two cultural narratives and concepts. One of these is, above all, the idea of economic success and dominion, but a partial correspondence of *fazer a América* and the 'American Dream' exists in the implication of the arrival of migrants in a new homeland and their aspiration to material prosperity.

6. *Telenovela*: American Dream Visions

América, the *telenovela* scripted by Glória Perez,[41] condenses historical and conceptual formations as well as shifts and similarities. The signifier of 'Sonho Americano' is used in a flexible relation to its US original. It therefore requires a conceptual link; accordingly, the following discussion shall employ a coupling of the two concepts – 'American Dream/Sonho Americano' – as an analytical tool.

---

[40] Dagmar Bechtloff, "Imago Mundi Cartographica," 100.

[41] Jayme Monjardim, Marcos Schechtman et al., *América* (screenplay by Glória Perez, producer Vera Daflon; Rio de Janeiro: TV Globo, 14 March–5 November 2005; ca. 203 episodes, 60 min. per episode).

The plot of the *telenovela* concerns the emigration of an undocumented Brazilian woman, Sol, to the USA via Mexico, after being deported twice. For her 'American Dream/Sonho Americano', Sol leaves her Brazilian boyfriend behind. In order to support her family in Brazil, she has to do odd jobs in the USA while living among other Latin American migrants in Miami, on the margin of the new host society. Sol finally falls in love with an Anglo-American who had been an acquaintance before and whom she originally marries in order to obtain a green card. At the end of the *telenovela*, the protagonist is deported to Brazil, starting a new life together with her US husband and their newborn son. *América* is complemented by a wide range of other narrative threads, all of which include certain types of aspirational realization, either as national Brazilian dreams, as American dreams in the USA, or as transnational 'American Dreams/Sonhos Americanos'.

The similarities between the signified dream constellations in different languages often produce moments of ambiguity in which the viewer does not know to which concept the signifier is linked and which one is being evoked. Recurring to the above-mentioned ideas of the transformative force of translation, I shall refer in particular to one specific scene in the *telenovela* under examination. In order to be more precise about the similarities in question, I will refer to verbal/iconic usages (such as *sonho americano*), symbolic linkage (as in such symbols of the American dream as the Statue of Liberty and the Empire State building), and thematic matters (the different realizations of dreams, as in the Brazilian vs American dream). The 'American Dream/Sonho Americano' is constantly mentioned in the *telenovela*, always in relation to desires about a future life in the USA or in Brazil. These recurrent references depict it as a dream realized in a country where everybody has everything, where young girls will become famous actresses, and where nobody has to suffer from hunger. On a metaphoric level, they partly echo the Pilgrims' early claims as well as the European immigrants' later hopes for economic security (as in the first episode of *América*). This is emphasized by several flashbacks during the protagonist's border-crossings into the USA or conversations about her 'dream mission'. The possibilities for realizing a Brazilian type of American Dream are limited to a more connotative referential scheme, such as alluding to possible constructions of a future life in that country, but without the verbal component of the 'dream'.

The symbolic linkages are strongly guided by the artifact of a snow globe, given to the protagonist in her childhood by her friend's aunt, who had emigrated to the USA. It contains miniatures of the Statue of Liberty and the

Empire State building, two of the main symbols of the 'American Dream'. Whereas the former refers specifically to the immigrants' dream, the latter signals economic prosperity as well as vertical US exceptionalism. In the course of the narrative, the object is literally transported to the USA by Sol when she emigrates there as an adult. When her 'American Dream/Sonho Americano', aimed at making it in the USA, finally shatters, the snow globe disappears. Again, possible forms of a Brazilian American Dream are depicted through the linkage to a national saint and to the double sense of constructing a home – in its immediate physical, domestic sense as well as in its meaning of a homeland.

Finally, the thematic references described may be considered as frequently fluid subcategorizations of latent references to the Brazilian American Dream. First, they depict the 'American Dream/Sonho Americano' in the USA, portrayed by Brazilian and Latin American expatriates living in a migrants' pension in Miami. Secondly, the Mexican owner Consuelo, together with family and guests from other parts of Latin America, represents a further element in the dream constellations conveyed (the Hispano-American version of the American Dream), while also evoking the above-mentioned Bolivarian dream of a unified Latin America. Thirdly, the Hispano-American dream-narrative is set up in contrast to the national 'Brazilian Dream/Sonho Brasileiro', that of the protagonist's former boyfriend Tião in the Brazilian hinterland. He follows the dream of his father as he builds a house with his wife in the place where he was born, in order to raise his future children there. The complexity of this dream configuration can be observed in the suppressed signified of 'American Dream' economic prosperity in this Brazilian version and possible mixtures with a Hispano-American one. Thus, some evidence of the transnational routes of the 'American Dream/Sonho Americano' is manifest in the decision of the rich upper-class woman Haydée from Rio de Janeiro to finally abandon the city for her old love Tony, a US citizen of Brazilian origin who lives in Miami. An additional case is that of the US-born Mexican Conchita leaving her country: for a romantic marriage with the Brazilian cowboy Carrerinha, whom she met in Miami, she emigrates to a small village in the rural area of São Paulo state in Brazil.

One sequence of scenes merges a large number of the similarities proposed and may therefore function as a trans-allegory: Still eighty episodes before the end of *América*, this sequence is taken from episode 123 depicting the 'American Dream/Sonho Americano' in a revealing constellation. In one scene, Sol works as a *tableau vivant* of the Statue of Liberty in Miami. With white make-up, she represents several of the 'American Dream/Sonho Americano' signifieds at the same time. She is a personification of the statue, virtually embodying the American Dream while she holds its main symbols, the torch and a copy of the Declaration of Independence, in her hands. In addition, the 'American Dream/Sonho Americano' refers metonymically to all Brazilians and other Latin Americans who come to the USA, and who are often doomed to do odd jobs. Further, on a metaphoric level, Sol is transformed into one of the icons of her childhood American Dream, that of the snow globe which contained the miniatures of the Statue of Liberty and the Empire State building. Ironically, Sol enacts the Statue of Liberty and is indirectly trapped in the – absent – material dream of prosperity, as people have to pay for gazing at her. Finally, irony is implied in the process of whitening through the white make-up with its implication of an enforced process of americanization. During the realization of the 'American Dream' it echoes the changing destiny of the European immigrants who came to the USA, recalling that, at the end of the nineteenth century, migrants from Southern Europe with a rather dark complexion were often refused entry.

The 'American Dream/Sonho Americano' constellation becomes even more obvious if one considers the continuation of the scene. While 'working' as the statue, Sol's former Brazilian boyfriend Tião and his new Brazilian girl-friend Simone pass by without recognizing her, thereby illustrating the invisibility of the American Dream to the Brazilian couple. Moreover, as they are in Miami only on vacation, they demonstrate that their own Brazilian American Dream will come true at home in Brazil when they build a house of their own and establish a family (with Simone already pregnant by Tião). The intended juxtaposition of the dream constellation – Sol's private dream vs the professional dream which she embodies for money – becomes even more salient in the next scene, when Sol begins to cry after recognizing the couple: while she is trapped in the 'American Dream/Sonho Americano', it literally dissolves as tears roll down her face. The vanishing of the dream is further accentuated by a melodramatic building-up of this moment, as a cloudburst completely washes away the peel of her 'American Dream/Sonho Americano', on the literal as well as on the metaphorical level. This is the case because Sol, unable to continue working, will receive no payment. Simultaneously, this can be considered an anticipation of the end of Sol's 'American Dream/Sonho Americano' twenty episodes later, when she realizes that it is over and all that is left is for her to return home to Brazil.

One might argue that the construction of ambiguous subject-positions and layered meanings is emphasized by a kind of oscillation between melodramatic consolidation and postmodern irony at the very end of the *telenovela*: Sol is deported back to Brazil, but returns with a US husband, a university lecturer, and their child. This could be conceived of as a possible continuation of the 'American Dream/Sonho Americano' – except that this 'Sonho Americano' is reduced to a metonym of the fulfilment of romantic love. From a different perspective, one might also interpret this final twist as suggesting the most successful dream, the return to one's home country, as stressed and complemented by Tião's and Simone's fulfilment of their Brazilian American Dream. On another level, an ironic distance is evoked: in one of the parallel narrative threads, the undocumented Latin American migrants in the Miami pension all win a green card in the lottery. They are thus allowed to remain in the USA, as they are granted the opportunity to legalize their 'American Dream/Sonho Americano'. This solution parodies the high improbability for the large majority of undocumented migrants in the USA to stay there on a legal basis.

7. Conclusion

The interpretation of a Brazilian *telenovela* as a cultural translation of the American Dream has established two dimensions of similarity. The first one, that of historical narrative, elucidates the fact that the US myth of exceptionalism is tied to the American Dream through references to equal opportunity, migration, hope of economic success, while prone to changes of fortune and reschedulings through circumstance. In the case of Brazil, the more recent narrative of exceptionalism is likewise linked to a certain notion of economic success. In the second dimension, a conceptual one, a similarity exists between the idea of the American Dream and that of *fazer a América*, with both describing, at least in part, processes of historical immigration linked to material prosperity. In addition, the resignification of the concept of *fazer a América* in Brazilian Portuguese describing migration from Brazil to the USA thus conflates historical processes of migration with present-day ones. As a consequence, semantic overdetermination is at work in the expression 'Sonho Americano' owing to certain similarities between US-American and Brazilian exceptionalism and the linkage between *fazer a América* and 'American Dream', emphasized by its resignification.

In the concrete example of the *telenovela América*, several of the constellations mentioned lead to a juxtaposition and even conflation by suggesting the coupling of the two concepts 'American Dream/Sonho Americano' along with that of the Brazilian American Dream. Condensed in a scene where the Brazilian protagonist Sol professionally represents the Statue of Liberty, the two signifiers transgress linguistic borders before summoning their respective signifieds. Both are materialized in the visions, dreams, or nightmares of historical and contemporary migrants. Engaging in dialogue with each other, they unite synchronic and diachronic meanings by also recalling the dreams of the Hispano-American migrants.

As a concluding remark, it may be proposed that something new can be observed in the different forms of similarities presented here: The visualization of the 'Sonho Americano', the Brazilian element of cultural difference in the American Dream, transcends the referential integrity of its established version. This raises the question of whether the USA is still the privileged country for best fulfilling the 'American Dream' – perhaps Brazil is an alternative.

WORKS CITED

Alencar, Mauro. *A Hollywood Brasileira: Panorama da Telenovela no Brasil* (Rio de Janeiro: Senac, 2002).

América, dir. Jayme Monjardim, Marcos Schechtman et al., screenplay by Glória Perez, producer Vera Daflon (Rio de Janeiro: TV Globo, 14 March–5 November 2005; ca. 203 episodes, 60 min. per episode).

Antiásov, Marat. *Panamericanismo: Doctrinas y Hechos* (Moscow: Progreso, 1986).

Appadurai, Arjun. "Disjuncture and Difference in the Global Economy," in *The Anthropology of Globalization: A Reader*, ed. Jonathan Xavier Inda & Renato Rosaldo (Oxford, Malden MA & Carlton, Victoria: Blackwell, 2003): 47–65.

——. *Modernity at Large: Cultural Dimensions of Globalization* (Minneapolis: U of Minnesota P, 1996).

Martín–Barbero, Jesús. *De los medios a las mediaciones: Comunicación, cultura y hegemonía* (Mexico City: Gustavo Gili, 1987).

Barros de Andrade, Roberta Manuela. *O Fascinio de Scherazade* (São Paulo: Annablume, 2003).

Bechtloff, Dagmar. "Imago Mundi Cartographica: Frühneuzeitliche Vor- und Darstellungen der Neuen Welt in Europa und Amerika," in *Amerika – Amerikas: Zur Geschichte eines Namens von 1507 bis zur Gegenwart*, ed. Ursula Lehmkuhl & Stefan Rinke (Stuttgart: Akademischer Verlag, 2008): 63–84.

Benjamin, Walter. "The Task of the Translator: An Introduction to the Translation of Baudelaire's *Tableaux Parisien*," tr. Harry Zohn, in *The Translation Studies Reader*, ed. Lawrence Venuti ("Die Aufgabe des Übersetzers," in *Sprache und Geschichte*, 1927; tr. 1969; London: Routledge, 2000): 75–86.

Bhabha, Homi K. *The Location of Culture* (New York & London: Routledge, 1994).

Bolívar, Simón. "Carta desde Jamaica," *Ideas en torno de Latinoamérica*, ed. Leopoldo Zea, vol. 1 (1814; Mexico City: Universidad Nacional Autónoma de México, 1986): 19–36.

Borchmeyer, Florian. *Die Ordnung des Unbekannten: Von der Erfindung der neuen Welt* (Berlin: Matthes & Seitz, 2009).

Costa, Sérgio. "Der Kampf um Öffentlichkeit: Begriffe, Akteure, politische Dynamiken," in *Jahrbuch Lateinamerika: Analysen und Berichte: Medien und ihre Mittel*, vol. 28, ed. Wolfgang Gabbert et al. (Münster: Westfälisches Dampfboot, 2004): 13–31.

Del Priore, Mary, & Carla Beozzo Bassanezi. *História das mulheres no Brasil* (São Paulo: Contexto, 1997).

Del Priore, Mary, & Lucy Murray. "A América no Teatro do Mundo: Uma Cartografia de Imagens," in *América Latina: Imagens, imaginação e imaginário*, ed. Bessone Tavares, Maria Tánia & Tereza Aline P. Queiroz (São Paulo: EDUSP, 1997): 499–512.

Dunkerley, James. *The United States and Latin America: The New Agenda* (London: Institute of Latin American Studies, 1999).

Ferreira Costa, Vanessa, & Marluce Zacariotti. "*Telenovela* e Merchandising Social: Ficção e Realidade," in *UNIrevista* 1.3 (2006): 1–13.

Foucault, Michel. "Nietzsche, Genealogy, History," tr. Donald F. Bouchard & Sherry Simon, in *Language, Counter-Memory, Practice: Selected Essays and Interviews*, ed. Donald F. Bouchard ("Nietzsche, La Généalogie, L'Histoire," in *Hommage à Jean Hyppolite*, 1971; New York: Cornell UP, 1977): 139–64.

Frederickson, George M. "Models of American Ethnic Relations: A Historical Perspective," in *Cultural Divides: Understanding and Overcoming Group Conflicts*, ed. Deborah A. Prentice (New York: Russell Sage Foundation, 1999): 23–34.

Freese, Peter. *The American Dream and the American Nightmare* (Paderborn: Universitätsverlag, 1987).

Freyre, Gilberto. *Casa Grande e Senzala* (1933; Rio de Janeiro: Record, 1998).

Fuisz, Lisbeth. "We are the People: The U.S. Government's Recent Recruitment of Literature for Nation Building," in *Moment to Monument*, ed. Andrea Ochsner et al. (Bielefeld: transcript, 2009): 111–21.

Hamburger, Ester. *O Brasil antenado: A sociedade da telenovela* (São Paulo: Jorge Zahar, 2005).

Kenny, Dorothy. "Equivalence," in *Routledge Encyclopedia of Translation Studies*, ed. Mona Baker & Gabriela Saldanha (1998; New York & London: Routledge, 2008): 77–80.

Lash, Scott, & Celia Lury. *Global Culture Industry* (Cambridge & Malden M A: Polity, 2007).

Lima, Oliveira. *Pan-Americanismo: Monroe – Bolívar – Roosevelt* (Rio de Janeiro: H. Garnier, 1907).

McLuhan, Marshall. *Understanding Media: The Extensions of Man* (New York: Mc-Graw–Hill, 1964).

——, et al. *The Medium is the Message: An Inventory of Effects* (New York: Bantam, 1967).

Martí, José. *Nuestra América* (1891; Guadalajara: Centro de Estudios Martianos, 2002).

Martín–Barbero, Jesús. *De los medios a las mediaciones* (Barcelona: Gustavo Gili, 1987).

Rial y Costas, Gundo. "The (Trans)migrant in the Spotlight: Space and Movement in Brazilian *Telenovelas*," in *Aesthetic Practices and Politics in Media, Music and Art: Performing Migration*, ed. Rocío Davis, Dorothea Fischer & Joana Kardux (New York & London: Routledge, 2011): 125–41.

Rinke, Stefan. "25.4.1507: Tauftag Amerikas: Die Prägkraft einer Namensgebung," in *Amerika – Amerikas: Zur Geschichte eines Namens von 1507 bis zur Gegenwart*, ed. Ursula Lehmkuhl & Stefan Rinke (Stuttgart: Akademischer Verlag 2008): 85–105.

Todorov, Tzvetan. *The Conquest of America: The Question of the Other*, tr. Richard Howard (*Conquête de l'Amérique*, 1982; New York: Harper & Row, 1984).

Vasallo Lopes, Immacolata. *Telenovela, internacionalização e interculturalidade* (São Paulo: Loyola, 2004).

——. *Vivendo com a telenovela: Mediações, recepção, teleficionalidade* (São Paulo: Summus, 2002).

Zweig, Stefan. *Brazil: A Land of the Future*, tr. Lowell A. Bangerter (*Brasilien: Ein Land der Zukunft*, 1941; tr. 1942; Riverside C A: Ariadne, 2000).

⌘

Curio(us) Translocations
—Site-Specific Interventions in Banglatown, London

KATHY–ANN TAN

Culture and tourism are destined once and for all to be together.[1]

All over the world now we find these 'attractions' – of little significance for the inward life of a people, but wonderfully saleable as a
tourist commodity.[2]

THIS ESSAY SETS OUT TO INVESTIGATE a particular mode of encounter with cultural difference that is performed in a specific site of postcolonial translocation – the tourist zone. In cities with large immigrant or minority populations, enclaves that have come to be known as China-
town, Little Italy, Little Vietnam, and Banglatown allegedly offer tourists a
taste of the 'authentic' (from culinary delights to cultural practices), yet at the
same time they are clearly inauthentic, 'disneyfied', 'exotic' re-inventions that
are often the result of urban regeneration and cultural-planning policies. I
explore how the popularity of tourist zones illustrates the fact that cultural difference sells – that it can effectively be packaged, sold, consumed – and thus
functions as a commodity. This raises questions with regard to the relation-

---

[1] Leo van Nispen, Director of the International Council on Monuments and Sites
(ICOMOS), quoted in Greg Richards, "Introduction" to *Cultural Tourism in Europe*,
ed. Richards (Wallingford: CAB International, 1996): 17. A comprehensive and seminal study with comparative transnational statistics, the book was subsequently reissued
by the Association for Tourism and Leisure Education (ATLAS) (2005), http://www
.tram-research.com/cultural_tourism_in_europe.pdf (accessed 26 February 2010).

[2] Daniel Boorstin, *The Image: A Guide to Pseudo-Events in America* (New York:
Harper & Row, 1964).

ships between tourists as consumers and local communities as producers of cultural experiences. Also examined are some of the negative outcomes of this process of commodification, such as cultural stereotyping, the imposition of homogeneity, and the erasure of diversity and internal differences in migrant communities. The elision of ethnic, religious, linguistic, gender, and class disparities in 'multicultural' urban districts and the reductive stereotyping and labelling of all migrants as 'them', however, ironically reifies the notion of difference and reinforces categories of 'us' and 'them'. In order to explore the nature of the tourist zone as a site of postcolonial translocation and to examine in greater detail the efficacy of art's potential intervention in the workings of cultural tourism, I shall be looking at *Curio*, an exhibition that attempted to disrupt the tourist zone of Banglatown in London's East End in 2002. It might be useful, however, to begin with a conceptual and contextual outline of the development of cultural tourism.

Within the scope of this essay, the term 'culture' will be understood to refer primarily to "the distinctive ideas, customs, social behaviour, products, or way of life" of a community, and not the "artistic and intellectual development"[3] of an individual.[4] More pertinently, the term 'cultural tourism' will be used to denote the following:

---

[3] "Culture," *Oxford English Dictionary* (2008), http://oed.com/view/Entry/45746 (accessed 10 March 2010).

[4] It is impossible to do justice in a few lines to the complex debate surrounding the concept of 'culture'. Kroeber and Kluckhohn's comprehensive 1952 survey of culture aptly illustrates this in its compilation of no fewer than 164 definitions of the term, grouped into seven different categories. See Alfred L. Kroeber & Clyde Kluckhohn, *Culture: A Critical Review of Concepts and Definitions* (Cambridge MA: Peabody Museum, 1952): 75–142. The seminal work of critics such as Richard Hoggart and Stuart Hall at the Birmingham Centre for Contemporary Cultural Studies (est. 1964), which first put cultural studies on the global map as an academic discipline, also contributed to a surge of interest in the study of culture(s) in the late 1960s.

Subsequent criticism has been levelled at the school of British cultural studies by academics such as Harold Bloom ("that incredible absurdity" – see Bloom, "Ranting against Cant," interview by Jennie Rothenberg in *Atlantic Unbound* [16 July 2003], http://www.theatlantic.com/past/unbound/interviews/int2003-07-16.htm [accessed 10 March 2010]) and Alan Sokal ("fashionable nonsense" – see Sokal & Jean Bricmont, *Fashionable Nonsense: Postmodern Intellectuals' Abuse of Science* [New York: Picador, 1998]: 206).

the activities of persons travelling to and staying in places outside their usual environment for not more than one consecutive year for leisure, business and other purposes not related to the exercise of an activity remunerated from within the place visited.[5]

In order to explore the dynamics of the specific cultural-tourism model as proposed by Eduard Delgado – one based on "the concepts of diversity (culture and creativity), interaction (trust) and context (distinction)"[6] and where community-engaged approaches work in partnership with artistic and cultural initiatives organized by urban-planning and development councils – 'culture' will also be regarded as an interactive and collaborative process and not merely as an entity that can accrue to individuals, unlike Pierre Bourdieu's notion of acquiring "cultural capital."[7]

Moving away from conceptual definitions of 'cultural tourism' and on to its contextual framework, a seminal phase of development occurred during the expansion of the middle class in the second half of the nineteenth century.[8] This led to the opening up of 'high' culture to a larger audience, and

---

Further illustration of the lack of critical consensus even today on the definition(s) of 'culture' can be found in Pierre Bourdieu, who held that it lacks sufficient scientific methods of enquiry – see Bourdieu, "Concluding Remarks: For a Sociogenetic Understanding of Intellectual Works," in *Bourdieu: Critical Perspectives*, ed. Craig Calhoun, Edward LiPuma & Moishe Postone (Chicago: U of Chicago P, 1993), and Terry Eagleton ("the golden age of cultural theory is long past") – see Eagleton, *After Theory* (London: Allen Lane, 2003): 1.

[5] World Tourism Organization (UNWTO) quoted in William F. Theobald, "Introduction" to *Global Tourism*, ed. Theobald (1994; Oxford: Butterworth–Heinemann, 1998): 14.

[6] Eduard Delgado, quoted in Greg Richards, *Cultural Tourism: Global and Local Perspectives* (Binghamton NY: Haworth, 2007): 330.

[7] See Pierre Bourdieu, "Cultural Reproduction and Social Reproduction," in *Power and Ideology in Education*, ed. Jerome Karabel & A.H. Halsey (Oxford: Oxford UP, 1977): 487–511.

[8] Prior to the nineteenth century, an earlier manifestation of cultural tourism in Europe was the Grand Tour that flourished between 1660 and 1840. Undertaken primarily by upper-class young men as an essential part of their liberal education, the Grand Tour was an expedition to the principal cities in Europe, especially France and Italy, that aimed at exposing the traveller to the artistic and cultural legacies of Western civilization. Lasting a period of several months to several years, the Grand Tour was a means of inculcating in these young men a cultural sensibility attuned to the intellec-

was one of the preconditions for the first boom in the tourism industry in the aftermath of the Second Industrial Revolution. Unlike the situation obtaining in the days of the Grand Tour, cultural consumption was no longer an elitist pursuit limited to the upper classes or aristocracy, as the success of the tour operator Thomas Cook (the first to offer predominantly middle-class travellers package tours to European destinations with a 'cultural slant' since the 1860s) illustrated. In the UK, the 1845 "Museums of Art in Corporate Towns Act" also led to the formation of local museums and galleries that were frequented by the local public.[9] Over a century later, a second boom in 'cultural tourism' could be ascribed to the increased affordability of air and rail travel from the late-1970s onwards. The result was a gradual merging of the spheres of high and popular culture, a move that led to a much broader clientele base. By the time the phrase 'cultural tourism' achieved widespread currency in the 1980s,[10] often interchangeably with other terms such as 'heritage tourism', 'arts tourism', and 'ethnic tourism', tour operators had established the fact that there was indeed a market for tourism directed towards experiencing the artistic and cultural heritage of a place.

What exactly, then, *is* cultural tourism? In 1991, the European Association for Tourism and Leisure Education and Research (ATLAS), interestingly, agreed on two slightly different definitions of the term – one technical, one

---

tual, fashionable, and social pursuits of well-to-do Europeans. Up until the nineteenth century, therefore, (high) culture played a central role in the refinement of the individual through different forms of education. For further reading, see James Buzard's essay "The Grand Tour and After (1660–1840)," in *The Cambridge Companion to Travel Writing*, ed. Peter Hulme & Tim Youngs (Cambridge: Cambridge UP, 2002): 37–52.

[9] Gareth Shaw, "Growth and Employment in the UK's Culture Industry," *World Futures* 33 (1991): 165–80.

[10] See Oliver Frey's "Creativity of Places as a Resource for Cultural Tourism," in *Enhancing the City: New Perspectives for Tourism and Leisure*, ed. Giovanni Maciocco & Silvia Serreli (Heidelberg: Springer, 2009): 1–15. The World Tourism Organisation (UNWTO) defines cultural tourism as the "movements of people motivated by cultural intents such as study tours, performing arts, festivals, cultural events, visits to sites and monuments, as well as travel for pilgrimages." See "Cultural Tourism and Poverty Alleviation," report on the forty-first meeting of the WTO Commission for East Asia and the Pacific, Siem Reap, World Tourism Organization (UNWTO) (7–9 June 2004), http://pub.world-tourism.org:81/WebRoot/Store/Shops/Infoshop/Products/1391/1391-1.pdf (accessed 26 February 2010): 1.

conceptual/practical – as part of its seminal Cultural Tourism Research Project. The technical definition reads: "all movements of persons to specific cultural attractions, such as museums, heritage sites, artistic performances, and festivals outside their normal place of residence." The conceptual or practical definition, however, reads:

> the movement of persons to cultural manifestations away from their normal place of residence, *with the intention to gather new information and experiences to satisfy their cultural needs.*[11]

The latter definition depicts the tour package as a commodity whereby the transaction between tour operator and client involves the act of purchasing and then "consuming the way of life of places visited."[12] Of course, the reverse also holds true – governments and other local organizations invest heavily in cultural tourism as a product whose 'purchase' will contribute to the prosperity of specific regions. In Europe, owing to the segmentation of the tourist industry into different niche markets in the 1970s and 1980s (winter and sun holidays, family and senior-citizen holidays, adventure holidays, active and luxury-spa holidays, and so on), a phenomenon that led to the creation of new opportunities for specialist cultural tourism operators, cultural tourism has become one of the largest sectors of tourism as a whole.[13]

   The definition of tourism by the World Travel Organisation, as mentioned previously, makes a distinction between the terms 'travel' and 'tourism'. For the latter, there has to be a displacement outside one's usual environment for a period of time in order for one to experience a host culture that is separate from one's own surroundings. An interesting variation of this model can be found in instances of cultural tourism at work in cities with a large immigrant population. The latter, as sites of transculturation (to use a term coined by Fernando Ortiz denoting "the process of transition from one culture to another"[14]) shift the parameters slightly, as the tourist need not necessarily travel

---

[11] Richards, *Cultural Tourism in Europe*, 24 (my emphasis).

[12] Dallen J. Timothy & Stephen W. Boyd, *Heritage Tourism* (Harlow: Pearson Education, 2003): 5.

[13] See the OECD (Organisation for Economic Co-operation and Development) report *The Impact of Culture on Tourism* (Paris: OECD, 2009). For a comprehensive overview of the development of cultural tourism, see also Melanie K. Smith, *Issues in Cultural Tourism Studies* (London: Routledge, 2003), especially Chapter 2, "Reconceptualising Cultural Tourism," 29–44.

[14] Fernando Ortiz writes:

large distances in to experience the 'Other'. Given that one central aspect of cultural tourism is the pursuit of authenticity – tourists assume and demand the 'real' experience; promoters and cultural entrepreneurs tout events as authentic fare; and the host culture shares with the tourist a slice of its everyday life – the easy availability of authentic difference on one's own doorstep brings not only cultural stereotyping much closer to home but also the marketing of difference and consumption of difference as a product.[15] The next section will look more closely at one conceptual art exhibition's attempt to dismantle some of the most common assumptions in encounters with cultural difference in the tourist zone. The aims of the exhibition reflected its efforts to create a new cultural tourism model, one very much akin to that proposed by Eduard Delgado according to which culture is "a human right, with roots in the most basic part of human dignity."[16] The project thus represented a dis-

---

I am of the opinion that the word transculturation better expresses the different phases of the process of transition from one culture to another because this does not consist merely in acquiring another culture, which is what the English word acculturation really implies, but the process also necessarily involves the loss or uprooting of a previous culture, which could be defined as a deculturation. In addition it carries the idea of the consequent creation of new cultural phenomena, which could be called neoculturation.

—Ortiz, *Cuban Counterpoint: Tobacco and Sugar*, tr. Harriet de Onís (*Contrapunteo cubano del tabaco y el azúcar*, 1940; tr. 1947; Durham NC: Duke UP, 1995): 102–103.

[15] Or, as Alan Clarke puts it: "For cultural tourism, folklore is often seen to be more important than the folk in the destination. The tourists themselves bring with them their own cultures and their own expectations of the cultures they will be able to consume"; Clarke, "The Cultural Tourism Dynamic," in *Developing Cultural Tourism: Proceedings of the Second DeHaan Tourism Management Conference*, Nottingham University Business School, http://www.nottingham.ac.uk/ttri/discussion/2004_3.pdf (accessed 26 February 2010): 5. Although I agree with most of Clarke's argument, I find it worrying that he does not question the striving for authenticity, or the authentic experience, in the cultural-tourism model. Clarke even goes so far as to ask "how this authenticity can be recognised and how it can be differently constituted through different relationships in the promotion, development and consumption of cultural tourism" (4), hence implying that authenticity remains the chief aim and yardstick of good cultural-tourist practice.

[16] Eduard Delgado, "Planificación cultural contra espacio público," *Karis* 11 (2001): 49–61, quoted in Jordi Pascual i Ruiz & Sanjin Dragojević, *On Citizen Participation in*

ruption of the tourist zone that tends to foster a 'society of the spectacle'[17] through its commodification and mass consumption of cultural difference.

⌘

Curio, an intermedia art exhibition organized by *terra incognita*, a street-level, non-profit arts organization based in London, was a four-week intervention by seven artists (Jananne Al-Ani, Eamon O'Kane, Mohini Chandra, Michèle Fuirer, Martin Parker, Erika Tan, and Chila Burman) into the commodification of difference in the tourist zone commonly known as 'Banglatown', an area between Whitechapel and Spitalfields in London's East End. Historically an industrial, working-class, poor area, home to immigrant communities as diverse as the Huguenot refugees escaping from Catholic persecution in France in the eighteenth century and Jews fleeing Eastern Europe a century later, the area now houses one of the largest Bangladeshi populations in Europe.[18] According to a census from 2001, approximately 70% of the residents in the area are of Bangladeshi origin.[19] The official rebranding of the district as 'Banglatown', initially part of a tourism strategy designed to boost the local economy, led to the formation of a new political entity when the local electoral ward was renamed "Spitalfields & Banglatown" in 2001.

Curio ran from 12 September to 9 October 2002, exactly a year after the 9/11 attacks. Calling for a revision of the dominant practices of cultural tour-

---

Local Cultural Policy Development for European Cities (Amsterdam: European Cultural Foundation, 2007): 11–12.

[17] Guy Debord, *La Société du spectacle* (Paris: Buchet–Chastel, 1967).

[18] For a more in-depth historical overview, see Paola Briata's case study of the Spitalfields area in "The Concept of 'Culture' in Multi-Ethnic Areas Regeneration Policies: Common Views, Weaknesses, Experiences, Perspectives," paper presented at *The Vital City: Diversity, Cohesion and the Richness of Cities: Tenth Anniversary Conference of the European Urban Research Association (EURA)*, University of Glasgow, http://www.gla.ac.uk/media/media_47901_en.pdf (accessed 10 March 2010). In particular, Briata critiques "the simplification of the immigrant culture that the 'disneyfication' of the area tends to present as homogeneous" (7). She also notes that "the project to transform Spitalfields into Banglatown was a cause of tension 'inside' the so-called Bangladeshi community, as well as 'outside' it. From an 'inside' point of view, not all the 'Bangladeshi community' appreciate the *exotic reinvention* of Spitalfields" (7).

[19] See *The New East End: Kinship, Race and Conflict*, ed. Geoff Dench, Kate Gavron & Michael Young (London: Profile, 2006).

ism as sketched out above (the harnessing of ethnicity as commodity; the establishment of cultural tradition as a central marker of identity; the pre-occupation with authenticity; the maintenance of distance; the reification of difference or 'Otherness'), the artistic intervention sought to challenge tour-ists' anticipated consumption of cultural difference and to subvert their acts of imagining 'realities' from their mythic presumptions of the area. As the exhi-bition's curator Alana Jelinek explains, the project's aim was to "explore how Otherness is created, portrayed and maintained; how we create an 'us' and a 'them' in order to enjoy those differences as exotica to consume."[20] The viewer's anticipations of the "spectacle of difference" were undermined and even frustrated by the artwork of the exhibition in the street, which was de-liberately not clearly tagged or indicated.

In contrast to art exhibited in a museum or gallery, which is accompanied by labels, signage, or brief explanatory notes that call attention to the piece's cultural significance, art situated in the street teasingly and unapologetically plays with the viewer's expectations of an encounter with the art object. Seve-ral of the installations that were part of the *Curio* project consisted of half-torn posters, makeshift signage, and small spray-painted stencils on a brick wall that could easily have been mistaken for graffiti. The intended effect on art viewers was one of slowing down the encounter, making them ponder what was, and what was not, part of the exhibition.[21] Many of the visitors who went to the exhibition actually remarked that this experience was confusing and irritating, yet refreshingly different. In contrast to a visit to an art gallery, therefore, where the viewer is given information about the painting, sculpture, or installation on display via the small signs that are placed next to the art-work, visitors to the *Curio* exhibition were left to their own devices in inter-preting the significance of a sound installation that deliberately interacted with the noise of traffic, a sticker pasted onto the back of a signpost, or a date sprayed on a wall. Interestingly, several of the artists reported that anonymous passers-by had also 'added' to their artwork – someone had, for example, lined up a group of gray plastic toy soldiers on the remains of a brick wall in the vicinity of one of Erika Tan's installations.

Unlike art displayed in an enclosed gallery space, therefore, the installa-tions themselves were not the primary focus of the exhibition. Rather, it was

---

[20] Alana Jelinek, in an unpublished interview with Mike Brennan.

[21] For that matter, as art-viewers mixed and mingled with tourists in the area, it also became increasingly difficult to separate the two groups of visitors.

the interaction of the artwork with its environment, and, very often, the reflection of the art public's gaze back onto itself, that triggered questions of
authority and perspective, disrupted notions of subject and object, and brought
ideas of spectacle and consumerism to the fore. The situation, hence contextualization, of the artworks in a specific site of transculturation, the tourist area
of Banglatown, also signalled the project's larger aims – to engage critically
with notions of cultural tourism, stereotype, authenticity, and fantasies of the
'Other'.[22] The temporal setting of the exhibition, exactly a year after 9/11, deliberately made its audiences reflect on how the dominant ideology of fear
instilled by mass media around the globe and the political rhetoric of the Bush
government's 'War on Terror' helped to disseminate the perception of terrorists as the 'Other', as well as the stereotype that all Muslims are terrorists.

The location of *Curio* in the largely working-class districts of Whitechapel
and Spitalfields was therefore a significant part of the project's artistic conceptualization. In line with the role that (high) culture played in forms of
education directed at the enhancement of the individual in the nineteenth
century, the East End was the location of the Anglican clergyman and social
reformer Samuel Barnett's 'Art-to-the-Poor' initiatives in the 1880s, where he
exhibited paintings in order to "stimulate moral sentiments, patriotism, and a
feeling for beauty among the residents of the East End slums and settlement
houses."[23] This attempt to foster an aesthetic sensibility in the lower and
working classes by projecting onto them moral codes of behaviour would
probably be castigated by critics today. Nevertheless, a similar problem of
externalization or projection lies behind the enthusiasm of cultural tourists
who flock to the East End in order to seek out confirmations of their preconceived notions of the area – Jack the Ripper, the real East End, the cockney
paradise, the Victorian slum, the curry houses, the birthplace of Asian cool.
Younger generations visit the area in a pilgrimage to the home of British hip-
hop and r&b mashed up with Eastern beats from the likes of Cornershop,

---

[22] *Curio* sought "to explore how Otherness is created, portrayed and maintained";
Jelinek, "Foreword," *Curio: Disrupting the Tourist Zone*, ed. Alana Jelinek (London:
terra incognita, 2003): 5.

[23] Andrew McClellan, "A Brief History of the Art Museum Public," in *Art and its
Publics: Museum Studies at the Millennium*, ed. McClellan (London: Blackwell,
2003): 9.

Asian Dub Foundation, and, more recently, a certain (DJ) Mumzy who self-professedly "puts the 'B(eat)' back in Bengali."[24]

In the four-week period of the *Curio* exhibition, the artists' installations were located at various points along Hanbury Street and its intersection with Brick Lane. Hanbury Street thus effectively became a site or space (in Henri Lefebvre's definition of the term, a social construction) where the viewer not only engaged with the artwork on display but was also confronted with the diasporic culture being marketed and consumed. With the bustling city at one end, and the more residential area, home to a, mostly immigrant, Bangladeshi community, at the other, Hanbury Street marks translocation as a process, or in the words of *Curio*'s curator, Alana Jelinek, "a journey from global capitalism, its symbols and manifestations, through cultural tourism to the local (or vice versa, depending on your perspective)."[25]

The following discussion will focus on five of the visual art exhibits, sound recordings, and interactive media installations that made up *Curio* – Erika Tan's "Random Acts of...," Michèle Fuirer's untitled mirror installations, Mohini Chandra's "Flow," Martin Parker's "Erika," and, last but not least, Eamon O'Kane's "Sign Series / Stay." The diverse cultural backgrounds, perspectives, and critical approaches of the artists who contributed to the project resulted in different manifestations of a shared view of the aims of the project that I described earlier. All of the artists sought to subvert the neat packaging, branding, marketing, and consumption of foreignness in Banglatown, thus critiquing the prevailing assumptions of cultural tourism and exposing the projected tourist fantasy that is mediated by notions of cultural and ideological difference. With the aim of working with the local community, the artists also underwent a mentoring programme whereby each paired up with a local young person in the months leading up to and during the exhibition:

> the plan was to ensure that [...] the work produced by the artists
> would reflect a relationship with individuals from the local area itself.

---

[24] Interestingly, the Baishakhi Mela in Brick Lane on 10 May 2009, an entertainment bonanza in celebration of the Bengali New Year organised by the Tower Hamlets Council (at which (DJ) Mumzy made an appearance), stated in the disclaimer on their website that "artists are subject to contract and overseas artists have or are in the process of confirming their visas. No one will perform at the Mela without a valid visa" (http://www.towerhamlets.gov.uk/news/council_news_-_dont_edit/april/international_artists_announce.aspx).

[25] Jelinek, "Foreword," 4–5.

The relationship would not interfere with the artists' processes of making but simply be a point of reflection and exchange.[26]

To this extent, *Curio* effectively offered a new model of cultural tourism that stressed the interactive and collaborative nature of tourism and not merely the consumption of cultural difference as a commodity or product.

Erika Tan's "Random Acts of…" included the 'camouflaging' of lamp-posts in military uniforms, the 'insulation' of electric power supplies in felt, the envelopment of electricity cabinets in custom-made, shroud-like covers, the stencilling of visuals and dates on brick walls, and the displaying of 'lost' notices on lampposts. Playfully defamiliarizing the inventory of the street – signage, manhole covers, sewage pipes, traffic lights, telecommunication mains – Tan's intervention worked on two levels. First, it was a direct act of inserting the heretofore unacknowledged narratives and stories that official versions (the 'grand narratives') of history had excluded. Hence, for example, the portraits of several of the women whom Jack the Ripper had murdered were stencilled on brick walls, together with the date (1888) of their deaths (see Fig. 11 overleaf). Second, because Tan's individual pieces were subject to the contingency (literally, "random acts") of theft and damage by both pas-sers-by and weather conditions, they challenged the authoritative acts of docu-mentation and preservation carried out by archives and art museums. Playful-ly referring to the popular image of London's East End as a neighbourhood rampant with poverty and crime due to a large migrant population predomi-nantly from the lower and working classes, Tan's installations pushed at the boundaries of what was 'permissible' behaviour on the street and what coun-ted as acts of vandalism.

As artistic interventions in the street, Tan's pieces also undermined the "utopian optimism underpinning museum rhetoric" which "endorse[s] a pro-found belief in the transcendent, life-enhancing potential of art," a belief that, as Andrew McClellan notes, "takes on added resonance in the wake of up-heavals such as world wars, social protest, and, most recently, 9/11."[27] Instead of an emphasis on the importance of preservation and an adherence to an 'etiquette of viewing' that characterize the unwritten code of conduct in muse-ums and art galleries, Tan's temporary pieces encouraged the spontaneous and contingent nature of participating in the artistic process of creation in

---

[26] Alana Jelinek, "Afterword," in *Curio: Disrupting the Tourist Zone*, ed. Jelinek (London: terra incognita, 2003): 46.

[27] McClellan, *Art and its Publics*, 1.

whichever way the passer-by saw fit. Accordingly, as already mentioned, a group of gray plastic toy soldiers had been added onto the remains of a brick wall in the vicinity of one of her installations. The piece that camouflaged a lamppost in army combat uniform, for example, also challenged the directive and transcendent potential of art – the streetlamp no longer illuminated

Fig. 11: Erika Tan, "Random Acts of…" (2002).
Reproduced by kind permission of Alana Jelinek.

the way for the pedestrian, but was transformed into an ambiguous object that alluded to the violence intrinsic in processes of racial and social discrimination rampant in London's East End. Passers-by were therefore confronted with the ambivalent nature of their presence as both art viewer and cultural tourist in the space. The art installations made them reflect on the extent to which they were implicated in the reiteration of difference by endorsing the neat packaging, branding, marketing, and consumption of foreignness in Banglatown. Erika Tan's series "Random Acts of…" thus critiqued the prevailing assumptions of cultural tourism and exposed the projected tourist fantasy that is mediated by notions of cultural and ideological difference.

Michèle Fuirer chose to expose the tourist's projection onto the area by startling her viewers in a moment of self-recognition wherein they were presented with the imperative to reflect on the very nature of the gaze. Her work

Fig. 12: Michèle Fuirer, "Mirror Series: Speculate" (2002).
Reproduced by kind permission of Alana Jelinek.

for the exhibition consisted of five convex mirrors (the type used so that drivers know if they can pull out of a tight corner), each 'labelled' with the words 'curious', 'survey', 'regard', 'speculate', and 'spectate' respectively.

Reflecting the spectator's gaze back on her-/himself, the convex mirrors challenge the viewing process as the conferring of the gaze from viewer (subject) to artwork (object) is inverted. Instead of the viewer looking at the artwork, the process became one of the artwork looking at the viewer. Viewers saw not only themselves in the convex mirrors but also their surroundings, hence their location within the exhibition itself. They became, in other words, part of the art, thus collapsing the distance between subject and object. As Richard Stemp comments, "by looking at tourism and the crossing of cultural boundaries, the exhibition created its own subject: people coming to look, to experience something different and something new."[28] Instead of simply reflecting, and thus reinforcing, the old stereotypes based on perceived (ethnic, cultural, and class) differences, therefore, Fuirer's mirrors worked on the principle of refraction: i.e. by breaking up and dispelling the conventional perceptions of the area and its inhabitants.

Located a hundred metres away from one of Fuirer's convex mirrors, Mohini Chandra's strategic situation of her sound installation "Flow" at the intersection between Hanbury Street and Brick Lane effectively mapped out the cross-currents of people and traffic that traverse the space in terms of a conceptual soundscape (see Fig. 13 overleaf). With the aid of a software program designed to convert the activity on the street into the sound of flowing water, Chandra piped the sounds through speakers placed strategically at traffic lights and on the tops of signposts. From a steady trickle if there were fewer passengers and less traffic on the road to a gushing, burbling stream during rush hour, the digitally manipulated sounds became a part of the urban soundscape inhabited by other sounds like the conversations of passers-by, the noise of traffic, and the music played in roadside shops and restaurants. Barely audible at times and swelling to unbearable cacophony at others, "Flow" also alluded to the 'watery metaphors' often used in the social and political realms of contemporary public discourse about immigration[29] – 'wave of migration', 'flow of migrants', 'flood of refugees and asylum seekers', etc.

In an effort to explode white-liberal Britain's fantasy of moral supremacy, therefore, Mohini Chandra's piece represented an attempt to reverse these

---

[28] See Richard Stemp's essay "Where's the Art?" in *Curio: Disrupting the Tourist Zone*, ed. Alana Jelinek (London: terra incognita, 2003): 18–25.

[29] Interestingly, watery metaphors are also often used in fiscal discussions – e.g., liquid assets, flooding the market, floating a loan, cash flows, trickle-down effect. Discourses concerned with the impact of migrants on the social-welfare and healthcare system, as well as wage levels, employment, and growth, of a country are thus especially rampant with these metaphors.

watery metaphors. One major allusion in the piece was the Conservative MP Enoch Powell's 1968 'Rivers of Blood' speech, in which he condemned mass immigration from the Commonwealth countries to the UK as well as the Labour Government's implementation of the Race Relations Act which prohibited discrimination on the grounds of race and ethnic origin in matters of housing, employment, or public services.[30] Another reference in Mohini's piece was an allusion to Margaret Thatcher's 1978 interview with Granada TV in which she expressed the view that British people were "afraid that this country might be rather swamped by people with a different culture."[31] In directly juxtaposing leisure and tourism with exile and migration in the current context of global migration and mobility, Chandra also explores the tensions in diasporic communities – the experience that people who often 'belong'

Fig. 13: Mohini Chandra, "Flow" (2002).
Reproduced by kind permission of Mohini Chandra.

---

[30] "As I look ahead, I am filled with foreboding. Like the Roman, I seem to see 'the River Tiber foaming with much blood'. That tragic and intractable phenomenon which we watch with horror on the other side of the Atlantic but which there is interwoven with the history and existence of the States itself, is coming upon us here by our own volition and our own neglect. Indeed, it has all but come. In numerical terms, it will be of American proportions long before the end of the century. Only resolute and urgent action will avert it even now." Enoch Powell, "Rivers of Blood," Conservative Association meeting, Birmingham. 20 April 1968, *Daily Telegraph Online* (6 November 2007), http://www.telegraph.co.uk/comment/3643823/Enoch-Powells-Rivers-of-Blood -speech.html (accessed 26 February 2010).

[31] I am indebted to Annie E. Coombes' essay "Curious Encounters: The View from the Street" in Jelinek, *Curio: Disrupting the Tourist Zone*, 7–10, for mentioning these references.

to more than one place and community are nevertheless constantly placed 'outside' and excluded from forms of legal belonging such as citizenship.

Following up on the fear of the 'Other' and the subsequent allocation of fixed roles and stereotype to the immigrant, Martin Parker's sound installation "Erika" was a similar experimental attempt to expose and dispel these labels. His installation consisted of three recordings of his conversations with his mother (Erika), which was available on the menu at Meraz Cafe on 56 Hanbury Street, off Brick Lane (see Fig. 14). In the sound clips, Erika reflects the immigrant woman's journey from her native Germany to an adopted England.

Fig. 14: Martin Parker, "Erika" (2002) (extract).
Reproduced by kind permission of Martin Parker.

While it is impossible to reproduce on paper or transcribe what Erika's speech sounds like (one of the clips is titled "Na, bin gegang, plenty in Pictures..."), her language can best be described as a creole mix of German dialect and colloquial English. Interestingly, Erika does not give up her German mother tongue completely, yet acquires English phrases and colloquialisms such as 'the pictures' ('the cinema'). As Juliette Brown astutely observes, this could be interpreted as Erika's "resistance to assimilation," and her "rejection of the limitations of the role created for the migrant."[32] Erika's responses to her son Martin's questions about her childhood in Germany, the war, and her emigration to England constitute an act of oral documentation that literally enacts an act of translocation in the sense of straddling both cultures, languages, and countries. Martin Parker's sound installation also represents a transgressing of the personal into the realm of the public as Erika's stories and personal experiences become part of the larger collective tapestry of family lore, history, and experience shared by listeners who come to the restaurant and order her sound clips off the menu.

Interestingly, Meraz Café's menu itself was reworked for the duration of the *Curio* project. As already mentioned above, one could order a delicious Indian "Handi" meal (a meal slow-cooked in a Handi, or copper-bottomed dish), sip a cup of *chai*, and order any of Erika's sound clips for free. One would then receive a portable Discman with the three sound clips on a disc. Accordingly, the prices of Erika's three sound snippets are listed not in pounds and pence, but minutes and seconds. Almost as if they were doing their bit for the *Curio* exhibition, the menu also contains a disclaimer professing, "We at Meraz Café do not believe in commercialism and therefore the range and the variety have been kept simple for you."

Last but not least, Eamon O'Kane's "Stay/Sign Series" (see Fig. 15 overleaf) playfully inverted the tourist's urge to visually document her/his trip in a series of pictorial souvenirs. Brief slogans and longer quotations were printed on stickers that were pasted under makeshift "Diversion" ("Umleitung") traffic signs, beside "To Let" property signs and on the back of signposts, as well as on cups and mugs that were used in cafés. A video sequence titled "STAY: Simply to Authenticate Yourself" (with the word 'stay' replacing the directive 'stop' on a stop sign) was also first screened in the local arts and community centre at the 'non-tourist' end of Hanbury Street, and then later shown nightly on a small portable television on top of a fridge in the "Pizza n' Spice" takeaway, frequented mostly by the local community. The video sequence and signage featured quotations from various theorists on the nature of tourism and travel.

Collectively, O'Kane's signage and video installation undermined the art viewer's passive expectations to be fed information about the artwork. By literally giving his viewers only the sign(age) without the signified, O'Kane's

---

[32] Juliette Brown, "Tourism and the Global Cultural Theatre," in *Curio: Disrupting the Tourist Zone*, ed. Alana Jelinek (London: terra incognita, 2003): 31.

installation also highlighted the problematical notion of mediation – to what extent are we fed signs and signifiers in the form of advertising slogans and visuals, and then swayed into (re-)producing the signifieds that are already predetermined by marketing ploys? O'Kane's "Stay/Sign Series" therefore playfully critiques the tourist's desire for authenticity and the quest for the ultimate authentic experience, by making the viewer reflect on the ideological implications of such a drive.

Fig. 15: Eamon O'Kane, "Stay/Sign Series" (2002).
Reproduced by kind permission of Alana Jelinek.

Undermining the tourist's impulse to document, consume, and experience the local customs and fare and yet remain apart as an objective onlooker, *Curio* effectively represented not only a playful intervention into the tourist zone of Banglatown but also a more serious critique of the very political and economic power-structures that have come to establish dominant notions of cultural, religious, and ideological difference, as well as of the assumptions rooted in the discourse of cultural tourism. It suggested the possibility of an alternative model of cultural tourism, one that foregrounds the interactive and two-way process between tourists and host cultures and not merely the con-sumption of cultural difference as a product. Moreover, unlike its precursors in a long tradition of art as intervention, *Curio* did not presuppose a fixed agenda or seek to drive home a single message to its viewers. Rather, it sought to generate interaction and communication between people of different racial, socio-economic, and religious backgrounds who visit, or work and live in, the vicinity, all in the context of a temporary street-level project that vanished without a trace six weeks later. As it turned out, however, *Curio* left its mark, long after it vacated Banglatown.

Works Cited

Bloom, Harold. "Ranting against Cant," interview by Jennie Rothenberg in *Atlantic Unbound* (16 July 2003), http://www.theatlantic.com/past/unbound/interviews /int2003-07-16.htm (accessed 10 March 2010).

Boorstin, Daniel. *The Image: A Guide to Pseudo-Events in America* (New York: Harper & Row, 1964).

Bourdieu, Pierre. "Concluding Remarks: For a Sociogenetic Understanding of Intellectual Works," in *Bourdieu: Critical Perspectives*, ed. Craig Calhoun, Edward LiPuma & Moishe Postone (Cambridge: Polity, 1993): 263–75.

——. "Cultural Reproduction and Social Reproduction," in *Power and Ideology in Education*, ed. Jerome Karabel & A.H. Halsey (Oxford: Oxford UP, 1977): 487–511.

Briata, Paola. "The Concept of 'Culture' in Multi-Ethnic Areas Regeneration Policies: Common Views, Weaknesses, Experiences, Perspectives," paper presented at *The Vital City: Diversity, Cohesion and the Richness of Cities: Tenth Anniversary Conference of the European Urban Research Association (EURA)*, University of Glasgow, http://www.gla.ac.uk/media/media_47901_en.pdf (accessed 10 March 2010).

Brown, Juliette. "Tourism and the Global Cultural Theatre," in *Curio*, ed. Jelinek, 29–31.

Buzard, James. "The Grand Tour and After (1660–1840)," in *The Cambridge Companion to Travel Writing*, ed. Peter Hulme & Tim Youngs (Cambridge: Cambridge UP, 2002): 37–52.

Clarke, Alan. "The Cultural Tourism Dynamics," in *Developing Cultural Tourism: Proceedings of the Second DeHaan Tourism Management Conference*, Nottingham University Business School, http://www.nottingham.ac.uk/ttri/discussion/2004_3 .pdf (accessed 26 February 2010): 4–12.

Coombes, Annie E. "Curious Encounters: The View from the Street," in *Curio*, ed. Jelinek, 7–10.

"Cultural Tourism and Poverty Alleviation," report on the forty-first meeting of the WTO Commission for East Asia and the Pacific, Siem Reap, *World Tourism*

Organization (UNWTO) (7–9 June 2004), http://pub.world-tourism.org:81/Web
Root/Store/Shops/Infoshop/Products/1391/1391-1.pdf (accessed 26 February 2010).

"Culture," *Oxford English Dictionary* (2008), http://oed.com/view/Entry/45746 (accessed 26 February 2010).

Dallen, J. Timothy, & Stephen W. Boyd. *Heritage Tourism* (Harlow: Pearson Education, 2003).

Debord, Guy. *La société du spectacle* (Paris: Buchet–Chastel, 1967).

Dench, Geoff, Kate Gavron & Michael Young, ed. *The New East End: Kinship, Race and Conflict* (London: Profile, 2006).

Disclaimer, *Tower Hamlets Council* (2009), http://www.towerhamlets.gov.uk/news
/council_news_-_dont_edit/april/international_artists_announce.aspx (accessed 26
February 2010).

Eagleton, Terry. *After Theory* (London: Allen Lane, 2003).

Frey, Oliver. "Creativity of Places as a Resource for Cultural Tourism," in *Enhancing
the City: New Perspectives for Tourism and Leisure*, ed. Giovanni Maciocco &
Silvia Serreli (Heidelberg: Springer, 2009): 1–15.

Jelinek, Alana. "Afterword," in *Curio*, ed. Jelinek, 45–47.

——. "Foreword," in *Curio*, ed. Jelinek, 4–6.

——, ed. *Curio: Disrupting the Tourist Zone* (exh. cat.; London: terra incognita,
2003).

Kroeber, A.L., & Clyde Kluckhohn. *Culture: A Critical Review of Concepts and Definitions* (Cambridge M A : Peabody Museum, 1952).

McClellan, Andrew, ed. *Art and its Publics: Museum Studies at the Millennium* (London: Blackwell, 2003).

Organisation for Economic Co-operation and Development (O E C D). *The Impact of
Culture on Tourism* (Paris: O E C D , 2009).

Ortiz y Fernández, Fernando. *Cuban Counterpoint*, tr. Harriet de Onís (*Contrapunteo
cubano del tabaco y el azúcar*, 1940; tr. 1947; Durham N C : Duke U P , 1995): 102–
103.

Pascual i Ruiz, Jordi, & Sanjin Dragojević. *On Citizen Participation in Local Cultural
Policy Development for European Cities* (Amsterdam: European Cultural Foundation, 2007).

Powell, Enoch. "Rivers of Blood," Conservative Association meeting, Birmingham.
20 April 1968. *Daily Telegraph Online* (6 November 2007), http://www.telegraph
.co.uk/comment/3643823/Enoch-Powells-Rivers-of-Blood-speech.html   (accessed
26 February 2010).

Richards, Greg, ed. *Cultural Tourism in Europe* (Wallingford: C A B International,
1996).

——, ed. *Cultural Tourism in Europe* (Wallingford: C A B International, 1996), reissued by the Association for Tourism and Leisure Education (A T L A S) (2005),

http: //www.tram-research.com/cultural_tourism_in_europe.pdf (accessed 26 February 2010).

——. *Cultural Tourism: Global and Local Perspectives* (Binghamton NY: Haworth, 2007).

Shaw, Gareth. "Growth and Employment in the UK's Culture Industry," *World Futures* 33 (1991): 165–80.

Smith, Melanie K. *Issues in Cultural Tourism Studies* (London: Routledge, 2003).

Smith, Stephen L.J. *Tourism Analysis: A Handbook* (Harlow: Longman, 1995).

Sokal, Alan D., & Jean Bricmont. *Fashionable Nonsense: Postmodern Intellectuals' Abuse of Science* (New York: Picador, 1998).

Stemp, Richard. "Where's the Art?," in *Curio*, ed. Jelinek, 18–25.

Theobald, William F., ed. *Global Tourism* (1994; Oxford: Butterworth–Heinemann, 1998).

⌘

Notes on Editors and Contributors

DIANA BRYDON (Fellow of the Royal Society of Canada 2008) is Canada Research Chair in Globalization and Cultural Studies at the University of Manitoba where she teaches Canadian and postcolonial literary, cultural, and global studies. By examining national and global imaginaries, she brings cultural perspectives to cross-disciplinary research collaborations investigating "Globalization and Autonomy" and "Building Global Democracy" (www.buildingglobaldemocracy.org). With Marta Dvořák, she has co-edited *Crosstalk: Canadian and Global Imaginaries in Dialogue* (2012). She is co-writing "Globalization and Autonomy: Conversing Across Disciplines," with William D. Coleman and Louis W. Pauly, and in 2011 she received funding from the Social Sciences and Humanities Research Council of Canada for "Brazil/Canada Knowledge Exchange: Developing Transnational Literacies." This project works with English teachers and teachers-in-training in Canada and Brazil to develop site-specific pedagogies and research production appropriate to the challenges of ethical cross-cultural engagement. The participants in the project hope to deepen understanding of what transnational literacy can mean in such circumstances while learning together how to make transnational, interdisciplinary partnerships work.

LARS ECKSTEIN is Professor of Anglophone Literatures and Cultures at the University of Potsdam. His publications include the monographs *Re-Membering the Black Atlantic: On the Poetics and Politics of Literary Memory* (2006) and *Reading Song Lyrics* (2010), as well as a number of edited collections, among them *English Literatures Across the Globe: A Companion* (2007); *The White Backlash: Conservatisms in Contemporary British Writing* (with Dirk Wiemann; themed issue of the journal *Hard Times* 89, 2011); *Romanticism Today* (with Christoph Reinfandt, 2009); *Multi-Ethnic Britain 2000+* (with Barbara Korte, Ulrike Pirker, & Christoph Reinfandt, 2008), and *The Cultural Validity of Music in Contemporary Fiction* (with Christoph Reinfandt, 2006).

PALOMA FRESNO–CALLEJA is a lecturer in the Department of English at the University of the Balearic Islands (Spain), where she teaches postcolonial literatures. Her research focuses on multiculturalism, identity-politics, gender, and diaspora in New Zealand and Pacific literatures and film. Some of her recent publications have appeared in the *Journal of Commonwealth Literature*, the *Journal of Postcolonial Writing*, *Australasian Drama Studies*, and *Studies in Australasian Cinema.*

LUCIA KRÄMER is assistant professor for British literary and cultural studies at Leibniz Universität Hannover. She received her PhD for a study of fictional biographies, *Oscar Wilde in Roman, Drama and Film* (2003), and has published widely on various aspects of the reception of Oscar Wilde. Her current main research interests include the theory and practice of adaptation, as well as Indian cinema and its reception in Britain (the subject of her postdoctoral thesis). She has also recently co-edited (with Wolfgang Funk) a compilation of articles on the issue of authenticity, *Fiktionen von Wirklichkeit: Authentizität zwischen Materialität und Konstruktion* (2011).

GESA MACKENTHUN teaches American studies at the University of Rostock. Her research centres on the analysis of colonial discourse in the Americas and on postcolonial theory. Her publications include *Fictions of the Black Atlantic in American Foundational Literature* (2004), *Metaphors of Dispossession: American Beginnings and the Translation of Empire, 1492–1637* (1997), and (ed. with Bernhard Klein) *Sea Changes: Historicizing the Ocean* (2004). She is editor of the DFG graduate school conference volumes on "Cultural Encounters and the Discourses of Scholarship": *The Fuzzy Logic of Encounter: Cultural Encounters and the Discourses of Scholarship* (with Sünne Juterczenka, 2009), *Human Bondage in the Cultural Contact Zone* (with Raphael Hörmann, 2010), and *Embodiments of Cultural Encounters* (with Sebastian Jobs, 2011). Her current research deals with nineteenth-century travel writing in the Americas and the concurrent scholarly discourses about antiquity.

THOMAS MARTINEK studied English and music at the University of Vienna and the University of Music and Performing Arts Vienna. He is currently employed as Senior Lecturer at the English department of the University of Vienna and as a secondary-school teacher in Vienna. His main research areas

are postcolonial theory, Nigerian and other African literature, theoretical approaches to the short story, and foreign language teaching. He is working on a
dissertation about contemporary Nigerian short stories and has published
articles on Ben Okri, Biyi Bandele (www.litencyc.com), and Wole Soyinka
(*Kindlers Literatur-Lexikon*).

SANDRA MEYER studied English and German at the universities of Heidelberg and Duisburg–Essen, where she received her MA in 2007. She is a research associate and lecturer at the University of Duisburg–Essen, where she
is currently writing a doctoral dissertation on the construction and representation of traumatized identities in the works of British author Kate Atkinson.
She uses an interdisciplinary approach combining narrative theory, recent
trends within the field of research on identity formation, and findings of psy-
chotherapy. Her prior fields of interest are contemporary literature, literary
and cultural theory, narratology, identity studies, trauma studies, postcolonialism, Victorianism, children's literature, and film studies. She is a member of
GNEL/ASNEL and of the Postcolonial Studies Association (PSA).

THERESE–M. MEYER is a lecturer in English literature at Martin-Luther-Uni-
versität Halle–Wittenberg. She is the author of *Where Fiction Ends* (2006),
an analysis of the textual construction of fictional author identities in Canadian and Australian literary scandals. Her research interests include contemporary international literatures in English and (post)colonial literatures in
English, especially from the Caribbean, Australia, New Zealand, and Canada.
Her second book project is a genre study of the Australian convict novel.

MARGA MUNKELT, in addition to teaching English and American language
and literature at the University of Münster, was a Visiting Professor in the
Department of English at the University of New Mexico, Albuquerque, USA,
for several years. Her main research interests are drama, Shakespeare studies
(with emphasis on editorial theory and practice, theatre history, and performance criticism), and Mexican-American/Chicano/a studies. She has edited
Shakespeare and published widely in all her research fields. Among her books
are a monograph on stage directions in Shakespeare's early printings and an
edition of *Mexican-American Short Stories*. Her articles have appeared,
among others, in such journals as *Analytical and Enumerative Bibliography*,
Romanische Studien, *Shakespeare Studies*, and *Theatre History Studies* as
well as in several anthologies and encyclopedias. One of her current projects
is a monograph on Mexican-American literature.

LYNDA NG recently received her doctorate from the University of New South Wales, Australia. Her dissertation explores the relationship between genre and nation in contemporary British and Australian fiction. She has published essays on nationalism, postcolonialism, and Australian literature. Her current projects are a monograph on the transnational dimensions of literature within the current late-capitalist environment and an edited collection of essays centred on Alexis Wright's *Carpentaria* that examines the interaction between indigeneity and globalization.

CLAUDIA PERNER is a lecturer in the department of Anglophone Studies at the University of Duisburg–Essen. She co-hosted the GNEL/ASNEL Summer School in 2007 and was a member of the executive board of GNEL/ASNEL between 2005 and 2009. Her research interests include film, fundamentalism, globalization theory, cosmopolitanism, as well as interfaces of postcolonial studies, English studies, and American studies. Her publications include an article on Mohsin Hamid's novels featured in *ARIEL* 41.3–4 (2010) and an article on Tristan Egolf's *Lord of the Barnyard* in the collection *Burning Books: Addressing Fundamentalism in Literature and Popular Culture* (ed. Catherine Pesso–Miquel & Klaus Stierstorfer, 2010). She is currently preparing the publication of her doctoral dissertation on US-American 'inoutside perspectives' in twenty-first-century anglophone novels.

KATHARINA RENNHAK is Professor of English Literature at the Bergische Universität Wuppertal. Previous positions include a visiting assistant professorship at the University of Texas at Austin and an interim professorship at Ludwig Maximilian University, Munich. She is especially interested in the link between literature and culture in the eighteenth, twentieth, and twenty-first centuries, in literary and critical theory (especially in narrative theories and in theories of identity, power, and gender), and in the relationship between British and Irish literary cultures and histories. Her publications include the monograph *Sprachkonzeptionen im metahistorischen Roman: Diskursspezifische Ausprägungen des* Linguistic Turn *in Critical Theory, Geschichtstheorie und Geschichtsfiktion 1970–1990* (2002) as well as the edited collections *Revolution und Emanzipation* (with Virginia Richter, 2004) and *Women Constructing Men: Female Novelists and Their Male Characters, 1750–2000* (with Sarah S.G. Frantz, 2010). Her second monograph, on narrative crossgendering and the construction of masculine identities in British and Irish women writers' novels around 1800, is forthcoming.

GUNDO RIAL Y COSTAS holds a PhD in Latin-American studies from the Freie Universität Berlin. He has also studied Spanish and English at King's College London and anthropology in Mérida, Mexico. Further, he was a research fellow at the media centre of the Universidade de São Paulo in Brazil. He has published academic articles in English, German, Portuguese, and Spanish on social and cultural transformations in the Americas. His work has been presented at international congresses in Austria, Brazil, Germany, Holland, Hungary, and Portugal. Among his latest publications are articles in *Revista Iberoamericana* 41 (2011) and *Revista Electrónica Celpcyro* 11 (2012) and several essay-contributions to edited collections, such as *Aesthetic Practices and Politics in Media, Music and Art: Performing Migration*, ed. Rocío G. Davis, Dorothea Fischer–Hornung & Johanna C. Kardux (2011) and *Fronteiras da Integração: Dimensões Culturais do Mercosul*, ed. Ligia Chiappini & Jan David Hauck (2011).

MARKUS SCHMITZ is an assistant professor affiliated to the Chair of English, Postcolonial and Media Studies at the English Department of the University of Münster. He read Middle Eastern studies, political science, and international law at the universities of Bochum and Cairo, and cultural studies at the University of Potsdam. His dissertation *Kulturkritik ohne Zentrum: Edward W. Said und die Kontrapunkte kritischer Dekolonisation* ("Cultural Criticism without a Centre: Edward W. Said and the Counterpoints of Critical Decolonization") was published in 2008. He has taught and published on transnational literatures and postcolonial audiovisual representations, comparative cultural theory, critical cosmopolitanism, and cultural resistance. His current research project revolves around counter-discursive strategies of critical correlation in contemporary Arab-American writing, audiovisual arts, and criticism.

MARK STEIN is Chair of English, Postcolonial and Media Studies at the University of Münster (www.wwu.de/ptts) and Chair of the Association for the Study of the New Literatures in English (www.gnel.de). In research and teaching, he takes an interest in anglophone cultural production (esp. literatures and film) from around the globe, with particular emphasis on diaspora, transnationalism, and transmigrancy. Special emphasis is placed on postcolonial and transcultural phenomena. He is a member of the AfroEuropeans research group. His publications include *Edward Said's Translocations: Essays in Secular Criticism* (ed. with Tobias Döring, 2012), *Hybrid Cultures – Nervous States: Britain and Germany in a (Post)Colonial World* (ed. with Ulrike

Lindner, Maren Möhring, & Silke Stroh, 2010), *African Europeans* (special issue of *Wasafiri*, ed. with Lyn Innes, 2008), *Cheeky Fictions: Laughter and the Postcolonial* (ed. with Susanne Reichl, 2005).

SILKE STROH studied at the universities of Aberdeen and Frankfurt, where she completed her doctorate on "(Post)Colonial Scotland? Literature, Gaelicness and the Nation" (on both Gaelic and English literature) in 2006. Having taught at the universities of Frankfurt and Giessen, she is currently an assistant professor in English, postcolonial and media studies at the University of Münster, working on a postdoctoral thesis on diasporic and transmigrant identities in British colonial settler cultures. She is the author of *Uneasy Subjects: Postcolonialism and Scottish Gaelic Poetry* (2011), as well as co-editor of *Transcultural Identities: Britain* (with Britta Freitag; themed issue of *Der fremdsprachliche Unterricht Englisch* 95, 2008) and *Hybrid Cultures – Nervous States: Britain and Germany in a (Post)Colonial World* (with Ulrike Lindner, Maren Möhring, & Mark Stein, 2010). She has also published articles on anglophone Scottish, Asian British, African, and Canadian literature and culture as well as on postcolonial theory, ecocriticism, and strategies for teaching transcultural competence in EFL (English as a foreign language) classes.

KATHY–ANN TAN is an assistant professor in the American Studies Department at the University of Tübingen, where she teaches courses on North American literature, fictions of globalization, and diasporic writing, especially Caribbean Canadian literature. Her first book, *The Nonconformist's Poem: Radical "Poetics of Autobiography" in the Works of Lyn Hejinian, Susan Howe and Leslie Scalapino* (2008), reflects her early interest in the experimental work of women poets associated with the L=A=N=G=U=A=G=E school. Her current research interest span the fields of globalization, citizenship studies, and postcolonial theory while maintaining a literary focus, hence her second book project (postdoc thesis) on "Sites of Contestation – Resistant Citizenship and Denizenship in North American Fiction."

PETRA TOURNAY–THEODOTOU is an associate professor of English at the European University Cyprus, where she teaches postcolonial, British, African-American, and women's literature. She obtained both her MA and PhD in English and Spanish language and literature from the Rheinisch-Westfälische Technische Hochschule Aachen. Her publications include essays and book chapters on nineteenth- and twentieth-century literature – Spanish (Gustavo

Adolfo Bécquer, Manuel Rivas), Latin-American (Carlos Fuentes, Jorge Luis Borges), and British (John Banville, Lawrence Durrell, Zadie Smith, Caryl Phillips, Leone Ross, Bernardine Evaristo, Eve Makis, Monica Ali) – as well as a monograph on the Spanish poet Gustavo Adolfo Bécquer.

DARIA TUNCA works in the English Department of the University of Liège. Her research focuses on stylistic approaches to African literatures, with a particular emphasis on contemporary Nigerian fiction. She has published articles in such international journals as the *Journal of Postcolonial Writing* and *Postcolonial Text*, and, with Bénédicte Ledent, she has co-edited the volume of essays *Caryl Phillips: Writing in the Key of Life* (2012). She maintains bibliographical websites on Chris Abani, Chimamanda Ngozi Adichie, and Ben Okri (all accessible via www.L3.ulg.ac.be/bibliographies).

JESSICA VOGES was a student of English and American literature, comparative literature, and media studies at the University of Potsdam, with the main focus on postcolonial studies. She is currently working on her doctoral dissertation at the University of Münster, examining the performative aspects of laughter in black British literature.

ROLAND WALTER is associate professor of English, comparative literature, and literary theory at the Universidade Federal de Pernambuco, Recife, Brazil. He is the author of three books, *Magical Realism in Contemporary Chicano Fiction* (1993), *Narrative Identities: (Inter)Cultural In-Betweenness in the Americas* (2003), and *Afro-América: Diálogos Literários na Diáspora Negra das Américas* (2009). He has also edited the e-book *As Américas: Encruzilhadas Glocais* (2007), co-edited the book *Narrações da Violência Biótica* (with Ermelinda Ferreira, 2010), and published widely in journals throughout the Americas on diverse aspects of inter-American literatures. Recent publications include "Identities on the Move: Of Cultural Fissures and Fusions in Black Canadian Literature" (*Canadian Review of Comparative Literature-CRCL* 36.1, 2009) and the "Foreword" to *The Function of Contemporary Travel Narratives in the French, Anglo, and Latin Americas: Mixing and Expanding Cultural Identity* (ed. Jean–François Coté, 2011). From 1997 to 2006 he was associate editor of *Multi-Ethnic Literature of the United States* (*MELUS*) and, since 2003, has been an associate researcher in the Groupe Interdisciplinaire de Recherche sur les Amériques (GIRA), Montreal.

DIRK WIEMANN is Professor of English literature at the University of Potsdam. His research interests include cultures of republicanism in seventeenth-
century England, Victorian contagion narratives, and (post)secularism in contemporary Britain and India. He has published a monograph on *Genres of
Modernity: Contemporary Indian Novels in English* (2008) and is co-editor
of *Discourses of Violence – Violence of Discourses* (with Johannes Anger-
müller, Anke Bartels & Agate Stopinska, 2007), among others. His numerous
articles focus on theatre and politics in the English Republic; Indian and
British cinema; Indian writing in English; cultures of memory; John Milton;
Thomas Hobbes; and autobiography as fiction.

⌘